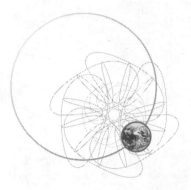

REAL WORLD ADOBE INDESIGN CS2

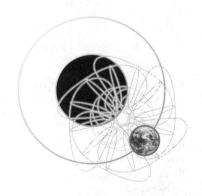

Real World
Adobe InDesign CS2

by

Olav Martin Kvern
&
David Blatner

Adobe

PEACHPIT PRESS

for Micki McNaughton
&
Gabriel and Daniel

REAL WORLD ADOBE INDESIGN CS2
Olav Martin Kvern and David Blatner

Copyright © 2006 by Olav Martin Kvern and David Blatner

PEACHPIT PRESS
1249 Eighth Street
Berkeley, California 94710
(800) 283-9444
(510) 524-2178
(510) 524-2221 (fax)

Find us on the Web at: *www.peachpit.com*
Peachpit Press is a division of Pearson Education
Real World Adobe InDesign CS2 is published in association with Adobe Press

Project editor: Lisa Brazieal
Indexer: Jan Wright
Cover art direction: Charlene Charles-Will
Cover design: Gee + Chung Design
Cover illustration: Ron Chan
Cover production: Ellen Reilly
Interior design, illustration, and production: Olav Martin Kvern and David Blatner

CREDITS
Thanks to the Seattle Gilbert and Sullivan Society and their photographer, Ray O. Welch, for giving us permission to use some of their archival photographs as example images. Special thanks to the late Ed Poole for the free use and abuse of his moustache.

ISBN 0-321-32202-9
9 8 7 6 5 4 3 2

Printed and bound in the United States of America

CONTENTS

We're desktop publishers—just like you. We've been through the long shifts (some of them longer than 70 hours), entering and editing text, setting type, drawing paths, importing images, and trying to get files to print. On most of those late nights and early mornings, we could have been home in bed if we had known just one key piece of information. But we weren't. There was no one there to tell us.

We're here to tell you.

If some piece of information in this book saves you one late night, one early morning, or gets your document to print on the first pass through the imagesetter instead of the second or third, we will have succeeded in our purpose.

InDesign is a watershed of important, new technologies that have, until recently, been at the edge of our page layout "radar": support for OpenType and Unicode, direct export of prepress-quality PDF files, integral PostScript/PDF screen rendering, multi-line composition, XML, transparency, optical kerning, and solid scripting support, to name just a few of them. Adobe has always said that InDesign is "the future of page layout"—but we think they're selling themselves a bit short. With InDesign, the future is here today.

And, to our eyes, at least, it looks pretty cool.

How This Book Was Produced

To answer the question we've been asked so many times: Yes, we produced this book in Adobe InDesign CS2. Some chapters were written in Microsoft Word, saved as Rich Text Format (RTF) files, and imported into InDesign templates. Other chapters were written or edited using InDesign's Story Editor feature. Screen captures were produced using Snapz Pro (for Mac OS X) and SnagIt (for Windows). Other graphics were produced using either InDesign's drawing tools, Adobe Photoshop, or Adobe Illustrator.

David laid out chapters using a Macintosh 17-inch PowerBook G4 running Mac OS X. Olav laid out chapters on a homebuilt AMD Athlon XP system running Windows XP and on a Macintosh Power-Book G4, also running Mac OS X.

The book is set entirely in Robert Slimbach's Minion Pro (an Adobe OpenType face, which was particularly useful when moving files from Windows to Macintosh, and *vice versa*), except for code samples—set in Lucas de Groot's TheSansMonoCondensed, and a few example characters in other fonts.

Acknowledgments

Thanks to Adobe's InDesign team and all the other folks at Adobe who helped support this book—including Will Eisley, Michael Wallen, Bur Davis, Angie Hammond, Whitney McCleary, Tim Cole, Matt Phillips, Mark Niemann-Ross, Thomas Phinney, Lonn Lorenz, Molly Ruf, Eric Menninga, David Stephens, Peter Boctor, Jonathan Brown, Alan Stearns, Dov Isaacs, Zak Williamson, Roey Horns, Paul Sorrick, and Christine Yarrow.

We appreciate the growing web of InDesign users and trainers with whom we love to trade cool tips and tricks, including Sandee Cohen, Claudia McCue, Steve Werner, Anne-Marie Concepción, Deke McClelland, Scott Citron, Diane Burns, Avery Raskin, Dave Saunders, Branislav Milic, Rufus Deuchler, Mordy Golding, Christopher Smith, Ray Robertson, and Shane Stanley.

Thanks to Jan C. Wright, Queen of Indexing, for our index, and thanks to all our friends at Peachpit Press for their patience, support, patience, professionalism, patience, and understanding (and did we mention patience?), including publisher Nancy Ruenzel, our editor Nancy Davis, Lisa "stay calm" Brazieal, Pam Pfiffner, Rachel Tiley, and Charlene Will.

DAVID: "My deepest appreciation to my wife and partner, Debbie Carlson, as well as to our sons Gabriel and Daniel, who ensured that sanity wouldn't gain the upper hand. My thanks, too, go to the Flip-Side Coffee House and to Delerium."

OLE: "Thanks to Max Olav Kvern, for covering my back when the brain-sucking evil undead Elmore zombies attack, and to the Anime Night gang for keeping me something like sane."

Olav Martin Kvern
okvern@ix.netcom.com

David Blatner
david@moo.com

Workspace

Come on in! Let us show you around. We'll be your tour guides to the world of InDesign. We're here to tell you what's what, what's where, and how it fits together. This chapter is all about InDesign's user interface—the myriad windows, palettes, menus, and other gadgets InDesign displays on your screen. It tells you what they all are, and what we call them. This is important, because not everything in InDesign is clearly labeled—as you read through the techniques in this book, you need to know that we mean this button *over here*, and not that button *over there*.

This chapter also contains lots of tips and tricks for working with InDesign's user interface. These are the "little things" that make all the difference between enjoying and hating the time you spend working with InDesign (or any other program, for that matter). The point is to get you up to speed with all of these new tools so that you can get on with your work.

Ready? Let's start the tour.

A Note About Keyboard Shortcuts: Throughout this book, we will refer to keyboard shortcuts using the format: Mac OS/Windows, as in "Command-Z/Ctrl-Z" (this is not necessarily in our order of platform preference, but it is in alphabetical order).

1

Another Note About Keyboard Shortcuts: Since you can redefine most of the keyboard shortcuts in InDesign, we can't guarantee that your keyboard shortcuts will match ours. And we can't follow every keyboard shortcut in the text with the disclaimer, "...or the shortcut you've defined for this action." So, as you read this, bear in mind that we're using the shortcuts from the default keyboard shortcut set. If you want to return to InDesign's default keyboard shortcuts, see "Customizing Keyboard Shortcuts," later in this chapter.

Yet Another Note About Keyboard Shortcuts: A few of InDesign's default keyboard shortcuts—especially those for selecting tools—do not use a modifier key (by "modifier key," we mean Command, Control, Option, Ctrl, Alt, Shift, and so on). If you're editing text, you can't use these keyboard shortcuts. If you do, you'll end up entering characters in the text.

The keyboard shortcut to switch to the Pen tool, for example, is "P." If you press the shortcut while the cursor is in text, you'll enter the character "P." If you use InDesign to set type (as most of us do), you'll almost certainly want to add a modifier key to the unmodified keyboard shortcuts you use most often.

Unfortunately, you can't modify the "hide all palettes" shortcut. It's hard wired to the Tab key.

Layout and Story Windows

When you open or create an InDesign document, you view and work on the publication using one or more windows (see Figure 1-1). InDesign windows come in two flavors: *layout windows* give you a view of a page or spread; *story windows* show a section of text in a document. You can have multiple windows of either type open at once. We'll cover story windows in more detail in "The Story Editor," in Chapter 3, "Text."

The view of the document you see in a layout window can be magnified or reduced, and each layout window can be set to a different magnification. Since magnification is primarily a way of moving around in your publication, we'll cover it later in this chapter, in "Publication Navigation."

Title Bar   At the top of a window you'll see the title bar. The appearance of the title bar differs slightly between the Windows and Mac OS versions of InDesign, and between Windows 2000 and Windows XP).

FIGURE 1-1
InDesign Windows

Windows version

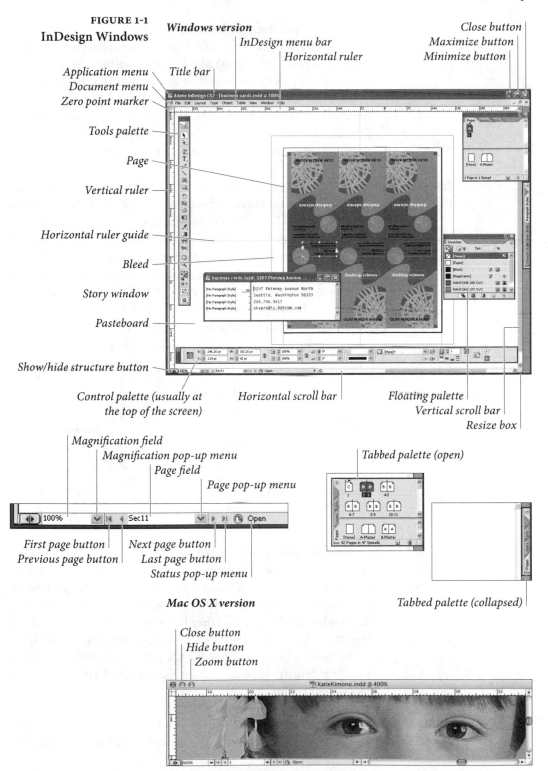

Application menu
Document menu
Zero point marker

Title bar

InDesign menu bar
Horizontal ruler

Close button
Maximize button
Minimize button

Tools palette

Page

Vertical ruler

Horizontal ruler guide

Bleed

Story window

Pasteboard

Show/hide structure button

Control palette (usually at the top of the screen)

Horizontal scroll bar

Floating palette
Vertical scroll bar
Resize box

Magnification field
Magnification pop-up menu
Page field

Page pop-up menu

First page button
Previous page button

Next page button
Last page button
Status pop-up menu

Tabbed palette (open)

Tabbed palette (collapsed)

Mac OS X version

Close button
Hide button
Zoom button

In Windows, you'll see the title, control menu, and close/minimize/maximize buttons (click them to close, hide, or enlarge a publication window, respectively). On the Mac OS, you'll see the close/minimize/maximize buttons followed by the title (the name of your file).

To close a window, press Command-W/Ctrl-W (or Ctrl-F4 in Windows). To close all windows, press Command-Option-Shift-W/Ctrl-Alt-Shift-W. If you have unsaved changes in any of the documents you're closing, InDesign will ask if you want to save them.

Pasteboard   Like most other page layout programs, InDesign is built around the metaphor of the traditional layout table. In the days before this desktop publishing fad came along, we would lay out our pages on a table, drafting board, desk, or on the dashboard of a speeding 1972 Volvo. As we did our layout, we'd place our waxy galleys of type and artwork on the pasteboard, an area off the page. We would then move the items onto our layout as they were needed. The pasteboard is the same in InDesign—an area off the page on which you place and graphic elements for future use (see Figure 1-2).

FIGURE 1-2
Pasteboard

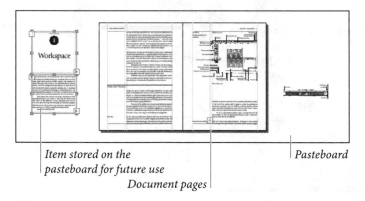

Item stored on the
pasteboard for future use
                         Document pages

                                           Pasteboard

The pasteboard is not a fixed size, as it is in FreeHand or PageMaker, and it's not shared between spreads—each spread has its own pasteboard (as in QuarkXPress). You can use areas of the pasteboard for temporary storage of the elements you're working with—just drag the elements off the page, and they'll stay on the pasteboard until you need them (again, this is just like an old-fashioned layout board).

By the way, you can also make the pasteboard above and below your page larger; we cover that in "Guides and Pasteboard Preferences," later in this chapter.

Scroll Bars   The most obvious, least convenient, and slowest way to change your view of your publication is to use a scroll bar (that is, to click in a

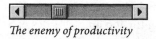

The enemy of productivity

scroll bar, drag a scroll handle, or click the scroll arrows). For more on better ways to get around, see "Publication Navigation," later in this chapter.

Page Field and Page Buttons

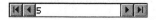

The Page field/pop-up menu and its attached navigation buttons give you a way to get from one page to another. Click the Previous Page button to move to the previous page in your publication, or click the Next Page button to move to the next page. Alternatively, you can click the First Page button to go to the first page in the publication, or the Last Page button to go to the last one.

If you know exactly which page you want to go to, choose the page number from the Page pop-up menu or enter the page number in the Page field. You can jump directly to the page number field by pressing Command-J/Ctrl-J. By the way, if your document has more than 100 pages, don't freak out if the Page pop-up menu doesn't list them all; to save space and time, it rounds off some page ranges. If you want it to show all the pages, hold down Command/Ctrl when selecting the pop-up menu.

Magnification Field

Enter a magnification percentage in this field, or choose one from the attached pop-up menu, and InDesign magnifies or reduces the view of the publication you see in the publication window. There are better ways to do this, as shown in "Publication Navigation," later in this chapter.

To make the cursor "jump" into the Magnification field, press Command-Option-5/Ctrl-Alt-5. Enter a percentage and press Enter to change the publication window's magnification.

These views aren't the only magnifications available—if you use the Zoom tool, you can achieve any magnification you want (from 5 to 4,000 percent). For more on using the Zoom tool, see "Zooming," later in this chapter.

Status Pop-Up Menu

The Status pop-up menu interacts with both Adobe Version Cue and Adobe Bridge, which you may or may not have installed (Bridge is part of both the Creative Suite and standalone packages; Version Cue is a suite-only feature).

If your document is being managed by Version Cue, you can choose Versions or Alternates to view the corresponding states of the document. Choose Reveal in Finder (Mac OS) or Reveal in Explorer (Windows) to open the folder containing the document. Choose Reveal in Bridge to display the folder containing the document in Bridge.

Rulers Pressing Command-R/Ctrl-R displays or hides InDesign's rulers—handy measuring tools that appear along the top and left sides of a publication window (see Figure 1-3). The rulers are marked off in the units of measurement specified in the Units & Increments Preferences dialog box. The actual increments shown on the rulers vary somewhat with the current magnification; in general, you'll see finer increments and more ruler tick marks at 800% size than you'll see at 12% size.

As you move the cursor, lines in the rulers (we call them "shadow cursors") display the cursor's position on the rulers (see Figure 1-4).

To change the units of measurement used by a ruler, Control-click/Right-click the ruler to display the Context menu. Choose a new measurement system from the menu, or choose Custom to enter a custom measurement increment (if you do this, InDesign displays the Custom Measurement Unit dialog box, where you can enter the measurement unit you want to use). If your document has a 15-point leading grid, for example, you could set the custom ruler to 15 points; the ruler would then indicate the number of "lines" down the page.

FIGURE 1-3
Rulers

The Context menu on the rulers is the quickest way to change measurement units.

Points
Picas
Inches
Inches decimal
Millimeters
Centimeters
Ciceros
Custom
(16 points)

FIGURE 1-4
Shadow Cursors

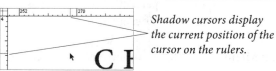

Shadow cursors display the current position of the cursor on the rulers.

Zero Point The intersection of the zero measurement on both rulers is called the zero point. In InDesign, the default location of the zero point is at the upper-left corner of the spread, page, or binding spine (it's an option in the Grids Preferences dialog box). To change the location of the zero point, use the zero point marker (see Figure 1-5).

To move the zero point, drag the zero point marker to a new position. As you drag, intersecting dotted lines show you the position of the zero point. Stop dragging, and the rulers will mark off their increments based on the new position of the zero point marker.

To reset the zero point to the default location, double-click the zero point marker.

To lock the position of the zero point, use the Context menu. Point at the zero point, then hold down Control and click (Macintosh) or click the right mouse button (Windows). Choose Lock Zero Point from the Context menu (see Figure 1-6). To unlock the zero point, display the Context menu and choose Unlock Zero Point.

FIGURE 1-5
Moving the Zero Point

Position the cursor over the zero point marker.

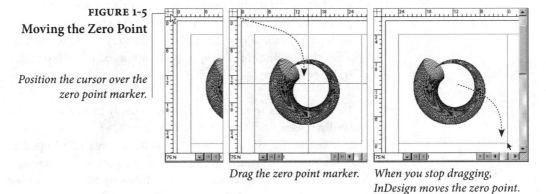

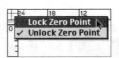

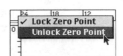

Drag the zero point marker.   *When you stop dragging, InDesign moves the zero point.*

FIGURE 1-6
Locking the Zero Point

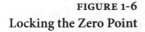

Unlocked zero point.   *Choose Lock Zero Point from the Context menu.*   *Locked zero point.*   *To unlock the zero point, use the Context menu.*

Managing Multiple Windows

If you want to open more than one window on a publication, choose "New Window" from the Window menu. The new window covers the original window, so you'll have to drag and resize windows to see both views at once, or choose Tile Windows from the Window menu (see Figure 1-7). Choose Cascade from the Window menu to stack the open publication windows on top of each other.

To switch from an active publication window to an inactive publication window, you can click any part of the inactive window, or you can choose a window name from the listing of open windows at the bottom of the Window menu. Press Command-~ (tilde)/Ctrl-F6 to switch from one open window to the next.

Sometimes it's easier to display pages in multiple windows than it is to scroll or zoom from page to page. Think about using multiple windows in the following situations:

► When you find yourself jumping back and forth between two or more locations in a publication.

► When you need to copy an object or objects from one page to another page that's several pages away. Dragging the objects from one publication window to another is faster than scrolling and dragging or cutting and pasting.

► When you're trying to fit copy into a story that spans several pages. You can make one publication window focus on the end of the story, and, as you edit and format text, you can see exactly when the last line of the copy appears at the end of the last text frame (see Figure 1-8).

There's no trick to removing a view—simply close the window, and it disappears from your Windows menu.

You can also have as many different documents (files) open as you like. You switch from one publication to another by choosing a window name from the bottom of the Window menu, or by clicking on their windows, just as you'd switch among applications.

FIGURE 1-7
Window Views

When you choose Cascade from the Window menu, InDesign stacks up the open windows. To bring any window to the front, click its title bar.

In either view, you can rearrange and resize windows to create custom views.

Use the Tile view when you want to drag objects from one window to another or from one publication to another.

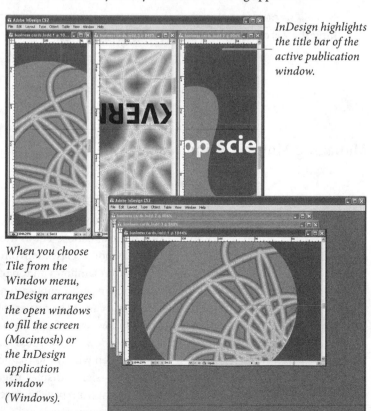

InDesign highlights the title bar of the active publication window.

When you choose Tile from the Window menu, InDesign arranges the open windows to fill the screen (Macintosh) or the InDesign application window (Windows).

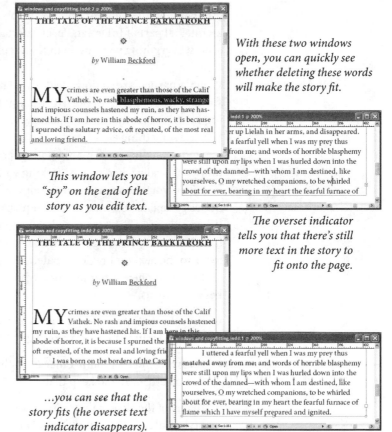

FIGURE 1-8
Using Views
for Copyfitting

This window shows you the text at the beginning of the story.

With these two windows open, you can quickly see whether deleting these words will make the story fit.

This window lets you "spy" on the end of the story as you edit text.

The overset indicator tells you that there's still more text in the story to fit onto the page.

When you delete the text in this window...

...you can see that the story fits (the overset text indicator disappears).

As we noted earlier, to close all open windows, hold down Option as you click the Close box (Macintosh) or hold down Alt as you click the Close button (Windows). Or press Command-Option-Shift-W/ Ctrl-Alt-Shift-W to close all of the open windows.

InDesign's Palettes

Can you see your page? If not, it's probably due to InDesign's omnipresent palettes—there are plenty of them. Don't rush out to buy a larger screen—you don't have to have all of the palettes open all of the time. The best way to work with InDesign's palettes is to have the minimum number of them open at once, to combine palettes into functional groups and workspaces, and to learn and master the keyboard shortcuts for working with and navigating through palettes. That's what this part of the book is about.

InDesign's palettes work two ways—they display information about the document or the selected object, and they provide controls for changing the publication and the objects in it. The palettes are an integral part of InDesign's user interface and are the key to doing almost everything you can do in the program.

All About Focus

When a particular window, field, or control is active, we say it has "focus"—it's receiving any keystrokes you might press. If you're pressing keys, and yet no text is appearing in the selected text frame, it's because something else—another window or field—has focus.

Understanding and manipulating palette focus is very important—especially when you're working with text.

When you choose a menu option or click a button in a palette, InDesign applies the change and returns focus to your page layout. When you press Tab to move ahead one field (or Shift-Tab to move back one field), InDesign applies any change you made and shifts focus to the next (or previous) palette field.

InDesign offers a number of keyboard shortcuts for controlling keyboard focus:

▶ Press Enter/Return to apply a value you've entered in a palette field and return focus to your page.

▶ Press Shift-Return/Shift-Enter to apply the value you've entered in a palette field and keep that palette field in focus.

▶ In any of the "list" palettes (the Swatches palette or Character Styles palette, for example), hold down Command-Option/Ctrl-Alt and click in the list. This transfers focus to the list—you can press the up and down arrows, or even type the name of a list item to select that item from the list (see Figure 1-9).

▶ You can return to the last-used palette field by pressing Command-Option-~/Ctrl-Alt-~ (tilde; that's the key in the upper-left corner of the keyboard). If you want to change this, look for the "Activate last used field in palette" feature in the Views and Navigation product area of the Keyboard Shortcuts dialog box (see "Keyboard Shortcuts," later in this chapter).

FIGURE 1-9
Palette Lists and Focus

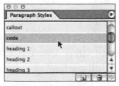

Hold down Command-Option/ Ctrl-Alt and click to give a list focus. When a list has focus, InDesign displays a dark border around it.

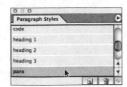

Once a list has focus, you can select list items by typing—it's often quicker than scrolling.

Displaying and Hiding Palettes

You can use keyboard shortcuts to show and hide palettes and save yourself lots of mouse movement (see Table 1-1). If a palette's open, but behind other palettes in the same group, pressing the keyboard shortcut brings the palette to the front of the group. To close a palette, press the shortcut again, or click the Close button on the palette's title bar.

Hiding All Palettes. Press Tab, and all of the palettes currently displayed disappear; press it again, and they reappear. This shortcut won't work when you have text selected or have an active text cursor in a text frame (it'll enter a tab character, instead). You'd think that you could use the keyboard shortcut to switch to the Selection tool (hold down Command/Ctrl) and then press Tab to hide the palettes, but you can't.

Zipping and Unzipping Palettes. With all these palettes, it's easy to run out of room on your screen to see anything *but* the palettes. While you can use keyboard shortcuts to display the palettes, you might like this better: you can shrink a palette down to just its tab and title bar by clicking the zoom box (on the Mac OS) or the Minimize button (in Windows). You can also double-click the palette's tab to do the same thing.

This is called "zipping" a palette. The title bar stays on the screen (see Figure 1-10). When you want to display the entire palette, click the zoom box again if you're a Macintosh user, or click the Maximize button if you're using Windows. The palette expands to its full size. In addition, you can:

▶ Double-click the tab of the front most palette in a group.

▶ Click the tab of any palette in a group that is not the front most palette in the group.

▶ Press the keyboard shortcut for the palette.

You can't zip palettes that are attached to the side of the screen (see "Side tabs," below).

Displaying options. Many of InDesign's palettes can be set to display all of the available options for a particular feature, or a subset of those options. The Stroke palette, for example, can display all stroke attributes (stroke weight, stroke type, end cap type, join, and arrowheads) or the stroke weight only. To expand this kind of palette to show all its features, select Show Options from the palette menu.

To display this palette:	Press:
Align	Shift-F7
Attributes	None/Alt-W, B
Character	Command-T/Ctrl-T
Character Styles	Shift-F11
Check Spelling	Command-I/Ctrl-I
Color	F6
Control	Command-Option-6/Ctrl-Alt-6
Find/Change	Command-F/Ctrl-F
Glyph	None/Alt-T, G
Gradient	None/Alt-W, D
Index	Shift-F8
Info	F8
Layers	F7
Links	Command-Shift-D/Ctrl-Shift-D
Object Styles	Command-F7/Ctrl-F7
Pages	F12
Paragraph	Command-Option-Shift-T/ Ctrl-Alt-Shift-T
Paragraph Styles	F11
Pathfinder	None/Alt-W, F
Story	None/Alt-T, R
Stroke	F10
Swatches	F5
Table	Shift-F9
Tabs	Command-Shift-T/Ctrl-Shift-T
Text Wrap	Command-Option-W/Ctrl-Alt-W
Tools	None/Alt-W, T
Transform	F9
Transparency	Shift-F10

Resizing palettes. To resize a palette, drag the Resize box at the palette's lower-right corner (see Figure 1-11). If a palette doesn't have a Resize box, you can't resize it. In Windows, you can drag the sides of some of the palettes to resize them (this works for the "list" palettes, like Paragraph Styles, Character Styles, Pages, and Swatches).

FIGURE 1-10
Zipping and Unzipping Palettes

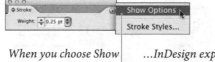

When you choose Show Options from a palette menu...

...InDesign expands the palette to display additional options.

Here's another (and possibly quicker) way to accomplish the same thing. Position the cursor over a palette tab...

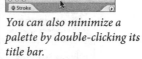

...and double-click the tab (or click the arrows). The palette shrinks to the next smaller size (if one is available).

Click again, and InDesign shrinks the palette further (if possible).

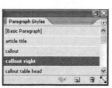

You can also minimize a palette by double-clicking its title bar.

FIGURE 1-11
Resizing Palettes

In Windows, you can also drag the borders of the palette to resize the palette.

To change the size of a palette, drag the resize box.

Snapping palettes into position. When you drag a palette near to the edge of another palette, InDesign snaps the edge of the palette you're moving to the closest edge of the other palette. This makes it easy to arrange and resize palettes in relation to other palettes.

Grouping and separating palettes. When you first launch InDesign, you'll notice that some palettes are combined. For example, Paragraph Styles and Character styles are grouped together. You can rearrange any of these "tabbed" palettes, pull tabbed palettes apart, or combine the palettes in any groups you want (see Figure 1-12). We all have different ways of working, and tabbed palettes give us a way of customizing InDesign to fit our particular habits and needs.

FIGURE 1-12

**Combining Or
Separating Tabbed
Palettes**

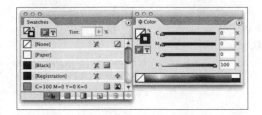

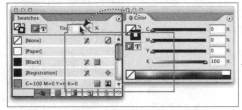

*Position the cursor over
a palette tab. then drag
the palette into another
palette group.*

*Stop dragging. InDesign
combines the palettes.*

To split a palette group...

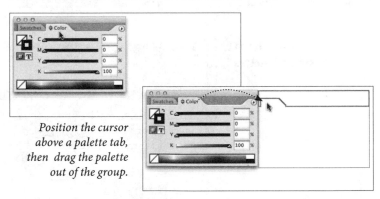

*Position the cursor
above a palette tab,
then drag the palette
out of the group.*

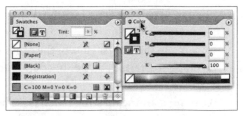

*Stop dragging. InDesign
splits the palette group.*

To combine palettes, drag the tab of one palette into the area at
the top of another palette. When you combine two or more palettes,
you create a "palette group." A palette group behaves as if it is a single
palette—the palettes move, resize, and zip/unzip as a unit.

In any palette group, only one palette can be "on top" at a time; only the tabs of the other palettes in the group are visible. To display another palette in the group, click the palette's tab or press the keyboard shortcut for the palette.

Docking palettes. Another way to customize the layout of InDesign's palettes is to "dock" one palette to another. When you do this, both palettes remain visible (in contrast to grouped palettes, where only the uppermost palette is visible), and move, hide, display, or resize as a single palette.

To dock one palette with another, drag the tab of a palette into the area at the bottom of another palette. As you drag, InDesign highlights the bottom of the target palette. Stop dragging and release the mouse button, and InDesign joins the palettes (see Figure 1-13).

FIGURE 1-13
Docking Palettes

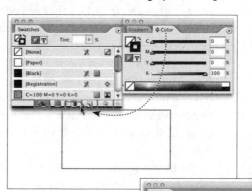

Drag the tab of one palette into the bottom of another palette. InDesign displays a highlight when the palettes are ready to dock.

Stop dragging and release the mouse button. InDesign docks the two palettes.

Side tabs. Another way to show and hide palettes is to use InDesign's side tabs feature. When you drag a palette tab within a few pixels of the left or right edge of the screen (on the Mac OS) or the sides of the application window (Windows), InDesign collapses the palette and displays the rotated palette tab at the edge of the workspace (see Figure 1-14). You can also drag the palette tab into any other side tab to add it to that palette group.

FIGURE 1-14
Side Tabs

You don't have to use the
right side; the left side will
also work.

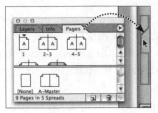

Drag the palette tab into the area at the
edge of the screen (on the Mac OS) or to
the edge of the application window (in
Windows).

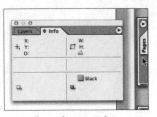

Drop the palette, and
InDesign creates a side tab.

To collapse all of the palettes in a palette group, hold down Option/Alt as you drag the palette tab (see Figure 1-15).

You can't collapse the Tools palette, the Control palette, or the Tabs palette into side tabs. You also can't turn the names of the palettes "right side up" when they're collapsed into the side; you just have to turn your head 90 degrees to read them.

To expand a side tab, click the palette's tab or press the palette's keyboard shortcut (see Figure 1-16). To collapse the palette again, click its tab (or press the keyboard shortcut again). To collapse all of the palettes on one side of the screen, hold down Option (Mac OS) or Alt (Windows) as you click a palette tab. Or, even more fun, press Command-Option-Tab/Ctrl-Alt-Tab to hide or show all the side tab palettes.

To turn a palette back into a floating palette, drag the palette's tab away from the edge of the screen or window (see Figure 1-17). Hold down Option/Alt and drag a palette group to convert the entire group to a floating palette group.

Small Palette Rows. To reduce the height of each item in any of the "list" palettes (like the Paragraph Styles, Character Styles, Links, and Layers palettes), choose Small Palette Rows from the palette's pop-up menu (see Figure 1-18).

FIGURE 1-15
**Adding a Palette Group
to a Side Tab**

*(Again, you can also drag
the palettes to the left side
of the screen).*

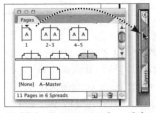

Hold down Option/Alt and drag the
palette tab to the edge of the screen
(Mac OS) or application window
(Windows).

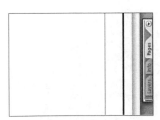

InDesign moves the entire
palette group into the side tab.

FIGURE 1-16

Expanding a Side Tab

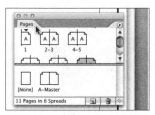

Click the palette tab...

...and InDesign expands the side tab.

FIGURE 1-17

Converting a Side Tab to
a Floating Palette

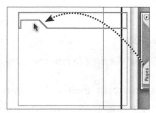

*Drag the palette tab away
from the edge of the screen.*

*When you release the palette,
InDesign converts the side tab
into a floating palette.*

FIGURE 1-18

Small Palette Rows

*Choose Small Palette
Rows from a list
palette menu...*

*...and InDesign
reduces the height of
each list entry.*

Overriding Units of Measurement. Being able to switch from one measurement system to another is great, but what do you do when you want to enter a value in a measurement system other than the one currently selected? Do you have to go to the Units & Increments Preferences dialog box and switch to another measurement system? No—all you need to do add a "measurement override" when you enter the value. Want to enter 115.3 points in a field that's currently showing decimal inches? It's easy: enter "115.3 pt," or even "0p115.3" in the field, and InDesign will take care of the conversion for you. You can use these shortcuts in any numeric field in any InDesign palette or dialog box. Table 1-2 shows you how to enter measurement overrides.

You can also cycle through measurement units by pressing Command-Option-Shift-U/Ctrl-Alt-Shift-U when any measurement field has focus (note, though, that this changes the measurement system in all fields and rulers).

When you want:	Enter:	Example:
points	pt	136 pt
points	0p	0p136
picas	p	1p
picas and points	p	1p6
inches	i*	1.56i
millimeters	mm	2.45mm
ciceros	c	3c
ciceros and didots	c	3c4

* or "in" if you feel the need to type the extra character.

Doing Arithmetic in Fields. You can add, subtract, multiply, or divide in any numeric field in any InDesign palette or dialog box. Want an object to be half its current width? Type "/2" after the value in the W (width) field in the Transform palette and press Enter. Want an object to move two picas to the right? Enter "+2p" (yes, all of the measurement unit overrides shown above work with these operations) after the value shown in the X field in the Transform palette. Enter "*" to multiply, or "-" to subtract. You get the idea.

You can also enter percentages as part of any arithmetic operation. For example, if you replace a value with "25%" and press Enter, InDesign enters one quarter of the value for you.

A Quick Tour of the Palettes

Here's a quick description of the palettes you'll see as you work with InDesign. Most of the rest of the book is taken up by descriptions of how you use the palettes—this section is your formal introduction to the palettes and to the gadgets they contain.

Align palette. Use the Align palette to arrange objects relative to other objects. To display or hide the Align palette, press F8 (see Figure 1-19). To align two or more objects, select them and then click the alignment button corresponding to the alignment you want.

Note that the Align palette's distribution options include the ability to space objects a specific distance apart, including objects of differing sizes/shapes. For more on working with the Align palette, see Chapter 8, "Transforming."

Attributes palette. Have you been looking for the object-level overprinting options in the Stroke palette or the Color palette? You won't find them there, because they're in the Attributes palette (see Figure 1-20). We're not sure why. Choose Attributes from the Window menu to display the Attributes palette.

FIGURE 1-19
Align Palette

Align right edges
Align horizontal centers
Align left edges

Align top edges
Align vertical centers
Align bottom edges

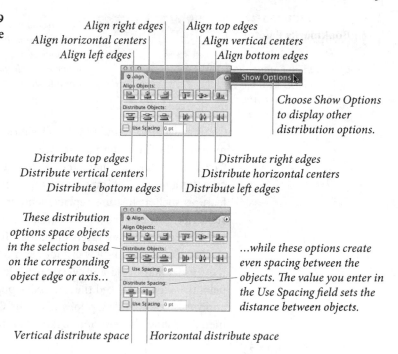

Choose Show Options
to display other
distribution options.

Distribute top edges
Distribute vertical centers
Distribute bottom edges

Distribute right edges
Distribute horizontal centers
Distribute left edges

These distribution
options space objects
in the selection based
on the corresponding
object edge or axis...

...while these options create
even spacing between the
objects. The value you enter in
the Use Spacing field sets the
distance between objects.

Vertical distribute space | Horizontal distribute space

FIGURE 1-20
Attributes Palette

The options in the Attributes palette control the
overprinting/knockout qualities of the fill or stroke
of an object.

Book palette. In a way, a book palette isn't really a palette, even
though it looks pretty much like any of the other palettes (see Figure
1-21). A book palette is really a book *document*—an InDesign file that
contains a list of references to other InDesign files. Books are a way
to associate a group of files together for the purpose of numbering
pages, generating a table of contents or index, printing, or exporting
as PDF. For more on books, see Chapter 8, "Long Documents."

If you close a palette group containing a book palette, InDesign
closes the book palette.

FIGURE 1-21
Book Palette

Bookmarks palette. The Bookmarks palette displays PDF bookmarks you've added to your document—you can add bookmarks
manually, or by creating a table of contents (see Figure 1-22). You can
create, edit, rearrange, and delete bookmarks using the Bookmarks
palette. For more on bookmarks, see Chapter 13, "Interactive PDF."

FIGURE 1-22
Bookmarks Palette

You can add and manage bookmarks with the Bookmarks palette.

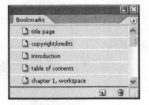

Bookmarks in InDesign documents can be exported to PDF, but you can also use the Bookmarks palette for document navigation–double-click a bookmark to jump to the bookmark's destination page.

Character palette. You'll find InDesign's character formatting commands in the Character palette (see Figure 1-23). Press Command-T/Ctrl-T to display the Character palette. The Character palette menu contains a number of important typesetting commands, controlling features such as ligature replacement, small caps, superscript, and subscript. However, because most of these features are duplicated in the Control palette, we rarely open the Character palette anymore.

You can choose to show or hide several Character palette options: the Horizontal Scale and Vertical Scale fields, the Baseline Shift field, the Skew field, and the Language pop-up menu. To hide these controls, choose Hide Options from the Character palette's pop-up menu. To show these options again, choose Show Options.

FIGURE 1-23
Character Palette

Press Command-T/Ctrl-T to display the Character palette.

Character palette menus

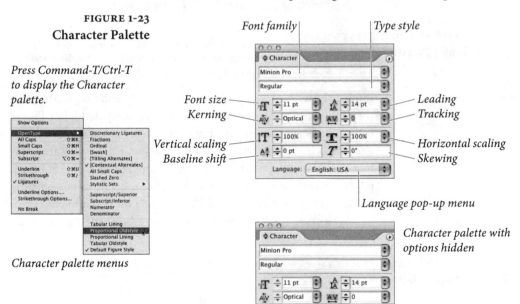

Character palette with options hidden

Character Styles palette. Use the Character Styles palette to create, edit, and apply InDesign's character styles (see Figure 1-24).

To create a character style, select text that has the formatting attributes you want and choose New Style from the Character Styles palette menu (or Option/Alt-click the Create New Style button at the

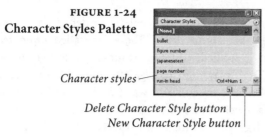

FIGURE 1-24
Character Styles Palette

Character styles

Delete Character Style button
New Character Style button

The Character Styles palette menu provides options for working with character styles.

bottom of the palette). InDesign displays the New Character Style dialog box. At this point, you can enter a name for the style, or otherwise tinker with the style's definition. When you close the dialog box, note that InDesign does not apply the style to the selected text.

To edit a style, hold down Command-Option-Shift/Ctrl-Alt-Shift and double-click the style name, or point at the style name, display the context menu, and then choose Edit. This opens the style for editing, but does not apply it to the selected text. You can also double-click the style name to edit the style, but this applies the style to the selected text or to the document default.

To delete a character style, select the style (you might want to deselect any selected text or text frames before you click on the style) and choose Delete Styles from the palette's pop-up menu (or drag it on top of the delete button in the palette).

For more on character styles, see Chapter 4, "Type."

Check Spelling palette. As you'd expect from its name, you use this palette to check the spelling of the text in a publication (see Figure 1-25). To display this palette, press Command-I/Ctrl-I (or choose Check Spelling from the Edit menu).

For more on the Check Spelling palette, see Chapter 3, "Text."

FIGURE 1-25
Check Spelling Palette

When InDesign finds a suspicious-looking word during a spelling check, the word appears in the Not in Dictionary field.

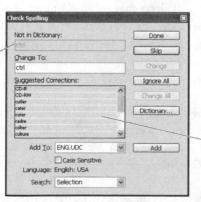

You've heard the rumor, and it's true: InDesign pushes the boundaries of user interface design (and possibly common sense) by providing the Check Spelling palette.

InDesign displays a list of spelling alternatives in the Suggested Corrections list.

Color palette. You can use the Color palette to define and apply colors interactively (see Figure 1-26). These are called *unnamed colors* because they're applied without first making a swatch in the Swatches palette. To display the Color palette, press F6 (or choose Color from the Windows menu). You won't find colors from standard color libraries—such as Pantone or TruMatch—here. They're in swatch libraries (which you can load using the Swatches palette).

To define a color, choose the color model you want to work with from the Color palette's menu, then adjust the color parameters in the Color palette. Tip: You can switch from one color model to the next by Shift-clicking in the color bar at the bottom of the palette.

The Color palette interacts with the Swatches palette. When you select a color swatch in the Swatches palette, InDesign loads the Color palette with the color definition of the swatch. The Swatches palette returns the favor: when you choose New Swatch from the Swatches palette menu, or click the New Swatch button at the bottom of the Swatches palette, InDesign creates a new swatch with the color definition currently in the Color palette.

For more on defining, editing, and applying colors, see Chapter 9, "Color."

FIGURE 1-26
Color Palette

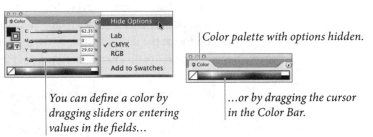

Color palette with options hidden.

You can define a color by dragging sliders or entering values in the fields...

...or by dragging the cursor in the Color Bar.

Control palette. The Control palette is similar to the Measurements palette in QuarkXPress or the Control palette in PageMaker—it's a single palette that collects a number of frequently-used controls in one place. The cool part is that it's context sensitive—it changes the controls it displays as you select different objects. This is very handy, as it means you get several palettes for the price (in screen pixels) of one (see Figure 1-27).

Data Merge palette. Use the Data Merge palette to mark placeholders for (very simple) database publishing (see Figure 1-28). For more on using the Data Merge palette, see Chapter 7, "Importing and Exporting."

Dictionary palette. InDesign's hyphenation and spelling features depend on dictionaries. When a word isn't in a dictionary, InDesign

FIGURE 1-27
Control Palette

The options in the Control palette change based on the selection.

When multiple objects are selected, alignment buttons appear

Control palette in object mode.

Control palette in character mode.

Control palette in paragraph mode.

When text is selected, the Control palette can be displayed in either Character or Paragraph mode.

FIGURE 1-28
Data Merge Palette

Data Merge palette before you select a data source file.

After you select a data source, the palette displays the field names in the data records.

has no idea how to spell the word, and has to make guesses about where the word should be hyphenated. With the Dictionary palette, we can help InDesign learn new words, or change the way that it treats words it already knows (see Figure 1-29).

FIGURE 1-29
Dictionary Palette

Find/Change palette. As you'll see in Chapter 3, "Text," InDesign's ability to search for, find, and change text is an extremely powerful word processing and formatting tool. The key to using this feature is yet another palette: the Find/Change palette (see Figure 1-30). Press Command-F/Ctrl-F to display the Find/Change palette (or choose Find/Change from the Edit menu).

FIGURE 1-30
Find/Change Palette

The pop-up menus associated with the Find what and Change to fields make searching for special characters easy.

Enter the text you want to search for in the Find what field...

...then enter the text you want to replace it with in the Change to field (if necessary).

In this example, we specified a search range (the current document), and specified formatting (click the More Options button to display the Find Style Settings and Change Style Settings options).

The "alert" icons tell you that formatting attributes have been set.

You can find and change any formatting InDesign can apply.

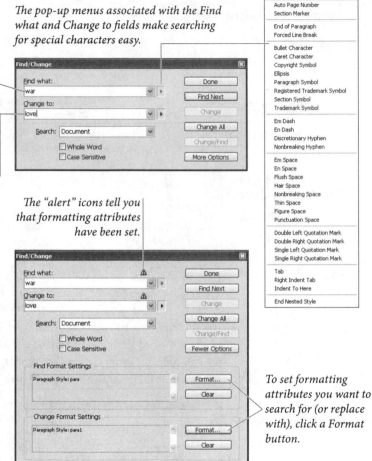

To set formatting attributes you want to search for (or replace with), click a Format button.

Flattener Preview palette. If you wander anywhere near Seattle, you'll hear David shouting repeatedly that this should not be called the Flattener Preview palette because it doesn't preview anything! It's really a Flattener *Alert* palette—it alerts you to areas of your page involving transparency which may cause issues at print time (see Figure 1-31). We explore the Flattener *Alert* palette in Chapter 10, "Printing."

Glyphs palette. You know that the character you want is somewhere within a certain font...but where? In the past, we've had to resort to KeyCaps, PopChar, or the Windows Character Map utility to find

FIGURE 1-31
**Flattener Preview
(Alert !) Palette**

special characters, but now there's no need to leave InDesign. Just display the Glyphs palette (choose Glyphs from the Type menu), and you can easily browse all of the characters of any font available to InDesign (see Figure 1-32).

And we do mean *every* character. Many fonts include characters which aren't normally available due to the limitations of the Mac OS or Windows character encoding. Once you've found the character you're looking for, you can double-click the character to insert it at the current text cursor location (or to replace the selected text). For more on the Glyphs palette, see Chapter 4, "Text."

FIGURE 1-32
Glyphs Palette

The Glyphs palette menu provides various ways of sorting/filtering the character display.

Select a font and font style, and InDesign will display every character in the font.

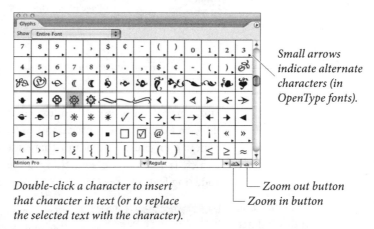

Small arrows indicate alternate characters (in OpenType fonts).

Double-click a character to insert that character in text (or to replace the selected text with the character).

Zoom out button
Zoom in button

Gradient palette. InDesign's ability to apply gradients to the fill and stroke of paths and text characters is one of the program's signature features, and the Gradient palette is one of the ways you create, edit, and apply gradients (see Figure 1-33). For more on gradients, see Chapter 5, "Drawing."

FIGURE 1-33
Gradient Palette

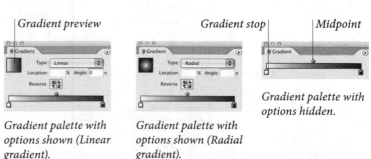

Gradient preview

Gradient stop

Midpoint

Gradient palette with options hidden.

Gradient palette with options shown (Linear gradient).

Gradient palette with options shown (Radial gradient).

Hyperlinks palette. InDesign offers the ability to attach hyperlinks to page items or to text. These hyperlinks can take you to another page, a specified chunk of text, or to a web page or email address. The hyperlinks you add to InDesign pages will function when you export your pages as PDF, but they can also be used inside InDesign itself.

You use the Hyperlinks palette (see Figure 1-34) to create hyperlinks, define hyperlink destinations, navigate using hyperlinks, and control hyperlink appearance and attributes. For more on working with hyperlinks, see Chapter 13, "Interactive PDF."

FIGURE 1-34
Hyperlinks Palette

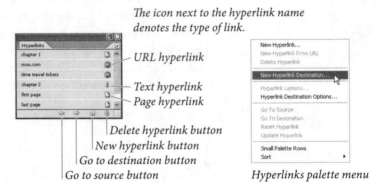

The icon next to the hyperlink name denotes the type of link.

URL hyperlink

Text hyperlink
Page hyperlink

Delete hyperlink button
New hyperlink button
Go to destination button
Go to source button

Hyperlinks palette menu

Index palette. You use the Index palette (see Figure 1-35) to create, edit, and delete index entries and index topics, view an index, and generate an index. We admit that indexing makes our heads spin (which is really quite something to see). For more on InDesign's indexing features, see Chapter 8, "Long Documents."

FIGURE 1-35
Index Palette

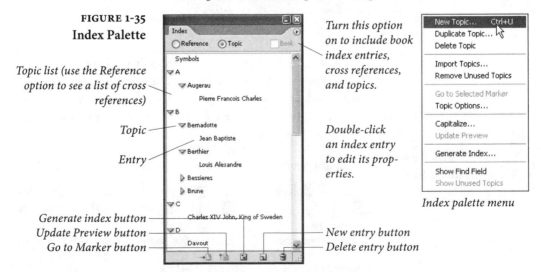

Topic list (use the Reference option to see a list of cross references)

Topic

Entry

Turn this option on to include book index entries, cross references, and topics.

Double-click an index entry to edit its properties.

Index palette menu

Generate index button
Update Preview button
Go to Marker button

New entry button
Delete entry button

Info palette. The Info palette displays information about the selected object, or, if no objects are selected, about the current location of the cursor (see Figure 1-36).

▶ When no object is selected, it shows you information about the document itself.

▶ When you select a character, it shows you the Unicode value of the character.

▶ When you select a frame or line, the Info palette displays the stroke and fill colors; you can determine whether it shows the color's swatch name or the color definition (like "Red" versus "0C/100M/100Y/0K" by clicking on the tiny fill and stroke icons in the File Info palette.

▶ When you place the cursor in a text frame, the palette displays a count of characters, words, lines, and paragraphs in the entire story—or however much text is currently selected.

▶ Click on a placed image, and the palette shows the image's file type (EPS, TIFF, PSD, or whatever), resolution (both the image resolution and the effective resolution, which will be different if you have scaled the picture larger or smaller), and color space (RGB, CMYK, or Grayscale). InDesign can't extract the information from some file types, notably EPS and PDF.

FIGURE 1-36
Info Palette

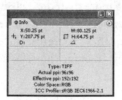

Layers palette. Layers give you a way to control the stacking order of objects in your publication and also help you control the speed with which InDesign draws and redraws your publication's pages. Layers can be hidden, or locked. To work with layers, you use the Layers palette (see Figure 1-37). To display the Layers palette, press F7 (or choose Layers from the Window menu).

The following are quick descriptions of each control in the Layers palette.

▶ Show/Hide button. If you see an "eye" icon on this button, the layer is visible. Click the icon to hide the layer. To show the layer again, click the button.

FIGURE 1-37
Layers Palette

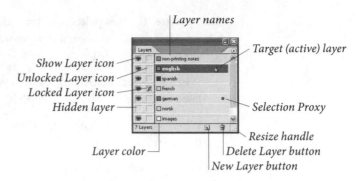

Layer names

Show Layer icon
Unlocked Layer icon
Locked Layer icon
Hidden layer

Target (active) layer

Selection Proxy

Resize handle
Delete Layer button
New Layer button

Layer color

▶ Lock/Unlock button. To lock a layer, click this button. When a layer is locked, a pencil with a red slash through it (as in the international "prohibited" symbol) appears on this button. To unlock the layer, click the button again.

▶ Layer color swatch. The color shown on this button determines the color of the selection handles of objects assigned to this layer.

▶ Target layer icon. This icon shows you which layer is active. Any new objects you create, objects you paste into the publication, or groups you create will appear on this layer.

▶ Layer name. The name of the layer.

▶ Selection Proxy. The Selection Proxy represents the items you've selected. If the selection contains objects from more than one layer, you'll see more than one Selection Proxy in the palette. Clicking a layer does not move the selection to that layer, as it would in some other programs. Instead, you move objects from layer to layer by dragging the Selection Proxy up or down in the list of layers.

▶ New Layer button. Click this button to create a new layer. The new layer appears at the top of the list of layers.

▶ Delete Layer button. Click this button to delete the selected layer. InDesign will display a dialog box that asks if you want to delete the layer. If you do, click the Yes button—InDesign deletes the layer and any objects assigned to the layer. If you don't want to delete the objects, click No.

▶ Resize handle. Drag this icon to change the size of the palette.

Double-click a layer to display the Layer Options dialog box, where you can change the layer color, layer name, and other layer options.

For more on working with layers, see Chapter 2, "Page Layout."

Library palette. Use the Library palette (or palettes, as you can have multiple libraries open at once) to store and retrieve commonly used items (see Figure 1-38). Does your company or client have a logo they like to plaster all over every publication you lay out? Put it in a library. You open library files just as you open InDesign documents or book files—using the Open and New options on the File menu.

When you close a palette group containing a library palette, InDesign closes the library palette.

FIGURE 1-38
Library Palette

Library palette in Thumbnail view.

Library palette in List view.

Library palette menu

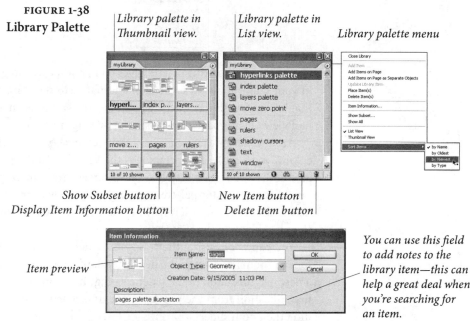

Show Subset button
Display Item Information button

New Item button
Delete Item button

Item preview

You can use this field to add notes to the library item—this can help a great deal when you're searching for an item.

When you click the Display Item Information button, InDesign displays the Item Information dialog box.

When you click the Show Subset button, InDesign displays the Subset dialog box. Specify the parameters you want and click the OK button, and InDesign displays the library items that match.

Links palette. InDesign keeps track of all the images (and sometimes your text files, too) that you import into your document in the Links palette. This palette lets you manage these files and is the gateway to the XMP "metadata" information that can be stored inside Photoshop and Illustrator images (see Figure 1-39). We cover the Links palette in all its glory in Chapter 7, "Importing and Exporting."

FIGURE 1-39
Links Palette

Navigator palette. This palette gives you another way to get around in your publication—it's a kind of alternative to scrolling and zooming. When you display the Navigator palette, you'll see in it a thumbnail view of your page or page spread (see Figure 1-40).

Around the spread, you'll see a red rectangle (you can change the color if you want). This rectangle is the View box and represents the area of the publication visible on your screen. You can drag the View box in the Navigator palette to change your view of the publication. As you drag, InDesign scrolls your view of the publication to match the area shown in the View box.

You can zoom using the Navigator palette. Click the Zoom buttons to zoom in or out to the next "standard" magnification, or enter a new magnification in the palette's Magnification field (or choose a magnification from the pop-up menu associated with the field). Or drag the Zoom slider.

FIGURE 1-40
Navigator Palette

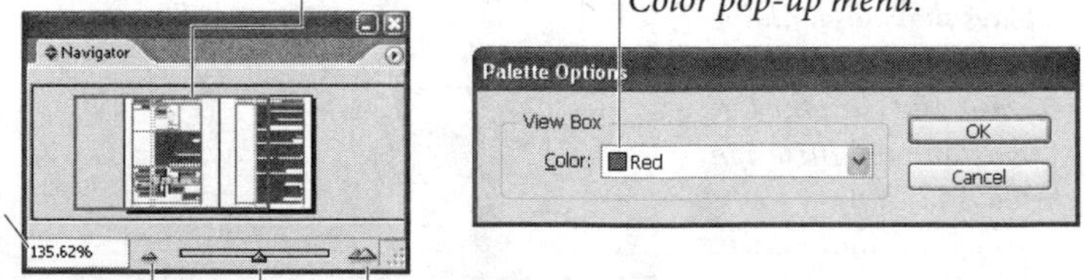

The View Box represents the area of your screen.

Drag the View box to scroll your view of the publication.

To change the color used to display the View Box, choose Palette Options from the palette menu. Choose a color from the Color pop-up menu.

Enter a magnification percentage in the Magnification field, or …
…click this button to zoom to the next lower magnification preset (e.g., from 200% to 100%), or …
…drag the Zoom slider to change the magnification percentage (as you drag, the View Box will change size), or …

…click this button to zoom to the next higher magnification preset (e.g., from 100% to 200%).

If you don't use the Navigator palette, turn it off—you'll get faster screen redraw.

When you've set the Navigator palette to display all of the spreads in your document, you can also scroll from spread to spread using the palette scroll bar.

We use the Zoom tool, Hand tool, Pages palette, and keyboard shortcuts to move from place to place in our publications, rather than the Navigator palette, but you should give the palette a try—you might like it better than we do.

If you don't use the Navigator palette, turn it off to get faster screen redraw. It takes InDesign time to draw the little page preview in the palette.

Object Styles palette. InDesign's object styles can control almost every attribute that can be applied to a page item—fill color, stroke color, paragraph style, text frame insets, and drop shadow settings are all examples of formatting you can control using object styles (see Figure 1-41). Object styles are very powerful, and they're discussed in more detail in Chapter 6, "Where Text Meets Graphics."

FIGURE 1-41
Object Styles Palette

PageMaker toolbar. The PageMaker toolbar is just a palette containing buttons for common tasks (see Figure 1-42). If you prefer clicking a button to pressing keyboard shortcuts, using the menus, or for some reason do not like the Control palette, you might like this feature. We don't actually have any use for it.

FIGURE 1-42
PageMaker Toolbar

Pages palette. The Pages palette is for creating, rearranging, and deleting pages and master pages (see Figure 1-43). It's also a great way to navigate from one page to another, and it's where you apply master pages to document pages. The following are brief descriptions of the controls found in the Pages palette.

▶ Spread and page icons. These icons represent the document pages and master pages in your publication. You can drag these pages around in the Pages palette to change the page order, or apply master pages to document pages (or other master pages), or create new master pages (by dragging document pages into the master page area of the palette).

▶ **New page button.** Click this button to create a new document page.

▶ **Delete page button.** Click this button to delete the selected page or pages.

▶ **Master/Document page separator.** This bar separates the master pages in your publication (at the bottom of the palette) from the "normal" publication pages (at the top). You can drag the separator up or down to change the size of these areas.

▶ **Resize box.** Drag this icon to resize the Pages palette.

FIGURE 1-43
Pages Palette

Pages display the prefix ("B" or "C," in this example) of the master page applied to them.

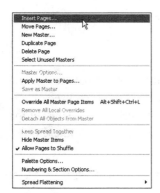

Pages palette menu

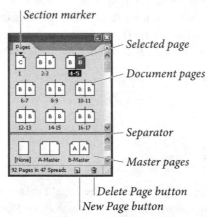

Section marker

Selected page

Document pages

Separator

Master pages

Delete Page button

New Page button

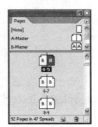

Another way to view the Pages palette. This view means you have to scroll a lot more, but, hey, it looks like QuarkXPress.

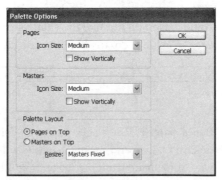

Choose Palette Options from the Pages palette menu, and InDesign displays the Palette Options dialog box. Use the options in this dialog box to change the arrangement of the controls in the Pages palette.

Paragraph palette. You use the controls in the Paragraph palette to specify paragraph formatting. To display the Paragraph palette, press Command-Option-Shift-T/Ctrl-Alt-Shift-T (see Figure 1-44).

When you choose Hide Options from the Paragraph palette menu, InDesign hides the Paragraph Space Above, Paragraph Space Below, Drop Cap Characters, and Drop Cap Lines fields, and the Hyphenate

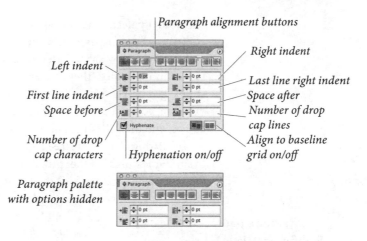

FIGURE 1-44
Paragraph Palette

Paragraph alignment buttons

Right indent

Left indent

First line indent

Space before

Last line right indent

Space after

Number of drop cap lines

Number of drop cap characters

Hyphenation on/off

Align to baseline grid on/off

Paragraph palette with options hidden

Paragraph palette menu

checkbox and shrinks the palette to a smaller size. To display these options again, choose Show Options from the menu. As with the Character palette, we tend to keep the Paragraph hidden and just use the paragraph-formatting features in the Control palette.

For more on working with paragraph specifications, see Chapter 4, "Type."

Paragraph Styles palette. InDesign's paragraph styles are the most powerful text formatting feature in the program, and the Paragraph Styles palette is the way you work with them (see Figure 1-45).

▶ New Paragraph Style button. Click this button to create a new paragraph style. If you have text selected, the new paragraph style will have the formatting attributes of the first paragraph in the selection.

▶ Delete Paragraph Style button. Click this button to delete the selected paragraph style (or styles).

FIGURE 1-45
Paragraph Styles Palette

Paragraph styles

New Paragraph Style button
Delete Paragraph Style button

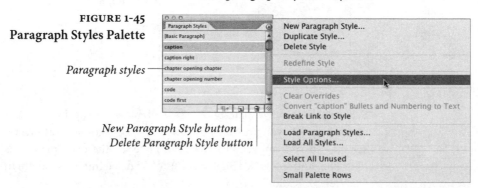

Pathfinder palette. The buttons in the Pathfinder palette give you the ability to merge shapes, or use one shape to cut an area out of another, or to create a new shape based on the area of intersection between two or more shapes. They're great for creating complex paths out of simple geometric shapes. If you need to draw a doughnut shape, for example, you can simply draw one circle inside another, select both circles, and then click the Subtract button in the Pathfinder palette.

The Pathfinder palette (see Figure 1-46) is InDesign's counterpart to similar features in other programs—Pathfinder in Illustrator, Path Operations in FreeHand, or the Merge features in QuarkXPress; we cover it in Chapter 5, "Drawing."

FIGURE 1-46
Pathfinder Palette

Use the Pathfinder palette to create shapes by combining other shapes.

Scripts and Script Label palettes. The Scripts palette gives you a way to run scripts without leaving InDesign (see Figure 1-47). What? You don't want to have to know about programming to use InDesign? Relax—you don't have to do any programming to simply run scripts, and many useful scripts are available online.

The Script Label palette is a bit more obscure, and you probably won't need to use it unless you write scripts or are working with a scripter. We'll defer any further discussion of these palettes and scripting until Chapter 12, "Scripting."

FIGURE 1-47
Scripts palette and Script Label palette

Double-click a script in the Scripts palette to run the script. No, really, you don't need to know how to program to use scripting.

Separation Preview palette. We're still blown away by this palette, which lets you preview process- and spot-color separations on screen—so you can see just the cyan plate, or the cyan plate plus PMS 286, and so on (see Figure 1-48). We'll delve into this palette in Chapter 10, "Color."

FIGURE 1-48

Separations
Preview palette

States palette. InDesign documents can include rich media elements such as buttons, sounds, and movies. The States palette helps you control button objects, such as rollovers (see Figure 1-49). Look to Chapter 13, "Interactive PDF," for more on this palette.

FIGURE 1-49

States palette

Story palette. You've heard that InDesign features hanging punctuation (which, in InDesign, goes by the name "Optical Margin Alignment"), but you haven't been able to find the control for it? Relax—it's in the Story palette (see Figure 1-50). Actually, there's nothing else in the Story palette. To display the Story palette, choose Story from the Type menu.

For more on the Story palette, see Chapter 4, "Type."

FIGURE 1-50

Story palette

Stroke palette. A stroke is the outline of a path; the Stroke palette controls the formatting of that outline (see Figure 1-51).

The basic Stroke palette is minimalist: there's only the Weight option to play with. Choose Show Options from the Stroke palette menu, however, and InDesign expands the palette to include options controlling the line cap, miter limit, line join, stroke type, gap color, and arrowhead properties of a path. What these options really mean is discussed more fully in Chapter 5, "Drawing."

Swatches palette. Swatches can be colors, tints of colors, mixed inks, or gradients. They're a way of storing the values in the Color palette or the Gradient palette for future use. The Swatches palette gives you a way to organize, edit, and apply swatches in your publications

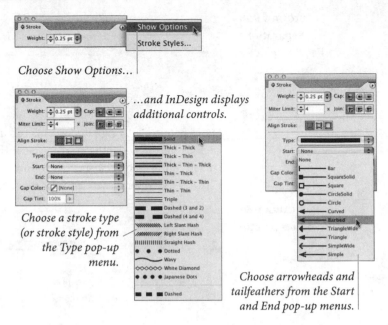

FIGURE 1-51
Stroke Palette

Choose Show Options...

...and InDesign displays additional controls.

Choose a stroke type (or stroke style) from the Type pop-up menu.

Choose arrowheads and tailfeathers from the Start and End pop-up menus.

(see Figure 1-52). To display the Swatches palette, press F5 (or choose Swatches from the Window menu).

While you can get by without the Swatches palette—by using the Color palette and the Gradient palette to apply fill and stroke attributes—we don't recommend it. Here's why: When you apply a fill or stroke using the Swatches palette, you create a relationship between the object's formatting and the swatch. If you later find you need to change the definition of the swatch, the appearance of any objects formatted using the swatch will change. Swatches, like paragraph and character styles, are a feature that can really save your sanity when your client/boss/whatever changes their mind about a color scheme an hour before your publication deadline.

▶ **Fill, Stroke, and Text buttons.** Click these buttons to apply a swatch to the corresponding attribute of an object (they're the same as the buttons in the Tools palette).

▶ **Tint field.** Enter a value in this field (or choose a value from the attached pop-up menu) to apply a tint of the selected color to the selection. This does not create a new tint swatch.

▶ **Show All button.** Click this button to display all of the swatches in the publication.

▶ **Show Colors button.** Click this button to display all of the color and tint swatches in the publication (and hide any gradient swatches).

- ▶ **Show Gradients button.** Click this button to display all of the gradient swatches in the publication (and hide any color or tint swatches).

- ▶ **New Swatch button.** Click this button to create a new swatch.

- ▶ **Delete Swatch button.** Click this button to delete the selected swatch or swatches.

- ▶ **Resize box.** Drag this icon to resize the Swatches palette.

For more on working with color swatches, see Chapter 9, "Color." For more on gradient swatches, see Chapter 5, "Drawing."

FIGURE 1-52
Swatches Palette

Use the default "None" swatch to remove the fill or stroke (or both).

The default "Registration" swatch prints on all separations.

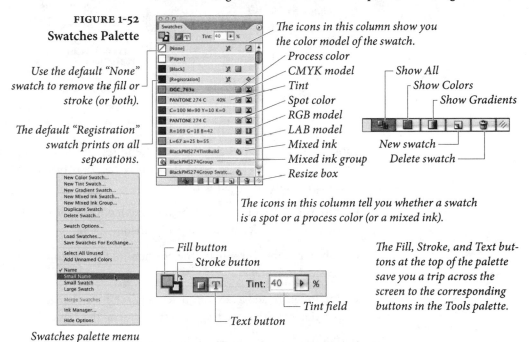

The icons in this column show you the color model of the swatch.

Process color
CMYK model
Tint
Spot color
RGB model
LAB model
Mixed ink
Mixed ink group
Resize box

Show All
Show Colors
Show Gradients

New swatch
Delete swatch

The icons in this column tell you whether a swatch is a spot or a process color (or a mixed ink).

Fill button
Stroke button

Tint field

Text button

The Fill, Stroke, and Text buttons at the top of the palette save you a trip across the screen to the corresponding buttons in the Tools palette.

Swatches palette menu

If you choose to use the Small Swatch or Large Swatch views, be aware that colors whose swatches are very similar in appearance can have very different color definitions.

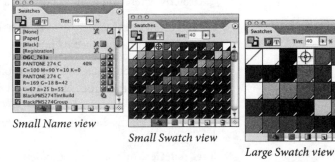

Small Name view

Small Swatch view

Large Swatch view

Table palette. This one is a monster (see Figure 1-53). Sure, you can set up your tables using the dialog boxes you can summon using the commands on the Table menu, but we think you'll often turn to the Table palette, which packs many of the most important table controls into a much smaller space.

FIGURE 1-53
Table Palette

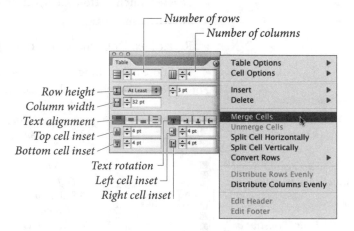

Tabs palette. Use InDesign's Tabs palette to set tab stops and paragraph indents (see Figure 1-54). To display the Tabs palette, press Command-Shift-T/Ctrl-Shift-T.

▶ Tab Alignment buttons. Set the alignment of the selected tab stop (or set the default tab stop alignment).

▶ Tab stop icons. These mark the positions of the tab stops in the selected paragraph.

▶ Tab Ruler. To add a tab stop, delete a tab stop, or change the position of a tab stop, drag a tab stop icon on the Tab Ruler.

▶ Tab Position field. Enter a value in this field when you know exactly where you want to position a tab stop.

▶ Tab Leader field. Enter up to two characters in this field to apply a tab leader to the selected tab stop.

▶ Snap Palette button. Click this button to align the Tab Ruler's zero point at the left edge of the text frame.

For more on the Tabs palette, see Chapter 4, "Type."

Tags palette. You use the Tags palette to control the way that objects in your page layout correspond (or "map") to elements in the XML structure of your document (see Figure 1-55). If you're confused

FIGURE 1-54
Tabs Palette

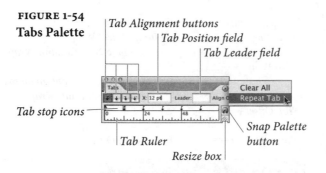

Tab Alignment buttons
Tab Position field
Tab Leader field
Tab stop icons
Tab Ruler
Resize box
Snap Palette button

What the symbols on the tab ruler mean:

↓ Left tab stop
↓ Right tab stop
↓ Centered tab stop
↓ Character tab stop
◀ Left indent
◣ First line indent
◀ Right Indent

FIGURE 1-55
Tags Palette

Tags provide a link between objects and elements in the XML structure of your document. The Tags palette is where you create, manage, and apply tags.

Choose Map Tags to Styles to associate specified paragraph styles with XML tags.

If the names of your tags and the names of your paragraph styles match, you can click the Map by Name button to automatically match tags to styles.

about what we mean by this, we understand. Please see Chapter 14, "XML," for more on using XML in InDesign.

Text Wrap palette. When you need to tell text to avoid an object—an imported graphic, an InDesign path, or another text frame, you use the Text Wrap palette (see Figure 1-56). We discuss text wrap in Chapter 6, "Where Text Meets Graphics."

Transform palette. Look: In two-dimensional page layout and illustration programs, there's just no escape from basic geometry. So you might as well just learn to like working with numbers. Sometimes, they're the best way to get the job done. And it's not difficult—especially with InDesign's Transform palette (see Figure 1-57). Note that because these features also appear in the Control palette, we often just leave the Transform palette closed.

FIGURE 1-56
Text Wrap Palette

Wrap Around
Bounding Box

Contour Wrap

Jump Object Wrap

Jump to Next Column Wrap

No Wrap

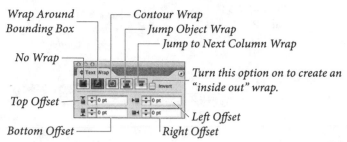

Turn this option on to create an
"inside out" wrap.

Top Offset

Bottom Offset

Left Offset

Right Offset

*If you select Contour Wrap
when you have an imported
graphic selected, you can
match the shape of the text
wrap to the shape of the
clipping path.*

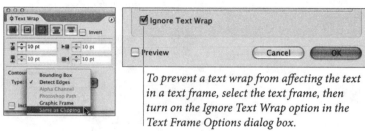

*To prevent a text wrap from affecting the text
in a text frame, select the text frame, then
turn on the Ignore Text Wrap option in the
Text Frame Options dialog box.*

FIGURE 1-57
Transform Palette

Horizontal location (X)

Width

Height

Proxy

Vertical location (Y)

Horizontal Scaling

Rotation Angle

Shear Angle

Vertical Scaling

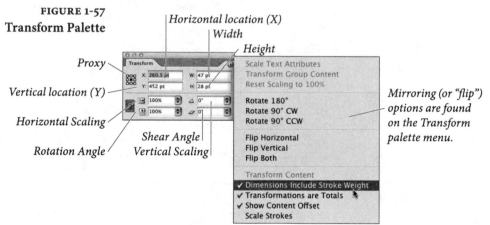

*Mirroring (or "flip")
options are found
on the Transform
palette menu.*

The Transform palette shows you the horizontal (X) and vertical
(Y) location of the selected object (or the cursor). The coordinates
that appear in the X and Y fields are shown in the current units of
measurement, and are relative to the current location of the zero
point. The W (for width) and H (for height) fields show you the size
of the selection. The Vertical and Horizontal scaling fields show you
any scaling applied to the object, the Rotation field shows you the
current rotation angle, and the Shear field shows you the skewing
angle applied to the object. Not only do these fields give you information on the selection, they can also be used to change its location, size,
rotation angle, or skewing angle.

As an object moves to the right, relative to the horizontal zero
point, the object's X coordinate increases. As an object moves *down*
on the page, the value of its Y coordinate increases. Note that this

means that the vertical (Y) axis of InDesign's coordinate system is upside down compared to the graphs you created in junior high school (see Figure 1-58).

A "proxy" represents something else—the Proxy in InDesign's Transform palette represents the selection (see Figure 1-59). The squares at the edges and in the center of the Proxy represent the corners, sides, top, and center of the selection's bounding box, and control the way that changes in the Transform palette affect the selected object or objects.

FIGURE 1-58
InDesign's
Coordinate System

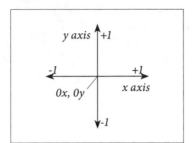

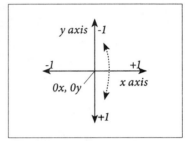

"Classical" geometric coordinates: y values increase as you go up the vertical axis.

InDesign coordinates: y values increase as you go down the vertical axis.

FIGURE 1-59
The Proxy

The Transform palette's Proxy "stands in" for the selection.

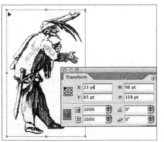

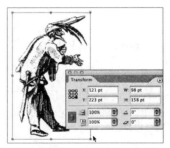

Select a point on the Proxy, and InDesign displays the location of the point of the selection (the upper-left corner, in this example).

Select a different point on the Proxy, and you'll see different values in the X and Y fields (in this example, I've selected the lower-right corner).

While the X and Y fields display the current cursor position when you move the Selection tool or the Direct Selection tool, they don't change when you're using any other tool. So you can't use the X and Y fields for positioning information as you draw a path with the Pen tool, or create a text frame with the Type tool.

Note for PageMaker users: Unlike PageMaker's Control palette, whose Proxy features both "move" and "stretch" modes, InDesign's Proxy is always in "move" mode. Entering a new X coordinate for a side handle, for example, will always move the handle to that location without resizing the selected object. You'll have to simulate the effect of "stretch" mode using the W(idth) or H(eight) fields, or the Scaling fields.

Transparency palette. Don't rush to the Layers palette looking for transparency options (as in Photoshop)—InDesign's Transparency palette (see Figure 1-60) contains the controls you're looking for.

FIGURE 1-60
Transparency Palette

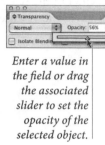

Enter a value in the field or drag the associated slider to set the opacity of the selected object.

Choose a transparency blending mode from the pop-up menu.

Trap Presets palette. InDesign's trap presets are collections of trapping settings you can apply to a page or range of pages in a document. The Trap Styles palette displays a list of the presets you've defined (see Figure 1-61). For more on trapping, see Chapter 6, "Color."

FIGURE 1-61
Trap Presets Palette

You use the Assign Trap Presets dialog box to apply trapping styles to pages and ranges of pages.

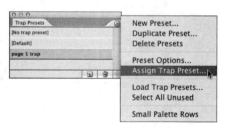

The Trap Presets palette is odd in that the pages it affects are not necessarily the ones that you see in the current window. Almost every other palette affects the selected page item or text.

Saving and Loading Workspaces

Once you've gotten your palettes set up just the way you want them, you can save them—their locations and their states—to a workspace. You can then load that workspace to return to that arrangement.

This means that you can set up special palette configurations for specific tasks—you might want to have one set of palettes for working with paths; another for entering text and typesetting, and still another for creating bookmarks and hyperlinks. You might even want to have different workspaces for different clients or documents. With InDesign's workspace management, you can dramatically reduce the number of palettes you have up on your screen at any one time while making palette use more efficient.

To save a workspace, choose Save Workspace from the Workspace submenu of the Window menu. InDesign displays the Save Workspace dialog box. Enter a name for the workspace and press the OK button to save the workspace. InDesign adds the workspace name to the list of available workspaces (see Figure 1-62).

FIGURE 1-62

Saving a Workspace

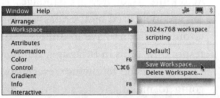

To save the current arrangement of InDesign's palettes, choose Save Workspace from the Workspace menu.

Enter a name for your workspace.

The new workspace appears on the Workspace menu. To switch to a different workspace, simply choose it from the menu.

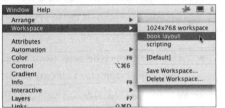

It takes only seconds to switch from one workspace to another, so you can set up workspaces optimized for specific layout tasks.

To apply a workspace, choose the workspace name from the Workspace submenu of the Window menu. After a (relatively) brief pause, InDesign resets your palettes to the configuration saved in the workspace. You can assign keyboard shortcuts to the workspaces in the Load Workspace features in the Window Menu area of the Edit Keyboard Shortcuts dialog box (see "Keyboard Shortcuts," later in this chapter).

To delete a workspace, choose Delete Workspace from the Workspace submenu of the Windows menu. InDesign displays the Delete Workspace dialog box. Choose a workspace from the Name pop-up menu and click the Delete button. InDesign deletes the workspace and closes the dialog box.

Once you have your workspaces set up the way you like them, it's a good idea to back up the file containing them. It's called "Active-Workspace.xml" and you can find it by searching your hard drive.

There's no practical way to edit a workspace once you've saved it; you just have to make a new one and delete the old one. You *could* edit the XML of the workspace settings file, but doing so would probably take longer than re-creating the workspace from scratch. (Ole experimented with this for far longer than he should have.)

Using the Tools Palette

If the publication window is the layout board where you collect the galleys of type, illustrations, and photographs you want to use in your publication, the Tools palette is where you keep your waxer, X-Acto knife, T-square, and bandages. (Note to youngsters: the foregoing are tools used by the Classical Greeks in the early days of page layout. You don't have to understand how they work to use the corresponding tools in InDesign. But it helps.)

Some of the following descriptions of the tool functions aren't going to make any sense unless you understand how InDesign's points and paths work, and that discussion falls in Chapter 5, "Drawing." You can flip ahead and read that section, or you can plow through this section, get momentarily confused, and then become enlightened when you reach the descriptions of points and paths. It's your choice, and either method works.

You can break InDesign's toolbox (as shown in Figure 1-63) into six conceptual sections.

▶ Selection tools (the Selection, Direct Selection, and Position tools) select objects. You can do different things with the objects depending on the selection tool you've used.

▶ Tools for drawing basic shapes (the Rectangle, Polygon, Ellipse, and Line tools) and their equivalent frames (Rectangle Frame, Polygon Frame, and Ellipse Frame tools) draw complete paths containing specific numbers of points in specific positions on the path.

▶ Path-drawing and editing tools (the Pen, Add Point, Delete Point, Convert Point, Gradient, Pencil, Eraser, Smooth, and Scissors tools) draw paths point by point (or, in the case of the Scissors tool, delete points or split paths).

▶ Transformation tools (the Rotate, Shear, Scale, and Free Transform tools) change the rotation angle, size, and skewing angle of objects on your pages.

▶ The Type tool and Path Type tool let you enter and edit text (the latter along a path).

▶ Navigation tools (the Zoom and Hand tools) help you move around in your publication.

The tool descriptions below are brief and are only intended to give you a feeling for what the different tools are and what they do.

FIGURE 1-63
The Tools Palette

Click the Adobe Online button to connect with Adobe's web site (and download updated plug-ins, if you want).

Swap fill/stroke (Shift-X)
Fill (X)
Stroke(X)
Default fill/stroke (D)
Formatting affects container
Apply Color (,)
Apply Gradient (.)

Formatting affects text
Apply None (/)
Preview Mode (W)
Normal View Mode (W)

Some of the "slots" in the Tools palette are occupied by more than one tool. How can you tell? When you see a tiny arrow in the corner of a tool icon, more tools lurk beneath the surface. To select a "hidden" tool…

…position the cursor over a tool, then hold down the mouse button.

InDesign displays a "flyout" menu containing the available tools.

Choose a tool from the menu and release the mouse button.

* *Hold down Command/Ctrl to switch to the Selection tool temporarily.*
** *Hold down Option-Space-bar/Alt-Spacebar and drag to switch to the Hand tool temporarily.*

	Tool name	Shortcut		Tool name	Shortcut
▶	Selection	V*	⬜	Rectangle	M
▷	Direct Selection	A	⊠	Rectangle Frame	F
	Position	Shift-A	◯	Polygon	
	Pen	P	◯	Polygon Frame	
	Add Point	+	↻	Rotate	R
	Delete Point	-	⊠	Free Transform	E
▷	Convert Point	Shift-C		Scale	S
T	Type	T		Shear	O
	Path Type	Shift-T	⬜	Gradient	G
	Pencil	N	✂	Scissors	C
	Smooth			Eyedropper	I
	Eraser			Measure	K
╲	Line	\		Button	B
◯	Ellipse	L		Hand	H**
⊗	Ellipse Frame		🔍	Zoom	Z

To learn more about entering text with the Type tool, see Chapter 3, "Text." For more on drawing objects with the drawing tools, see Chapter 5, "Drawing." For more on working with the Transformation tools, see Chapter 8, "Transforming."

Talking about InDesign's tools and their use can get a little confusing. When you select a tool in the Tools palette (or press the keyboard shortcut to select a tool), what does the cursor become? In this book, we will sometimes use phrases like "select a tool and drag," or "drag the tool on the page." We hope this is clear—from our point of view, the cursor *is* the tool.

Hiding the Tools palette. Sometimes, you want to hide all of the palettes except the Tools palette. To do that, make sure that the cursor isn't in a text frame, and then press Shift-Tab. InDesign hides all open palettes, but leaves the Tools palette open. If you've hidden all of the palettes including the Tools palette, you can display it by choosing Tools from the Window menu.

Tools Palette Keyboard Shortcuts. You can choose most of the tools in the Tools palette using keyboard shortcuts such as "F" for the Frame tool (no Command/Ctrl or other modifier key necessary). This is usually faster than going back across the screen to the palette. Note, however, that you can't press these while you're editing text. That's why we like to add additional keyboard shortcuts (see "Keyboard Shortcuts," later in this chapter) to the tools we use most often; for example, on David's system, Command-Shift-1/Ctrl-Shift-1 switches to the Selection tool when he's editing text.

Hidden Tools/Tool Variants. To save some of your precious screen real estate, some of the slots in the Tools palette contain more than a single tool. You can tell by looking at the tool icon—when you see a tiny triangle on a tool icon, you know that other tools are lurking beneath it.

To use one of the "hidden" tools, position the cursor over a tool icon and hold down the mouse button (the left mouse button, for Windows users). InDesign displays a short pop-up menu, or "flyout," containing the available tools. Choose one of the tool icons, and that tool will be displayed in the Tools palette.

For each of the basic shape tools, InDesign offers a corresponding frame drawing tool. There's really very little difference between the path drawn by the Rectangle tool and a frame drawn by the Rectangular Frame tool, and paths can be converted to frames—and frames to paths—very easily. There's no penalty for drawing a path one way or another, as there is in some other programs.

InDesign Home Page   When you click the button at the top of the Tools palette, InDesign displays the InDesign home page at adobe.com (www.adobe.com/products/indesign/). This is where you can find technical support documents or download new plug-ins. You'll also find columns, articles, and white papers on various topics related to InDesign. Do we ever click this? No. But we wouldn't want to stop you from doing it.

Selection Tool   You use the Selection tool to select and transform objects. Press V to select the Selection tool (when the cursor is not in text). When any other tool is selected in the Tool palette, you can temporarily switch to the Selection tool by holding down Command/Ctrl. In Windows, you can get the Direct Selection tool temporarily by pressing Tab while you're holding down Ctrl. To switch back to the Selection tool, press Tab again (assuming that you're still holding down the Ctrl key). When you release Command/Ctrl, the cursor turns back into whatever tool you were using before you summoned the Selection/ Direct Selection tool.

On either the Mac OS or in Windows, once you have the Selection tool selected in the Tool palette, you can press Control-Tab (yes, that's Control for Mac OS users, too, not Command) to switch to the Direct Select tool, or *vice versa*. See "Selecting and Deselecting," in Chapter 2, "Page Layout," for more about making selections.

Direct Selection Tool   How many selection tools does a page layout application really need? We don't know, but InDesign has two—one for everyday selection; another for selecting objects on Sundays and holidays. No, seriously, the Direct Selection tool (press A) is for selecting objects that are inside other objects, such as the following.

▶ Individual points on paths. For more on editing the shape of a path, see Chapter 5, "Drawing."

▶ Component paths of compound paths. For more on working with compound paths, see Chapter 5, "Drawing."

▶ Objects inside groups. For more on selecting objects inside groups, see Chapter 2, "Page Layout."

▶ Objects pasted inside other objects. For more on working with path contents, see Chapter 8, "Transforming."

Position Tool   PageMaker users will recognize their old friend, the Cropping tool, in InDesign's Position tool—and for good reason, as this tool was part of the "PageMaker Plug-in Pack" that was available for InDesign CS. The Position tool gives you a way to adjust the cropping and positioning of imported graphics inside frames. You can use the Direct Selection tool to do the same thing, of course, but it'll take you a few more steps.

Pen Tool   You use the Pen tool to draw paths containing both straight and curved line segments (that is, paths containing both curve and corner points). Illustrator users will recognize the Pen tool immediately, because it's pretty much identical to Illustrator's Pen tool (maybe there's something to all this "cross-product" talk, after all). Click the Pen tool to create a corner point; drag to create a curve point. Press P to select the Pen tool.

Under the Pen tool, you'll find the following tools:

▶ Add Point tool (press + to switch to this tool). When you click the Add Point tool on a selected path, InDesign adds a point at that location on the path. (Adobe calls this tool the Add Anchor Point tool.)

▶ Delete Point tool (press – to switch to this tool). When you click the Delete Point tool on a point on a selected path, InDesign deletes the point. (Adobe calls this tool the Delete Anchor Point tool.)

▶ Convert Point tool. When you click the Convert Point tool on a point on a selected path, InDesign converts the point to the other kind of point—if the point you click is a corner point, InDesign converts it to a curve point; if it's a curve point, InDesign converts it to a corner point. You can also use the Convert Point tool to adjust the direction handles of a point. (Adobe calls this tool the Convert Direction Point tool.)

For more (much more) on working with the Pen tool (and its variants) to draw and edit paths, see Chapter 5, "Drawing."

Type Tool   You enter and edit text using the Type tool. To create a text frame, select the Type tool and drag the tool in the publication window; a text frame appears with a flashing text-insertion point (or text cursor) in its first line. To edit text, select the Type tool and click in the text frame. For more on entering, editing, and formatting text, see Chapter 3, "Text." To select the Type tool, press T. Note that when you have the Selection or Direct Select tool chosen in the Tool palette, you can switch to the Type tool automatically by double-clicking any text frame. InDesign places the text cursor as close as possible to where you double-clicked.

Path Type Tool   Use the Path Type tool to enter and edit text on a path (Adobe calls this the "Type on a Path" tool). To add text to a path, select the Path Type tool and click the tool on a path. A flashing text insertion point (or text cursor) appears on the path. At this point, text you enter will flow along the path. See Chapter 6, "Where Text Meets Graphics." To select the Path Type tool, press Shift-T.

Pencil Tool   If you're one of the millions of computer users who find the Pen tool—and the whole process of drawing by manipulating points, line segments, and control handles—confusing, give the Pencil tool a try. With the Pencil tool (press N), you can sketch free form paths. As you drag the tool, InDesign creates a path that follows the cursor, automatically placing points and adjusting curve control handles as it does so.

If you don't like something about a path you've drawn using the Pencil tool, you can adjust it using any of InDesign's other drawing tools (including that scary Pen tool). You might want to start with the other tools that share the same space in the Tools palette: the Smooth tool and the Eraser tool (see below).

Smooth Tool   We like power tools. A good belt sander, for example, can reduce just about anything to a smooth, rounded blob in mere seconds. The Smooth tool is something like that. Select a path—any path—and drag the Smooth tool over it. It'll get smoother. Not smooth enough yet? Drag again.

As you drag the Smooth tool, InDesign adjusts the points and control handles that define the path to create a smoother transition from one line segment to another. InDesign often removes points during this process. If you continue to repeat the smoothing process, we think you'll eventually end up with a simple curve between two points.

Eraser Tool   The Eraser tool erases line segments and points. To use the Eraser tool, select a path, then drag the eraser tool over part of the path. InDesign splits the path and removes the line segments and points where you dragged the Eraser tool.

Line Tool   Use the Line tool to draw straight lines—paths containing two corner points. If you hold down Shift as you drag the Line tool, the lines you draw will be constrained to 0-, 45-, and 90-degree angles. Press \ (backslash) to select the Line tool.

Ellipse Tool   Use the Ellipse tool to draw ellipses and circles. Hold down Shift as you drag the Ellipse tool, and InDesign draws circles. Press L to select the Ellipse tool.

Rectangle Tool   Use the Rectangle tool to draw rectangles. If you hold down Shift as you drag, you draw squares. Press M to select the Rectangle tool.

If you need a rectangle with rounded corners, draw the rectangle using the Rectangle tool, then choose Corner Effects from the Object menu to display the Corner Effects dialog box (you can also get to this dialog box via the context menu, or by pressing Command-Option-R/Ctrl-Alt-R). The Corner Effects dialog box can provide a variety of other corner shapes, as discussed in Chapter 5, "Drawing."

Polygon Tool

The Polygon tool makes it easy to draw equilateral polygons, such as pentagons, hexagons, and dodecagons. (Polygons are closed geometric objects that have at least three sides; they're equilateral if all sides are the same length.) You can also use the Polygon tool to draw stars (also called starbursts).

To change which polygon the Polygon tool draws, double-click the tool in the Tools palette. InDesign displays the Polygon Settings dialog box (see Figure 1-64). Enter the number of sides you want in the Number of Sides field. If you want the polygon to be a star polygon, enter a percentage (from 0 to 99 percent) in the Star Inset field. If you don't want the polygon to be a star polygon, enter 100 percent in the Star Inset field.

FIGURE 1-64
Polygon Settings

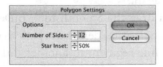

Rotate Tool

To rotate the selected object (or objects), select the Rotate tool from the toolbox (press R) and then drag the tool on your page. When you select the Rotate tool, InDesign displays the transformation center point icon on or around the selected object. The center point icon sets the center of rotation (the point you'll be rotating around), and corresponds to the selected point on the Proxy in the Transform and Control palettes. Drag the transformation center point icon to a new location (or click one of the points in the Proxy) to change the center of rotation.

Hold down Shift as you drag the Rotate tool to constrain rotation to 45-degree increments (that is, as you drag the Rotate tool, InDesign snaps the selection to 0, 45, 90, 135, 180, 225, 270, and 315 degree angles).

Scale Tool

To scale (or resize) an object, select the object (press S), select the Scale tool, and then drag the tool in the publication window. When you select the Scale tool, InDesign displays the transformation center point icon on or around the selected object. The location of the center point icon sets the center of the scaling transformation, and corresponds to the selected point on the Proxy in the Transform and Control palette. Drag the transformation center point icon to a new location (or click one of the points in the Proxy) to change the point you're scaling around.

Hold down Shift as you drag a corner handle to retain the object's proportions as you scale it. When you scale an object that has a stroke and Scale Strokes is turned on in the Transform palette, the stroke may appear disproportional (thicker in some places and thinner in others) and the stroke weight in the Strokes and Control palettes appears incorrect. You can fix both of these problems by choosing Reset Scaling to 100% from either the Transform or Control palette menus.

Shear Tool   Shearing, or skewing, an object alters the angle of the vertical or horizontal axes of the object. This makes it appear that the plane containing the object has been slanted relative to the plane of the publication window. To shear an object, drag the Shear tool (press O) in the publication window. As you drag, InDesign shears the object.

When you shear an object, InDesign distorts the stroke weights of the paths in the selection. The Reset Scaling to 100% feature mentioned above will fix this distortion, too.

Free Transform Tool   The Free Transform (press E) tool is a combination of the Scale and Rotate tools, plus some aspects of the Selection tool, all bundled into a single tool. What the tool does depends on the position of the cursor.

▶ When the cursor is above one of an object's selection handles, the Free Transform tool acts as the Scale tool. Drag the Free Transform tool, and you scale the object around its center point.

▶ When the cursor is just outside one of the selection handles, the Free Transform tool behaves as if it were the Rotate tool. Drag the tool to rotate the object around its geometric center.

▶ When the Free Transform tool is inside the bounds of the selection, it acts as a "move" tool—drag the tool to move the object.

For more on working with the Free Transform tool, see Chapter 8, "Transforming."

Eyedropper Tool   The Eyedropper tool (press I) can pick up formatting attributes (from the fill and stroke of a path to the character and paragraph formatting of text) and apply them to other objects. You can also use the Eyedropper tool to sample a color in an object on an InDesign page-including imported graphics and add it to your Swatches palette.

To "load" the Eyedropper tool, click the tool on an object (the object doesn't have to be selected). If you have an item selected when you click, InDesign applies the attributes of the item under the cursor to the selected item. Then click the "loaded" Eyedropper tool on an object to apply the formatting (see Figure 1-65).

Double-click the Eyedropper tool to display the Eyedropper Options dialog box. Use the settings in the three panels of this dialog box to define the attributes sampled and affected by the Eyedropper tool (see Figure 1-66).

FIGURE 1-65
Eyedropper Tool

Select an object or a series of objects and then choose the Eyedropper tool from the Tools palette.

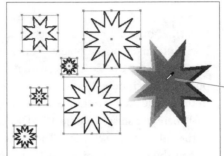

Position the Eyedropper tool over an object that has the formatting you want to apply.

To format text using the Eyedropper tool, select the text using the Type tool.

Click the Eyedropper tool. InDesign applies the formatting of the object beneath the cursor to the selected objects.

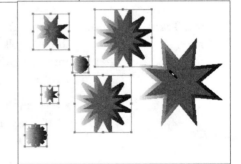

Here's another method.

Select the Eyedropper tool from the Tools palette.

Position the cursor over an object and click. InDesign loads the Eyedropper tool with the formatting attributes of the object.

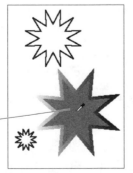

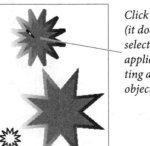

Click another object (it doesn't have to be selected). InDesign applies the formatting attributes to the object.

FIGURE 1-66
Eyedropper
Tool Options

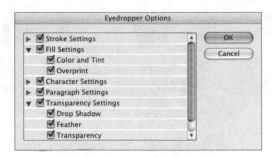

Measure Tool

The Measure tool—which is usually hidden under the Eyedropper tool—gives you a way to measure distances and angles in a layout window (see Figure 1-67).

To measure the distance between two points, select the Measure tool (press K) and drag it from one point to the other. When you drag the Measure tool, InDesign displays the Info palette. The D field in the Info palette shows the distance between the two points.

To measure an angle, select the Measure tool and drag it between two points—this creates one side of the angle. Next, hold down Option/Alt and drag from one of the end points of the line created by the Measure tool. This creates the other side of the angle. The Info palette displays the angle in the Angle field (it also displays the length of the two sides of the angle in the D1 and D2 fields).

FIGURE 1-67
Measure Tool

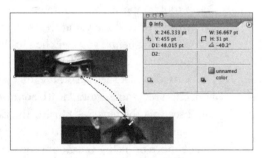

Drag the Measure tool between two points, and the Info palette will show you the distance between the points.

Gradient Tool

Use the Gradient tool to apply gradients, or to adjust gradients you've applied. When you drag the Gradient tool above an existing gradient, you're setting the location of the beginning and ending points of the gradient (see Figure 1-68). We discuss drawing gradients and blends in Chapter 5, "Drawing."

Button Tool

In Chapter 13, "Interactive PDF," we'll look at how the Button tool lets you draw buttons on your page that control sounds, movies, hyperlinks, and other rich media.

FIGURE 1-68
Gradient Tool

Once you've applied a gradient to a path, you can use the Gradient tool to change the gradient.

To edit a gradient, select an object and drag the Gradient tool.

When you stop dragging, InDesign changes the appearance of the gradient.

 The Gradient tool affects the formatting of either the fill or the stroke, depending on the state of the Fill or Stroke button.

Scissors Tool

The Scissors tool cuts paths or points. Select a path, choose the Scissors tool (or press C), and then click the path. InDesign splits the path at the point at which you clicked.

Hand Tool

The Hand tool lets you scroll around your page; we explore how best to use it in "Publication Navigation," later in this chapter. Note that double-clicking on the Hand tool sets your view to Fit Spread in Window.

Zoom Tool

Use the Zoom tool to change the magnification in a publication window. To switch to the Zoom tool, press Z (obviously, this shortcut will work a lot better if you're not editing text). To switch to the Zoom tool temporarily, hold down Command-Spacebar/Ctrl-Spacebar (when you're done using the tool, InDesign will select the tool you were using before you switched to the Zoom tool).

Once you've switched to the Zoom tool (regardless of the method you've used), click the tool on the area you want to magnify, or drag a selection rectangle around it. To zoom out, hold down Option/Alt—you'll see that the plus ("+") inside the Zoom tool changes to minus ("-")—and then click or drag to zoom out.

For more on using the Zoom tool, see "Publication Navigation," later in this chapter. Note that double-clicking on the Zoom tool jumps to 100-percent View, though pressing Command-1 is probably easier and faster.

Fill and Stroke

The Fill and Stroke buttons, or "selectors," near the bottom of the Tools palette control what part (the fill or the stroke) of the selected path or text is affected when you apply a color. To make a selector active, click it. InDesign brings the active selector to the front. Here are two very useful shortcuts:

▶ Swap colors—apply the color assigned to the fill to the stroke, or vice versa—click the swap fill and stroke icon (or press Shift-X).

▶ Press X (when you're not editing text) to switch between the Fill selector and the Stroke selector.

Beneath the Fill and Stroke buttons, you'll see two very small buttons—the Formatting Affects Container button and the Formatting Affects Text button. When you have a text frame selected with one of the selection tools, you can apply a fill or stroke to either the text frame or to the characters of text inside the text frame. Click the former button to apply the formatting to the text frame; click the latter to apply it to the text.

As your eye proceeds down the Tools palette, you'll find three more buttons—they're shortcuts for applying colors or gradients, or for removing a fill or stroke from an object. Click the Apply Color button to apply the current color (in the Color palette or Swatches palette) to the fill or stroke of the selected object. The state of the Fill and Stroke selector determines which part of the object is affected. Click the Apply Gradient button to apply the current gradient (in the Swatches palette or the Gradient palette), and click the Apply None button to remove the fill or stroke from the selected object.

As you'd expect, InDesign has shortcuts for these buttons, too.

▶ To apply the most recently used color to the current fill or stroke (which attribute is affected depends on which selector is active), press , (comma—again, this won't work when text is selected).

▶ Press . (period) to apply the current gradient.

▶ Press / (slash) to remove the fill or stroke from the selected object or objects.

For more on applying colors, see Chapter 9, "Color."

Context Menus

Context menus are menus that pop up at the location of the cursor, and change according to the location of the cursor and the object you have selected (see Figure 1-69). On the Macintosh, you summon a context menu by holding down Control as you click the mouse button. In Windows, click the right mouse button.

Context menus give you a great way to do a lot of things—from changing the formatting of the selected objects to changing your magnification. Let's face it—your attention is where the cursor is, and there's a limited amount of it. Dragging the cursor across the screen to reach a menu or button is distracting, time-consuming, and tiring.

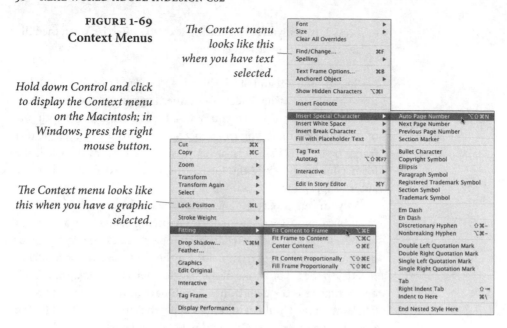

FIGURE 1-69
Context Menus

The Context menu looks like this when you have text selected.

Hold down Control and click to display the Context menu on the Macintosh; in Windows, press the right mouse button.

The Context menu looks like this when you have a graphic selected.

The only thing wrong with InDesign's context menus is that you can't add more commands to them.

In addition, some commands—such as Fit Selection In Window—appear only on the context menus.

Context menus also show the shortcut keys for the commands on the menu—a handy reminder.

Keyboard Shortcuts

We hate it when software manufacturers change the keyboard shortcuts we know and love. Especially when they change an easy-to-reach, frequently used shortcut to one that's difficult to use (PageMaker users, you know exactly what we're talking about). InDesign gives us something we'd like to see in every application—editable keyboard shortcuts. This means that we can make the program's keyboard shortcuts work the way we think they ought to.

For the most part, the keyboard shortcuts you can redefine are those that correspond to menu commands—you can't redefine some of the keyboard shortcuts that modify mouse actions.

To define or redefine a keyboard shortcut, follow these steps (see Figure 1-70 on the following page).

1. Choose Keyboard Shortcuts from the Edit menu. InDesign displays the Keyboard Shortcuts dialog box.

FIGURE 1-70
Editing Keyboard
Shortcuts

When you select an option from this pop-up menu...

...InDesign displays a list of the available commands.

When you select a command, InDesign displays the shortcut in this field.

Click the New Set button, or choose the QuarkXPress 4.0 shortcut set from the Set pop-up menu.

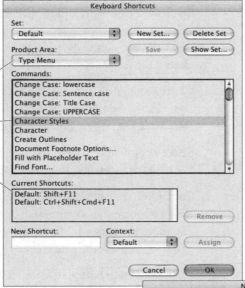

If you're creating a new set, InDesign displays the New Set dialog box. Enter a name for your set and click the OK button.

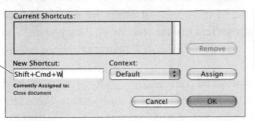

If you loaded the QuarkXPress 4.0 set, and don't want to edit any shortcuts, click the Save button, then close the dialog box.

Select an option from the Product Area pop-up menu.

Select a command.

If a keyboard shortcut is already assigned to a command, InDesign displays the name of the command here. Assigning the shortcut removes the conflicting shortcut.

Select the existing shortcut. Click the Remove button. InDesign deletes the shortcut.

Enter the new shortcut and click the Assign button.

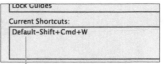

InDesign assigns the shortcut to the command.

2. To create a new shortcut set, click the New Set button. To use an existing set, choose the set's name from the Set pop-up menu (if that's all you want to do, you can skip to Step 7). To delete a set, choose the set's name and click the Delete Set button.

3. Choose an option from the Product Area pop-up menu. InDesign fills the Commands list with the available commands for the corresponding area of the program.

4. Select a command from the list. InDesign displays the current shortcut (or shortcuts) assigned to the command.

5. To remove a selected shortcut, click the Remove button. To assign a shortcut to a command, or to replace an existing short-cut, move the cursor to the New Shortcut field and press the keys you want to use for the shortcut.

6. Click the Assign button to assign a shortcut to the command, or (if you had a shortcut selected) click the Replace button to replace the selected shortcut. Note that a single command can have multiple shortcuts assigned to it. If you want, you can save your changes without closing the dialog box by pressing the Save button.

7. Once you've changed all of the shortcuts you want to change, click the OK button to close the dialog box and save the set.

Keyboard shortcut sets are saved in the Shortcut Sets folder in your InDesign folder. Want to take your keyboard shortcuts with you to another machine? Take the shortcuts file from your machine and copy it into the Shortcut Sets folder of the copy of InDesign you'll be using. Open the Keyboard Shortcuts dialog box and choose your shortcut set from the Sets pop-up menu.

To return to InDesign's default keyboard shortcuts, all you need to do is choose the Default set from the Set pop-up menu.

To view or print a complete listing of the shortcuts in a set, select the set from the Set pop-up menu, then click the Show Set button. InDesign creates a text file containing a list of the shortcuts in the set and then opens it using the default text editor on your system (SimpleText on the Macintosh, Notepad in Windows). You can print or save this file for your reference.

Setting the context. You can have the same keyboard shortcut mean different things in different contexts. For example, you might want Command-T/Ctrl-T to open the Text Frame Options dialog box when you're editing text and open the Table Options when your cursor is in a table. It's easy: Just select from the Context menu before you click the Assign button in step 6 above.

A few thoughts on making up your own shortcuts. There are two approaches to making up your own keyboard shortcuts. The first is assign shortcuts using a key that has something to do with the name of the command—like "P" for "Print." Usually, these shortcuts are easy to remember. Another, and, in our opinion, better, approach is to analyze the way you work with commands, and then take the commands you use most often and assign them shortcuts that are easy to reach with one hand (usually the left hand, given that the shortcuts for copy, cut, and paste are all located on the left side of the keyboard).

What's the most frequently used keyboard shortcut? For us, it's got to be Fit Page In Window, because we navigate by zooming in with the Zoom tool, then zooming out to the Fit Page In Window view, and then zooming in on another part of the spread. The default shortcut for the Fit Page In Window view, Command-0/Ctrl-0 doesn't work for us. It's a long reach for the left hand, and 0 (zero) is a difficult key to hit without looking at the keyboard. Consider using Command-Shift-W/Ctrl-Shift-W—it's an easy, one-handed reach.

Similarly, after years of getting used to pressing Command-M/ Ctrl-M for the Paragraph palette (and the Paragraph dialog box in MS Word), the Macintosh operating system grabbed this shortcut for it's own—now Command-M minimizes the current document window. If you use Minimize as much as we do (like, never), then you can assign the Command-M keyboard shortcut back to the Paragraph palette (it's in the Type Menu product area in the Keyboard Shortcuts dialog box). This removes the shortcut from Minimize and adds it to the Paragraph palette. Yes, you can have more than one keyboard shortcut that does the same thing!

Setting Preferences

Why do applications have Preferences dialog boxes? It's simple: there's often more than one "right" way to do something. Rather than dictatorially decide to limit users, InDesign gives you a choice. Preferences are one way you can control the appearance and behavior of the program. (Defaults are another—see "Setting Defaults," later in this chapter.) They're a place where you can customize the program to better fit your work habits and personality.

To display InDesign's Preferences dialog box, choose General from the Preferences submenu (under the InDesign menu on the Macintosh, or the File menu in Windows), or press Command-K/Ctrl-K. The Preferences dialog box contains a number of panels—each listed along the left side for you to click on. Better yet, you can press Command-Down Arrow/Ctrl-Down Arrow to go to the next panel, or Command-Up Arrow/Ctrl-Up Arrow to display the previous panel. You can even access the first ten panels by pressing Command-1/Ctrl-1, Command-2/Ctrl-2, and so on. Or you can reach any panel of the Preferences dialog box directly, using the corresponding item of the Preferences submenu.

We refer to each panel in the Preferences dialog as a separate dialog box—for example, we'll say "the General Preferences dialog box" rather than "the General panel of the Preferences dialog box."

The settings in the Preferences dialog box affect the active publication—or, if no publication is open, control the preferences settings for any new publications you create. Changes you make to the preferences of one publication do not affect other publications.

General Preferences

The General Preferences dialog box (see Figure 1-71) is the "kitchen sink" of the Preferences dialog box universe—it contains the things that didn't fit anywhere else.

Page Numbering. The options on the View pop-up menu change the way InDesign displays page numbers in the Pages palette. When you choose Absolute Numbering, InDesign numbers the pages sequentially, starting with page one, and pays no attention to the page numbering options of any of the sections in the publication. Choose Section Numbering to have InDesign display page numbers based on the page numbering options you've set up in the Section Options dialog box for each section. For more on setting up sections and numbering pages, see Chapter 2, "Page Layout."

Tool Tips. If you're having trouble remembering the names of the tools in InDesign's palettes or their associated keyboard shortcuts, choose Fast or Normal from the Tool Tips pop-up menu. When you do, InDesign displays a small window containing a tool's name when your cursor passes over the tool (see Figure 1-72). Tool tips do not work for every tool or control in every palette. Once you're familiar with InDesign, turn this option off—showing tool tips does slow down the application.

FIGURE 1-71
General Preferences

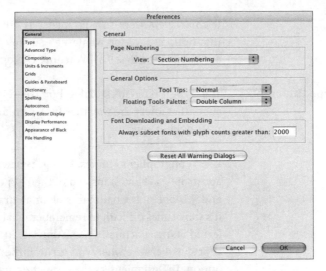

FIGURE 1-72
Tool Tips

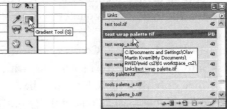

With Tool Tips on, InDesign displays information about the user interface item beneath the cursor.

Floating Tools Palette. You can choose to display the Tools palette in one of three arrangements: Single Row, Double Column, or Single Column. Choose the option you like best.

Always Subset Fonts with Glyph Counts Greater than 2000. Whew. This one takes a bit of rapid-fire explaining. When InDesign sends a font to a printer (or into an exported file), you can choose to include all of the characters in the font, or to include only those characters of the font that are used in the document. The latter option is called a font "subset" (see Chapter 7, "Importing and Exporting").

While we generally think that you should include all of the characters in a font (you never know when you might need them, and disk space/network bandwidth are both cheap these days), we have to say that some fonts are *huge.* Some OpenType fonts actually include *tens of thousands* of character glyphs. Turning this option on lets us download complete character sets of standard Western fonts without forcing us to download all of Kozuka Gothic Pro just because Ole felt the need to spell out "furi kuri" in Katakana.

フリクリ

Reset All Warning Dialogs. Many of InDesign's warning dialog boxes include a "never ask me this question again" option (if only telemarketers were so equipped!). If you have adamantly checked this option, and, for whatever reason, want to see the dialog box again, click the Reset All Warning Dialogs button.

Type Preferences

The Type Preferences dialog box (see Figure 1-73) contains preferences that affect the way that InDesign formats and displays text in your publications.

Use Typographer's Quotes. Using "typewriter" quotation marks and apostrophes (" and ') instead of their typographic equivalents (", ", ', and ') is one of the hallmarks of amateur desktop publishing design. It's sometimes difficult to remember what keys to press to get the preferred marks. Fortunately, you don't need to remember these obscure shortcuts because when you turn on the Use Typographer's Quotes option, InDesign enters the correct quotation marks for you as you type normal straight quotes.

Automatically Use Correct Optical Size. This setting only comes into play when you're working with multiple master fonts—and then only with those fonts that have a defined optical size axis (not all multiple master fonts do). If your font fits this description, feel pleased that you're among a tiny handful of people on the planet, and that turning on Automatically Use Correct Optical Size forces the font to use an optical size axis that matches the point size of the text, regardless of the optical size axis setting of the instance of the font.

FIGURE 1-73
Type Preferences

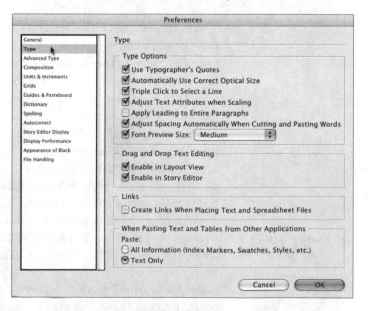

When this option is off, InDesign uses the optical size axis setting of the font instance.

Triple Click to Select a Line. When the Triple Click to Select a Line checkbox is on, triple-clicking the Type tool in text selects the line you're clicking on and quadruple-clicking selects the paragraph; when this option is off, triple-click to select a paragraph and quadruple-click to select the entire story. Since we can't agree on the "correct" setting for this option, we leave it up to you.

Adjust Text Attributes When Scaling. In earlier versions, scaling a text frame using the Transform palette, the Scale tool, or the Free Transform tool would change the appearance of the text, but would not affect its underlying point size (see Figure 1-74).

When the Adjust Text Attributes When Scaling option is on, scaling a text frame scales the point size of the text, the way almost everyone on the planet expects. When it's off, InDesign leaves the point size unchanged, but applies scaling to the entire text frame (see Chapter 9, "Transforming"). There is one benefit to turning this off: You can always reset the text frame to 100 percent size in the Control palette or Transform palette, returning the text to its original, pre-scaled size. When you turn this preference on, it's hard to get back to the original size later (you can, of course, use Undo).

FIGURE 1-74
Scaling Text Attributes (Or Not)

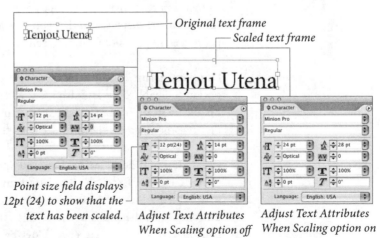

Original text frame
Scaled text frame

Point size field displays 12pt (24) to show that the text has been scaled.

Adjust Text Attributes When Scaling option off

Adjust Text Attributes When Scaling option on

Apply Leading to Entire Paragraphs. While you might, in rare instances, want to vary the leading of lines in a paragraph, you'd probably prefer to use a single leading value for all lines in a paragraph (if you're coming to InDesign from QuarkXPress, Frame-Maker, or Microsoft Word this is the behavior you expect).

By default, InDesign applies leading at the character level, which means that you might accidentally create uneven leading between lines of a paragraph. To force InDesign to use a single leading value for an entire paragraph, turn on the Apply Leading to Entire Paragraphs option. When you do this, the largest leading value in the paragraph sets the leading of the paragraph. Note that this doesn't affect any leading that you set while this preference was turned off—only leading you apply from here on out. That means you can get the best of both worlds: Leave it turned on most of the time and turn it off on the rare occasions that you want to adjust leading on a line-by-line basis (see Chapter 4, "Type").

Adjust Spacing Automatically when Cutting and Pasting Words. What should InDesign do when you paste a word into text? Should it add space before and after the word, if necessary? If you think it should, turn this option on. Note that InDesign will not insert space before sentence-ending punctuation, regardless of the state of this option. This option also controls whether InDesign removes extra spaces when you press Delete.

Font Preview Size. This option turns the font preview in the various font menus (in the Control palette, Type menu, and Character menu) on or off, and controls the size of the text used in the menus. We have to mention that turning this option off will dramatically speed up the font menu display, and that you should select typefaces based on printed examples, not from a screen.

Drag and Drop Text Editing. Turn on the Enable in Layout View option to enable drag and drop text editing in layout view; turn on Enable in Story Editor to make it work in the story editor. For more on drag and drop text editing, see Chapter 3, "Text."

Create Links When Placing Text and Spreadsheet Files. When you imported text or Excel files into InDesign 1.x and 2, InDesign always maintained a link to the original file on disk (unless you manually unlinked it in the Links palette). This caused all sorts of confusion, so Adobe made it a preference. Now, by default, imported non-picture files are *not* linked. If you want them to be linked, then turn on the Create Links When Placing Text and Spreadsheet Files option. We discuss this in more depth in Chapter 3, "Text."

When Pasting Text and Tables from Other Applications. When you switch from one application to another, copied text typically appears on the Clipboard as both RTF and plain text. RTF carries formatting with it; plain text doesn't. If you want to retain the RTF formatting when you paste text into InDesign from Microsoft Word or some other program, turn on the All Information (Index Markers, Swatches, Styles, etc.) option. To have pasted text take on the attributes of the text or text frame you're pasting it into, turn on the Text Only option.

Advanced Type Preferences

The options in the Advanced Type Preferences dialog box provide additional control over text formatting (see Figure 1-75). For more on superscripts, subscripts, and small caps, see Chapter 4, "Type."

FIGURE 1-75
Advanced Type Preferences

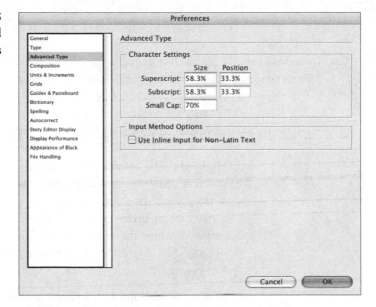

Character Settings. When you apply Superscript or Subscript to text, InDesign scales the selected characters and shifts their baseline position. (This doesn't apply to OpenType formatting.) How can you control the amount of scaling and baseline shift? That's where the options in this section come in. The Size fields are percentages of the size of the selected characters (you can enter from 1 to 200 percent); the Position fields are percentages of the leading (you can enter from –500 to 500 percent). When you apply Small Caps formatting to text, InDesign scales the selected characters by the percentage you enter in the Small Cap Size field (from one to 200 percent).

Note that these settings affect all superscript, subscript, and small caps formatting you've applied throughout your current document. (This is the way that QuarkXPress handles these formatting attributes, but it's unlike PageMaker, where superscript, subscript, and small caps formatting options are set at the character level.) For more on working with superscript, subscript, and small caps, see Chapter 4, "Type."

Use Inline Input for Non-Latin Text. When you're entering characters that are outside the range of the Western character set (like Japanese, Chinese, or Korean), you can use one of (at least) two methods to get the characters into the text frame. You can use the Input Method Editor (or IME) that comes with your operating system (usually typing characters in a separate floating window), or you can use the inline text entry method (where you type right in the text frame). We think it's much easier to type "inline," along with all the other text, so we turn on this preference.

Composition Preferences

Composition is the process of making type fit in the columns and pages in your publication. The options in the Composition Preferences dialog box (see Figure 1-76) relate to various aspects of InDesign's text composition features. To really understand how composition works, see Chapter 4, "Type."

Highlight. The options in the Highlight section help you spot composition problems before they become printed mistakes. All three options work the same way: when they spot a composition problem (a place where InDesign has had to break your rules to lay out a publication, or where InDesign lacks the font to properly compose a piece of text), they "highlight" the text by drawing a colored bar behind it (see Figure 1-77).

▶ **Keep Violations.** In the Keep Options dialog box (choose Keep Options from the Paragraph palette's menu, or press Command-Option-K/Ctrl-Alt-K), you'll see a variety of settings that determine the way a paragraph deals with column and page breaks. These settings, collectively, are called "keeps." InDesign will sometimes have to disobey your keeps settings in order to compose a publication. Keeps violations are very rare, but you can easily spot them by turning on the Keep Violations option. When you do, InDesign highlights the problem paragraphs.

▶ **H&J Violations.** When InDesign composes the text in your publications, it tries to follow the guidelines you've laid out for each paragraph (using the Justification dialog box), but, sometimes, it just can't. In those cases, InDesign applies word spacing that's looser or tighter than the minimum or maximum you've specified. This is known as an "H&J violation." When you turn on the

FIGURE 1-76
**Composition
Preferences**

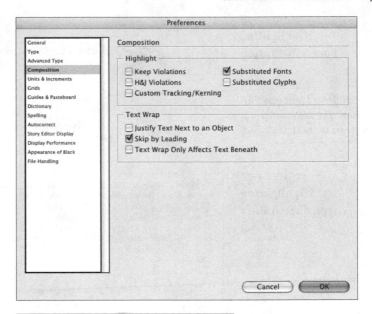

**FIGURE 1-77
Highlighting
Composition Problems**

"Scarcely had I pronounced these words when a thick, black cloud cast its veil over the firmament, and dimmed the brilliancy about us; and the hiss of rain and growling of a storm filled the air. At last my father appeared, borne on a meteor whose terrible effulgence flashed fire upon the world. 'Stay, wretched

When you turn on the H&J Violations option in the Highlight section of the Text Preferences dialog box, InDesign highlights lines of text that break the spacing rules you entered in the Justification dialog box.

H&J Violations option, InDesign highlights the problem lines by displaying a yellow bar behind the text. The intensity of the tint used to draw the bar gives you a rough indication of the severity of the "violation"—the more saturated the yellow, the greater the variation from your settings.

▶ **Substituted Fonts.** When you turn on the Substituted Fonts option, InDesign highlights text formatted using fonts you do not currently have loaded. This makes it very easy to spot that space character you accidentally formatted using Hobo before you left your office. The highlight color is pink. See Figure 1-78.

▶ **Substituted Glyphs.** InDesign has various features that replace characters in your text with other characters, such as ligatures, swashes, ordinals, and so on (most of these options are on the Character palette menu). To see the places where InDesign has applied these special characters, turn on the Substituted Glyphs option. The highlight color is purple. See Figure 1-79.

FIGURE 1-78
Highlighting Font Substitution

Font (Poetica Chancery) present

Highlighted font substitution. The substituted text appears in the default font.

Font missing

FIGURE 1-79
Highlighting Glyph Substitution

Highlighted glyph substitution

▶ **Custom Tracking/Kerning.** To see the places in your text that have had custom kerning or tracking applied to them, turn on the Custom Kerning/Tracking option. When you do this, InDesign highlights any text containing manual kerning (i.e., kerning that was not applied by one of the automatic kerning methods), or tracking values other than zero with a blue-green tint. See Figure 1-80.

Justify Text Next to an Object. When an object bearing a text wrap appears in the *middle* of a column of text, should InDesign justify the text around the wrapped object? If so, turn on Justify Text Next to an Object. Note that this option has no effect on text wraps that do not split a line into two or more parts. The authors suggest that you never create a design that would cause you to care about this option one way or the other. See Figure 1-81.

FIGURE 1-80
Highlighting Custom Tracking and Kerning

The paragraph style applied to this paragraph specifies a tracking value.

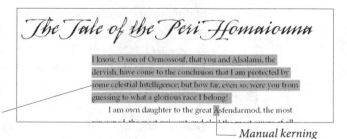

Manual kerning

FIGURE 1-81
**Justifying Text Next
to an Object**

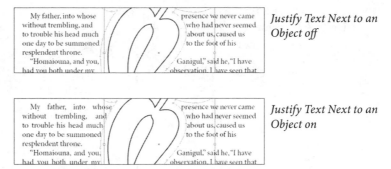

*Justify Text Next to an
Object off*

*Justify Text Next to an
Object on*

Skip by Leading. When a text wrap breaks a text column, and the text in the text column is aligned to a baseline grid, should the text continue to align to the baseline grid, or should it get as close to the text wrap boundary as possible? We like to turn Skip by Leading on to make sure the text aligns to the baseline grid. For more on this topic, see Chapter 6, "Where Text Meets Graphics."

Text Wrap Only Affects Text Beneath. Many QuarkXPress users get confused when using text wrap (runaround) in InDesign because text can wrap even when the wrapping-object is underneath the text frame (in the page's stacking order or layer order). If you don't like this behavior, you can turn on the Text Wrap Only Affects Text Beneath checkbox. There are pros and cons to both methods. For more on this topic, see Chapter 6, "Where Text Meets Graphics."

Units & Increments Preferences

We've all got favorite units of measure—Ole is partial to furlongs and stone, while David prefers cubits—so we should be able to choose the measurement system we use to lay out our pages. That's what the Units & Increments Preferences dialog box is for (see Figure 1-82).

Ruler Units. The Origin pop-up menu sets the default location of the ruler zero point. Choose Spread to have InDesign position the zero point at the upper-left corner of the spread. Choose Page, and InDesign locates the zero point at the upper-left corner of the page. If you have three or more pages in a spread, you might want to choose Spine to place the ruler zero point at the binding spine.

Use the Horizontal and Vertical pop-up menus to select the measurement units (inches, inches decimal, picas, points, millimeters, and ciceros) you want to use for the rulers. In addition to the measurement systems, you can use custom increments for either or both rulers. When you choose Custom, you can enter a value in the field attached to the pop-up menu (see "Rulers," earlier in this chapter).

FIGURE 1-82
**Units & Increments
Preferences**

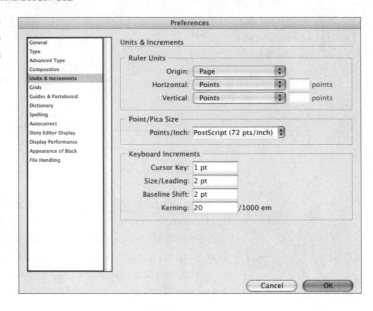

As you set up a publication's measurement units, there are two things you should keep in mind:

▶ You can use the Context menu to change ruler units—Control-click (Macintosh) or right-click on the ruler in the document window, and InDesign displays a Context menu containing the same options as you see in the Units & Increments Preferences dialog box.

▶ You can always override units of measurement in any field in any palette or dialog box in InDesign. For more on entering measurement unit overrides, see "Overriding Units of Measurement," earlier in this chapter.

Point/Pica Size. This option changes the definition of the size of a point (and, therefore, the size of a pica). The modern (i.e., post-desktop publishing) standard for the size of a point is 72 points per inch.

If using your old Compugraphic E-scale is more important to you than anything else in life, feel free to set this option to something other than PostScript (72 pts/inch). Just don't tell us about it, or insist that we should do the same.

Keyboard Increments. What happens when you push an arrow key? That depends on the settings you've entered in the following fields.

▶ **Cursor Key.** When you have an object selected using the Selection or Direct Select tool, you can move it by pressing the arrow keys. How far do you want it to move with each key press? Enter that value in this field.

▶ **Size/Leading.** When you have text selected (using the Type tool), you can increase or decrease the size and/or leading of the text by pressing keyboard shortcuts (by default, you press Command-Shift->/Ctrl-Shift-> to increase the size of the text; Command-Shift-</Ctrl-Shift-< to decrease the size; Option-Up arrow/Alt-Up arrow to increase the leading; or Option-Down arrow to decrease the leading). How much larger or smaller should the point size or leading get with each key press? Enter the amount you want in this field.

▶ **Baseline Shift.** When you have selected text using the Type tool, you can increase baseline shift by pressing (by default) Option-Shift-Up Arrow/Alt-Shift-Up Arrow, or decrease baseline shift by pressing Option-Shift-Down Arrow/Alt-Shift-Down Arrow. How much baseline shift should each key press apply? Enter the amount you want in this field.

▶ **Kerning.** When the text cursor is between two characters, you can apply kerning by pressing Option-Left Arrow/Alt-Left Arrow or Option-Right Arrow/Alt-Right Arrow. When a range of text is selected with the text tool, pressing this shortcut applies tracking. Enter the kerning amount you want to apply (in thousandths of an em) in this field.

Grids Preferences   InDesign can display two different types of grid: baseline and document. You control various aspects of their appearance using the options in this dialog box (see Figure 1-83). Both grids are very similar to the guides (ruler guides, margin guides, and column guides), and have a similar effect on items on your pages.

Baseline Grid. The baseline grid is an array of horizontal guides that mark off the page in units equal to a specified leading amount (note that the baseline grid isn't really a "grid," as it has no vertical lines).

▶ **Color.** Choose a color for the baseline grid using the Color pop-up menu.

▶ **Start.** Enter a value in the Start field to set the distance from the top of the page at which you want the baseline grid to begin.

▶ **Increment Every.** Enter a distance—in general, the leading value of your publication's body text—in the Increment Every field.

FIGURE 1-83
Grids Preferences

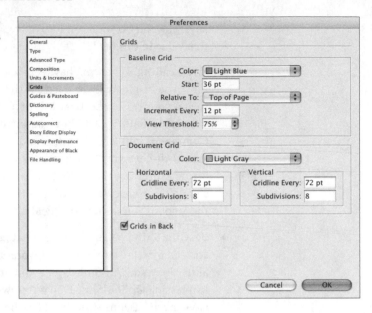

▶ **View Threshold.** Set the magnification at which the grid becomes visible in the View Threshold field.

Document Grid. The document grid is a network of horizontal and vertical guidelines spaced a specified distance apart (it's like graph paper).

▶ **Color.** Choose a color for the grid using the Color pop-up menu.

▶ **Gridline Every.** Enter the distance you want between grid lines in this field.

▶ **Subdivisions.** Just as the document grid divides the page, subdivisions divide the grid into smaller sections. The number you enter in this field sets the number of subdivisions between each grid line. If you don't want to subdivide the document grid, enter 1 in this field. InDesign displays the grid subdivision lines using a tint of the color you specified for the document grid.

Grids in Back. Turn on the Grids in Back option to make both grids appear at the bottom of the stacking order rather than on top of your page objects.

Guides and Pasteboard Preferences

Use the Guides and Pasteboard Preferences dialog box (see Figure 1-84) to set the color for displaying margin, column, bleed, and slug guides, as well as the preview color of the pasteboard. Why isn't there an option for setting the color of ruler guides? Because you don't have to use the same color for all of your ruler guides—you specify

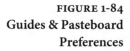

FIGURE 1-84
Guides & Pasteboard
Preferences

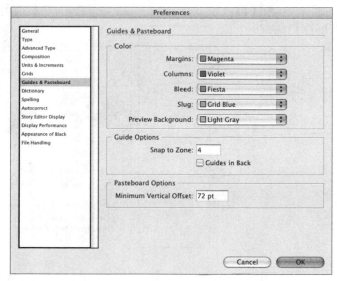

the color using the Ruler Guides dialog box. (Tip: Changing your pasteboard color to black before showing a client boosts the apparent contrast and looks cool. You could also change the preview color for each stage of a job—first draft could be pink, second draft green, and so on. But remember that any color other than neutral gray may make your page or images look like they have a slight color cast on screen; that's just the way the human eye works.)

Snap to Zone. Use the Snap to Zone option to set the distance, in screen pixels, at which guides begin to exert their mysterious pull on objects you're drawing or dragging.

Guides in Back. Turn on Guides in Back to position the guides at the bottom of the stacking order of the layer they're on. We've never figured out a good reason to turn this feature off.

Minimum Vertical Offset. The Minimum Vertical Offset field sets the distance from the top or bottom of the page to the outside edge of the pasteboard. To make your pasteboard taller, increase this value; to make it shorter, decrease the value. This is the equivalent of the old Pasteboard XTension for QuarkXPress (but without the associated bugs and troubles).

Dictionary Preferences

You can choose a language from the Dictionary pop-up menu to set the default dictionary used by the text in the publication (see Figure 1-85). Of course, you can always override this setting for one or more words by selecting a language in the Character or Control palette.

FIGURE 1-85
Dictionary Preferences

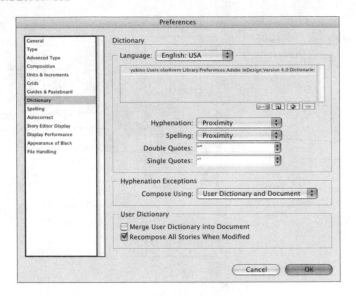

Some languages offer more than one option for hyphenation vendor and spelling vendor—if you're working with one that does, you'll see more than one choice on the corresponding pop-up menus. You can add additional dictionaries for each language by clicking the New Dictionary or Add Dictionary buttons.

Double Quotes. Enter the pair of characters you want to use for double quotes, or select them from the pop-up menu.

Single Quotes. Enter the pair of characters you want to use for single quotes, or select them from the pop-up menu.

Compose Using. When you add a word to the user dictionary (including changes you make to hyphenation points), InDesign adds the word to the user dictionary's exceptions list. Choose User Dictionary to use the exceptions list in the current user dictionary; choose Document to use the hyphenation exceptions stored in the document; or choose User Dictionary and Document to use both exception lists.

User Dictionary Options. Choose Merge User Dictionary into Document to copy the hyphenation and spelling exceptions list from the user dictionary into each document you open. Clearly, this isn't an option you want to turn on if you frequently open documents created by other people.

Choose Recompose All Stories When Modified to recompose all stories in a document when the user dictionary changes (or when you change the setting of the Compose Using pop-up menu). Recomposing all stories in a document can be a time-consuming process; most of the time, we think you should leave this option turned off.

Spelling Preferences

The options in the Spelling panel of the Preferences dialog box give you control over InDesign's spelling checker and dynamic spelling feature (see Figure 1-86).

Spelling. There's not much to the options in the Spelling section. Turn on Misspelled Words to check for spelling errors. Turn on Repeated Words to check for "the the" and other repetitions. Turn on Uncapitalized Words to check for common capitalization errors, and turn on Uncapitalized Sentences to find sentences that do not start with a capital letter.

Dynamic Spelling. Turn on the Enable Dynamic Spelling option to have InDesign mark possible spelling errors in text (this feature is vary similar to the dynamic spelling features in Word or other word processors). You can specify the colors InDesign uses to mark misspelled words, repeated words, uncapitalized words, and uncapitalized sentences using the pop-up menu associated with each type of spelling error. For more on dynamic spelling, see Chapter 3, "Text."

FIGURE 1-86
Spelling Preferences

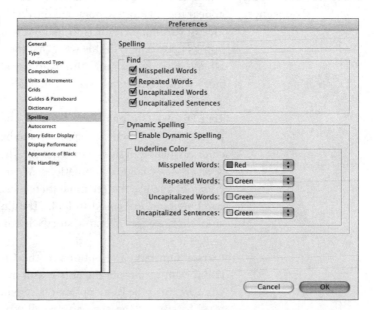

Autocorrect Preferences

InDesign's Autocorrect feature can fix misspelled words as you type. To turn the Autocorrect feature on or off, and to add or remove words from the list of misspellings and their corresponding corrections (see Figure 1-87). For more on using the Autocorrect feature, see Chapter 3, "Text."

FIGURE 1-87
Autocorrect Preferences

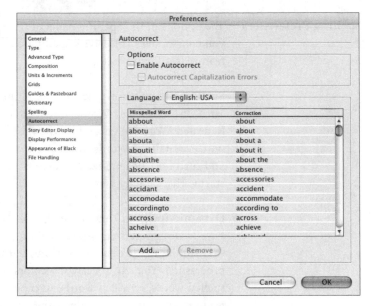

Story Editor Display Preferences

The options in the Story Editor Preferences dialog box control the appearance of Story windows in the document (see Figure 1-88). The idea of the Story Editor is to make text editing easier on your eyes, but it's up to you to decide what that means. They're your eyes, after all. We have many more things to say about the Story Editor and story windows, as you'll see in Chapter 3, "Text."

Text Display Options. The options in the Text Display Options section set the font, font size, spacing, and background and foreground colors displayed in story windows. The Theme pop-up menu contains several preset color combinations. We always choose the Data Seventy font and use the Terminal theme, because, by crikey, that's how computers are supposed to look. The Enable Anti-Aliasing option smooths the edges of text in story windows.

Cursor Options. The options in the Cursor Options section control the appearance of the cursor as it moves through text in a story window. Turn the Blink option on to make the cursor blink, or turn it off to prevent the cursor from blinking. We had actually finally

FIGURE 1-88
Story Editor Display
Preferences Dialog Box

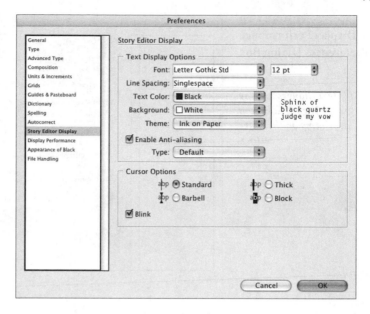

expunged the memory of the 1980s Block cursor from our minds when Story Editor brought it all back for us.

Display Performance Preferences

The options in the Display Performance Preferences dialog box control the way that InDesign draws text and graphics on your screen. The choices you make here can dramatically speed up—or slow down—drawing and redrawing the screen (see Figure 1-89).

Default View Settings. Choose an option on the Default View pop-up menu to set the default view setting for the document. Perhaps we're just middle-of-the-road guys, but we like to choose Typical.

Preserve Object-Level View Settings. The Preserve Object-Level View Settings option tells InDesign to save any display settings you've applied to images when you save the document and then reopen it. When it's turned off, InDesign forgets all the display settings. While it seems like a good idea to turn this on, it can increase the time it takes to open your documents, so we usually leave it off.

Adjust View Settings. You can apply one of three display settings—which are named "Optimized," "Typical," and "High Quality"—to any InDesign window or object, and you can define the parameters of each setting. Note that the names of these settings do not necessarily apply to the quality of the display; "High Quality" can be redefined to produce a lower quality display than "Optimized." (We urge you not to do this, as you will only drive yourself mad.)

FIGURE 1-89
Display Performance Preferences Dialog Box

This text changes to Gray Out or High Resolution, depending on the slider setting.

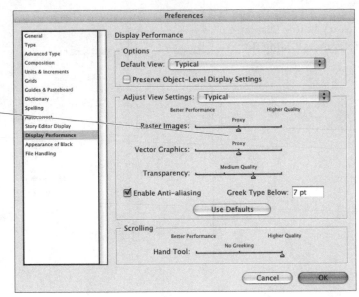

To edit the parameters of a view setting, choose the setting and then adjust the values of the options.

▶ **Raster Images.** This slider defines the method InDesign uses to draw imported bitmap images (TIFF, JPEG, GIF). Note that images saved in the EPS (including DCS) and PDF formats are considered "vector graphics." See Figure 1-90.

Choose Gray Out to draw every image as a gray box.

Choose Proxy to have InDesign construct a low-resolution screen version of the imported graphic and use that image for display at all magnification levels.

When you choose High Resolution from the Raster Images slider, InDesign gets its information about how to render an image from the original file that's linked to your publication, which means that InDesign renders the best possible display of the image for the current magnification.

This setting has no effect on the way the images print.

▶ **Vector Graphics.** Choose an option from the slider to define the method InDesign uses to display vector graphics (EPS and PDF). See Figure 1-91.

Choose Gray Out to draw every graphic as a gray box.

Choose Proxy to have InDesign construct a low-resolution screen version of the imported graphic and use that image for display at all magnification levels.

When you choose High Resolution from the Vector Graphics slider, InDesign gets its information about how to render the

FIGURE 1-90
**Raster Images
View Settings**

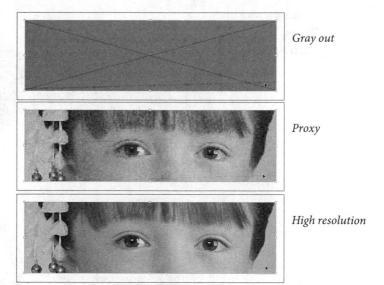

Gray out

Proxy

High resolution

FIGURE 1-91
**Vector Graphics
View Settings**

Proxy

High Resolution

graphic by reinterpreting PostScript/PDF instructions in the graphic file. InDesign then renders the best possible view of the graphic for the current screen resolution. Note, however that this process can be very time consuming.

This setting has no effect on the way the images print to a PostScript printer.

▶ **Transparency.** The Transparency slider controls the appearance of transparency on your screen—it has nothing to do with the way that transparency prints. Choose Off to omit previews for transparency altogether, or choose Low Quality, Medium Quality, or High Quality to control the accuracy of the preview (see Figure 1-92).

FIGURE 1-92
**Transparency
View Settings**

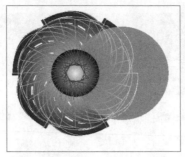

Off

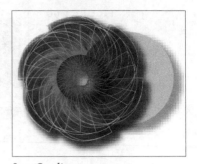

Low Quality

Medium Quality

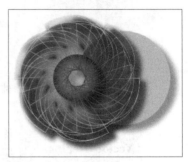

High Quality

▶ **Enable Anti-Aliasing.** Anti-aliasing smooths the edges of InDesign objects by adding pixels around the edges of the object. See Figure 1-93.

▶ **Greek Type Below.** It takes time to draw text characters, and, frankly, it's not always worth doing. You might have noticed that when you zoom out to the 12.5% page view, InDesign doggedly attempts to give the best preview it can of the (now very tiny) text on your pages. To tell InDesign not to bother, and to speed up your screen redraw, use greeking.

**FIGURE 1-93
Anti-Aliasing**

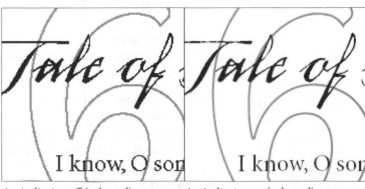

Anti-aliasing off (enlarged)   *Anti-aliasing on (enlarged)*

FIGURE 1-94
Greeking

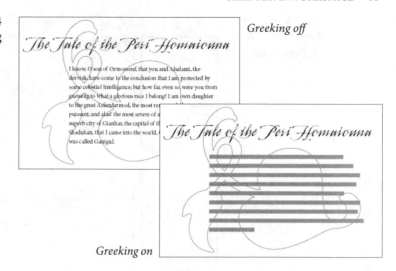

Greeking off

Greeking on

When you enter a value in the Greek Type Below field that's greater than zero, InDesign displays text characters that are equal to or smaller than that value as a gray bar (see Figure 1-94).

The value shown in the field is in points, but it doesn't refer to the point size of the text. Instead, it refers to the size of the text as it appears on your screen at the current magnification. The advantage of using this option is that the gray bar draws much faster than the actual characters. Greeking has no effect on text composition.

▶ **Use Defaults.** Click this button to return the options for the selected display setting to their default value.

Appearance of Black Preferences

What is the color "black" in your documents? Is it always 100 percent black ink (or "100K black")? Or is it sometimes a "rich black," a color made up of large percentages of other inks? The options in the Appearance of Black panel of the Preferences dialog box control the on-screen, exported, and printed appearance of both 100K black and rich black colors. The best way to understand what the settings in the Appearance of Black panel of the Preferences dialog box (see Figure 1-95) is to look at the example graphics in the dialog box (Example of 100K Black and Example of Rich Black).

On Screen. When you choose Display All Blacks Accurately, InDesign will display 100K black as a dark gray and rich black(s) as RGB black (the darkest color your monitor can represent). When you choose Display All Blacks As Rich Black, both 100K black and rich black(s) will appear as RGB black.

FIGURE 1-95
**Appearance of
Black Preferences**

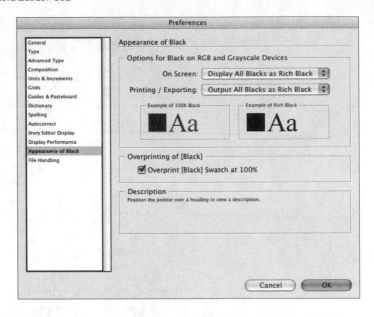

Printing/Exporting. When you choose Output All Blacks Accurately and print to a non-Postscript printer or export to an RGB file format, InDesign will print (or save) 100K black as gray and rich black(s) as RGB black. Choose Output All Blacks As Rich Black, and InDesign will print (or save) both 100K black and rich black(s) as RGB black.

Overprint [Black] Swatch at 100%. If you always want objects colored with the [Black] swatch to overprint, turn this option on. This setting overrides any changes you might make in the Print dialog box. Note that this setting only affects that swatch; it has no effect on any other black swatch (even solid black!), which will print solid black and still knock out whatever is behind it even if this option is on (see Chapter 10, "Color").

File Handling   The File Handling panel (see Figure 1-96) contains options for setting the location of InDesign's temporary files and for Version Cue, (Adobe's workflow management program).

Document Recovery Data. As you work with InDesign, the program saves information about your preference settings and keeps a record of changes you make to your document. While this makes for a lot of disk-writing activity, it also gives you InDesign's multiple undo and document recovery features.

To change the folder InDesign uses to store its temporary files, click the Choose button. InDesign displays a dialog box. Locate and select the folder you want to use and click the OK button.

FIGURE 1-96
File Handling
Preferences Dialog Box

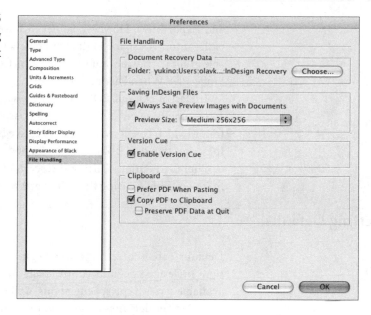

FIGURE 1-96
File Handling
Preferences Dialog Box

Why would you want to change the location? InDesign's temporary files—in particular the SavedData file, can get quite large. You might want to move them to a larger capacity drive to free disk space on your system drive, or to a faster drive to improve performance.

Save Document Preview Image. Turn this option on to save a preview image of the document with the document file. The preview slightly increases the file size. We usually leave this turned off.

Enable Version Cue. Turn this option on and restart InDesign to enable Version Cue, Adobe's project management and collaboration system for the Adobe Creative Suite. When this option is on, a Version Cue button appears in the Save As and Open dialog boxes.

Clipboard. When you copy some data out of an application and switch out of that application, the program writes data to the system Clipboard so that it can be pasted into other applications. Applications often post multiple data formats to the Clipboard in the hope that at least one of them will be readable by the application you want to paste the data into.

Some applications (notably Illustrator) can put PDF format data on the system Clipboard. InDesign can paste this data as an imported PDF graphic. Whether this is a good thing is debatable—personally, if we want an Illustrator PDF file in InDesign, we'd much rather save it to disk and import it using Place (see Chapter 7, "Importing and Exporting"). However, sometimes we want to paste Illustrator paths into InDesign as editable objects (rather than as a non-editable graphic). If you want to paste paths from Illustrator, turn off the Prefer PDF When Pasting option.

InDesign can put PDF data on the Clipboard, too. This lets you copy something out of InDesign and paste it elsewhere, such as Illustrator (which can convert the PDF into editable objects). If you want InDesign to put PDF data on the Clipboard, turn on the Copy PDF to Clipboard option. Turn on Preserve PDF Data at Quit to prevent InDesign from clearing the Clipboard when you quit.

Setting Defaults

"Defaults" are the settings you begin with when you start InDesign. InDesign's defaults control page size, fill type and stroke color, available styles, type specifications, and other details. InDesign has two kinds of defaults—application defaults and document defaults. Application defaults determine the appearance and behavior of all new publications; document defaults control the specifications of objects you create in a particular publication.

Neither document defaults nor application defaults change any existing objects or publications—you can change the defaults at any time without harming publications you've already laid out.

When you create a new InDesign publication, do you immediately add a set of colors to the Colors palette, change the default line weight, display the rulers, and add styles to the Style palette? If you do, you probably get tired of making those changes over and over again. Wouldn't it be great if you could tell InDesign to create new documents using those settings?

You can. To set InDesign's application defaults, close all publications (without closing InDesign), then, with no publication open (what we like to call the "no pub state," or, as our good friend Steve Broback would say, "Utah"), add or remove styles and colors, set type specifications, and otherwise make the changes you've been making in each new publication.

The next time you create a new InDesign publication, it'll appear with the settings you specified.

Some document properties cannot be set as application defaults—you cannot, for example, create a new layer or add master pages.

Reverting to InDesign's Original Defaults

You may occasionally want to delete your preferences and start over from scratch. For example, if you think something has become corrupted or if someone from the Paranoids Society broke into your office at night and changed your preferences in some unpleasant way. (You have to watch out for those folks; they're everywhere!)

InDesign has several preferences files, but you can delete the two important ones (InDesign SavedData and InDesign Defaults) by holding down Command-Control-Shift/Ctrl-Alt-Shift while launching InDesign. The files are reset to the factory defaults. However, this won't reset your palette positions, as their locations are saved in a different preference file (named ActiveWorkspace.xml). You can find this file (and other preferences) on the Macintosh in User>Library> Preferences>Adobe InDesign>Version 4. In Windows, simply search for the file named "InDesign SavedData," then open the folder containing the file you've found (where, exactly, it goes depends on your version of Windows and your personal settings).

Publication Navigation

InDesign offers three ways to change your view of the publication: zooming, scrolling, and moving from page to page. Zooming changes the magnification of the area inside the publication window. Scrolling changes the view of the publication in the publication window without changing the magnification.

Zooming   When you zoom in and out on a page, you are using an electronic magnifying glass, first enlarging a particular area of a page and then reducing your screen view so that you are seeing the entire page or pages at once. InDesign lets you magnify or reduce your screen view from 5 percent to 4,000 percent. (Note that if InDesign let you magnify beyond 4000 percent, you would effectively be able to see detail at a finer resolution than an imagesetter can output your document— like performing adjustments at quantum level.)

Zooming with the View menu. The View menu offers InDesign's "standard" magnifications, or views, and provides keyboard shortcuts for most of them (see Table 1-3). In fact, some of the keyboard shortcuts in the table should probably just be committed to memory, as they don't appear in the View menu—such as Command-2/Ctrl-2 to zoom to 200-percent view, and Command-Option-2/Ctrl-Alt-2 to zoom back to the last magnification you used.

All of these commands except Fit Page in Window and Fit Spread in Window center the object you've selected in the publication window. If you don't have an object selected, these shortcuts zoom in or out based on the center of the current view. Fit Page In Window

TABLE 1-3
View Shortcuts

To zoom to this view:	Press:
Actual size (100%)	Command-1/Ctrl-1
200%	Command-2/Ctrl-2
400%	Command-4/Ctrl-4
50%	Command-5/Ctrl-5
Fit Page in Window	Command-0/Ctrl-0
Fit Spread in Window	Command-Option-0/Ctrl-Alt-0
Zoom in	Command-+/Ctrl-+
Zoom out	Command-- (minus)/Ctrl--(minus)
Last zoom	Command-Option-2/Ctrl-Alt-2

centers the current page in a publication window. This makes Fit Page In Window the perfect "zoom-out" shortcut.

Fit Selection In Window. Another view command we use all of the time is Fit Selection In Window. Don't bother looking for it on the View menu—it's not there. Instead, it appears on the context menu when you have an object selected. It does just what it says—zooms (in or out) on the current selection and centers it in the publication window (see Figure 1-97). Press Command-Option-=/Ctrl-Alt-= to zoom to the Fit Selection In Window view. When text is selected, this shortcut fits the text frame containing the text in the window.

FIGURE 1-97
Fit Selection in Window

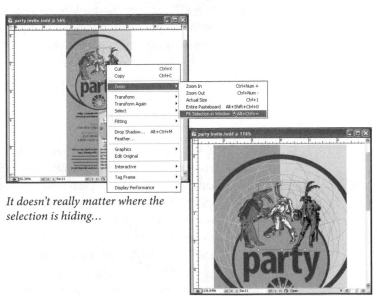

It doesn't really matter where the selection is hiding...

..."Fit Selection in Window" will find it and make it more visible.

Zooming with the Zoom tool. Another zooming method: choose the Zoom tool, point at an area in your publication, and click. InDesign zooms to the next larger view size (based on your current view—from 100% to 200%, for example), centering the area you clicked on in the publication window. Hold down Option/Alt and the plus ("+") in the Zoom tool changes to a minus ("-"). Click the Zoom tool to zoom out.

Switching to the Zoom Tool. Press Command-Spacebar/Ctrl-Spacebar to temporarily switch from any tool to the Zoom tool to zoom in; or hold down Command-Option-Spacebar/Ctrl-Alt-Spacebar to zoom out.

The Best Way to Zoom. To zoom in, press Command/Ctrl and hold down Spacebar to turn the current tool (whatever it is) into the Zoom tool, then drag the Zoom tool in the publication window. As you drag, a rectangle (like a selection rectangle) appears. Drag the rectangle around the area you want to zoom in on, and release the mouse button. InDesign zooms in on the area, magnifying it to the magnification that fits in the publication window (see Figure 1-98).

To zoom out, use one of the keyboard shortcuts—Command-0/Ctrl-0 (for Fit Page In Window) is especially handy. It's even better if you redefine the shortcut to make it easier to reach with one hand—why take your hand off of the mouse if you don't need to?

Entering a magnification percentage. To zoom to a specific magnification percentage, enter the percentage in the Magnification field

FIGURE 1-98
Drag Magnification

Hold down Command-Spacebar/Ctrl-Spacebar to switch to the Zoom tool.

Drag the Zoom tool around the area you want to magnify.

InDesign zooms in on the area you defined by dragging.

and press Return/Enter. To "jump" into the Magnification field, press Command-Option-5/Ctrl-Alt-5. InDesign zooms to the percentage you specified (centering the selection, if any, as it does so).

Scrolling

As we said earlier in this chapter, we rarely use the scroll bars to scroll. So how do we change our view of our publications? We use the Hand tool (also known as the "Grabber Hand"), or we let InDesign do the scrolling for us as we move objects.

Scrolling with the Hand tool. So how do *you* use the Hand tool? As usual, there are several ways. Sure, you can always click on the Hand tool in the Tools palette, or press H to switch to the Hand tool. If you want to drive yourself a little batty, try remembering that you can hold down the Spacebar to get the Hand tool, but only when you're *not* editing text. If you *are* editing text, the Spacebar just types a space character, so instead, hold down the Option/Alt key to switch to the Hand tool. What to do? Use the keyboard shortcut which always works, no matter what tool you have selected: Option/Alt-spacebar (see Figure 1-99).

Scrolling as you drag objects. Don't forget that you can change your view by dragging objects off the screen. If you know an object should be moved to some point outside your current view, select the object and do one of the following things:

▶ To scroll down, drag the cursor into the scroll bar at the bottom of the publication window. Don't drag the cursor off the bottom of the screen—InDesign won't scroll if you do this (for some unknown reason).

▶ To scroll to the right, move the cursor into the vertical scroll bar, or drag the cursor off of the left edge of the screen.

▶ To scroll to a point above your current view, drag the cursor into the horizontal ruler.

▶ To scroll to the left, drag the cursor into the vertical ruler (or off the screen, if the ruler is not visible).

The window scrolls as long as the mouse button is down. Sometimes it's the best way to get something into position.

InDesign won't let you drag objects to an area in the publication window that is behind a palette. If you drag the cursor into any palette other than the Library palette, InDesign displays the "prohibited" symbol. When you drop objects you're dragging into an area covered

FIGURE 1-99
Using the Hand Tool

Hold down Option-Spacebar/Alt-Spacebar to switch to the Hand tool, then drag the Hand tool to scroll.

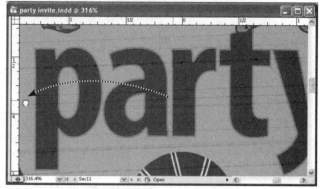

When the publication window looks the way you want it to, stop dragging.

by a palette, InDesign bounces the objects back to their original locations. You can't hide palettes while you're dragging objects, so you might want to hide the palettes before you begin dragging.

Scrolling with a Scroll Wheel. If your mouse has a scroll wheel, InDesign probably supports it (no promises—there are lots of different mice out there). Move the scroll wheel to scroll the window up and down, or hold down Option/Alt as you move the scroll wheel to scroll the window from side to side.

Jump to Page   Sure, you can use the scroll bars (or even the Hand tool) to navigate from one page to the next. But we don't recommend this unless you're being paid by the hour and need to maximize your income. Instead, you can use the page-navigation features in the Layout menu, their accompanying keyboard shortcuts, or the buttons in the lower-left corner of the document window. By now, you probably already know that we'd recommend learning the keyboard shortcuts. In fact, one of the best navigation keyboard shortcuts doesn't appear in the menu: Command-J/Ctrl-J, for Go To Page (it jumps to the page field in the lower-left corner of the window).

Because two of the page-navigation features in the Layout menu have odd names (Go Back and Go Forward) and are set apart in the menu, most people don't know what they do. That's a pity, because these are two of the coolest ways to navigate your document. InDesign is forever watching what pages you're working on and lets you return to them quickly. For example, let's say you're working on page 9 when you jump to page 25 to make a quick change and then jump to page 81 to see how the change affected the end of the story. Now you can press Command-Up Arrow/Ctrl-Up Arrow (Go Back) to jump back to page 25, and press it again to return to page 9. Want to return to page 25? Press Command-Down Arrow (Go Forward). We find this amazingly helpful.

Place Icons

When you place (that is, import) a file, InDesign changes the cursor into an icon called a "place icon," or "place gun" (see Figure 1-100). You can click the place icon to specify the position of the upper-left corner of the incoming file, or you can drag the place icon to define the width and height of the file.

▶ To "unload" a place icon without placing the file, click the place icon on any of the tools in the toolbox. Or press Command-Z/Ctrl-Z to undo the place operation.

▶ If you had a frame selected, InDesign places the file in that object. This is, in general, a very useful feature, but it can sometimes mean that imported files end up in frames you didn't want to fill with the file. When this happens to you, press Command-

FIGURE 1-100
Place Icons

Text place icon (manual flow)
Text place icon (semi-automatic flow)
Text place icon (autoflow)
Graphic place icon
Image place icon
Text place icon (in frame)
Text place icon (autoflow, in frame)
Image place icon (in frame)
Graphic place icon (in frame)

Z/Ctrl-Z (or choose Undo from the Edit menu), and InDesign will display the loaded place icon. Now you can click or drag the place icon to place the file.

We'll talk more about place icons in the next chapter, again in Chapter 3, "Text," and in Chapter 7, "Importing and Exporting."

Managing InDesign's Plug-Ins

Everything you see in InDesign is provided by a plug-in. The "application" itself is little more than a plug-in manager. The functions we traditionally think of as being central to a page layout application—things like text composition, text editing, or basic drawing tools—they're all plug-ins. We're not kidding.

This means that you can turn plug-ins on and off to customize InDesign to the way that you work and the publications you work with. Specifically, you can turn off the plug-ins you don't use.

To define the plug-ins InDesign will load the next time you start the program, choose Configure Plug-ins from the InDesign menu (on the Macintosh), or from the Help menu (in Windows). InDesign displays the Configure Plug-ins dialog box (see Figure 1-101).

Why would you want to turn plug-ins off? Simple—to reduce the amount of memory taken up by InDesign and to increase the speed of the application (slightly).

Some plug-ins are required by InDesign—they're the ones with the little padlock next to them. But all of the other plug-ins are fair game. Never use the Navigator palette? Turn it off!

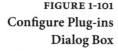

FIGURE 1-101
Configure Plug-ins
Dialog Box

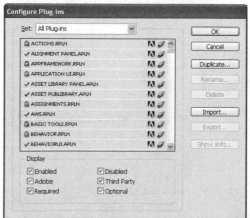

Before you add a new plug-in or set of plug-ins, save your current plug-in set. This way, if you decide you don't want to use the new plug-in, you can easily revert to the "snapshot" you've taken of your plug-in configuration. We've used this tip several times in the making of this book.

Getting Help

If you installed InDesign's online help system, you can display information on the meaning and use of specific InDesign features. Select InDesign Help from the Help menu (or press Help/F1) to open the help system (see Figure 1-102).

FIGURE 1-102

InDesign's Help System

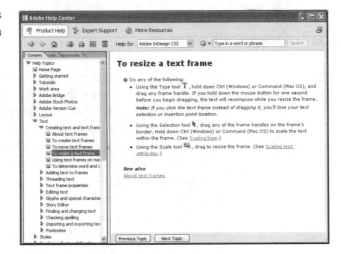

On with the Tour

At this point in the InDesign tour, we've seen most of the sights. Don't worry if you're a little confused—it's hard to take it all in at once. In the following chapters, we'll help you put the tools in context—so far, we've just talked about what the tools *are*. In the rest of the book, we'll talk about that you can *do* with them.

Page Layout

Now that you know what's what, and what's where, in InDesign, it's time to create an InDesign publication and set up some pages. As you work your way through the process of defining the page size, margins, column layout, and master pages for your new publication, think ahead. How will the publication be printed? How will it be bound? Will you need to create a different version of the publication for a different paper size (such as switching from US Letter to A4 for an international edition)? Will you need to create a different version of the publication for online distribution?

We know that having to think about these things and make design decisions early in the process can be boring. And InDesign makes it relatively easy to make changes to your layout late in the production process. Easy, but not without a certain amount of trouble. How high is your threshold of pain? Will it decrease as your deadline approaches? You decide.

Creating a New Publication

When you choose New from the File menu, InDesign displays the New Document dialog box (see Figure 2-1). You use the controls in this dialog box to set up the basic layout of the pages in your publication. Don't worry—you're not locked into anything; you can change these settings at any time, or override any of them for any page or page spread in your publication. Getting them right at this point, however, might save you a little time and trouble later on.

▶ **Number of Pages.** How many pages do you want? We tend to start with one page and add pages as we go along, but you might want to think ahead and add a bunch at once.

Note: To enter the starting page number of the document, you use section options (in the Pages palette; see "Defining Sections," later in this chapter).

FIGURE 2-1
The New Document Dialog Box

Choose a page size from this pop-up menu...

...or enter a custom page size using these fields.

Enter page margin settings in the fields in this section. Note that the margin settings of individual pages override these settings.

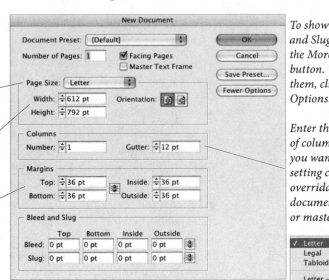

To show Bleed and Slug, click the More Options button. To hide them, click Fewer Options.

Enter the number of columns you want. This setting can be overridden on document pages or master pages.

If you turn off the Facing Pages option, the "Inside" and "Outside" fields change to read "Right" and "Left."

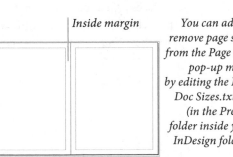

Inside margin

Outside margin

You can add or remove page sizes from the Page Size pop-up menu by editing the New Doc Sizes.txt file (in the Presets folder inside your InDesign folder).

▶ **Facing Pages.** If you're creating a single-sided document—like an advertisement, poster, or handbill—leave Facing Pages turned off. Turn it on for books and magazines, which usually have both left- (*verso*) and right-hand (*recto*) pages.

▶ **Master Text Frame.** Should InDesign create a text frame on the master page? If so, turn the Master Text Frame option on. The width and height of this "automatic" text frame are defined by the area inside the page margins; its column settings correspond to the column settings for the page.

▶ **Page Size.** Pick a page size according to the final size of your printed document (after trimming), not the paper you're print-ing on. The Page Size pop-up menu lists most of the standard sizes, but you can always enter your own page width and height (when you do this, the Page Size pop-up menu changes to "Custom"). If you often use a custom page size, see "Changing Default Page Sizes" below, for more on adding page sizes.

▶ **Columns.** When you specify that a document should have more than one column, InDesign adds column guides. Next, enter the amount of space to leave between columns in the Gutter field. Column guides can be overridden on both document pages and master pages.

▶ **Margins.** Use the fields in the Margins section of the dialog box to specify the size of the margins on all four sides of a page. When you turn on the Facing Pages option, "Left" and "Right" change to "Inside" and "Outside." You can always change your margin guides later, on a specific page or for a master page.

▶ **Bleed and Slug.** When objects can extend beyond the edge of the page and into the pasteboard, they "bleed." The objects will be clipped off at the edge of the paper when your commercial printer cuts your printed pages.

You define the bleed area outside the page edges by entering values in the Bleed fields in the New Document or Document Setup dialog box. If you can't see the Bleed fields, click the More Options button.

In addition to the bleed area, you can extend the printing area of the page by creating a "slug" area. (Here in rainy Seattle, we are very familiar with slugs.) In general, the slug behaves exactly as the bleed does—objects extending into or placed in the slug area will print even when they extend beyond the edges of the page. The slug area is usually slightly outside the bleed area, but you can set it up any way you want.

So what's the difference between the bleed and the slug? Usually, people put things in the bleed area that have to do with their design, and put job tracking and other document information in the slug area. But the real difference, from an InDesign point of view, is that they have independent printing controls. You might choose to include the slug area when printing proofs and then omit the slug when printing your final version.

To define the slug area, use the Slug fields in the Document Setup dialog box. If you can't these fields, click the More options button.

The size of the bleed, the slug, the page size, and the size of the paper (that is, the paper, film, or plate size you use when you print your final copy) all affect each other. In InDesign, the page size you define in the Document Setup dialog box should be the same as the final size of the document's page after it's been printed and trimmed by a commercial printer. You define the paper size in the Print dialog box when it's time to print your publication. When you're printing to an imagesetter, the paper size is a defined area on the imagesetter's film roll (or sheet, or plate).

If your publication's page size (without the bleed and/or slug) is the same as the paper size you've chosen in the Print Options dialog box, you can expect InDesign to neatly clip off any elements that extend beyond the edge of the page. Choose a larger paper size than your publication's page size when you want to print bleeds (choose Letter.Extra when you're printing a letter-size publication with a bleed, for example).

Document Presets

Do you find that you frequently have to change the settings in the New Document dialog box? If you have particular page sizes and margin settings that you use all of the time, consider making a document preset. The easiest way to make one is to type all the values (page size, margin, bleed and slug settings, and so on) into the New Document dialog box, click the Save Preset button, and give your preset a name.

The next time you want to create a document based on that preset, you can select the name from the Document Preset pop-up menu at the top of the New Document dialog box. You can also make, delete, or edit document presets by choosing Define from the Document Presets submenu (under the File menu). The Define Document Presets dialog box also lets you save presets to disk or load presets from disk—very helpful if you need to send a document preset to someone else in your workgroup.

By the way, for those who care about terminology, the difference between a *preset* and a *style* has to do with how InDesign behaves when you later change the preset or style. Let's say you save a Document Preset, make three new documents based on that preset, and then change the definition of the preset. InDesign doesn't change the documents you already made. Now let's say you define a paragraph style in a document, apply it to three paragraphs, and then go back and change the style definition. InDesign applies the change to all of the paragraphs formatted using that style. (We cover paragraph styles in Chapter 4, "Type.") This change in terms affects several features that existed in InDesign 2.x—"printer styles" are now "printer presets," "trap styles" are now "trap presets," and so on.

Skip the dialog box. If you a specific document preset all of the time, why in the world should you have to look at the New Document dialog box every time you create a layout? You don't. You can bypass the dialog box by holding down the Shift key while selecting the preset name from the Document Presets submenu (under the File menu). Or, instead of pressing Command-N/Ctrl-N to create a new document, press Command-Option-N/Ctrl-Alt-N. This creates a new document using the settings you used most recently.

Changing Default Page Sizes

The Page Size pop-up menu in the New Document dialog box lets you pick from among 10 common document sizes, such as Letter and A4. Don't like these default sizes? You can add your own by using a text editor (such as Windows Notepad or BBEdit) to edit the text file called New Doc Sizes.txt, which is inside the Presets folder (inside the InDesign folder). It's important to save the file as a text-only file (no formatting), or else it may cause trouble. When you're done editing, open the New Document dialog box to see the change.

Setting New Document Defaults

The Document Preset feature is great, but some people create the same kind of document day in and day out. If you're one of those folks, you should probably change the values in the default New Document dialog box (the way it first opens). You can do this by choosing Define from the Document Presets submenu (under the File menu) and editing the Default preset.

But wait, there's more! If you always want your new documents to have certain paragraph styles, character styles, and colors, create them while no documents are open. Every new document you build from then on will have these settings.

Opening Publications

You know, we've often been asked why we bother writing about the process of opening documents. Doesn't everyone know the drill by now? Nevertheless, we'll cover it because some readers might be new to computing altogether, and because InDesign offers a couple of slightly unusual options.

Choose Open from the File menu, or press Command-O/Ctrl-O, and InDesign displays the Open a File dialog box (see Figure 2-2). Locate and select the InDesign document you want to open, then click the Open button and InDesign opens the selected document in a new window.

There are two "twists" InDesign adds to the standard process. The first has mainly to do with publications you've saved as templates (also known as "stationery" on the Macintosh), or documents you want to treat as templates (later in the chapter, we'll describe templates). To open a copy of the file, turn on the Open Copy option. InDesign opens an untitled copy of the file you selected. To open a template file for editing, turn on the Open Original option.

The second twist has to do with opening files created in previous versions of InDesign. Unlike most programs, InDesign doesn't just open earlier version's files—rather, it actually converts them to InDesign CS2 files. It takes longer than you might expect (though usually not too long), and the file opens with "[Converted]" in the title bar. You can't save converted files; you have to use Save As. Perhaps this is a safety measure so you won't accidentally replace an earlier version, but it can be frustrating at times.

QuarkXPress and PageMaker Files. InDesign can also open PageMaker or QuarkXPress files. Select the file you want to convert, and then click the Open button. (To do this in Windows, choose the file type you want to open from the Files of Type pop-up menu, or choose All Documents.) InDesign converts the file and opens it as a new, untitled InDesign publication. However, before you convert a file, we strongly encourage you to open it in QuarkXPress or PageMaker, make sure the images are all linked properly and available on a local hard drive, and perform a Save As to save a clean copy of the file for conversion.

How well does this conversion process work? That depends on the publication you're trying to open, but you should never expect the conversion process to be perfect. There are simply too many differences in the capabilities of the different products.

FIGURE 2-2
**The Open a File
Dialog Box**

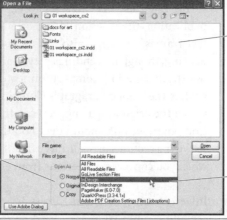

Locate and select a file.

*Choose Normal to open the
publication; choose Original
to open and edit a file you've
saved as an InDesign
template file; and choose
Copy to open a file as an
untitled publication.*

*Click the Open button to
open the publication.*

*The option you choose from
the Files of Type menu
determines which files you
see in the file list.*

*The Mac OS X standard
Open a File dialog box.*

*You can control the appearance of the files
in the view using this pop-up menu.*

*On either platform, you can
click the Use Adobe Dialog
button to display this version
of the Open a File dialog box.
Some people like it.*

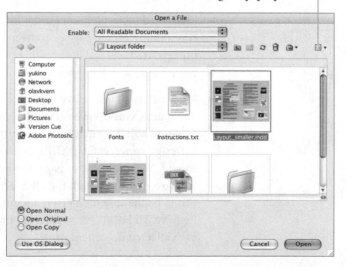

InDesign usually manages to capture the basic geometry of a publication, the position of imported graphics, and the content of text frames. InDesign also does a good job of converting text formatting, though line endings may change due to InDesign's different (we think superior) composition features. (The conversion process applies the Adobe Paragraph Composer to the text; if you want to match the original spacing, you can try changing this to Single Line Composer; we talk about how to do this in Chapter 4, "Type.") The following sections provide more detail on what you can expect to see when you convert publications from other page layout programs.

QuarkXPress Files   InDesign can open QuarkXPress 3.3-4.11 documents and templates, including multi-language QuarkXPress Passport files. This useful ability is subject to a number of terms and conditions, which we'll outline in this section. First, InDesign cannot open:

▶ QuarkXPress 5.x or 6.x files (but you can open QuarkXPress 4.x documents saved from version 5.x)

▶ QuarkXPress documents (any version) created using XTensions that require you have the XTension to open the document (the infamous Pasteboard XT, for example)

▶ QuarkXPress book or library documents

Provided the document you want to convert does not fall into one of the above accursed categories, InDesign will convert the document setup, pages, and page items into their InDesign equivalents as best it can. However, as you might expect, there are still a number of details you need to be aware of.

▶ **Misplaced Objects.** Ruler guides and page objects can shift a tiny amount on the page or pasteboard during the conversion process. It's rare, and it's usually no more than a point or two, but we have seen it happen.

▶ **Master Page items.** As we'll see later in this chapter, InDesign and QuarkXPress have very different philosophies when it comes to handling items on master pages. For the most part, InDesign converts QuarkXPress master pages and items as it should, but some master page items on document pages will get local overrides to match the QuarkXPress method. If you find this to be the case for a given document, you'll have to choose Remove All Local Overrides from the Pages palette menu for each affected document page.

► **Fancy borders.** InDesign converts most strokes (borders) without trouble, but it ignores the "fancy" border styles ("Yearbook," for example), replacing them with the Solid stroke type.

► **First Baselines.** InDesign and QuarkXPress use different methods to calculate the position of the first baseline of text in a text frame, so you can expect to see the position of the text in converted text frames move up or down on the page (depending on the settings in the First Baseline section of the Text tab of the Modify dialog box in QuarkXPress and the First Baseline section of the Text Frame Options dialog box in InDesign).

► **Special characters.** In QuarkXPress, the default size of the em space is the width of two zeros, though there is a preference to use a standard em space (where the em space equals the current size of the font). InDesign always uses the standard em space, so you may see minor differences in kerning, tracking, and so on. QuarkXPress "flex space" characters convert to standard word spaces. Some uppercase characters with accents display and print differently in InDesign than they do in QuarkXPress.

► **Superior type style.** InDesign does not have a "superior" formatting attribute. InDesign applies the superscript type style to text formatted using this attribute.

► **Kerning and Tracking Tables.** QuarkXPress lets you build custom kerning pairs and tracking tables, while InDesign does not (we're hoping this will appear in a future version). If your document uses these, text will reflow accordingly. If you really need custom kerning, we suggest using a font-editing program like FontLab to build the kerning pairs directly into the font.

► **Other Contrast images.** QuarkXPress can adjust the colors in TIFF and JPEG files using a blunt and unfriendly instrument called Other Contrast. Few people use this because Photoshop is a much better tool. However, if your QuarkXPress document does include this, it's simply ignored by InDesign. Similarly, if you've applied a special halftone screen to an image in QuarkXPress, InDesign ignores that.

► **Colors.** QuarkXPress 4.x HSB and LAB colors are converted to RGB colors; QuarkXPress 3.x HSB colors are converted to LAB colors. Although InDesign can handle QuarkXPress's multi-ink colors, it has no equivalent for Hexachrome colors, so they are converted to RGB.

▶ **OLE/Publish and Subscribe.** InDesign has no ability to handle images imported using Publish and Subscribe (which doesn't even exist in Mac OS X anymore) and Windows' OLE.

▶ **Gradients.** Most of QuarkXPress's special effect blend (gradient) types—such as Mid-Linear Blend and Diamond Blend—are ignored and replaced with a plain linear or radial gradient.

▶ **XTension Formatting.** Quark XTensions add functionality to QuarkXPress, but InDesign may not be able to replicate any formatting created or applied by an XTension—for example, custom underlines, special box types, and so on.

PageMaker Files   As you convert, or prepare to convert, publications from PageMaker to InDesign, keep the following in mind.

▶ **Pasteboard items.** Any objects on the pasteboard in a Page-Maker publication are placed on the pasteboard of the first spread in the converted publication.

▶ **Master page items.** All master page items are assigned to a layer named "Master."

▶ **Ruler guides.** All ruler guides in the PageMaker publication are converted and are placed on a new layer named "Guides."

▶ **Non-printing objects.** If you've suppressed the printing of an object in PageMaker (to do this, you select the object and choose Non-Printing from the Element menu), InDesign converts the item and sets it to non-printing.

▶ **Book list.** The book list of the PageMaker publication is not copied to the InDesign version of the publication.

▶ **Leading.** PageMaker has three leading methods: Top of Caps, Proportional, and Baseline. InDesign's leading method is most similar to PageMaker's Baseline leading method. When you convert a PageMaker publication, you can expect text in paragraphs using the other PageMaker leading methods to shift up or down on the page (usually down).

In addition, the position of the first baseline of text in an InDesign text frame is determined by the Offset pop-up menu in the First Baseline section of the Text Frame Options dialog box. By default, InDesign applies the Ascent option—which can make text in converted PageMaker publications shift vertically. If you've been using the Baseline leading method in your Page-

Maker publications (as we think you should), choose Leading from the Offset pop-up menu to restore the position of your text baselines to their original position.

▶ **Font and type style conversion.** When, during the process of converting a PageMaker publication, InDesign encounters a font change or type style change, it tries to map the PageMaker formatting into its InDesign equivalent. This isn't always possible. When you apply the font "Minion" and type style "Bold" to text in a PageMaker publication, PageMaker applies Minion Semibold—and that's what InDesign applies. When you apply the type style "Bold" to Minion Bold or Minion Black however, InDesign displays an error message and applies Minion Bold. The conversion is actually better than we'd expected, given the differences in specifying fonts in the two programs—but you'll have to closely check converted publications against your original PageMaker versions.

InDesign does not support the PageMaker type style Shadow, and formats any text using that type style as plain text. InDesign converts text formatted using the Outline type style to text formatted with a hairline (.25 point) stroke and a fill of the color "Paper." You'll also notice that the position and thickness of the bar in text using the Underline or Strikethrough type styles changes slightly in the InDesign version of the publication.

▶ **Tracking.** InDesign removes all kerning applied by PageMaker's Expert Tracking command (the tracks "Very Loose," "Loose," "Normal," "Tight," and "Very Tight"). InDesign's "tracking" is the same as PageMaker's Range Kerning feature, not PageMaker's Expert Tracking feature.

▶ **Text effects.** InDesign converts text formatted using PageMaker's goofy "Shadow" effect to plain text. Text formatted using PageMaker's "Outline" text effect is converted to text with a .25 point stroke and a fill of the color "Paper."

▶ **Long document features.** InDesign converts PageMaker index entries and topics to InDesign entries and topics. PageMaker's "See Herein" and "See Also Herein" index entires are converted to "See" or "See Also"entires. PageMaker tables of contents are converted to InDeign tables of contents.

▶ **Colors.** Colors defined using the HLS and Hexachrome color models are converted to RGB colors. Tints are converted to new colors in the Swatches palette (tints based on colors defined using the HLS or RGB model will become new RGB colors; tints based on process colors will become new process colors).

▶ **OLE/Publish and Subscribe.** Files imported into PageMaker using using (pre Mac OS X) Publish and Subscribe and Windows' OLE will be omitted.

▶ **Image control settings.** InDesign doesn't have a set of features corresponding to those found in PageMaker's Image Control dialog box, and any settings you've applied to images using these controls will be removed from the images in the converted version of the publication. Note that InDesign doesn't have a way to apply halftone screen settings to individual images.

▶ **Masks and masked objects.** If you've used an object to mask other objects in a PageMaker publication, those objects will be pasted into the masking object in the InDesign publication (you can select them using the Direct Selection tool).

▶ **Fill patterns.** PageMaker features a variety of goofy fill patterns (making possible what Edward Tufte dubbed "chartjunk") that date from the early Stone Age of desktop publishing. InDesign doesn't have a similar feature, so these anachronisms are converted to solid fills during the conversion process.

▶ **Imported graphics.** Even if an image is embedded in a PageMaker publication, InDesign requires an up-to-date link to the original version of the graphic. If InDesign can't find the original graphic, it uses the screen preview image in the PageMaker publication (if any such image exists).

If you've placed a PDF in the PageMaker publication you're converting, InDesign will always place the first page of that PDF in the InDesign version of the publication—regardless of the page you selected to place in PageMaker.

Saving Publications

To save a publication, choose Save from the File menu (or press Command-S/Ctrl-S). To save a publication under a different name, choose Save As (or press Command-Shift-S/Ctrl-Shift-S), and InDesign will display the Save File As dialog box. Use this dialog box to set a location for the new file, assign a file name, and decide whether the file should be saved as a publication file or as a template.

If you're trying to save the file in a format other than an InDesign file, use the "Export" command. For more on exporting publications or parts of publications in file formats other than InDesign's native format, see Chapter 7, "Importing and Exporting."

Save with an Extension. Windows users always save files with file-name extensions because Windows requires these in order to figure out what files are associated with which applications. InDesign publications, for example, have the four-letter .indd file name extension. InDesign templates (see below) use .indt. We want to encourage Mac OS users to use these suffixes, too. In today's multi-platform world, you just never know when your Mac OS InDesign file will need to be opened on a Windows machine. File-name extensions are ugly, but they're a fact of life.

Saving As a Template

Here's a process we've gone through many times, and we bet you have, too. Stop us if you've heard this one before. You need to base a new publication on the design of a publication you've already laid out. You want to open the older publication, then save it under a new name, and then change its content. You open the publication, replace a few elements and delete others, and edit and format text. Then you save the file.

And only then do you realize that you haven't renamed the publication, and that *you've just written over a publication you probably wanted to keep.* You can undo many stupid actions in InDesign—but an inadvertent "Save" isn't one of them.

Has this ever happened to you? If not, please accept our hearty congratulations. If so, you should know that the ability to save or open a file as a template is something that was developed for marginally competent people like us. When you try to open a file that was saved as a template, InDesign automatically opens a copy of the file. If, at that point, you try to save the file, InDesign will display the Save As dialog box. Which means you can proceed with your plan to save the publication under a new name. Remember? Your plan?

To save an InDesign publication as a template, choose Save As from the File menu. In the Save As dialog box, enter a name for the template file and then choose InDesign Template from the Format pop-up menu (on the Macintosh) or the Save As Type pop-up menu (in Windows). Click the Save button to save the template file.

You can also create a template by locking the file. On the Macintosh, select the file in the Finder, choose Get Info from the File menu (or press Command-I), and then turn on either the Locked or the Stationery checkbox in the Get Info dialog box. In Windows, right-click on the file's icon on the desktop, choose Properties, and turn on the Locked feature in the Properties dialog box.

Actually, any InDesign file can act as a template, no matter how you've saved it. When you open any publication via the Open dialog box and turn on the Open Copy option, InDesign opens it in a new, untitled publication, just as though it were a template.

Saving for InDesign CS   InDesign CS2 gives you a way to "save back" to InDesign CS, the previous version. The way it does this is not to write a file in the InDesign CS format—instead, you can export a file using the InDesign Interchange, or INX format, and then open those files in InDesign CS. To make this work, however, InDesign CS must be updated using the 3.0.1 patch dated April, 2005 (or later—it's a bit confusing, because two patches were named "3.0.1").

To do this, choose Export from the File menu, select the InDesign Interchange format, and then export the file. For more on the INX file format, see Chapter 7, "Importing and Exporting."

Do not use INX to deliver InDesign CS2 files to a printer or service bureau for final printing. We've heard many horror stories of printers who have only InDesign CS asking InDesign CS2 users to give them INX files for printing. This is not a good idea, because conversion is not perfect. Using INX to "save backwards" from InDesign CS2 to InDesign CS does a pretty good job of transferring the basic geometry of a document from one version to another, but there will be differences in the appearance of the file.

If your printer doesn't have InDesign CS2, give them a PDF file, rather than an INX file. Using a PDF is best, in any case, because it freezes the layout as it appears on your system. This means that you don't have to worry about the layout changing when it's printed.

Crash Recovery

It will happen. At some point, your computer will suddenly stop working. A wandering child, dog, or co-worker will trip over the power cord, or accidentally press the reset switch. A storm will leave your area without electrical power. Or the software we jokingly refer to as the "operating system" will fail for some unknown reason.

At this point, it's natural to assume you've lost work—and maybe that you've lost the file forever. That is, after all, the way things work in most other programs.

But it's not true for InDesign. InDesign keeps track of the changes you've made to a document—even for an untitled document you haven't yet saved. When you restart InDesign after a system or application failure, the program uses the contents of a folder named "InDesign Recovery" to reconstruct the publication or publications that were open when you crashed—even if you hadn't saved them yet. Because of this automatic "backup"system, you'll be right back where you left the program.

If you don't want to recover the most recent changes you made to a publication before a crash (which you might want to do if you felt that your changes caused the crash), delete the files in the folder. This folder appears in different places on different operating systems, so the best way to find it is to use your operating system's Search utility to find a folder called "InDesign Recovery."

You should also delete these files if InDesign is crashing on startup as it tries to read the recovery information (this is pretty rare). In this case, a file has been damaged and cannot be opened—you'll have to try opening the original document (or rebuild the document from from scratch, if you hadn't saved the file).

Setting Basic Layout Options

As we stated earlier, you can always change the margins, columns, page size, and page orientation of a publication. You change the margin and column settings using the Margins and Columns dialog box, and you can apply these changes to any page, page spread, or master page in a publication.

Changing Page Size and Orientation

Page size and page orientation affect the entire document (you can't mix page sizes and page orientations in a file), and you use the Document Setup dialog box (press Command-Option-P/Ctrl-Alt-P to display this dialog box, or choose Document Setup from the File menu) to change these settings. To change the page size, choose a new page size for the publication from the Page Size pop-up menu (or enter values in the Width and Height fields); to change the page orientation, click the orientation button corresponding to the page orientation you want.

Usually, InDesign centers the page items on the new page size—that is, each page grows equally on all four sides. However, if you have turned on the layout adjustment feature (from the Layout menu), InDesign moves objects and guides on your pages when you change the page size or page orientation, sometimes in unexpected ways. See "Adjusting Layouts," later in this chapter, for more on this topic.

Specifying Margins and Columns

You aren't stuck with the margin and column setup you specified in the New Document dialog box—you can change margin and column settings for any page, at any time. To change margin and column settings, navigate to the page you want to change, then choose Margins and Columns from the Layout menu (see Figure 2-3). Click the OK button to close the dialog box, and InDesign applies the new margin and column settings. While you can make these changes to any page, it's likely that you'll most often be making changes to master pages.

You can also create columns of unequal width by dragging the column guides on the page (see "Adjusting Column Guides," later in this chapter).

What happens to the objects on a page when you change the margin and column settings for that page? Do they reposition themselves relative to the new margins? Or do they stay put? That depends on the settings in the Layout Adjustment dialog box. See "Adjusting Layouts," later in this chapter, for more on adjusting layouts.

FIGURE 2-3
Margins and Columns
Dialog Box

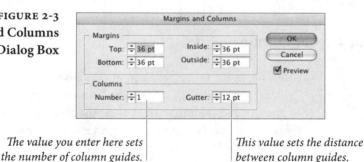

The value you enter here sets the number of column guides.

This value sets the distance between column guides.

Guides

InDesign can display three types of guides: margin guides, column guides, and ruler guides. Guides are nonprinting guidelines you can use for positioning objects on the pages and pasteboard of an InDesign publication. Margin guides appear inside the page margins for a particular page. Column guides are actually pairs of guides that move as a unit. The space between the two guides making up the column guide is the gutter, or column spacing. This built-in spacing makes these guides good for—you guessed it—setting up columns. A ruler guide is a horizontal or vertical guideline you can use as an aid to aligning or positioning page items.

You use guides to mark a position on the page or pasteboard. The most important thing about guides is not just that they give you a visual reference for aligning objects to a specific location, but that they can exert a "pull" on objects you're moving or creating. To turn on that "pull," choose Snap to Guides from the View menu. When this option is on (it's on by default), and you drag an object within a certain distance of a guide, InDesign snaps the object to the guide.

This is one of our favorite psychocybernetic illusions—as an object snaps to a guide, your nervous system tells you that your hand can feel the "snap" as you drag the mouse. Turning on Snap to Guides can't physically affect the movement of your mouse, of course, but the illusion is very useful.

When you want to drag an object freely, without having it snap to any guides it encounters on its path across the publication window, turn Snap to Guides off. Do not try to align an object to a guide while Snap to Guides is turned off, however—there aren't enough pixels available on your screen to allow you to do a good job of this at any but the highest magnifications (see Figure 2-4).

Objects do not snap to guides when guides are hidden. This includes guides that are on a hidden layer.

FIGURE 2-4
Don't Trust Your Screen

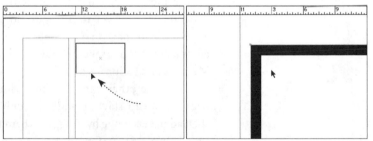

When InDesign's Snap to Guides feature is turned off, it's easy to think that you've gotten an object into perfect alignment with a guide...

...but zooming in will often show you that you've missed the guide. Turning on Snap to Guides can help.

Hiding and Displaying Guides

Tired of looking at all of the guides? To hide all guides, choose Hide Guides from the View menu (press Command-;/Ctrl-;). To display the guides again, choose Show Guides (or press the keyboard shortcut again).

Note that you can also make guides disappear by changing the view threshold associated with the guides (see Figure 2-5). For the document grid, baseline grid, margin guides, and column guides, you set the view threshold using the Preferences dialog box (see Chapter 1, "Workspace"). For individual ruler guides, use the View

FIGURE 2-5
Guide View Threshold

The View Threshold of these
ruler guides is set to 100%...

...the View Threshold
of these ruler guides is
set to the default: 5%.

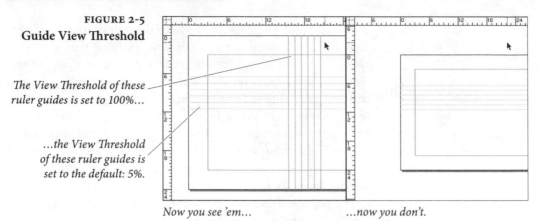

Now you see 'em...   *...now you don't.*

Threshold field in the Ruler Guides dialog box (select a guide and choose Ruler Guides from the Layout menu or the context menu).

Adjusting
Column Guides

While column guides are very similar to ruler guides, they have an important distinction: they can affect text flow. When you click the text place icon in a column created by column guides, InDesign flows the text into the column. By contract, ruler guides have no effect on text flow. For more on flowing text, see Chapter 3, "Text."

The method you use to adjust the position of column guides depends on what you're trying to do. If you're trying to divide the area inside the page margins into equal columns, select the page and enter a new value in the Number field in the Columns section of the Margins and Columns dialog box (from the Layout menu).

If, on the other hand, you're trying to get columns of unequal width, you can start by adding evenly-spaced column guides, and then adjust each one by dragging them to the left or right on the page (see Figure 2-6). You might have to unlock the column guides first; see "Locking and Unlocking Column Guides," below.

You can't adjust the distance between the column guides (the "gutter") by dragging—instead, you'll have to go to the Margins and Columns dialog box. To change the gutter width, enter a new value in the Gutter field (see Figure 2-7). When you open the Margins and Columns dialog box after you've set up a custom column guide arrangement, InDesign displays "Custom" in the Number field. Do not enter a number in this field, or InDesign will move your column guides so that they again evenly divide the space between the margins. If you change the gutter width without touching the Number field, InDesign leaves your column guides in their original positions, but changes the space inside each guide.

You should also bear in mind that text frames can, by themselves contain multiple columns of equal width, independent of the Mar-

FIGURE 2-6

FIGURE 2-6
Creating Columns of
Unequal Width

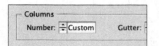

When you create columns of unequal width, InDesign displays "Custom" in the Number field of the Margins and Columns dialog box.

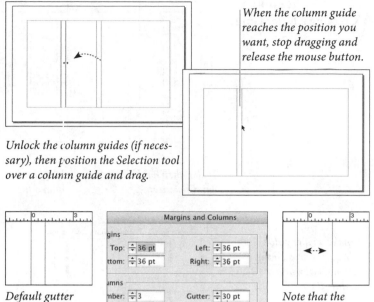

When the column guide reaches the position you want, stop dragging and release the mouse button.

Unlock the column guides (if necessary), then position the Selection tool over a column guide and drag.

FIGURE 2-7
Adjusting Gutter Width

Default gutter width of 1 pica.

Note that the gutter is resized evenly around its center point.

Choose Margins and Columns from the Layout menu, then enter a new value in the Gutter field. Click the OK button to close the dialog box.

gins and Columns setting. For more on this topic, see Chapter 3, "Text." Sometimes it's easier to work with a single multi-column text frame than with multiple single-column text frames.

Locking and Unlocking
Column Guides

One of David's biggest gripes about column guides in previous versions of InDesign was that they could not be locked. He was forever moving column guides accidentally, and so ended up avoiding them. In InDesign CS2, you can lock and unlock column guides, just as you can ruler guides. To lock the column guides, choose Lock Column Guides from the Guides and Grid submenu of the View menu; to unlock the guides, choose Unlock Column Guides.

Creating a New
Ruler Guide

To create a new ruler guide, position the cursor over one of the rulers (for a horizontal ruler guide, move the cursor to the vertical ruler; for a vertical ruler guide, use the horizontal ruler), and then click-and-drag. As you drag, InDesign creates a new ruler guide at the position of the cursor. When you've positioned the ruler guide where you want it, stop dragging. InDesign adds a ruler guide (see Figure 2-8). You can also hold down the Shift key while dragging a guide to make it snap to the nearest increment in the ruler.

FIGURE 2-8
Creating a Ruler Guide

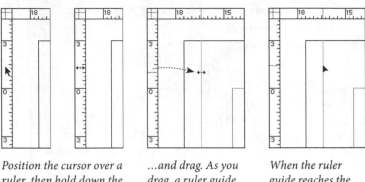

*Position the cursor over a
ruler, then hold down the
mouse button...*

*...and drag. As you
drag, a ruler guide
follows the cursor.*

*When the ruler
guide reaches the
position you want,
stop dragging.*

*To make a ruler guide snap
to the tick marks on the
ruler, hold down Shift as
you drag the ruler guide.*

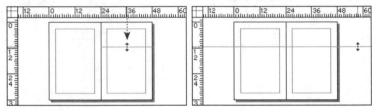

*Drag a ruler guide on a page to limit
the guide to that page...*

*...or drag the cursor outside the
spread (or hold down Command/
Ctrl) to create a guide that crosses
pages in the spread.*

Ruler guides can spread across a single page or the entire pasteboard. If you let go of the mouse button while the cursor is over the
page, you get a page guide; if the cursor is over the pasteboard, you
get a pasteboard guide. Or, you can hold down Command/Ctrl as
you drag the guide to force the guide to cross the whole pasteboard.
To adjust this type of ruler guide, drag the guide on the pasteboard or
with the Command/Ctrl key held down—if you drag it on a page or
without the modifier key, InDesign will limit the guide to that page.

You can also double-click a ruler to create a new ruler guide—
InDesign creates a guide at the point at which you clicked. While
this sounds appealing, we actually find it quite difficult to double-
click exactly where we want the guide to be; it's often more precise
to drag.

Using Create Guides   Want to add a regular grid of ruler guides to your page? Try the Create
Guides Option on the Layout menu (see Figure 2-9). The options in
the Create Guides dialog box are pretty straightforward—enter the
number of rows and columns you want, and enter the distance you
want between the rows and columns. You can also choose to create
the guides within the page margins, which is a nice touch. In addi-

FIGURE 2-9
Using Create Guides

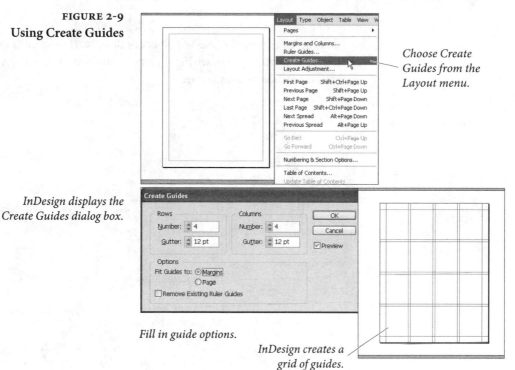

*Choose Create
Guides from the
Layout menu.*

*InDesign displays the
Create Guides dialog box.*

Fill in guide options.

*InDesign creates a
grid of guides.*

tion, you can choose to remove all existing ruler guides from the page as you create the new guides.

Disappearing Guides?

If your guides are mysteriously disappearing immediately after you draw them, you're probably in Preview mode. In Preview mode, guides appear only as long as they're selected. Once you deselect a guide, it disappears (just like all of the other nonprinting objects). Click the Normal View Mode button (or press W) to view your guides.

Snapping Guides to Objects

You can snap a guide to any control handle of an object. To do this, select the object with the Selection or Direct Selection tool, and then drag a guide out and drag the cursor on top of any side or corner handle—the guide will snap to the handle. You can even snap a guide to a point along a bézier curve.

Adding Ruler Guides Around an Object

Another way to position ruler guides around a selected objectis to use the AddGuides script—one of the scripting examples on the InDesign CD—can do this for you (Ole wrote it). Install the script (see Chapter 12, "Scripting" for installation instructions), then run it by double-clicking the script name in the Scripts palette. The script will display a dialog box you can use to set the positions of the ruler guides (see Figure 2-10). When you click the OK button, InDesign adds guides around the selected object or objects. This script is especially useful when you're setting up a publication for use with InDesign's layout adjustment features.

FIGURE 2-10
Add Guides Script

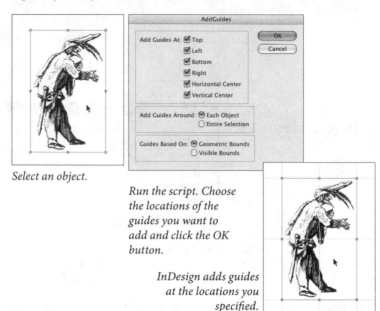

Select an object.

Run the script. Choose the locations of the guides you want to add and click the OK button.

InDesign adds guides at the locations you specified.

Selecting Ruler Guides

To select a ruler guide, click on the guide using one of the selection tools, or drag a selection rectangle over the guide. This differs from PageMaker and QuarkXPress, where you cannot select a ruler guide as you would any other object. You can select multiple ruler guides at once by dragging a selection rectangle (a *marquee*) over them or Shift-clicking on each guide. If the selection marquee touches an object, InDesign selects the object, in preference to any ruler guides touching the selection rectangle—you cannot select both ruler guides and objects in the same selection. When a ruler guide is selected, it displays in the layer color of the layer it's on.

Editing Ruler Guides

To change the location of a ruler guide, do one of the following.

▶ Drag the guide (using the Selection or Direct Selection tool).

▶ Select the ruler guide and then enter a new position in the X field (for a vertical guide) or in the Y field (for a horizontal guide) of the Transform palette or Control palette.

▶ Select the guide and press an arrow key to "nudge" the guide one direction or another.

You can also select more than one ruler guide at a time, and use the techniques above to move them, as a unit, to a new location (see Figure 2-11).

FIGURE 2-11
Moving Multiple Guides

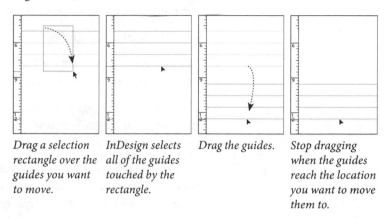

Drag a selection rectangle over the guides you want to move.

InDesign selects all of the guides touched by the rectangle.

Drag the guides.

Stop dragging when the guides reach the location you want to move them to.

Moving a Ruler Guide to a Specific Layer

You can assign a ruler guide to a layer as you would any other selected object—drag the Proxy that appears in the Layers palette up or down, then drop it on the layer to which you want to send the guide (see Figure 2-12). The guide will appear on top of other objects. (You can move the guides behind the objects on the layer by turning on the Guides in Back option in the Guides Preferences dialog box, but we can't think of any good reason to do this.)

FIGURE 2-12
Guides and Layers

These guides are on the "text" layer and are selected.

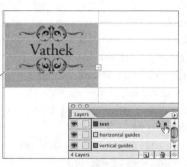

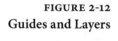

Drag the selection proxy (representing the guides) to another layer.

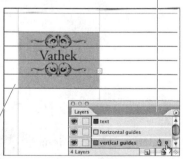

At this point, the guides appear to be in front of the text—guides always come to the front when selected.

The guides are actually behind the text, as you can see when we deselect them.

Setting Guide Options

When you create a ruler guide, InDesign applies the default guide color (which you specified in the Guides Preferences dialog box) and a default view threshold (usually 5%) to the guide, but you can change these options if you want (see Figure 2-13).

1. Select the ruler guide (or guides).

2. Choose Ruler Guides from the Layout menu or the context menu to display the Ruler Guides dialog box.

3. Choose one of InDesign's preset colors from the Color pop-up menu, or (if you're really finicky) select Custom to create a custom guide color.

4. You can also change the view threshold of the selected ruler guide by entering a new value in the View Threshold field. The percentage you enter is the percentage magnification at and above which you want the ruler guide to appear. Enter 5% to make the guide visible at all magnifications. If you change this to 100%, the guide will be visible at 100-percent view or higher (closer), but will be invisible at anything less than 100-percent view.

5. Click the OK button to close the Ruler Guides dialog box. InDesign displays the guide (or guides) in the color you chose.

Why would you want to assign different colors to guides? Guides are such useful tools that we find we use *lots* of them. Color coding guides for different tasks makes it easier for us to see what's going on. One set of guides, for example, might be used for aligning captions in one illustration; another set might be used in a different illustration. Applying colors, changing view thresholds, and assigning guides to layers helps control the way that InDesign draws the guides in the publication window.

Note that guides always take on the layer selection color of their layer when they're selected.

FIGURE 2-13
Setting Guide Options

Select a guide, then choose Ruler Guides from the context menu or the Layout menu.

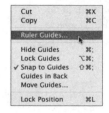

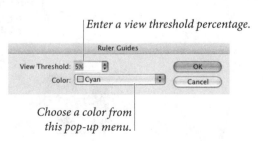

Enter a view threshold percentage.

Choose a color from this pop-up menu.

Locking Ruler Guides   To lock the position of a selected ruler guide, choose Lock Position from the Object menu (or press Command-L/Ctrl-L), or display the Context menu and choose Lock Position. Once you've locked the position of a ruler guide, you can change the color of the guide, move the guide to another layer, change its view threshold, or copy the guide, but you can't change its position.

To unlock the guide, select the guide and choose Unlock Position from the Object menu, or choose Unlock Position from the Context menu. Of course, you can also lock the position of guides by locking the layer containing the guides.

To lock all guides, press Command-Option-;/Ctrl-Alt-; (or choose Lock Guides from the Grids & Guides submenu of the View menu or the Context menu). When you do this, you're locking more than guide position—you won't be able to select a guide until you choose Unlock Guides (from the Grids & Guides submenu of the View menu or from the Context menu) or press the keyboard shortcut again.

Deleting Ruler Guides   To delete a ruler guide (or guides), select the guide (or guides) and press the Delete key. Trying to drag the guide onto a ruler or out of the publication window (the technique used in PageMaker and QuarkXPress) simply scrolls your view of the publication window. So don't bother dragging the guide; just press Delete.

Copying Ruler Guides   You can also copy selected ruler guides and paste them into other spreads or publications. When you paste, the guides appear in the positions they occupied in the original spread (that is, they're not pasted into the center of the publication window as page objects are), provided the page sizes are the same (see Figure 2-14). If the page sizes are not the same, InDesign gets as close to the original positions as it can.

FIGURE 2-14
Copying Ruler Guides

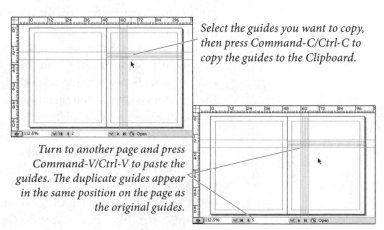

Select the guides you want to copy, then press Command-C/Ctrl-C to copy the guides to the Clipboard.

Turn to another page and press Command-V/Ctrl-V to paste the guides. The duplicate guides appear in the same position on the page as the original guides.

But wait! It gets better! You can use InDesign's Step and Repeat feature to duplicate ruler guides (see Figure 2-15). For more on Step and Repeat, see Chapter 9, "Transforming." This is a great way to create custom grids, though the Document Grid feature (see below) is even better.

FIGURE 2-15
**Duplicating
Ruler Guides**

*Select the guides you want to
duplicate, then press
Command-Shift-V/Ctrl-
Shift-V to display the Step
and Repeat dialog box.*

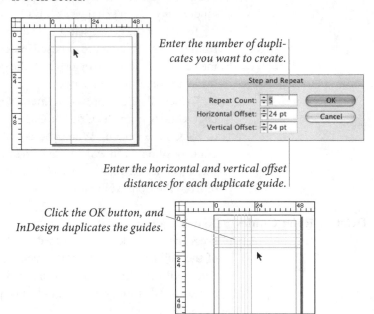

*Enter the number of dupli-
cates you want to create.*

*Enter the horizontal and vertical offset
distances for each duplicate guide.*

*Click the OK button, and
InDesign duplicates the guides.*

Grids

InDesign can display two different grids: the document grid and the baseline grid. Both grids are arrangements of guidelines spaced a specified distance apart. (Note that the baseline grid is not truly a grid, as it has no vertical guidelines.) You'll find the settings for both grids in the Grids Preferences dialog box, as described in Chapter 1, "Workspace."

To display a grid, choose the corresponding option (Show Document Grid or Show Baseline Grid) from the View menu, or from the context menu (when nothing is selected, and when a tool other than the Type tool is active). You can also hide or show the document grid by pressing Command-'/Ctrl-'.

If the magnification of the current publication window is below the view threshold of the baseline grid (again, this setting is in the Grids Preferences dialog box), you'll have to zoom in to see the grid (see Figure 2-16).

As we mentioned earlier, the grids aren't very useful without the relevant "snap." The regular Snap to Guides option (from the View

FIGURE 2-16
Setting the View
Threshold of the
Baseline Grid

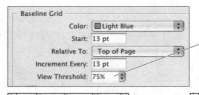

You can set the magnification at (and above) which the baseline grid becomes visible using the View Threshold field in the Grids Preferences dialog box.

 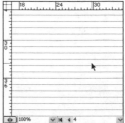

If you've chosen Show Baseline Grid from the View menu, but the baseline grid has not appeared...   *...it's because you haven't zoomed in enough to cross the view threshold. Once you do, you'll see the grid.*

menu) affects the baseline grid guides when they're visible, but not the document grid—you'll need to use the Snap to Document Grid feature (on the View menu) for that. In fact, when the Snap to Document Grid option is turned on, objects snap to the document grid even when the grid is not visible. (David likes this because the document grid is useful for aligning objects but distracting to his eye.)

Normally, only frames and lines snap to the baseline grid, but the feature's name implies that you can also snap the baselines of text to these guides—a very useful typesetting feature. We discuss working with text leading grids and the baseline grid in Chapter 4, "Type."

Pages and Spreads

We considered naming this section "The Great Pages Palette Workout," because that's what it is. You won't get far in InDesign without mastering the Pages palette, the primary tool for creating, arranging, deleting pages, and applying master pages (see Figure 2-17). It's also a great way to move around in your publication.

Selecting Pages
and Spreads

The question "what page am I working on?" seems so simple, but in InDesign it can be somewhat complex. InDesign makes a distinction between *targeting* a page or spread and *selecting* a page or spread. The distinction may be new to you:

▶ A page (or spread) is targeted if it is the page onto which the next new objects will be placed, such as objects pasted into a document.

FIGURE 2-17
Pages Palette

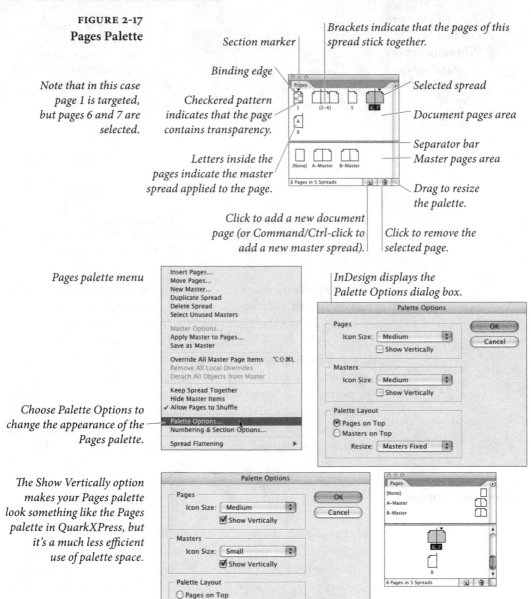

Section marker

Binding edge

Note that in this case page 1 is targeted, but pages 6 and 7 are selected.

Checkered pattern indicates that the page contains transparency.

Brackets indicate that the pages of this spread stick together.

Selected spread

Document pages area

Separator bar
Master pages area

Letters inside the pages indicate the master spread applied to the page.

Click to add a new document page (or Command/Ctrl-click to add a new master spread).

Drag to resize the palette.

Click to remove the selected page.

Pages palette menu

InDesign displays the Palette Options dialog box.

Choose Palette Options to change the appearance of the Pages palette.

The Show Vertically option makes your Pages palette look something like the Pages palette in QuarkXPress, but it's a much less efficient use of palette space.

▶ A page (or spread) is selected if the next page action—such as duplicating the spread or changing its margins—will affect that page or spread.

The target page and the selected page can be different pages—you can be viewing one page while your actions affect another. By default, the page you are looking at is the one that is targeted. But if you're zoomed back so that more than one page or spread is visible on screen, you can target *and* select any page or spread by clicking on it.

To select a page, click the page icon in the Pages palette (see Figure 2-18). To select a spread, click the spread name—the text beneath the page icons. You can also select one page in the spread, then hold down Shift and select the other page or pages, but it's slower. Note that you must select all of the pages in a spread in order to use the Spread Options option on the Pages palette menu—InDesign does not make it available when you select a single page of the spread.

To select more than a single spread at a time, select the first spread, then hold down Shift as you select the other spreads. Hold down Command/Ctrl as you click pages to select non-contiguous pages or spreads.

Double-click a page icon (or the page numbers beneath the spread) to select that page or spread, display it in the publication window, *and* target it (see Figure 2-19). Tip: You can hold down Option/Alt as you double-click a page icon, and InDesign changes the page view to the Fit Page in Window view.

This goes for master pages, too. For example, while looking at your document pages, you can select a master page in the Pages palette (click on it once), open the Margins and Columns dialog box (from the Layout menu) and make changes. The changes are applied to the master page, which then ripple through to the document pages that you see on screen.

FIGURE 2-18
Selecting Pages and Spreads

Click a page icon to select the page.

Click the label of a spread (the name or page numbers beneath the spread icon) to select the spread.

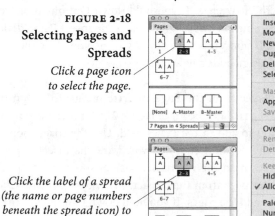

When you select a page (rather than a spread), InDesign changes the options on the Pages palette menu, making some commands unavailable.

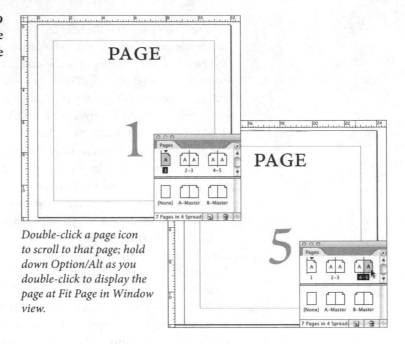

*Double-click a page icon
to scroll to that page; hold
down Option/Alt as you
double-click to display the
page at Fit Page in Window
view.*

Adding Pages

To add a page to your publication, do any of the following.

Click the Add Page button. InDesign adds a page to the publication and displays the new page in the publication window (see Figure 2-20). At the same time, InDesign applies the most recently applied master page to the new page. If you hold down Option/Alt as you click the Add Page button, InDesign displays the Insert Pages dialog box (see below). If you press Command/Ctrl as you click the Add Page button, InDesign adds a new master page.

Choose Insert Pages from the Pages palette menu. InDesign displays the Insert Pages dialog box (see Figure 2-21). Enter the number of pages you want to add in the Pages field. Use the Insert pop-up menu to select the position at which you want the inserted pages to appear. If you want to apply a master page or spread to the pages, choose that master page from the Master Page pop-up menu. Click the OK button to add the pages. If you hold down Option/Alt, InDesign turns the Cancel button into the Reset button. Click the Reset button, and the controls will be set back to the state they were in when you opened the dialog box.

FIGURE 2-20
The Add Page Button

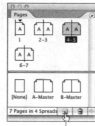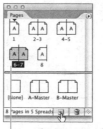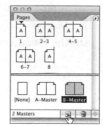

Click the Add Page button...

...and InDesign adds pages after the selected page or spread.

Hold down Command/ Ctrl as you click to add a new master spread.

FIGURE 2-21
Using the Insert Pages Dialog Box

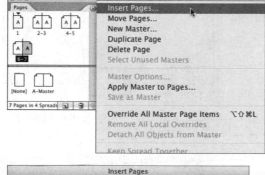

Choose Insert Pages from the Pages palette menu.

Enter the number of pages you want to add.

Use these controls to tell InDesign where you want to add the pages.

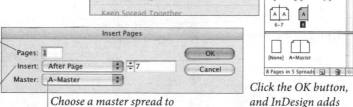

Choose a master spread to apply to the new pages.

Click the OK button, and InDesign adds pages to the document.

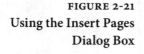

Drag a master spread icon into the document pages area of the Pages palette. This creates a new document page or page spread and applies the master page to it (see Figure 2-22). To create a page without applying a master page to it, drag and drop the None master page in the document pages area.

Hold down Option/Alt as you drag a page or page spread icon. Just as you can copy an object on a page by Option/Alt-dragging it on the page, you can duplicate document or master pages by Option/Alt-dragging them in the Pages palette (see Figure 2-23).

Choose Duplicate Spread from the Pages palette's menu. This duplicates the selected spread (including any page objects on the spread's pages) and adds it to the current section (see Figure 2-24).

FIGURE 2-22
Drag a Master Spread into the Document Pages Area

Select a master spread icon.

Drag the master spread out of the masters area and into the document pages area.

Drop the master spread icon. InDesign adds a new spread.

FIGURE 2-23
Drag and Drop Duplication

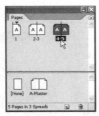 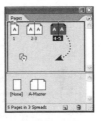 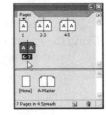

Select a page or spread icon.

Hold down Option/ Alt and drag.

Drop the icon where you want to add the page (or spread).

FIGURE 2-24
Duplicating a Spread

Select a spread icon (not an individual page icon).

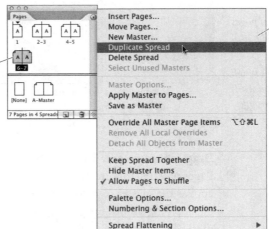

Choose Duplicate Spread from the Pages palette menu.

InDesign duplicates the spread.

Arranging Pages

Ordinarily, the pages in your publication are arranged into spreads according to the state of the Facing Pages option in the New Document and Document Setup dialog boxes. If you've turned the Facing Pages option on, InDesign arranges the majority of pages into two-page spreads (the first page is a single page spread). If the Facing Pages option is off, InDesign makes each page in the publication into a single page spread.

But you're not limited to these arrangements of pages and spreads. At any point, in any section of your publication, you can create a spread—also called an "island spread"—containing anything from one to ten pages.

An island spread pays no attention to the default arrangement of pages, but follows its own whim. It doesn't matter what you do—you can add or remove pages that precede the island spread in a section, and the island spread will remain unchanged.

To create an island spread, select a spread and then choose Keep Spread Together from the Pages palette menu. InDesign displays brackets around the name of the spread to indicate that it's an island spread (see Figure 2-25). Selecting more than a single spread before you choose Keep Spread Together converts all of the spreads to separate island spreads; it does not join them into a single island spread.

When you drag a page or spread into an island spread, InDesign adds the pages of the spread to the island spread. When you drag a page out of an island spread, InDesign does not set the page as an island spread (that is, the pages of the island spread do not inherit the spread's "island" quality).

FIGURE 2-25
Creating an "Island Spread"

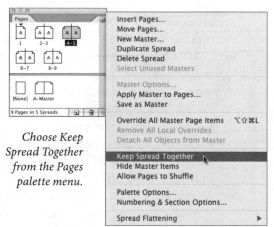

Select a spread in the Pages palette.

Choose Keep Spread Together from the Pages palette menu.

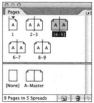

InDesign converts the spread to an island spread.

Brackets around the spread's label indicate that the spread is an island spread.

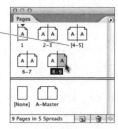

To add a page to an island spread, select a page icon...

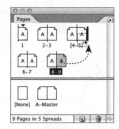

...and drag it into or adjacent to the island spread.

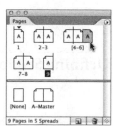

InDesign adds the page to the island spread.

Shuffling Pages   Usually, when you drag pages around in the Pages palette, InDesign shuffles all the pages around to accommodate the change. That is, if you add a page in a facing pages document between pages 3 and 4, the left-hand page 4 gets shuffled over to become a right-hand page 5, which pushes page 5 over, and so on. However, you can cause all kinds of curious mayhem if you turn off the Allow Pages to Shuffle feature in the Pages palette menu. When this is off, InDesign won't shuffle the pages; rather it just moves and adds pages. For example, in the scenario above, the new page would be added to the spread of either pages 2 and 3, or the spread of 4 and 5 (creating a pseudo-island three-page spread).

Which spread gets the page is subtle: As you drag a page between two spreads in the Pages palette, you'll see a dark vertical line. If you move the cursor a little closer to the spread on the left, the dark line will jog to the left a pixel or two. Move the cursor to the right, and the line jogs to the right. That's the only indication as to which spread (the one to the left or to the right) the page will be added.

Perhaps you want the first page of your facing-pages publication to begin on a left-hand page? Turn off Allow Pages to Shuffle, then drag the first page to the left until you see a tiny black arrow pointing to the left. There may only be a single screen pixel on which this happens, so watch closely. When you let go, the page moves over.

Here's one more time you might want to turn off the Allow Pages to Shuffle feature: If you have a facing pages document and you want to bleed an object into the inside of a spread (that is, the object looks like it's bleeding into the binding), you'll need to separate the left- and right-pages in the spread. Turn off Allow Pages to Shuffle, then drag one of the pages away from the spread until you see a dark vertical bar. When you let go, the pages will be separated. Of course, if you're going to bleed into the binding, you first need to make sure your printer and their imposition software can handle this correctly.

While dragging pages around the Pages palette can be fun, it's often faster and more precise to choose Move Pages from the Pages submenu (under the Layout menu) or from the Pages palette menu

Defining Sections

Sections are ranges of pages that have unique properties—for instance, they often have a different page numbering style. Using sections, you can combine front matter numbered using lowercase roman numerals starting with page one (or *i*) and regular pages numbered using Arabic numerals and also beginning with page one (1). Another example would be a magazine layout containing a special advertising section that has a page numbering system that differs from that used in the rest of the magazine. A third example: A book or catalog that has consistent page numbering throughout, but has different headers listed along the top of the page in different sections.

InDesign's sections features makes setting up these sorts of variations easy. You can have multiple sections in an InDesign publication, and each section can have its own starting page number, page numbering system, and page numbering prefix. By default, every InDesign file has one section already, beginning on the first page.

To define a new section, follow these steps (see Figure 2-26).

1. Select the page icon in the Pages palette that represents the first spread in the section.

2. Choose Numbering & Section Options from the palette's menu. InDesign displays the Numbering & Section Options dialog box.

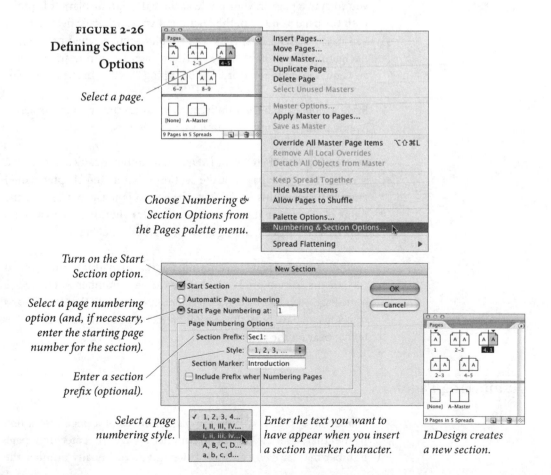

FIGURE 2-26
Defining Section Options

Select a page.

Choose Numbering & Section Options from the Pages palette menu.

Turn on the Start Section option.

Select a page numbering option (and, if necessary, enter the starting page number for the section).

Enter a section prefix (optional).

Select a page numbering style.

Enter the text you want to have appear when you insert a section marker character.

InDesign creates a new section.

3. Make sure the Section Start checkbox is on, and then use the controls in the New Section dialog box (see descriptions below) to specify the page numbering options of your new section, then click OK. InDesign adds a little black triangle above the page icon in the Pages palette to indicate a section start.

When you want to edit a section, you can repeat the process above or just double-click the black triangle icon in the Pages palette.

Page Numbering. If you want InDesign to continue the page numbering from the previous section, choose the Automatic Page Numbering option. Otherwise, turn on the Start Page Numbering At option and enter a starting page number in the associated field.

Section Prefix. If you want, you can enter a label for the section in the Section Prefix field (you can enter up to eight characters). When you turn to a page in your publication, InDesign displays this prefix with the page number in the document window's Page field. Or, you can use the prefix to specify a particular section when printing or navigating. If you have three sections, each beginning with page 1, you could jump to the third one by typing "Sec3:1" in the Page field.

Style. Choose the page numbering style you want (roman numerals, Arabic numerals, or upper- or lower-case letters).

Section Marker. If you want InDesign to automatically enter text on some or all of the pages of the section (such as the chapter name), enter that text in this field. Most of the time, you use this field for the name of the section itself—but you can enter anything (up to around 100 characters). See "Adding Section Marker Text," below.

Include Prefix when Numbering Pages. Turn this option on to include the section prefix text before the page number wherever the Auto Page Number special character appears. Note that this means that you can have both the section prefix text and the section marker text appear on the page.

Numbering Pages

While you can always type the page number of a page into a text frame, there's an easier way to number a page. By entering a page number marker, you can have InDesign automatically number the page for you. If you move the page, or change the page numbering for the section containing the page, InDesign updates the page number.

To enter a page number marker, click the Type tool in a text frame and do one of the following:

▶ Display the Context menu, then choose Auto Page Number from the Insert Special Character submenu.

▶ Choose Auto Page Number from the Insert Special Character submenu of the Type menu.

▶ Press Command-Shift-Option-N/Ctrl-Shift-Alt-N.

If you're on a master page, you'll see the master page prefix (if you're on master page "A," for example, you'll see an "A"); if you're on a document page, you'll see the page number itself (see Figure 2-27).

FIGURE 2-27
Inserting Page Numbers

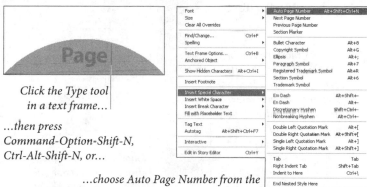

Click the Type tool in a text frame...

...then press Command-Option-Shift-N, Ctrl-Alt-Shift-N, or...

...choose Auto Page Number from the Insert Special Character submenu of the Context menu.

InDesign inserts a page number marker at the location of the text cursor.

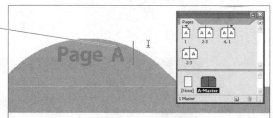

If the text frame is on a master spread, you'll see a letter corresponding to the prefix of the master spread.

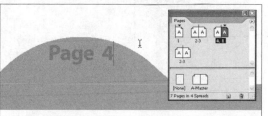

On the document pages, InDesign displays the page number.

Adding Section Marker Text

To have InDesign automatically enter the section marker text in a story, click the Type tool in a text frame and choose Section Name from the Insert Special Characters submenu (under the Type menu or the context menu). InDesign inserts the text you entered in the Section Marker field of the Numbering & Section Options dialog box (see Figure 2-28). If you're on a master page, however, you'll just see the word "Section." Later, when you change the contents of the Section Marker field, InDesign changes the text on the document pages.

David recently completed a book in which each file contained 10 or 20 sections. At first, he though he would have to create over 10

FIGURE 2-28
Inserting Section Marker Text

Click the Type tool in a text frame. (In this example, we've added a section marker to a text frame at the edge of the page; we then rotated the text frame 90 degrees.)

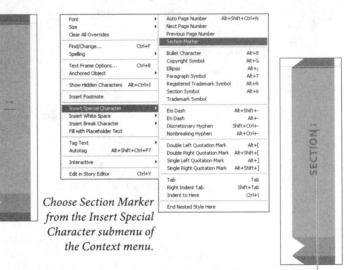

Choose Section Marker from the Insert Special Character submenu of the Context menu.

If you're on a master page, you'll see the word "Section" where you entered the section marker.

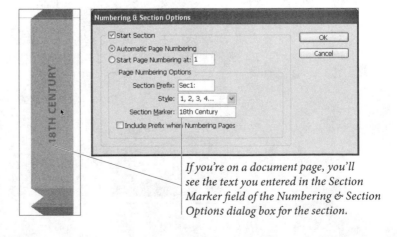

If you're on a document page, you'll see the text you entered in the Section Marker field of the Numbering & Section Options dialog box for the section.

master pages for each document—each one identical except for the running head that indicates the section name. Using section marker text, however, he found he could insert a Section marker on a single master page and then simply update the Section field (in the Section & Numbering dialog box) for each section.

Most of the time, you'll probably want to enter automatic page number and section marker characters on your master pages—but you can also enter them on document pages.

Working with Master Spreads

Master spreads (also called master pages) are the background on which you lay out your publication's pages. When you assign a master spread to a document page, InDesign applies the margin and column settings of the master spread to the page. Any page items on the master spread also appear on the document page, on the layers they occupy on the master spread. Master page items cannot be edited on document pages unless you choose to override the items from the master pages (see "Overriding Master Items").

You lay out master spreads using the same techniques you use to lay out document pages. Repeating page elements, such as page numbers, headers and footers, and background images, are all great candidates for master spread page items. In addition, you can place empty text and graphic frames on a master spread to provide a text layout template for document pages.

Creating Master Spreads

To create a new master spread, use any of the following techniques:

► Hold down Command/Ctrl as you click the Add Page button at the bottom of the Pages palette. InDesign adds a new master spread to the publication (see Figure 2-29). You can display the New Master dialog box by holding down Command-Option/Ctrl-Alt while you click.

► Choose New Master from the Pages palette menu. InDesign displays the New Master dialog box (see Figure 2-30).

► Drag a spread from the document pages section of the Pages palette into the master pages section (see Figure 2-31). If you've already laid out a document page using the layout you'd like to use as a master page, this is the easiest way to transfer that layout to a master page. This is called "creating a master spread by example." When you do this, InDesign creates a new master

FIGURE 2-29
Command/Ctrl-Click the Add Page Button to Create a Master Spread

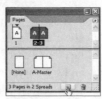 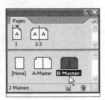

Hold down Command/Ctrl and click the Add Page button.

InDesign adds a new master spread. This new master spread is not based on the selected master spread.

FIGURE 2-30
Choose New Master to Create a Master Spread

Choose New Master from the Pages palette menu.

InDesign displays the New Master dialog box.
Enter a prefix for the master spread.

Enter a name for the master spread, if you want.

Choose an existing master spread from this pop-up menu to base the new master spread on that spread.

Enter the number of pages in the master spread.

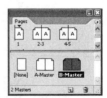

Click the OK button, and InDesign creates a new master spread.

FIGURE 2-31
Basing a Master Spread on a Document Spread

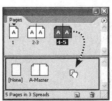 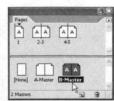

Drag the page spread into the master spreads area of the Pages palette.

InDesign creates a new master spread with the same margins, guides, and page objects.

page with the margins, column guides, ruler guides, and content of that document page. The new master spread is based on the master spread applied to the example document pages (see "Basing One Master Spread on Another").

▶ Hold down Option/Alt as you drag and drop an existing master spread icon in the master pages area of the Pages palette. InDesign creates a copy of the master spread (see Figure 2-32).

▶ Choose Duplicate Master Spread from the Pages palette menu. This has the same effect as the above method (see Figure 2-33).

FIGURE 2-32
One Way to Duplicate a Master Spread

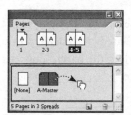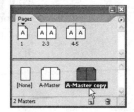

Hold down Option/Alt key as you drag a master spread.

InDesign creates a copy of the master spread.

FIGURE 2-33
Another Way to Duplicate a Master Spread

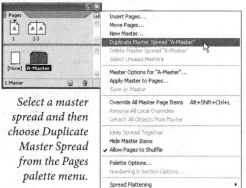

Select a master spread and then choose Duplicate Master Spread from the Pages palette menu.

InDesign creates a new master spread with the margins, guides, and objects of the selected master spread.

Basing One Master Spread on Another

Imagine that you produce a catalog, and that, over the course of a year, you produce seasonal issues of the catalog. The basic design elements—the section, margins, columns, and page numbering—remain the same throughout the year, but the colors used, and the page footers change with each issue. Do you have to create a new set of master spreads for each issue? Not when you have InDesign's ability to base a master spread on another master spread, you don't.

When you base a new master spread on an existing master spread, the new master *inherits* the properties of the existing master spread. This is part of the reason that we refer to the relationship between the original style and the new style as a "parent/child" relationship. Once you've applied a master spread to another master spread, you can add to it or work with (override) page elements on the pages of the "child" spread, just as you can from any document page (see "Overriding Master Items," below).

Here's how inheritance works: When you change any of the attributes defined by the "parent" spread, those changes appear in the "child" spread. When the attributes between a "child" spread and its "parent" spread differ, those attributes are controlled by the definition found in the "child" spread. Take a look at the (somewhat overwrought) example in Figure 2-34 on the next page, and you'll see what we mean.

You can base one master page on another by picking a master page from the Based on Master pop-up menu in the New Master dialog box. Or drag the parent master on top of the child master in the Pages palette.

Applying Master Pages and Master Spreads

To apply a master page or master spread to a document page (or even to another master page), do one of the following.

▶ Drag and drop the master page spread icon or master page icon on a page icon. Usually, this just affects a single page, but if you move the cursor carefully around the icons until a thick black line appears around the whole spread, the master page is applied to all pages in the spread. This is a slow and tedious process which you'll perform once and then never do again.

▶ Select a master page in the Pages palette and then choose Apply Master to Pages from the Pages palette menu (see Figure 2-35). Enter the page, or pages, to which you want to apply the master spread. To enter non-contiguous pages, enter commas between the page numbers ("1, 3, 10, 12, 22"), or enter page ranges ("55-73"), or mix ranges and individual pages ("1, 3, 7-13, 44"). This is a reasonably speedy method if you know exactly what pages you want to change.

▶ Select the page or pages to which you want to apply the master page in the Pages palette, and then Option/Alt-click on the master page. Remember that you can Shift-click to select contiguous pages or Command/Ctrl-click to select noncontiguous pages. This is the fastest method, period.

FIGURE 2-34
Basing One Master Spread on Another

TimeTravelTickets offers time travel to great performances in history. Their catalog is divided into sections based on the century of the performance, each section is divided into the categories "Theatre," "Music," and "Dance." We've set up master spreads to reflect the organization of the catalog.

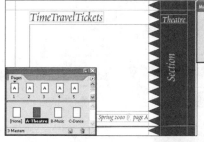
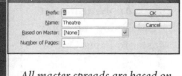

All master spreads are based on master spread "A" (which we'll apply to all of the pages in the "Theatre" category).

Master spread "A" applied to a document page.

Enter the text of the bleed tab.

Master spread "B" uses a different color scheme and replaces the word "Theatre" with "Music," but is otherwise identical to master spread "A."

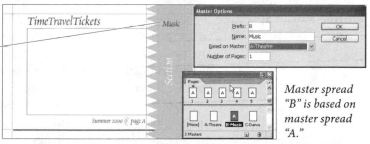

Master spread "B" is based on master spread "A."

Here's an example of master spread "B" in another section (note the differing section text).

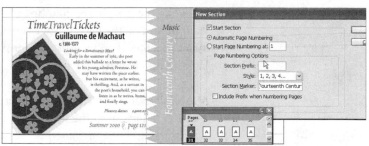

Ready to update the catalog? Enter a new season and year in the page footer of the "parent" master spread...

See how easy it was to update all of the catalog's master spreads for a new season? While a layout like this takes time to set up initially, it can save you lots of time and trouble in the long run.

...and that change will be reflected in all of the "child" master spreads.

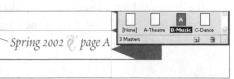

FIGURE 2-35
Applying Master
Spreads Using the Apply
Master to Pages Option

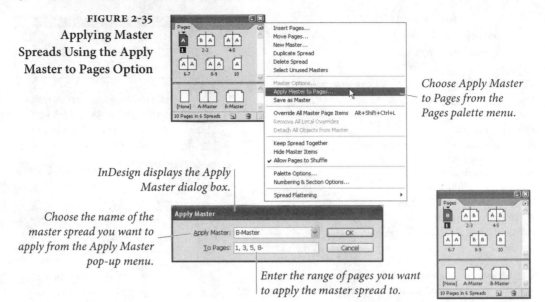

*Choose Apply Master
to Pages from the
Pages palette menu.*

*InDesign displays the Apply
Master dialog box.*

*Choose the name of the
master spread you want to
apply from the Apply Master
pop-up menu.*

*Enter the range of pages you want
to apply the master spread to.*

Editing Master Spreads

To edit the items on a master spread, display the master spread. There are several ways to do this, but the two easiest methods are either to double-click the master spread's label in the Pages palette or press Command/Ctrl-J (to jump to the Page field), type the prefix (like "B" for the "B-Master") and press Enter.

Once you're viewing a master page, you can edit the master spread's margins guides, ruler guides, and page items just as you would any items and attributes of a document spread. If you're changing the margins or columns of a master page, you'll probably want to turn on the Layout Adjustment feature so that your changes affect page items on your document pages (see "Adjusting Layouts," later in this chapter).

Master Options. You can also select a master page and then choose Master Options from the Pages palette menu to change the master page's prefix, name, or based-on status. Shortcut: double-click on the master page (to view it) and then Option/Alt-click on the master page's label in the Pages palette to open the same dialog box.

**Deleting
Master Spreads**

To remove a master spread from a publication, choose the master spread in the Pages palette, then choose Delete Master Spread from the Pages palette menu. You can also drag the master page to the Delete button at the bottom of the Pages palette.

Hiding Master Items   Are the items from your master page too distracting? Do you wish you could just make them all go away for a little while? No problem: Select Hide Master Items from the View menu. Later, when you want to see the completed page, select Show Master Items. If you use this a lot, don't forget to assign your own keyboard shortcut to it (it doesn't have one by default).

Copying Master Spreads Between Documents   Those folks at Adobe love to drag-and-drop. So, it's not surprising that you can drag-and-drop master pages from one document into another. First, have the two document windows side by side. Select the document with the master you want to copy, and drag the master page icon from the Pages palette over the document window of the other document. When you let go of the mouse button, the master page is copied over.

Similarly, you can copy one or more pages between documents by dragging them in the same manner, and InDesign copies any master pages that were applied to those document pages. However, this is less reliable than dragging over the master page itself. (For example, if the two documents have master pages with the same name, the master page isn't brought across.)

Overriding Master Items

Want to modify or delete a master page item from a document page, but leave all of the other master pages items alone? Wait! Don't cover the master page item with a white box! There's a better way. InDesign calls it "overriding" a master page item.

To override a master page item, hold down Command-Shift/Ctrl-Shift and click the master page item (or, if you're using the Type tool, click inside the master page item). InDesign "unlinks" the master page item, so you can select it, format it, or delete it as you would any other page item (see Figure 2-36). You can also override everything on any page(s) selected in the Pages palette by choosing Override All Master Page Items from the palette menu.

Notice that we put "unlink" in quotation marks above, indicating that the objects aren't really unlinked from their master page. You can return an overridden master page item to its original state by selecting the object and choosing Remove Selected Local Overrides from the Pages palette menu (see Figure 2-37). If you've made some terrible mistake, you can return one or more pages' worth of overridden objects by selecting the pages in the Pages palette and choosing Remove All Local Overrides from the palette menu.

*If you click on the master spread item
you want to change, nothing happens.
This is probably a good thing, as
it prevents you from accidentally
changing master items.*

*Instead of using copy and paste to
move the master page item from the
original master page, hold down
Command-Shift/Ctrl-Shift...*

*...and click the object. InDesign copies
the object to the current page and
marks it as a "local override."*

Now you can edit or format the text.

Maintaining Some Links. Overridden items are not entirely free of
the influence of their master page counterpart. For example, if you
override a frame and then move it on the document page, the position of that item (it's xy coordinates) is no longer linked to the position of the master page item. However, if you change the fill of the
master page item, those changes *do* flow through to the overridden
master page—there is still some connection there. Okay, now if you
change the fill of that object on the document page, the "fill link" is
broken but changes you make to the stroke on the master page still
flow through.

If you want to totally unlink an object from the master page, so
that nothing you do on the master will affect the item on the document page, first override the item, and then—while it's still selected—
choose Detach Selection from Master from the Pages palette menu
or deselect everything and select Detach All Objects from Master
(also from the Pages palette menu).

Reapplying Master Pages. When you reapply the master page to a
document page containing overridden or detached items, the original master page items reappear on the document page, but the overridden page items are not deleted. This isn't usually a good thing—it's
easy to end up with stacks of duplicated objects (which is probably
not what you want).

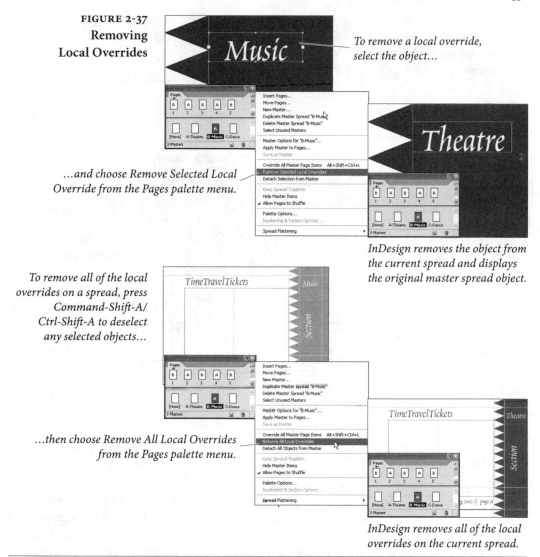

FIGURE 2-37
Removing
Local Overrides

To remove a local override,
select the object...

...and choose Remove Selected Local
Override from the Pages palette menu.

InDesign removes the object from
the current spread and displays
the original master spread object.

To remove all of the local
overrides on a spread, press
Command-Shift-A/
Ctrl-Shift-A to deselect
any selected objects...

...then choose Remove All Local Overrides
from the Pages palette menu.

InDesign removes all of the local
overrides on the current spread.

Layers and Master Pages

In older page layout software (such as QuarkXPress or PageMaker),
objects on master pages are always displayed behind document page
objects. This means that page numbers often end up being hidden by
items on your document pages, and that you may have to copy the
master page item to your document page to get it to display or print.

In InDesign, objects on master pages are arranged according to
the layer they're on. This means that you can put page numbers on
the uppermost layer in a publication without worrying about them
being obscured by images or other page items on the document
pages (see Figure 2-38).

FIGURE 2-38
Using Layers to Control
the Stacking Order of
Master Spread Items

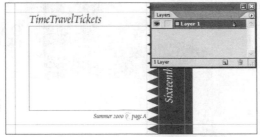

With only a single layer...

Master page text hidden behind the background image.

...master spread objects (in this example, the page header and footer) appear behind document page objects (the image).

Master page text appears in front of the background image.

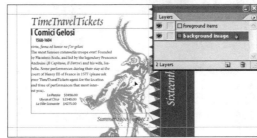

To avoid this problem, put your master spread items on at least one layer. If you do this, you'll be able to control their stacking order.

Adjusting Layouts

What happens when you change the margins of a page, or apply a different master page? Should the items on the affected pages move or resize to match the new page geometry? Or should they stay as they are? You decide. Choose Layout Adjustment from the Layout menu to see the Layout Adjustment dialog box (see Figure 2-39). Here's a quick walk-through of the controls here.

Enable Layout Adjustment. Turn this option on, and InDesign adjusts the position and size of the objects on the affected pages according to the settings in this dialog box. With this option off, InDesign does not change object positions or sizes when you apply master pages, change page size, or otherwise change page geometry.

Layout Adjustment sometimes changes your file in ways you may not expect. For instance, let's say you have a normal, single-column document with a master text frame. If you change the number of

FIGURE 2-39
Adjusting Layouts

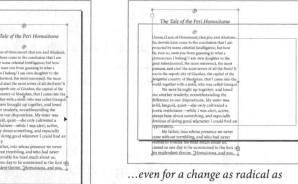

When the Enable Layout Adjustment option is off, InDesign does not change the position or size of page objects when you change the geometry of the page…

…even for a change as radical as changing page orientation.

Turn on the Enable Layout Adjustment option, and InDesign changes the position and size of page objects in response to changes in page size, orientation, column setup, or margins.

The options in the Layout Adjustment dialog box give you a way to "fine tune" the automated adjustment process.

Here's the layout, as adjusted by InDesign.

Ruler guide positions are very important to the layout adjustment feature. In this example, changing the page size changes the shape and position of the graphics—all because of their relationship to the ruler guides that surround them.

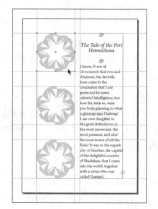

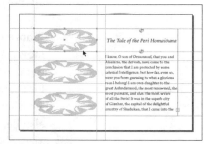

As the ruler guides move, InDesign resizes the graphics you've "stuck" to the ruler guides.

columns to three while Layout Adjustment is enabled, InDesign replaces the single text frame with three threaded frames. However, Layout Adjustment has no effect on the number of columns in multi-column text frames.

Snap Zone. How close to a guide does an object have to be to be affected by layout adjustment? That's what you're telling InDesign by the value you enter in this field. Objects within the specified distance will move or resize; objects outside that range won't.

Allow Graphics and Groups to Resize. When this option is turned off, InDesign will not resize graphic frames or groups of objects while adjusting layouts. When it's on, InDesign looks at graphic frames and groups and if they extend to the edges of the column or margin, will resize them to match the new page layout. Note that InDesign never scales text in a text frame; it may resize the frame itself, but not the text inside it. It will, however, scale graphics inside of graphic frames when this option is on. This is quite powerful, but also quite dangerous. For example, if you have a picture that spans from the left margin to the right margin in a single-column document, and you use Margins and Columns to split the page into two or more columns, this option will scale that picture down into the left-most column—probably not what you were hoping for.

Allow Ruler Guides to Move. Should ruler guides move when you change the layout of the page or spread? If you'd like the ruler guides to move, turn this option on; if not, turn it off. How far guides move when you make a layout change depends on a host of issues. (That's a nice way of saying that we've tried to figure it out and we're baffled. The best we can say is that InDesign tries to maintain the general look and feel of the page, so if you increase the left margin, the guides all move a bit to the right.)

Ignore Ruler Guide Alignments. When this option is off, InDesign moves and resizes objects to match the positions of ruler guides in the new page layout. When it's on, InDesign does not consider the locations of ruler guides when resizing or moving objects—only the location of margin guides and page edges. The effect of this option also depends on the state of the Allow Ruler Guides to Move option (described above).

Ignore Object and Layer Locks. What should InDesign do while adjusting your layout when it encounters a locked object, or an object on a locked layer? When you turn this option on, InDesign will treat the objects as if they were unlocked. To leave locked objects alone, turn this option off.

It's All in the Guides. The key thing to remember is that InDesign bases all layout adjustment decisions on the positions of margin guides, ruler guides, column guides, and page edges. InDesign cannot know that you want an object to change its size or position unless you somehow associate the object with a guide or a page edge.

Selecting and Deselecting

Before you can act on an object, you have to select it (see Figure 2-40). Sounds simple, but in InDesign you can quickly get in a messy situation if you don't pay attention to what, exactly, is selected on your page and how you selected it. That's why we recommend that even experienced users read through this carefully.

The Selection Tool. You select objects or groups of objects with the Selection tool by clicking on them, dragging the selection rectangle (marquee) over the page so that part of the marquee touches the object, or by Shift-selecting (select one object, hold down Shift, and select another object). When you select an object or group of objects using the Selection tool, InDesign displays the object's selection handles and the object's bounding box—the smallest rectangular area capable of enclosing the selection. The selection handles on the bounding box also correspond to the points on the proxy in the Transform palette.

FIGURE 2-40
Selecting Objects

Bounding box

Selection handles

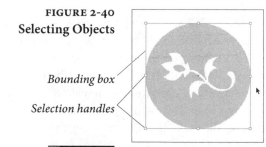

When you select an object using the Selection tool, InDesign displays the objects's selection handles and bounding box.

When you select an object using the Direct Selection tool, InDesign displays the points on the object's path.

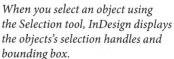

Proxy

The proxy in the Transform palette and Control palette represents the selection handles of the selected object.

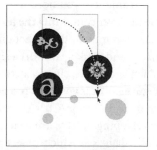

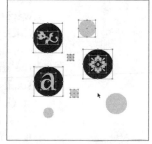

When you drag a selection rectangle around an object or objects...

...InDesign selects all of the objects that the selection rectangle touched.

You can also select everything on the current spread by choosing Select All from the Edit menu (or pressing Command/Ctrl-A) while using either selection tool.

The Direct Selection Tool. As we noted in "Using the Tools Palette" in Chapter 1, "Workspace," when you click an object using the Direct Selection tool, InDesign displays the points on the object's path—whether it's a line or a frame. You can also use the Direct Selection tool to select objects nested inside other objects (see "Selecting Inside Objects," below). The most common example is selecting a picture inside a graphic frame—the frame and the picture are two separate objects in InDesign, and you can use the Direct Selection tool to select the frame (by clicking on its edge) or the picture (by clicking anywhere inside the frame).

You can drag a selection marquee using the Direct Selection tool, too, just as you can with the Selection tool—InDesign selects the points on the objects within the selection, even if they're in more than one object. To select all the points on a line or frame, hold down Option/Alt while you select with the Direct Selection tool.

Deselecting. To deselect all selected objects, click an uninhabited area of the page or pasteboard, or, better yet, press Command-Shift-A/Ctrl-Shift-A. We've developed this keyboard shortcut into something of a nervous tic; it's incredibly useful because there are so many times you need to make sure everything is deselected. For example, when you create a new color, InDesign applies that color to whatever you have selected on the page. If you don't want this, you'd better deselect everything first!

Selecting Through Objects

Sometimes, you have to select an object that's behind another object. You might, for example, need to select and edit a background graphic behind a text frame. Do you need to drag the text frame out of the way? Or hide the layer containing the text frame? There's a better way: Click the Selection tool on the object on top of the stack, then press Command/Ctrl and click again. InDesign selects the next object in the stack. Each successive click selects the next object down in the stack (see Figure 2-41). If you click too far, you can move back up the stack by Command-Option/Ctrl-Alt-clicking.

When overlapping objects are exactly or nearly the same in size, it can be difficult to see which object in a stack is selected. Don't start dragging objects out of the way—look for clues. The color of the selection handles, the state of the Fill and Stroke buttons in the

FIGURE 2-41
**Selecting Through
Objects**

*Want to select an object
that's behind other objects?
You don't need to drag
objects out of the way.
Instead, hold down
Command/Ctrl and click
the Selection tool above the
object you want to select.*

Text frame selected

Background graphic selected

*The first click selects the object on
top of the stack of objects...*

*...but each subsequent click selects the
next object in the stack.*

Toolbox, and the Stroke palette all provide information that can help
you determine which object is selected.

Keyboard Selections

InDesign also has menu items and keyboard shortcuts for selecting
objects on your page. The menu items live in the Select submenu,
under the Object menu, but we only use them if we forget the keyboard shortcuts (below). Note that these features differ from the click-
through method; Command/Ctrl-click selects through an object to
one directly beneath it. The Select features select from among all the
objects on a spread. For example, if you have four small frames, one
in each corner of a page (whether they're overlapping or not), you can
select among them with these shortcuts.

▶ To select the topmost object, based on the stacking order on the
page (see "Stacking Objects," later in this chapter) press Com-
mand-Option-Shift-] / Ctrl-Alt-Shift-] or choose First Object
Above from the Select submenu.

▶ To select the object *behind* the currently selected object in a
stack of objects, press Command-Option-[/ Ctrl-Alt-[or choose
Next Object Below from the Select submenu. Once you reach
the bottom of a stack of objects, InDesign stops. Pressing the
keyboard shortcut again does nothing.

▶ To select the object above the currently selected object in a stack
of objects, press Command-Option-] / Ctrl-Alt-] or choose Next
Object Above from the Select submenu.

▶ To select the bottommost object on the page, press Command-
Option-Shift-[/ Ctrl-Alt-Shift-[or choose Last Object Below
from the Select submenu.

Selecting Inside Objects

Sometimes, you need to select an object that you've pasted inside another object, or to select an object inside a group. The Direct Selection tool, as you might expect, is the tool you'll use to do this, and the process is called "subselection." (When Ole selects an object that's inside another object, he actually says the object is "subselected." David, who felt subselected through much of his childhood, prefers the term "select-challenged.")

Selecting objects inside groups. You don't have to ungroup a group of objects to select and edit the objects in the group—you can work with them just as if they were outside the group. To do this, select the Direct Selection tool and click the element that you want to edit. InDesign selects the object. You can then change its attributes, text, shape, or position. Deselect the subselected item, and it goes back to being part of the group (see Figure 2-42).

If you want to drag a single object inside a group, select it with the Direct Selection tool, and then hold down Command/Ctrl while you drag. (Don't drag a point or control handle; that actually moves the point!) Of course, you can always move an object by selecting it and then pressing the arrow keys or adjusting the values in the X and Y fields of the Control palette.

Selecting embedded objects. One of the trickiest things to master in InDesign is the process of selecting and working with objects you've pasted inside other objects.

First, when you click on an object inside a path using the Direct Selection tool, InDesign selects the object (see Figure 2-43). To work with the bounding box of the item (to move or resize the embedded object, for example), press V to switch to the Selection tool, or E to switch to the Free Transform tool. We use this select-then-press-V technique all the time.

FIGURE 2-42
Subselecting Objects Inside Groups

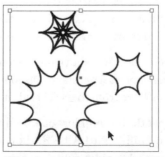

Click the group with the Selection tool to select the group, or...

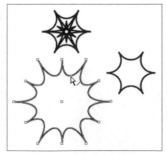

...click one of the objects in the group with the Direct Selection tool.

FIGURE 2-43
Subselecting Path Contents

Select the Direct Selection tool from the Tools palette (or press A), position the tool over the object you want to select…

…and click. InDesign selects the object.

To work with the bounding box of the subselected object, press V (to switch to the Selection tool).

Second, when you Option/Alt-click on any object, you select one level higher in the hierarchy. What the heck does that mean? Here's an example. Lets' say you have a path grouped with a frame, and this group has been pasted inside another frame using the Paste Into feature (in the Edit menu). Click the path with the Direct Selection tool to select a segment or point on the path; then Option/Alt-click to select the whole path; then Option/Alt-click again to select the group; then Option/Alt-click again to select the frame (see Figure 2-44). Don't drag as you click—holding down Option/Alt will make a copy of the selected object. To move a group inside a frame, Option/Alt-click the object, press V to switch to the Selection tool, and then hold down Command/Ctrl as you drag the group (see Figure 2-45).

Third, you can use the Select submenu (under the Object menu or the context menu). Choose Content to select the next embedded object ("down the hierarchy") or choose Container to select the containing object ("up the hierarchy," just like Option/Alt-clicking). Once you're inside a group, you'll see the Select Next Object in Group and the Select Previous Object in Group options.

Finally, you can use buttons on the control palette to navigate the object hierarchy (see Figure 2-46). These buttons do pretty much the same things as the options on the Select submenu, but we find we use them a great deal more often than we use the menu.

FIGURE 2-44
Subselecting
Nested Groups

If all you want to do is select an object inside the group, it's easy—just click the Direct Selection tool on the object. But what if you want to select the entire group?

Click the Direct Selection tool inside the containing frame. InDesign selects the frame.

Hold down Option/Alt and click again. InDesign subselects the objects in the group.

Switch to the Selection tool (press V) to work with the group's bounding box.

FIGURE 2-45
Moving a
Subselected Group

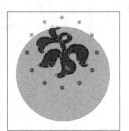

Hold down Option/Alt and click inside the frame until all of the group objects are selected.

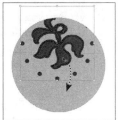

Press V, then hold down Command/Control and drag.

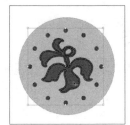

The cursor must be over one of the group objects, or you'll end up moving the containing frame.

Note that you can also press E to switch to the Free Transform tool and then drag the center point.

Stacking Objects

Page items on an InDesign page can be arranged in front of or behind each other. You can imagine that every object exists on an invisible plane that it cannot share with other objects, if you like. These planes can be shuffled to place one object above another, or behind another.

FIGURE 2-46
Control Palette
Selection Buttons

Select Container button.

Click the Select Content button to select the group within the circle.

Select Content button.

We've pasted a group of star polygons inside this circle.

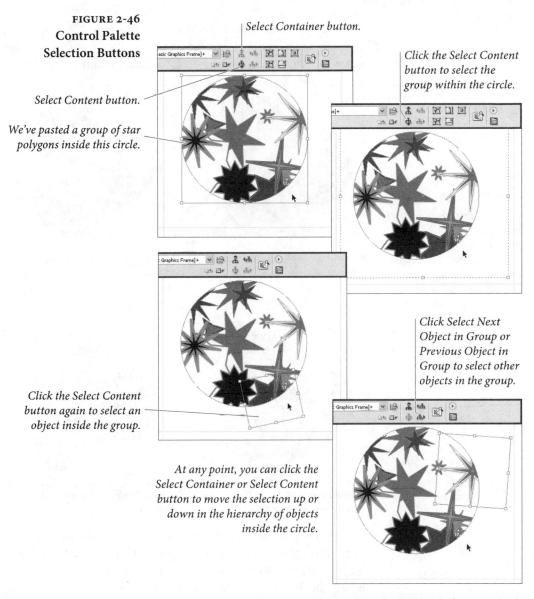

Click Select Next Object in Group or Previous Object in Group to select other objects in the group.

Click the Select Content button again to select an object inside the group.

At any point, you can click the Select Container or Select Content button to move the selection up or down in the hierarchy of objects inside the circle.

Simple stacking isn't the only way to control the front-to-back order of objects on a page—layers are another, and usually better, method (we cover layers in the next section). Arranging objects on a single layer, however, is very similar to tasks we perform every day as we stack and sort physical objects (our lives, for example, seem to revolve around stacks of paper).

Each layer in InDesign has its own stacking order and you can move an object to the front, or send an object to the back of the layer it occupies (see Figure 2-47). To bring an object to the front, Choose Bring to Front from the Arrange submenu (under the Object menu or the context menu). Or you can press Command-Shift-] / Ctrl-Shift-]. To send an object to the back, choose Send to Back from the Arrange submenu. Alternately, you can press Command-Shift-[/ Ctrl-Shift-[.

FIGURE 2-47
Bring to Front and Send to Back

Note that bringing an object to the front or sending it to the back only changes its position in the stacking order of the current layer. Objects on other layers can still appear in front of objects brought to the front; objects on layers behind the current layer will still appear behind objects sent to the back.

To bring an object to the front, select the object...

...and then press Command-Shift-]/Ctrl-Shift-]. InDesign brings the selected object to the front of the current layer.

To send an object to the back of the current layer, select the object...

...and then press Command-Shift-[/Ctrl-Shift-[.

You can also choose to bring objects closer to the front or send them farther to the back in the stacking order of objects on a layer (see Figure 2-48). To bring an object closer to the front (in front of the next higher object in the stacking order), choose Bring Forward from the Arrange submenu (under the Object menu or the context menu) or press Command-] / Ctrl-]. To send an object backward, choose Send Backward or press Command-[/ Ctrl-[.

Text Wrap and Stacking Order

In QuarkXPress, text wrap is affected by the stacking order of objects on the page. If a text box is above a wrapped object, the text avoids the text wrap area; if it's behind/below the wrapped object, the text ignores the text wrap. While there is nothing inherently logical or intuitively obvious about this behavior, many people have gotten used to it.

FIGURE 2-48
**Bring Forward
and Send Backward**

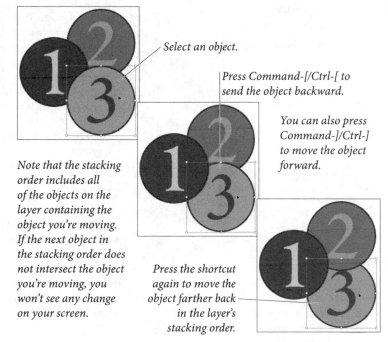

Select an object.

Press Command-[/Ctrl-[to send the object backward.

You can also press Command-]/Ctrl-] to move the object forward.

Note that the stacking order includes all of the objects on the layer containing the object you're moving. If the next object in the stacking order does not intersect the object you're moving, you won't see any change on your screen.

Press the shortcut again to move the object farther back in the layer's stacking order.

To make InDesign behave this way, turn on the Text Wrap Only Affects Text Beneath option in the Composition panel of the Preferences dialog box. Once you've done this, the stacking order of objects on the page will have an effect on text wrap (see Figure 2-49).

For more on working with text wrap, see Chapter 6, "Where Text Meets Graphics."

Layers

InDesign's layers are transparent planes on which you place page items. You've probably heard that layers are a way to organize your publication (that's what all the marketing materials say, after all). But there's far more to InDesign's layers than just organization—layers give you control over what parts of your publication display and print, and whether they can be edited or not.

Layers Basics   InDesign's layers have a few characteristics you should understand before you start using them. First, layers affect an entire document—not individual pages or page spreads. Next, layers created in one document do not affect layers in another document. As far as we can tell, there's no technical limit to the number of layers you can have in a publication; it's possible to make hundreds or more of them if you

FIGURE 2-49
Stacking Order
and Text Wrap

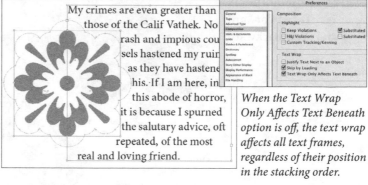

The text frame is in front of the wrapped object.

When the Text Wrap Only Affects Text Beneath option is off, the text wrap affects all text frames, regardless of their position in the stacking order.

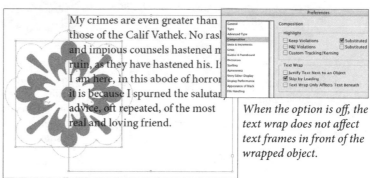

Note that you can also prevent a text wrap from affecting a text frame by turning on the Ignore Text Wrap option in the Text Frame Options dialog box.

When the option is off, the text wrap does not affect text frames in front of the wrapped object.

have enough memory. But just because you can do that doesn't mean that you should. Too many layers can make a publication difficult to manage.

Layers are especially useful when you're working with pages containing slow-drawing graphics, when your publication features complicated stacks of objects, or when you want to add a nonprinting layer of comments or instructions to a publication. Layers are also helpful when you want to create "conditional" layers containing differing text or graphics (you could create multiple versions of the publication in different languages, for example, and store all of the versions in a single publication).

The Layers Palette   You use the Layers palette to create, edit, rearrange, and delete layers (see Figure 2-50). To display the Layers palette, choose Layers from the Window menu (or press F7). If you're familiar with the Layers palettes found in Illustrator and PageMaker (and, to a more limited extent, Photoshop or QuarkXPress), you'll be right at home with the InDesign Layers palette. The Layers palette is chock full o' features; let's look at them one at a time.

FIGURE 2-50
Layers Palette

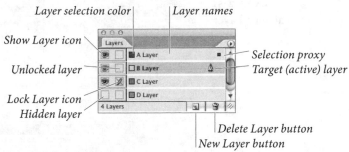

Layer selection color | Layer names

Show Layer icon

Unlocked layer

Lock Layer icon
Hidden layer

Selection proxy
Target (active) layer

Delete Layer button
New Layer button

To reduce the amount of vertical space taken up by the Layers palette...

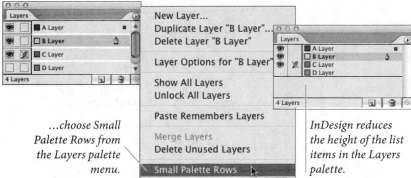

...choose Small Palette Rows from the Layers palette menu.

InDesign reduces the height of the list items in the Layers palette.

New Layer. To create a new layer, click the New Layer button at the bottom of the palette or select New Layer from the Layers palette menu (see Figure 2-51). InDesign normally adds new layers at the top of the Layers palette, but you can tell the program to add the layer immediately beneath the currently-selected layer by holding down Command-Option/Ctrl-Alt as you click the New Layer button.

If you want to name the layer (we think you should) or change any other options, hold down the Option/Alt key when you click this button to display the New Layer dialog box. (You can also get to this dialog box by double-clicking the layer after creating it.) We cover the controls in this dialog box in "Layer Options," below.

Delete Layer. Click the Delete Layer button to delete the selected layer or layers (to select more than one layer, hold down Command/Ctrl as you click each layer name). If the layer you have selected contain objects, InDesign warns you that deleting the layer will delete the objects, too.

Show/Hide column. When you see an "eye" icon in the left-most column of the Layers palette, the layer is visible. When there's no icon in this column, all of the objects on the layer are hidden (invisible). Click once in this column to change from one state to another. You

FIGURE 2-51
Creating a Layer

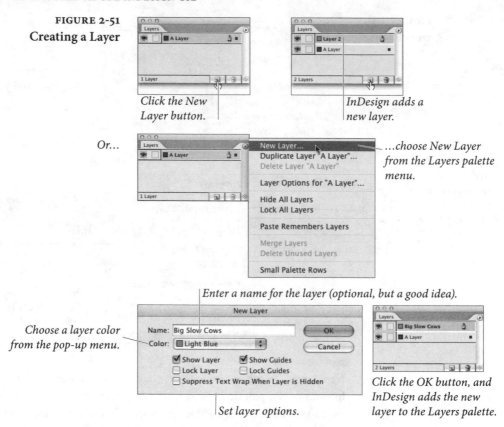

Click the New
Layer button.

InDesign adds a
new layer.

Or...

...choose New Layer
from the Layers palette
menu.

Enter a name for the layer (optional, but a good idea).

Choose a layer color
from the pop-up menu.

Set layer options.

Click the OK button, and
InDesign adds the new
layer to the Layers palette.

can't select or edit objects on hidden layers, and objects on hidden layers don't print.

Often, you want to hide all the layers in a publication except one. It's easy: hold down Option/Alt as you click in that layer's Show/Hide column (or choose Hide Others from the Layers palette menu). Clicking again in the column while holding down Option/Alt will show all layers, which is equivalent to choosing Show All Layers from the Layers palette menu (see Figure 2-52).

Lock/Unlock column. Click in the second column to lock a layer. InDesign displays the "lock" icon (a pencil with a red line through it) in that column. To unlock the layer (and remove the icon), click on it (see Figure 2-53).

You can't select objects on locked layers (so you can't move or format them, either), and you can't assign objects to locked layers. When you want to lock all of the layers in a publication except one, hold down Option/Alt and click in the lock/unlock column (or choose Lock Others from the Layers palette menu). To unlock

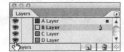

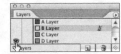

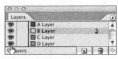

FIGURE 2-52
Showing and Hiding Other Layers

To hide all but one layer, follow these steps.

Point at the layer's Visibility icon, hold down Option/Alt...

...and click. InDesign hides all of the other layers.

Press Option/Alt and click again to make the layers visible.

FIGURE 2-53
Locking and Unlocking Other Layers

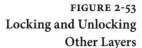

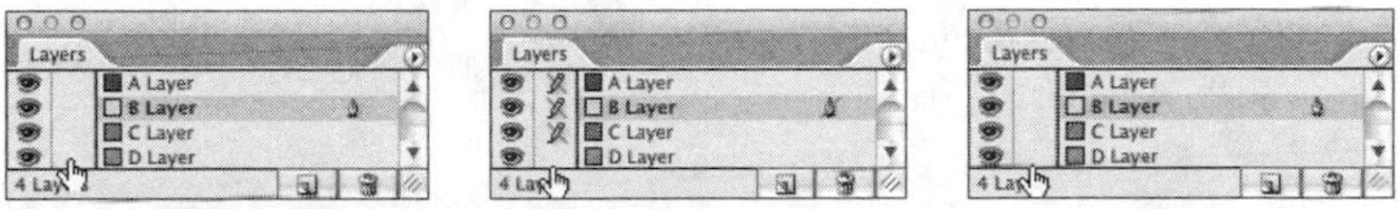

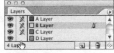

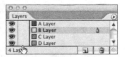

Point at the layer's Lock/Unlock icon, hold down Option/Alt...

...and click. InDesign locks all of the other layers.

Press Option/Alt and click again to unlock the layers.

every locked layer, hold down Option/Alt and click the lock/unlock column (this is the same as choosing Unlock All Layers from the Layers palette menu).

Target layer icon. The target layer icon (it looks like a little fountain pen nib) shows you which layer is the "target layer"—the layer on which InDesign will place any objects you create, import, or paste. Making a layer the target layer does *not* assign any currently selected objects to that layer.

Selection Proxy. When you select an object on your page, InDesign highlights the name of the layer containing the object and sets that layer as the target layer. In addition, InDesign displays a small square to the right of the layer name. This square is the Selection Proxy, which represents the layer or layers containing the selected objects (just as the proxy in the Transform palette "stands in" for the bounding box of the selection). To move objects from one layer to another, drag the Selection Proxy to another layer (see Figure 2-54).

While this method of moving objects from one layer to another makes it difficult to accidentally move objects, it also makes it difficult to move objects from multiple layers to a single layer. To accomplish this, you'll have to make multiple trips up and down the Layers palette, selecting and moving the selection proxy for each layer in the selection.

Note that you can also copy an object from one layer to another by holding down Option/Alt and dragging the Selection proxy. Plus, you can even move objects to a locked or hidden layer—to do this, press Command/Ctrl as you drag the selection proxy to the layer.

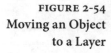

FIGURE 2-54
**Moving an Object
to a Layer**

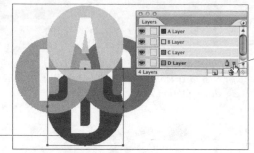

*Move the cursor over
the selection proxy
representing the object.*

*This object is on the layer
named "D layer."*

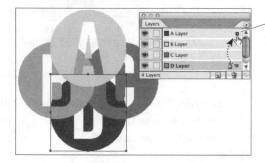

*Drag the selection
proxy to another layer.*

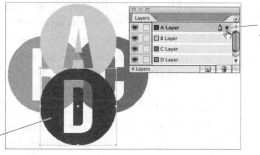

*Drop the selection
proxy. InDesign moves
the object to the layer.*

*Object is now on the
layer named "A layer."*

To copy objects as you move them to a hidden or locked layer, hold
down Command-Option/Ctrl-Alt as you drag.

Layer Options   Here's a quick rundown of each of the controls in the New Layer and
Layer Options dialog boxes.

Layer name. InDesign assigns a default name to each layer you create,
but we think it's better to enter a layer name that means something in
the context of your publication. It's far easier to remember that the
enormous, slow drawing image of grazing Herefords is on the layer

you've named "Big Slow Cows" than it is to remember that you've placed the image on the layer named "Layer 51."

Layer color. Each layer has its own color that helps you see which objects are on which layers. When Show Frame Edges (in the View menu) is turned on, InDesign uses the layer color for the outlines of frames and other objects. When you select an object, its selection handles appear in the selection color of that layer. If you don't pick a color yourself, the program picks one for you automatically. To change a color later, either double-click a layer in the Layers palette, or select a layer and choose Layer Options from the Layers palette menu. We have never felt the need to change a layer's selection color in an actual project, but it's nice to know that you can.

Show Layer. Should the layer be visible, or hidden? This option performs the same task as the show/hide column in the Layers palette.

Lock Layer. Should the layer be locked or unlocked? This option performs the same task as the lock/unlock column.

Show Guides. Remember that you can put ruler guides on layers. But should those guides be visible or hidden? If you want to hide just this layer's guides, turn off the Show Guides option.

Lock Guides. Should the guides on this layer be locked or unlocked? By default they're unlocked; turn this option on to lock 'em.

Suppress Text Wrap When Layer is Hidden. People complained to high heaven because InDesign 2 couldn't turn off the text wrap on objects that were on hidden layers. Fortunately, now you can. This is helpful if you're trying out a number of different designs, each on its own layer. As you hide a layer, you don't want its graphics to affect the other layers!

Paste Remembers Layers. This option doesn't appear in the Layer Options dialog box; rather it's in the Layers palette menu. The Paste Remembers Layers option takes care of a question: "If I copy objects from several layers and then paste, where should the pasted objects end up?" Should they be placed on the target layer (in a stack corresponding to their layer order)? Or should they be placed on the layers they originally came from?

We think you'll turn this option on and leave it on. If you do this, you'll be able to copy layers between publications. To do this, select objects on different layers in one publication, then copy them, and then switch to another publication and paste. When you paste, the layers will appear in the publication's Layers palette.

If layers with the same names already exist in the publication, InDesign moves the incoming objects to the corresponding layers, which is why you might want to turn the Paste Remembers Layers option off. If you don't, and if the layer stacking order is not the same as it was in the publication you copied the objects out of, the appearance of the pasted objects might change.

Deleting Layers

To delete a layer, select the layer and choose Delete Layer from the Layers palette menu or click the Delete Layer button. As we noted earlier, if there are any objects on the layer, InDesign warns you first (because deleting a layer also deletes its objects). To delete all of the unused layers (layers that have no objects assigned to them) in a publication, choose Delete Unused Layers from the Layers palette menu.

Changing Layer Stacking Order

To change the stacking order of layers, drag the layer up (to bring the layer closer to the front) or down (to send the layer farther to the back) in the Layers palette. As you drag, InDesign displays a horizontal bar showing the position of the layer. When the layer reaches the point in the list at which you want it to appear, stop dragging and InDesign moves the layer (and all the objects on it) to a new location (see Figure 2-55).

Merging Layers

To combine a series of layers into a single layer, select the layers and then choose Merge Layers from the Layers palette menu. InDesign merges the layers into a single layer—the first layer you selected (see Figure 2-56). Note that merging layers sometimes changes the stacking order of objects on the merged layers.

Moving Layers from One Publication to Another

To move a layer from one publication into another publication, make sure you've turned on the Paste Remembers Layers option (on the Layers palette menu), then copy an object from that layer and paste it into the publication that lacks that layer. When you paste, InDesign adds the layer to the list of layers.

Here's a bonus tip: You can select all the objects on a layer by Option/Alt-clicking on the layer in the Layers palette. Now copy and paste these objects to effectively copy the whole layer to another document.

FIGURE 2-55
**Changing Layer
Stacking Order**

*The selected object is on the
layer named "A layer."*

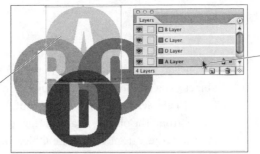

*Move the cursor over
the layer you want to
move.*

*Drag the layer to a
new position in the
Layers palette.*

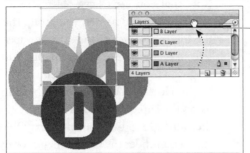

*The layer named "A layer"
is now the layer closest
to the front.*

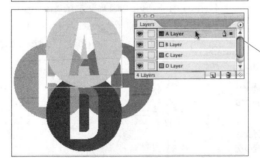

*When the layer
reaches the location
you want, stop drag-
ging. InDesign changes
the layer stacking
order.*

FIGURE 2-56
Merging Layers

*Select a series of layers and
choose Merge Layers from
the Layers palette menu.*

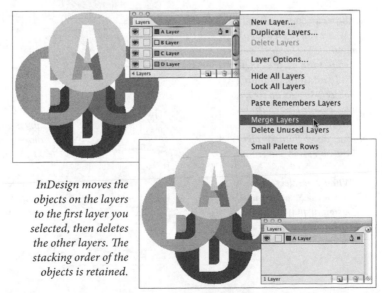

*InDesign moves the
objects on the layers
to the first layer you
selected, then deletes
the other layers. The
stacking order of the
objects is retained.*

Grouping Objects

What does it mean to "group" objects in a page layout program? When you group objects, you're telling the application to treat the objects as a single object. The objects in the group move and transform (scale, skew, and rotate) as a unit.

To group the objects in a selection, press Command-G/Ctrl-G (or choose Group from either the Object menu or the context menu). Note that you can't have objects in a group when they're each on different layers, so when you group the objects, the group moves to the top-most layer of the selection (see Figure 2-57). To ungroup a selected group, press Command-Shift-G/Ctrl-Shift-G (or choose Ungroup from the Context menu or the Object menu).

To select (or "subselect") an object inside a group, click the object using the Direct Selection tool. You can then select another object in the same group by choosing Next Object in Group from the Select submenu (under the Object menu) or by clicking the Next Object in Group or Previous Object in Group buttons in the Control palette. By the way, don't forget that you can group together groups—each group acting as a single object in the larger group.

FIGURE 2-57
Grouping and Ungrouping Objects

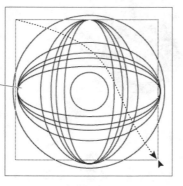

Select the objects you want to group.

Groups can come in handy when you've created an assemblage of objects you want to treat as a single object. In addition, grouping objects speeds up screen redraw—InDesign draws selection handles for one object, rather than for all of the objects in the group.

When you select a group with the Selection tool, InDesign displays a dashed line around the group.

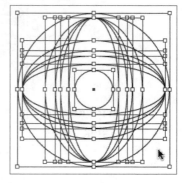

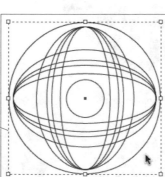

Press Command-G/Ctrl-G. InDesign groups the objects. You can move, scale, shear, or rotate the group as you do any other single object.

To select an object inside the group, switch to the Direct Selection tool and click the object.

To ungroup, select a group and press Command-Shift-G/Ctrl-Shift-G.

Locking Object Positions

When you want to keep somebody from changing the location of an object, you can lock it by selecting it and then pressing Command-L/Ctrl-L (or choose Lock Position from the context menu or the Object menu). When an object is locked, you can select it, but you can't change its position on the page or pasteboard. You can, however, move the object to another layer (we're not sure why; perhaps it's a bug). When you try to drag a locked object, the cursor turns into a "padlock" icon (see Figure 2-58).

If you're looking for a super industrial-strength lock—a way to keep from selecting and formatting objects—lock the layer that contains the object (see "Layers," earlier in this chapter). Unfortunately, even graphics and text on locked layers can still be changed if you try hard enough: changes made with the Find/Change palette and the Links palette still affect locked objects and layers (which is usually what you want, anyway).

FIGURE 2-58
**Locking and
Unlocking Objects**

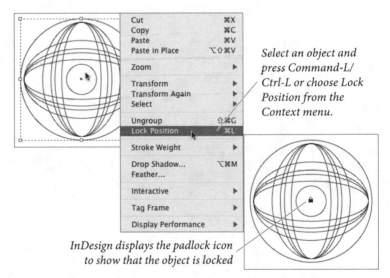

*Select an object and
press Command-L/
Ctrl-L or choose Lock
Position from the
Context menu.*

*InDesign displays the padlock icon
to show that the object is locked*

Deleting Objects

Deleting objects on your page is simple: Just select one or more items with the Selection or Direct Selection tools and press the Delete key. If you want a slower method, choose Clear from the Edit menu instead. If you're really trying to kill time, and you're using the Mac OS, you can drag the object from the page into the operating system's Trash icon. Why? Because you can.

A Good Foundation

The authors admit that they are not spectacularly organized persons. In general, we respond to events when something or someone catches fire, whacks one of us upside the head, or threatens some form of legal action.

We've found, however, that being methodical every now and then can save a lot of trouble later. Setting up master pages, defining layers, creating layout grids, and positioning ruler guides are not the most glamorous parts of InDesign, but they're a good place to expend a little organizational energy.

Far from cramping your creative style, paying attention to basic layout options—at the very beginning of the production process, if possible—sets the stage on which you produce and direct the play of your publications.

CHAPTER 3

Text

Text is the stream of characters that inhabit the text frames of your publication. Text is not about what those characters look like (that's "type," the topic of the next chapter)—it's about the characters themselves, and the text frames that hold them.

There are areas of overlap between these definitions, of course. Changing the number of columns in a text frame, for example, definitely changes the appearance of the text, but we've put it in this chapter because it's an organizational change, not one that changes the appearance of individual characters.

Text in an InDesign publication is contained in text frames (see Figure 3-1). Text frames are similar to the text "boxes" found in QuarkXPress, and they're also similar to the text "blocks" found in PageMaker (yes, text blocks are text frames—they just hide the frame from your view). In our opinion, InDesign's text frames present a "best of both worlds" approach—you get the flexibility and fluidity of PageMaker's text blocks combined with the precision of QuarkXPress' text boxes.

Text, in a word, is what publications are really all about. A picture might be worth a thousand words, but they're not very specific words. When you create a poster for a concert, for example, the text is what tells the viewer where the concert will be presented, at what time, and on which date. The point of using an image, color, or a stylish layout in a publication is to get people to *read the text*.

FIGURE 3-1
Text Frame Anatomy

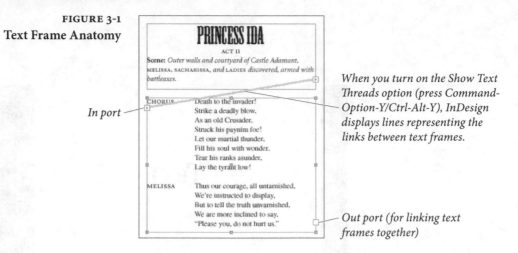

In port

When you turn on the Show Text Threads option (press Command-Option-Y/Ctrl-Alt-Y), InDesign displays lines representing the links between text frames.

Out port (for linking text frames together)

This chapter is all about how to get text into your InDesign documents—how to create and edit text frames, enter text, edit text, and import text files. It's also about checking the spelling of the text in your publication; and about finding and changing text. We'll even go a little bit off the deep end with a description of InDesign's tagged text import and export format.

Creating Text Frames

Before you can add text to your InDesign publication, you've got to have something to put it in: a text frame. To create a text frame, you can use any of the following methods.

▶ Draw a frame using one of the frame drawing tools (the Rectangular Frame, Ellipse Frame, or Polygonal Frame tools). QuarkXPress users may think these tools only make "picture boxes" because they have an "X" in them. Not so, they're just generic frames. To convert the frame to a text frame, choose Text from the Content submenu of the Object menu, or click inside the frame using the Type tool (see Figure 3-2).

▶ Draw a frame using the Rectangle, Ellipse, or Polygon tools, and then convert it to a text frame by choosing Text from the Content submenu of the Object menu (or click the Type tool inside the frame; see Figure 3-3). Remember that the only difference between these tools and the frame tools is that these tools create shapes (usually with stroked borders). Use the frame tools when you know a frame will contain pictures or text.

FIGURE 3-2
Converting a Graphic
Frame to a Text Frame

Select a frame
drawing tool.

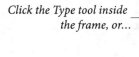

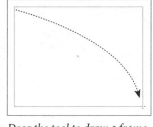

Drag the tool to draw a frame.

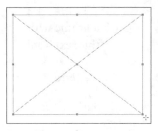

InDesign sets the content type
of the new frame to "Graphic."

Click the Type tool inside
the frame, or...

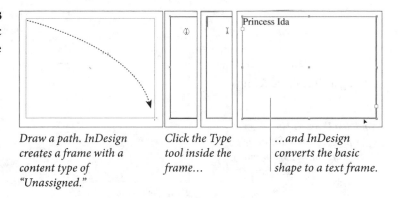

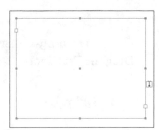

...select Text from the Content
submenu of the Object menu.

InDesign converts the graphic
frame to a text frame.

FIGURE 3-3
Converting a Basic
Shape to a Text Frame

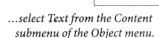

Princess Ida

Draw a path. InDesign
creates a frame with a
content type of
"Unassigned."

Click the Type
tool inside the
frame...

...and InDesign
converts the basic
shape to a text frame.

▶ Click the Type tool inside any empty frame. If the frame is an
empty graphic frame, clicking it with the Type tool converts it to
a text frame (see Figure 3-4).

▶ Drag the Type tool to create a frame whose height and width are
defined by the area you specified by dragging (see Figure 3-5).

▶ Drag a text place icon. The text place icon appears whenever you
import a text file, or when you click the in port or out port of a
text frame (see Figure 3-6). For more on text place icons, and the
in port and out port of a text frame, see "Importing Text" later
in this chapter.

FIGURE 3-4
**Click a Frame with
the Text Tool**

*You've probably figured
this out already, given the
previous illustrations, but
what the heck.*

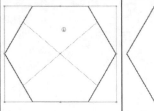 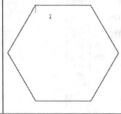 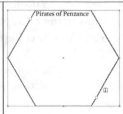

*Position the Type tool
over any empty frame
(the frame does not
have to be selected).*

*Click the Type tool
inside the frame.
InDesign converts the
frame to a text frame.*

Enter or place text.

FIGURE 3-5
Drag the Text Tool

Select the Type tool.

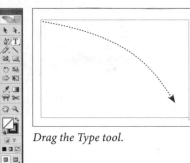

Drag the Type tool.

*InDesign creates a text frame
that's the width and height you
specified by dragging.*

FIGURE 3-6
Drag a Text Place Icon

*You "load" a text place icon
by placing a text file or by
clicking the in port or out
port of a text frame.*

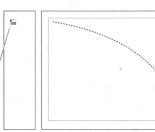 

Drag the text place icon…

*…to create a text frame that's the
width and height you specified by
dragging.*

▶ Deselect all (Command-Shift-A/Ctrl-Shift-A) and then paste text
into the publication (or drag it out of another application and
drop it into the publication, which accomplishes the same thing).
InDesign creates a text frame containing the text (see Figure
3-7).

▶ Drag a text file (or series of text files) out of your operating system's file browser (the Finder on the Macintosh, or the Windows
Explorer in Windows) and drop it into an InDesign publication
(see Figure 3-8).

FIGURE 3-7
Paste Text

Copy text out of another application...

...and paste it into InDesign.

FIGURE 3-8
Drag and Drop Text Files

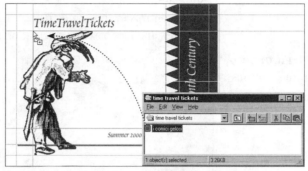

Drag a text file (or files) out of a Finder window (on the Mac OS) or Explorer window (in Windows) into the InDesign publication window.

Drop the file. InDesign places the file in your publication.

Note that InDesign does not require you to create a text frame *before* you add text, as (for example) QuarkXPress does. Most of the text frame creation methods described previously dynamically create a text frame as you enter, import, or paste text.

Once you've created a text frame, you can change its size, shape, and rotation angle just as you would any other object you've created (see Chapter 5, "Drawing" and Chapter 9, "Transforming"). You can also change the shape of the text frame using InDesign's drawing and path editing tools (see Chapter 5, "Drawing").

Text can also appear *on* a path—for more on this topic, see Chapter 6, "Where Text Meets Graphics."

Setting Text Frame Options

Text frames have attributes that are not shared with graphics frames or with frames whose content is set to "Unassigned." To view and edit these attributes, choose Text Frame Options from the Type menu, or press Command-B/Ctrl-B. or hold down Option/Alt as you double-click the frame with either the Selection or the Direct Selection tool. InDesign displays the Text Frame Options dialog box (see Figure 3-9).

The controls in this dialog box set the number of columns, inset distances, and first baseline calculation method for the text frame.

FIGURE 3-9
Text Frame Options

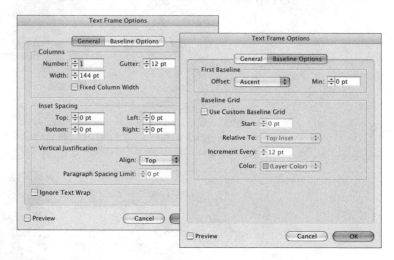

The Measure of Columns

InDesign text frames can contain up to 40 columns—enter the number of columns you want in the Number field. To define the distance between columns, or "gutter," enter a value in the Gutter field.

Column width. When we think of the typesetting specifications for a block of text, we think first of the typeface, then the point size, the leading, and the measure, or column width—in that order. When we see a line of type, our thoughts go something like this: "That's Bodoni Book, eleven-on-fifteen, on a fourteen pica measure." The length of the lines of text is roughly as important as the character shapes, their size, and their leading.

QuarkXPress lets you set the number of columns in a text frame, but it doesn't let you specify the width of the columns—instead, you have to work with the width of the text box to get the column width you want. InDesign recognizes the importance of column width in typesetting by giving you the ability to determine the width of a text frame by the width of its columns. When you type the number of columns in the Text Frame Options dialog box and click OK, InDesign divides the current width of the text frame into columns for you (as QuarkXPress does). However, if you specify a value in the Width field, then the program changes the width of your text frame so that the columns will fit.

The Fixed Column Width option tells InDesign what to do with your text frame when it gets wider or narrower. When you turn this option on, you'll notice that when you resize the text frame it snaps to widths determined by the fixed widths of the columns (and gutters) it contains (see Figure 3-10). If you leave this option turned off, the column widths change when you resize the frame.

FIGURE 3-10
Fixed Column Width

When you turn on the Fixed Column Width option…

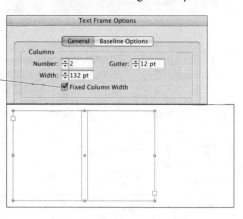

…InDesign resizes the text frame based on the column width you entered (rather than evenly dividing the width of the text frame into columns of equal width).

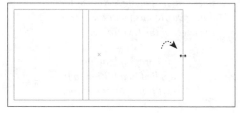

If you resize a text frame that has a fixed column width…

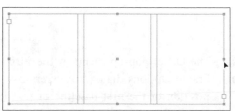

…InDesign will "snap" the frame widths based on that column width. No matter how narrow you make the frame, it will always contain at least one column of that width.

Setting Text Frame Insets The values you enter in the Inset Spacing section of the Text Frame Options dialog box control the distances InDesign will push text from the edges of the text frame. You can enter an inset distance from 0 to 720 picas or 120 inches. (Unfortunately, you can't enter negative values to make the text hang out of the text frame.)

Inset distances work in conjunction with (and in addition to) the margins of the paragraphs in a text frame (see Figure 3-11). In general, we prefer to work with the text inset values set to zero, and use the left and right indent values of individual paragraphs to control the distance from the edges of the text to the edges of the text column. However, these inset features are sometimes helpful when you need to move all the text in a frame up or down slightly without moving the frame itself.

FIGURE 3-11
Text Frame Insets

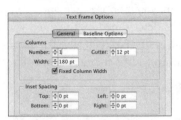 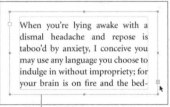

By default, InDesign applies no inset—note that this differs from most versions of QuarkXPress, which apply a one point inset by default.

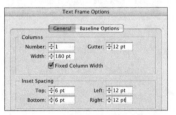 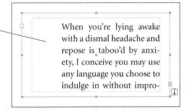

Enter inset distances in the fields in the Inset Spacing section of the dialog box to push text away from the edges of the text frame.

When you select the text frame with the Selection tool, InDesign displays the text inset boundary.

Paragraph indents are applied in addition to the text frame inset distances.

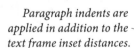

Setting First Baseline Position

The Offset pop-up menu in the First Baseline section of the Text Frame Options dialog box offers five methods for calculating the position of the first baseline of text in a text frame: Ascent, Cap Height, Leading, x Height, and Fixed (see Figure 3-12).

If you use either the Ascent or Cap Height method, the tops of characters in your text frames will touch (or come close to touching) the top of the text frame (provided, of course, that the top frame inset is zero). Choosing x Height is similar: the tops of the lower-case char-

FIGURE 3-12
First Baseline Position

Example font is Minion Pro; example leading is 24 points.

All baseline distances calculated using Neo-Atlantean super science, and will vary from font to font.

If you use the Fixed or Leading options, you can know exactly where the first baseline of text will fall in relation to the top of the text frame, regardless of the font or the point size of the text.

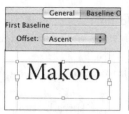

Distance from the top of the text frame to the first baseline: 17.44775390625 points.

Distance from the top of the text frame to the first baseline: 15.6000316143036 points.

Distance from the top of the text frame to the first baseline: 10.4640212059021 points.

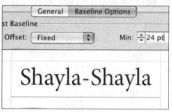

Distance from the top of the text frame to the first baseline: 24 points.

Distance from the top of the text frame to the first baseline: 24 points.

acters will bump up against the top of the frame (and the ascenders and uppercase letters will pop out the top of the frame). These settings come at a price, however: it's almost impossible to calculate the distance from the top of the frame to the baseline of the first line of text in the frame (without resorting to scripting).

In addition, using these methods means that InDesign will vary the leading of the first line when you enter characters from different fonts in the line, or change the size of characters, or when you embed inline graphics in the line.

Is that bad? It is, if you care about type.

It's important that you know exactly where the first baseline of text in a text frame will appear, relative to the top of the text frame. Why? Because if you know the position of the first baseline, you can snap the top of the text frame to your leading grid—and rest secure in the knowledge that the first baseline will fall neatly on the next baseline.

To control the location of the first baseline of text in a text frame, choose either Leading or Fixed from the Offset menu in the First Baseline section. When you choose Leading, the first baseline is one leading increment from the top of the text frame—regardless of the size of the characters (or the height of inline graphics) in the line. When you choose Fixed, you can specify exactly how far from the top of the frame the first baseline should fall using the Min field.

The Min field for the Offset settings other than Fixed means, "between the Min value and what the Offset would be ordinarily, use the larger value."

For more on leading, see Chapter 4, "Type."

Ignoring Text Wrap

In a typical magazine spread, some text wraps around graphics; some text doesn't. Imagine that you want the body text of an article to wrap around an image—but you want to place a headline on top of the same image. To keep text in a text frame from obeying a text wrap, select the frame, open the Text Frame Options dialog box, and then turn on the Ignore Text Wrap option (see Figure 3-13).

Note that in this case (where the text was on top of the offending graphic) you could also turn on the Text Wrap Only Affects Text Beneath option in the Composition Preferences dialog box. This preference affects all text wraps in your file (see Chapter 6, "Where Text Meets Graphics").

FIGURE 3-13
Ignoring Text Wrap

When you try to place a text frame on top of a graphic that has a text wrap, InDesign pushes the text out of the frame.

Unless, that is, you display the Text Frame Options dialog box (select the text frame and press Command-B/Ctrl-B) and turn on the Ignore Text Wrap option.

Once you do this, text in the text frame ignores the text wrap.

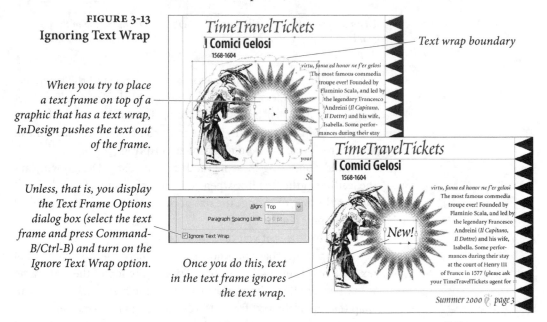

Text wrap boundary

Vertical Justification

Just as the alignment of a paragraph controls the horizontal position of the paragraph in a column, vertical justification controls the vertical position of the text in a text frame (see Figure 3-14). To set the vertical justification method used for a text frame, select the text frame, display the Text Frame Options dialog box, and then choose a method from the Align pop-up menu.

FIGURE 3-14
Vertical Justification

When you choose Center from the Align pop-up menu, you might want to choose the Cap Height or Ascent option from the Offset pop-up menu (in this case, choosing Leading is not a good idea, as it pushes the text away from the visual center of the text frame).

When you choose Justify from the Align pop-up menu, InDesign adds space to force the text to fill the height of the frame. The method InDesign uses is based on the value you enter in the Paragraph Spacing Limit field (you can enter values from 0 to 8640 points).

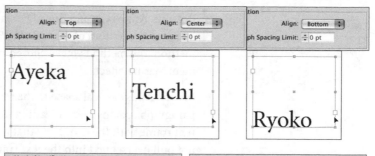

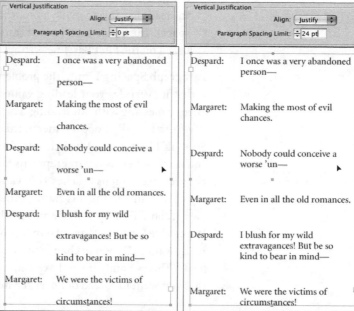

When you enter zero, InDesign applies leading to make the text fill the height of the text frame.

When you enter a value, InDesign applies paragraph spacing up to that amount before changing the leading.

► **Top.** Aligns the text to the top of the text frame, positioning the first baseline of text in the frame according to the method you've selected from the Offset pop-up menu (see above).

► **Center.** Vertically centers the text in the text frame. InDesign centers the text between the bottom of the text frame and the top of the first line of text (taking the baseline options into account). The problem is that in small text frames the text may be mathematically centered, but not actually appear centered—especially single lines of all-capitals text, or in fonts that have no ascenders or descenders. In these relatively rare cases, you may have to tweak the First Baseline or Baseline Shift settings to center the text.

▶ **Bottom.** Aligns the baseline of the last line of text in the text frame to the bottom of the frame. When you choose this method, the method you've chosen from the Offset pop-up menu has no effect.

▶ **Justify.** Adds vertical space to the text in the text frame (using paragraph spacing and/or leading to add this space) to fill the text frame with the text. Note that using the Justify method will not pull overset text into the text frame (that is, it won't lessen the leading value to make more text fit in the frame; it only adds space). The first line of the text frame will remain where it was, based on the First Baseline setting.

Paragraph Spacing Limit. The problem with vertically justified text is that it overrides your leading values, and we don't take kindly to anyone messing with our leading. Fortunately, when you choose Justify from the Align pop-up menu, InDesign activates the Paragraph Spacing Limit control, which sets the maximum amount of space you'll allow between paragraphs in the text frame. Once the space between paragraphs reaches this value, InDesign adjusts the leading of each line in the text frame, rather than adding space between paragraphs. To keep InDesign from changing leading at all, enter a large value (up to 8640 points) in this field. On the other hand, if you really want InDesign to change the leading instead, enter zero in this field. (This is handy if you have a long list of single-line paragraphs that you want to spread out over the height of a text frame.)

Linking and Unlinking Text Frames

You can link one text frame to another to make the text continue—or "flow"—from frame to frame. In InDesign, the controls for linking and unlinking text frames are the "in port" and "out port" icons on the text frames themselves. This means that the process of linking text frames in InDesign is similar to working with the "window-shade handles" on PageMaker text blocks, and should feel familiar to PageMaker users. There's no need to go to the Toolbox to get a special "linking" tool, as there is in QuarkXPress.

Text frames come with their own somewhat obscure terminology. Any continuous series of text characters is a *story*. A story can be as small as a single, unlinked text frame, or as large as a series of hundreds of text frames containing tens of thousands of words and spanning hundreds of pages. When you link text frames together, you're *threading* stories through the text frames. When you place text to create a series of linked text frames, you're *flowing* text.

The text in a story has a direction—it has a beginning, a middle, and an end. When we speak, in this section, of a particular text frame appearing before or after another, we're talking about its position in the story, not relative to its position on the page.

The way that InDesign displays the in port and out port of a text frame tells you about the text frame and its position in a story (see Figure 3-15).

▶ When the in port or out port is empty, no other text frame is linked to that port. When both ports are empty, the text you see in the text frame is the entire story.

▶ When you see a plus sign (+) in the out port, it means that not all of the text in the story has been placed. The remaining (or "overset") text is stored in the text frame, but is not displayed.

▶ When you see a triangle in the in port or the out port (or both), InDesign is telling you that the text frame is linked to another text frame.

FIGURE 3-15
In Ports and Out Ports

This text frame is at the start of a story, because the in port is empty.

This text frame contains all of the text in a story. How can you tell?

The in port is empty, and... *...the out port is also empty.*

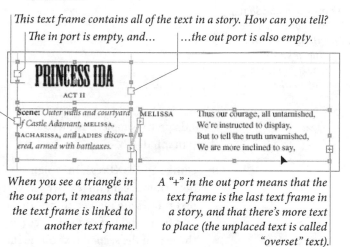

When you see a triangle in the out port, it means that the text frame is linked to another text frame.

A "+" in the out port means that the text frame is the last text frame in a story, and that there's more text to place (the unplaced text is called "overset" text).

Linking Text Frames

To link one text frame to another, choose the Selection or Direct Selection tool, then click either the in port or the out port of a text frame. InDesign displays the text place icon. Place the cursor over another frame (when you do this, InDesign displays the text link icon, which either looks like a little chain or like some text inside big parentheses, depending on what type of frame you're hovering over) and then click. InDesign links the two frames (see Figure 3-16). That

FIGURE 3-16
Linking Text Frames

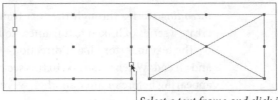

Select a text frame and click its out port.

At this point, you can also create a new text frame by dragging the text place icon. The new frame will be linked to the text frame you clicked.

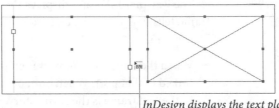

You can also click the in port to load the text place icon.

InDesign displays the text place icon.

Position the text place icon over a frame.

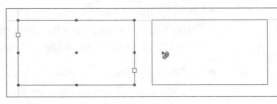

InDesign changes the text place icon to the link icon.

If you've turned on the Show Text Threads option (on the View menu), InDesign will display a line linking the out port of one text frame with the in port of another.

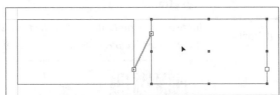

Click the link icon on the frame. InDesign links the two frames.

sounds pretty simple, but there are a number of details you should keep in mind:

► Unlike QuarkXPress, InDesign can link two text frames when both frames contain text. When you do this, the stories in the text frames are merged into a single story. If the text in the first text frame did not end with a carriage return, InDesign will run the text in the second text frame into the last paragraph of the first text frame (see Figure 3-17).

► Unlike PageMaker's text blocks, InDesign frames can be linked when they're empty. This means you can easily set up text layouts without having the copy in hand and without resorting to a "dummy text" placeholder.

► The port you click (the in port or the out port) sets the position of the link in the sequence of linked text frames making up the story. If you click the out port, the text frame you link to will

FIGURE 3-17
Linking Stories

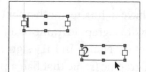 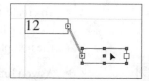

Two unlinked text frames.

Click the out port of one of the frames to load the text place icon.

If the first frame did not end with a carriage return, InDesign runs the text from the first paragraph of the second frame into the last paragraph of the first frame.

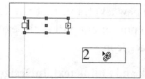

Click the text place icon on the other frame.

InDesign links the two frames.

come after the current text frame. If you click the in port and then another frame, this second frame will come earlier in the story (see Figure 3-18).

▶ When you click the out port of a text frame that contains more text than it can display (that is, an out port that displays the "+" symbol), the additional text will flow into the next text frame in the story (see Figure 3-19).

FIGURE 3-18
Controlling the Order of Text Frames in a Story

Two unlinked text frames.

When you load the text place icon by clicking the out port...

...and link to another text frame...

...that frame becomes the next frame in the story.

If, on the other hand, you load the text place icon by clicking on an in port...

...the frame you link to becomes the previous text frame in the story.

FIGURE 3-19
Placing Overset Text

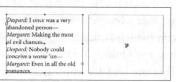 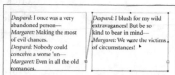

This text frame contains overset text. When you link it to another text frame...

...InDesign places the overset text in the following text frame (in this example, all of the text in the story has been placed).

▶ You don't have to link to another text frame—you can also create a link to a graphic frame or a frame whose content type has been set to "None." In InDesign 1.0, you could link a text frame to a graphic frame that had a picture in it and InDesign would discard the picture and fill the frame with text. InDesign no longer lets you link to a frame when there's a picture in it.

▶ To create a new text frame that's linked to an existing text frame, click the in port or out port of the existing frame and then drag the text place icon.

Link icon   *Unlink icon*

▶ As you link and unlink text, InDesign changes the appearance of the cursor to give you a clue (or, as a more formal author would say, a "visual indication") about what you're doing or are about to do.

▶ What if you have a "loaded" text place cursor and then realize that you need to scroll, or turn to another page? Do you need to "unload" the text place cursor (see below) before issuing other commands? Probably not—you can scroll, zoom, turn pages, create or modify ruler guides, and create new pages while InDesign displays the text place cursor.

▶ To "unload" the text place cursor (disable it, like if you change your mind midstream), click on any tool in the Toolbox (or just press a key to switch tools, like "V" for the Selection tool).

▶ To view the links between text frames, choose Show Text Threads from the View menu. InDesign displays lines connecting text frames in the selection (see Figure 3-20).

Unlinking Text Frames   To break a link between text frames, double-click the in port or out port on either side of the link (see Figure 3-21). When you break a link between text frames that have text content, the text usually becomes overset text (which is stored in the last text frame in the story).

Alternatively, you can click the out port of one frame and then click the next frame in the thread (see Figure 3-22). When you move the text place icon over the next frame, InDesign displays the Unlink Text icon (which is subtly different than the Link Text icon). When you click the Unlink Text icon on the frame, InDesign breaks the link. This method accomplishes the same thing, but is slower and involves more mouse movement than double-clicking—however, some people like it better.

FIGURE 3-20
Viewing Text Threads

To view the links between selected text frames...

...choose Show Text Threads from the View menu.

InDesign displays lines linking the text frames.

FIGURE 3-21
Unlinking Text Frames

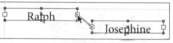

Select a text frame and double-click the out port (or in port).

InDesign breaks the link at the point at which you clicked.

FIGURE 3-22
Another Method

Select a text frame then click the out port (or in port). InDesign displays a text place icon.

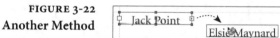

Move the text place icon over the next (or previous, if you clicked an in port) text frame. InDesign displays the unlink icon.

InDesign breaks the link between the two text frames.

By the way, when you break a link in the middle of multiple frames, the links before and after the break stick around. That is, if boxes A, B, C, and D are linked together, and you break the link between B and C, then C and D will stay linked together (even though there won't be any text in them).

Cutting and Pasting Text Frames

What happens to links when you delete or cut a linked text frame or series of linked text frames? First, InDesign does not delete any text in the story—the only time it does that is when you select all of the frames in the story and delete them. Otherwise, InDesign always flows the text contained by the frames you've deleted into the remaining frames in the story. If you want to delete text, you have to select it using the Type tool first. For more on selecting text, see "Editing Text," later in this chapter.

When you cut or copy a series of linked text frames, then paste, InDesign maintains the links between the duplicated frames—but not between the duplicates and the original frames or any other frames in the publication (see Figure 3-23). The copies of the frames contain the same text as the originals.

An interesting side effect of this behavior is that you can copy text frames from a story that are not linked to each other, and, when you paste, the text frames will be linked. This can come in handy when you're trying to split a story that is in multiple frames (as you can see in Figure 3-24).

FIGURE 3-23
Cutting and Pasting Linked Frames

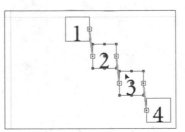 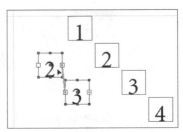

In this example, we've selected the second and third text frames in a story. When we copy and paste…

…InDesign retains the link between the two copied frames.

FIGURE 3-24
More About Copying and Pasting

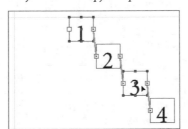 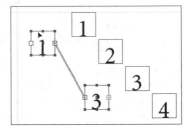

In this example, we've selected the first and third text frames in a story. When we copy and paste…

…InDesign retains the link between the two copied frames—even though the original frames were not directly connected to each other.

Adding a New Frame to a Story

It's easy to add a text frame in the middle of a sequence of linked text frames. Just follow these steps (see Figure 3-25).

1. Use the Selection tool to click the out port at the point in the story at which you want to add the new frame.

2. Drag the text place icon to create a new text frame, or click an existing, empty, unlinked frame.

InDesign only lets you link to empty and unlinked frames unless you're adding frames to the beginning or end of your thread.

FIGURE 3-25
**Adding a New Frame
to a Story**

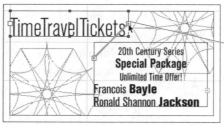

*Click the out port of a text
frame at the point at which
you want to add the new
frame (or click the in port
of the following frame).*

*InDesign displays the
text place icon.*

Drag the text place icon.

*InDesign creates a new
text frame and adds the
text frame to the story.*

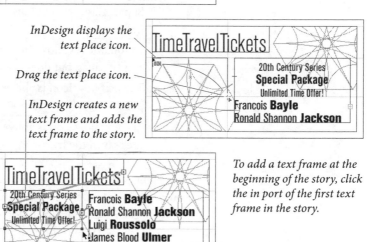

*To add a text frame at the
beginning of the story, click
the in port of the first text
frame in the story.*

Flowing Text

When you select Place from the File menu (and then choose a text
file), or use the Selection tool to click the in port or out port of a
text frame, your cursor changes to the text place icon. You can drag
this text place cursor to create a text frame, or you can click on an
existing frame to flow text into it. Flowing text is all about the care,
maintenance, and feeding of the text place icon (see Table 3-1 for
more on text place icons).

Once you've "loaded" the text place icon, you can use one of four
text flow methods: Manual text flow, Semi-automatic text flow, Automatic text flow, or Super Autoflow. These determine what happens
when you click or drag the text place icon. Here's the lowdown.

▶ **Manual text flow.** By default, InDesign uses the manual text
flow method. When you click the text place icon on your page,
or drag the text place icon, InDesign creates a new text frame
and flows the text into it (see Figure 3-26). When you click the
text place icon in between column guides, the width of the text
frame is determined by the width of the column you clicked in;

TABLE 3-1
Text Place Icons

Icon:	What it means:
	Manual text flow. Click to flow text into a frame; click in a column to create a frame that's the width of the column, or drag to create a frame.
	Semi-automatic text flow. InDesign "reloads" the text flow icon after each click or drag.
	Super Autoflow text flow. Click to place all of the text in the story (InDesign adds pages as necessary).
	Automatic text flow. InDesign flows the story to all empty pages, but does not add pages.
	The text flow icon is above a guide or grid "snap" point.
	The text flow icon is above a frame; clicking will place the text in the frame.

the height of the frame is the distance from the point at which you clicked the text place icon to the bottom of the column (see Figure 3-27). In a one-column document, the text frame reaches from the page's left to right margins. InDesign then flows the text into the new text frame. When you click the text place icon on an existing text frame or series of linked text frames, InDesign flows the text into the frame or frames. In either case, once InDesign is done flowing the text, the text place icon disappears and you're back to whatever tool you had selected before you loaded the text place icon. To continue placing text, click the out port to reload the text place icon.

▶ **Semi-automatic text flow.** Semi-automatic text flow is almost exactly like manual text flow—the difference is that InDesign reloads the text place icon after you've placed some text. The advantage? You don't have to click the out port of a text frame to reload the text place icon. To turn on semi-automatic text flow, hold down Option/Alt when the text place icon is visible. InDesign displays the semi-automatic text place icon when you do this (the cursor looks like a half-solid and half-dotted curvy line; see Figure 3-28).

▶ **Automatic text flow.** Automatic text flow—which you get if you hold down both Option/Alt and Shift—places as much text in the story as can fit on the pages in your document (the cursor looks like a solid down arrow). InDesign adds text frames as

FIGURE 3-26
Manual Text Flow

Load the text place icon (by placing a text file or clicking the in port or out port of any text frame).

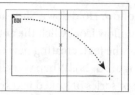

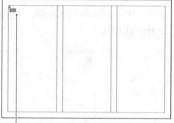

InDesign displays the manual text flow icon. Drag the icon.

InDesign flows text into the area you defined by dragging.

FIGURE 3-27
Manual Text Flow and Column Guides

Load the text place icon. InDesign displays the manual text flow icon.

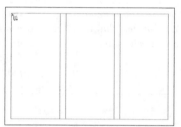

Click the manual text flow icon in a column.

InDesign flows the text into the column. Click the out port to reload and place more text.

FIGURE 3-28
Semi-Automatic Text Flow

Load the text place icon. InDesign displays the manual text flow icon.

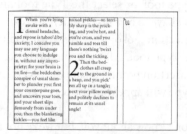

Hold down Option/Alt to switch to the semi-automatic text flow icon, then click the icon in a column.

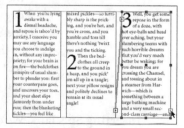

InDesign flows the text into the column, then automatically reloads the text place icon.

Click the the semi-automatic text flow icon in the next column. InDesign creates a new text frame and links it to the previous text frame.

Repeat this process until you've placed all of the columns of text you want to place.

necessary on each subsequent column or page (and links them together, of course), but it won't add additional pages to your document.

▶ **Super Autoflow.** Hold down Shift, and the text place icon turns into the autoflow icon. Click the autoflow icon, and InDesign places all of the text, creating new frames and pages as necessary (see Figure 3-29). When you click the autoflow icon in a text frame or series of linked text frames, InDesign duplicates that frame (or frames) on any new pages it creates, automatically links the frames, and places the text in the frames. When you click the autoflow icon in a column, InDesign creates a new text frame in each column (adding pages until it has placed all of the text in the story).

FIGURE 3-29
Super Autoflow

Load the text place icon. InDesign displays the manual text flow icon.

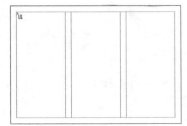

Hold down Shift to switch to the Super Autoflow text flow icon, then click the icon in a column.

InDesign flows the text into the available columns or text frames, and continues adding new text frames and pages until there's no more text left to place.

Entering Text

The simplest way to get text into the text frames in your InDesign publications is to type it. To do this, create a text frame by dragging the Type tool, or select the Type tool and click in a frame (again, it doesn't have to be a text frame). You can also double-click with either the Selection tool or the Direct Selection tool to automatically switch to the Type tool. All these methods place a blinking text cursor (or "text insertion point") inside the text frame. Type, and the characters you type will appear in the text frame.

Inserting Special Characters

We don't know about you, but we're not getting any younger, and we have trouble remembering exactly which keys to press to produce certain special characters. If you're like us, you'll appreciate the list of common characters in Table 3-2. InDesign lists these shortcuts in the Insert Special Character submenu (under the Type menu, or in the Context menu, see Figure 3-30). InDesign also offers (in the same places) the Insert White Space submenu (which lists various white spaces such as an Em Space) and the Insert Break Character

TABLE 3-2
Entering Special Characters

Special character:	What you press:
Bullet (•)	Option-8/Alt-8
Column break	Keypad Enter
Copyright symbol (©)	Option-G/Alt-G
Discretionary hyphen	Command-Shift--/Ctrl-Shift--
Ellipsis (…)	Option-;/Alt-;
Em dash (—)	Option-Shift--/Alt-Shift--
Em space	Command-Shift-M/Ctrl-Shift-M
En dash (–)	Option--/Alt--
En space	Command-Shift-N/Ctrl-Shift-N
Even page break	undefined*
Figure space	undefined*
Flush space	undefined*
Frame break	Shift-Keypad Enter
Hair space	undefined*
Indent to here	Command-\/Ctrl-\
Next page number	Command-Option-Shift-] Ctrl-Alt-Shift-]
Non-breaking hyphen	Command-Option--/Ctrl-Alt--
Non-breaking space	Command-Option-X/Ctrl-Alt-X
Odd page break	undefined*
Page break	Command-Keypad Enter Ctrl-Keypad Enter
Page number	Command-Option-Shift-N Ctrl-Alt-Shift-N
Paragraph symbol (¶)	Option-7/Alt-7
Previous page number	Command-Option-Shift-[Ctrl-Alt-Shift-[
Punctuation space	undefined*
Trademark (™)	undefined*
Left double quote (")	Option-[/Alt-[
Left single quote (')	Option-]/Alt-]
Right double quote (")	Option-Shift-[/Alt-Shift-[
Right single quote (')	Option-Shift-]/Shift-Alt-]
Section symbol (§)	Option-6/Alt-6
Thin space	Command-Option-Shift-M Ctrl-Alt-Shift-M
Registered trademark (®)	Option-R/Alt-R

You can define the undefined shortcuts (or redefine any of the others) by selecting Keyboard Shortcuts from the Edit menu.

FIGURE 3-30
**Entering Special
Characters Using the
Context Menu**

*Click the Type tool
in a text frame.*

*In this example, the section
marker text (in the Section
Options dialog box) is
"Sixteenth Century."*

*Display the context
menu and choose
a special character
from the Insert
Special Character
submenu.*

*InDesign enters
the character.*

*You can also use
the context menu
to enter space
characters...*

*...and break
characters.*

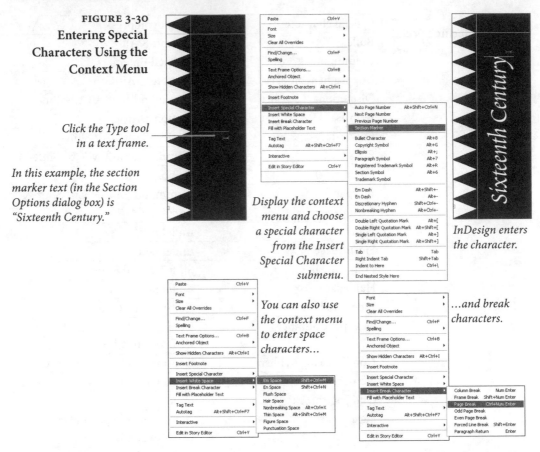

submenu (which lists Forced Line Breaks, Column Breaks, and other
interruptions of the text flow).

Inserting Glyphs   We're sometimes stumped when it's time to type a dagger (†) or a cir-
cumflex (^). And we often spend time hunting through KeyCaps (on
the Mac OS) or Character Map (in Windows) looking for the right
character in a symbol font (such as Zapf Dingbats).

If you also have this problem, you'll love the Glyphs palette. To
open this palette, choose Glyphs from the Type menu (see Figure
3-31). A "glyph" is the word for a specific shape of a character. For
instance, there may be three different glyphs in a font that all look
like the character "A" (one regular A, one with a swash, and one in
small caps).

The Glyphs palette is easy to use: while the text cursor is blinking in a text frame, choose the font (if different than the one you're
currently using), then double-click a character from the list of characters in the font. InDesign places the character at the location of the
cursor.

FIGURE 3-31
Inserting Characters Using the Glyphs Palette

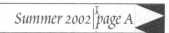

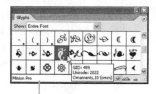

Click the Type tool in a text frame.

Choose Glyphs from the Type menu.

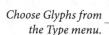

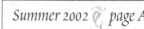

Select a font family and type style, then double-click a character …

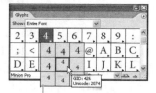

…and InDesign inserts the character.

Click these buttons to reduce or enlarge the size of the character display.

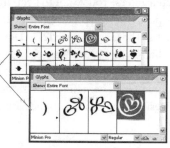

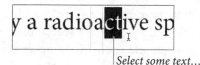

If you've selected an OpenType font, you can choose alternate character glyphs from the pop-up menus associated with each character.

The Show menu provides a number of ways to sort and display the glyphs available in the font. One of our favorites, Alternates for Selection, appears when you have text selected.

Select some text…

…and choose Alternates for Selection from the Show menu.

If the font contains alternate glyphs for the selected characters, they will appear in the Glyphs palette.

Double-click the alternate glyph to replace the selected characters.

Now here's the cool part: If a character can be found inside a font, you can use it—even if the character is outside the range of characters supported by your system. For instance, many fonts have a ½ character, but there's no way to type it on the Mac OS. This seems like a silly feature—after all, why would fonts contain characters that would be inaccessible to any other program? We don't know, mate, but they do. Fonts have all kinds of foreign-language characters, weird punctuation, and even ornaments that simply can't be used in QuarkXPress or other programs. But the Glyphs palette makes it easy to get to them. Characters such as "fi" and "fl" ligatures, which aren't part of the Windows character set, suddenly become available (without switching to an "expert" font). It's well worth your time to trawl through your fonts just to see if there's anything you can use that you haven't been using.

Missing characters. You've got to keep in mind that just because one font has a particular glyph doesn't mean that another font will, too. When you use the Glyphs palette, InDesign remembers the Unicode value for that glyph. When you change fonts, the program tries to find the same Unicode value in the new font. If the font designer didn't include that character, or assigned it to a different Unicode value, InDesign displays the dreaded pink highlight instead of the character.

Glyph Sets. You've spent hours looking, and you've finally found the perfect ornament characters for your publication. Unfortunately, they're in three different fonts. Wouldn't it be great if you could save those three characters in a special place to access them later? That's where glyph sets come in. To make a new glyph set to store your characters, choose (surprise!) New Glyph Set from the Glyphs palette menu (see Figure 3-32). Then, the next time you find a character you love, click it and choose your set from the Add to Glyph submenu (in the palette menu). You can mix and match fonts in a set, and have as many different sets as you want.

InDesign lists your glyph sets in the Show pop-up menu in the Glyphs palette; once you select a set, you can insert a glyph into the current text frame by double-clicking it.

By default, glyphs in a set remember what font they came from. So, when you insert a glyph from a set, InDesign assigns the proper font automatically. However, sometimes you want to insert a character in the current font of the selected text. You might want to include the one-half (½) symbol in your set, but want it to appear in the current font when you insert it. To do this, select the name of the glyph

FIGURE 3-32
Glyph Sets

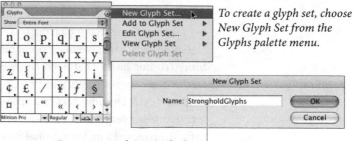

To create a glyph set, choose New Glyph Set from the Glyphs palette menu.

Enter a name for your glyph set and click the OK button.

To add a character to a glyph set, select the character and then choose the glyph set from the Add to Glyph set submenu of the Glyphs palette menu.

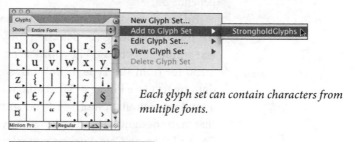

Each glyph set can contain characters from multiple fonts.

To display the glyph set in the Glyphs palette, choose the glyph set's name from the Show pop-up menu.

To make changes to the glyph set, select the glyph set name from the Edit Glyph Set submenu of the Glyphs palette menu. InDesign displays the Edit Glyph Set dialog box.

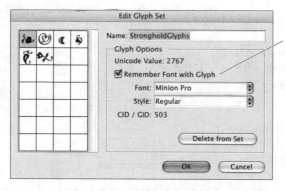

To associate a specific glyph with a specific font, select the glyph and check this option (and choose the appropriate font and font style, if necessary)

set from the Edit Glyph Set submenu of the palette menu, select the character, and turn off the Remember Font with Glyph checkbox. InDesign indicates that this character can be in any font with a little "u" symbol in the palette.

Dummy Text The client wants to see the new layout. But the writer won't give you the text. You're stuck—a layout looks, so, well, incomplete without text. And the client, a singularly humorless individual, cannot be appeased by whatever snatches of text from Gilbert & Sullivan,

Brecht, or Edgar Rice Burroughs come easily to mind. What you need is something that looks like text, but isn't really text at all.

Graphic artists have been prepared for this eventuality for *centuries* (rumor has it that even *Gutenburg's* writers couldn't deliver text in time for an important meeting)—we use something called "dummy text." Dummy text is a meaningless stream of fake Latin text that *looks* very much like real text (it's so realistic that it's used to fill the pages of a major national newspaper). It's just the thing you need to survive your meeting and get that approval your business depends on.

InDesign makes it easy to add dummy text to a text frame—select the text frame using the Selection tool, or click the Type tool in a text frame and choose Fill with Placeholder Text from the context menu (or from the Type menu). InDesign fills the text frame with dummy text (see Figure 3-33). By the way, InDesign's dummy text is a random compilation of words taken from the Lorum Ipsum text that many designers have used over the years. If you're using the Mac OS, and turn on Caps Lock as you select Fill with Placeholder Text, InDesign will, instead, fill the box with random words from an oration by Cicero.

Even better: If you save a text file in the InDesign folder with the name "Placeholder.txt" the program will use this text instead of the fake Latin stuff. This probably isn't actually useful, but it's nice to know it's possible, ain't it?

FIGURE 3-33
Filling a Frame with Dummy Text

Select a text frame with the Selection tool, or click the Type tool in a text frame.

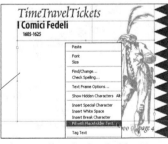

Choose Fill with Placeholder Text from the context menu (or from the Type menu)...

...and InDesign fills the selected frame with dummy text.

Importing Text

Most of the time, the text you work with in a page layout program isn't originally written using that program—it's written using a word processing program (such as Microsoft Word) or text editors (such as BBEdit). To get the text into InDesign, you must either copy-and-paste or import (or "place") the text files.

Pasting text. A surprising number of people find their primary source of text is their e-mail program or Web browser. The best way to get text from there to InDesign is copy and paste. In earlier versions of InDesign, the program would always try to maintain any formatting applied to the text. By default, InDesign now ignores all text formatting when you paste text from another program. If you want to retain the formatting, turn on the All Information option in the When Pasting Text from Other Applications section of the Type panel of the Preferences dialog box. Note that this only affects text pasted from other programs. To paste text that was copied from within InDesign without its formatting, choose Paste Without Formatting from the Edit menu (or press Command/Ctrl-Shift-V).

Placing text. InDesign can import text files in a variety of formats, including Microsoft Word, Microsoft Excel, text-only (ASCII or Unicode), Rich Text Format (RTF), and InDesign tagged text. You can view the complete list of available import filters in the Files of Type pop-up menu in the Place Document dialog box in Windows.

If you don't see your word processor or text editor listed as one of the available import filters, don't despair. InDesign can import text in common "interchange" formats, such as text-only and RTF, and chances are good that your word processor or text editor can save text in one of those formats.

In addition, InDesign's tagged text filter can import formatted text from any application that can write a text-only file. The tagged text format is something like RTF—it's a text-only format that uses special codes to define the typesetting of the text in the file (see "Working with InDesign Tagged Text," later in this chapter).

To place a text file, follow these steps (see Figure 3-34).

1. Choose Place from the File menu (or press Command-D/Ctrl-D). InDesign displays the Place dialog box.

2. Locate and select the text file you want to import.

3. Check Show Import Options to set up the import options you want (if necessary), and/or check Replace Selected Item.

  ▶ **Show Import Options.** Turn on the Show Import Options checkbox to display another dialog box containing more import options for the specific type of file you're placing. This dialog box appears after you click the Open button to import the text file. We rarely turn this checkbox on; instead, if we want to see the Options Import dialog box we take a shortcut:

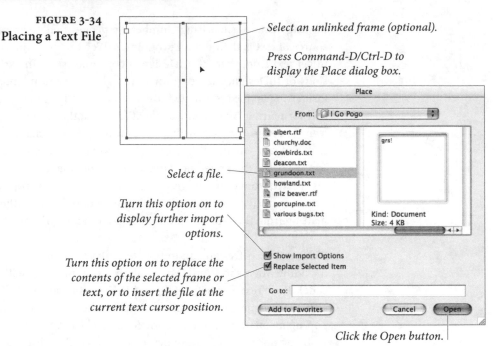

FIGURE 3-34
Placing a Text File

Select an unlinked frame (optional).

Press Command-D/Ctrl-D to
display the Place dialog box.

Select a file.

Turn this option on to
display further import
options.

Turn this option on to replace the
contents of the selected frame or
text, or to insert the file at the
current text cursor position.

Click the Open button.

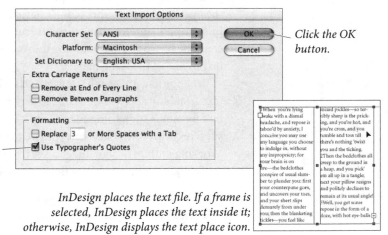

If you turned on the Show
Import Options option or
held down the Shift key when
clicking Open, InDesign
displays the Import Options
dialog box for the file format
you're importing.
Turn this option on to
have InDesign replace any
"straight quotes" in the text
file with proper typographic
quotation marks.

Click the OK
button.

InDesign places the text file. If a frame is
selected, InDesign places the text inside it;
otherwise, InDesign displays the text place icon.

Hold down the Shift key while clicking the Open button or
while double-clicking a text file in the Place dialog box.

▶ **Replace Selected Item.** If you had a frame selected before you
displayed the Place dialog box, InDesign makes the Replace
Selected Item option available. Turn this option on to replace
the contents of the frame (if any) with the text file. If you
had text selected, or if you had clicked the Type tool in a text
frame, turning the Replace Selected Item option on inserts
the text from the file into the text frame.

4. Click the Open Button. If Show Import Options was on (or you held down the Shift key), InDesign displays a dialog box containing options for the type of file you selected (see below).

5. If no frames were selected, InDesign displays the Text Place cursor and waits for you to click on a frame or drag one out (see "Flowing Text," earlier in this chapter). If the incoming text file contains fonts that aren't currently loaded, InDesign warns you of their presence. If you had selected a frame before opening the Place dialog box, and you turned on the Replace Selected Item checkbox, InDesign fills the frame with the file you selected—even if it was a graphic frame with a picture in it! This can be very annoying if you had forgotten to deselect all frames first. Fortunately, you can always press Command-Z/Control-Z to undo the Place and reload the Text Place cursor.

Word and RTF Import Options

InDesign imports the text formatting in Word and RTF text files, without any page layout ("page geometry") information saved in the file. This means that InDesign imports paragraph indents, but does not import page margins. For a more complete list of the formatting imported—or not—by the Word and RTF import filters, see the Filters ReadMe.pdf file (you'll find it in your InDesign folder).

When you turn on the Show Import Options option and place a Word or RTF file, InDesign displays the corresponding Import Options dialog box (see Figure 3-35).

Table of Contents Text. Turn this option on to import the table of contents text (if any) in the Word/RTF file. However, the table of contents entries lose their special qualities. The page numbers appear as

FIGURE 3-35
RTF Import Options

If you find yourself repeatedly making the same choices in this dialog box, click Save Preset—your preset will show up in the Preset pop-up menu. This is especially helpful when using the Customize Style Import mapping feature.

they were in the document the last time the file was saved, and do not change as you place the text on the pages of your InDesign publication. The table of contents also loses its navigational (i.e., hyperlink) properties. To InDesign, it's just text. InDesign's Table of Contents feature is not linked with this at all; if you're going to build a table of contents with the InDesign feature, you might as well leave this checkbox turned off.

Index Text. Turn this option on to import an index (or indices) you've inserted in the Word/RTF document. Note that individual index entries that you make in Word are imported whether this option is on or off; this only controls whether any built indexes get imported. We usually leave this turned off.

Footnotes/Endnotes. When you turn on this option, InDesign places any footnotes or endnotes at the end of the story. Leave this option off to omit any footnote or endnote text.

Use Typographer's Quotes. Turn on the Use Typographer's Quotes option to convert any straight quotes (i.e., foot and inch marks) to proper typographic quotation marks and apostrophes.

Remove Styles and Formatting from Text and Tables. When you turn this option on, InDesign strips out any text formatting in your file (paragraph and character styles, font, size, color, and so on) and places the text using the current default formatting.

Preserve Local Overrides. Turn this option on to retain bold, italic, underline, and other local formatting in the incoming text.

Convert Tables To. If you've chosen to remove text and table formatting (see above), you can choose Unformatted Tables or Unformatted Tabbed Text to tell InDesign how to deal with tables.

Preserve Styles and Formatting form Text and Tables. When you turn this option on, InDesign will import text formatting used in the Word/RTF document. How, exactly, it does this is, is determined by the controls that become available when you choose this option, which are described in the following paragraphs.

Manual Page Breaks. What should InDesign do when it finds a page break setting? (In Word, you can set up automatic page breaks in the Line and Page Breaks tab of the Paragraph dialog box, or by pressing Shift-Enter.) We typically want InDesign to ignore these, so we choose No Breaks. However, if those breaks are there for a good reason, you can choose Preserve Page Breaks or Convert to Column Breaks to have InDesign automatically apply the page and column break settings (which is usually done manually using the Start Paragraph pop-up menu in the Keep Options dialog box).

Import Inline Graphics. If you want to include graphics from the Word file, turn this option on. While this can be very useful for importing equations and other Word graphics, be aware that the many of the graphics embedded in Word/RTF documents are not suitable for high resolution printing. Most of the time, we think you'll be better off saving the graphics as separate files (in a format suitable to your production/printing process, as described in the file format discussion in Chapter 7, "Importing and Exporting") and then placing them in InDesign.

Import Unused Styles. When this option is turned on, InDesign will import character and paragraph styles that are not used in any of the text in the incoming document. When it's off, InDesign does not attempt to import the unused styles.

Import Styles Automatically. The two pop-up menus below this option tell InDesign what to do when character and paragraph styles in the Word document match the names of existing styles in the InDesign document. For both character and paragraph styles, you can choose to use the InDesign style definition, redefine the InDesign style to match the Word style, or to create a new style for each style name conflict. If you choose to take the latter approach, InDesign will automatically generate a new name for each style.

Customize Style Import. To get more control over style import, turn this option on and click the Style Mapping button. When you do this, InDesign displays the Style Mapping dialog box (see Figure 3-36).

Tip: Beware the Fast Save. It's so seductive. It's hard to resist the natural impulse to turn on the Allow Fast Saves option in Word's Options dialog box (it's on by default; see Figure 3-37). It sounds like such a good idea. Faster saves mean you spend less time waiting for Word to save files—and saving time is good, right?

Not in this case, it isn't. The Word file format is very complicated, and using this option sometimes produces files that import filters

FIGURE 3-36
**Mapping Styles
on Import**

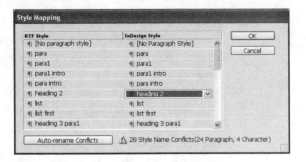

FIGURE 3-37
**Word's Allow Fast
Saves Option**

Turn it off! Stop it before it kills again!

can't read. Heck, when you turn this option on, Word sometimes writes files that *Word* can't read.

If you're having trouble importing a Word file, open the file in Word (if you can) and save it under another file name—it's very likely the person who gave you the file had forgotten to turn off the Allow Fast Saves option.

Text-Only Import Options

Text-only files often arrive full of extra characters—usually spaces and carriage returns added to change the appearance of text on screen. Text prepared for online viewing, for example, often contains a carriage return at the end of each line, as well as carriage returns between paragraphs. The options in the Text Import Options dialog box give you a way to have the import filter do some of the clean-up for you (see Figure 3-38).

Character Set. If you're seeing odd characters in the text files you import, it might be that the character set of the computer used to create the files is not the same character set as the one in use by your copy of InDesign. As you import a text file, you can choose a character set that matches the character set of the text file.

Platform. Windows and the Mac OS use different character sets and also use different ways of ending a paragraph. If you're using Windows and know that the text file you're placing came from the Mac OS—or vice versa—choose the appropriate platform from this pop-up menu.

FIGURE 3-38
Text Import Options

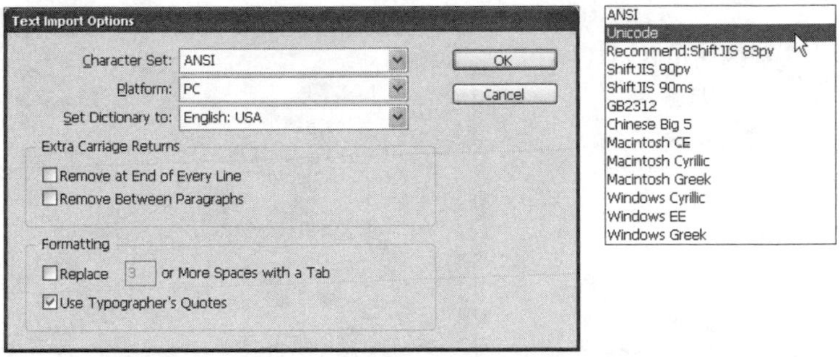

Set Dictionary To. Use this pop-up menu to apply a default spelling and hyphenation dictionary to the incoming text.

Extra Carriage Returns. The people who prepare the text files for you want to help. They really do. That's why they entered all of those carriage returns (to force a page break). And why they entered all of those spaces (to center the headline). They are trying to do some of the formatting so that you don't have to. The only trouble, of course, is that they usually make a mess that you're left to fix. InDesign's Text Import filter can solve many of the problems your co-workers create. The options in the Extra Carriage Returns section of the Text Import Options dialog box help you clean up the extraneous carriage return characters.

Use Typographer's Quotes. We recommend turning on the Use Typographer's Quotes option so that InDesign converts the straight quotes to proper typographic quotation marks and apostrophes.

Extra Spaces. Why do people enter extra spaces in text? Usually, they're trying to indicate to you, their trusted typesetter, that they want to enter some amount of horizontal space. In other words, a tab. InDesign can replace some number of spaces in the incoming text file with tabs—just enter a value for the number of contiguous space characters you want replaced. Note that this approach often enters multiple tab characters in the story, but that problem is easily cleaned up using Find and Change.

Excel Import Options

Use the options in the Excel Import Options dialog box to specify the range of cells you want to import and the formatting applied to those cells (see Figure 3-39). See Chapter 6, "Where Text Meets Graphics," for more on what you can do with tables. Remember that InDesign can only import Excel tables, not charts. If you need to import a graphic chart from Excel, you should probably export it as a PDF file

FIGURE 3-39
Excel Import Options

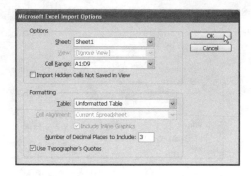

(and possibly even open that PDF in Illustrator to fine-tune it before saving and importing into InDesign).

View, Sheet, and Cell Range. Use these options to define which custom view, worksheet, and range of cells you want to import. By default, the Cell Range field selects the filled cells of the worksheet you've selected.

Import Hidden Cells Not Saved in View. Turn this option on to import any cells in the Excel file that have been formatted as hidden cells.

Table. By default, InDesign tries to match as much of Excel's table formatting as possible. However, if you'd prefer to handle formatting your table in InDesign, set the Table pop-up menu to Unformatted Table. Or, you can also import the table data as straight tab-delimited text by selecting Unformatted Text.

Cell Alignment. How do you want InDesign to align the text from the cells you're importing? The default setting is Current Spreadsheet, which tells InDesign to copy the alignment from Excel. However, unless you have done a lot of formatting in your Excel spreadsheet that you want to keep, we recommend changing this to Left and then applying your alignment once the table is built in InDesign.

Import Inline Graphics. Turn this option on to include any inline graphics in the spreadsheet. As with importing graphics embedded in Word/RTF files, this can be useful or dangerous, depending on the graphics and on your printing process. Again, we think it's best to save the graphics as separate files, in a high-quality graphics format, and then place them in InDesign (see Chapter 7, "Importing and Exporting," for more on file formats).

Decimal Places. You can choose the number of decimal places you want to use in the imported spreadsheet cells. For example, a spreadsheet cell might be 3.1415926, but if you specify only three decimal places, only 3.142 shows up in the table (it rounds off to the nearest decimal digit).

Use Typographer's Quotes. Unless there's a good reason to stick with straight quote marks in your Excel data, turn on the Use Typographer's Quotes to get curly quotes.

Tagged Text Import Options

InDesign's Tagged Text import filter gives you a great way to get formatted text from any application that can create a text-only file. You can use FileMaker Pro, vi on a UNIX workstation, or even the original Quark word processor for the Apple II to save a tagged text file. For more on creating tagged text files, see "Working with InDesign Tagged Text," later in this chapter. When you import a tagged text file, you can set some import options (see Figure 3-40).

Use Typographer's Quotes. Okay, we've already described this feature more times in this section than it's worth. We're going to assume you now know what it does.

Remove Text Formatting. Just because someone went through all the difficulty of making a tagged text file doesn't mean you can't strip out the styles and import simple text. To do this, turn on the Remove Text Formatting option.

FIGURE 3-40
**Tagged Text
Import Options**

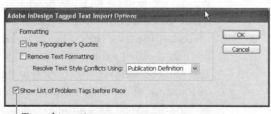

Turn this option on...

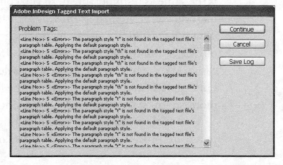

...and InDesign will list any errors it finds in your tagged text file. It will also list a number of things that aren't errors, but might be good to know about.

Remove Text Style Conflicts Using. If the name of an incoming style (character or paragraph) matches a style that already exists in the publication, which style definition should InDesign use? Choose the Publication Definition option to apply the formatting defined by your document (this is what we almost always use), or Tagged File Definition to import the style defined in the tagged text file. When you choose the latter method, InDesign adds the style to the publication and appends the word "copy" to the style's name. This does not affect the formatting of any text in the publication tagged with the original style.

Show List of Problem Tags Before Place. If you're not getting the formatting you expect from your tagged text files, turn this option on to have InDesign display a list of errors. If InDesign does find errors, you can choose to place the file, or to cancel the place operation. You can write the error list to a text file by clicking the Save Log button.

Text Files and File Linking

When you imported a text file (or a Microsoft Word file, or anything else from disk) in InDesign 2, the publication maintained a link to the text file itself, and added the link to the Links palette (to display the Links palette, press Command-Shift-D/Ctrl-Shift-D or choose Links from the File menu). This is similar to what programs have done for many years with graphics. If you later edited the Microsoft Word document (or RTF file, or whatever), InDesign recognized that it had changed and let you update the file.

Today, you have the option of linking to text files on disk or not. You can choose by turning on or off the Create Links When Placing Text and Spreadsheet Files option in the Text Preferences dialog box. (Is it just us, or are these feature names getting longer?)

Linking to text files sounds cool, but watch out: Updating the file is the same as re-importing it, so you completely lose any edits or formatting you've applied in InDesign. Instead, we recommend embedding your text files. You can do this by having this preference turned off before importing. Or, if you have already imported the file, you can break the link to the disk file by selecting the file's name in the Links palette and choosing Embed File from the palette menu. (For more on links, see Chapter 7, "Importing and Exporting.")

However, if you have a workflow in which you need to edit text in a word processor and have it update on your InDesign page, this text-linking feature can be a great help—as long as you never make edits or formatting changes in InDesign.

Exporting Text

When you need to get your text back out of an InDesign publication and back into some other program—a text editor, word processor, or database—you can export the text in a variety of text formats. To export a story, follow these steps (see Figure 3-41).

1. Select the story you want to export (click the Type tool in the story) and choose Text from the Export submenu of the File menu (or press Command-E/Ctrl-E). InDesign displays the Export dialog box.

2. Choose an export format for the text from the Format pop-up menu. Note that some of the items in this pop-up menu, like EPS or PDF, don't export your story; they export the whole page (or document). To export the text, choose Text Only (which will export the text without any formatting), Rich Text Format (RTF), or Adobe InDesign Tagged Text (which we'll discuss in "Working With InDesign Tagged Text," later in this chapter).

3. Specify a name and location for the file.

4. Click the Save button to export the story.

FIGURE 3-41
Exporting Text

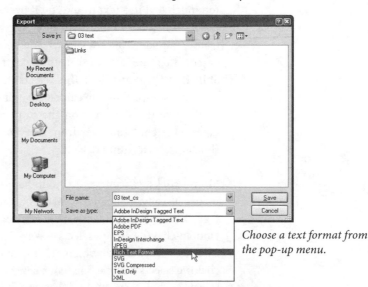

Choose a text format from the pop-up menu.

Editing Text

Once you've entered or imported text, chances are good you're going to have to change it. InDesign includes most common word processing features, such as the ability to move the cursor through text using keyboard shortcuts, check the spelling of text, or find and change text and formatting. Fortunately, InDesign now has a Story Editor feature (which PageMaker users have come to know and love)—so your text editing can be done either on the page or in a story window.

Moving the Cursor Through Text

When we're entering text, one of the last things we want to do is take our hands away from the keyboard. We don't want to have to use the mouse to move the text cursor or select text. That's why we like to use keyboard shortcuts to move the cursor and select text—they keep our hands where they belong: on the keyboard.

InDesign comes with a fairly complete set of keyboard shortcuts, as shown in Table 3-3. Note that some of the shortcuts have several keys associated with them—pick the combination that works best for you. You can always change the shortcuts by choosing Keyboard Shortcuts from the Edit menu. David changed his so that they better matched those in QuarkXPress, which he has become used to.

Whatever keyboard shortcuts you use, remember that you can typically add Shift to them to select text as you move. For example, Command-End/Ctrl-End jumps to the end of a story, so adding Shift to that will select the text to the end of the story. Let's say you've got too much text in a text frame and it overflows, producing an overset mark. You could make the frame bigger or link the text to a new frame, but sometimes it's faster and more convenient to place the cursor after the last word in the text frame and press Command-Shift-End/Ctrl-Shift-End. This selects the overset text (even though you can't see it). Now you can delete it or cut it.

We like the shortcuts on the numeric keypad, even though it takes our right hand away from the "home row." To use the keypad shortcuts, turn Num Lock off.

Mouse clicks. Of course, if you do happen to have one hand on the mouse already, you can use various combinations of clicks to select text. *Which* clicks, exactly depends on your preferences settings. Double-clicking always selects a word. If you've turned on the Triple Click to Select a Line option in the Type Preferences dialog box, triple-clicking selects a single line (not a sentence), and quadruple-clicking selects a whole paragraph; if that option is off, triple-clicking selects a paragraph and quadruple-clicking selects the entire story.

TABLE 3-3
Moving the Cursor
Through Text

Hold down Shift as you press
these shortcuts to select text
as you move the cursor.

To move the cursor:	Press
Right one character	Right arrow, Keypad 6
Left one character	Left arrow, Keypad 4
Right one word	Command-Right arrow Ctrl-Right arrow, Ctrl-Keypad 6
Left one word	Command-Left arrow Ctrl-Left arrow, Ctrl-Keypad 4
Up one line	Up arrow, Keypad 8
Down one line	Down arrow, Keypad 2
Up one paragraph	Command-Down arrow Ctrl-Down arrow, Ctrl-Keypad 8
Down one paragraph	Command-Down arrow Ctrl-Down arrow, Ctrl-Keypad 2
End of line	End, Keypad 1
Start of line	Home, Keypad 7
Start of story	Command-Home/Ctrl-Home, Keypad 7
End of story	Command-End/Ctrl-End, Keypad 1

The Keyboard Dance. Selecting text in InDesign—whether you're in a story window or a document window—is in most ways the same as any other program. There is one difference, however, which drives us crazy. When you select text using keyboard shortcuts, InDesign remembers where the cursor was when you started—but it only remembers as long as you hold the modifier keys down. This is a subtle thing, and much more difficult to explain than to show.

Here's an example. You place the text cursor at the beginning of this paragraph and then Command-Shift-Down Arrow/Ctrl-Shift-Down Arrow to select the whole paragraph. Suddenly, you realize that you don't want to select the last character (the paragraph return character), so you press Shift-Left Arrow to deselect it. What happens next depends on whether or not you raised your hand from the keyboard. If you keep the Shift key down between the two shortcuts, InDesign will deselect the last character (which is what you want). If you let go of the keyboard before pressing Shift-Left Arrow, then InDesign sees this as a whole new selection and *adds* one character to the *left* of the paragraph (the last character in the previous paragraph) to your selection (which is *never* what you want).

At that point, getting the selection you want requires you to extend the selection to the right (perhaps by pressing Shift-Right Arrow) and then deselect the characters (Shift-Left Arrow, twice). This what we call doing they keyboard dance. It's so bad that we sometimes take our fingers off the keyboard and use the mouse.

Confused? Try it for yourself and you'll see why we hesitate before letting go of a modifier key before we're absolutely certain that the selection is the one we hoped for.

Showing and Hiding "Invisibles"

Sometimes, the best tools are the simple ones. When you're handed another person's file to clean up, choose Show Hidden Characters from the Type menu (or press Command-Option-I/Ctrl-Alt-I). InDesign displays the carriage returns, tabs, spaces, and other invisible characters in the text (see Figure 3-42).

FIGURE 3-42 Showing Hidden Characters

Dragging and Dropping Text

You can move text from place to place using the drag and drop techniques you're probably familiar with from other word processors and text editors. (If you're not familiar with this feature, just think of it as a way to cut/copy and paste by moving a tool, rather than using a menu command.)

By default, drag and drop text editing is turned on for the Story Editor view and turned off for layout view. To change these settings, check or uncheck the corresponding options in the Type panel of the Preferences dialog box. To use drag and drop text editing (see Figure 3-43), follow these steps.

1. Select some text.

2. Position the cursor over the selected text until you see the drag and drop icon.

3. Drag the text to a new location (to copy the text, hold down Option/Alt as you drag—see Figure 3-44). This location can be pretty much anywhere—in the same story, in another story, in a text frame in another window or document. As you drag, InDesign displays a vertical bar to show you the destination for the text. To create a new text frame as you drop the text, hold down Command/Ctrl as you drag (see Figure 3-45).

4. Release the mouse button to drop the text.

FIGURE 3-43
Drag and Drop
Text Editing

> The King of Elfland's Daughter, by Lord Dunsany (pen name of Edward John Moreton Drax Plunkett, 18th Baron Dunsany). G.P.Putnam & Sons Ltd., London, 1924. Cloth Hardcover.
>
> Lord Dunsany () influenced H. P. Lovecraft, Clark Ashton Smith, and other fantasy authors.

Select some text, then move the cursor over the selection. If drag and drop text editing is active, you'll see the drag and drop icon.

> The King of Elfland's Daughter, by Lord Dunsany (pen name of Edward John Moreton Drax Plunkett, 18th Baron Dunsany). G.P.Putnam & Sons Ltd., London, 1924. Cloth Hardcover.
>
> Lord Dunsany () influenced H. P. Lovecraft, Clark Ashton Smith, and other fantasy authors.

Drag the text to a new location. As you drag, InDesign displays a vertical bar to show the destination of the text.

> The King of Elfland's Daughter, by Lord Dunsany (, 18th Baron Dunsany). G.P.Putnam & Sons Ltd., London, 1924. Cloth Hardcover.
>
> Lord Dunsany (pen name of Edward John Moreton Drax Plunkett) influenced H. P. Lovecraft, Clark Ashton Smith, and other fantasy authors.

Stop dragging and release the mouse button, and InDesign moves the text to the location of the vertical bar.

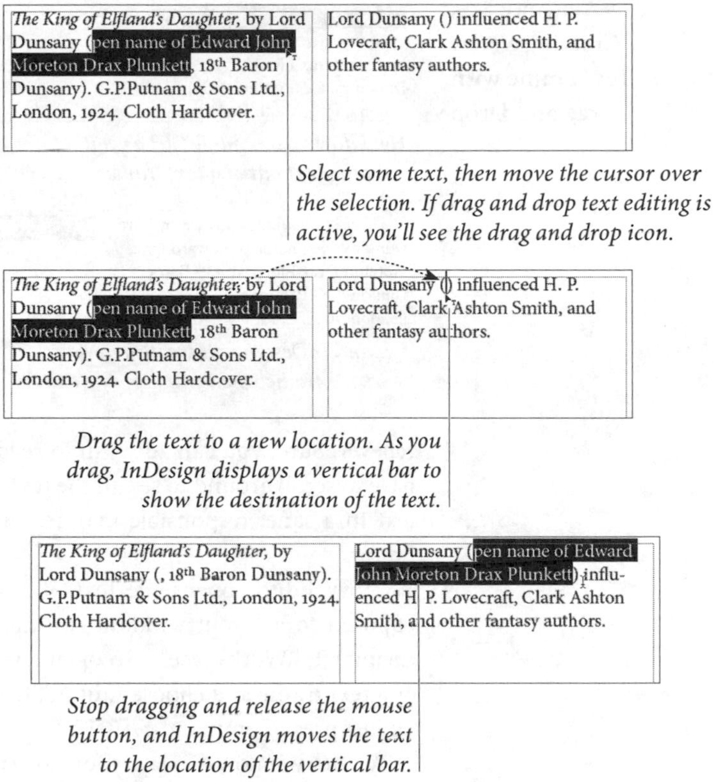

FIGURE 3-44
Copying Text with
Drag and Drop

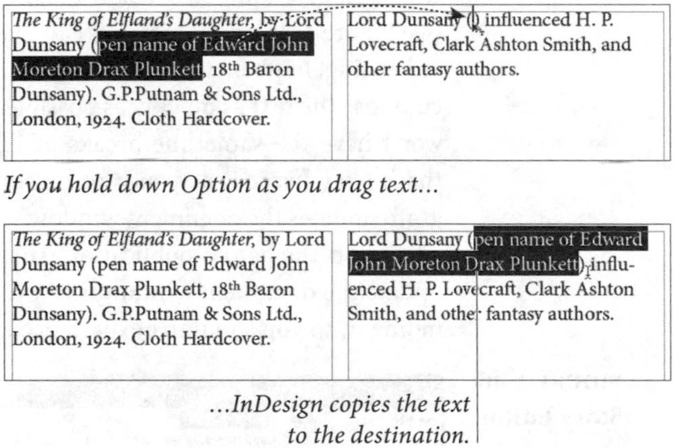

> The King of Elfland's Daughter, by Lord Dunsany (pen name of Edward John Moreton Drax Plunkett, 18th Baron Dunsany). G.P.Putnam & Sons Ltd., London, 1924. Cloth Hardcover.
>
> Lord Dunsany () influenced H. P. Lovecraft, Clark Ashton Smith, and other fantasy authors.

If you hold down Option as you drag text...

> The King of Elfland's Daughter, by Lord Dunsany (pen name of Edward John Moreton Drax Plunkett, 18th Baron Dunsany). G.P.Putnam & Sons Ltd., London, 1924. Cloth Hardcover.
>
> Lord Dunsany (pen name of Edward John Moreton Drax Plunkett) influenced H. P. Lovecraft, Clark Ashton Smith, and other fantasy authors.

...InDesign copies the text to the destination.

Story Editor

Reading and editing text on-screen is never any fun, and it's even worse when it's that legal notice you set in 8-point Garamond Extra Condensed Light, all caps, and reversed out of a dark background. Eyestrain is one of the occupational hazards of graphic design, and tiny, tinted text will usually require two of your preferred pain

FIGURE 3-45
**Creating a New
Text Frame with
Drag and Drop**

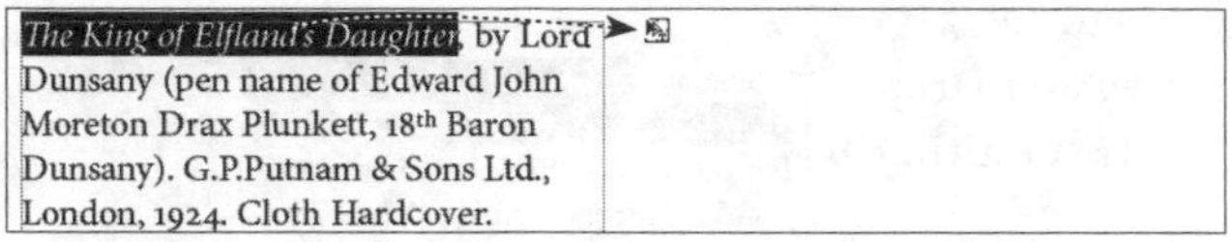

The King of Elfland's Daughter, by Lord
Dunsany (pen name of Edward John
Moreton Drax Plunkett, 18th Baron
Dunsany). G.P.Putnam & Sons Ltd.,
London, 1924. Cloth Hardcover.

*Hold down Command/Ctrl as you
drag text out of a text frame...*

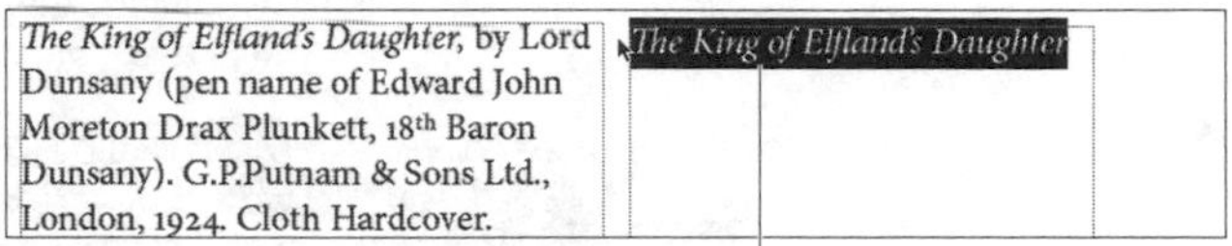

The King of Elfland's Daughter, by Lord
Dunsany (pen name of Edward John
Moreton Drax Plunkett, 18th Baron
Dunsany). G.P.Putnam & Sons Ltd.,
London, 1924. Cloth Hardcover.   *The King of Elfland's Daughter*

*...and InDesign will create a new text
frame when you drop the text.*

reliever. Sure, you can zoom in to read it more easily, but then you
have to scroll around to see all the text. Isn't there a way to view your
text in a sane, responsible manner? There is—it's called the Story
Editor.

Story Editor opens the text of a story in a story window (as
opposed to a layout window—we discussed the window types in
Chapter 1, "Workspace"). To open a story window, select some text
or a text frame and choose Edit in Story Editor from the Edit menu
(or just press Command-Y/Ctrl-Y).

A story window displays your story in a single column of readable
text, ignoring font, size, color, indents, and most other formatting
(see Figure 3-46). It also ignores calculation-intensive features—such
as kerning, hyphenation, and justification options—so InDesign can
compose the text as quickly as possible. The text in the story window
won't have the same line breaks as in the document window. But
that's okay because as you type or edit in a story window, the program updates the document window so you can see the effect of your
editing in the actual publication. InDesign only takes the time to
update the document window when you stop typing or editing for a
moment, so you shouldn't experience much of a slowdown.

FIGURE 3-46
Story Editor

*Clicking the paragraph
style name will not select
the paragraph, as it does in
PageMaker.*

*The vertical depth in the
left column is in inches,
mm, points, or whatever the
measurement system is*

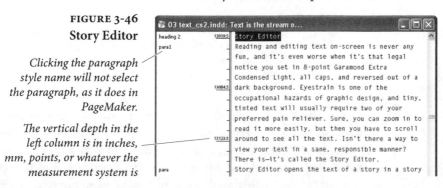

When you open or select a story window, some InDesign features are unavailable. For example, almost every tool in the Tool palette becomes grayed out. You can still use all the text-related features: apply paragraph and character styles, change text formatting, and so on. However, most of the formatting you can apply doesn't appear in the story window (though you can see it in the document window if it's visible in the background). The only formatting that Story Editor does display are the bold and italic versions of fonts and small caps—plus, it may list the paragraph style for each paragraph in a column along the left side of the window (that's an option).

Multiple Windows

You can have as many story windows open as you want. If you select three text frames in the publication and press Command-Y/Ctrl-Y, InDesign opens each story in its own window. Story windows, like layout windows, appear at the bottom of the Window menu. To move from one window to the next, you can press Command-F6/Ctrl-F6, or Command-`.

As you edit in a story window, InDesign doesn't change the view in the layout window, so the layout window might be displaying page 3 of a long story while you're making changes to page 23 in a story window. If you click the layout window, it comes to the front and you'll notice that even the text cursor can be in one place in one window and somewhere else in the other window. However, pressing Command-Y/Ctrl-Y while you're in a story window switches to the layout window containing the text, updates the layout window view so it displays the text you're editing, *and* matches the cursor position and/or text selection.

The New Window feature (in the Arrange submenu, under the Window menu) works on Story Editor windows, too. That means you can have two or more story windows open on the same story, each looking at a different chunk of text. This is helpful when you need to refer to text in one part of the story while editing another.

Footnotes in the Story Editor

The Story Editor displays footnotes as an icon—click the icon to expand and edit the footnote (see Figure 3-47). You can also choose to expand all footnotes by choosing Expand All Footnotes from the Story Editor submenu of the View menu, or hide them all by choosing Collapse All Footnotes.

Story Editor Options

The Story Editor is designed to be utilitarian, not pretty. However, you can spruce it up a bit, making it appear comfortable to your eye, by changing settings in the Story Editor Preferences dialog box (see Figure 3-48).

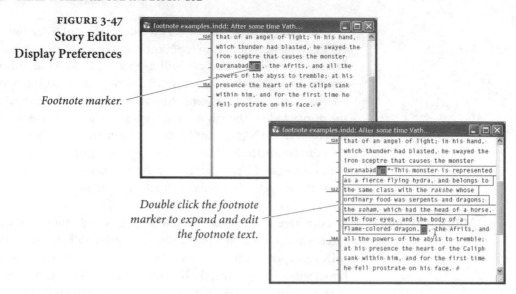

Footnote marker.

*Double click the footnote
marker to expand and edit
the footnote text.*

*We trust that you will use
these settings responsibly.*

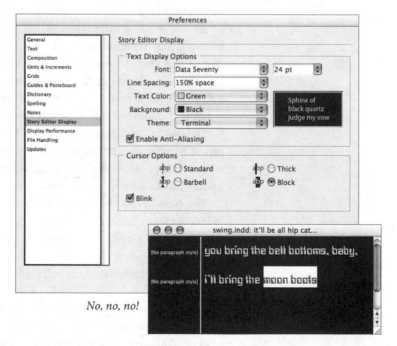

No, no, no!

Text Display Options. You can select any font and size you want, though it behooves you to pick something as readable as possible (David likes 16-point Georgia). You should also choose line spacing (*a.k.a.*, leading), the text color, whether text should be anti-aliased, and a background color for your story windows. The Theme pop-up menu offers several text color and background color combinations, but you don't have to use these. We suggest you set somebody else's computer to the Terminal theme, making them think they're having flashbacks to their old CP/M or DOS computer (pick Letter Gothic font and turn off anti-aliasing for the best effect). Remember that these settings have no effect on the printed appearance of your text; they're just for the story windows.

Cursor Options. We've never met anyone who wanted to use anything other than the normal, thin cursor (called Standard here). But, just in case you happen to fall into that category, you can choose Thick, Barbell, or Block. (The Block option really complements the "DOS look" described above.) And if a blinking cursor drives you mad, turn off the Blink option.

Paragraph styles column. You can also edit the size of the left column in a story window (where the paragraph style names appear). If you never use paragraph styles—shame on you!—you might as well minimize that column by dragging the vertical divider bar all the way to the left.

Using Adobe InCopy

We don't ordinarily talk about buying additional programs in this book, but we need to make a quick exception for Adobe InCopy, a word processor that is designed to work especially well with InDesign—sort of a Story Editor on steroids. While it's not part of the Creative Suite, it's well worth buying if you work with text heavy publications, especially if you're collaborating with other people.

InCopy lets you write or edit stories using all the text-formatting available in InDesign, using the same paragraph and character styles, with the knowledge that what you set in InCopy will appear the same in InDesign. InCopy lets you see your stories in story mode (like Story Editor), layout mode (as though you're seeing the layout in InDesign, but can only edit the story), or galley mode (like story, but you actually see the line breaks).

When you install InCopy, a number of plug-ins are added to InDesign's InCopyWorkflow plug-ins folder. These are called the Live Edit plug-ins (some folks call them the "bridge" plug-ins) and they allow you to set up an InDesign layout for editing from within InCopy. The plug-ins add an Assignments palette for managing InCopy stories, plus a Note tool, menu and palette to let InDesign users exchange notes with InCopy users.

Checking Spelling

Toward the end of a project, we fall prey to the delusion that everything, every last word, on all of our pages, is misspelled. We find ourselves staring blearily at relatively simple words. Is "dog" really spelled "D-O-G?" In our typical pre-deadline panic, we don't know. Everything looks wrong.

We don't know what we'd do without psychotherapy—and, of course, the spelling checkers in the page layout and word processing programs we use.

InDesign can check the spelling of any text in an InDesign text frame, and can also catch duplicated words ("the the") and possible capitalization errors. InDesign uses the language dictionary or dictionaries associated with your text to perform the spelling check.

To check spelling, follow these steps (see Figure 3-49).

1. Press Command-I/Ctrl-I (or choose Check Spelling from the Edit menu) to display the Check Spelling palette (note that this really is a palette, even though it looks like a dialog box—which means you can leave it open while editing text).

2. Define the scope of the spelling check using the Search pop-up menu at the bottom of the palette. Note that InDesign can check the spelling of all of the open publications, if you want, or you can restrict the spell check to the current story, or—if you have one or more words highlighted—even just to the selected words.

3. Click the Start button to start checking the spelling of text in the range you've chosen. When InDesign finds a potential misspelled word, the word appears in the Not in Dictionary field,

FIGURE 3-49
Checking Spelling

InDesign scrolls to display any suspect words it finds while checking spelling.

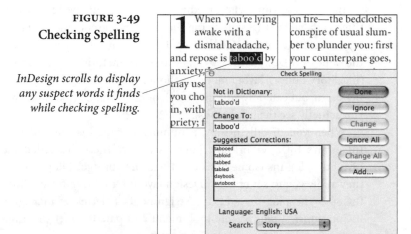

and a number of possible corrections appear in the Suggested Corrections list. At this point, you can:

▶ Skip the word without making any change. To do this, click the Ignore button. InDesign continues with the spell check. To have InDesign ignore every occurrence of the word, click the Ignore All button.

▶ Replace the word with one of the suggestions. Select the suggestion, and InDesign enters the suggested word in the Change To field. Click the Change button to replace the selected word with the suggestion. Click the Change All button to replace every instance of the selected text with the text in the Change To field.

▶ Enter replacement text in the Change To field. Click the Change button to replace the selected word with the text you've entered, or click the Change All button to replace every instance of the selected text.

▶ Add the word to the user dictionary. This is a good thing to do with technical terms and names that appear frequently in your publications. For more on entering words in the dictionary, see "Adding Words to the User Dictionary."

After you've taken any of the above actions, InDesign continues with the spelling check.

4. When you've finished checking the spelling of the publication (or publications), you can click the Done button to close the Check Spelling palette.

Adding Words to the User Dictionary

We use lots of words in our publications that aren't found in InDesign's dictionary. Even quite common, household words such as "Kvern" and "Blatner" will provoke an angry query from the spelling checker. You can allay InDesign's fears by entering these words in a separate dictionary, the "user dictionary." When InDesign can't find a word in its dictionary, it consults the user dictionary before questioning the spelling of the word. If a word appears in both the standard dictionary (which can't be edited) and the user dictionary, InDesign favors the word in the user dictionary.

You can add a word to the user dictionary in two ways: from within the Check Spelling palette or from the Dictionary palette (see Figure 3-50). When you're checking your document's spelling and a "misspelled" word pops up, you can temporarily open the Dictionary

FIGURE 3-50
**Adding a Word to the
User Dictionary**

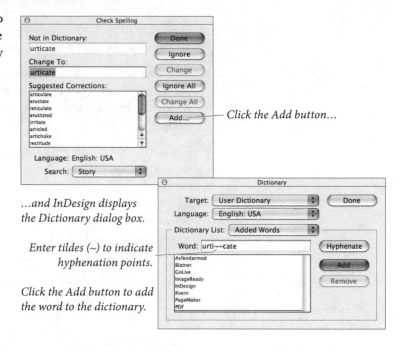

— *Click the Add button...*

*...and InDesign displays
the Dictionary dialog box.*

*Enter tildes (~) to indicate
hyphenation points.*

*Click the Add button to add
the word to the dictionary.*

palette by clicking the Add button. If you want to add or remove items from your user dictionary without first checking spelling (or without even having the word on your page), you can open the Dictionary palette by choosing Dictionary from the Edit menu.

1. Enter the word you want to add in the Word field of the Dictionary palette, if necessary (if you're in the middle of a spelling check, InDesign enters the word displayed in the Not in Dictionary field for you, though you can edit it if you want).

2. Click the Hyphenate button when you want to view the word's hyphenation points (for more on hyphenation, see Chapter 4, "Type"). InDesign displays the hyphenation points (or the proposed hyphenation points) in the word.

   Hyphenation points are ranked—the best hyphenation point is indicated by a single tilde ("~"), the next best point is indicated by two tildes ("~~"), and, at the least good hyphenation points, you'll see three tildes ("~~~"). You can enter hyphenation points in words you're adding to the user dictionary, or change the hyphenation points of words already in the user dictionary.

   If you do not want InDesign to hyphenate the word, enter a tilde before the first character of the word.

3. Choose either the User Dictionary or your document's name from the Target pop-up menu. Generally, you'll want to add

words to the user dictionary which can be used by all your documents. However, if you choose your current file, then the word will only appear spelled correctly in that document, and no others. This might come in handy if you're building an annual report for a medical company and you don't want to add "fluoxetine" to your general user dictionary.

4. Click the Add button to add the word to the user dictionary.

Removing Words From the User Dictionary

Obviously, once you add a word to your user dictionary you can remove it: Just choose Dictionary from the Edit menu, select the word you want to remove, and click the Remove button. But you can also tell InDesign to remove a word from the regular dictionary by adding it to the Removed Words list.

1. Open the Dictionary palette and choose a Target. (If you choose User Dictionary, the change will affect all your documents; if you choose just the open document from the Target pop-up menu, the word is only removed from this document.)

2. Select Removed Words from the Dictionary List pop-up menu.

3. Type the word in the Word field (if you're in the middle of checking your document's spelling, it should show up here automatically).

4. Click the Add button. This *adds* the word to the list of words that should be *removed*.

At this point, the word will appear as incorrect when you check its spelling. Later, if you want to take it off the "removed" list, you can open the Dictionary dialog box, select the word, and click Remove.

Dynamic Spelling. You can also check the spelling of text without going to the Check Spelling dialog box. To do this, turn on Dynamic Spelling (using either the Enable Dynamic Spelling option in the Spelling Preferences dialog box or the corresponding option on the Spelling submenu of the Edit menu). After you do this, InDesign will mark suspect words in your document using the colors you assigned in the Preferences dialog box. If you're working with a long document, it can take some time for InDesign to apply the highlight.

Once you've done this, you can use the Context menu to change suspect words to any of a list of likely replacement candidate words, add the word to the dictionary, or direct InDesign to ignore the word (see Figure 3-51).

FIGURE 3-51
Dynamic Spelling

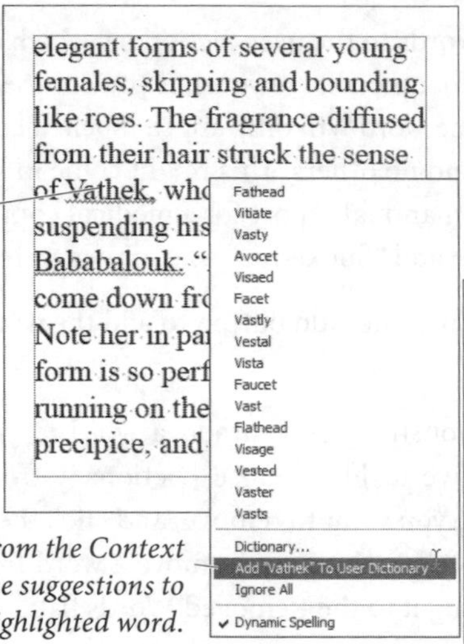

To deal with one of the marked words, click the Type tool inside the word and then display the Context menu.

elegant forms of several young females, skipping and bounding like roes. The fragrance diffused from their hair struck the sense of Vathek, who suspending his Bababalouk: " come down fr Note her in pai form is so perf running on the precipice, and

Fathead
Vitiate
Vasty
Avocet
Visaed
Facet
Vastly
Vestal
Vista
Faucet
Vast
Flathead
Visage
Vested
Vaster
Vasts

Dictionary…
Add "Vathek" To User Dictionary
Ignore All
✓ Dynamic Spelling

When you have turned on the Dynamic Spelling option, InDesign will mark questionable words (i.e., words that are not found in the dictionary).

elegant forms of several young females, skipping and bounding like roes. The fragrance diffused from their hair struck the sense of Vathek, who, in an ecstasy, suspending his repast, said to Bababalouk: "Are the Peris come down from their spheres? Note her in particular whose form is so perfect, venturously running on the brink of the precipice, and turning back her

Choose one of the actions from the Context menu. Select one of the suggestions to replace the highlighted word.

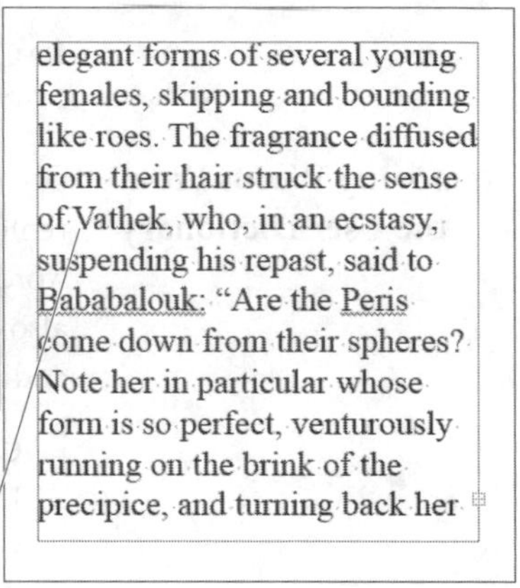

In this example, we've told InDesign that the word is spelled correctly, so InDesign removes the highlight from the word.

Autocorrect. If you enter a lot of text using InDesign, and you habitually type "hte," for "the," (or "pargraph," for "paragraph," as Ole does), you'll love the autocorrect feature (see Figure 3-52). As you type, autocorrect will change the text you've typed to fix common typing errors. You can also use Autocorrect to change capitalization errors ("Indesign" to "InDesign," for example). Autocorrect has no effect on text you have already entered.

To turn this feature on or off, use the Enable Autocorrect option in the Autocorrect Preferences dialog box, or choose Autocorrect from the Spelling submenu of the Edit menu. To have Autocorrect catch errors of capitalization, turn on the Autocorrect Capitalization Errors option.

As you can see by looking at the Autocorrect Preferences dialog box, InDesign has a large list of common misspelled words and their corresponding corrections. If you commonly type certain words wrong, check the list; if you don't see the error there, you can add it to the list.

To add the error, click the Add button. InDesign displays the Add to Autocorrect List dialog box (see Figure 3-53). Enter the typo in the Misspelled Word field, and enter the correct text in the Correction Field. Click the OK button, and InDesign adds the error to the Autocorrect list.

To remove a word from the Autocorrect list, select the word and click the Remove button.

FIGURE 3-52
Autocorrect

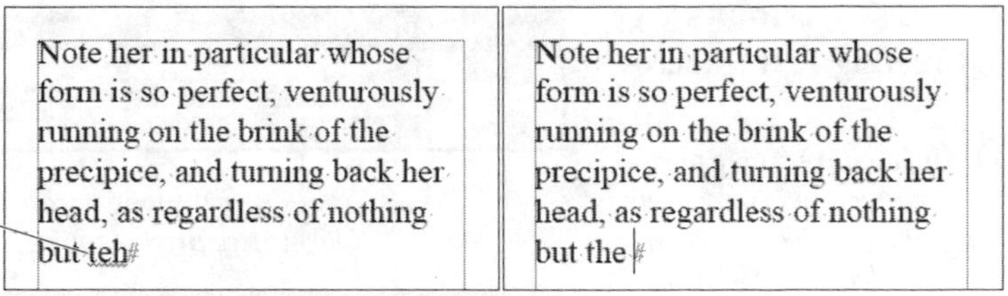
Note her in particular whose form is so perfect, venturously running on the brink of the precipice, and turning back her head, as regardless of nothing but teh#
Note her in particular whose form is so perfect, venturously running on the brink of the precipice, and turning back her head, as regardless of nothing but the #

When the Autocorrect feature is on, InDesign will correct misspelled words as you type.

FIGURE 3-53
Add to Autocorrect

Add to Autocorrect List
Misspelled Word: paragarph
Correction: paragraph
OK
Cancel

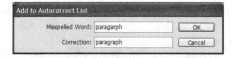

Click the Add button in the Autocorrect panel of the Preferences dialog box to add a word to the list of misspelled words.

Do you find yourself typing a phrase over and over again? A phrase that you're really tired of typing? If so, did you know that you can use InDesign CS2's Autocorrect feature to make your life easier?

Let's say you frequently have to type the phrase "H.M.S. Pinafore, or, The Slave of Duty," in your documents. It's an irritating and awkward phrase to type, as it includes more changes in capitalization and punctuation than run-of-the-mill body text. Wouldn't it be great to reduce the number of keystrokes it takes to type this phrase?

Try this: Open the Autocorrect panel of the Preferences dialog box and click the Add button. Enter a short phrase that you would not type in normal circumstances (something like "xa" will work) in the Misspelled Word field, then enter the "problem" phrase in the Correction field. Close the dialog box. InDesign adds the item to the list of words used by Autocorrect. Close the Preferences dialog box.

Once you've done this, every time you type "xa" (or whatever combination you've entered for your shortcut), InDesign will insert the phrase. You've just reduced a large number of keystrokes to two. See Figure 3-54 for an example.

Footnotes

InDesign CS2 adds the ability to add footnotes to text, a capability requested by InDesign users[1] since version 1.0. While InDesign's footnotes don't do everything that one could possibly want in such a feature. they're able to handle a broad range of footnote needs.

[1] Though we have never found a use for them, ourselves.

FIGURE 3-54
Creating Text "Macros"

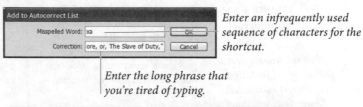

Enter an infrequently used sequence of characters for the shortcut.

If you have a long phrase that you type frequently, you can use the Autocorrect feature to save keystrokes.

Enter the long phrase that you're tired of typing.

After you click the OK button, InDesign adds the misspelled word and the correction.

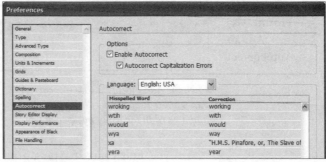

When you type the shortcut, InDesign replaces it with the longer phrase.

Time Travel Tickets is proud to offer excellent seats in Gilbert and Sullivan's xa#

Time Travel Tickets is proud to offer excellent seats in Gilbert and Sullivan's "H.M.S. Pinafore, or, The Slave of Duty," #

What are the limitations? The biggest one is that you're limited to one footnote numbering style in a document. If your publications feature one footnote numbering style for body text, and another style for sidebars, you'll have to take care of one of the footnote styles manually (as you have in previous versions).

The other significant (in our opinion) limitation is that the width of the footnote text is based on the width of the column containing the footnote reference marker. This means that you cannot easily create a three-column layout with footnote text that spans the three columns (a fairly common newsletter layout for footnotes).

In addition, footnote text is not affected by text wrap.

Finally, footnotes go to the bottom of the column, which is not necessarily the bottom of the page. This means that if we want to add a graphic between the footnote reference and the footnote text, we'd have to resort to text wrap or an inline graphic just to fool the footnote into landing at the bottom of the page.

As usual, we've written an introduction to a section without fully defining our terms. When we say "footnote reference marker," we mean the number or symbol that appears in the body text. When we say "footnote text," we're referring to the text that appears at the bottom of the column. These two parts make up a "footnote."

Creating a Footnote   To create a footnote, follow these steps (see Figure 3-55).

1. Position the text cursor at the point at which you want to add the footnote marker. You cannot add footnotes to footnote text or text in a table.

2. Choose Insert Footnote from the Context menu (or the Type menu). When you do this, InDesign inserts a footnote marker (a number or symbol) and positions the text cursor in the footnote text. The footnote text is usually at the bottom of the column containing the marker, but can appear elsewhere in some cases.

3. Enter the text for the footnote.

When you are done editing the footnote text, you can return to the footnote marker (in the body text) by choosing Go to Footnote Reference from the Context menu.

To select all of the text in a footnote, press Command-A/Ctrl-A Editing footnote text is something like editing text in a table cell, except for a key difference: you can view and edit footnote text in the Story Editor (see "Story Editor," later in this chapter).

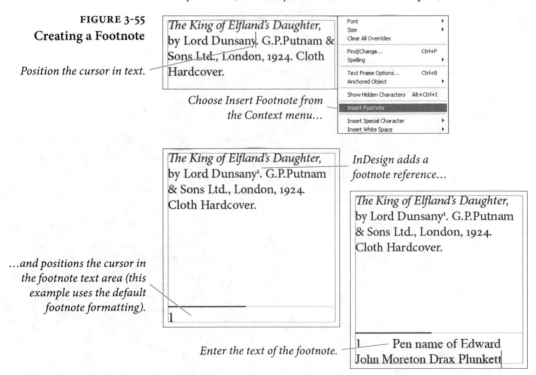

FIGURE 3-55
Creating a Footnote

Position the cursor in text.

Choose Insert Footnote from the Context menu...

InDesign adds a footnote reference...

...and positions the cursor in the footnote text area (this example uses the default footnote formatting).

Enter the text of the footnote.

If you happen to delete the footnote number in the footnote text, you can reinsert it by choosing Footnote Number from the Insert Special Character submenu of the Context menu.

To delete a footnote, delete the footnote marker.

Footnote Options

To control the appearance and behavior of the footnotes in a document, choose Document Footnote Options from the Type menu. The Footnote Options dialog box appears (see Figure 3-56).

Numbering Style. Choose the numbering style you want to use.

Start At. Use this option to set the starting number for the footnotes in each story in the document. If you're continuing footnote numbering from another document, this option comes in handy.

FIGURE 3-56
Footnote Options

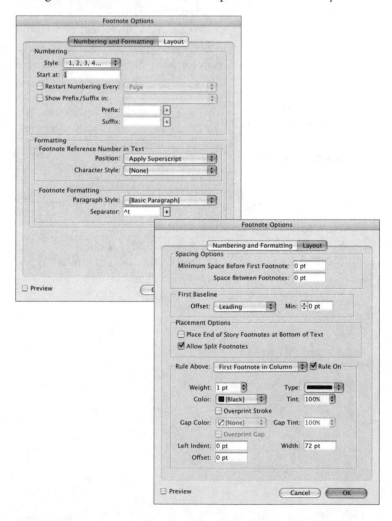

Restart Numbering Every. You can choose to have footnote numbering restart every page, spread, or section. This is a good thing, as some numbering systems (such as asterisks) are designed to restart every page.

Show Prefix/Suffix In. "Prefix" and "suffix," in this case, refer to characters that can be placed before or after the figure number. These characters can appear in the footnote reference, the footnote text, or in both places (see Figure 3-57). You can also enter the character(s) you want to use, or choose a predefined character from a list.

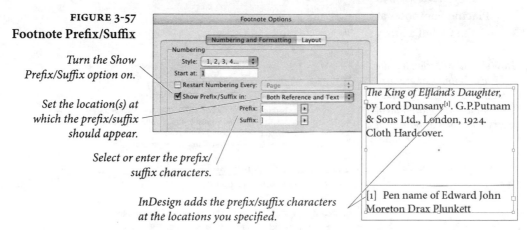

FIGURE 3-57
Footnote Prefix/Suffix

Turn the Show Prefix/Suffix option on.

Set the location(s) at which the prefix/suffix should appear.

Select or enter the prefix/ suffix characters.

InDesign adds the prefix/suffix characters at the locations you specified.

Character Style. This option specifies the character style applied to the figure reference number.

Position. Sets the position of the figure number reference character. You can choose subscript, superscript, or normal position.

Paragraph Style. Choose the paragraph style you want to apply to the footnote text.

Separator. Defines the character between the figure number and the body of the footnote text.

Minimum Space Before First Footnote. Use this option to specify the minimum amount of space between the first footnote in a column and the bottom of the text in the column.

Space Between Footnotes. How much vertical space do you want to insert between footnotes? Enter it here.

First Baseline Offset. This option is very similar to the corresponding option in the Text Frame Options dialog box—it controls the method used to calculate the position of the first baseline of text in a footnote (see the discussion of first baseline offsets earlier in the chapter).

Place End of Story Footnotes at Bottom of Text. Turn this option on, and InDesign will place the footnotes at the end of the story immediately after the end of the text, rather than at the bottom of the last text column (see Figure 3-58).

FIGURE 3-58
**Placing Footnotes at
the End of a Story**

*How should InDesign handle
the last footnote or group of
footnotes in a story? That's
the point of the Place End of
Story Footnotes at Bottom of
Text option.*

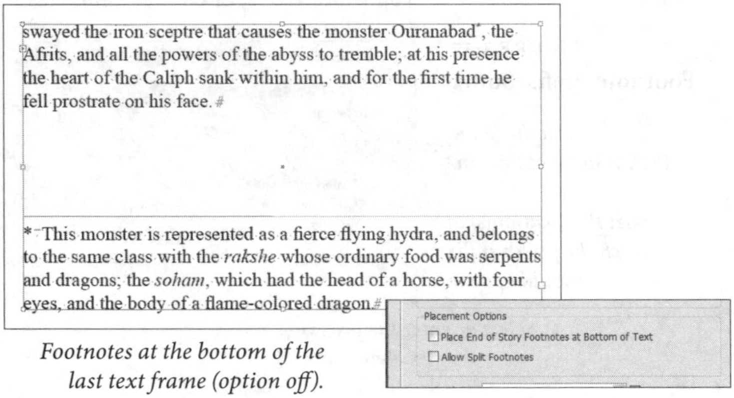

swayed the iron sceptre that causes the monster Ouranabad*, the Afrits, and all the powers of the abyss to tremble; at his presence the heart of the Caliph sank within him, and for the first time he fell prostrate on his face. #

*‾This monster is represented as a fierce flying hydra, and belongs to the same class with the *rakshe* whose ordinary food was serpents and dragons; the *soham*, which had the head of a horse, with four eyes, and the body of a flame-colored dragon.#

Placement Options
☐ Place End of Story Footnotes at Bottom of Text
☐ Allow Split Footnotes

*Footnotes at the bottom of the
last text frame (option off).*

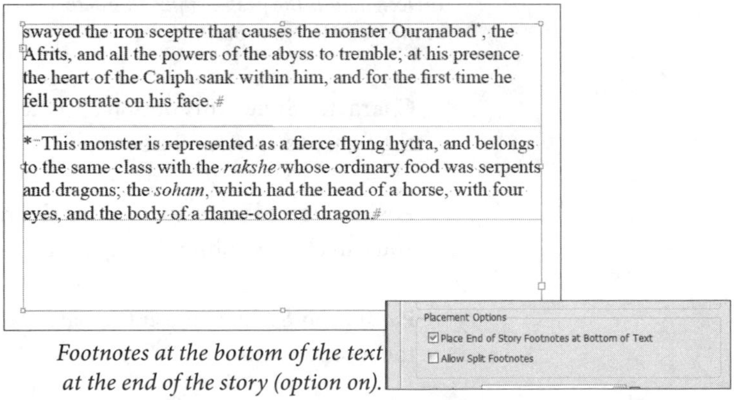

swayed the iron sceptre that causes the monster Ouranabad*, the Afrits, and all the powers of the abyss to tremble; at his presence the heart of the Caliph sank within him, and for the first time he fell prostrate on his face. #

*‾This monster is represented as a fierce flying hydra, and belongs to the same class with the *rakshe* whose ordinary food was serpents and dragons; the *soham*, which had the head of a horse, with four eyes, and the body of a flame-colored dragon.#

Placement Options
☑ Place End of Story Footnotes at Bottom of Text
☐ Allow Split Footnotes

*Footnotes at the bottom of the text
at the end of the story (option on).*

Allow Split Footnotes. When this option is true, InDesign will split footnotes across columns and pages. When it's false, InDesign will attempt to fit all footnotes into the column containing the footnote text reference (see Figure 3-59). If it's not possible (due to the location of the reference) to fit the footnote in that column, InDesign will push the footnote text to the last column in the frame. If that won't work, InDesign will attempt to push the reference and the footnote to the next column capable of holding them both.

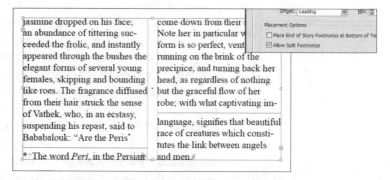

FIGURE 3-59
Splitting Footnotes (or Not)

When you turn the Allow Split Footnotes option on, InDesign will split footnote text among columns (depending on the length of the footnote text and the location of the footnote reference marker).

Turn the Allow Split Footnotes option off, and InDesign will push the footnote (both the marker and the footnote text) to the next column capable of containing it. With this option off, long footnotes and short columns can easily result in overset text.

Rule Above. To add a dividing line above the footnote text, turn on the Rule Above option. Most of the controls in this section correspond to paragraph rule options (see Chapter 4, "Type" for more on paragraph rules), but some of them are specific to footnotes.

Choose First Footnote in Column from the pop-up menu to control the settings for the rule above the top of the first footnote only; choose Continued Footnotes to specify the formatting of the rules above all subsequent footnote sections, including footnotes continued in other columns.

The width of a paragraph rule can be set by either the width of the text or the width of the column, but the width of a footnote rule is determined by the value in the Width field.

Find and Change

Economists and productivity experts keep telling us that personal computers have not lived up to their promise of increased productivity. Workers, they say, are no more productive than they were before the microcomputer revolution.

They are, of course, wrong—or maybe they've never worked as typists or typesetters. Since the advent of word processing and desktop publishing software, we "text workers" have been enjoying a productivity increase that is nothing short of mind boggling. Although we're not sure "enjoying" is quite the right word.

One of the key innovations made possible by the text processing renaissance is the ability to find text in a document and, if necessary, to change it to something else—and all in an automated fashion. It doesn't matter what you call it—"find and change" or "search and replace," it's a kind of text-manipulation tool we didn't have in the "good ol' days."

Find and change is all about pattern recognition. Most of what we do in InDesign (or in life, for that matter) is repetitive. We work our way through text, selecting each occurrence of "f f i" and changing it to "ffi" (the ligature). Or we select each bullet character we've typed, and replace it with a character from Zapf Dingbats. In each case, we're searching for one pattern in our text and replacing it with another.

Finding and changing text is all about working with strings. A *string* is any range of text—a single character, a word, or a phrase. Strings can also contain special, nonprinting characters, such as tab characters, em spaces, or carriage returns.

There are at least four different ways to perform a search-and-replace mission.

▶ Search for a text string and replace it with a different text string.

▶ Search for formatting and replace that formatting with other formatting.

▶ Search for a text string and apply formatting to it.

▶ Search for formatting, and replace it with a string.

Finding Text   If you need to find some text, follow these steps (see Figure 3-60).

1. Open the Find/Change palette (press Command-F/Ctrl-F).

2. Enter the string you want to find in the Find What field.

3. Choose one of the options on the Search pop-up menu to set the scope of the search: Story, To End of Story, Document, or All Documents. Story always begins the search from the beginning of the story, while To End of Story only searches from the cur-

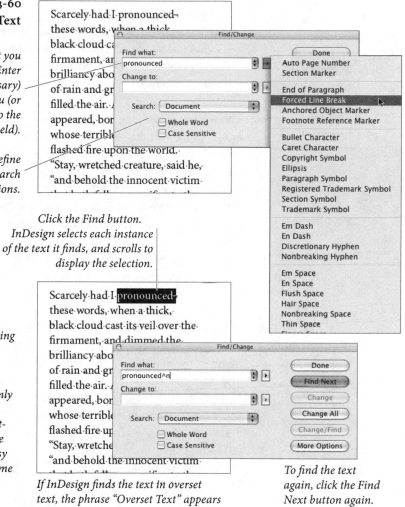

FIGURE 3-60
Finding Text

Enter the text you want to search for. Enter metacharacters (if necessary) using the pop-up menu (or simply type them into the Find What field).

Use these controls to define the search range and search options.

Click the Find button. InDesign selects each instance of the text it finds, and scrolls to display the selection.

firmament^p
^p^t^8
Evangelion
Misato

Once you've entered a string in the Find What field, the string will appear on the pop-up menu associated with the field (but only for the rest of the current InDesign session—restarting the program clears the menus). This makes it easy to search again for the same string.

If InDesign finds the text in overset text, the phrase "Overset Text" appears above the Find What field.

To find the text again, click the Find Next button again.

rent text cursor position onward. All Documents means every currently open document; this is helpful when you need to find something that may appear in multiple chapters of a book.

4. Turn on the Whole Word checkbox if you want to find only exact matches for the text you entered in the Find What field (if you've entered "dog" and want to find only that word, and not "dogged" or "underdog"). Turn on the Case Sensitive option to find only text with the same capitalization as the word you entered (this way, you'll find "dog," but not "Dog").

5. Click the Find Next button. InDesign finds an occurrence of the string you entered in the Find what field and displays it in

the publication window, turning pages and scrolling to display the text, if necessary. You can continue clicking the Find Next button to find the next occurrence of the text in the specified search range until, eventually, you'll return to the first instance InDesign found.

About metacharacters. You can't enter invisible characters—such as tab characters, line-end characters, or carriage returns—in the Find What or Change To fields. To get around this, you enter codes—known as "metacharacters"—representing those characters. We've listed all those codes in Table 3-4, but if you don't have this book sitting next to your computer all the time InDesign makes the process of entering metacharacters easy—they're on the pop-up menus attached to the Find What and Change To fields.

To enter a metacharacter in the Find What or Change To fields, you can either enter it directly (if you know the code) or choose it from the pop-up menus associated with the fields.

Wildcard Metacharacters

Imagine that you need to find all of the part numbers in a publication. Your part numbers start with the string "IN" and are always followed by four letters, a hyphen, and four numbers. How can you find all of the strings?

You can use InDesign's "wildcard" metacharacters—these give you a way to find patterns containing unspecified characters. To match any single, character, type "^?" in the Find What field. Enter "^9" to find any single digit, or "^$" to find any single letter.

To find all of the part numbers in the example, you'd enter "IN^$^$^$^$-^9^9^9^9" in the Find What field. Note that using wildcard metacharacters also helps you avoid finding the strings you don't want to find—if, in our example, we'd used the wildcard-laden string "IN^?^?^?^?^?^?^?^?^?" we'd run the risk of finding the word "INdubitable," which appears in our imaginary catalog many times, rather than the part numbers.

Be careful—entering these wildcard characters in the Change To field results in text being replaced by the metacharacter codes themselves, which is almost certainly *not* what you want. That's why the wildcards don't appear on the Change To field's pop-up menu.

Replacing Text

To replace one text string with another, you enter text in both the Find What and Change To fields of the Find/Change palette (see Figure 3-61). Once you've done this, you have two choices:

TABLE 3-4
Metacharacters

To search for this character:	Enter:
Automatic page number	^#
Section marker	^x
Bullet	^8
Caret	^^
Copyright	^2
Return (end of paragraph marker)	^p
Forced line break	^n
End nested style	^\
Inline graphic	^g
Paragraph	^7
Registered trademark	^r
Section symbol	^6
Tab	^t
Right indent tab	^y
Indent to here	^i
Em dash	^_
Em space	^m
En dash	^=
En space	^>
Flush space	^f
Hair space	^|
Nonbreaking space	^s
Thin space	^<
White space	^w
Discretionary hyphen	^-
Nonbreaking hyphen	^~
Double left quotation mark	^{
Double right quotation mark	^}
Single left quotation mark	^[
Single right quotation mark	^]
Any character	^?
Any digit	^9
Any letter	^$

▶ You can choose to have InDesign replace all instances of the
string in the Find What field with the string you entered in the
Change To field throughout the search range by clicking the
Change All button.

FIGURE 3-61
Replacing Text

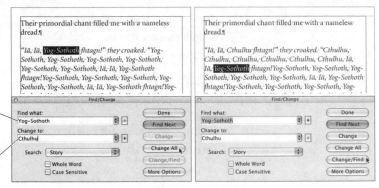

Enter the text you want to find in the Find What field.

Enter the replacement text in the Change To field.

Click the Find Next button to find the first instance of the text.

Click the Change button to replace the selection with the text in the Change To field, or click the Change All button to change all occurrences of the text in the Find What field...

...or click the Change/Find button to make each change yourself.

▶ You can find each occurrence of the string in the specified search range and decide to replace it or not. To do this, click the Find Next button, view the found text, and then click the Find Next, Change, or Change/Find button. The Find Next button moves on to the next instance of the string *without* making any changes; the Change button replaces the selected text with the contents of the Change To field, and waits to see what you'll do next. The Change/Find button replaces the string, then finds the next instance and waits.

Note that the Case Sensitive checkbox determines the case of characters it's replacing, too. However, when the Case Sensitive option is turned off, InDesign still pays attention to the capitalization of the word: If the word it finds is capitalized, then it will replace it with a capitalized word, even if the word you typed in the Change To field was in all lowercase.

Find/Change Keyboard Shortcuts

As we noted earlier, Command-F/Ctrl-F opens the Find/Change palette. But if you're a hard core Find/Change fiend, you're going to want to control this powerful feature using keyboard shortcuts whenever possible. Here are a few shortcuts we find useful; you can, of course, change them by selecting Keyboard Shortcuts from the Edit menu and looking in the Text and Tables Product Area.

▶ You can load the Find What field by selecting one or more characters in a story and pressing Shift-F1. This also finds the next occurrence, but the next occurrence is whatever you selected, so you'll want the following shortcut.

▶ You can find the next occurrence of the Find What field by pressing either Command-Option-F/Ctrl-Alt-F or Shift-F2.

▶ You can load the Replace With field by selecting some text and pressing Command-F2/Ctrl-F2. Then, to actually replace any selected text with this, press Command-F3/Ctrl-F3. Even better, press Shift-F3 to replace, then find the next occurrence.

Finding and Changing Formatting Attributes

What do you do when you want to find all of the occurrences of the word "Zucchini" formatted as 10-point Helvetica bold? And, for that matter, change the word's formatting to 12-point Adobe Caslon italic? It's easy—use the Find Format Settings and Change Format Settings controls at the bottom of the Find/Change dialog box (if you can't see these settings, it's because you need to expand your Find/Change dialog box—click the More Options button, and InDesign expands the dialog box to display these options).

To choose the formatting attributes you want to find, click the Format button in the Find Style Settings field. InDesign displays the Find Format Settings dialog box (see Figure 3-62). This dialog box is another of those multi-panel extravaganzas InDesign will no doubt be famous for. And, as in the other dialog boxes, the best way to get through it is to hold down Command/Ctrl as you press the up or down arrow key.

The ten panels of the Find Format Settings dialog box give you the ability to specify almost any formatting that can be applied to text in InDesign. Navigate through the panels until you find the formatting options you want, then use them to specify the formatting you want to find. When you're done, click the OK button to return to the Find/Change dialog box. InDesign displays a list of the options you've chosen in the field in the Find Format Settings section.

Note that when you first set up the Find Format Settings dialog box, all the pop-up menus and fields are blank. Let's say you select a format—such as 6-point text—and then change your mind; you can simply select the field and press Delete to make it blank again. This comes in handy when searching for fonts. If you select the font Palatino, the styles field automatically changes to "Roman," which means InDesign will *only* search for the roman characters and won't find italic or bold text in that font. However, if you delete "Roman" from that field, the program searches for all cases of Palatino, no matter what the style.

To set up the formatting options you want to apply to any text you find, click the Format button in the Change Format Settings field. This displays the Change Format Settings dialog box, which is

FIGURE 3-62
**Find and Change
Formatting Attributes**

*In this example, we're
replacing one bullet
character with another.*

*Click the More Options
button (which then becomes
the Fewer Options button) to
display Find/Change
formatting options.*

*Unicode value of the
replacement bullet
character.*

*Click the Format button to display the
Find Format Settings dialog box.*

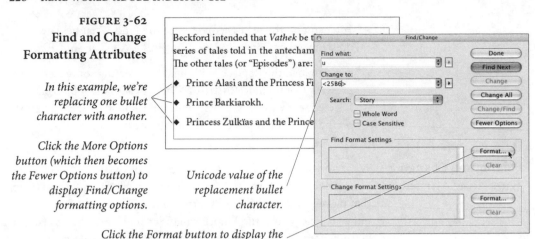

*Use the panels of the Find Format Settings dialog
box to specify the formatting you want to find.*

*Click the other Format button, then use the Change
Format Settings dialog box to specify the formatting
you want to apply.*

*The Find Format Settings
and Change Format
Settings dialog boxes
contain the same set
of panels and options.*

*When you've specified
formatting, InDesign
displays an alert icon.*

*When you're ready to
change text, click the
Change All button, or
click Find Next to step
through the find/change
process.*

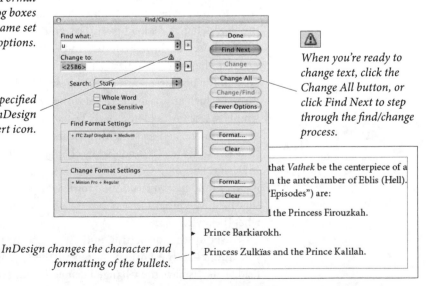

*InDesign changes the character and
formatting of the bullets.*

identical in all but name to the Find Format Settings dialog box. Use the Change Format Settings dialog box to specify the formatting you want to apply, then return to the Find/Change dialog box. InDesign displays the formatting you've chosen in the field in the Find Format Settings section.

When you've specified formatting in the Find Format Settings section, InDesign displays a yellow "alert" triangle above the Find What field. When you enter formatting in the Change Format Settings field, InDesign displays the yellow triangle above the Change To field.

To clear the formatting you've set in either the Find Format Settings or the Change Format Settings dialog boxes, click the Clear button in the corresponding section of the Find/Change dialog box.

Once you've specified the formatting you want to find and/or change, you can use the Find/Change dialog box in the same manner as you would when finding/changing text strings.

Note that when you have specified formatting in the Find Format Settings or Change Format Settings dialog boxes, you can:

► Leave the contents of the Find What and Change To fields empty. When you do this, InDesign searches for any instances of the formatting you've specified in the Find Format Settings dialog box, and replaces it with the formatting you've entered in the Change Format Settings dialog box.

► Enter text in both the Find What and Change To fields. In this case, InDesign searches for an instance of the string you entered in the Find What field that has the formatting specified in the Find Format Settings section, and replaces the text it finds with the string you entered in the Change To field. InDesign applies the formatting from the Change Format Settings section to the replacement text.

► Enter text in only the Find What field and leave the Change To field blank. When you do this, InDesign searches for the string you entered in the Find What field (and any formatting you've specified in the Find Format Settings section), and changes the formatting of the found text to the formatting specified in the Change Format Settings section (but won't change the text string itself).

► Enter text only in the Change To field and leave the Find What field blank. In this case, InDesign searches for the formatting you entered in the Find Format Settings area, and replaces any text it finds with the string you entered in the Change To field (plus any formatting you've specified in the Change Format settings section). While you aren't likely to use this find/change method (it's pretty obscure), it's nice to know it's available.

Automating Run-in Headings

If you've been in this business for a while, you've probably seen that bane of the desktop publisher's existence—a run-in heading. What's a run-in heading? It's a heading that starts a paragraph of body text. The text of the heading "runs into" the body text. You'll often see them used for paragraphs starting with "Note:" or "Warning:" or "Tip:" or the like (you'll even see them scattered through this book).

The trouble is, writers and editors usually want to keep the heading as a separate paragraph so that they can view it as a heading level in the outline mode of their word processing program. It's only when the text reaches you for layout that it needs to be formatted using run-in headings.

Luckily, in InDesign, you can use the Find and Change feature to make this change. First, you must define the heading style to match the body text style, and then specify a nested character style for the first sentence (the "run-in" character style). We discuss paragraph styles and nested character styles in Chapter 4, "Type."

Then, to make the headings "run in" to the body text paragraphs, type the paragraph metacharacter ("^p") into the Find What field, and specify the heading paragraph style. In the Replace With field, type whatever separator (usually a period or colon, followed by a space) you want to use for the run-in heading. When you click Change All, the carriage returns in the heading style are deleted and replaced with the separator characters (see Figure 3-63).

InDesign now automatically formats the first sentence of the paragraph with your run-in character style, because that's what you told it to do with the nested character style. Voilá! A run-in heading.

Goodbye, Paragraph!

We frequently work with publications containing notes written to us by other people—you know, things like, "Ole, this section still needs work." We don't want to see that paragraph in the printed version of the piece (and we have, believe us!), so we tag these paragraphs with a paragraph style named "Comment."

When we're laying out the publication, we remove all of the paragraphs tagged with this style name. Do we hunt through the text, laboriously selecting each paragraph and pressing the Delete key? No way—we use an unexpected and probably unintended feature of InDesign's Find/Change dialog box. Here's the easy way to delete paragraphs tagged with a particular style (see Figure 3-64).

FIGURE 3-63
Automating
Run-In Headings

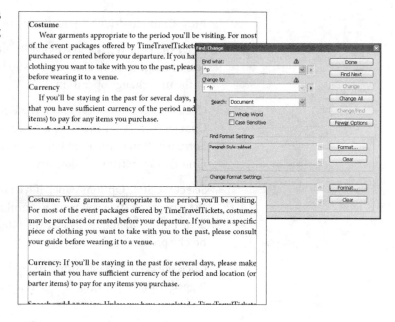

FIGURE 3-64
Removing All
Paragraphs Tagged
with a Specific
Paragraph Style

This text contains paragraphs tagged with the style "editorial comment"— they're left over from the writing process. To remove them all, display the Find/Change dialog box...

...make sure that the Find What and Change To fields are empty...

...then click the Format button and choose the style name from the Paragraph Style pop-up menu in the Style Options panel of the Find Format Settings dialog box...

...and click the Change All button. InDesign removes all paragraphs tagged with the paragraph style you selected.

1. Press Command-F/Ctrl-F to display the Find/Change palette.

2. Leave the Find What and Change To fields empty. Choose a search range from the Search pop-up menu to define the scope of the find/change operation.

3. Click the Clear buttons in both the Find Format Settings and Change Format Settings areas, if necessary. Then, click the Format button in the Find Format Settings section to open the Find Format Settings dialog box.

4. Select the Style Options panel, if it's not already visible. Choose the paragraph style you want to annihilate from the Paragraph Style pop-up menu, then close the Find Format Settings dialog box by pressing OK.

5. Click the Change All button. InDesign deletes every paragraph tagged with the paragraph style from the search range.

Working with InDesign Tagged Text

It's been pointed out to us that we live on another planet. This planet, everyone agrees, is one very much like Earth. In fact, almost everything is the same—right down to the existence of a desktop publishing program named "InDesign." At that point, however, things get different. Disturbingly, subtly different.

The most recent reason for the "Kvern and Blatner are alien weirdos" talk around our offices is that one of the features that excites us most about InDesign is rarely mentioned in the marketing materials. Or on the back of the box. It's not the typesetting features, nor it it the ability to place native Photoshop and Illustrator files. We think those are great features, but they're not it.

What is this mystery feature? It's the ability to save and read tagged text. To explain why this is so important, we've got to explain a little bit about what tags are.

The Land That WYSIWYG Forgot

Tags have been around for a long time. Before desktop publishing appeared, the world of typesetting was ruled by dedicated typesetting systems. As we set type on these machines, we didn't see anything that looked like the type we were setting. Instead, we saw the text of our newspapers, books, and magazines surrounded (and sometimes obscured) by cryptic symbols: typesetting tags and codes.

To see what these symbols meant, we had to print the file. Only then would we see our type with its formatting applied. (If you have ever messed around with HTML text, you have played with a kind of tagged text, where <B> means make the text bold, but you can't actually see the bold text until you open it in a Web browser.)

Then came the Macintosh, PageMaker, the LaserWriter, and WYSIWYG (What you See Is What You Get) publishing. This revolution made it easier for more people to set type—in part because it freed us from having to learn and use the obscure codes and tags of the dedicated typesetting systems. These days, modern desktop publishing programs are better typesetting systems than anything we had in the old days—and you can see what you're doing.

Why Bother with Tags?

Why should you mess with tags in this day and age? It turns out that they can make some jobs easier, and sometimes they can make it possible to do things that wouldn't be practical to do using menus, dialog boxes, and the Character and Paragraph palettes.

The tagged text export filter takes formatted InDesign text and turns it into tags in a text file. The tagged text import filter reads tags—strings of text you've entered in the text file—and turns them into formatted ("WYSIWYG") text. There's a key point to make here: InDesign's tagged text export filter is the only text export filter that doesn't change the appearance of the text you're exporting.

Here are some of the reasons you might want to use tags:

▶ If you have employees using text editors (such as BBEdit on the Macintosh) instead of full-featured word processors, they cannot apply formatting such as bold or italic or paragraph styles. However these programs are small, fast, and can do lots of things word processors cannot. In short, we want to be able to take advantage of all of InDesign's text formatting features, but create and manage our text using a program that speaks nothing but ASCII (text only) format. You can do that with tagged text.

▶ Any application that can save files in text-only format can be used to create formatted text for use in InDesign. This means that your catalog clients can use FileMaker database to mark up their text—Visual Basic, Microsoft Excel, and Microsoft Access are other obvious choices. It might even help your old uncle who lives in a cave and uses nothing but EDLIN.

▶ You can store frequently used formatted text as tagged text files. It's far quicker to place a tagged text file than it is to open another InDesign publication and copy/paste the text you want. In addition, the tagged text file takes up far less disk space than an InDesign publication or InDesign library file.

Getting Started with Tagged Text

To learn how tags work, the best thing you can do is to export some formatted text from InDesign (select the story, choose Export from the File menu, and change the Format pop-up menu to InDesign Tagged Text) and then use a text editor to look at the file (you can't, unfortunately, place a tagged text file in InDesign without converting the tags to formatting).

While it is possible to open these tagged text files in a word processor like Microsoft Word, those programs often assume that because there are tags in the file, it must be HTML (so you either get errors or things get really weird). That's why text editors (such as Windows Notepad or BBEdit) are better—they just deal with plain text and never try to format anything.

The "official word" on tagged text is the Tagged Text.pdf file, which you'll find inside the Adobe Technical Info folder on your InDesign installation CD. This guide includes basic instructions and a list of most of the tags you can use.

One thing that's implied by the tagged text documentation, but not explicitly stated, is that you can enter any character using its Unicode value. To do that, use the form "<0xnnnn>", where *nnnn* is the hexadecimal form of the code (as seen in the Glyphs palette).

What Tags Can Contain

InDesign's tags can specify basic character formatting (such as font, point size, color, or baseline shift), paragraph formatting (such as indents, tabs, and paragraph space before and after), and styles (both paragraph styles and character styles). Any formatting that can be applied to text can be applied using tags. Even tables can be exported or imported as tagged text. (That means you can program your database to export fully formatted InDesign tables.)

Tag Structure

InDesign tags are always surrounded by open (<) and close (>) angle brackets (which most of us also know as "greater than" and "less than" symbols). The first characters in a tagged text file must state the character encoding (ASCII, ANSI, UNICODE, BIG5, or SJIS), followed by the platform (MAC or WIN). So the typical Windows tagged text file begins with <ASCII-WIN>, and the Macintosh version begins with <ASCII-MAC>. If InDesign doesn't see one of these tags at the start of the file, InDesign won't interpret the tags in the file, and all the tags show up as part of your text. Here are a few more details about tagging conventions.

▶ Any characters you enter outside a tag will appear as characters in the imported text.

▶ Enter an empty tag to return the formatting affected by the tag to its default state. For example:

```
Baseline <cBaselineShift:3>Shift<cBaselineShift:> text following
should be back to normal.
```

Paragraph Style Tags

If you're a long-time PageMaker user, you may have worked with PageMaker's style tags to apply paragraph formatting to text files. InDesign's tagged text format is different than PageMaker's, but you can create a "minimalist" tagged text file that's almost as easy to work with as PageMaker's paragraph style tags. Here's the header for an example tagged text file:

```
<ASCII-WIN>
<DefineParaStyle:heading><DefineParaStyle:subhead><DefineParaStyle:para>
<ColorTable:=<Black:COLOR:CMYK:Process:0,0,0,1>>
```

Note that the paragraph style definitions in this tagged text file do not contain any formatting—our assumption is that you'll set up corresponding paragraph styles in your publication. Then all you need to do is paste the appropriate header at the top of a text file, and then enter the paragraph style tags for each paragraph. If, when preparing a file for import into PageMaker, you entered "<heading>" then enter "<ParaStyle:heading>" for InDesign.

Here's an example (very simple) text file marked up with Page-Maker paragraph tags:

```
<heading 1>TimeTravelTickets
<subhead>Travel through time to experience the greatest artistic
performances in history!
<para>We are pleased to announce our Summer, 2006 series.
```

Here's the same text, marked up with InDesign tags:

```
<ASCII-WIN>
<DefineParaStyle:heading><DefineParaStyle:subhead><DefineParaStyle:para>
<ParaStyle:heading>TimeTravelTickets
<ParaStyle:subhead>Travel through time to experience the greatest
artistic performances in history!
<ParaStyle:para>We are pleased to announce our Summer, 2006 series.
```

A few things to note about converting PageMaker paragraph style tags to InDesign tagged text:

▶ For each paragraph style used in the file, you must include a (blank) paragraph style definition with exactly the same name in the InDesign tagged text file header.

▶ While PageMaker paragraph style tags don't require that you tag each paragraph, you should tag each paragraph in the InDesign version of the file.

▶ InDesign's tagged text import filter is fragile, and can crash the program when it encounters a tag it doesn't understand. Always save your work before importing a tagged text file (yes, even a tagged text file exported from InDesign).

▶ This would be a great process to automate using a search and replace tool or a script. (As you might expect, Ole has already done this.)

What About XPress Tags? InDesign 1.5 could import text files marked up using QuarkXPress' tagged text format, but InDesign has forgotten how to do that since then. We decry this loss of capability (many publishing systems are built around XPressTags). Em Software (www.emsoftware.com) has created XTags, an InDesign import/export filter pair that supports not only QuarkXPress' native set of tags, but adds additional tags.

After Words

In academic circles, debate continues on whether we're born with the ability to understand language, or whether it's something we're taught. We don't know the answer, and, most of the time, we don't even know which side of the argument we want to be on. What we do know is that language is the most important technology humans have developed.

In this chapter, we've shown how to get words into InDesign, how to organize them in your publications, and how to get them out again. Next stop—typesetting with InDesign!

CHAPTER 4

Type

Ole's sordid tale: "Late night. The pale glow from the monochrome monitor of my Compugraphic phototypesetter. The smell of the office standard 'French Vanilla' coffee—warming, now, for several hours and resembling nothing so much as battery acid. The gentle snoring of one of the staff writers, who is curled up in the warmth of the unit that holds the spinning filmstrips containing the fonts I'm using to set his story.

"These are the things I think of when I hear the word 'typesetting'—they're memories from my job at Seattle's free rock and roll newspaper *The Rocket*, circa 1982. Desktop publishing didn't exist yet, and digital (as opposed to photo) typesetting systems—with their WYSIWYG displays—were rare. The codes and characters I saw on my screen wouldn't look anything like type until they were printed, one character at a time, on a strip of photographic film and developed. I could set just about any kind of type using that machine, provided the characters would fit on a piece of film not more than seven inches wide, and provided I didn't need to use characters from more than six fonts."

When desktop publishing systems appeared, we found that they couldn't do everything Ole could do with his Compugraphic—but that being able to see what our type would look like *before we printed it* more than made up for any deficiencies in precision, automation, and flexibility. These days, page layout programs are far more capable than Ole's trusty EditWriter. Does that mean, however, that there's no more room for improvement? For surprising new features? Is typesetting "done"?

Not a chance—InDesign offers a number of improvements and surprises in the area of typesetting. It's an evolutionary product—not a revolutionary one, but, on its release, InDesign be came the best desktop typesetting program, and raised the bar for its competition.

In this chapter, we'll walk through InDesign's typesetting features. We'll start with character formatting (font, point size, kerning, and baseline shift are examples of character formatting), move on to paragraph formatting (indents, tabs, space above and below, and composition), and then dive into formatting using character and paragraph styles. Along the way, there may be a joke or two.

Selecting and Formatting Text

Generally, when you want to change the formatting of some text, you have to select it with the Type tool. However, there are two caveats to this statement. First, because paragraph formatting (which we'll discuss later) always applies to an entire paragraph, you don't have to select every character in the paragraph before applying it—you can simply place your text cursor anywhere in the paragraph.

Second (and more interesting) is that you can apply text formatting to text frames you've selected using the Selection tool or the Direct Selection tool. When you do this, InDesign applies the formatting to all of the text in the text frame, including any overset text. InDesign won't let you use this method to apply formatting to text frames that are linked to other text frames. Tired of using the Type tool to select and format every photo caption on a page? Use the Selection tool to select them all and apply your formatting—it's easier, and it's quicker (see Figure 4-1).

The ability to apply formatting with the Selection tools is very powerful, but it's also slightly dangerous. Let's say you set a single character to Zapf Dingbats somewhere in your text frame. If you select the text frame using the Selection tool and then apply a new font, every character—including that dingbat—gets changed.

The only warnings that InDesign gives you that some of the text in the selected text frame uses a different font are: the Font field in the Character palette is blank, and the Font submenu (under the Type menu) has hyphens next to each font.

FIGURE 4-1
**Formatting the
Text in Text Frames**

*Use the Selection tool to select
the text frames you want to
format…*

*…and apply formatting. InDesign
applies the formatting to all of the
text in the text frames. That's all
there is to it. In this example, we've
changed character attributes (font,
font style, and leading) and paragraph attributes (alignment).*

Character Formatting

Character formatting is all about controlling the appearance of the
individual letters in your publication. Font, type size, color, and leading are all aspects of character formatting. (Longtime QuarkXPress
users won't think of leading as a character format, but we'll cover
that next.)

We refer to all formatting that can be applied to a selected range of
text as "character" formatting, and refer to formatting that InDesign
applies at the paragraph level as "paragraph" formatting. Tab settings,
indents, paragraph rules, space above, and space after are examples of
paragraph formatting. There are areas of overlap in these definitions.
Leading, for example, is really a property that applies to an entire
line of text (InDesign uses only the largest leading value in a line to
set the leading for that line), but we'll call it "character" formatting,
nonetheless, because you can apply it to individual characters.

In addition to these distinctions, InDesign's paragraph styles can
include character formatting, but apply to entire paragraphs. See
"Styles," later in this chapter.

Character Formatting Controls

InDesign's character formatting controls are found in both the Character palette and the Control palette (see Figure 4-2). The controls in the palettes are substantially the same, so we'll discuss them once.

To display the Character palette and shift the focus to the palette's Font field, press Command-T/Ctrl-T. If the palette is already visible when you use this keyboard shortcut, InDesign hides it; you may need to press it twice.

To display the Control palette, press Command-Option-6/Ctrl-Alt-6. If the palette is already open, but is displaying the paragraph controls, press Command-Option-7/Ctrl-Alt-7.

Font Family and Font

Selecting a font in InDesign is a little bit different than selecting a font in most other page layout programs. To InDesign, fonts are categorized as font "families," and each family is made up of one or more type styles. A font family is a set of typefaces designed to have a common "look." A "font," then, is specified by its font family and type style. In this book, we've used the font family Minion Pro, and the type style Regular for the body text—so the font of the body text is "Minion Pro Regular."

InDesign's user interface for selecting fonts mirrors this approach. When you choose a font from the Font submenu of the Type menu, you must select both the font family and a specific type style (that is, you can't simply select the font family).

FIGURE 4-2
Character Formatting Controls

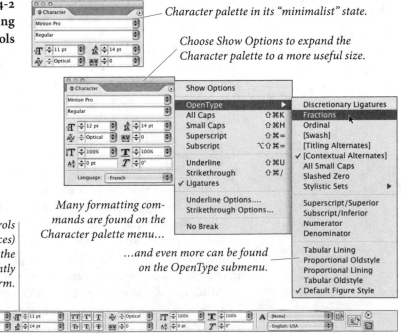

Character palette in its "minimalist" state.

Choose Show Options to expand the Character palette to a more useful size.

Many formatting commands are found on the Character palette menu...

...and even more can be found on the OpenType submenu.

The same controls (including the menu choices) are also available on the Control palette—in slightly rearranged form.

Note that InDesign does not have "type styles" in the same way that other programs do—it makes no assumption that the selected font family has a "bold" or "italic" member, and will never *generate* a fake bold or italic version of a font. The names that appear on the Type Style pop-up menu are all taken from the fonts themselves—if you don't have a font for a particular type style, you won't see it listed in the Type Styles menu (see Figure 4-3).

To select a font family or type style, you can type into the appropriate field—you don't have to use the menu. As you type the name of a font family or type style, InDesign will display the available font or fonts that match the characters you typed. For instance you can type "T" and it will guess "Tekton" (if you have that font installed); if you meant "Times" then you may have to type "Ti" or even "Tim". Note that you can also press the up and down arrow keys, which is especially helpful in the Style field to move from Regular to Bold to Italic, and so on.

Font Style Keyboard Shortcuts. Although InDesign won't generate a bold or italic weight, you can type Command-Shift-B/Ctrl-Shift-B to make your text bold and Command-Shift-I/Ctrl-Shift-I to make it italic. If a font doesn't have a bold or italic version, InDesign will not change the text.

Symbols and Dingbats. Sometimes, when you change to a symbol font (such as Zapf Dingbats), you may encounter font substitution (the dreaded pink highlight). This happens because InDesign is attempting to map the character from one font to another. To avoid this problem, hold down Shift as you apply the font.

FIGURE 4-3
Selecting a Font

Select a font family...

...and then select a type style. InDesign will not generate fake bold or italic type styles.

The number of type styles available varies from family to family.

You can also choose the family and style from the Font pop-up menu in a single step.

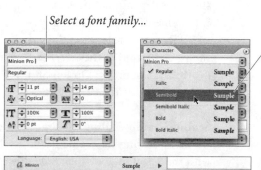

Duplicate Font Names. Many people have more than one font with the same name on their systems—such as a TrueType and a PostScript version of Times Roman. While most programs just pick one of them (and you never know which you're getting), InDesign displays both, including either T1 or TT in parentheses after the font name.

Size   You can change the size of text by entering the point size you want in the Size field of the Character or Control palette, or choose a point size from the attached pop-up menu (see Figure 4-4). If you type the size, you can specify it in .001-point increments. After you've entered the size you want, apply the change by pressing Return/Enter or by pressing Tab to move to another field.

FIGURE 4-4
Point Size

Click the "nudge" buttons, or...

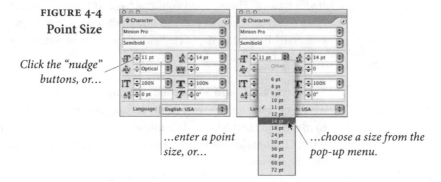

...enter a point size, or...

...choose a size from the pop-up menu.

Size Adjustment Keyboard Shortcuts. You can increase the size of selected type by pressing Command-Shift->/Ctrl-Shift->, or decrease the size by pressing Command-Shift-</Ctrl-Shift-<. The amount that InDesign increases or decreases the point size when you use these shortcuts depends on the value in the Size/Leading field in the Units & Increments Preferences dialog box.

To increase or decrease the size of the selected text by five times the value entered in the Size/Leading field, you can add the Option or Alt key: Command-Option-Shift->/Ctrl-Alt-Shift->, or Command-Option-Shift-</Ctrl-Alt-Shift-<.

Scaling Text by Scaling the Frame. You can also scale text in a text frame by scaling the frame itself. To do this, select the text frame with the Selection tool, then hold down the Command/Ctrl key and drag a corner or side handle. Hold down Command-Shift/Ctrl-Shift as you drag to scale proportionally (a good thing, as far as text is concerned).

Leading Text characters—usually—sit on an imaginary line, which we call the baseline. Leading (pronounced "ledding") is the vertical distance from the baseline of one line of text to the next text baseline. When you hear "10 on 12" or see "10/12", it means "10-point text on 12-point leading." In InDesign, leading is measured from the baseline of the current line of text to the baseline of the line of text above (see Figure 4-5). When you increase the leading in a line of text, you push that line farther from the line above it, and farther down from the top of the text block.

FIGURE 4-5
Leading

Leading is the distance from the baseline of one line to the baseline of the line above it.

Character
Minion Pro
Regular
11 pt
13 pt
Optical
0
100%
100%
0 pt
0°
Language: English: USA
For
accursed

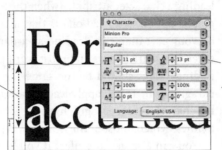

You set the leading of selected characters using the Leading control—enter a value, click the arrows, or choose a value from the pop-up menu. You can also choose Auto from the pop-up menu to base the leading on the point size of the text.

In InDesign—as in PageMaker or FreeHand—leading is an attribute of individual characters, but the largest leading value in a line predominates (see Figure 4-6). This differs from QuarkXPress, where leading is a paragraph attribute (although if you use QuarkXPress's relative leading mode, the largest leading in a line predominates).

For those of us who came to desktop publishing from typesetting, the idea of leading being a character attribute seems more natural than QuarkXPress' method of setting it at the paragraph level. Fortunately, InDesign lets you have it both ways: When you turn on the Apply Leading to Entire Paragraphs option in the Text tab of the Preferences dialog box, the program automatically sets the leading of

FIGURE 4-6
The Largest Leading in a Line Wins

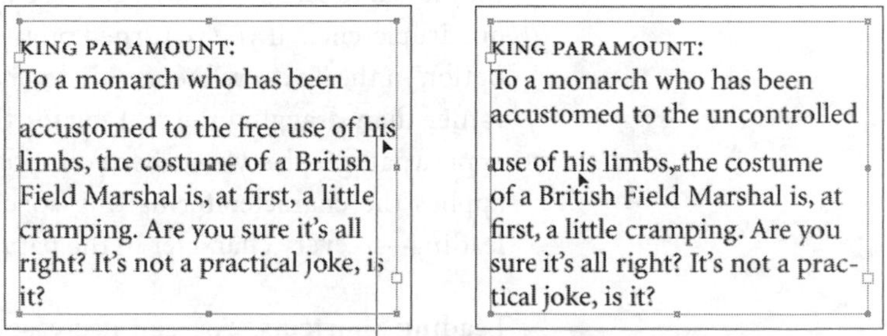

KING PARAMOUNT:
To a monarch who has been
accustomed to the free use of his
limbs, the costume of a British
Field Marshal is, at first, a little
cramping. Are you sure it's all
right? It's not a practical joke, is
it?
KING PARAMOUNT:
To a monarch who has been
accustomed to the uncontrolled
use of his limbs, the costume
of a British Field Marshal is, at
first, a little cramping. Are you
sure it's all right? It's not a practical joke, is it?

This word has a larger leading value than the other characters in the line.

When the word moves to another line (due, in this example, to a change in the text), the larger leading is applied to that line.

every character in a paragraph to the same value. QuarkXPress users will probably want to turn this option on.

However, this preference only affects paragraphs that you change *after* you set it. For instance, you could have it on most of the time, then turn it off in order to vary the leading of lines within a paragraph—something you sometimes have to do to optically balance display copy—and then turn the preference back on again.

How to Avoid Wacky Leading. The main disadvantage of making leading a character attribute (when the Apply Leading to Entire Paragraphs option is turned off) is that it requires a bit more vigilance on your part than the "leading-as-a-paragraph-attribute" approach taken by QuarkXPress and most word processors. Most of the time, leading values should be the same for all of the characters in the paragraph. If, as you apply leading amounts, you fail to select all of the characters in a paragraph, you'll get leading that varies from line to line—which, most of the time, is a typesetting mistake.

You can also get this effect if you leave your paragraph's leading set to the default Auto leading, which always sets the leading to some percentage (usually 120%) of the text size—or, more specifically, some percentage of the largest character on a line. This is true even when Apply to Entire Paragraph is turned on. We strongly urge you not to use Auto leading (except for inline frames and graphics, as discussed in Chapter 6, "Where Text Meets Graphics").

If you've seen paragraphs where the leading of the last line of the paragraph is clearly different from that of the lines above it, you know exactly what we're talking about (see Figure 4-7).

It's simple—the carriage return, that sneaky invisible character, can have a different leading value than the other lines in the paragraph. When the person formatting the text selected the paragraph, they failed to select the carriage return. To avoid this, triple-click (or quadruple-click, if you've turned on the Triple Click to Select a Line option in the Text Preferences dialog box) the paragraph to select it, rather than dragging the text cursor through the text. Or you can apply a paragraph style—when you apply a paragraph style, InDesign applies the character formatting specified in the style—including leading—to every character in the paragraph.

Leading Shortcuts. You can decrease the leading of selected type by pressing Option-Up arrow/Alt-Up arrow or increase the size by pressing Option-Down arrow/Alt-Down arrow (yes, this does seem counterintuitive). The amount that InDesign increases or decreases the leading depends on the value you entered in the Size/Leading

FIGURE 4-7

That Crazy Carriage Return

In this example, the carriage return character carries an Auto leading value and point size left over from previous paragraph formatting (the leading of the rest of the text in the paragraph is 13 points).

To avoid this problem, select the entire paragraph before applying character formatting—this selects the carriage return character.

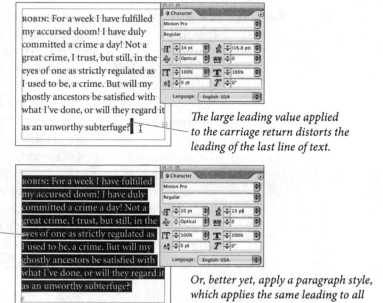

The large leading value applied to the carriage return distorts the leading of the last line of text.

Or, better yet, apply a paragraph style, which applies the same leading to all characters in the paragraph.

field in the Units & Increments Preferences dialog box (for more on units and increments, see Chapter 1, "Workspace").

To increase the leading of the selected text by five times the value in the Size/Leading field, press Command-Option-Up arrow/Ctrl-Alt-Up arrow. To decrease the leading by the same amount, press Command-Option-Down arrow/Ctrl-Alt-Down arrow.

Leading Techniques. Here are a few tips and tricks for adjusting your leading.

▶ Increase leading as you increase line length (the column width). Solid leading (such as 12 point text on 12 points leading) produces almost unreadable text for all but the narrowest of lines.

▶ Use extra leading for sans serif or bold type.

▶ Fonts with a small x-height (the height of the lowercase "x" in relation to the height of the capital letters) can often use a smaller leading value than those with a large x-height.

▶ Decrease leading as point size increases. Large display or headline type needs less leading than body copy. You can often get by with solid leading or less—just make certain that the descenders of one line don't bump into the ascenders of the line below.

Kerning   The goal of kerning—the adjustment of the space between characters—is to achieve even spacing. InDesign offers both pair kerning (the adjustment of the space between adjacent characters) and tracking (or "range kerning")—the adjustment of all of the inter-character spaces in a series of characters.

For each space between any pair of characters in a publication, InDesign applies the total of the pair kerning and tracking values (so if you set kerning to 50 and tracking to –50, you will not see any change in the composition of the text).

InDesign adjusts kerning using units equal to one-thousandth of an em. An *em* is equal in width to the size of the type—for instance, in 18 point text, an em is 18 points wide, and so each unit in the kerning or tracking fields equals 18/1000 point (about .00025 inch). You can enter values from –1000 (minus one em) to 10000 (plus 10 ems) in the Kerning and Tracking fields.

Manual Kerning   To adjust spacing between a pair of characters, move the text insertion point between the characters and apply manual kerning (see Figure 4-8). Use any of the following techniques.

▶ Enter a value in the Kerning field of the Character palette or Control palette. If the kerning field already contains a value entered by one of the automatic kerning methods (see below), you can replace the value by typing over it, or add to or subtract from it (by typing a "+" or "-" between the value and the amount you want to add or subtract).

▶ Click the arrow buttons attached to the Kerning field. Click the up button to increase the kerning amount by the value you entered in the Kerning field in the Units & Increments Preferences dialog box, or click the down button to decrease kerning by the same amount.

▶ Press a keyboard shortcut (see Table 4-1).

To remove all kerning and tracking from the selected text, press Command-Option-Q/Ctrl-Alt-Q (this sets tracking to zero and sets the kerning method to Metrics).

You can't apply pair kerning when you have a range of text selected—if you try, InDesign displays an error message. When you want to apply a kerning value to a range of text, use Tracking.

Automatic Kerning   InDesign offers two automatic kerning methods: pair kerning based on kerning pairs found in the font itself (choose Metrics from the Kerning pop-up menu), and kerning based on the outlines of the

FIGURE 4-8
Kerning Text

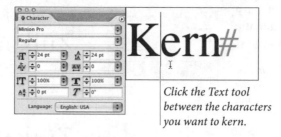

*Click the Text tool
between the characters
you want to kern.*

*Enter a value in the Kerning
field, or choose a value from
the associated pop-up menu,
or click the arrows, or press a
kerning keyboard shortcut.*

*InDesign adjusts the spacing
between the characters.*

characters (choose Optical). To see the difference between the two methods take a look at Figure 4-9.

► **Metrics.** When you turn on the Metrics automatic kerning method, InDesign reads the kerning pairs built into the font by the font's designer (or publisher). These kerning pairs cover—or attempt to cover—the most common letter combinations (in English, anyway), and there are usually about 128 pairs defined in a typical font.

You'd think that using the kerning pairs defined in the font would be the perfect way to apply automatic kerning to your text. Who, after all, knows the spacing peculiarities of a given font better than its designer? Would that this were true! In reality,

TABLE 4-1
**Kerning Keyboard
Shortcuts**

To change kerning by:	Press:
+20/1000 em*	Option-Right arrow/ Alt-Right arrow
-20/1000 em*	Option-Left arrow/Alt-Left arrow
+100/1000 em**	Command-Option-Right arrow/ Ctrl-Alt-Right arrow
-100/1000 em**	Command-Option-Left arrow/ Ctrl-Alt-Left arrow
Reset Kerning	Command-Option-Q/ Ctrl-Alt-Q

* This is the default value in the Kerning field of the Units & Increments Preferences dialog box.

** Or five times the default kerning amount.

FIGURE 4-9
Automatic
Kerning Methods

Choose Optical or
Metrics from the
Kerning pop-up menu.

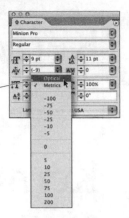

Automatic kerning using the Metric method.

Zülkaïs & Kalilah

   0   0   -23   0

Automatic kerning using the Optical method.

Zülkaïs & Kalilah

-15   12   6   21

very few fonts contain well-thought-out kerning pairs (often, pair kerning tables are simply *copied* from one font to another), and the number of kerning pairs defined per font is inadequate (a really well-kerned font might contain several *thousand* pairs, tweaked specifically for the characters in that typeface).

We really need a better method—a method that can adjust the spacing between *every* character pair, while taking into account the peculiarities of the character shapes for a particular font. We also need a kerning method that can automatically adjust the spacing between characters of different fonts. With InDesign's Optical kerning method, we get both.

▶ **Optical.** What's new and different about kerning text in InDesign is the Optical kerning method, which considers the composed shapes of the characters and applies kerning to even out spacing differences between characters.

If you've ever worked with PageMaker's Expert Kerning dialog box, you'll understand the basic technology behind Optical Kerning, but you'll be surprised by the speed with which InDesign automatically kerns your type.

In general, the kerning applied by InDesign when you use the Optical kerning method looks looser than that applied by the Metrics kerning method. That's okay—once you've accomplished even spacing, you can always track the text to tighten or loosen its overall appearance. Because tracking applies the same kerning value to all of the text in the selection, in addition to any pair kerning, the even spacing applied by the Optical kerning method is maintained.

Viewing Automatic Kerning Amounts. As you move your cursor through the text, you'll be able to see the kerning values applied to the text in the Kerning field of the Character palette or Control palette. Kerning values specified by Optical kerning or Metrics kerning are displayed surrounded by parentheses; manual kerning values you've entered are not (see Figure 4-10).

FIGURE 4-10
How You Can Tell It's
Automatic Kerning

*InDesign displays
automatic kerning
amounts in parentheses.*

Changing Word Spacing. It's not entirely true that you can't apply kerning when more than one character is selected. You can select a range of text and select Metrics, Optical, or 0 (zero) from the pop-up menu attached to the Kerning field.

If you want to increase the spacing between words but don't want to change the letterspacing of a range of text, press Command-Option-\ or Ctrl-Alt-\ (backslash) to add the base kerning increment (as defined by the value in the Kerning field in the Units & Increments Preferences dialog box) after each space character in the range. Hold down Shift as you press this shortcut, and InDesign adds kerning by five times the base kerning amount. To decrease word spacing, press Command-Option-Delete/Ctrl-Alt-Backspace (add Shift to the shortcuts to multiply the effect by five).

This keystroke works simply by changing the kerning after each space character. You can always go back and change the kerning, or use Find/Change to remove it.

Tracking   Tracking, in InDesign, applies the same kerning value to every character in a selected range of text (see Figure 4-11). When you change the tracking of some text, InDesign applies the tracking in addition to any kerning values applied to the text (regardless of the method—manual or automatic—used to enter the pair kerning). Note that this is the same as the definition of tracking used by QuarkXPress, and is different from the definition used by PageMaker. In PageMaker, tracking also applies kerning, but the amount of kerning applied varies depending on the point size of the selected text and the tracking table in use. In PageMaker, InDesign's tracking would be called "range kerning."

Just as you cannot apply kerning using the Kerning field when you have multiple characters selected, you can't change the Tracking field when the text insertion point is between two characters—you have

FIGURE 4-11
Tracking

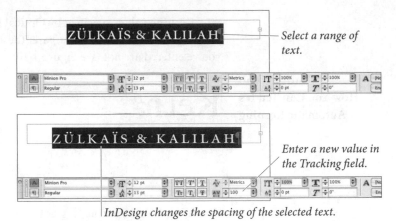

Select a range of text.

Enter a new value in the Tracking field.

InDesign changes the spacing of the selected text.

to have one or more characters selected. (Actually, you *can* change it, but it doesn't do anything.)

Note that the default keyboard shortcuts for tracking are exactly the same as those for kerning; which one you get depends on whether or not you have a range of text selected.

Tracking Tips. The following are a few of our favorite tracking tips.

▶ If you're setting text in all capitals or the small caps style, add 20 or 50 units of tracking to the text. Do not add tracking to the last character of the last word in the text, as that will affect the amount of space after the word, too.

▶ Printing white text on a black background often requires a little extra tracking, too. That's because the negative (black) space makes the white characters seem closer together.

▶ Larger type needs to be tracked more tightly (with negative tracking values). Often, the larger the tighter, though there are aesthetic limits to this rule. Advertising headline copy will often be tracked until the characters just "kiss."

▶ A condensed typeface (such as Futura Condensed) can usually do with a little tighter tracking. Sometimes we'll apply a setting as small as -10 to a text block to make it hold together better.

▶ When you're setting justified text and you get bad line breaks, or if you have an extra word by itself at the end of a paragraph, you can track the whole paragraph plus or minus one or two units without it being too apparent. Sometimes that's just enough to fix these problems.

Horizontal and Vertical Scaling

Enter a value in the Horizontal Scaling field or the Vertical Scaling field (or both) to change the size of the selected text (see Figure 4-12). When the values you enter in these fields are not equal, you're creating fake "expanded" or "condensed" type. We say "fake" because true expanded or condensed characters must be drawn by a type designer—when you simply scale the type, the thick and thin strokes of the characters become distorted.

Note that entering values in these fields does not affect the point size of the type.

FIGURE 4-12
Squashing and Stretching Type

Select some text.

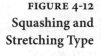

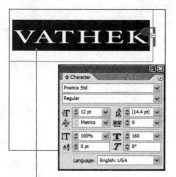

Enter a scaling value in the Horizontal Scaling field (and/or Vertical Scaling field).

InDesign squashes and stretches the characters of the selected text.

Baseline Shift

Sometimes, you need to raise the baseline of a character or characters above the baseline of the surrounding text (or lower it below the baseline). In pre-DTP typesetting, we would accomplish this by decreasing or increasing the leading applied to the character. However, that won't work in modern programs—remember, in InDesign the largest leading in the line predominates. Instead, you use the Baseline Shift field in the Character palette or Control palette (see Figure 4-13).

Enter an amount in the Baseline Shift field to shift the baseline of the selected text by that amount. As you'd expect, positive values move the selected text up from the baseline; negative values move the selected text down from the baseline.

While it's tempting to use Baseline Shift to adjust numbers in formulae, registered trademark symbols, and so on, it's better to use the Superscript or Subscript features (see "Superscript and Subscript," later in this section).

Baseline Shift Keyboard Shortcuts. You can apply baseline shift using your keyboard. To do this, select some text and press Option-Shift-Up arrow/Alt-Shift-Up arrow to move the baseline of the text

FIGURE 4-13
Baseline Shift

Select the character or
characters you want to
shift...

...then enter a baseline shift
distance in the Baseline Shift
field (positive values move
the baseline up; negative
values move it down).

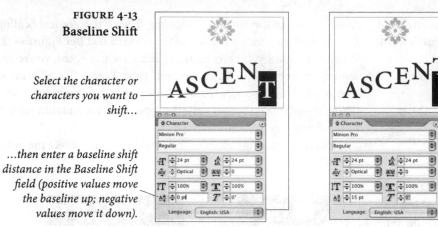

InDesign shifts the baseline of the
selected character or characters.

up two points—or whatever value you've entered in the Baseline Shift field of the Units & Increments Preferences dialog box, or Option-Shift-Down arrow/Alt-Shift-Down arrow to shift the baseline down by the same distance.

To shift the baseline of the selected text *up* by a distance equal to five times the value you entered in the Units & Increments Preferences dialog box, press Command-Option-Shift-Up arrow/Ctrl-Alt-Shift-Up arrow. To shift the baseline down by the same amount, press Command-Shift-Down arrow/Ctrl-Alt-Shift-Down arrow.

Skewing   When you apply skewing to a range of characters in an InDesign text frame, InDesign slants the vertical axis of the type by the angle you enter here (see Figure 4-14). You can enter from –85 degrees to 85 degrees. Positive skew values slant the type to the right; negative values slant it to the left.

This might be useful as a special text effect, but you shouldn't count on it to provide an "italic" version of a font family that lacks a true italic type style. Why? Because there's more to an italic font than simple slanting of the characters (see Figure 4-15).

Language   The language you choose for a range of text determines the dictionary InDesign uses to hyphenate and check the spelling of the text (see Figure 4-16). Because language is a character-level attribute, you can apply a specific language to individual words—which means you can tell InDesign to stop flagging "frisson" or "gemütlichkeit" as misspelled words, if you want. The only languages that show up in the Language pop-up menu in the Character palette or Control

FIGURE 4-14
Skewing Text

Select some text.

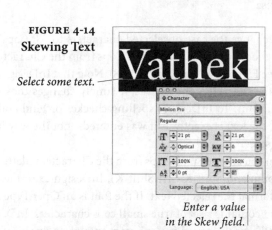
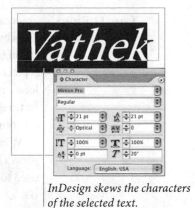

*Enter a value
in the Skew field.*

*InDesign skews the characters
of the selected text.*

FIGURE 4-15
**Real and Fake
Italic Characters**

AaBbCcDdEeFf

Real: Minion Pro Italic

*Note the differences in
character shapes.*

AaBbCcDdEeFf

*Fake: Minion Pro
Regular with 10 degree
skewing.*

palette are those for which you have a dictionary installed. If the
language you're looking for isn't in this list, then you can use the
InDesign installer to install that dictionary for you.

FIGURE 4-16
Assigning a Language

*Select a word or phrase, then
select a language from the
Language pop-up menu.*

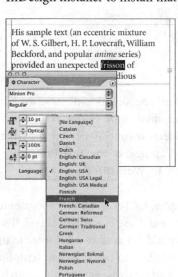
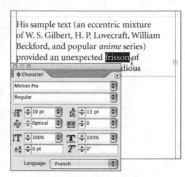

*InDesign will use the language
you selected when composing text
or checking spelling.*

Case Options

You can change the case of selected characters to All Caps or Small Caps by choosing All Caps or Small Caps from the Character palette menu (see Figure 4-17 and Figure 4-18). Note that InDesign does not replace the characters themselves; it simply changes they way they look and print. To InDesign's spelling checker or Find and Change features, the text is exactly as it was entered—not the way it appears on your screen.

When you choose Small Caps from the Character palette menu (or press Command-Shift-K/Ctrl-Shift-K), InDesign examines the font used to format the selected text. If the font is an OpenType font, and if the font contains a set of true small caps characters, InDesign uses true small caps. InDesign is also smart enough to do this if you have a non-OpenType font that has an "Expert" version. If the font is not

FIGURE 4-17
All Caps

Select the text you want to capitalize, then choose All Caps from the Character palette or Control palette menu.

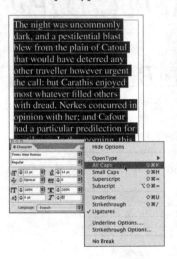

InDesign displays (and prints) the selected text in all caps.

an OpenType font, doesn't have an Expert font available, or doesn't contain small caps characters, InDesign scales regular uppercase characters down to 70 percent (or whatever value you entered in the Small Cap field of the Text Preferences dialog box, as described in Chapter 1, "Workspace").

Changing Case

If Chapter 3, "Text," was all about entering text, why didn't we put the Change Case command there? Because, frankly, that chapter is already laid out and we don't want to upset our indexer.

In addition to being able to temporarily change the case of characters using the case options, you can have InDesign change the case of the characters by typing new characters for you using the Change Case submenu (which you'll find on the Type menu and on the context menu when text is selected).

FIGURE 4-18
Small Caps

Select some text...

...then choose Small Caps from the Character palette or Control palette menu

If you're using an OpenType font (as in this example), InDesign displays the small caps version of the selected characters (if the OpenType font contains small caps alternate characters).

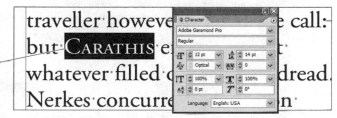

If you're using a PostScript Type 1 or TrueType font, InDesign displays scaled, capitalized versions of the selected characters.

Adobe Garamond Pro (OpenType)

THESE ARE TRUE SMALL CAPS

Adobe Garamond (PostScript Type 1)

THESE ARE NOT TRUE SMALL CAPS

If you're using a PostScript Type 1 font, don't use the Small Caps character formatting option; instead, change the font of the text to an "expert set."

To change the case of selected characters, choose an option: Uppercase, Lowercase, Title Case, or Sentence Case. Uppercase and Lowercase are self-explanatory. Sentence Case capitalizes the first letter of each sentence. Title Case is very simpleminded: it capitalizes the first character of each word in the selection, even if the word is "the," "and," or another preposition or article (see Figure 4-19).

Underline

When you choose Underline from the Character palette menu, click the Underline button in the Control palette, or press Command-Shift-U/Ctrl-Shift-U, InDesign applies an underline to the selected text (see Figure 4-20).

Custom Underlines. Fortunately, you can customize the underline style in each instance that you use it. The trick is to select Underline Options from the Character palette menu (or the Control palette menu when it's displaying character formatting). The Underline Options dialog box is pretty self-explanatory, letting you set the thickness, offset from the text baseline, color, and line style of the underscore. You can't save these settings as a style or preset, but you

FIGURE 4-19
Changing Case

Select some text.

InDesign's Title Case command capitalizes the first character of each word (you'll have to fix articles and prepositions yourself).

Choose a case conversion option from the Change Case submenu (on the Type menu or the context menu).

InDesign converts the case of the selected text. This conversion, unlike the All Caps and Small Caps formatting options, actually replaces the characters in the text.

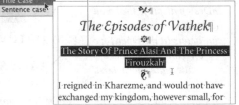

FIGURE 4-20
Underline

Select the text you want to underline.

By default, stroke weights are based on the size of the text.

Choose Underline from the Character palette menu.

InDesign applies an underline to the selected text.

Use the Underline Options dialog box to specify the appearance of the underline.

Here's a quick way to display the Underline Options dialog box: hold down Option/Alt as you click the Underline button on the Control palette.

can build them into the definition of a character style (we cover character styles later in this chapter).

Breaking at Spaces. InDesign's underline also includes any spaces in the selection. Some designs require that underlines break at spaces in the text. You could laboriously select each space and turn off the underline attribute, by why not use Find/Change to do the work for you? Find a space in the selection with the Underline attribute, then replace it with a space with Underline turned off.

Breaking at Descenders. At some point, we said that there was no way to break underlines at descenders. We lied. You can apply a white one-point stroke to the characters. The stroke overlaps the underline. It's a thing of beauty. If you need to do this to a lot of text, use Find/Change to search for characters with descenders (such as the "j" or the "y") and use the Format button in the Change To area to give them a stroke.

Strikethrough

When you choose Strikethrough from the Character palette menu (or click the Strikethrough button in the Control palette or press Command-Shift-?/Ctrl-Shift-?), InDesign applies the strikethrough text effect to the selected text (see Figure 4-21). To remove the Strikethrough text effect, select the feature or press the keystroke again.

FIGURE 4-21
Strikethrough

By default, the stroke weight of the Strikethrough effect varies based on the size of the text.

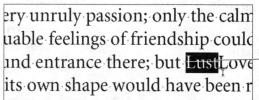

Select some text…

…then choose Strikethrough from the Character palette menu or click the Strikethrough button on the Control palette.

You can use the Strikethrough Options dialog box to to specify the appearance and position of the strikethrough rule.

To display the Strikethrough Options dialog box, hold down Option/Alt as you click the Strikethrough button in the Control palette, or choose Strikethrough Options from the Control palette menu.

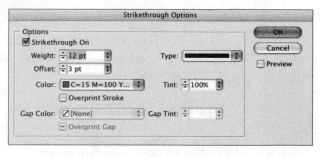

Custom Strikethrough. The strikethrough style isn't particularly consistent; it changes its thickness and distance from the baseline depending on the font. However, you can control the strikethrough style by selecting Strikethrough Options from the Character or Control palette menu. The options here are very similar to those in the Underline Options dialog box: You can adjust the thickness, color, offset (from the baseline), and style of the line. If you're applying a colored strikethrough on top of black text, you may want to set it to overprint so that it won't knock out a fine white line—which would be difficult to register on press. If so, make sure you like the result by turning on Overprint Preview (from the View menu).

Highlighting Text. Want to make some text look as if it's been highlighted with a felt "highlight" marker? You can simulate the effect using a custom strikethrough (see Figure 4-22). Make your strikethrough larger than the text it's supposed to cover, then turn on the Overprint Stroke checkbox. (If you don't overprint the stroke, you won't be able to see the text through the "highlight." You'll have to turn on Overprint Preview from the View menu. The highlight color cannot match the color of the type, because overprinting doesn't work with overlapping areas of a single color.)

FIGURE 4-22
Creating a "Highlight" Effect

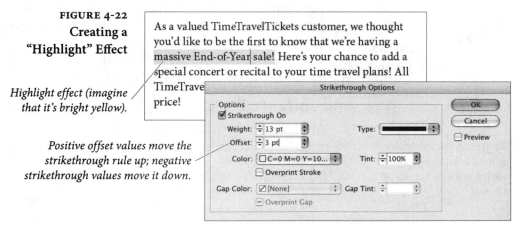

Highlight effect (imagine that it's bright yellow).

Positive offset values move the strikethrough rule up; negative strikethrough values move it down.

You can also create interesting highlight effects by mixing a custom strikethrough with a custom underline. For instance, you could make a line appear above and below some text, sort of like putting the text in a stripe.

Ligatures   Some character combinations are just trouble—from a typesetting standpoint, at least. In particular, when you combine the lowercase "f" character with "f," "i," or "l," the tops of the characters run into each other. To compensate for this, type designers provide ligatures—special characters "tied" ("ligature" means "tie") together.

When you choose Ligatures from the Character palette's menu, InDesign replaces some of the character combinations in the selected range of text with the corresponding ligatures (see Figure 4-23).

If the font you've selected is not an OpenType font, InDesign replaces only the "fl" and "fi" character combinations. In Windows, InDesign uses these ligature characters if they're available in the font (and they are, for most PostScript Type 1 fonts), even though they are not part of the Windows character set—that is, there is usually no way to type them. If the font you've selected is an OpenType font, InDesign makes the ligature substitutions are suggested by the font.

OpenType fonts can also feature discretionary ligatures—for more on this topic, see "OpenType Fonts," later in this chapter.

FIGURE 4-23
Ligatures

Select some text and then choose Ligatures from the Character palette menu.

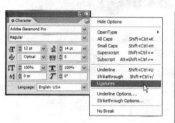

If you're using an OpenType font, InDesign uses additional ligatures defined in the font. In this example, InDesign applies the "ffi" and "ffl" ligatures.

Ligatures off
Adobe Garamond Pro (OpenType)
file difficult reflect affliction

Adobe Garamond (PostScript Type 1)
file difficult reflect affliction

Ligatures on
Adobe Garamond Pro (OpenType)
file difficult reflect affliction

Adobe Garamond (PostScript Type 1)
file difficult reflect affliction

Superscript and Subscript

While you can always create superscript or subscript characters (for use in fractions or exponential notation) by changing the point size and baseline shift of selected characters, InDesign provides a shortcut: the Superscript and Subscript text effects (see Figure 4-24).

When you select Superscript or Subscript from the Character palette menu, InDesign scales the selected text and shifts its baseline. (You can also press Command-Shift-=/Ctrl-Shift-= or Command-Option-Shift-=/Ctrl-Alt-Shift-=.) InDesign calculates the scaling and baseline shift by multiplying the current text size and leading by the values you've set in the Size fields (Superscript or Subscript) in the Text Preferences dialog box (see "Text Preferences" in Chapter 1, "Workspace").

Note that InDesign does not display the effective point size or baseline shift values in the corresponding fields of the Character palette when you select the text. If you are using an OpenType font that has true Superscript and Subscript characters, you'd be better

FIGURE 4-24
**Superscript and
Subscript**

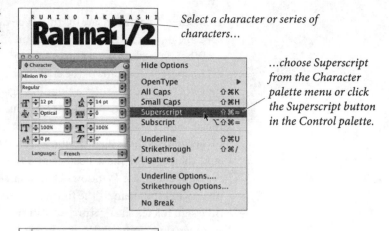

*Select a character or series of
characters...*

*...choose Superscript
from the Character
palette menu or click
the Superscript button
in the Control palette.*

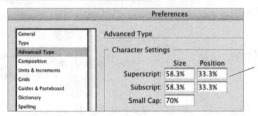

*InDesign scales the
text and shifts its
baseline...*

*Tip: To display the Text
panel of the Preferences
dialog box, hold down
Option/Alt and click the
Superscript or Subscript
button in the Control palette.*

*...according to the
values you entered in
the Text Preferences
dialog box.*

off using the Superscript/Superior and Subscript/Inferior formatting
in the OpenType submenu (see below).

No Break   This one is really easy to explain: To prevent a range of text from
breaking across lines, select the text and turn on the No Break option
in the Character palette's menu (see Figure 4-25).

FIGURE 4-25
No Break

*It should be obvious that
applying No Break to large
amounts of text can make
your text disappear (as it
cannot be composed in a
single column). Right?*

*InDesign will not break
the text when it falls
at the end of a line.*

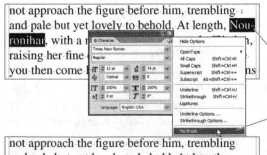

*Select the text you
want to keep from
breaking across lines
(in this example, a
name).*

*Choose No Break
from the Character
palette menu or
Control palette
menu.*

OpenType Fonts

We've mentioned OpenType fonts a few times in the chapter so far; however, we should probably take a moment to discuss them. The OpenType font specification was created jointly by Microsoft and Adobe as a way to represent a font with only a single file on both Macintosh and Windows (so you can move the font cross-platform). The characters are encoded using the international standard Unicode, so each font can have hundreds, or even thousands of different characters—even the very large character sets in non-Roman languages such as Japanese.

OpenType fonts act just like PostScript Type 1 or TrueType fonts in programs like Microsoft Word or QuarkXPress, but InDesign can perform special tricks with them, such as replacing characters with swashes (fancy versions of a letter), or with ligatures for character pairs such as ct and ffi. InDesign ships with several OpenType fonts, including Adobe Garamond Pro, Adobe Caslon Pro, Caflisch Pro, and Kozuka Mincho Pro (a Japanese typeface).

Most of the special OpenType typesetting features in InDesign are hidden in the OpenType submenu in the Character palette's menu (see Figure 4-26). If a font doesn't support one of these features, it appears in the menu within square brackets ("[Swash]").

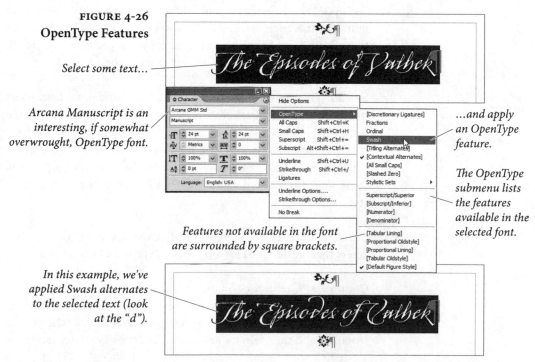

FIGURE 4-26
OpenType Features

Select some text...

Arcana Manuscript is an interesting, if somewhat overwrought, OpenType font.

...and apply an OpenType feature.

The OpenType submenu lists the features available in the selected font.

Features not available in the font are surrounded by square brackets.

In this example, we've applied Swash alternates to the selected text (look at the "d").

Alternate Characters

The OpenType features work by replacing one or more glyphs with another single glyph. "fi" and "fl" ligatures that we discussed earlier are a great example of this, but they're only the beginning.

Discretionary Ligatures. Font designers love making ligatures, but they recognize that users won't usually want to use more esoteric ligatures (such as "ct" or "st") in everyday text. If you select some text and turn on the Discretionary Ligatures feature, InDesign uses these lesser-known ligatures (if they're available in the font). We usually turn this off except when we're trying to make something look "old fashioned," or when using a script typeface (such as Caflisch Pro).

Fractions. Changing fake fractions (such as $^1/_2$) to real fractions (½) has long been a thorn in the side of anyone laying out cookbooks or construction manuals. Fortunately, you can now just turn on the Fractions feature and anything that looks like a fraction will convert to the proper character automatically. (In some OpenType typefaces, only very basic fractions such as ½, ¼, and ⅔ are converted. In others, even arbitrary fractions such as $^{355}/_{113}$ are changed (sadly, not in this font). It depends on the design of the font.) This feature has no effect on non-fractions, so we usually just turn this on and leave it on.

Ordinal. "First," "second," and "third" are all examples of ordinal numbers. InDesign can automatically set the "st", "nd", and "rd" (or the "o" and "a" in Spanish) to superscript when you turn Ordinal on in the OpenType submenu. "3rd," for example, becomes "3rd".

Swash. When you need to give a character a little more flair, select it and turn on the Swash feature. Swashes are typically used at the beginning or ending of words or sentences. You can see if a particular OpenType font has any swash characters by opening the Insert Glyph palette and looking for Swash in the Show pop-up menu; some fonts (such as Adobe Caslon Pro) have swashes in their italic styles only.

Titling Alternates. Some OpenType fonts have special "titling" characters that are designed for all-uppercase type set at large sizes.

Contextual Alternates. Some OpenType fonts—mostly script faces—have contextual ligatures and connecting alternates, which are very similar to ligatures. Set a paragraph in Adobe Caflisch Pro, for instance, and then select it and turn on Contextual Alternates. The result looks more like handwriting, because the alternate characters connect to each other.

All Small Caps. When you turn on the Small Caps feature (which we described in "Case Options," earlier), InDesign leaves uppercase characters alone. All Small Caps, however, forces uppercase characters to appear as lowercase small caps. This is useful when formatting acronyms such as DOS, NASA, or IBM.

Raised and Lowered Characters

Typesetting a treatise on Einstein's theory of relativity? If so, you'll be mighty happy about InDesign's ability to use true superscripts and subscripts instead of the faked scaled versions that you get with the Superscript and Subscript features in the Character palette's menu. You have four choices in the OpenType submenu (each one is mutually exclusive of the others):

▶ Superscript/Superior

▶ Subscript/Inferior

▶ Numerator

▶ Denominator

However, note that most OpenType fonts only have a small set of characters designed to be superscript or subscript, so you can't set any and all characters you want in these styles. For example, if you set the word "turkey" to Superscript/Superior style, only every other character changes. In some cases you'll get the same result when you choose Denominator or Subscript/Inferior.

Formatting Numerals

We like "old style" numerals (you know, the kind with descenders: 1234567890) better than full-height "lining figures" (1234567890), and we've always gotten them by changing the font of the characters to an "expert" version of whatever font we were using (if one was available). So we were very happy to see that there are four different ways InDesign can format numerals: Proportional Oldstyle, Tabular Oldstyle, Proportional Lining, and Tabular Lining (see Figure 4-27).

The default style is Tabular Lining, which works well for financial tables (such as those found in an annual report), because numbers have equal widths and align from one line to the next. If you choose Tabular Oldstyle from the OpenType submenu, the numerals line up, but InDesign uses old style characters. Proportional Lining numerals are all the same height, but vary in width. David prefers this style for everything other than tables, especially when interspersing num-

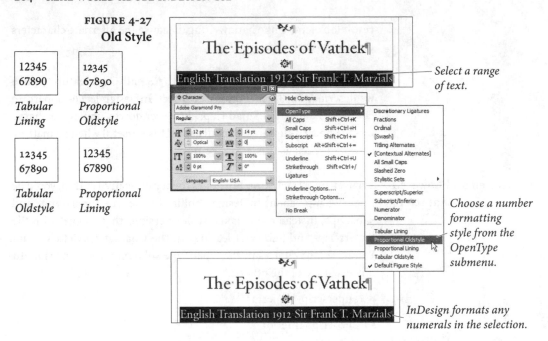

FIGURE 4-27
Old Style

12345
67890

*Tabular
Lining*

12345
67890

*Proportional
Oldstyle*

12345
67890

*Tabular
Oldstyle*

12345
67890

*Proportional
Lining*

Select a range
of text.

Choose a number
formatting
style from the
OpenType
submenu.

InDesign formats any
numerals in the selection.

bers and uppercase characters. Ole would rather use Proportional Oldstyle, which uses old style figures of varying widths.

The last OpenType numeral formatting option is Default Figure Style, which applies the figure style defined as the default by the type designer (so the effect varies from font to font).

Filling and Stroking Characters

Most page layout programs give you the ability to apply an "outline" type style to text. When you do this, you get a stroke around the text that varies in size depending on the point size of the text. But what if you want to apply a stroke of a particular width to the text? What if you want to apply a fill of a different color?

With InDesign, you can fill or stroke text as you would any other path. Once you've selected text (you can use the Selection tool to select unlinked text frames), you can set the fill color, or the stroke color and stroke weight (see Figure 4-28).

You can even apply gradients to the fill and stroke of the type—without converting the type to outlines. However, while gradients are easy to apply, it's not always easy to get the effect you're looking for. The reason is that gradients are based on the bounding box of the text frame (the bounding box is the smallest imaginary rectangle inside which the frame will fit). While we think that the

FIGURE 4-28
Character Fill and Stroke

Select an unlinked text frame using the Selection tool, then click the Formatting Affects Text button.

You can also select characters using the Text tool, then apply a fill and/or stroke to the text using the same controls you use to apply a fill or stroke to any path.

You can also click the Formatting Affects Text button in the Swatches palette.

Format the text using any of the fill and stroke formatting tools. In this example, we used the Swatches palette to apply a tint to the fill and stroke of the text, and then used the Stroke palette to set the stroke weight.

A character without a fill quickly becomes unreadable as you increase the stroke weight.

Note that the fill retains the shape of the character as you increase stroke weight. This works because InDesign strokes the characters and then fills them.

gradient-in-text feature is kind of fun, in the real world we usually convert the text to outlines first (see "Converting Text to Outlines" in Chapter 6, "Where Text Meets Graphics").

Paragraph Formatting

What makes a paragraph a paragraph? InDesign's definition is simple—a paragraph is any string of characters that ends with a carriage return. When you apply paragraph formatting, the formatting applies to all of the characters in the paragraph. Paragraph alignment, indents, tabs, spacing, and hyphenation settings are all examples of paragraph formatting.

You don't have to select all of the text in a paragraph to apply paragraph formatting—all you need to do is click the Text tool in the paragraph. To select more than one paragraph, drag the cursor through the paragraphs you want format. The selection doesn't have to include all of the text in the paragraphs, it only has to *touch* each paragraph.

If what you're trying to do, however, is apply character formatting (such as font or point size) to all of the characters in the paragraph, you should quadruple-click (or triple-click, if you've turned off the Triple Click to Select a Line option in the Text Preferences dialog box) the paragraph with the Text tool—that way, you'll select all of the characters, including the invisible carriage return character. (Note that you can force a line break without creating a new paragraph—called a "soft return"—by typing Shift-Return/Shift-Enter.)

You can find all of InDesign's paragraph formatting features in the Paragraph palette. To display the Paragraph palette, press Command-M/Ctrl-M. These features are duplicated in the Control palette—if the Control palette is displaying character formatting, then click the palette's Paragraph Formatting Controls button or press Command-Option-7/Ctrl-Alt-7 to switch to paragraph formatting.

Alignment Click the alignment buttons at the top of the Paragraph palette or in the Control palette to set the alignment of the selected paragraphs (see Figure 4-29).

InDesign supports the usual set of paragraph alignments—left aligned (also known as "rag right"), right aligned (also known as "rag left"), centered, and justified, but also adds a couple of variations on the justified alignment you might not be familiar with.

In addition to the standard "justified" alignment, which treats the last line of the paragraph as if it were left aligned, InDesign offers the force justified, right justified, and center justified alignments. These each tell InDesign to treat the last line of the paragraph differently. When you force justify the text, the last line is spread out all the way to the right margin, even if it's only a single word. In some cases, when the Paragraph Composer is turned on (see "Multi-line Composition," later in this chapter), turning on force justify actually reflows the paragraph significantly.

Right justified and center justified treat the last line as right aligned and center aligned, respectively. In the old days of typesetting, these alignments were known as "quad right" and "quad center."

Finally, the Align Towards Spine and Align Away from Spine options. The former aligns the text to the spine and leaves the outside of the text ragged; the latter does the opposite.

Indents Paragraphs can be indented using the Left Indent and Right Indent fields in the Paragraph or Control palette (see Figure 4-30). You can enter values from zero (0) to 720 picas in these fields, but you can't enter negative numbers to make the edges of the paragraph "hang" outside the edges of the column or text frame.

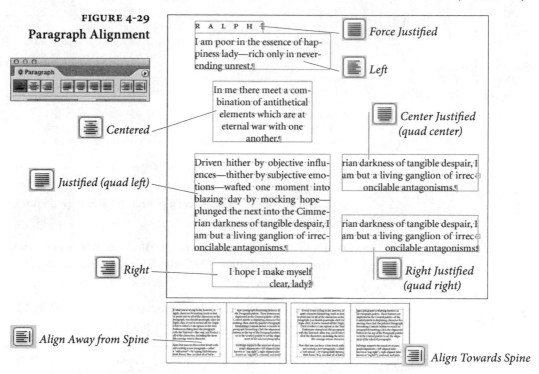

FIGURE 4-29
Paragraph Alignment

Centered

Justified (quad left)

Right

Align Away from Spine

Force Justified

Left

Center Justified
(quad center)

Right Justified
(quad right)

Align Towards Spine

Note that the left and right indents are always added to the text inset, as specified in the Text Frame Options dialog box. If you have a left inset of 6 points and a left indent of 12 points, then the left edge of the paragraph will sit 18 points from the edge of the frame.

There's also a special indent, called First Line, that applies to the first line of the paragraph alone. The value you enter in the First Line field sets the distance between the first line indent and the left indent. The First Line indent may be positive or negative, but cannot be a negative number greater than the left indent (see Figure 4-31). You should *never* create an indent by typing five spaces at the beginning of a paragraph to indent; instead, use First Line indent.

How large your First Line indent should be depends on your design and on the typeface you're working with. Typically, the larger the x-height of the font, the larger first-line indent you should use. Book designers often use a one- or two-em indent, so in an 11-point type, the indent might be 11 or 22 points.

FIGURE 4-30
Paragraph Indents

Left indent

Right indent

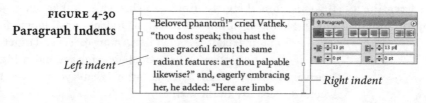

FIGURE 4-31
First Line Indent

Don't use tab characters to apply a first line indent...

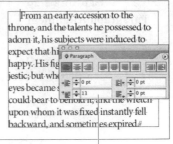

...use the First Line Indent field.

To change an indent value, select a paragraph and then do one of the following things:

► Display the Paragraph or Control palette, then enter a value in the First Line Left Indent, Left Indent, Right Indent, and/or the Last Line Right Indent fields (see Figure 4-32).

► Display the Tabs palette (press Command-Shift-T/Ctrl-Shift-T), and drag one of the indent icons (see Figure 4-33).

FIGURE 4-32
Setting an Indent

Click the Text tool in the paragraph you want to format.

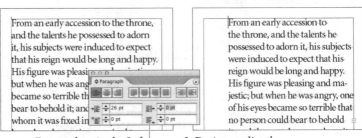

Enter values in the Left, Right, First, or Last fields.

InDesign applies the indents you've specified.

FIGURE 4-33
Indents on the Tabs Palette

Left indent   *Right indent*

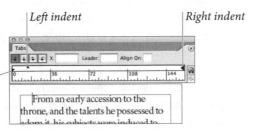

First Line indent

Creating a Hanging Indent

If you learn nothing else from this chapter, we'd like you to come out of it knowing how to set a hanging indent—a paragraph format you use for numbered lists, bullet lists, or any of several other situations. Use hanging indents, rather than breaking and indenting each line using carriage returns and tabs—you'll thank yourself for it later, when you need to edit the text.

To create a hanging indent that adapts when you change the width of a text block, edit copy, or change formatting in other ways, follow these steps (see Figure 4-34).

1. If you haven't already done this, type a bullet, a number, or some other character, followed by a tab at the beginning of the paragraph.

2. While the cursor is still blinking in the paragraph, press Command-Shift-T/Ctrl-Shift-T to display the Tabs palette. Hold down Shift and drag the Left indent icon to the right—leaving the First Line indent marker in position. Press the same keystroke to make the palette go away.

You can also set your hanging indent using the Paragraph or Control palette—to do this, enter a positive left indent and a negative first-line indent. Either way, there's no need to set a tab stop because InDesign assumes the left indent is the first tab stop.

Here's one other way to create a hanging indent: Set the Left indent for the paragraph where you want the bullet to be, then set a

FIGURE 4-34
Setting a
Hanging Indent

Click the Text tool in a paragraph, then press Command-Shift-T/ Ctrl-Shift-T to display the Tabs palette.

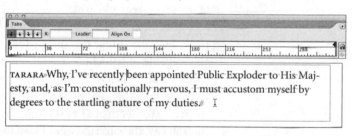

Hold down Shift and drag the Left indent icon to the right of the First Line indent marker.

As you drag, InDesign displays a vertical guide that follows the location of the Left indent icon.

Stop dragging, and InDesign applies a hanging indent to the selected paragraph.

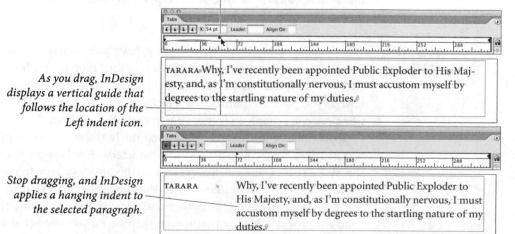

tab stop (see "Tabs," below, for more on this) where you want the Left indent for the rest of the paragraph to be. Now place the text cursor immediately after the tab character and press Command-\ or Ctrl-\ (backslash). This is the keyboard shortcut for the Indent Here character (you can also get this character from the Insert Special Character submenu in the Type menu or the Context menu). This invisible character causes the rest of the lines in a paragraph to indent to this place. If you want to delete it, you can place the cursor after it (since it's invisible and has no width, you might have to use the arrow keys to position it) and then press Delete.

While the Indent Here character is easy to type, we like using the negative First Line indent trick more because we can use it in a paragraph style.

Tabs   A classic Ole anecdote: "Whiz! Clunk. Whiz! Clunk. Ding! My father brought home a large, black typewriter—a machine so antiquated that even his school district (he was a high school math teacher) didn't want it anymore. It was a behemoth, a leviathan among typewriters. I couldn't lift it, and typing a letter took the entire strength of my seven-year-old arm.

"My brother and I were fascinated by the movement of the carriage. For one thing, the spring that pulled it was massive—probably capable of launching a small aircraft—so pressing the Tab key was, by itself, pretty exciting. But what really caught our attention were the tabs themselves: thick slabs of metal you 'set' by pushing them into the teeth of a bar set below the carriage. With each press of the Tab key, the carriage would leap to the right—then a protruding part would slam into one of the tabs. Bam! Unstoppable force meets immovable object. The rear of the typewriter would jump half an inch to the right. This was cool."

Tabs, Mice,   Tabs come to desktop typesetting from typewriters, by way of word
and History   processing (with a stopover along the way at the Linotype machine). They solve a problem that didn't exist in hand-set metal type—namely, how do you position characters at precise locations in a line of type when you can't simply slide them into place with your finger?

There are two methods of controlling the horizontal position of text in a line. First, you can use space characters—word spaces, thin spaces, en spaces, and em spaces. This method places characters at *relative* positions in the line—where they appear depends on the width of the spaces and of the other characters in the line. Tabs, by contrast, provide *absolute* position on the line—a tab stop set at 6 picas will remain at that position, regardless of the text content of the line.

Before we go any further, we'd better make sure we're using the same terminology. *Tab stops* are formatting attributes of paragraphs. *Tab characters* are what InDesign enters in a line of text when you press the Tab key. Tab characters push text around in a line; tab stops determine the effect of the tab characters. Each tab stop has a position (relative to the left edge of the text frame), an alignment (which specifies the composition of the text following a tab character), and, potentially, a leader (a tab leader is a series of repeated characters spanning the distance from beginning of the tab character to the beginning of the following text). Put tab stops and tab characters together, and you get *tabs*, the feature.

A Little Tab Dogma

Look. We try to be reasonable. We try not to insist that everyone work the way that we do, or that our way of doing things is necessarily the best way (in fact, we sometimes know it's not). But tabs are different—if you don't do it our way, you'll be causing yourself needless pain. Let's review the rules:

► Use tabs, not spaces, to move text to a specific position in a line of text.

► Use a First Line indent, not a tab, when you want to indent the first line of a paragraph.

► Do not force lines to break by entering tab characters (or multiple tab characters) at the end of a line! If you do, you'll find tab characters creeping back into the text as editing changes force text recomposition. To break a line without entering a carriage return, use the "soft return" (press Shift-Return/Shift-Enter).

► Don't use multiple tab characters when you can use a single tab character and an appropriately positioned tab stop. While there are some cases where you'll have to break this rule, putting two or more tab characters in a row should be the exception.

Types of Tab Stops

InDesign features five types of tab stop (see Figure 4-35).

Left, Right, and Centered Tab Stops. InDesign's left, right, and centered tab stops are the same as the basic tab stops you'll find in any word processor.

FIGURE 4-35
Tab Stop Alignment

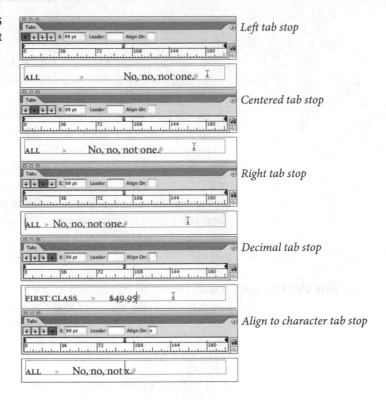

Left tab stop

Centered tab stop

Right tab stop

Decimal tab stop

Align to character tab stop

▶ Left tab stops push text following a tab character to a specific horizontal location in a column, and then align the text to the left of the tab stop position.

▶ Right tab stops push text to a location and then align the text to the right of the tab stop position.

▶ Centered tab stops center a line of text at the point at which you've set the tab stop.

Decimal Tab Stops. Decimal tab stops push text following a tab character so that any decimal point you've entered in the text aligns with the point at which you set the tab stop. Actually, the Decimal tab stop will use *any* non-numeric character. This turns out to be very useful when trying to align a column of numbers when some of them have footnotes, asterisks, or other symbols after them, because the numbers form to the left and the symbols "hang" off to the right. If there's no number followed by a character, InDesign treats the decimal tab stop as a right tab stop.

Align to Character Tab Stops. Align to character tab stops are just like decimal tab stops, but align to a character you specify (rather than a decimal point). If the character is not found in the text, the program treats the tab stop as a right tab stop.

Setting Tab Stops   To set a tab stop, follow these steps (see Figure 4-36).

1. If you haven't already entered tab characters in the text, enter them.

2. Select the text you want to format.

3. Display the Tabs palette (press Command-Shift-T/Ctrl-Shift-T), then click the Magnet button to snap the Tabs palette into position at the top of the text frame (if possible).

4. Click in the tab ruler and drag. As you drag, the X field shows you the position of the tab icon (relative to the left edge of the text frame). Then click one of the tab stop alignment buttons to determine the type of tab stop.

   If you want to add a tab leader, enter one or two leader characters in the Leader field in the Tabs palette (if you can't see this field, you'll need to increase the width of the palette).

You can also add a tab stop at a specific location on the tab ruler. To do this, enter the position you want in the X field in the Tabs palette and then press Enter. InDesign adds the tab stop. The new tab stop uses the current tab stop alignment, or you can click on a different one to change it.

FIGURE 4-36
Setting a Tab Stop

Click a tab stop button.

Drag the tab stop into position on the tab ruler.

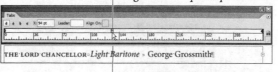

As you drag, InDesign displays a vertical guide that follows the location of the tab stop icon.

When the tab stop icon is in position, stop dragging.

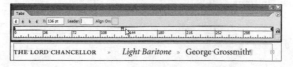

Removing Tab Stops. To remove a tab stop, drag the tab stop icon off the tab ruler (see Figure 4-37). Note that this doesn't remove any tab characters you've typed in your text, though it does make them behave differently (because you've taken away their tab stop).

FIGURE 4-37
Removing a Tab Stop

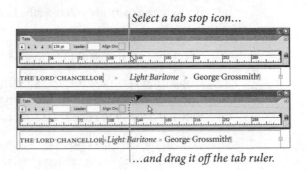

Select a tab stop icon…

…and drag it off the tab ruler.

Editing Tab Stops. To change a tab stop's position, drag the tab stop on the tab ruler (see Figure 4-38). Alternatively, you can select the tab stop (click on it), then enter a new value in the x field or give it a leader. Don't forget that if you want to move the tab stop by a specific amount, you can add a + or – character after the value that appears in the x field and then type the amount you want to move it ("+14mm").

To change a tab stop's alignment (from left to decimal, for instance), select the tab stop on the tab ruler and then click the tab stop button corresponding to the alignment you want. Or you can Option/Alt-click on the tab stop to rotate through the alignment types.

FIGURE 4-38
Editing a Tab Stop

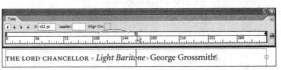

To change the position of a tab stop, drag the tab stop icon on the tab ruler.

To change the alignment of a tab stop, select the tab stop icon…

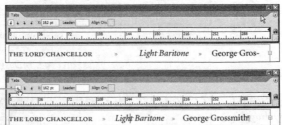

…and click one of the tab stop alignment buttons.

Repeating Tab Stops. To create a series of tab stops spaced an equal distance apart, select a tab stop on the tab ruler and choose Repeat Tab from the Tabs palette menu (see Figure 4-39). InDesign repeats the tab across the width of the current column. The distance between the new tab stops is equal to the distance between the tab stop you selected and the previous tab stop (or indent) in the column. InDesign also deletes all the tab stops that were already to the right of the tab stop you clicked (which can be frustrating if you've placed tab stops there and weren't expecting them to disappear).

FIGURE 4-39
Repeating a Tab Stop

Select the tab stop icon you want to repeat...

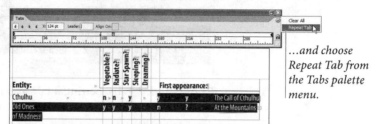

...and choose Repeat Tab from the Tabs palette menu.

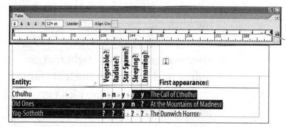

InDesign repeats the tab stop across the width of the tab ruler.

Working with Tab Leaders. A tab leader is a series of repeated characters that fill the area taken up by the tab character (see Figure 4-40). The most common tab leader character is a period—think of all of the "dot" leaders you've seen in tables of contents.

Characters in a tab leader are not spaced in the same fashion as other characters—if they were, the characters in tab leaders on successive lines would not align with each other. That would be ugly. Instead, characters in a tab leader are monospaced—positioned as if on an invisible grid. This means you'll see different amounts of space between the last character of text preceding a tab leader and the first tab leader. It's a small price to pay.

In InDesign, you can format the characters in a tab leader by selecting the tab character and applying formatting, just as you would any other character. For instance, dotted tab leaders typically look like a bunch of periods. To make them look more like traditional dot leaders, add a space after the period (in the Leader field), then select the tab character and reduce its size slightly.

FIGURE 4-40
Applying a Tab Leader

Select some text. ———

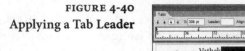

Select a tab stop.

Enter the character or characters you want to use for the tab leader in the Leader field. Press Return/Enter...

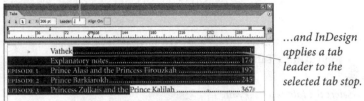

...and InDesign applies a tab leader to the selected tab stop.

Right-aligned Tabs. Setting a tab stop precisely at the right margin can be a bother; it's an even bigger bother when your art director says, "make that column narrower." Instead of using tab stops, try using a right-aligned tab character, which you can enter by pressing Shift-Tab (or add with the Insert Special Characters submenu in the Type menu). The text that follows the right-aligned tab character always aligns with the right margin, even when you change the right indent or the width of the text frame.

The right aligned tab picks up the tab leader settings from the last tab stop in the line.

Adding Space Before and After Paragraphs

When you want to add extra space between paragraphs, don't use carriage returns (not even one). If you do, you're certain to end up with unwanted carriage returns at the tops of text frames when text recomposes due to editing or formatting changes. Instead of typing carriage returns, use the Space Before and Space After fields in the Paragraph or Control palette. When you add space using these controls, InDesign removes the space when the paragraph falls at the top of a text frame (see Figure 4-41). If you need to add space before a paragraph at the top of a text frame, use First Baseline offset (see Chapter 3, "Text").

In addition, adding an exact amount of space is easier when you use the Paragraph or Control palette. Want to add four picas of vertical space above the paragraph? Enter it in the Space Before field. There's no need to guess how many carriage returns it would take to make up that vertical distance.

Align to Grid

When you have more than one column of text on a page, it's important that the baselines of the text line up across the columns. The idea

FIGURE 4-41
**Space Before
and Space After**

*If you try to use
carriage returns to
add vertical space...*

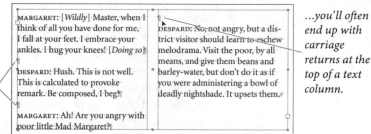

*...you'll often
end up with
carriage
returns at the
top of a text
column.*

*To avoid this problem,
use paragraph space
before (or after).*

Select some paragraphs...

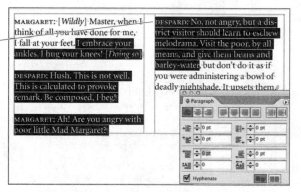

*...then enter
a value in the
Space Above
(or Space
Below) field.*

*If a paragraph falls at the
top of a text frame, InDesign
does not apply the paragraph
space above.*

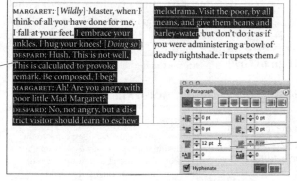

is that the leading should be consistent with an underlying "leading grid"—an invisible set of rules for where the baselines of text should lay. Many designers even work with leading grids on pages with a single column.

Unfortunately, in most page designs, you'll find elements that have to have leading values that differ from the leading applied to the body text. Inline graphics, paragraph rules, and headings are all examples of the sort of elements we're talking about. When one of these elements appears in a column of text, the leading of the lines in that column gets thrown off.

You need a way to compensate for leading variations inside a column of text. "Leading creep," the misalignment of baselines in adjacent text columns, is one of the hallmarks of amateur typesetting, so you want to avoid it.

While you could adjust the space above and below such intrusions to compensate, there's an easier way: use InDesign's Align to Baseline Grid command. Select a paragraph and click the Align to Baseline Grid button in the Paragraph palette, and InDesign forces the baselines of the lines in the paragraph onto the baseline grid (see Figure 4-42). You can change the leading and position of the document baseline grid in the Grids panel of the Preferences dialog box. To see this grid, select Show Baseline Grid in the View menu.

FIGURE 4-42
Align to Grid

This is all very pretty...

...but it throws the leading of the following paragraph off of the leading grid.

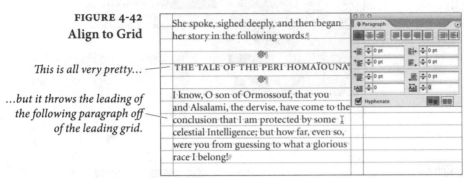

To fix this problem, select the paragraph and click the Align Baseline to Grid button.

InDesign snaps the baselines of the text in the paragraph to the baseline grid.

The baseline grid can also be calculated for individual text frames. To activate a custom baseline grid, select the text frame and press Command-B/Ctrl-B to display the Text Frame Options dialog box. Click the Baseline Options tab, and then turn on the Use Custom Grid option. Use the controls to set up your custom baseline grid (see Figure 4-43). Whe you specify a custom grid, the Align to Grid option aligns the text baselines with the baseline grid applied to the text frame, rather than to the document basline grid.

FIGURE 4-43
Custom Basline Grid

To set up a custom baseline grid for a text frame, select the frame, then open the Text Frame Options dialog box . Click the Baseline Options tab, then turn on the Use Custom Baseline Grid option.

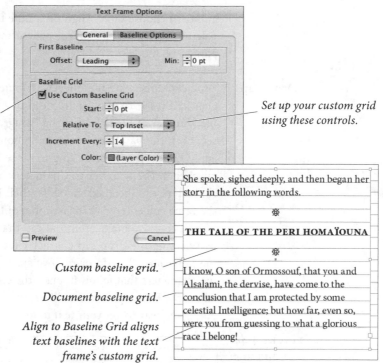

Set up your custom grid using these controls.

Custom baseline grid.

Document baseline grid.

Align to Baseline Grid aligns text baselines with the text frame's custom grid.

Why We Rarely Use Align to Baseline. While there's no doubt that a careful study and practice of baseline grids can make your documents better looking, we rarely use the Align to Baseline Grid feature. The reason: you can get the same result by making sure your leading, Space Before, and Space After always add up to an even multiple of the leading value.

For example, if your body text has 15-point leading, then make sure your headings also have 15- or 30-point leading. If you use Space Before or Space After, make sure those values are set to a multiple of 15, such as: 15, 30, or 45 points. Finally, snap the tops of your frame to the baseline grid and set the First Baseline setting to Leading, and you can't go wrong.

Only Align First Line to Grid. Often, sidebars in magazines or newsletters are set in a different font and leading than the main body text, and they're placed in their own text frame. You can make the first baseline of that sidebar align with the leading grid by using the Only Align First Line to Grid feature. This forces the first line of a selected paragraph to snap to the baseline grid, but then leaves the rest of the paragraph alone. To align the first baseline of a paragraph to the baseline grid, first align the whole paragraph to the baseline grid and then choose Only Align First Line to Grid from the Paragraph palette menu (or the Control palette menu when the palette is in paragraph mode).

Drop Caps

Drop caps are a paragraph-level attribute in InDesign (as they are in QuarkXPress). To apply a drop cap to a paragraph, enter a value in the Number of Lines field of the Paragraph or Control palette (this sets both the baseline shift and the point size of the drop cap). To apply the drop cap formatting to more than one character, enter a number in the Number of Characters field. InDesign enlarges the characters you specified and shifts their baseline down according to the value you entered in the Number of Lines field (see Figure 4-44).

You can also make an initial cap that drops down *and* raises up by selecting the drop cap character (or characters) and increasing the point size. To add or remove space between the drop cap and the characters that follow it, place the cursor after the drop cap and adjust the Kerning value (see "Kerning," earlier in this chapter). The only good way to get your text to follow the shape of a drop cap ("A"

FIGURE 4-44
Drop Caps

Select a paragraph.

Enter the number of lines you want to "drop" the initial character(s).

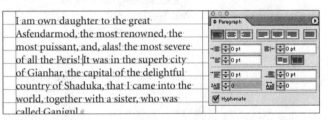

Enter the number of characters you want to apply the drop cap format to, if necessary.

or "W," for example) is to convert the character to an outline, cut it out of the text frame, place it above or below the frame, and then apply a text wrap.

If you find yourself often applying character formatting to your drop caps—changing size, font, color, *etc.*—then you should consider using nested character styles, described later in this chapter.

Type in the Margin. In InDesign, the edges of text frames are usually inviolable (apart from the adjustments applied by optical margin alignment). There's no margin release, no handy command for moving one line a bit over the edge. Or is there? Instead of a single-character drop cap, specify a two-character drop cap. Add a space to the left of the first character in the paragraph—if your paragraph is justified, this should be a space that doesn't get wider, such as an en space (Command-Shift-N/Ctrl-Shift-N). Place the cursor between the space and the drop cap and apply negative kerning until the left edge of the character moves outside of the text frame. Note, also, that using optical margin alignment may provide the effect you're looking for without all of the extra work.

Nested Styles

When we look at the formatting in our documents, we see patterns. In this book, for example, a paragraph containing a run-in heading starts with our "run-in heading" character style and then reverts to the formatting of our body text. A period separates the heading from the body text. To apply this formatting, we have to select the first sentence and apply the character style. Wouldn't it be nice if we could tell our page-layout application to apply that pattern of formatting for us?

With InDesign's nested styles, we can do just that. Nested styles give you a way to automatically apply character formatting to portions of a paragraph—the first character, the first sentence, or just the third word. Nested styles rely on you first creating a character style; we discuss how to do this later in this chapter. You might want to skip forward, read that section, and then return to this explanation.

Nested styles are perfect for automatically applying a style to a drop cap, a run-in heading (where the first sentence is styled differently from the rest of the paragraph), or any structured paragraph. Catalogs, for example, often have structured paragraphs—such as a paragraph that contains an item number followed by a title, followed by a description, followed by a price. With nested styles, you can tell InDesign to apply a different character style to each element.

You can apply a nested style as local formatting, but it's generally better to define a nested style as part of a paragraph style. To apply a nested style to one or more selected paragraphs in a story, choose Drop Caps and Nested Styles from the Paragraph or Control palette menu (or press Command-Option-R/Ctrl-Alt-R). We'll discuss how to define a paragraph style later in this chapter.

The Drop Caps and Nested Styles dialog box contains two sections: formatting for drop caps and formatting for paragraphs.

Drop Caps. Earlier in this chapter, we discussed the process of applying a drop cap to paragraph—the Drop Caps section of this dialog box is an alternate way to do the same thing.

Many designs specify that the first line of text following a drop cap be formatted a particular way—small caps are quite commonly used. With nested styles, you can accomplish this easily by adding a forced line break, as shown in Figure 4-45.

FIGURE 4-45
Drop Caps and Nested Styles

By including the drop cap as part of the paragraph's nested style definition, we can automatically apply a character style to the drop cap (which is a good thing to do, in any case).

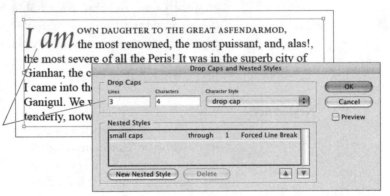

Nested Styles. The Nested Styles section is where you build a set of rules for InDesign to follow while formatting a paragraph. Here's how you make a nested style (see Figure 4-46).

1. Display the Drop Cap and Nested Style dialog box (choose Drop Caps and Nested Styles from the Paragraph palette menu or the Control palette menu). Click the New Nested Style button.

2. Select the character style you want to apply from the first pop-up menu. Of course, you have to have defined at least one character style for this to work.

3. To activate the second option, click the word "through." Select either "up to" or "through" from this pop-up menu. Choose "through" if you want to apply the style up to *and including* a given character, or "up to" to apply the style to the text but *not* to the delimiting character.

FIGURE 4-46
Applying Nested Styles

*This text and needs
to be formatted.*

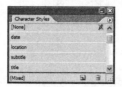

*We've created character
styles to assist us in
formatting the text.*

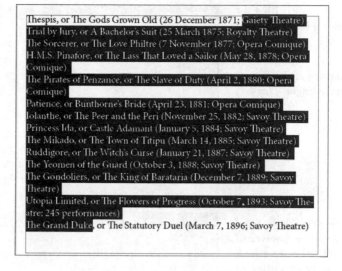

Thespis, or The Gods Grown Old (26 December 1871; Gaiety Theatre)
Trial by Jury, or A Bachelor's Suit (25 March 1875; Royalty Theatre)
The Sorcerer, or The Love Philtre (7 November 1877; Opera Comique)
H.M.S. Pinafore, or The Lass That Loved a Sailor (May 28, 1878; Opera Comique)
The Pirates of Penzance, or The Slave of Duty (April 2, 1880; Opera Comique)
Patience, or Bunthorne's Bride (April 23, 1881; Opera Comique)
Iolanthe, or The Peer and the Peri (November 25, 1882; Savoy Theatre)
Princess Ida, or Castle Adamant (January 5, 1884; Savoy Theatre)
The Mikado, or The Town of Titipu (March 14, 1885; Savoy Theatre)
Ruddigore, or The Witch's Curse (January 21, 1887; Savoy Theatre)
The Yeomen of the Guard (October 3, 1888; Savoy Theatre)
The Gondoliers, or The King of Barataria (December 7, 1889; Savoy Theatre)
Utopia Limited, or The Flowers of Progress (October 7, 1893; Savoy Theatre; 245 performances)
The Grand Duke, or The Statutory Duel (March 7, 1896; Savoy Theatre)

*We apologize, in advance,
for the complexity of this
illustration (which continues
on the next page). We can't
help it—this stuff is nothing
short of magical.*

We want to format the text according to the following rules:

1. Apply the "title" style to the text up to the comma.
2. Leave the comma and "or" in the paragraph's default style.
3. Format the subtitle (the text up to the open parenthesis).
*4. Format the open parenthesis character
using the paragraph's default style.*

Example line —— Thespis, or The Gods Grown Old (26 December 1871; Gaiety Theatre)¶

5. Format the date (the text up to the semicolon).

*6. Format the semicolon character
using the paragraph's default style.*
*7. Apply the "location" character
style to the theater name.*
*8. Format the close parenthesis character
using the paragraph's default style.*

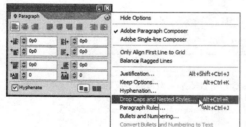

*Rather than work our way through the text and apply
character styles manually, we choose Drop Caps and
Nested Styles (from the Paragraph palette or the Control
palette menu).*

*InDesign displays the
Drop Cap and Nested
Styles dialog box.*

*Click the New Nested Style
button. InDesign creates a
new nested style. Choose
a character style from
the first pop-up menu.*

FIGURE 4-46
**Applying Nested Styles
(continued)**

*The following pop-up menus
set the length of the text
style range.*

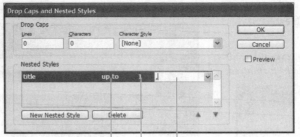

*Choose "up to" or "through"
from this pop-up menu.*

*Enter the number of
delimiter characters.*

*Enter a delimiter character (or
choose one of the preset delimtiers
from the pop-up menu).*

*Following the title, we want
to leave the comma and
the word "or" in the default
character formatting for
the paragraph. Click New
Nested Style and leave the
Style pop-up menu set to
"[No character style]".*

*We entered a
space here.*

*At this point, we're ready to
set up the formatting for the
subtitle. The character at the
end of the subtitle text is an
open parenthesis, so we enter
that character and set the
range to "up to."*

*We create a further six
character styles to cover all
of the rules we've defined.
When we're done, we have
formatted all of the text. No
selecting, no clicking, and
no keyboard shortcuts. This
process takes far longer to
explain than it does to do.*

*It's even better when you
make the nested styles
part of a paragraph style,
as we'll demonstrate
later in this chapter.*

THESPIS, or *The Gods Grown Old* (26 December 1871; Gaiety Theatre)
TRIAL BY JURY, or *A Bachelor's Suit* (25 March 1875; Royalty Theatre)
THE SORCERER, or *The Love Philtre* (7 November 1877; Opera Comique)
H.M.S. PINAFORE, or *The Lass That Loved a Sailor* (May 28, 1878; Opera
Comique)
THE PIRATES OF PENZANCE, or *The Slave of Duty* (April 2, 1880; Opera
Comique)
PATIENCE, or *Bunthorne's Bride* (April 23, 1881; Opera Comique)
IOLANTHE, or *The Peer and the Peri* (November 25, 1882; Savoy Theatre)
PRINCESS IDA, O
THE MIKADO, OI
RUDDIGORE, or
THE YEOMEN OF
THE GONDOLIEL
Theatre)
UTOPIA LIMITEI
Theatre; 245 per
THE GRAND DUI

4. Click the setting in the third column to change it from "1" to some other number, if necessary. If you want to apply your character style "up to the third word," for example, you would change this number to "3."

5. Click the last column to activate the pop-up menu, then enter a delimiter character (or choose one from the pop-up menu). To apply the style up to the first en space in the paragraph, for example, choose En Spaces from the pop-up menu. You can enter any character you want into this field—including many of the find/change metacharacters.

6. If you want another style to follow the one you just made, start at Step 1 again.

End Nested Style Here. What if you want to apply a character style to some portion of your paragraph, but there's no obvious "stopping point" you can target? For example, each paragraph may require the style up to a different point. No problem: Just choose End Nested Style Character from the last pop-up menu in Step 5, above. Then place the text cursor at that point in the paragraph and choose End Nested Style Here from the Insert Special Character submenu (under the Type or context menu). This is an invisible character, so it won't reflow your text. If a paragraph doesn't contain one of these special characters, InDesign applies the character style you specify to the entire paragraph.

Multi-Line Composition

Composition—the method our desktop publishing program uses to fit text into a line—isn't glamorous. It's not going to be the focus of any glossy magazine advertisement. In fact, most people never consciously notice good or bad composition. We are convinced, however, that readers perceive the difference between well spaced and poorly spaced text. Good spacing not only improves readability, it also conveys an aura of quality to the publication or organization. In short, it's worth caring about.

There are four basic ways to fit text onto a line:

▶ Controlling the spacing between the letters.

▶ Controlling the spacing between the words.

▶ Adjusting the size of the characters themselves.

▶ Breaking the words at line endings by hyphenating.

If you're serious about type, you already know that a large part of your typesetting time is spent fixing bad line breaks and lines with poor word and letter spacing. In our experience, fully one third of our typesetting and production time in QuarkXPress or other programs is spent "walking the lines"—fixing spacing problems.

Other desktop publishing programs use a "single line composer" to compose lines of text. As the program arranges the characters on each line, it only considers the spacing of that line, which means that adjacent lines may have dramatically different spacing. The greater the variation of letter and word spacing among lines in a paragraph, the harder it is to read (and the less appealing it is to look at).

InDesign, however, has both a single-line composer and a multi-line composer, which can examine an entire paragraph's worth of lines at a time.

How does it work? The multi-line composer (called Adobe Paragraph Composer) creates a list of possible line break points in the lines it examines. It then ranks the different sets of possible break points, considering the effect of each break point on spacing and hyphenation. Finally, it chooses the best of the alternatives. You'd think that this would take a lot of time—but it doesn't. When you use the default settings, you get composition speed that's equal to that of a single-line composition system, and you get better-looking text (see Figure 4-47).

Multi-line composition takes some getting used to because characters *preceding* the cursor will sometimes *move* as you enter or edit text—something you won't see in most page layout, word processing, or illustration programs. You really can't be certain of the position of the line breaks in a paragraph until you've entered the last word in the paragraph. Luckily, it doesn't take long to adjust to this behavior—especially when the results are so much better than what you're accustomed to.

FIGURE 4-47
Multi-Line Composition

Note the extreme variation in word and letter spacing from line to line in the text composed using the Single-line composer.

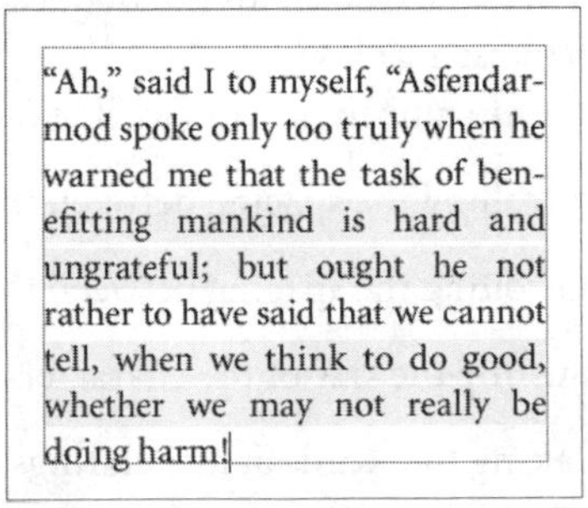

> "Ah," said I to myself, "Asfendar-mod spoke only too truly when he warned me that the task of ben-efitting mankind is hard and ungrateful; but ought he not rather to have said that we cannot tell, when we think to do good, whether we may not really be doing harm!

Single-line composition.

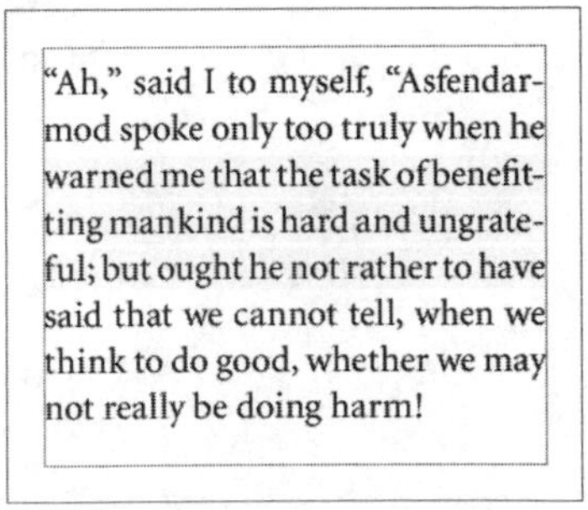

> "Ah," said I to myself, "Asfendar-mod spoke only too truly when he warned me that the task of benefit-ting mankind is hard and ungrate-ful; but ought he not rather to have said that we cannot tell, when we think to do good, whether we may not really be doing harm!

Multi-line composition.

In some rare cases you might want or need to turn the Adobe Paragraph Composer off and exercise manual control over the line breaks in a paragraph—when lines absolutely must break a particular way. Also, single-line composition is faster than multi-line, so if quality isn't an issue, you might consider turning it off.

Multi-line composition is on by default; to use the single-line composition method, select a paragraph and choose Adobe Single-line Composer from the Paragraph or Control palette menu (or in the Justification dialog box). To turn multi-line composition back on again for the paragraph, choose Adobe Paragraph Composer.

(If you used InDesign 1.5, you might be looking for the Multi-line Composer controls in the Preferences dialog box. They're not there—Adobe took them out in version 2.)

Hyphenation Controls

If you're tired of having your favorite page layout program hyphenate the word "image" after the "m," you'll like InDesign's hyphenation controls. To set the hyphenation options for a paragraph, choose Hyphenation from the Paragraph or Control palette's menu. InDesign displays the Hyphenation dialog box (see Figure 4-48). QuarkXPress users are used to having both hyphenation and justification settings in one dialog box; in InDesign they're broken into two. Also, in QuarkXPress, you have to make and save an H&J setting first, and then apply it to a paragraph. In InDesign, you select a paragraph and change its hyphenation and justification settings.

The first checkbox in the Hyphenation Settings dialog box, simply labeled Hyphenate, controls whether the selected paragraph or paragraphs will be hyphenated. This is identical to turning on and off the Hyphenate checkbox in the Paragraph palette. Then there are seven other controls that determine the hyphenation rules.

Words with at Least. You can direct InDesign's hyphenation system to leave short words alone using the Words with at Least option. If you don't want words like "many" to hyphenate, you can set this to 5 or higher.

FIGURE 4-48
**Hyphenation Settings
Dialog Box**

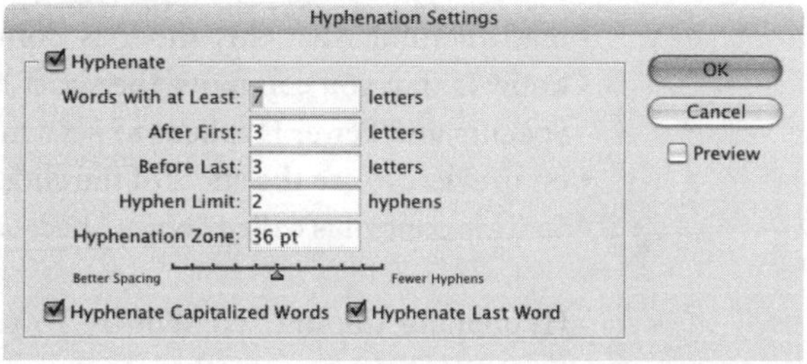

After First. The value you enter here sets the minimum size, in characters, of the word fragment preceding a hyphen. Many typesetters dislike two-letter fragments, so they increase this value to three.

Before Last. The value you enter here sets the minimum size, in characters, of the word fragment following a hyphen. Some people don't mind if the "ly" in "truly" sits all by itself on a line. You care about type, so you set this to at least three.

Hyphen Limit. You can limit the number of consecutive hyphens you'll allow to appear at the left edge of a column of text using the Hyphen Limit field. Enter a value greater than one to allow consecutive hyphens.

Hyphenation Zone. Another way to limit the number of hyphens in a paragraph is the Hyphenation Zone setting. The idea is that there is an invisible zone along the right margin of each paragraph. If InDesign is trying to break a word at the end of a line, it looks to see where the hyphenation zone is. If the word *before* the potentially hyphenated word falls inside the zone, then InDesign just gives up and pushes the word onto the next line (without hyphenating it). If the previous word does not fall into the zone, then InDesign will hyphenate the word.

That's the concept, at least. As it turns out, InDesign's composition algorithms are complex enough that the hyphenation zone is often overridden by other factors, especially when using the Paragraph Composer. In addition, the Hyphenation Zone setting doesn't have any effect at all on justified text. In general, for non-justified text, larger amounts mean fewer hyphens but more variation in line lengths ("rag").

Hyphenation Slider. Someone, somewhere must have complained that InDesign's hyphenation controls weren't flexible enough, because those wacky engineers at Adobe have added the Hyphenation Slider to the Hyphenation Settings dialog box. We're sure there's a lot of math behind what this slider is doing, but all you really need to know is that you can move the slider back and forth between Better Spacing and Fewer Hyphens to get a more pleasing appearance (turn on preview to see the effect of the slider).

This control is called "Nigel" because it goes all the way to eleven.

Hyphenate Capitalized Words. To prevent capitalized words (i.e., proper names) from hyphenating, turn off this option.

Discretionary Hyphens. There's another way to control hyphenation: Use a discretionary hyphen character. When you type a discretionary hyphen (Command-Shift-hyphen/Ctrl-Shift-hyphen) in a word, you're telling InDesign that you wouldn't mind if the word hyphenates here. This doesn't force the program to hyphenate the word at that point; it just gives it the option. This is much better than typing a regular hyphen because if (or when) your text reflows, you won't be stuck with hyphens littered in the middles of your paragraphs—the discretionary hyphen "disappears" when it's not needed. Another way to get a discretionary hyphen is to use the Insert Special Character submenu (in the Type menu or the context-sensitive menu).

By the way, longtime QuarkXPress users know that in that program you can place a discretionary hyphen before a word to make it not break. That's also true in InDesign, but, if you want a word (or phrase) not to hyphenate, select the text and turn on the No Break option in the Character palette's menu. If it's a word that you think should never be hyphenated, or should always be hyphenated differently than InDesign thinks, you can add it to your user dictionary (see "Adding Words to the User Dictionary" in Chapter 3, "Text").

Controlling Word and Letter Spacing

When InDesign composes the text in your publications, it does so by following the spacing rules you've laid down using the controls in the Justification dialog box (choose Justification from the Paragraph palette menu or press Command-Option-Shift-J/Ctrl-Alt-Shift-J to display the dialog box; see Figure 4-49). Contrary to popular opinion, this dialog box controls all text composition, not only that of justified text.

This dialog box offers six controls: Word Spacing, Letter Spacing, Glyph Scaling, Auto Leading, Single Word Justification, and Composer. The important thing to remember is that you will never find a set of spacing values that will work for all fonts, point sizes, and line lengths. In addition, the text that you are typesetting plays a role. Spacing settings that work for one writer's copy may not work for copy composed by a different author, even when the typesetting

FIGURE 4-49
Justification Dialog Box

	Minimum	Desired	Maximum	
Word Spacing:	80%	100%	133%	OK
Letter Spacing:	0%	0%	0%	Cancel
Glyph Scaling:	100%	100%	100%	☐ Preview
Auto Leading:	120%			
Single Word Justification:	Full Justify			
Composer:	Adobe Paragraph Composer			

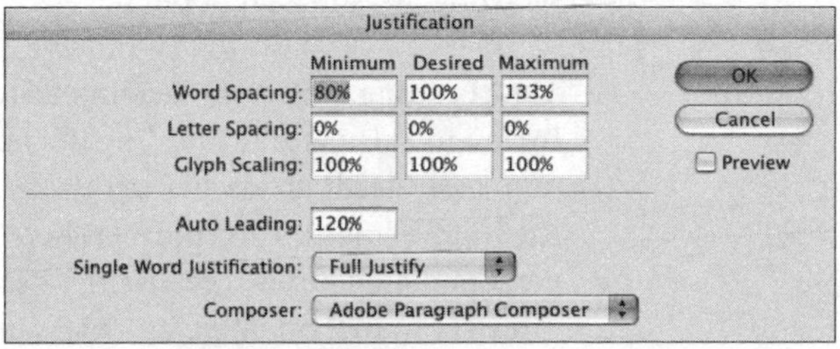

specifications are exactly the same. You just have to experiment to discover the settings that work best for you and your publications.

InDesign's default settings give you a reasonable starting point. The spacing values encourage wide word spacing over narrow word spacing, and attempt to discourage letter spacing.

Word Spacing. You can adjust the amount of space InDesign places between words by changing the Minimum, Desired, and Maximum percentages. In non-justified text, only the Desired value matters. In InDesign, the values in the word spacing fields are *percentages of* the standard word space (the width of the space is defined by the font's designer, and is stored in the font). The defaults tend to encourage wide word spacing over narrow word spacing in justified text.

Letter Spacing. You can adjust the amount of space the program places between each character in your paragraphs by changing the Minimum, Desired, and Maximum percentages. Again, in non-justified text, only the Desired value makes a difference. These percentages represent the *amount of variation* from a standard spacing unit—the "spaceband" defined in the font. By default, the percentages are all set to zero, which discourages adjusting letter spacing at all.

Glyph Scaling. QuarkXPress and PageMaker both allow you to set the letterspacing and wordspacing values. The Glyph Scaling option, however, is something new, different, and, potentially, more than a little strange.

When you enter anything other than 100% in any of the Glyph Scaling fields, you give InDesign permission to horizontally scale the characters in the paragraph to make them fit. We are always opposed to distorting character shapes (our opposition doesn't extend to Multiple Master typefaces, which are designed to be squashed and stretched). You can also enter larger values to use Glyph Scaling as a wacky design effect, but you'll have to endure the scowls of typesetting purists (see Figure 4-50). We're not even purists, and we're scowling just thinking about it.

Auto Leading. The Auto Leading feature is easy: This controls how InDesign calculates the leading of characters that have a leading of Auto (see "Leading," earlier in this chapter, for why we almost never use Auto leading). This control is here, rather than in one of the Preferences dialog boxes, because the base autoleading percentage is a property of individual paragraphs (unlike QuarkXPress, where the autoleading percentage is set at the document level).

FIGURE 4-50
Glyph Scaling

Watch out—abuse of the Glyph Scaling option can result in obvious differences in the shape of characters from line to line. (It can also lead to blindness, madness, and, eventually, death.)

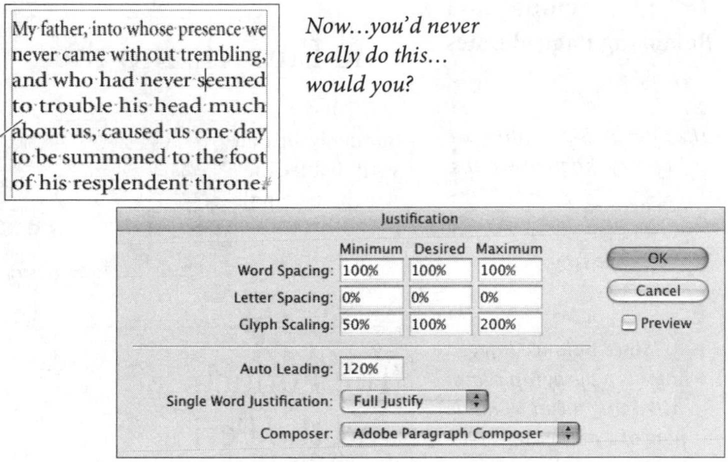

My father, into whose presence we never came without trembling, and who had never seemed to trouble his head much about us, caused us one day to be summoned to the foot of his resplendent throne.
Now…you'd never really do this… would you?
Justification
Minimum Desired Maximum
Word Spacing: 100% 100% 100%
Letter Spacing: 0% 0% 0%
Glyph Scaling: 50% 100% 200%
OK
Cancel
Preview
Auto Leading: 120%
Single Word Justification: Full Justify
Composer: Adobe Paragraph Composer

Single Word Justification. What do you want InDesign to do when a word in the middle of a paragraph is so long (or a column so narrow) that only that one word fits on the line? If the line isn't justified, it's no big deal. But if the line is justified, do you want InDesign to add letterspacing to spread the word out across the line? Or make it flush left, flush right, or centered? That's what the Single Word Justification pop-up menu controls.

Composer. Earlier in this chapter, we discussed the Paragraph Composer and how it's different from the Single Line composer. Here's one more place you can specify which InDesign should use.

Balance Ragged Lines

Sometimes headlines or headings are way out of balance—and we don't just mean the political slant. We mean that the lines are of wildly varying length. The first line fills the column; the second line contains a single short word. This is, at best, unsightly; at worst, it makes the text hard to read.

InDesign's Balance Ragged Lines feature can help you make the line widths in a paragraph more even. To do this, choose Balance Ragged Lines from the Paragraph palette or Control palette menu. (Note that this feature only works on non-justified paragraphs.) Take a look at Figure 4-51 to see the effect of Balance Ragged Lines.

If the last line of the paragraph is significantly narrower than the other lines, the program breaks the text so that the last line is wider.

Balance Ragged Lines generally produces an inverted pyramid shape—that is, the first line is longer than the second line, the third line is shorter than the second line, and so on. This matches Ole's expectations, but is the opposite of what David expects.

FIGURE 4-51
Balancing Ragged Lines

*The lines of this heading are
of very different widths.*

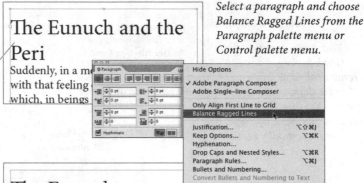

Select a paragraph and choose
Balance Ragged Lines from the
Paragraph palette menu or
Control palette menu.

*Since Balance Ragged
Lines is a paragraph-level
attribute, it can be made
part of a paragraph style.*

*InDesign changes the line
breaks in the paragraph to
make the width of the lines
more even.*

**Highlighting
Typographic
Problems**

Like PageMaker, InDesign can "flag" text composition problems—
cases where the program has had to break your rules for composing
text, or where substituted fonts appear in your publication. Choose
Composition from the Preferences submenu of the Edit menu, then
turn on the options in the Highlight section of the Composition
Preferences dialog box. Lines in which InDesign has had to violate
composition rules you've established (using the Justification and
Keep Options dialog boxes) are highlighted in yellow; substituted
fonts are highlighted in pink (see Figure 4-52). We usually work with
these turned on so we can quickly identify "problem" lines.

FIGURE 4-52
**Highlighting Loose
and Tight Lines**

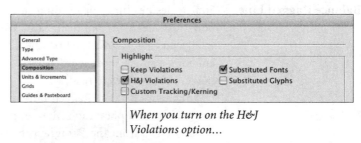

*When you turn on the H&J
Violations option…*

*…InDesign highlights lines
that break the spacing ranges
you set in the Justification
dialog box.*

*InDesign uses three shades
of yellow to highlight loose
or tight lines—darker
shades indicate more
severe spacing problems.*

**Paragraph
Keep Options**

A *widow* is the last line of a paragraph that winds up all by itself at the top of a column or page. An *orphan* is the first line of a paragraph that lands all by itself at the bottom of a column or page. Widows and orphans are the bane of a typesetter's existence.

Designers sometimes also refer to the single-word last line of a paragraph as either a widow or an orphan. To avoid the confusion, we often just use the word *runt*.

All typographic widows and orphans are bad, but certain kinds are really bad—for example, a widow line that consists of only one word, or even the last part of a hyphenated word. Another related typographic horror is the heading that stands alone with its following paragraph on the next page.

Fortunately, InDesign has a set of controls that can easily prevent widows and orphans from sneaking into your document. These controls—along with a setting that lets you force a paragraph to begin at a particular place—live in the Keep Options dialog box, which you can find by selecting Keep Options from the Paragraph palette's menu, or by pressing Command-Option-K/Ctrl-Alt-K (see Figure 4-53). There are three parts to this dialog box: Keep with Next, Keep Lines Together, and Start Paragraph.

**FIGURE 4-53
Keep Options**

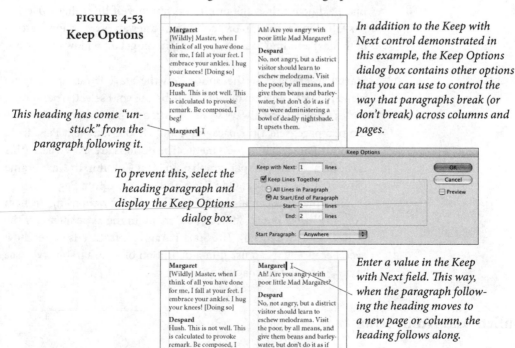

This heading has come "un-stuck" from the paragraph following it.

To prevent this, select the heading paragraph and display the Keep Options dialog box.

In addition to the Keep with Next control demonstrated in this example, the Keep Options dialog box contains other options that you can use to control the way that paragraphs break (or don't break) across columns and pages.

Enter a value in the Keep with Next field. This way, when the paragraph following the heading moves to a new page or column, the heading follows along.

Keep with Next. The Keep With Next Lines feature helps you ensure that headings and the paragraphs that follow them are kept together. If the paragraph is pushed onto a new column, a new page, or below an obstructing object, the heading follows. It's rare that we need to type more than 1 in the Lines field.

Keep Lines Together. The Keep Lines Together feature is the primary control over widows and orphans. When you turn on the Keep Lines Together checkbox and choose All Lines in Paragraph, InDesign not break the paragraph across column or pages. For example, if a paragraph spans across two pages, enabling All Lines In Paragraph results in that entire paragraph being pushed onto the next page to keep it together.

You can control the number of lines that should be kept together at the beginning and end of the paragraph by choosing At Start/End of Paragraph. The value you type in the Start field determines the minimum number of lines that InDesign allows at the beginning of a paragraph. For example, a Start value of 2 means that if at least two lines of that paragraph cannot be placed on the page, then the entire paragraph is pushed over to the next page. The value specified in the End field determines the minimum number of lines that InDesign lets fall alone at the top of a column or after an obstruction. Setting both Start and End to 2 means you'll never get an widow or orphan.

Start Paragraph. Use the options on the Start Paragraph pop-up menu to force a column or page break before your selected paragraph. For example, if you always want a particular paragraph to sit at the top of a page, select the paragraph and choose On Next Page from the Start Paragraph pop-up menu. The options are: Anywhere (this is the default value for paragraphs), In Next Column, In Next Frame, On Next Page, On Next Odd Page, and On Next Even Page.

Note that you can also get a similar effect by choosing an item from the Insert Break Character submenu in the Type menu (or the context-sensitive menu). The Start Paragraph feature is better, however, because you can use it in a definition of a paragraph style (see "Styles," later in this chapter).

Bullets and Numbering

As the human attention span has grown shorter under the stresses of modern life, lists of one sort or another have come to dominate our texts. Abraham Lincoln could spend several days delivering a single perfect paragraph to an informed audience; we must convey the same information in an executive summary that takes no more than nanoseconds to parse. InDesign aids and abets this diminution of the human intellect by providing the Bullets and Numbering feature, which provides:

▶ Bullets.

▶ Numbering.

Bullets and Numbering is a paragraph level attribute that applies a bullet character or a numeral to the start of the afflicted paragraph. Applying a bullet is fairly straightforward; numbering is a bit more complicated in that you need to be able to tell InDesign where to start a numbering sequence.

Applying Bullets and Numbering

To apply bullets or numbering, follow these steps (see Figure 4-54).

1. Select a range of text.

2. Choose Bullets and Numbering from the Paragraph palette or Control palette menu. You can also click the Bulleted List button or the Numbered List button in the Paragraph view of the Control palette. InDesign displays the Bullets and Numbering dialog box.

3. Choose the type of formatting (bullets or numbering) from the List Type pop-up menu.

4. At this point, the dialog box changes to display options for the type of list you've selected (as described below).

5. Once you've got the inserted characters to look the way you want them to (turn on the Preview option), click the OK button to apply the list formatting to the selected paragraphs.

Note that when you insert characters using the Bullets and Numbering feature, you cannot select the characters and change their formatting as you would with other text. Instead, you'll have to select the paragraphs and return to the Bullets and Numbering dialog box. This takes a bit of getting used to.

Bullets

The options in the Bullet Character section of the dialog box control the glyph used for the bullet. This section works very much like the Glyphs palette described earlier in this chapter—the dialog contains a short list of characters, but you can click the Add button choose characters from any of the available fonts and add them then to the

FIGURE 4-54
**Applying Bullets
and Numbering**

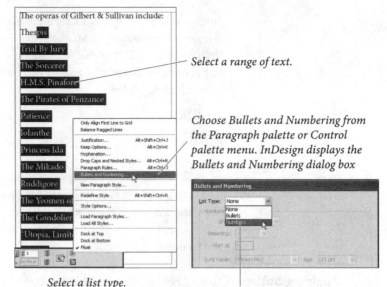

Select a range of text.

*Choose Bullets and Numbering from
the Paragraph palette or Control
palette menu. InDesign displays the
Bullets and Numbering dialog box*

Select a list type.

*Set up the formatting
options for the list, then
click the OK button.*

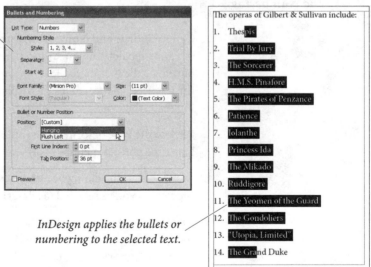

*InDesign applies the bullets or
numbering to the selected text.*

list (see Figure 4-55). The settings for Font Family, Font Style, Size,
and Color set the formatting used for the bullet character.

Numbering   The options in the Numbering Style section of the dialog box control
the type of numbered list to use (which you select from the Style
pop-up menu), a separator character to enter between the number
and the body of the paragraph (Separator), and the number at which
to start the list (the Start At field)—see Figure 4-56. The settings for
Font Family, Font Style, Size, and Color set the formatting used for
the bullet character.

FIGURE 4-55
Bullet Options

Select a bullet character.

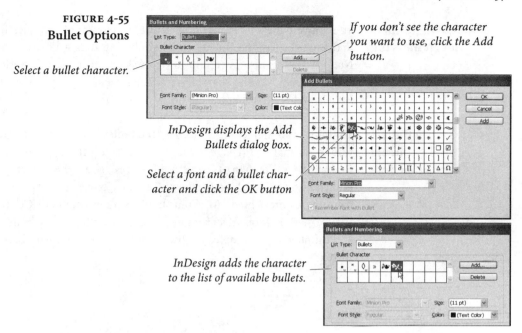

If you don't see the character you want to use, click the Add button.

InDesign displays the Add Bullets dialog box.

Select a font and a bullet character and click the OK button

InDesign adds the character to the list of available bullets.

FIGURE 4-56
Numbering Options

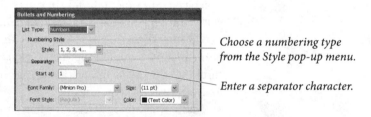

Choose a numbering type from the Style pop-up menu.

Enter a separator character.

Bullet or Number Position

For either bullets and numbering, you can specify the location of the inserted character (the bullet or number) using the controls in the Bullet or Number Position section of the dialog box (see Figure 4-57). For either type of list, you can choose to format the paragraph as flush left or apply a hanging indent by choosing the appropriate option from the Position pop-up menu. The fields for the Left Indent, First Line Indent, and Tab position set the corresponding options for the selected paragraphs.

Note that the tab stop created by Bullets and Numbering is always a left-aligned tab; you cannot use this feature to create right-aligned numbered lists (a failing, in our opinion).

FIGURE 4-57
Positioning Options

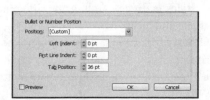

Removing Bullets and Numbering

To remove bullets or numbering, select the paragraphs in question and then display the Bullets and Numbering dialog box. Choose None from the List Type pop-up menu and click the OK button. InDesign removes the character and the formatting applied by the Bullets and Numbering feature.

Converting Bullets and Numbers to Normal Text

To change the characters inserted by the Bullets and Numbering feature to normal text (i.e., text you can select with the Type tool and format using InDesign's typesetting features), select the paragraphs and choose Convert Numbering to Text or Convert Bullets to Text from the Context menu (or from the Paragraph palette or Control palette menu). If you select a range of text that contains both bulleted and numbered paragraphs, choose Convert Bullets and Numbering to Text.

Styles

When you think about the text in your publication, chances are good you're thinking of each paragraph as being a representative of a particular kind of text. You're thinking, "That's a headline, that's a subhead, and that's a photo caption." Chances are also good that you're thinking of those paragraphs as having certain formatting attributes: font, size, leading, and indents.

That's what text styles do—they bundle all those attributes together so you can apply them to text with a single click. But there's more—if you then change your mind about the formatting, you can edit the style, and all the text with that style applied to it (that is, "tagged" with the style) is reformatted automatically.

Once you've created a text style for a specific kind of text, you'll never have to claw your way through the Character palette or Paragraph palette again to format that text. Unless, of course, you want to apply a local formatting override to your styled text, which you're always free to do.

Global versus Local Formatting. We've been using the term "local formatting." What are we talking about? The key to understanding text styles is understanding the difference between style-based formatting and local formatting.

Local formatting is what you get when you select text and apply formatting directly, using the Character palette or the choices on the Type menu. When you apply formatting using text styles, on the other hand, you're applying "global" formatting (that is, formatting specified by the selected style).

If local formatting has been applied to text that has had a paragraph style applied to it, you'll see a "+" after the style name in the Paragraph Styles palette when the text is selected (see Figure 4-58).

FIGURE 4-58
Styles and
Local Overrides

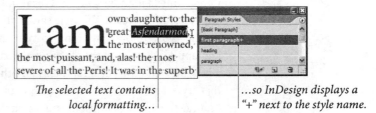

The selected text contains local formatting...

...so InDesign displays a "+" next to the style name.

Plus What? When you see that the text you've selected in a styled paragraph contains a local override, how can you tell what that local override is? If you have tool tips turned on, you can move the cursor over the style name, and InDesign will display a list of the local overrides. Or you can choose New Style from the Paragraph Styles palette menu. Look at the list of attributes in the Style Settings list at the bottom of the palette—it'll say "<stylename> + next: Same Style +" (where "<stylename>" is the name of the style applied to the paragraph) and a list of formatting. The items in the list are the local formatting (see Figure 4-59). Click Cancel (or press Command-period/Esc) to close this dialog box without actually creating a new style.

FIGURE 4-59
Local Formatting?
What Local Formatting?

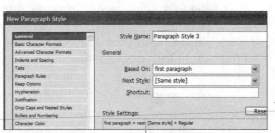

What does the "+" mean? To find out, choose New Style from the Paragraph Styles palette menu.

InDesign lists the formatting that varies from the formatting applied by the style.

Incorrect Style Order. Paragraph and character styles should appear in alphabetical order in their respective palettes. Sometimes, though, the palettes get confused and list them in a near-random order (probably the order in which you created the styles, which is silly). This happens most often when converting InDesign 2 files. If that happens, just edit any style (even making the tiniest change). When you click OK, InDesign should reorder the styles properly.

Styles Are More than Formatting. When you apply a style to a paragraph (which we call "tagging" a paragraph with a style), you're doing more than just applying the formatting defined by the style. You're telling InDesign what the paragraph is—not just what it looks like, but what role it has to play in your publication. Is the paragraph important? Is it an insignificant legal notice in type that's intentionally too small to read? The style says it all.

The most important thing to remember when you're creating and applying styles is that tagging a paragraph with a style creates a link between the paragraph and all other paragraphs tagged with that style, and between the paragraph and the definition of the style. Change the style's definition, and watch the formatting and behavior of the paragraphs tagged with that style change to match.

Character Styles

By now, most of us are used to the idea of paragraph styles, which give us a way to apply multiple paragraph formatting attributes to an entire paragraph with a single action. (If you're not familiar with paragraph styles, we discuss them in the next section.) Character styles are just like paragraph styles, except that they can be applied to ranges of text smaller than an entire paragraph (and, obviously, they lack paragraph formatting features, such as alignment). Applying a character style to a text selection establishes a link between that text and the definition of the style—edit the style, and the formatting of the text changes.

Use character styles for any character formatting you apply over and over again. Run-in headings, drop caps, and special ornamental characters are all good candidates for character styles. Each time you use a character style, you're saving yourself several seconds you would have spent fiddling with settings in the Character palette or the Type menu. It might not seem like much, but saving a few seconds several hundred times a day can add up.

Creating Character Styles. The easiest way to create a character style is to build it "by example" (see Figure 4-60).

1. Select some text that has the formatting you want your character style to have.

2. Hold down Option/Alt and click the New Style button at the bottom of the Character Styles palette (or select New Style from the Character Styles palette menu). InDesign displays the New Character Style dialog box.

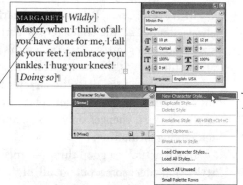

FIGURE 4-60
Creating a
Character Style

To create a new character style, select a range of text that has the formatting you want...

...Choose New Style from the Character Styles palette menu (or press Option/Alt and click the New Style button).

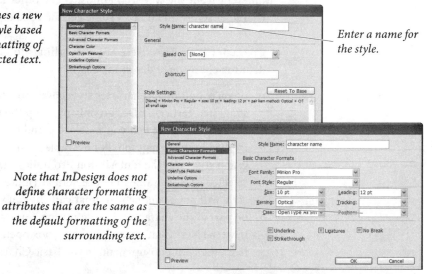

InDesign defines a new character style based on the formatting of the selected text.

Enter a name for the style.

Note that InDesign does not define character formatting attributes that are the same as the default formatting of the surrounding text.

InDesign adds the new character style to the list of character styles, but you have to apply it to the text manually.

3. At this point, if you want to create a relationship between this style and another character style, you can choose that style from the Based On pop-up menu (see "Creating Parent-Child Style Relationships," later in this chapter).

4. Now give your style a name. You can also assign a keyboard shortcut to the character style—the key used must use a modifier key (Command, Ctrl, or Shift and a number key from the numeric keypad; NumLock must be on to define the shortcut).

When you create a character style, InDesign does not automatically apply the style to the text you selected in Step 1.

QuarkXPress Users Beware: In QuarkXPress, a character style always defines *all* the character formatting of the text—font, color, size, and other attributes. InDesign's character styles, however, are defined by *differences* between the character formatting of the selected text and the default character formatting of the surrounding text. In InDesign you can create a character style which, when applied to text, changes only its size and color, but retains all other underlying formatting.

This is actually a good thing—it means you can create character styles that affect some, but not all, of the attributes of a selection. It's different from the way that almost every other application defines character styles, and it takes some getting used to.

Character Style Tips. Here are a few things to keep in mind when defining character styles in InDesign.

► If you're building a character style based on example text (as we suggested earlier), InDesign only picks up the formatting differences between the text you've selected and the paragraph style applied to the paragraph. For example, if the underlying paragraph style uses the font Minion Pro Italic, and the text you've selected uses the same font, the Font attribute of the character style will not be defined automatically. If you want the font to be part of the character style definition, you can add it once you have the New Character Style dialog box open (select the font from the Font pop-up menu in the Basic Character Formats tab).

► If you want your character style to be defined by *every* attribute of your text selection, you can use the CreateCharacterStyle script (see Chapter 12, "Scripting," for more on the example scripts that come with InDesign). Or you can create the character style from scratch (not from example text), specifying the font, size, color, leading, and all other formatting.

► Clicking the New Style button in the Character Styles palette creates a new character style based on whatever style was selected in the palette. It doesn't open a dialog box.

► If you want to "undefine" an attribute in a character style, select and delete the current value (see Figure 4-61).

Applying Character Styles. To apply a character style, select some text and do any one of the following things (see Figure 4-62).

► Click the character style name in the Character Styles palette.

FIGURE 4-61
Undefining Attributes

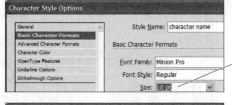

To prevent a character style from affecting a formatting attribute, select the attribute...

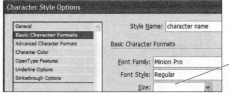

...and press Delete. When you apply the style, InDesign will leave this attribute unchanged.

FIGURE 4-62
Applying a Character Style

Select the text you want to format.

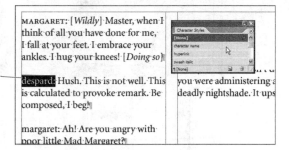

InDesign applies the character style to the text.

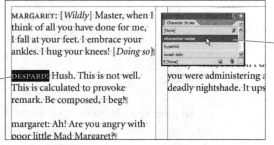

Click the character style name in the Character Styles palette.

▸ Press the keyboard shortcut you assigned to the character style.

▸ Point at the style name in the Character Styles palette and choose Apply from the context menu.

▸ PressCommand-Enter/Ctrl Enter to display the Quick Apply panel, type the name of the style, and then press Enter.

Again, applying a character style changes only those attributes that are defined in the style. This can cause grave confusion and hair-pulling if you're used to the way QuarkXPress does it. If you apply a character style that applies only the underline type style and color, for example—InDesign leaves all other character formatting as is (see Figure 4-63).

FIGURE 4-63
**Character Styles Affect
Only Defined Attributes**

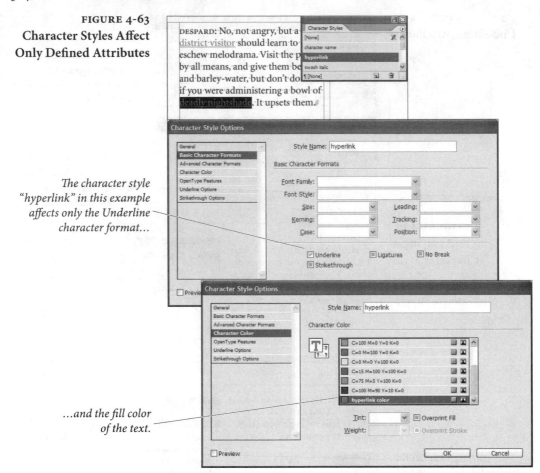

*The character style
"hyperlink" in this example
affects only the Underline
character format...*

*...and the fill color
of the text.*

To remove a character style from a text selection, click No Character Style in the Character Styles palette. Note that this does not change the formatting of the selected text—it simply applies the formatting applied by the character style as local formatting. This is sometimes useful when you want some text to be formatted using the formatting of a given character style, but you don't want it actually linked to that style (because you know the style definition might change). Selecting No Character Style breaks the link between text and its style definition.

If you want to remove a character style *and* reset the formatting to the publication's default formatting, hold down Option/Alt as you click No Character Style in the Character Styles palette.

Editing Character Styles. The great thing about styles is that you can always change them later, and those changes ripple throughout your document. To edit a character style, you can use any or all of the following approaches—all of them display the Character Style Options dialog box, which you can use to change the attributes of the style.

▶ Hold down Command-Option-Shift/Ctrl-Alt-Shift and double-click the style name in the Character Styles palette.

▶ Point at the style you want to edit in the Character Styles palette and choose Edit from the context menu.

▶ Select the style and choose Style Options from the Character Styles palette menu.

▶ Double-click the style name in the Character Styles palette.

The first two approaches above do not apply the style; the latter two apply the style to the selected text, or to the document default formatting when no text is selected. Be aware of this difference as you go to edit a style—otherwise, you run the risk of accidentally applying the character style.

Redefining Character Styles. Editing a character style through the Character Style Options dialog box works fine, but is kind of boring. For quick changes, try this: Find some text tagged with the character style you want to redefine, then apply local formatting to it (change it to the way you want the style to be defined). A "+" will appear next to the character style name in the Character Styles palette. Next, without deselecting the text, press Command-Option-Shift-C/Ctrl-Alt-Shift-C. InDesign automatically redefines the character style based on the selected text (see Figure 4-64).

FIGURE 4-64
**Redefining a
Character Style**

*Apply local formatting to
an instance of the character
style you want to redefine.*

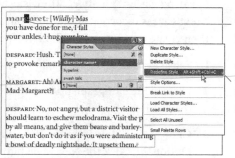

*Select a character or
characters...*

*...and choose Redefine
Style from the Character
Styles palette menu or the
Control palette menu.*

*InDesign updates the character
style's definition based on the
formatting of the selected text.*

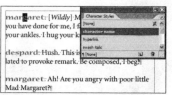

Alternatively, you can select the text and choose Redefine Style from the Character Styles palette menu. Or you could point at the style name in the palette and choose Redefine from the context menu. But the keyboard shortcut is more fun.

Deleting character styles. To remove a character style, press Command-Shift-A/Ctrl-Shift-A to deselect everything (do this so that you don't accidentally apply the character style to text), then select the character style and choose Delete Styles from the Character Styles palette menu (or click the Delete Style button in the palette).

InDesign displays the Delete Character Style dialog box, where you can select a replacement style (including no style). If you choose another character style, InDesign applies that character style to the text that had been formatted with the deleted style. If you choose no style, the formatting you applied throughout your document using the character style does not change in appearance, but becomes local formatting.

Paragraph Styles

Paragraph styles encapsulate all text formatting—both paragraph formatting and character formatting.

Basic Style. If you look at the Paragraph Styles palette, you'll a "Basic Paragraph" style. This is something like Word's (infamous) "Normal" style, and provides a kind default style for all text. We tend not to use this style, or base any other style on it, because we've found it can cause problems as we move text from document to document.

Creating Paragraph Styles. The easiest way (in our opinion) to create a text style is to format an example paragraph using local formatting, then create a new style based on that paragraph (see Figure 4-65).

1. Select a formatted paragraph.

2. Display the Paragraph Styles palette, if it's not already visible (press F11).

3. Choose New Style from the Paragraph Styles palette menu (or Option/Alt-click the New Style button) to open the New Paragraph Style dialog box.

4. Enter a name for the style in the Style Name field. You could leave the name set to the default, but we think it's better to enter a descriptive name—"heading 1" is quite a bit easier to remember than "Paragraph Style 6."

FIGURE 4-65
Defining a
Paragraph Style

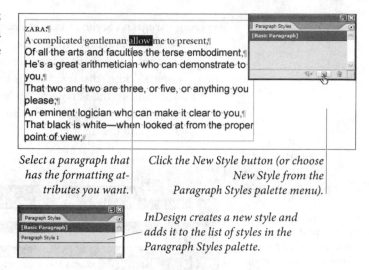

Select a paragraph that has the formatting attributes you want.

Click the New Style button (or choose New Style from the Paragraph Styles palette menu).

InDesign creates a new style and adds it to the list of styles in the Paragraph Styles palette.

You can also assign a Next Style (see "Next Styles" later in this chapter) and a keyboard shortcut to the style—the shortcut must use a modifier key (Shift, Command/Ctrl, Option/Alt, or some combination of the above) and a number key from the numeric keypad (NumLock must be on to define the shortcut).

5. Click the OK button.

When you're done, InDesign adds a new paragraph style. The style definition includes all the character and paragraph formatting applied to the first character in the selected "example" text.

That's all there is to it—you've created a paragraph style. InDesign does not apply the style to the selected paragraph, so you'll probably want to do that now (see "Applying Paragraph Styles," below).

If you work by the hour you might prefer to create a style by using the style definition dialog boxes, rather than basing your style on an example.

1. Choose "New Style" from the Styles palette menu. InDesign displays the New Style dialog box.

2. Work your way through the dialog box, setting the options as you want them for your new style. When everything looks the way you want it to, press Return/Enter to close the dialog box.

Creating a style this way is a little bit more awkward than simply basing a style on an example paragraph, but some people prefer it. We've met at least one person who likes setting tabs "without all that pesky text in the way."

Applying Paragraph Styles. To apply a paragraph style, select a paragraph or series of paragraphs (remember, you don't have to select the entire paragraph to apply paragraph formatting—for a single paragraph, simply clicking the Text tool in the paragraph will do) and click a style name in the Paragraph Styles palette (see Figure 4-66). Alternatively, if you've defined a keyboard shortcut for the paragraph style, you can press the shortcut.

FIGURE 4-66
Applying a
Paragraph Style

Select the paragraphs you want to format (remember, you don't need to select the entire paragraph).

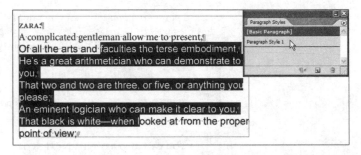

Click a style name in the Paragraph Styles palette. InDesign applies the paragraph style to the selected paragraphs.

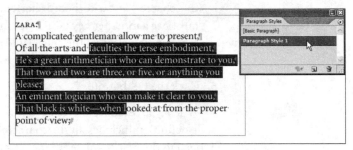

When you simply click a paragraph style to apply it, InDesign retains all the local formatting, so italic text remains italic. The one exception to this rule is when every character in the paragraph has local formatting—that stuff always gets removed.

To remove all local formatting as you apply a paragraph style, hold down Option/Alt as you click the paragraph style name. Any formatting applied using character styles is retained.

To remove all local formatting and remove formatting applied by character styles, hold down Option-Shift/Alt-Shift as you click the paragraph style name.

To remove all local formatting (not including character styles) after you've applied a style, click the Clear Override button at the bottom of the Paragraph Styles palette. To remove all local character formatting, hold down Command/Ctrl as you click the button; to remove paragraph formatting, hold down Command-Shift/Ctrl-Shift as you click.

To remove a paragraph style from a text selection, choose Break Link to Style from the Paragraph Styles palette menu. Note that this does not change the formatting of the selected paragraphs—it simply applies the formatting applied by the paragraph style as local formatting. As we said in the "Character Styles" section, you can think of this as breaking the link between the paragraph and the style definition.

To remove a paragraph style and reset the formatting to the publication's default formatting, hold down Option/Alt as you click No Paragraph Style in the Paragraph Styles palette.

Editing Paragraph Styles. To edit a paragraph style, you can use any or all of the following approaches—all of them display the Paragraph Style Options dialog box, which you can use to change the attributes of the paragraph style.

▶ Hold down Command-Option-Shift/Ctrl-Alt-Shift and double-click the paragraph style name in the Paragraph Styles palette.

▶ Point at the style you want to edit in the Paragraph Styles palette and choose Edit from the context menu.

▶ Select the style and choose Style Options from the Paragraph Styles palette menu.

▶ Double-click the style name in the Paragraph Styles palette.

The first two approaches above do not apply the style; the latter two apply the style to the selected text, or to the document default formatting when no text is selected. Be aware of this difference as you go to edit a style—accidentally setting the default font for a document to a style featuring hot pink dingbats can be a frustrating and embarassing experience.

Redefining Paragraph Styles. The easiest way to *create* a paragraph style is to base the style's definition on the formatting of an example paragraph. The easiest way to update the style definition? The same. Here's what you do (see Figure 4-67).

1. Pick any paragraph tagged with the style you want to change, and apply local formatting to it (a "+" will appear next to the style name in the Paragraph Styles palette).

2. Do one of the following things, and InDesign will redefine the style based on the selected text.

FIGURE 4-67
Redefining a
Paragraph Style

Change the formatting of an example paragraph tagged with the paragraph style you want to change. A "+" appears next to the style name in the Paragraph Styles palette.

Choose Redefine Style from the Paragraph Styles palette menu.

InDesign updates all instances of the style with the formatting of the selected paragraph.

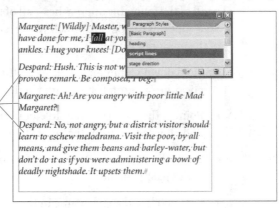

When the cursor is above a character style name, you can use the context menu to edit, duplicate, apply, or delete the character style.

▶ Choose Redefine Style from the Paragraph Styles palette menu.

▶ Press Command-Option-Shift-R/Ctrl-Alt-Shift-R.

▶ Point at the style name in the Paragraph Styles palette and choose Redefine Style from the context menu.

Next Style. If you're typing in InDesign, and the paragraph you're in is tagged with the "Heading" style, you probably don't want the next paragraph to be tagged with "Heading" too, right? You can force InDesign to automatically change the subsequent paragraph style with the Next Style pop-up menu in the New Paragraph Style or Modify Paragraph Style Options dialog box (see Figure 4-68). For example, if you want the subsequent paragraph to be "BodyText," then choose "BodyText" from the Next Style pop-up menu.

Note that this only works if the insertion point is at the end of a paragraph when you press Return/Enter. If the insertion point is

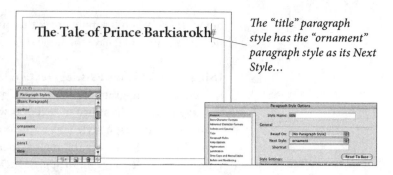

The "title" paragraph style has the "ornament" paragraph style as its Next Style…

In this example, we have set the Next Style option for each paragraph style to automatically apply the paragraph style we want when we press Return/Enter.

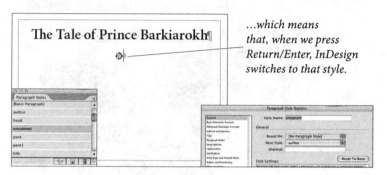

…which means that, when we press Return/Enter, InDesign switches to that style.

The "ornament" style, in turn, has the paragraph style named "author" as its next style, so pressing Return/Enter as we type text switches to the "author" style.

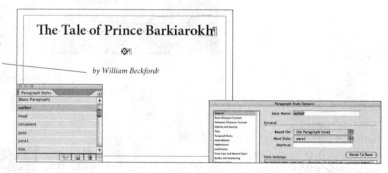

When we enter text following the "author" paragraph style, InDesign applies the "para1" style, which includes drop cap formatting.

The wonderful thing about the Next Style property is that all of these paragraph style assignments take place as we type; we never have to reach for the Styles palette.

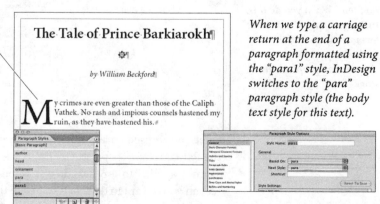

When we type a carriage return at the end of a paragraph formatted using the "para1" style, InDesign switches to the "para" paragraph style (the body text style for this text).

anywhere else, you'll simply break that paragraph in two, and both new paragraphs will have the same style as the original one.

Using Next Style on Existing Text. What if you want to apply a sequence of paragraph styles to text you've already entered or imported? Select the range of text you want to format, then point at the first paragraph style you want to apply. Choose Apply *style name* The Next Style from the context menu (where *style name* is the name of the style you want to apply). InDesign applies the sequence of paragraph styles (see Figure 4-69).

FIGURE 4-69
Applying
Sequential Styles

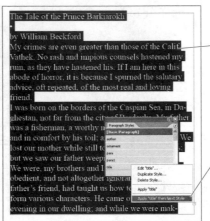

Select the text you want to format. The first paragraph selected should be the start of the "chain" of styles you want to apply.

Point at the first style name of the sequence in the Paragraph Styles palette, then choose Apply style name then Next Style from the context menu (where style name is the name of the style).

Note: You can also apply sequential styles by selecting a text frame with the Selection tool. When you do this, InDesign applies "next style" formatting to all of the text in the story, beginning with the first paragraph in the story.

InDesign applies the styles, formatting each paragraph as specified by the Next Style setting of each style.

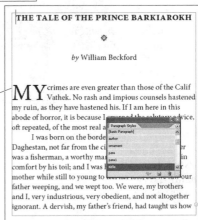

Selecting Unused Paragraph Styles. Choose Select All Unused from the Paragraph Styles palette menu to select all paragraph styles that are not applied to any text in the publication. Typically, the only reason you'd want to do this is to delete them all.

Deleting Paragraph Styles. To remove a paragraph style from your document, first deselect everything (press Command-Shift-A/Ctrl-Shift-A), then select the style name in the Paragraph Styles palette and choose Delete Styles from the palette's menu (or click the Delete Style button at the bottom of the palette). InDesign deletes the style.

InDesign gives you a choice of how to handle paragraphs already tagged with that style. You can choose No Paragraph Style to convert the formatting applied by the style to local formatting, or you can choose to apply another style. If you want to replace one style with another without deleting the original style, use the Find/Change palette (see Chapter 3, "Text").

Paragraph Styles and Nested Styles

As we mentioned in the discussion earlier in this chapter, nested styles really come into their own when combined with paragraph styles. Remember all of the work we did to set up the nested styles in our example? Now imagine putting all of that formatting power into a paragraph style. Imagine applying it with a single mouse click. Again, we think this stuff is very cool (see Figure 4-70).

FIGURE 4-70
Adding Nested Styles to a Paragraph Style

This raw text has been dumped into the document from a spreadsheet or database. Formatting a catalog full of this text would be very tedious, even if you used nested styles as local formatting.

If you add the nested style definitions to a paragraph style, however, you can apply massive amounts of formatting with a single mouse click, as we've done here.

Creating Parent-Child Style Relationships

One powerful feature of InDesign's character and paragraph styles is the ability to base one style on another, also called parent-child relationships (see Figure 4-71). You can base a style on another one by choosing a style from the Based On pop-up menu in either the New Style or the Modify Style dialog box (this works for either character or paragraph styles).

For example, in this book, there are body text styles for paragraphs that follow headings, paragraphs that are in lists, paragraphs that have run-in heads, and so on—but they're all based on one "parent" paragraph style. If we need to make the text size a half-point smaller, we could edit the parent style and the change would ripple throughout the book.

When one style is based on another, InDesign keeps track of the differences between the base style and the new style. Let's say you have a style called "Head1" and it's 18-point Futura with a 3 pica left indent, and a style called "Head2" that's based on "Head1," except that it's 12-point Futura. The difference between the two is the point size. If you change Head1's font, color, or anything *except* its point size, the edit ripples through to Head2. Nothing happens if you just edit the point size of Head1 because the "point size link" is broken between the two styles.

FIGURE 4-71
Using Based On

heading 1

heading 2

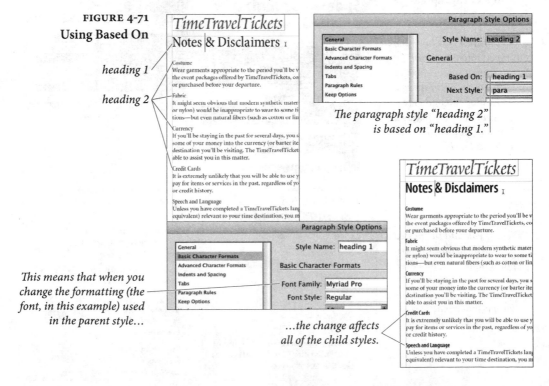

The paragraph style "heading 2" is based on "heading 1."

This means that when you change the formatting (the font, in this example) used in the parent style...

...the change affects all of the child styles.

Later, if you edit Head2 so that it has the same point size as Head1, then that link is reestablished, and changing Head1's size *will* ripple through to Head2.

Reset to Base. By the way, if your text cursor is in a paragraph when you create a new style, that paragraph's style becomes the "based on" style and any local formatting applied to the paragraph appears as the differences in the new style. If you don't want the local formatting, click the Reset to Base button. If you don't want your new style to be based on anything, make sure the Based On pop-up menu is set to No Paragraph Style.

Copying Styles from Other Publications

One of the great things about character and paragraph styles is that you can use them to unify standard formatting across a range of publications—the chapters of this book, for example. While you can't define a "master" style sheet and have all publications get their style definitions from it (as you can in FrameMaker), you can easily copy styles from one InDesign publication to another.

▶ To copy character styles from another publication, choose Load Character Styles from the Character Styles palette menu. InDesign displays the Open a File dialog box. Locate and select the InDesign publication file containing the styles you want and click the Open button. InDesign copies the character styles from that publication into the current document.

▶ To copy paragraph styles from one publication to another choose Load Paragraph Styles from the Paragraph Styles palette menu.

▶ To import both character and paragraph styles from another publication, choose Load All Styles from the palette menu of the Character Styles palette, the Paragraph Styles palette, or the Control palette.

When you import styles that have the same name as styles that already exist in the publication, InDesign overrides the attributes of the existing styles with the attributes of the incoming styles.

You can also move styles by copying text tagged with the styles you want from one publication and pasting it into another document (or dragging a text frame from one document into another). If the styles do not exist in the document you've pasted the text into, InDesign adds them. If the styles already exist, InDesign overrides the style definitions in the incoming text with the style definitions of the existing styles.

You can also synchronize style sheets among all the documents in a book when you use the Book palette, which we talk about in Chapter 8, "Long Documents."

Styles from imported text files. When you import a Microsoft Word or RTF file that includes paragraph or character styles that don't exist in the InDesign publication, those styles get added to the Character Styles and Paragraph Styles palettes. You can always tell one of these styles from those created in InDesign because the palettes display a little gray floppy disk icon next to the style name.

Libraries of Styles. One of our favorite uses for libraries (see "Library palette" in Chapter 1, "Workspace") is to save paragraph and character styles that we use in multiple documents. In a small text frame, we type a few words (usually the name of the style) and then apply one or more styles to them. Then we drag the text frame into a library (select Library from the New submenu, under the File menu, if you haven't already made one) and double-click on the library thumbnail to give it a name and description. Later, when we need that style in some other document, we can open the library file, drag that text frame into our document, and then delete the text frame—the styles remain. Of course, this works with libraries of color swatches, too.

Optical Margin Alignment

Ever since Gutenberg set out to print his Bible, typesetters have looked for ways to "balance" the edges of columns of text—particularly lines ending or beginning with punctuation. Because the eye doesn't "see" punctuation, it can sometimes appear that the left or right edges of some columns of type (especially justified type) are misaligned. Some other programs compensate for this problem by using a "hanging punctuation" feature, which pushes certain punctuation characters outside the text column. But there's more to making the edges of a column look even than just punctuation.

Some characters can create a "ragged" look all by themselves—think of a "W," at the beginning of a line, for example.

When you select an InDesign story (with either the Selection or the Type tool) and turn on the Optical Margin Alignment option in the Story palette (choose Story from the Type menu to display the Story palette), the program balances the edges of the columns based on the appearance of *all* of the characters at the beginning or end of the lines in the column. This adjustment makes the columns appear more even—even though it sometimes means that characters are extending *beyond* the edges of the column (see Figure 4-72).

The amount that InDesign "hangs" a character outside the text column depends on the setting you enter in the Base Size field of the Story palette (that's the field with the icon that looks like it would make a drop cap). In general, you should enter the point size of your body text in this field.

Unfortunately, it turns out that many designers don't like the look of Optical Margin Alignment. It's not that the feature is flawed; it's that designers (especially younger folks) have become accustomed to the lower quality of type set without this feature. Nevertheless, we encourage you to try turning it on and seeing how your readers like it—we think they'll find the text easier to read.

FIGURE 4-72
Optical Margin Alignment

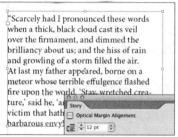

Optical Margin Alignment off

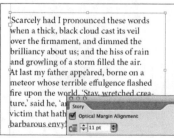

Optical Margin Alignment on

In this close-up view, you can clearly see the way that InDesign adjusts the characters at the edge of the text column.

Punctuation is positioned outside the column.

Some characters hang outside the column...

...others are moved farther inside the column.

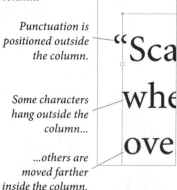

An Old Typesetter Never...

Late night. The sound of the espresso machine in the kitchen about to reach critical mass and melt down, destroying the office and civilization as we know it. The office is different, the equipment and the coffee are better, but we still seem to be up late at night setting type.

And, to tell you the truth, we're not sure we would have it any other way.

CHAPTER 5

Drawing

Using InDesign's drawing tools, you can draw almost anything—from straight lines and boxes to incredibly complex freeform shapes.

The drawing tools can be divided into three types: the Rectangle, Polygon, Oval, and Line tools are for drawing basic shapes; the Pencil, Smooth, Eraser, Pen, Add Point, Delete Point, and Convert Point tools draw or edit more complex paths (see Figure 5-1). The Scissors tool gives you a way of cutting paths.

Some of the path drawing tools (the Rectangle, Oval, and Polygon tools) have counterparts that draw frames (the Rectangular Frame, Oval Frame, and Polygonal Frame tools). The only thing different about these tools is that the "frame" versions draw paths whose content type has been set to "Graphic" (the "regular" versions of these tools draw paths whose content type is "Undefined"). That's it.

In this book, we'll use the default variant of the tool to refer to both tools—when we say "the Rectangle tool," we're referring to both the Rectangle tool and the Rectangular Frame tool.

FIGURE 5-1
Drawing Tools

Freeform path drawing tools

[Pen] Pen tool

[Pencil] Pencil tool

Path editing tools

[Add Point] Add Point tool

[Delete Point] Delete Point tool

[Convert Point] Convert Point tool

[Scissors] Scissors tool

[Smooth] Smooth tool

[Erase] Erase tool

Basic shape tools

[Rectangle] Rectangle tool

[Ellipse] Ellipse tool

[Polygon] Polygon tool

[Rectangle Frame] Rectangle Frame tool

[Ellipse Frame] Ellipse Frame tool

[Polygon Frame] Polygon Frame tool

[Line] Line tool

Which path drawing tools should you use? Don't worry too much about it—the basic shapes can be converted into freeform paths, and the freeform drawing tools can be used to draw basic shapes.

The paths you draw in InDesign are made up of points, and the points are joined to each other by line segments (see Figure 5-2). An InDesign path is just like a connect-the-dots puzzle. Connect all the dots together in the right order, and you've made a picture, or part of a picture. Because points along a path have an order, or winding, you can think of each point as a milepost along the path. Or as a sign saying, "Now go this way."

A Brief Note on Path Drawing Terminology. Adobe likes to refer to points on a path as "anchor points," and to control handles as "direction lines." We don't.

FIGURE 5-2
Parts of a Path

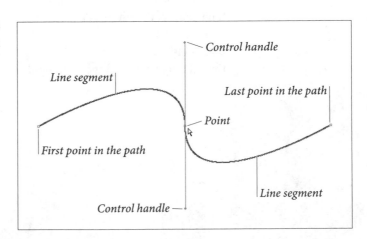

Drawing Basic Shapes

The basic shapes tools (the Rectangle, Polygon, Ellipse, and Line tools, and their frame-drawing counterparts) don't draw anything you couldn't draw using the Pen tool (discussed later in this chapter) or (even) the Pencil tool; they just make drawing certain types of paths easier. They're shortcuts.

The operation of the basic shapes tools is straightforward: drag the tool and get a path of the corresponding shape. If you want to draw a frame, you can either use the frame-drawing variant of the tool, or draw the path and then convert it to a frame.

To draw a rectangle, oval, polygon, or line, follow the steps below (see Figure 5-3).

1. Select the appropriate tool from the Toolbox.

   To specify the type of polygon you'll be drawing, double-click the Polygon tool and choose the shape you want in the Polygon Settings dialog box before you start drawing.

2. Position the cursor where you want one corner of the shape, then drag. InDesign draws a path, starting where you first held down the mouse button.

   To draw squares, hold down Shift as you drag the Rectangle tool. To draw circles, hold down Shift as you drag the Ellipse tool. When you hold down Shift as you drag, the Polygon tool produces equilateral polygons. Holding down Shift as you drag the Line tool constrains the angle of the line to 45-degree tangents from the point at which you started dragging.

   Hold down Option to draw a basic shape from its geometric center point.

3. When the basic shape is the size and shape you want it to be, stop dragging and release the mouse button.

FIGURE 5-3
Drawing a Basic Shape

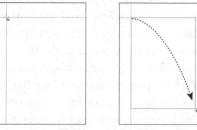 

Select a basic shape tool (in this example, the Rectangle tool).

Drag the tool on the page.

InDesign creates a basic shape.

You can also create rectangles and ellipses by specifying their width and height (see Figure 5-4).

1. Select the Rectangle tool or the Ellipse tool from the Toolbox.

2. Position the cursor where you want to place one corner of the basic shape, or hold down Option/Alt and position the cursor where you want to place the center point of the shape.

3. Click. InDesign displays the Rectangle dialog box (if you've selected the Rectangle tool) or the Ellipse dialog box (if you've selected the Ellipse tool).

4. Enter values in the Width and Height fields, then click the OK button.

FIGURE 5-4
Adding a Basic Shape "by the Numbers"

Select a basic shape tool.

You can control the origin of the basic shape by selecting a point on the Transform palette's Proxy before you click.

Click the tool on the page or pasteboard.

InDesign displays a dialog box (Rectangle, Polygon, or Ellipse). Enter the dimensions of the basic shape and click the OK button.

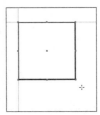

InDesign creates a basic shape using the dimensions you entered.

Points and Paths

Why is it that the most important things in life are often the most difficult to learn? Drawing by manipulating Bezier paths—the geometric construct used to represent path shapes in most of today's vector drawing programs—is one of those difficult things. When we first approached FreeHand and Illustrator, the process of drawing by placing points and manipulating control handles struck us as alien, as nothing like drawing at all. Then we started to catch on.

In many ways, we had been drawing lines from the point of view of everything *but* the line; in a Bezier-path-drawing program such as InDesign, we draw lines from the point of view of the line itself. This is neither better nor worse; it's just different and takes time to get used to. If you've just glanced at the Pen tool and are feeling confused, we urge you to stick with it. Start thinking like a line.

Thinking Like a Line
Imagine that, through the action of some mysterious potion or errant cosmic ray, you've been reduced in size so that you're a little smaller than one of the dots in a connect-the-dots puzzle. For added detail and color, imagine that the puzzle appears in a *Highlights for Children* magazine in a dentist's office.

The only way out is to complete the puzzle. As you walk, a line extends behind you. As you reach each dot in the puzzle, a sign tells you where you are in the puzzle and the route you must take to get to the next dot in the path.

Get the idea? The dots in the puzzle are points. The route you walk from one point to another, as instructed by the signs at each point, is a line segment. Each series of connected dots is a path. As you walk from one dot to another, you're thinking like a line.

Each point—from the first point in the path to the last—carries with it some information about the line segments that attach it to the previous and next points along the path.

Paths and their formatting (fill and stroke) attributes are different things. Even if the fill and stroke applied to the path is "None" or the stroke weight is 0 there's still a path there.

When you select a point, the point "fills in," becoming a solid square (see Figure 5-5). Note that this is the way that Illustrator displays a selected point, but the opposite of FreeHand's method.

FIGURE 5-5
Selected and
Unselected Points

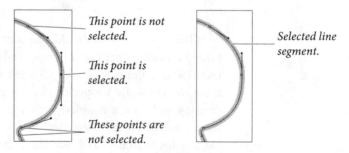

This point is not selected.

This point is selected.

These points are not selected.

Selected line segment.

Point Types
Points on an InDesign path are either *corner points* or *curve points*. Each type of point has its own special properties.

▶ A curve point adds a curved line segment between the current point and the preceding and following points along the path. Curve points have two control handles extended from them, and moving one control handle affects the position of the other control handle. One control handle affects the curve of the line segment following the curve point on the path; the other affects the curve of the line segment preceding the curve point. Curve points are typically used to add smooth curves to a path (see Figure 5-6).

▶ A corner point adds a straight line segment between the current point and the preceding point on the path (see Figure 5-7). Corner points are typically used to create paths containing straight line segments.

FIGURE 5-6
Curve Points

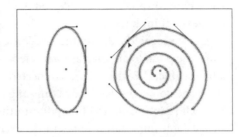

Curve points curve the line segments attached to the point. All of the points in this example are curve points.

FIGURE 5-7
Corner Points

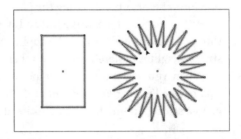

Corner points, by default, apply no curve to the line segments attached to the point. All of the points in this example are corner points.

What type of points should you use? Any type of point can be turned into any other type of point, and anything you can do with one kind of point can be done with the other kind of point. Given these two points (so to speak), you can use the kinds of points and drawing tools you're happiest with and achieve exactly the results you want. There is no "best way" to draw with InDesign's Pen tool, but it helps to understand how the particular method you choose works.

Winding   Paths have a direction, also known as "winding" (as in "winding a clock"). Path direction generally corresponds to the order in which you placed the points on the path (see Figure 5-8). In our connect-the-dots puzzle, path direction tells us the order in which we connect the dots.

To reverse the direction of a path, select the path and choose Reverse Path from the Object menu. InDesign reverses the direction of the path. You can also reverse the direction of a selected path using the Reverse Path path operation, as discussed in "Path Operations," later in this chapter.

FIGURE 5-8
Path Direction,
or "Winding"

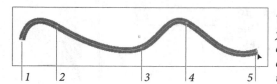

The order in which you create points determines the direction (or "winding") of the path.

1   2   3   4   5

Control Handles

You control the curvature of the line segments before and after each point using the point's control handles. Points can have up to two control handles attached to them. By default, new corner points have none and curve points have two. Note that each line segment has up to two control handles defining its curve—the "outgoing" control handle attached to the point defining the start of the line segment and the "incoming" control handle attached to the next point.

If you retract the control handle (by dragging it inside the point), the control handle has no effect on the curvature of the path. This doesn't necessarily mean that the line segment is a straight line, however—a control handle on the point at the other end of the line segment might also have an effect on the curve of the line segment.

The most significant difference between corner points and curve points is that the control handles attached to a corner point can be adjusted independently, while changing the angle of one control handle of a curve point changes the angle of the other control handle (see Figure 5-9). This difference, in our opinion, makes corner points more useful than curve points—you can do anything with a corner point you could do with a curve point or a connector point.

To convert a point from one point type to another, click the point using the Convert Point tool. If you click a curve point, this retracts both control handles. To convert a curve point to a corner point while leaving one of its control handles in place, drag the other control handle using the Convert Point tool (see Figure 5-10).

FIGURE 5-9
Curve Points vs.
Corner Points

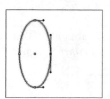 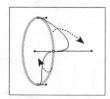 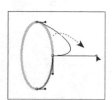

When you adjust one control handle on a curve point, InDesign adjusts the other control handle, as well.

To adjust the curvature of a line segment without changing the curve of the following line segment, use a corner point.

FIGURE 5-10
**Converting from One
Point Type to Another**

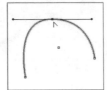
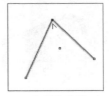
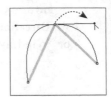

*Position the Convert
Point tool over a
curve point…*

*…and click. InDesign
converts the curve
point to a corner point.*

*To convert a corner point
to a curve point, drag the
Convert Point tool over
the point.*

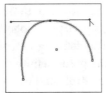
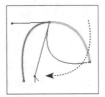
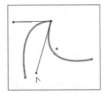

*To convert a curve
point to a corner point,
drag one of the control
handles using the
Convert Point tool.*

*InDesign converts the
curve point to a corner
point. As you drag the
control handle…*

*…InDesign adjusts the
curve of the correspond-
ing line segment, but
leaves the other line
segment unchanged.*

Drawing Paths with the Pencil Tool

The quickest way to create a freeform path on an InDesign page is
to use the Pencil tool. Click the Pencil tool in the Tools palette (or
press N), then drag the Pencil tool on the page. As you drag, InDesign
creates a path that follows the cursor, automatically placing corner
and curve points as it does so (see Figure 5-11).

FIGURE 5-11
**Drawing with
the Pencil Tool**

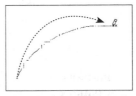

*Select the Pencil tool and position it
where you want the path to start.*

*Drag the Pencil tool on the page or
pasteboard.*

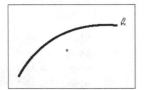

*When the path looks the way you
want it to, stop dragging.*

*As you drag the Pencil tool, InDesign
positions curve and corner points.*

Drawing Paths with the Pen Tool

You use the Pen tool and its variants (the Remove Point, Add Point, and Convert Point tools)—to create and edit paths.

When you *click* the Pen tool on a page, InDesign places a corner point. *Drag* the Pen tool, and InDesign places a curve point where you started dragging—you determine the length of the control handles (and, therefore, the shape of the curve) by dragging as you place the curve point (see Figure 5-12).

FIGURE 5-12
**Placing Curve
and Corner Points**

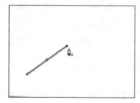

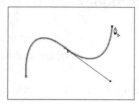

Drag the Pen tool...   *...and InDesign creates a curve point.*

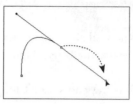

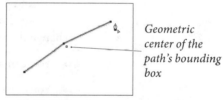

Geometric
center of the
path's bounding
box

Click the Pen tool...   *...and InDesign creates a corner point.*

To curve the line segment following a *corner* point, place the corner point, position the Pen tool above the point (this switches to the Convert Point tool), and then drag. As you drag, InDesign extends a control handle from the point (see Figure 5-13).

The trickiest thing about using the Pen tool this way is that you don't see the effect of the curve manipulation until you've placed the next point. This makes sense in that you don't need a control handle for a line segment that doesn't yet exist, but it can be quite a brain-twister.

FIGURE 5-13
**Dragging a Control
Handle Out of
a Corner Point**

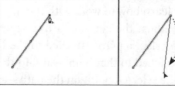

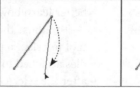

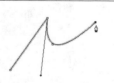

*Position the Pen tool
above a point (it will
change into the Convert
Point tool).*

*Drag a control handle
out of the point.*

*Click the Pen tool to add
a point. InDesign curves
the line segment connect-
ing the points.*

To convert a curve point you've just placed to a corner point, position the Pen tool above the point (to switch to the Convert Point tool) and then click the point. InDesign converts the point to a corner point and retracts the point's control handles.

You can change the position of points, as you'd expect, by selecting the point with the Direct Selection tool and then dragging the point to a new location.

Drawing Techniques

Now that you know all about the elements that make up paths, let's talk about how you actually use them.

Path Drawing Tips When you're drawing paths, don't forget that you can change the path after you've drawn it. We've often seen people delete entire paths and start over because they misplaced the last point on the path. Go ahead and place points in the wrong places; you can always change the position of any point. Also, keep these facts in mind:

▶ You can always add points to or subtract points from the path.

▶ You can change tools while drawing a path.

▶ You can split the path using the Scissors tool.

It's also best to create paths using as few points as you can—but it's not required. We've noticed that people who have just started working with Bezier drawing tools often use more points than are needed to create their paths. Over time, they learn one of the basic rules of vector drawing: Any curve can be described by two points and their associated control handles. No more, no less.

Manipulating Control Handles The aspect of drawing in InDesign that's toughest to understand and master is the care, feeding, and manipulation of control handles. These handles are fundamental to drawing curved lines, so you'd better learn how to work with them.

To adjust the curve of a line segment, use the Direct Selection tool to select a point attached to the line segment. The control handles attached to that point—and to the points that come before and after the selected point on the path—appear. If you don't see control handles attached to the point you selected, the curvature of the line segment is controlled by the points at the other end of the line segments. Position the cursor over one of the control handles and drag. The curve of the line segment associated with that handle changes as you drag. When the curve looks the way you want it to, stop dragging (see Figure 5-14).

To retract (delete) a control handle, drag the handle inside the point it's attached to.

You can also adjust the curve of a curved line segment by dragging the line segment itself. To do this, select the line segment (click the line segment with the Direct Selection tool, or use the tool to drag a selection rectangle over part of the line segment) and then drag. As you drag, InDesign adjusts the curve of the line segment (see Figure 5-15).

Adding Points to a Path

To add a point to an existing line segment, select the path, switch to the Pen tool, and then click the Pen tool on the line segment. InDesign adds a point to the path (see Figure 5-16).

You don't need to select the Add Point tool—InDesign will switch to it when you move the Pen tool above a line segment.

FIGURE 5-14
Adjusting Curve Points

Select a point using the Direct Selection tool.

Drag the control handle attached to the point to a new location.

InDesign curves the line segment.

FIGURE 5-15
Another Way to Adjust the Curve of a Line Segment

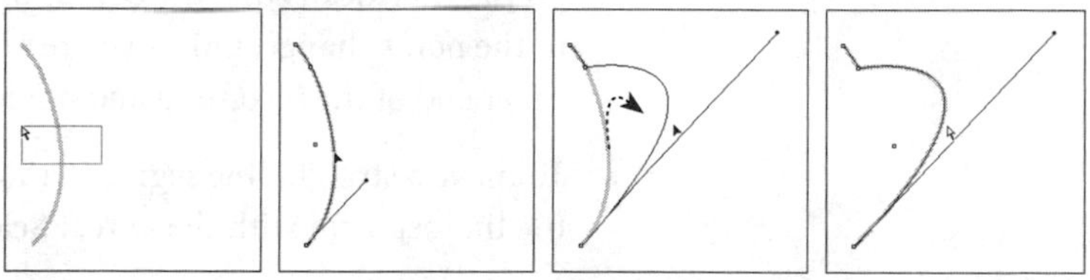

Select a line segment using the Direct Selection tool (drag a selection rectangle over the line segment).

Drag the line segment. As you drag, InDesign adjusts the curve of the line segment.

FIGURE 5-16
Adding a Point to a Path

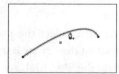 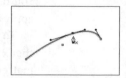

Position the Pen tool above a line segment. InDesign switches to the Add Point tool.

Click on the path, and InDesign adds a point to the path.

**Removing Points
from a Path**

To remove a point from a path, select the path, switch to the Pen tool, and then click the Pen tool on the point. InDesign removes the point from the path (see Figure 5-17).

FIGURE 5-17
**Removing a Point
from a Path**

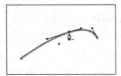

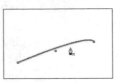

*Position the Pen tool above an
existing point on a path. InDesign
switches to the Delete Point tool.*

*Click the point, and InDesign
removes the point from the path.*

**Selecting and
Moving Points**

If you've gotten this far, you probably know how to select points, but here are a few rules to keep in mind.

▸ To select a point, click it with the Direct Selection tool, or drag a selection rectangle around it (using the same tool).

▸ You can select more than one point at a time. To do this, hold down Shift as you click the Direct Selection tool on each point, or use the Direct Selection tool to drag a selection rectangle around the points you want to select.

▸ You can select points on paths inside groups or compound paths by using the Direct Selection tool.

▸ When you move a point, the control handles associated with that point also move, maintaining their positions relative to the point. This means that the curves of the line segments attached to the point change, unless you're also moving the points on the other end of the incoming and outgoing line segments.

▸ To move a straight line segment and its associated points, select the line segment with the Direct Selection tool and drag.

**Opening and
Closing Paths**

Paths can be open or closed (see Figure 5-18). An open path has no line segment between the beginning and ending points on the path. You don't have to close a path to add contents (text or a graphic) or apply a fill to the path.

To close an open path, select the path, select the Pen tool, and then click the Pen tool on the first or last point on the path (it doesn't matter which). Click the Pen tool again on the other end point. InDesign closes the path (see Figure 5-19).

Another way to close an open path is to use the Close Path path operation, as discussed in "Path Operations," later in this chapter.

To open a closed path, select the Direct Selection tool and click the line segment between two points on the path (you can also drag a selection rectangle over the line segment). Press Delete, and InDesign removes the line segment, opening the path between the points on either side of the line segment (see Figure 5-20).

FIGURE 5-18
Open and Closed Paths

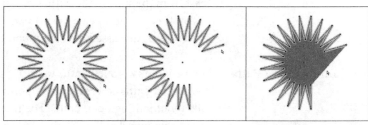

Closed path.   *Open path.*   *A path does not have to be closed to have a fill.*

FIGURE 5-19
Closing an Open Path

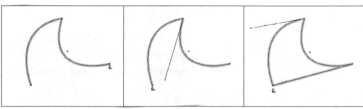

Move the Pen tool over an end point of an open path.   *Click the Pen tool, then move it over the other end point on the path.*   *Click on the end point. InDesign closes the path.*

FIGURE 5-20
Opening a Closed Path by Deleting a Line Segment

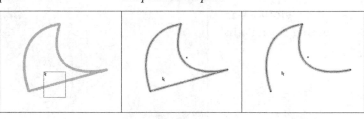

Select the Direct Selection tool, then drag a selection rectangle over a line segment.   *Press the Delete key to delete the line segment.*

FIGURE 5-21
Opening a Closed Path

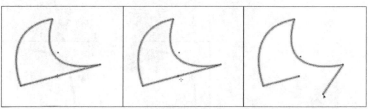

Click a line segment or point with the Scissors tool.   *InDesign opens the path. You can drag the path's end points apart, if necessary.*

To open a path *without* removing a line segment, select the Scissors tool and click the path. Click on a point to split the path at that point, or click a line segment to split the path at that location (see Figure 5-21).

The point closest to the start of the path (following the path's winding) becomes the point farther to the back, and the point farthest from the start of the path is on top of it.

Another way to open a closed path is to use the Close Path path operation, as discussed in "Path Operations," later in this chapter.

Joining Open Paths

You can join two open paths to create a single path, or you can join two closed paths to create a compound path. In this section, we'll talk about joining open paths. For more on joining closed paths to create compound paths, see the next section, "Compound Paths."

To join two open paths, follow these steps (see Figure 5-22).

1. Select the Pen tool.

2. Position the Pen tool above the start or end point of one of the open paths (you don't need to select a path). InDesign changes the cursor to show that it's ready to add a point to the path.

3. Click the Pen tool, then position the cursor over the start or end point of the second path. InDesign changes the cursor to show that it's ready to connect the current path to the point.

FIGURE 5-22
Joining Open Paths

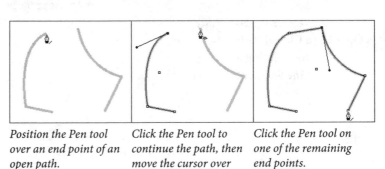

Position the Pen tool over an end point of an open path.

Click the Pen tool to continue the path, then move the cursor over the end point of another open path.

Click the Pen tool on one of the remaining end points.

Click on the other end point to close the path.

4. Click the Pen tool. InDesign joins the two paths.

5. Repeat this process for the other two end points to close the path.

Compound Paths

In the old days, not only did Ole have to walk miles to school in freezing cold weather, but he also had to work his way through an impossibly difficult series of steps just to create holes inside closed paths. While the process was kind of fascinating, it did nothing to improve his already gloomy outlook on life.

These days, creating holes in paths is easier—just make them into compound paths. Compound paths are made of two or more paths (which must be unlocked, ungrouped, and closed) that have been joined using the Make option on the Compound Paths submenu of the Object menu. Areas between the two paths, or areas where the paths overlap, are transparent. The following steps show you how to make a torus, or "doughnut" shape (see Figure 5-23).

1. Select the Ellipse tool from the Tools palette.

2. Draw two ovals, one on top of the other.

3. Fill the ovals with a basic fill.

4. Select both ovals.

5. Press Command-8/Ctrl-8 to join the two ovals.

FIGURE 5-23
Creating a
Compound Path

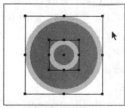

Choose Make from the Composite Paths submenu of the Object menu.

Select the paths you want to turn into a compound path.

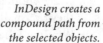

InDesign creates a compound path from the selected objects.

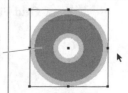

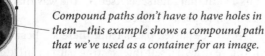

Compound paths don't have to have holes in them—this example shows a compound path that we've used as a container for an image.

If you decide you don't want the paths to be compound paths, you can change them back into individual paths. To do this, select the compound path and then choose Release from the Compound Paths submenu of the Object menu.

When you join paths with different lines and fills, the compound path takes on the stroke and fill attributes of the path that's the farthest to the back.

When you convert characters to paths, InDesign automatically converts the characters into compound paths.

Editing Compound Paths

You can subselect the individual points that make up a compound path in the same way that you subselect objects inside a group—select the Direct Selection tool and click on the point. Once a point is selected, you can alter its position (see Figure 5-24).

FIGURE 5-24
Editing a Compound Path

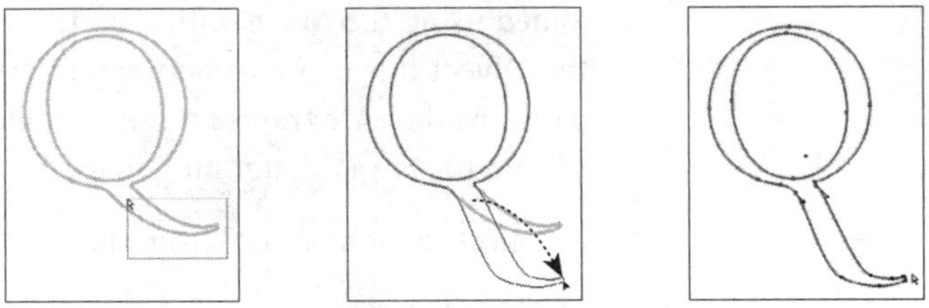

Use the Direct Selection tool to select some points.

Transform (move, scale, shear, or rotate) the points. In this example, we've dragged the points to a new location.

Splitting Compound Paths

To convert a compound path back into two or more normal paths, select the compound path and choose Release from the Compound Paths submenu of the Object menu (or press Command-Option-8/Ctrl-Alt-8). InDesign converts the compound path into its component paths. Note that the paths do not return to their original formatting when you do this.

Compound Paths and Even-Odd Fill

If you're familiar with Illustrator, FreeHand, or other drawing programs, you're probably used to having two options for filling paths. These options go by different names in different applications, but they're usually known as the "Even Odd Fill Rule" and the "Zero Winding Fill Rule." These rules control the way that the application fills a path that intersects itself, or the way that the interior areas of a compound path are filled.

If you've pasted paths from these applications into InDesign, or if you've drawn a self-intersecting path in InDesign, you've probably discovered that InDesign supports the Zero Winding Fill Rule, but not the Even Odd Fill Rule.

What the heck are we talking about? It's much easier to show than it is to describe (see Figure 5-25).

FIGURE 5-25
FIGURE 5-25
Fill Rules

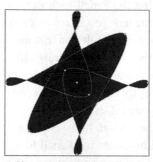

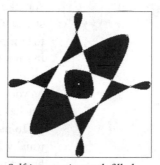

Self-intersecting path filled using the Zero Winding Fill Rule (InDesign).

Self-intersecting path filled using the Even Odd Fill Rule (Illustrator).

What can you do when you want the even/odd fill? Do you have to leave InDesign, create the path in a drawing program, and then import the path as a graphic?

This question drove Ole to the brink of madness before he discovered that you can simulate the effect of the Even Odd Fill Rule using compound paths and the Add path operation (we'll discuss path operations later in this chapter). See Figure 5-26.

1. Select the self-intersecting path.

2. Copy the path, then use Paste In Place (Command-Option-Shift-V/Ctrl-Alt-Shift-V) to create a duplicate of the object exactly on top of the original object.

3. Select both items and click the Add button on the Pathfinder palette (Intersect will also work). InDesign creates a compound path and fills it exactly as the original path would look if it had been filled using the Even Odd Fill Rule.

FIGURE 5-26
Simulating the Effect of the Even Odd Fill Rule

Select the path, then copy the path and paste the copy on top of the original using Paste In Place.

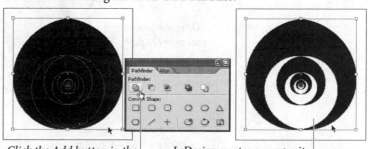

Click the Add button in the PathFinder palette.

InDesign creates a composite path that is filled using the Even Odd Fill Rule.

Smoothing Paths

You like using the Pencil tool. But your mouse hand isn't perfectly steady. Or the jerk you share office space with can't resist the urge to bump your arm while you're drawing. Either way, you need a way to smooth the path you've drawn in InDesign. Are you doomed to an after-hours workout with the Pen tool? Not with the Smooth tool on your side. This handy gadget can help you smooth out the rough patches in your InDesign paths.

To use the Smooth tool, select the tool from the Tools palette (it's usually hiding under the Pencil tool). Or select the Pencil tool and hold down Option/Alt to change the Pencil tool to the Smooth tool. Drag the tool along the path you want to smooth (see Figure 5-27). As you drag, InDesign adjusts the control handles and point positions on the path (sometimes deleting points as you drag).

To control the operation of the Smooth tool, double-click the Smooth tool in the Tools palette. InDesign displays the Smooth Tool Preferences dialog box (see Figure 5-28). The Fidelity slider controls the distance, in screen pixels, that the "smoothed" path can vary from the path of the Smooth tool (higher values equal more adjustment and greater variation from the existing path). The Smoothness slider controls the amount of change applied to the path (higher values equal greater smoothing).

FIGURE 5-27
Smoothing a Path

Select the Smooth tool from the Tools palette.

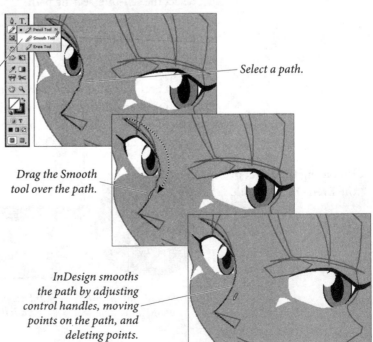

Select a path.

Drag the Smooth tool over the path.

InDesign smooths the path by adjusting control handles, moving points on the path, and deleting points.

FIGURE 5-28
Smooth Tool Preferences

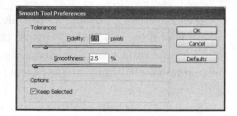

Erasing Paths

Imagine that you want to remove an arbitrary section of a path, and that the beginning and end of the section do not correspond to existing points on the path. In InDesign 1.0, deleting this section of the path would have involved splitting the path using the Scissors tool (at either end of the section you wanted to delete) and then deleting the path segment between the two points.

These days, it's much easier. Select the Erase tool from the Tools palette, then drag the tool over the area of the path you want to delete (see Figure 5-29).

FIGURE 5-29
Erasing Part of a Path

Select the Erase tool from the Tools palette (or press Shift-N until InDesign selects it for you).

Select a path.

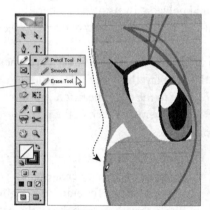

Drag the Erase tool over the parts of the path you want to erase.

When you drag the Erase tool over a line segment on a closed path, InDesign opens the path. When you drag over an open path, it gets split into two paths.

Path Operations

Path operations—which is what we call the commands represented by buttons on the Pathfinder palette—create paths from other paths, or change the shape of paths in some predefined way. The first row of buttons in the Pathfinder palette make it easy to create complex shapes by combining simple geometric shapes, and to create shapes that would be very difficult to draw using the Pen tool.

The Convert Shape operations provide a number of "utility" functions for working with paths. Why did they end up in the same palette with the Pathfinder path operations they have little or nothing in common with? Think carefully before you answer. Do you *really* want *another* palette?

The Pathfinder path operations work with the area(s) of intersection between two or more objects. These path operations can merge objects, or create new objects, or remove the area of one object from another object.

Many people have somehow gotten the impression that the path operations (in Illustrator, FreeHand, or QuarkXPress, for example) are "advanced" drawing techniques. "I can't draw," they say, "so I have no use for them. It's hard enough just using the Pen tool."

Nothing could be further from the truth—if you *can* draw, the path operations are a nice addition to your toolbox, but if you *can't* draw, or can't draw with the Pen tool, InDesign's path operations can quickly become your best friend. Think about it—even David can draw just about anything using rectangles, ellipses, and the occasional polygon. By using path operations, you can do the same, without ending up with stacks of overlapping shapes on your pages.

Applying Pathfinder Path Operations

To apply any of the Pathfinder path operations, select two or more paths, display the Pathfinder palette, and click the button corresponding to the path operation you want to apply (see Figure 5-30).

We'll cover what each of the path operations does, but first, a few ground rules:

▶ **Original shapes are deleted.** Path operations often consume the selected shapes and create a new shape. This shape is often a compound path. To retain the original shapes, you'll need to duplicate them before applying the path effect.

FIGURE 5-30
Applying a Path Operation

Select two or more objects...

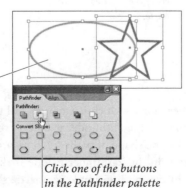
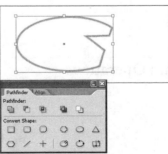

Click one of the buttons in the Pathfinder palette (Subtract, in this example).

InDesign applies the path operation to the selected objects.

▶ **Stacking order matters.** Most of the path operations affect either the foreground or background object in some predefined way. If you try a path operation and don't get the result you expect, undo, then shuffle the order of the objects (using Bring to Front, Send to Back, Bring Forward, and Send Backward from the Arrange submenu of the Object menu) and try again.

▶ **Formatting changes.** In general, the fill, stroke, layer, and other attributes of the foreground object define the formatting of the resulting object or objects. The exception is the Subtract path operation, where the background object defines the formatting of the result.

▶ **Path operations and text frames.** When you apply a path operation to a text frame, the shape of the frame is affected—not the text in the frame.

▶ **Alternatives to clipping paths.** You can sometimes use path operations to avoid clipping paths and nested objects, which can result in faster printing.

▶ **Watch out for path contents.** Performing path operations on objects that contain other objects—such as imported graphics—sometimes deletes the path content.

Add　The Add path operation creates a new path that has the outline of the selected objects, removing the area of intersection and any interior paths from the new object (see Figure 5-31). If the original paths are composite paths, any interior paths will be retained unless they intersect each other or fall within the area of intersection of the shapes.

FIGURE 5-31
Add Path Operation

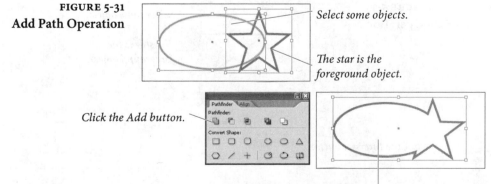

Select some objects.

The star is the foreground object.

Click the Add button.

The Add path operation creates a new path from the outline of the overlapping shapes.

Subtract   When you want to use one path to cut a hole in another, use the Subtract path operation. It's like a cookie cutter—the foreground object cuts a hole in the background object (see Figure 5-32). The resulting object takes on the fill and stroke of the background object.

FIGURE 5-32
Subtract Path Operation

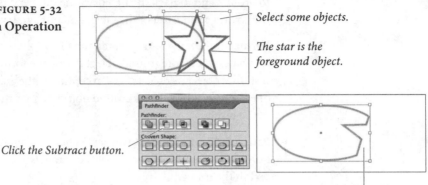

Select some objects.

The star is the foreground object.

Click the Subtract button.

The Subtract path operation removes the area of intersection from the background shape.

Intersect   The Intersect path operation creates a new object that is the shape of the area of intersection of the objects in the selection (see Figure 5-33). Intersect will display an error message if the objects do not share a common area of intersection.

As we've noted, path operations consume the selected objects. There are various ways to retain the original objects, but the quickest by far is to apply the path effect, copy the resulting path, undo (which restores the original paths), and then press Command-Option-Shift-V/Ctrl-Alt-Shift-V to paste in place. This trick is particularly useful when used with Intersect.

FIGURE 5-33
Intersect Path Operation

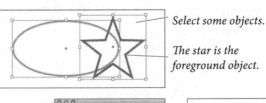

Select some objects.

The star is the foreground object.

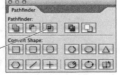

Click the Intersect button.

The Intersect path operation creates a new shape based on the area (or areas) of intersection of the original objects.

Exclude Overlap   The Exclude Overlap path operation creates a compound path from the selected objects, leaving any areas of intersection unfilled (see Figure 5-34).

FIGURE 5-34
Exclude Overlap
Path Operation

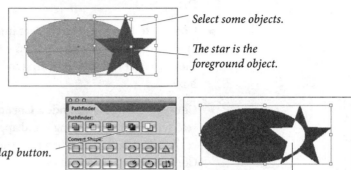

Select some objects.

The star is the foreground object.

Click the Exclude Overlap button.

The Exclude Overlap path operation creates a single shape from the objects—removing the area of intersection of the original objects.

Minus Back   The Minus Back path operation is the opposite of the Subtract path operation. When you click the Minus Back button in the Pathfinder palette, InDesign uses the background object to cut a hole in the foreground object (see Figure 5-35). The resulting object takes on the formatting attributes of the foreground object.

FIGURE 5-35
Minus Back
Path Operation

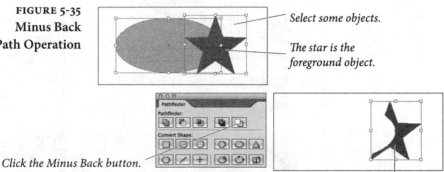

Select some objects.

The star is the foreground object.

Click the Minus Back button.

The Minus Back path operation creates a new shape by removing the area of the background objects from the foreground object.

Applying Convert   To apply any of the Convert Shape operations, select an object and
Shape Operations   click one of the buttons in the Pathfinder palette.

▶ **Convert to Rectangle.** Converts the selected object to a rectangle.

▶ **Convert to Rounded-Corner Rectangle.** Converts the selected object to a rectangle and applies the Rounded corner effect (using the current corner radius setting in the Corner Effects Dialog box).

▶ **Convert to Beveled-Corner Rectangle.** Converts the selected object to a rectangle and applies the Bevel corner effect (using the current corner radius setting in the Corner Effects Dialog box).

▶ **Convert to Inverse-Rounded-Corner Rectangle.** Converts the selected object to a rectangle and applies the Inverse Rounded corner effect (using the current corner radius setting in the Corner Effects Dialog box).

▶ **Convert to Ellipse.** Converts the selected object to an ellipse. If you have a square selected, the resulting ellipse will be a circle.

▶ **Convert to Triangle.** Converts the selected object to a triangle.

▶ **Convert to Polygon.** Converts the selected object to a polygon, using the current settings in the Polygon Settings dialog box.

▶ **Convert to Line.** Converts the selected object to a line.

▶ **Convert to Vertical or Horizontal Line.** Converts the selected object to a vertical or horizontal line.

▶ **Open Path.** Opens a closed path. Note that this operation does not remove the last line segment in the path—it simply opens the path at the first/last point in the path (see Figure 5-36).

▶ **Close Path.** Closes an open path.

▶ **Reverse Path.** Reverses the selected path.

FIGURE 5-36
Open Path

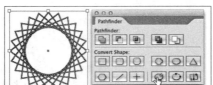 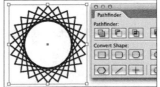

Select a path and click the Open Path button. | InDesign opens the path.

The path won't look any different, but it's now an open path... 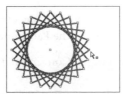 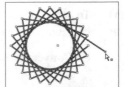 ...as you can see when you locate and move the first or last point on the path.

Corner Effects

InDesign can apply a number of distortions to the corners of the paths in your publication. These distortions are known as "Corner Effects," and are controlled by the settings you enter in the Corner Effects dialog box. The most common use of this feature is to add rounded corners to rectangles and squares.

To apply a corner effect, select a path and then choose Corner Effects from the Object menu. InDesign displays the Corner Effects dialog box. Choose the effect you want from the Effect pop-up menu, then enter a value in the Size field and then press Return to apply your change. InDesign changes the corners of the path based on the corner effect you selected (see Figure 5-37).

Strokes

Once you've created a path, you'll probably want to give the path some specific line weight, color, or other property. The process of applying formatting to a path is often called "stroking a path," and we refer to a path's appearance as its "stroke." Strokes specify what the outline of the path *looks like*.

To define a stroke for a path, select the path, then display the Stroke palette by pressing F10 (see Figure 5-38). Use the Type pop-up menu to choose the type of stroke you want to use—solid, dashed, or any of the "scotch" (i.e., multi-stroke) types.

In addition to the default stroke types, you can define custom dashed, striped, or dotted stroke styles. We'll talk more about stroke styles later in the chapter.

Weight   You can enter a line weight for the stroke of the selected path using the Weight field, or you can choose a predefined line weight from the pop-up menu associated with the field. To remove a stroke from a path, enter zero in the Weight field.

Historical Note: In the old days of desktop publishing, some programs created hairlines using the PostScript statement "0 setlinewidth," which generates a one-pixel wide stroke on a PostScript printer. Provided you were printing to a 300-dpi laser printer, this worked pretty well—you'd get a stroke that was approximately the width of a hairline (between .2 and .25 points). When imagesetters appeared, however, this approach led to strokes that were $1/1200$th of an inch wide or even smaller—stroke weights too fine to be printed on

FIGURE 5-37
Corner Effects

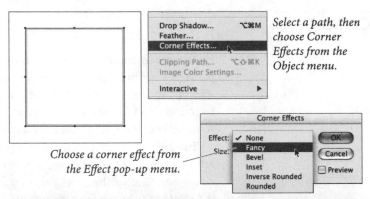

Select a path, then choose Corner Effects from the Object menu.

Choose a corner effect from the Effect pop-up menu.

InDesign's corner effects

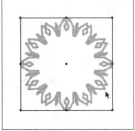

InDesign's corner effects can be applied to any corner point. Try them with polygons for interesting geometric shapes.

Enter a value in the Size field to set the size of the corner effect.

Shapes created by overlapping corner effects

most presses. So, we grizzled graybeards advised all of our younger cohorts to avoid entering zero for the weight of a stroke. In InDesign, at least, it doesn't matter—entering zero won't result in a "0 setline-width" stroke.

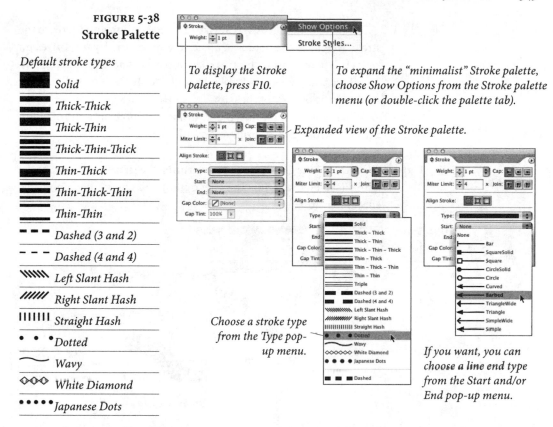

FIGURE 5-38
Stroke Palette

To display the Stroke palette, press F10.

To expand the "minimalist" Stroke palette, choose Show Options from the Stroke palette menu (or double-click the palette tab).

Expanded view of the Stroke palette.

Default stroke types

Solid
Thick-Thick
Thick-Thin
Thick-Thin-Thick
Thin-Thick
Thin-Thick-Thin
Thin-Thin
Dashed (3 and 2)
Dashed (4 and 4)
Left Slant Hash
Right Slant Hash
Straight Hash
Dotted
Wavy
White Diamond
Japanese Dots

Choose a stroke type from the Type pop-up menu.

If you want, you can choose a line end type from the Start and/or End pop-up menu.

Stroke Alignment

The three buttons in the Align Stroke section of the Stroke palette control the way that the stroke is positioned relative to the path. The options are Align Stroke to Center, Align Stroke to Inside, and Align Stroke to Outside, and they do just what they say (see Figure 5-39).

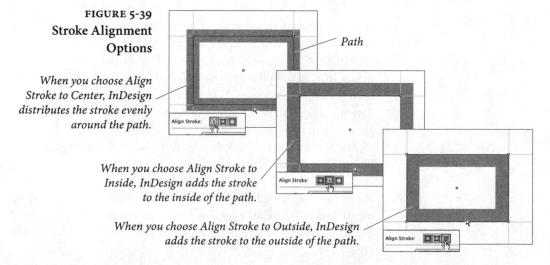

FIGURE 5-39
Stroke Alignment Options

Path

When you choose Align Stroke to Center, InDesign distributes the stroke evenly around the path.

When you choose Align Stroke to Inside, InDesign adds the stroke to the inside of the path.

When you choose Align Stroke to Outside, InDesign adds the stroke to the outside of the path.

If you're using the Align Stroke to Inside option and increase the stroke weight of the border of an ad in a magazine layout, InDesign keeps the stroke inside the area the advertiser is actually paying for.

When you use Align Stroke to Outside, InDesign will add the stroke to the outside of the path.

When you turn on the Align Stroke to Center option, InDesign adds the stroke evenly around the path.

Cap Select one of the Cap options to determine the shape of the end of the stroke (see Figure 5-40). The Cap option you choose has no visible effect on a closed path.

FIGURE 5-40
Cap Options

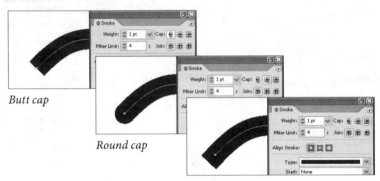

Butt cap

Round cap

Projecting cap

Join The Join option determines the way InDesign renders corners—the place where two line segments in a path meet in a corner point (see Figure 5-41).

Miter Limit When paths go around corners, some weird things can happen. Asked to corner too sharply, the stroke skids out of control, creating spiky elbows that increase the effective stroke weight of a path's corners. The value you enter in the Miter Limit field sets the distance, as a multiple of the stroke weight, that you'll allow the corner to extend before InDesign applies a beveled join to the corner (see Figure 5-42). If, for example, you enter "2" in the Miter Limit field, InDesign will flatten corners when the stroke weight of the corner is equal to or greater than two times the weight of the stroke.

The Miter Limit field is only available when you're using the Miter Join option, and applies only to corner points.

Dash If you want a dashed line, choose Dashed from the Type pop-up menu, and use the Dash and Gap fields that appear at the bottom of the Stroke palette to specify the appearance of the dashed stroke (see Figure 5-43).

FIGURE 5-41
Join Options

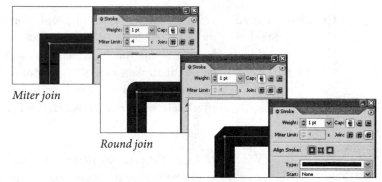

Miter join

Round join

Beveled join

FIGURE 5-42
Miter Limit

When angles get small, corners go out of control. In this example, a Miter Join creates a projecting "elbow."

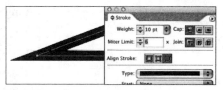

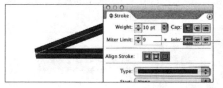

Increase the value in the Miter Limit field to cause corners with tight angles to be rendered using a Beveled miter join.

FIGURE 5-43
Applying a Dashed Stroke

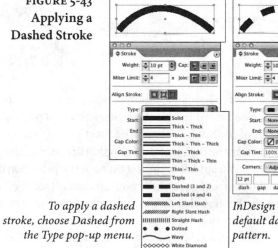

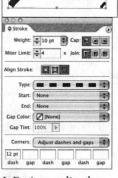

To apply a dashed stroke, choose Dashed from the Type pop-up menu.

InDesign applies the default dashed stroke pattern.

To edit the dashed stroke pattern, enter new values in the Dash and Gap fields (these fields use the current measurement units).

Creating Layered Strokes

We've heard a number of people complain that InDesign doesn't include their favorite "fancy" rules—if you can't find what you're looking for on the Type menu in the Stroke palette, and you can't create the stroke you want using stroke styles (discussed later in this chapter), you can make your own. To create a simple multi-stroke effect, follow these steps (see Figure 5-44).

1. Select a path.

2. Clone the path. To do this, press Command-C/Ctrl-C to copy the path, then press Command-Option-Shift-V/Ctrl-Alt-Shift-V. InDesign creates a copy of the selected path exactly on top of the original path.

3. Change the stroke weight, stroke type, or color of the copy of the path.

4. Select the original path and the clone and group them (note that you can't make them a compound path, as that would apply one of the two strokes to both paths and would undo your multi-stroke effect).

FIGURE 5-44
Creating a Complex Stroke by Stacking Paths

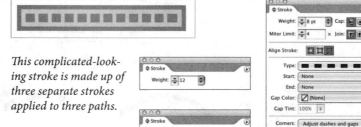

This complicated-looking stroke is made up of three separate strokes applied to three paths.

Arrowheads

You can add arrowheads or tailfeathers to any open path you want by choosing an arrowhead from the Start and End pop-up menus at the bottom of the Stroke palette. The Start pop-up menu applies to the first point in the path (according to the direction of the path); the End pop-up menu applies to the last point in the path. You don't have to make choices from both of the pop-up menus (see Figure 5-45).

To swap the arrowheads on the beginning and end of a path, select the path using the Direct Selection tool and choose Reverse Path from the Paths submenu of the Object menu (see Figure 5-46).

Overprint

You won't find this basic stroke option in the Stroke palette, so stop looking. Instead, it's in the Attributes palette (choose Attributes from the Window menu). Checking the Overprint Stroke option makes

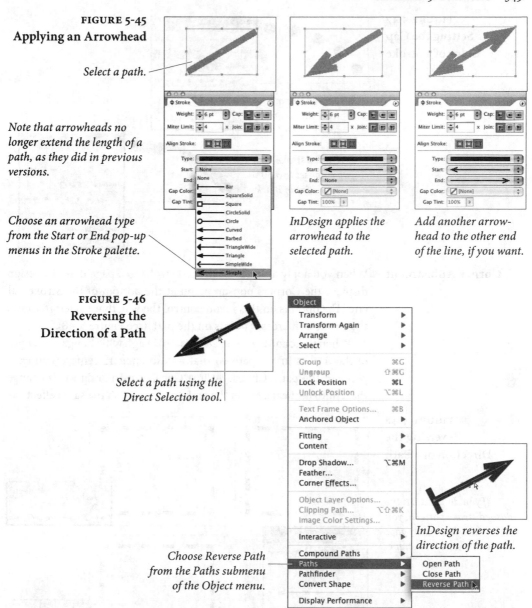

FIGURE 5-45
Applying an Arrowhead

Select a path.

Note that arrowheads no longer extend the length of a path, as they did in previous versions.

Choose an arrowhead type from the Start or End pop-up menus in the Stroke palette.

InDesign applies the arrowhead to the selected path.

Add another arrowhead to the other end of the line, if you want.

FIGURE 5-46
Reversing the Direction of a Path

Select a path using the Direct Selection tool.

Choose Reverse Path from the Paths submenu of the Object menu.

InDesign reverses the direction of the path.

the stroke overprint (rather than knock out of) whatever's behind it. This might not seem like much, but if you're creating color publications, you'll find it's one of the most important features in InDesign (see Chapter 10, "Color").

Gap Color and Gap Tint

When you choose a dotted, dashed, or striped stroke, InDesign displays the Gap Color and the Gap Tint pop-up menus at the bottom of the Stroke palette (see Figure 5-47). Use these controls to specify the color and tint of the "blank" areas in the stroke.

FIGURE 5-47
**Setting the Gap
Color of a Stroke**

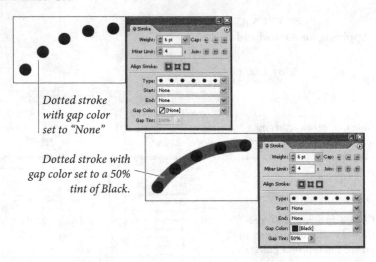

*Dotted stroke
with gap color
set to "None"*

*Dotted stroke with
gap color set to a 50%
tint of Black.*

Corner Adjustment
When you apply a dotted or dashed stroke to a page item, InDesign displays the Corners pop-up menu at the bottom of the Stroke palette. The options on this menu control the way that InDesign draws the stroke as it crosses points on the path (see Figure 5-48).

  When you choose Adjust Dashes, InDesign will change the length of the dashes in the path so that a dash appears centered on each point in the path. Choose Adjust Gaps, and InDesign will change the length of the dashes in the path to accomplish the same effect. As

FIGURE 5-48
**Reversing the
Direction of a Path**

*If you don't adjust the
dashed stroke pattern, you
run the risk of unsightly gaps
at the corners of the shape.*

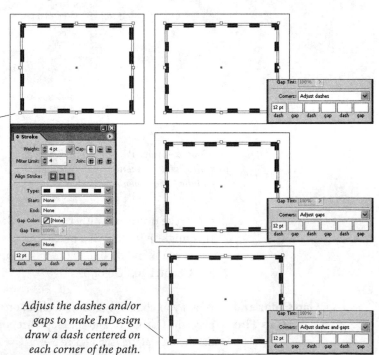

*Adjust the dashes and/or
gaps to make InDesign
draw a dash centered on
each corner of the path.*

you'd expect, choosing Adjust Dashes and Gaps changes the length of both dashes and gaps in the dash pattern, and choosing None does not adjust the position of dashes in the pattern at all.

Why adjust the dashes and/or gaps in a dash pattern? If you don't, you can easily end up with gaps at the corners of paths. It's particularly noticeable when you apply dashed strokes to rectangles.

Editing Strokes

Once you've applied a stroke to a particular path, you can change the stroke using any of the following methods. Again, there's no "right" way to edit a stroke—which method is best and quickest depends on how you work and which palettes you have open at the time you want to change the stroke.

▶ Display the Stroke palette, then make changes in the palette.

▶ Click the Stroke selector in the Color palette, then click a color in the palette (see Chapter 10, "Color," for more on applying colors using the Color palette).

▶ Use the Stroke button at the bottom of the Toolbox to apply or remove colors and gradients from the path.

▶ Select the path, then choose a new stroke weight from the Stroke Weight submenu of the Context menu.

▶ Use the Eyedropper tool to pick up the stroke of a path and apply that formatting to another path.

Removing Strokes

To quickly remove a stroke from a path, use one of the following techniques.

▶ Select the path, click the Stroke selector (at the bottom of the Toolbox), then click None.

▶ Select the path, display the Swatches palette, click the Stroke selector at the top of the palette, and then click the None swatch.

▶ Enter 0 in the Weight field of the Stroke palette.

Stroke Styles

If you've looked through the default strokes and haven't seen the stroke pattern you're looking for, you can probably create it using InDesign's stroke styles. This is provided that the stroke you're looking for is dashed, dotted, or striped—InDesign does not yet support strokes made up of arbitrary shapes. If you need a special skull and crossbones stroke for your pirate/goth/metal newsletter, you'll have to create it from scratch (using text paths, as shown in Chapter 6, "Where Text Meets Graphics").

To create a stroke style, follow these steps (see Figure 5-49)

1. Choose Stroke Styles from the Stroke palette menu. InDesign displays the Stroke Styles dialog box.

2. Click the New button to create a new stroke style. If you want to base your new stroke style on an existing style, select the style from the list of stroke styles before you click the button. InDesign displays the New Stroke Style dialog box.

3. Enter a name for the stroke style. Choose a stroke style type (Dash, Dotted, or Stripe) from the Type pop-up menu.

4. Set the options for the stroke style. The available options vary depending on the type of stroke style you selected.

    For each type, InDesign displays a preview of the stroke style with an associated Preview Weight field. As you would expect, changing the stroke weight using this field affects only the preview image of the stroke—the stroke style does not include the stroke weight. (We're hoping that the next version of InDesign will be able to store a stroke weight with a given stroke style.)

    In each of the stroke style types, the Pattern Length field controls the length of the pattern in the stroke style.

    Dash. Drag the cursor in the area below the ruler to set the length of the dashes in the stroke style, or enter values in the Start or Length fields. To make more than one dash in the pattern, click in the white area and drag. To remove a dash, point at the black area and drag it away from the ruler.

    You can also set the line cap and the way that InDesign handles the dash pattern around corners. These options work in exactly the same way as their counterparts in the Stroke palette, as discussed previously in this chapter.

    Dotted. When you choose Dotted from the Type pop-up menu, you can add dots to the pattern by clicking below the ruler, or by entering a value in the Center field. Either way, you're controlling the location of the center of the dot relative to the pattern length. You cannot scale the width or height of the dot—it's always a circle whose width is determined by the stroke weight. (If you're looking for an oval dot, use a dashed stroke with a rounded line cap.)

FIGURE 5-49
Defining a Stroke Style

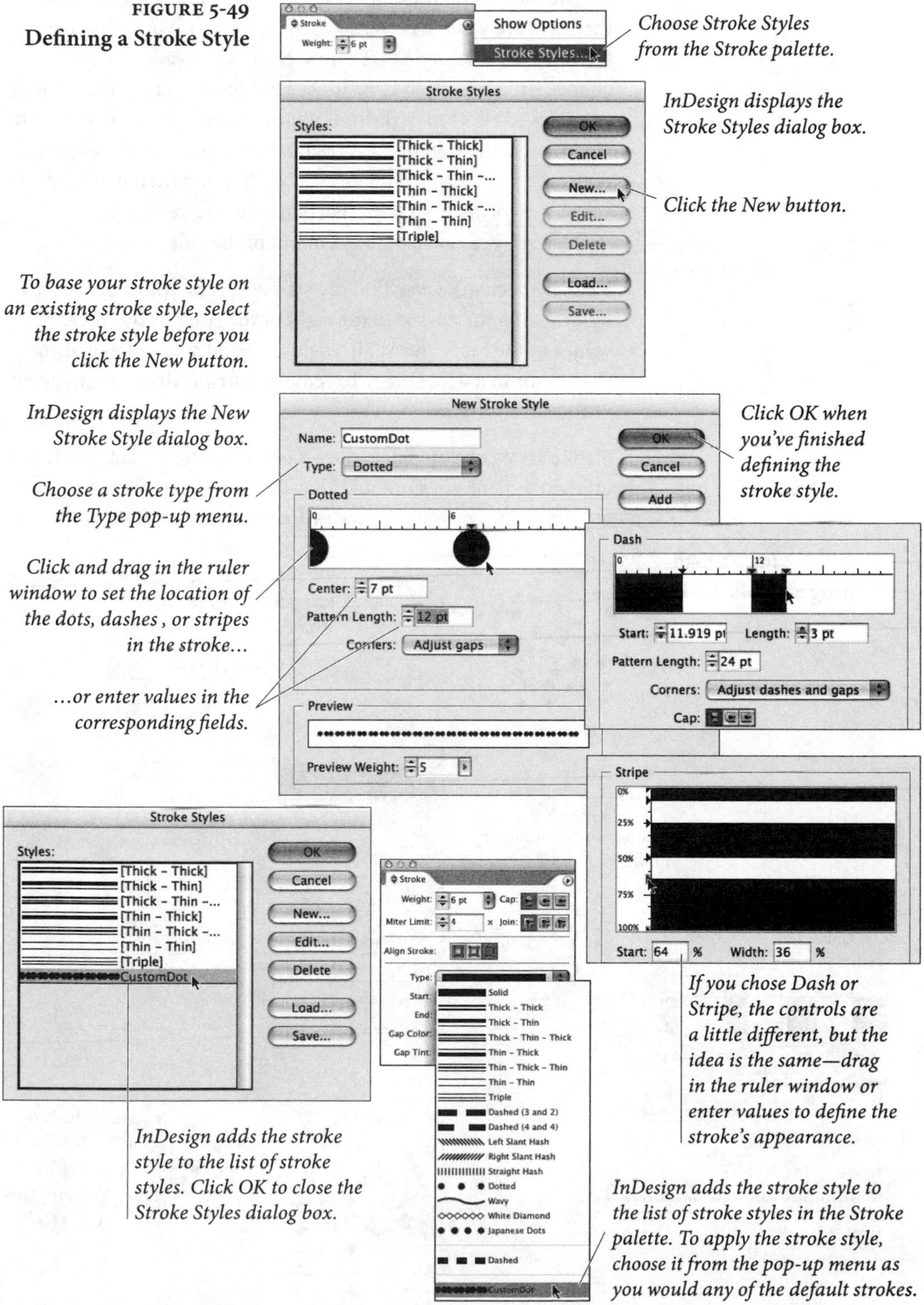
Stroke
Weight: 6 pt
Show Options
Stroke Styles...
Choose Stroke Styles from the Stroke palette.
Stroke Styles
Styles:
[Thick - Thick]
[Thick - Thin]
[Thick - Thin -...
[Thin - Thick]
[Thin - Thick -...
[Thin - Thin]
[Triple]
OK
Cancel
New...
Edit...
Delete
Load...
Save...
InDesign displays the Stroke Styles dialog box.
Click the New button.
To base your stroke style on an existing stroke style, select the stroke style before you click the New button.
New Stroke Style
Name: CustomDot
Type: Dotted
Dotted
Center: 7 pt
Pattern Length: 12 pt
Corners: Adjust gaps
Preview
Preview Weight: 5
OK
Cancel
Add
InDesign displays the New Stroke Style dialog box.
Click OK when you've finished defining the stroke style.
Choose a stroke type from the Type pop-up menu.
Click and drag in the ruler window to set the location of the dots, dashes, or stripes in the stroke...
...or enter values in the corresponding fields.
Dash
Start: 11.919 pt
Length: 3 pt
Pattern Length: 24 pt
Corners: Adjust dashes and gaps
Cap:
Stripe
0%
25%
50%
75%
100%
Start: 64 %
Width: 36 %
If you chose Dash or Stripe, the controls are a little different, but the idea is the same—drag in the ruler window or enter values to define the stroke's appearance.
Stroke Styles
Styles:
[Thick - Thick]
[Thick - Thin]
[Thick - Thin -...
[Thin - Thick]
[Thin - Thick -...
[Thin - Thin]
[Triple]
CustomDot
OK
Cancel
New...
Edit...
Delete
Load...
Save...
InDesign adds the stroke style to the list of stroke styles. Click OK to close the Stroke Styles dialog box.
Stroke
Weight: 6 pt
Cap:
Miter Limit: 4
x Join:
Align Stroke:
Type:
Start:
End:
Gap Color:
Gap Tint:
Solid
Thick - Thick
Thick - Thin
Thick - Thin - Thick
Thin - Thick
Thin - Thick - Thin
Thin - Thin
Triple
Dashed (3 and 2)
Dashed (4 and 4)
Left Slant Hash
Right Slant Hash
Straight Hash
Dotted
Wavy
White Diamond
Japanese Dots
Dashed
CustomDot
InDesign adds the stroke style to the list of stroke styles in the Stroke palette. To apply the stroke style, choose it from the pop-up menu as you would any of the default strokes.

The options on the Corners pop-up menu control the way that dots are adjusted around corners in paths you've applied the dotted stroke style to. Choose None for no adjustment, or choose Adjust Gaps to have InDesign increase or decrease the gap between dots to make dots appear at each point on the path. Note that adjusting the gaps results in uneven spacing between dots on a path, but is probably less distracting than having dots "miss" the corners of a path (particularly on a rectangle).

To remove a dot, drag the dot out of the ruler window.

Stripe. Specify the way that the stripes fill the width of the path by dragging the cursor to the right of the ruler or by entering values in the Start and Width fields. To add a new stripe, drag the cursor in a white area. To remove a stripe, drag the stripe out of the ruler window.

Stroke styles exist inside a document; creating a stroke style in a specific document does not add that stroke style to any other documents. You can copy stroke styles from one document to another.

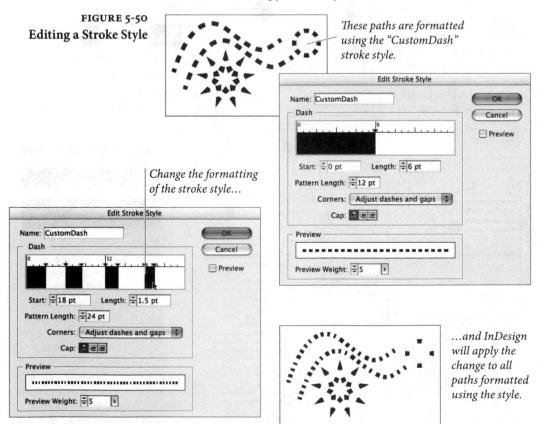

FIGURE 5-50
Editing a Stroke Style

These paths are formatted using the "CustomDash" stroke style.

Change the formatting of the stroke style...

...and InDesign will apply the change to all paths formatted using the style.

You can save and load stroke styles, and you can add stroke styles to all new documents. To add a stroke style to all new documents, create or load the stroke style when no documents are open.

Applying Stroke Styles

You apply stroke styles just as you would apply any of the default stroke types: select an object, then choose the stroke style from the Type pop-up menu in the Stroke palette.

Editing Stroke Styles

To edit a stroke style, choose Stroke Styles from the Stroke palette pop-up menu, select the style from the list of styles in the Stroke Styles dialog box, and click the Edit button. InDesign displays the Edit Stroke Style dialog box.

Make changes to the stroke style definition and close the dialog box, and InDesign will change the appearance of all of the objects you've applied the stroke style to (see Figure 5-50).

Deleting Stroke Styles

To delete a stroke style, choose Stroke Styles from the Stroke palette pop-up menu, select the style from the list of styles in the Stroke Styles dialog box, and click the Delete button.

When you delete a stroke style, InDesign will display a dialog box asking which stroke style you want to use to replace the stroke style you're deleting (see Figure 5-51). Choose a stroke style from the pop-up menu and click the OK button, and InDesign will replace all occurrences of the deleted style with the stroke style you've selected.

FIGURE 5-51
Deleting a Stroke Style

Saving Stroke Styles

To save the stroke styles in your document to a stroke styles file, choose Stroke Styles from the Stroke palette pop-up menu, select the styles you want to save from the list of styles in the Stroke Styles dialog box, and click the Save button. InDesign displays a standard file dialog box where you can choose a location and enter a file name for the saved stroke styles file. Saved InDesign stroke style documents have the file extension ".Inst".

Loading Stroke Styles

To load stroke styles from a saved stroke styles file, choose Stroke Styles from the Stroke palette menu to display the Stroke Styles dialog box, then click the Load button. InDesign displays a standard file dialog box. Locate and select the file you want to load stroke styles from and click OK to load the styles into the current document.

To copy a single stroke style from one document to another, select an object formatted with the stroke style, copy it, and then paste it into another document. InDesign will bring the stroke style along with the object, and you can then delete the object.

Fills

Just as strokes determine what the *outside* of a path looks like, fills specify the appearance of the *inside* of a path. Fills can make the inside of a path a solid color, or a linear or radial gradient. Any path you create can be filled, including open paths.

To apply a fill, select a path and do one of the following.

▶ Click the Fill selector at the top of the Swatches palette, then click a color swatch (see Figure 5-52).

▶ Click the Fill selector at the bottom of the Tools palette, then click the Apply Color button (or press comma). This applies the most recently selected color or swatch (see Figure 5-53).

▶ Drag a swatch out of the Swatches palette or Color palette and drop it on a path (see Figure 5-54). The path doesn't have to be selected.

▶ Click the Fill selector in the Color palette, then define a color in the palette (see Figure 5-55).

FIGURE 5-52
Applying a Fill (Swatches Palette Method)

Select an object.

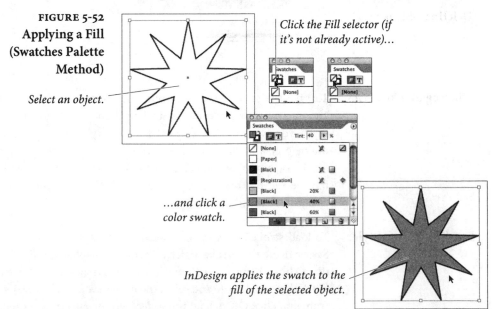

Click the Fill selector (if it's not already active)…

…and click a color swatch.

InDesign applies the swatch to the fill of the selected object.

FIGURE 5-53
Applying a Fill
(Tools Palette Method)

Click the Fill selector (if it's not already active)…

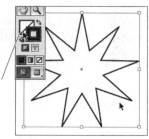

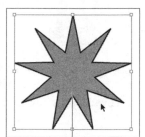

Click the Apply Color button.

InDesign applies the most recently selected swatch to the fill of the selected object.

FIGURE 5-54
Applying a Fill
(Drag and Drop Method)

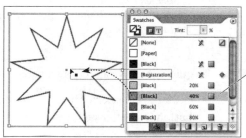

Drag a color swatch out of the Swatches palette…

…and drop it in the interior of a path.

Note that you don't need to select the object when applying a fill using drag and drop.

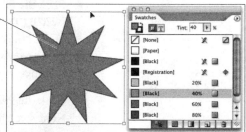

FIGURE 5-55
Applying a Fill
(Color Palette Method)

Select an object.

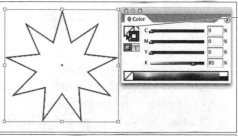

Click the Fill selector in the Color palette (if it's not already active).

Define a color. You can change color models, drag the sliders, enter values in the fields, or click anywhere in the color (as we have in this example).

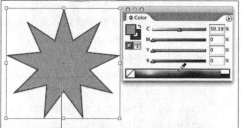

InDesign applies the color to the fill of the object.

> ▸ Select the Eyedropper too. Click an object formatted with the fill you want, then click on another object to apply the fill (see Figure 5-56).

FIGURE 5-56
**Applying a Fill
(Eyedropper Method)**

Use the Eyedropper tool to pick up the color you want from another path…

…and then click the Eyedropper tool on the path you want to format.

Removing Fills   To quickly remove a fill from a path, do one of the following:

> ▸ Click the Fill selector in the Tools palette, then click the None button (or, better yet, press X and then press /).

> ▸ Click the Fill button in the Color palette and then click the None swatch (if you can't see the None swatch, it's because you've hidden the Color palette's option—choose Show Options from the Color palette menu to expand the palette and display the options).

> ▸ Click the Fill button at the bottom of the Toolbox, then click the None swatch in the Swatches palette.

Gradients

A "gradient" is a type of fill or stroke that creates a graduation from one color to another—an effect also known as a "fountain," "blend," or "vignette." InDesign offers two types of gradients: "Linear" and "Radial." For either type of gradient fill, you can set the colors used in the gradient, the rate at which one color blends into another, and the colors used in the gradient (gradients can contain two or more colors). For Linear gradients, you can set the angle that the graduation is to follow.

Linear gradients create a smooth color transition (or series of transitions) from one end of a path to another; Radial gradients create a graduation from the center of a path to its edges. Gradients applied to paths are calculated relative to the geometric bounds of the path; gradients applied to text characters use the geometric bounding box of the text frame containing the text (not the individual characters themselves).

Applying Gradients

To apply a gradient to a path, follow these steps (see Figure 5-57).

1. Select the path using the Selection tool or the Direct Selection tool, or select text using the Text tool or Path Text tool.

2. Do one of the following.

    ▶   Click the Fill or Stroke selector in the Tools palette (to specify which part of the path you want to apply the gradient to). Click the Apply Gradient button at the bottom of the Tools palette.

    ▶   Display the Gradient palette (choose Gradient from the Window menu), and then click the gradient ramp.

    ▶   Click an existing gradient swatch in the Swatches palette (press F5 to display the Swatches palette). You can also drag the gradient swatch out of the Swatches palette and drop it on a path (the path doesn't have to be selected).

    ▶   Select the Eyedropper tool and click an object formatted with a gradient, then click the tool again on the selected path.

    ▶   Select the Gradient tool and drag the tool inside the path.

Gradient Controls

When you create or edit a gradient, you work with InDesign's gradient controls: the gradient ramp, gradient stop icons, and center point icons. What the heck are we talking about? See Figure 5-58.

Creating a Gradient Swatch

In our opinion, the best way to apply gradients is to use the Swatches palette. Just as applying a color from the Swatches palette establishes a link between the color swatch and the object you've applied it to, so applying a gradient swatch links the swatch and the objects you've formatted with it. This means that you can edit the definition of the gradient swatch and update the formatting of all of the objects you've applied the swatch to.

To create a gradient swatch, follow these steps (see Figure 5-59).

1. Select an object formatted using a gradient that has the attributes you want (this step is optional).

2. Display the Swatches palette, if it's not already visible, then choose New Gradient Swatch from the Swatches palette menu. InDesign displays the New Gradient Swatch dialog box. If you

FIGURE 5-57
Applying a Gradient

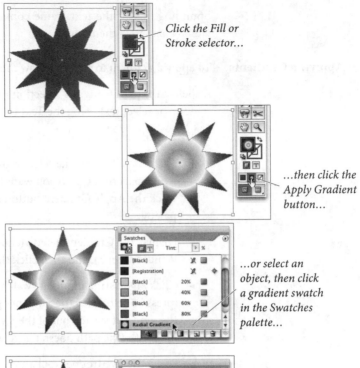

Click the Fill or Stroke selector...

...then click the Apply Gradient button...

...or select an object, then click a gradient swatch in the Swatches palette...

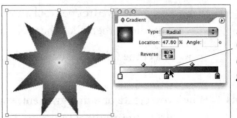

...or display the Gradient palette and click the gradient ramp...

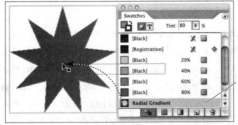

...or drag a gradient swatch out of the Swatches palette...

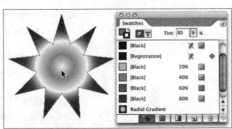

...and drop it on a path (the path does not have to be selected).

FIGURE 5-58
Gradient Controls

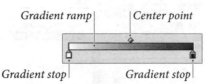

Gradient ramp | *Center point*

Gradient stop | *Gradient stop*

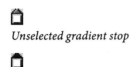

Unselected gradient stop

Selected gradient stop

To change the position of a center point, select it... | *...and then drag it to a new location on the gradient ramp.*

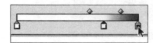 

To change the position of a gradient stop, select it... | *...and then drag it to a new location on the gradient ramp.*

To add a new gradient stop, position the cursor below the gradient ramp... | *...and click.*

To remove a gradient stop, select it... | *...and then drag it away from the gradient ramp.*

selected an object in Step 1, InDesign picks up the attributes of the gradient applied to the object and displays them in this dialog box. If you did not select an object, the controls in the dialog box reflect the document's default gradient formatting.

3. If you're creating a gradient based on the gradient applied to a selected object, enter a name for the gradient swatch (this step is optional) and click the OK button to save the gradient swatch. If you're creating a new gradient swatch "from scratch," specify the colors and gradient stop positions for the gradient. Once the gradient looks the way you want it to, click the OK button to save the gradient swatch. InDesign adds the gradient swatch to the list of swatches in the Swatches palette.

Using the Gradient Palette

You can also apply and edit gradients using the Gradient palette (see Figure 5-60). Like the New Gradient Swatch and Gradient Options dialog boxes, the Gradient palette contains a gradient ramp, with center points above the ramp and gradient stops below.

FIGURE 5-59
**Creating a
Gradient Swatch**

*Choose New Gradient
Swatch from the Swatches
palette menu.*

*InDesign displays the New
Gradient Swatch dialog box.*

*Enter a name for the
gradient (optional,
but a good idea).*

*Set up the gradient. If
you selected an object
formatted using a
gradient, that gradient's
properties will appear here.*

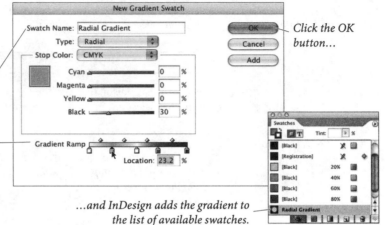

*Click the OK
button...*

*...and InDesign adds the gradient to
the list of available swatches.*

FIGURE 5-60
**Using the
Gradient Palette**

*You use the Gradient palette
to edit the gradient applied
to an object. You could,
as shown in this example,
change the location of the
center point between two
gradient stops.*

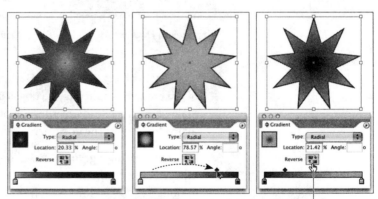

*One thing that the Gradient palette has that you
won't find elsewhere—the Reverse button, which
reverses the direction of the gradient.*

To apply a gradient, select a path, then display the Gradient palette, then click the gradient ramp. InDesign applies the gradient to the selected object.

To edit a gradient you've applied to a path, select the path, then display the Gradient palette (if it's not already visible). InDesign loads the gradient applied to the selected path into the Gradient palette. Adjust the gradient stop positions, or add gradient stops, or change the position of center points or colors, and InDesign applies the changes to the selected path.

Editing Gradients

To edit the color, gradient type, or angle of a gradient you've applied to an object, select the object and then display the Gradient palette. You can use any of the following techniques to change the gradient.

► Drag a gradient stop to a new position on the gradient ramp.

► Select the stop and enter a new value in the Location field.

► Add a new gradient stop by clicking below the gradient ramp.

► Change the position of the center point by dragging it above the gradient ramp. Or you can select the center point and enter a new value in the Location field.

► Remove a stop by dragging it away from the gradient ramp.

► Reverse the gradient ramp by clicking the Reverse button.

► Change the angle of a linear gradient by entering a new value in the Angle field.

► Change the color of a gradient stop using the Swatches palette. To do this, select the stop, then hold down Option/Alt and click a color swatch in the Swatches palette (see Figure 5-61).

► Change the color of a gradient stop to an unnamed color. To do this, select the gradient stop, then display the Color palette. Specify a color. As you change color values in the Color palette, InDesign changes the color applied to the gradient stop.

► Change the gradient type using the Type pop-up menu.

FIGURE 5-61
Getting a Swatch Color into a Gradient Stop

It's something every InDesign user has done at least once—you select a gradient stop, then click a color swatch in the Swatches palette, expecting to apply the color to the gradient stop. Instead, InDesign fills (or strokes) the path with the color. How the heck do you get a swatch color into a gradient stop?

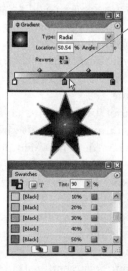

Select a gradient stop.

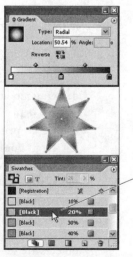

Hold down Option/Alt and click the color swatch in the Swatches palette. InDesign assigns the color to the gradient stop.

Applying a Gradient to Multiple Paths

To apply a gradient to more than one path, select the paths (which need not already have gradients applied to their fills or strokes), then drag the Gradient tool. The point at which you start dragging defines the starting point of the gradient (see Figure 5-62).

FIGURE 5-62

Applying a Gradient to Multiple Objects

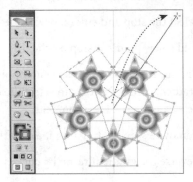

Select a series of paths. In this example, each path has been formatted using a radial gradient fill. Position the Gradient tool over the point at which you want to place the center point (for a radial gradient) or start (for a linear gradient), and then drag the tool.

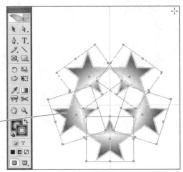

InDesign applies a single gradient to the selected paths.

Transparency

If this were an introductory logic class, rather than a somewhat illogical computer book, we could present the following syllogism: PostScript's basic drawing model does not allow for transparency; InDesign is a PostScript-oriented page layout program. Therefore, it follows that you cannot have transparent objects in InDesign. Right?

Well…not quite.

While PostScript itself does not handle transparency, InDesign's drawing model—the part of the software that draws elements on the screen—can. So how does InDesign print transparent objects to a PostScript printer? Simple: it cheats. When the time comes to print, InDesign does what Illustrator and FreeHand (and possibly Corel-DRAW, we have no idea) users have done for years—it uses clipping paths to create the illusion of transparency and/or rasterizes the transparent objects and sends the printer separated image data. All of this takes place in the background—InDesign does not change the objects in your document. Instead, it changes the way that the objects are sent to the printer.

The way that InDesign sends the transparent objects to the printer is defined by the Transparency Flattener settings for the spread containing the objects. Flattener settings are described in Chapter 11, "Printing." As a rule of thumb, however, transparent objects make documents somewhat harder to print, and putting one transparent object on top of another transparent object can make a document much harder to print.

This brings us to our patented "With Power Comes Responsibility" speech. It's very easy to come up with combinations of transparent objects and flattener settings that create a document that is impossible to print on any PostScript printer. It's also easy to create documents that can slow a printer to a crawl, or to produce files that take up enormous amounts of space on your hard drive.

This doesn't mean that you should avoid using transparency. That would be silly, given that there's sometimes no other way to create a specific creative effect. It's just that you must bear in mind that using the feature comes at a cost, and that you need to weigh the potential risks (slow printing, no printing) against the benefit (a cool layout).

If you're familiar with Photoshop's approach to transparency, you'll find InDesign's a bit different: In Photoshop, transparency is an attribute of layers; in InDesign, transparency is an attribute of individual page items. Transparency applies equally to the fill and stroke of an item; you cannot apply one level of transparency to the fill and another to the stroke.

Applying Transparency

To apply transparency to a page item, work your way through the following steps (see Figure 5-63).

1. Select a page item.

2. Display the Transparency palette, if it's not already visible (choose Transparency from the Window menu).

3. Choose an option from the Blending Mode pop-up menu, if necessary.

4. Drag the transparency slider or enter a value in the Opacity field.

Blending Modes

The transparency blending modes define the way that the colors in the transparent objects interact with objects that fall behind them (see Color Figure 10 on the color pages).

When you apply transparency, InDesign calculates the resulting color based on each color component of the foreground and background colors. For two overlapping process colors, for example, the

FIGURE 5-63
Applying Transparency
to an Object

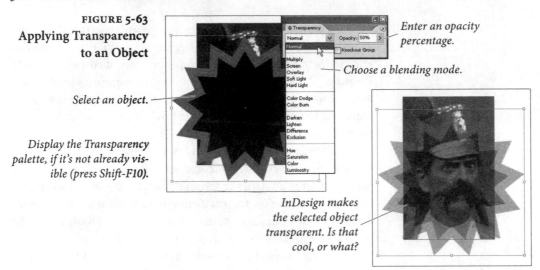

Select an object.

Display the Transparency
palette, if it's not already visible (press Shift-F10).

Enter an opacity
percentage.

Choose a blending mode.

InDesign makes
the selected object
transparent. Is that
cool, or what?

effect of the blending mode will almost certainly differ for each of the four inks. When we say that a blending mode behaves in a particular way for a specific gray percentage value, we mean the percentage of a color component.

The effect of a blending mode is dependent on the current color management settings. The ink values of the colors in a stack of transparent objects, for example, will never exceed the maximum ink coverage for the current color management profile. (For the sake of your press operator's sanity, don't try to prove us wrong.)

The following notes provide a quick description of the most useful of the blending modes. In these descriptions, the term "foreground color" refers to the color applied to the front-most object; "background color" refers to the color of the background object, and "resulting color" is the color you see where the two objects intersect.

Normal. The Normal blending mode adds the foreground color to the background color. If the foreground color is black, and the opacity percentage is 10%, then 10% black is added to the background color to produce the resulting color. The Normal blending mode at 100% opacity turns transparency off.

Multiply. The Multiply blending mode always results in a darker color. The one exception is when the foreground color is white or Paper color, in which case this blending mode has no effect at all. Multiply is very similar to overprinting one object over another (see Chapter 10, "Color," for more on overprinting), or overlapping lines when drawing with felt pens. We think the Multiply blend mode is the best choice for drop shadows (see below).

Screen. This blending mode almost always produces a resulting color that is lighter than the background color (unless the foreground color is black, which has no effect in this mode). The best real-world definition of this blending mode comes from Adobe's Russell Brown: Screen is like projecting two slides on the same screen. The result is always lighter than either of the two sources. If the background color is black or white, the background color remains unchanged.

Overlay. The Overlay blending mode compares the foreground and background colors, accentuating highlights and shadows in each by lightening light colors and darkening dark colors. If either the foreground or background color is 50-percent gray, then this mode has no effect. Overlay increases color contrast and can get out of hand quickly; we usually reduce the Opacity slider to temper the effect.

Soft Light. While most people describe the Soft Light blending mode as shining a soft spotlight on the background color, we like to think of this mode in terms of playing with semi-translucent colored acetate. Soft Light has no effect if the background color is black or white, but it subtly enhances any other color, making darker colors (in either the foreground or background) a little darker and lighter colors a little lighter.

Hard Light. The Hard Light mode is something like two blending modes in one: If the foreground color is lighter than 50-percent gray, the Hard Light mode lightens the background color similar to the Screen mode; if the foregrond color is darker than 50-percent gray, it darkens it using a method similar to the Multiply mode.

Darken. The resulting color is equal to the darker of the foreground and background colors.

Lighten. The resulting color is equal to the lighter of the foreground and background colors.

Hue. The Hue blending mode creates a new color by blending the color of the foreground object with the luminance (brightness) and saturation of the background. Putting a black object set to Hue over a colored object simply desaturates the background colors.

Saturation. The Saturation mode creates a new color by blending the foreground color's saturation and the hue (color) with luminance values of the background color.

Color. The Color mode is slightly different from the Hue mode; it combines the color and the saturation of the foreground color with with the luminance of the background color. Placing a solid color set to Color over an image colorizes the image, like a fake duotone.

Luminosity. Luminosity creates a new color by blending the brightness of the foreground color with the hue and saturation of the background color.

Transparency Options

So what about those options at the bottom of the Transparency palette? The meaning of the terms "Isolate Blending" and "Knockout Group" is hardly self evident. Both options apply only to groups.

Isolate Blending. When you turn on the Isolate Blending option, and objects in the group you've selected use blending modes other than the Normal blending mode, InDesign changes the way that the object in the group interact with objects behind the group. Regardless of the blending mode you've assigned to the group objects, InDesign treats them as if the Normal blending mode were assigned. *Inside* the group, blending modes behave as you specified (see Figure 5-64).

FIGURE 5-64
Isolate Blending

The selected group contains three circles. Each circle is filled with Black, set to 50% transparency, and uses the Multiply blending mode.

The half circle is outside and behind the group.

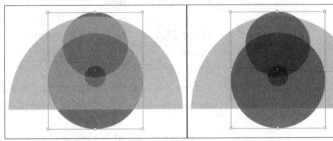

With Isolate Blending turned off, the foreground colors blend with the background colors according to their blending modes.

Turn Isolate Blending on, and InDesign changes the way that the foreground colors interact with the background colors.

Knockout Group. When you select a group containing transparent objects and turn on the Knockout Group option, InDesign makes the objects in the group opaque to each other (see Figure 5-65). In other words, the option should really be named "Knockout Objects Inside the Group," but there's not room in the palette. Objects *outside* the group are treated according to the state of the Isolate Blending option (see above). And yes, it is possible to have both Isolate Blending and Knockout Group turned on (see Figure 5-66).

FIGURE 5-65
Knockout Group

The selected group contains three circles. Each circle is filled with Black, set to 50% transparency, and uses the Multiply blending mode.

The half circle is outside and behind the group.

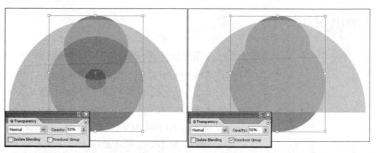

With Knockout Group turned off, the objects inside the group affect each other.

Turn on Knockout Group, and the objects in the group become opaque to each other, but are still transparent to any background objects.

FIGURE 5-66
Isolate Blending Plus Knockout Group

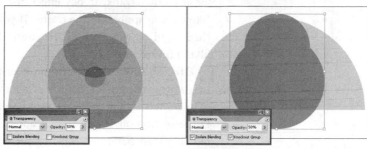

Both options off.

Objects inside the group knock each other out, and the group behaves as if the Normal blending option is applied to all members of the group.

Groups and Transparency

There's a difference between applying transparency to a group and applying transparency to the objects inside a group (see Figure 5-67). When you apply transparency to a group, InDesign will override the transparency settings for any objects in the group that have no transparency applied to them, but leaves transparent objects unchanged.

FIGURE 5-67
Applying Transparency to a Group

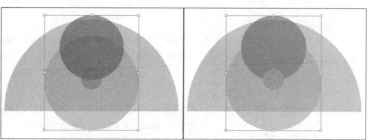

This group contains three circles. Each circle is filled with a tint of Black, and each uses the Multiply blending mode.

This is the same group of objects, but the 50% transparency has been applied to the group rather than to each individual object.

Drop Shadows

What is it about drop shadows? Does everyone want their page items to appear as if they are the highly mobile space battleship *Nadesico*, floating defiantly above the page? We're not sure, but we do know that these ubiquitous two-dimensional impersonations of three-dimensional space are something no graphic designer will leave home without—at least until clients stop asking for them.

Any object on an InDesign page can have a drop shadow, and you can control the offset distance, color, transparency, noise, and sharpness/blur of the shadow. Note that you cannot apply a drop shadow (or any other transparency effect, for that matter) to text in a text frame—you apply it to the frame. If you want a text *frame* to have a shadow, fill it with Paper; if you want the shadow on the characters, fill the frame with None.

Drop shadows come with many of the same cautions and warnings as transparency; used to excess, they can make a page difficult to print. Rather than repeat a rant here, we'll simply direct you back to the section on Transparency, above, on the benefits and dangers of using transparent objects in your page layouts. In short: It's OK, but use caution.

To apply a drop shadow follow these steps (see Figure 5-68).

1. Select an object.

2. Choose Drop Shadow from the Context menu or Object menu. InDesign displays the Drop Shadow dialog box.

3. Turn on the Drop Shadow option (that's why you're here, after all), and then use the controls in the dialog box to specify the appearance of the drop shadow. It helps to turn on the Preview option—this way, you can see what you're doing without having to close the dialog box.

4. When you're through adjusting the drop shadow settings, click the OK button to apply the drop shadow.

Drop Shadow Controls   The Opacity field and its associated pop-up menu control the opacity or transparency of the drop shadow (see Figure 5-69).

The Mode pop-up menu sets the transparency blending mode for the drop shadow. We've described all of the useful blending modes in the section on Transparency, above. The Multiply blending mode works well with drop shadows. On the other hand, you can create a

FIGURE 5-68
Applying a Drop Shadow

Typical Display

High Quality Display

Display performance settings have a big effect on the way that InDesign displays drop shadows, but not on how they print; that's up to the transparency flattener.

You can change the color mode to CMYK, RGB, or LAB, or swatches.

Select an object

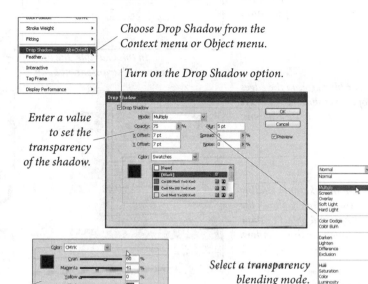

Choose Drop Shadow from the Context menu or Object menu.

Turn on the Drop Shadow option.

Enter a value to set the transparency of the shadow.

Select a transparency blending mode.

Click the OK button, and InDesign applies the drop shadow.

pretty cool glow around an object by making a light-colored drop shadow with zero offsets, and setting the Mode to Screen. For a color illustration of the blending modes, see Color Figure 10.

The X Offset and Y Offset fields define the distance (in horizontal and vertical measurement units, respectively) by which the drop shadow is offset from the selected object (see Figure 5-70).

A hard-edged shadow is probably not what you were looking for—what you need is a way to soften the edges of the shadow so that it looks more realistic. That's exactly what the Blur field does (see Figure 5-71). If you want a more realistic shadow (instead of a mathematically pure one), bump up the Noise field a little bit—just 4 or 5 percent noise makes a huge difference (see Figure 5-72). Noise values above 30 or 40 percent are mostly good for special grunge effects.

FIGURE 5-69
Shadow Transparency

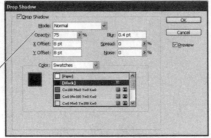
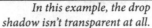

The blending mode and the Opacity field set the transparency of the drop shadow.

In this example, the drop shadow isn't transparent at all.

The blur around the edges of a drop shadow is always partly transparent.

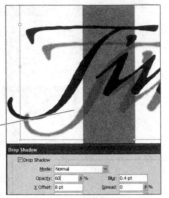
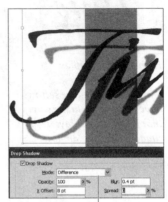

In this example, adding transparency allows the background object to show through the drop shadow.

You can use any of InDesign's blending modes to change the transparency of a drop shadow.

FIGURE 5-70
Drop Shadow Offset

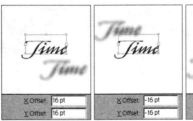

Use the X Offset (horizontal) and Y Offset (vertical) fields to position the shadow relative to the object.

Entering negative values in the X Offset field moves the shadow to the left; in the Y Offset field, negative values move the shadow up.

You can define the color of the drop shadow using swatches, or by creating a color using the RGB, CMYK, or LAB color models (switch among these color models using the Color pop-up menu).

The Spread field controls the intensity of the shadow. Technically, it controls how far out from the center of the shadow the darkest portion of the shadow will sit. Choosing 50 percent means the darkest area of the shadow takes up half the size of the shadow (which is determined by the Blur value).

FIGURE 5-71
Blur and Spread

Enter a value in the Blur field to control the diffusion of the drop shadow. Entering zero produces a hard-edged (but still bitmapped)shadow.

Entering a large blur value would make the shadow disappear altogether for this 24-point example text.

Increasing the Spread value makes the shadow more dense.

FIGURE 5-72
Shadow Noise

Feathering

The usual definition of feathering goes something like this: "feathering softens the edges of page items." This isn't really quite true. Feathering softens the *interior*—the fill or contents—of a page item around the edges of the page item. You can see the difference if you try applying a feather to some text; we keep expecting this would make the text look blurry, such as what you get with a drop shadow. Not so. Our disappointment aside, feathering is a useful addition to InDesign's path formatting features.

To apply the feathering effect to an object, follow these steps (see Figure 5-73).

1. Select an object.

2. Choose Feather from the Context menu or Object menu.

3. Turn on the Feather option.

4. Enter a value for feather width. This sets the distance from the edges of the object at which the feathering will take effect. Choose an option from the Corner pop-up menu (these options are described below). Turn on the Preview option if you want to see the effect before you close the dialog box.

5. Click the OK button to apply the effect.

FIGURE 5-73
Feathering

Select a page item.

Click the Feather option.

Enter a value for the width of the effect.

Choose a corner option from the Corners pop-up menu.

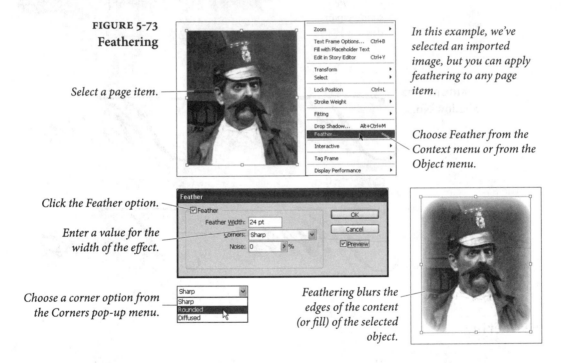

In this example, we've selected an imported image, but you can apply feathering to any page item.

Choose Feather from the Context menu or from the Object menu.

Feathering blurs the edges of the content (or fill) of the selected object.

Feather Corner Options

The options on the Corners pop-up menu control the appearance of the feathering effect as it approaches sharp corners at the edges of the object (see Figure 5-74).

Sharp. When you choose the Sharp option, the feathering effect follows the outline of the path as closely as possible.

Rounded. When you choose Rounded, InDesign rounds the edges of the feather effect as it nears sharp corners.

FIGURE 5-74
Feather Corner Options

While the Rounded corner option probably isn't a good match with the example star polygon, it's great for creating beveled buttons.

The edges of the Diffused ——— corner effect fade from opaque to transparent.

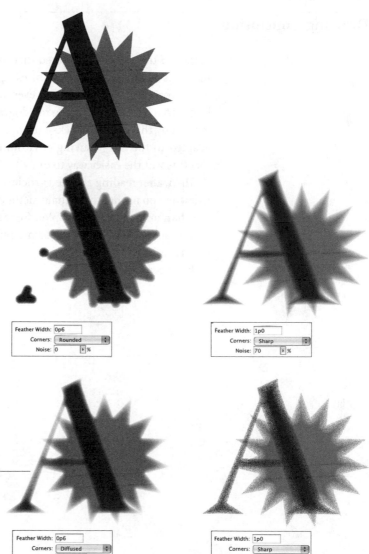

Diffused. This effect provides a general fade from opaque to transparent, based on the geometric center of the object, rather than on the shape of the path (as is the case for the Sharp and Rounded options). This is similar to the feathering effect in Illustrator.

Noise. Adding a little noise to your feather (such as four or five percent) makes the effect significantly more realistic, especially if you're blending an object into a photographic background. (Real life is noisy. But not too noisy.)

Drawing Conclusions

Earlier in this chapter, we noted that we found the process of drawing paths using Bezier curves confusing when we first encountered it. As we worked with the tools, however, we found that the parts of our brains that were used to using rapidographs (an obsolete type of pen favored by the ancient Greeks), triangles, curves, and rulers quickly adapted to the new drawing environment. Eventually, we realized that this was the easier way to draw.

Then, after reading a related article in a tabloid at the supermarket, it dawned on us that the archaic methods we'd learned were nothing less than an extraterrestrial plot, forced on us in classical antiquity by evil space gods, to some cosmic purpose which we cannot—as yet—reveal.

Just keep at it.

Where Text Meets Graphics

Usually, we think of text and graphics as occupying two different, but parallel, universes. But there's an area—a Twilight Zone, something like a Bermuda Triangle of page layout—where the boundary between text and graphics blurs, frays, or becomes thin.

In this strange dimension, text characters can be bound to paths, or become paths, graphics can be embedded in text and behave as if they were text characters, and nothing, nothing is what it seems.

In spite of the repeated warnings of our scientific colleagues, we must, for the sake of humanity, tell what we have discovered in this alien landscape.

Paragraph Rules

Ole laments, "I haven't looked at the PageMaker 3.0 documentation recently. I don't have to—it is forever burned into my memory.

"A feature of that manual's design was a rule drawn below a particular, and very common, heading. I know this, because I was one of the four people who put those rules there. For every one of those headings, one of us had to zoom in, measure from the baseline of the text in the heading, position a ruler guide, and then draw a rule. When the position of the heading changed, as it often did, we had to zoom in again, measure again, and move or redraw the rules.

"I still dream about it."

Which is part of the reason we like the paragraph rules feature found in PageMaker, QuarkXPress, and InDesign these days. Rules (or "lines") can be part of your paragraph's formatting (or, better yet, part of a paragraph style definition), and the rules you specify follow your paragraph wherever it happens to go.

Applying Paragraph Rules

To apply a paragraph rule to a paragraph, follow these steps (see Figure 6-1):

1. Select the paragraph (remember, you don't need to highlight the entire paragraph—all you need to do is click the Type tool somewhere inside the paragraph).

2. Choose Paragraph Rules from the Paragraph palette menu (or press Command-Option-J/Ctrl-Alt-J). InDesign displays the Paragraph Rules dialog box.

3. Choose the type of paragraph rule (Rule Above or Rule Below) from the Rule Type pop-up menu, then turn on the Rule On option.

4. Set the rule options you want using the controls in the panel. If you turn on the Preview option, you can watch InDesign apply the paragraph rule to the paragraph as you adjust the settings.

5. Click OK to apply the paragraph rule settings to the selected paragraph, or click Cancel to close the dialog box without applying the rule.

Ground Rules for Paragraph Rules

Paragraphs can have up to two rules attached to them. One rule can be positioned on or above the baseline of the first line of text in a paragraph (InDesign calls this the "Rule Above"); the other line can be positioned at or below the baseline of the last line of the paragraph

FIGURE 6-1
**Applying a
Paragraph Rule**

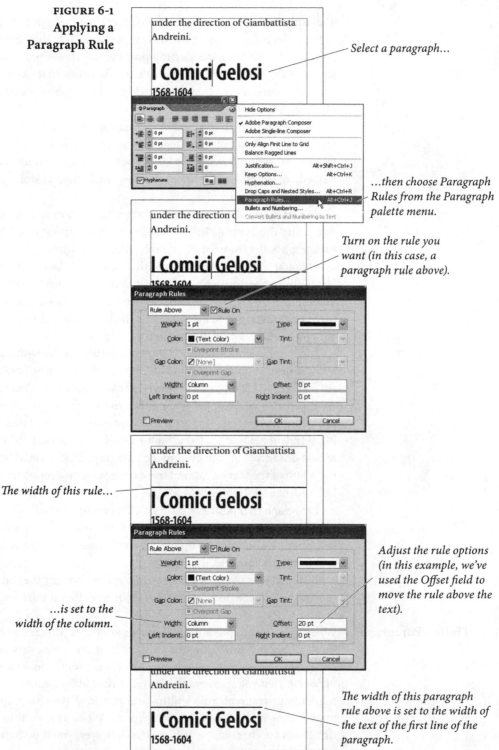

Select a paragraph…

…then choose Paragraph
Rules from the Paragraph
palette menu.

Turn on the rule you
want (in this case, a
paragraph rule above).

The width of this rule…

Adjust the rule options
(in this example, we've
used the Offset field to
move the rule above the
text).

…is set to the
width of the column.

The width of this paragraph
rule above is set to the width of
the text of the first line of the
paragraph.

(the "Rule Below"). You can't have two rules above a single paragraph, or two rules below, without trickery (see below). Note that these rule positions specify only the starting point of the rule—by manipulating the rule width, it's easy to create a rule below that extends far above the baseline, or a rule above that extends far below the baseline of the last line.

Paragraph rules, like any other paths you can draw in InDesign, can be up to 1000 points wide, and the stroke width can be specified in .001-point increments. Like other paths you can use dotted, dashed, or multi-line (striped) strokes, including custom stroke styles you've created.

You set the position at which InDesign starts drawing a paragraph rule using the controls in the Paragraph Rules dialog box (choose Paragraph Rules from the Paragraph palette menu).

Paragraph rules above grow *up* (that is, toward the top of the text frame) from the position you specify in the Offset field in the Paragraph Rules dialog box; rules below grow *down* (toward the bottom of the text frame) as you increase their stroke weight. InDesign draws paragraph rules *behind* the text in the text frame.

You can base the width of a paragraph rule on the width of the text column or on the width of the text in the first (for paragraph rules above) or last (for rules below) line of the paragraph. Paragraph rules can also be indented from either the width of the column or the width of the text—the value you enter in the Left Indent and Right Indent fields of the Paragraph Rules dialog box determines the indent distance. You can even make paragraph rules extend beyond the width of the text or column by entering negative numbers in the Left Indent and Right Indent fields.

Paragraph rule positions have no effect on the vertical spacing of text. If you want to make room above a paragraph for a paragraph rule above, or below a paragraph for a rule below, you can use paragraph space before and after.

You can't select or manipulate paragraph rules using the Selection tool or the Direct Selection tool. Everyone tries this at least once.

Tinting Paragraphs   When you want to put a tint behind a paragraph (which you might want to do for a sidebar, a line in a table, or for a note or warning paragraph in your text), paragraph rules are the way to go—provided, of course, that your paragraph isn't taller than 1000 points or so (the maximum paragraph rule width), and provided the paragraph fits inside a single text frame or text column. (When you want to put a tint behind a character, word, or line, however, you'll be better off using custom strikethrough rules and/or underlines.)

To use a paragraph rule to add a tint behind a paragraph, follow these steps (see Figure 6-2).

1. Calculate the height of the paragraph by adding up the leading of the lines in the paragraph.

2. Select the paragraph, then use the Paragraph Rules dialog box to apply a paragraph rule below. Use the Weight field to set the stroke width of the rule to at least the height of the paragraph.

3. Use the Color pop-up menu to set the color of the paragraph rule.

4. Enter a value in the Offset field to move the paragraph rule up or down behind the paragraph (remember, a negative value in the Offset field moves a paragraph rule below toward the top of the paragraph).

5. When the paragraph rule looks the way you want it to, click the OK button to apply it to the selected paragraph.

FIGURE 6-2
Placing a Tint Behind a Paragraph

Select a paragraph.

Display the Paragraph Rules dialog box and add a rule below.

Make the stroke weight of the rule at least equal to the sum of the leading of the lines in the paragraph.

Move the rule up or down by entering values in the Offset field (we usually start with the stroke weight, then add or subtract smaller values to fine-tune the rule position).

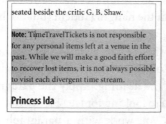

Putting a Box Around a Paragraph Using Paragraph Rules

Are you thinking what we're thinking? If the paragraph rule below overprints the paragraph rule above, and both rules fall behind the text in the paragraph, then you ought to be able to create a "box" around a paragraph by cleverly manipulating the width, height, and offset of the paragraph rules above and below. You can do just that, as shown in Figure 6-3.

Note that you can also accomplish this effect with a table containing a single cell to (see "Tables," later in this chapter) or with an anchored object (see "Inline Frames and Anchored Objects," much later in this chapter).

FIGURE 6-3
Using Paragraph Rules to Create a Box Around a Paragraph

Set the rule above so that it covers the area behind the paragraph.

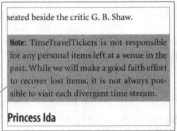

Set the rule below so it covers an area slightly smaller (in this example, two points smaller on all sides). Set the rule color to "Paper."

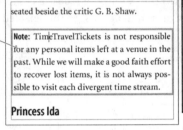

Note the values in the Left Indent, Right Indent, Weight, and Offset fields.

Hanging Your Head in a Bar

Here's an effect you see often—a heading, set in a hanging indent, and knocked out of a paragraph rule. There's no trick to it—you use the same approach described earlier, but this time you use a paragraph rule above and set the width of the rule so that it falls behind any text in the hanging indent (but not behind the text in the body of the paragraph).

To do this, set the right indent for the rule to at least the width of the body of the paragraph. Set the weight of the stroke to at least the height of the heading. Apply the paragraph rule, and you've got the effect you're looking for (see Figure 6-4).

When you work with a paragraph rule (or anything else) that extends beyond the edges of a text frame, InDesign sometimes forgets to redraw the rules when you edit text in the text frame. Don't worry—the rules are still there. To see them again, force InDesign to redraw the screen by pressing Shift-F5.

FIGURE 6-4
**Hanging Headings
and Paragraph Rules**

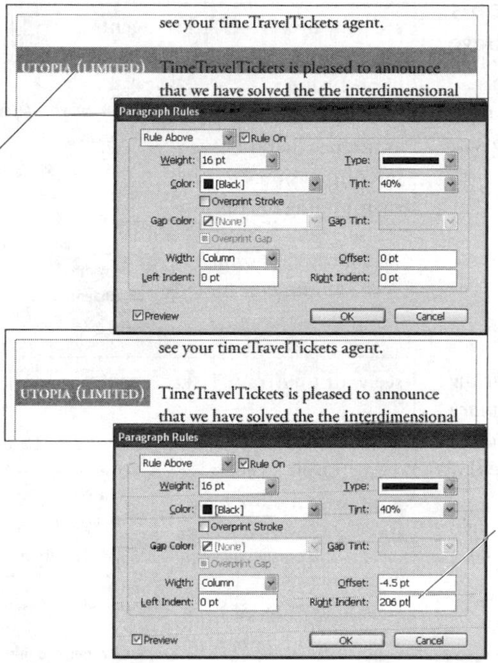

*Set the text color of
the heading to "Paper."*

*Add a paragraph rule
above that's (roughly)
the height of the
heading.*

*Set the value in the
Right Indent field to the
width of the body text
column (plus a bit, if
you want some space
between the heading
and the body copy).*

Two Rules Above   What can you do when one rule above isn't enough—when your design calls for two rules above your paragraph? A common design specification calls for two rules above a heading: a thin rule the width of the column and a thick rule the width of the text in the heading. How can you accomplish this using InDesign's paragraph rules? It's easy, as shown in the following steps (see Figure 6-5).

1. Select a paragraph.

2. For the paragraph rule below, choose Column from the Width pop-up menu, then enter a negative value in the Offset field that positions the rule above the tops of the characters in the first line of the paragraph (this will be something like the sum of the leading values in the paragraph). Set the line weight to a hairline (.25 points) or so.

3. For the rule above, choose Text from the Width pop-up menu, then set the stroke weight of the paragraph rule to something thicker than the stroke weight of the rule below (4 points, for example). Set the value in the Offset field so that the top edge of the rule above touches the bottom of the rule below.

More Than Two Rules   When you need to attach more than two rules above or below a paragraph, enter extra carriage returns before or after the paragraph, then

*For the paragraph
rule above...*

see your timeTravelTickets agent.

Utopia Limited
TimeTravelTickets is plea
announce that we have s
interdimensional technic
surrounding the openin

...enter a thick stroke weight...

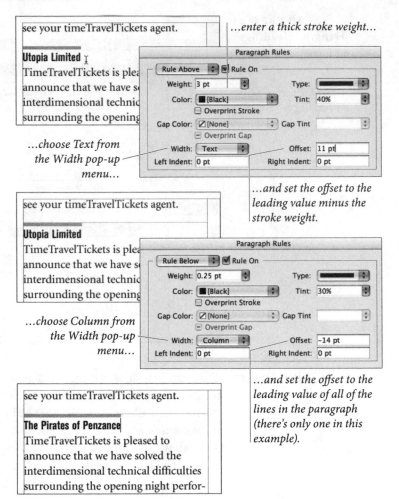

*...choose Text from
the Width pop-up
menu...*

*...and set the offset to the
leading value minus the
stroke weight.*

*For the paragraph rule below
(which we're going to place
above the paragraph—don't
get confused)...*

see your timeTravelTickets agent.

Utopia Limited
TimeTravelTickets is plea
announce that we have s
interdimensional technic
surrounding the openin

*...enter a thin stroke weight
(such as a hairline)...*

*...choose Column from
the Width pop-up
menu...*

*...and set the offset to the
leading value of all of the
lines in the paragraph
(there's only one in this
example).*

*When you change the **text**
in the first line, InDesign
changes the width of **the**
thicker **rule**.*

see your timeTravelTickets agent.

The Pirates of Penzance
TimeTravelTickets is pleased to
announce that we have solved the
interdimensional technical difficulties
surrounding the opening night perfor-

apply paragraph rules to the resulting "blank" paragraphs. You can
even set the leading of the empty paragraphs to zero, which keeps
the empty paragraphs from disturbing the leading of the other text
in the text column (see Figure 6-6). You can then use the Keep with
Next settings of the empty paragraphs to make them "stick" to the
original paragraph. Another solution is to use above line or anchored
objects, which is probably more effective.

*The range of possible design
effects is limited only by your
imagination. (Our imagina-
tions are running a little
thin, right at the moment.)*

Tables

Ole sees tables everywhere. He thinks they're the most common method of presenting text. This quirk is probably due to the time he spent typesetting a magazine devoted to horse racing (and its infamous "stud listing"), but he can be forgiven—tables really *are* everywhere. Looked at the business or sports section of a newspaper lately? Or a data sheet for that nifty new computer you want to buy? Or a calendar?

Tables are everywhere because they're a great way to present information that falls naturally into a set sequence of categories. If tables are so useful, why are they universally hated and despised by desktop publishing users? Since the dawn of the page layout era, creating tables has been a bother—programs that supported tables (Microsoft Word, FrameMaker, and Ventura Publisher, for example) didn't have the typesetting and color management features graphic arts professionals expect; popular page layout programs (such as PageMaker and QuarkXPress) lacked tools for tabular composition. Plug-ins and stand-alone table-editing programs attempted to provide the feature, but, frankly, never worked very well.

The desktop publishing field has been waiting for someone to "do tables right" in a page layout program.

InDesign can create and edit tables, or import tables from Word, Excel, or XML. How good is this feature? It's not perfect, but it's more than good enough to alleviate most of the pain of working with tables in a layout.

Table Anatomy

Tables are a matrix; a grid made up of *rows* (horizontal subdivisions) and *columns* (vertical subdivisions). The area defined by the intersection of a given row and column is called a *cell*. InDesign has a complete vocabulary of terms for the various parts of rows, columns, and cells, which we've attempted to explain in Figure 6-7.

Understanding InDesign Tables

Now that we've got the terminology out of the way, but before we dive into the details of working with tables in InDesign, there are a few conceptual points we'd like to make, as follows.

- ▶ Tables exist inside text frames. There is no "Table tool"—you create a text frame and then add a table to it, or convert text in the text frame to a table.

- ▶ From the point of view of the text frame (or story), a table acts like a single character (albeit a potentially *very large* one). Another way to look at a table is to think of it as a special type

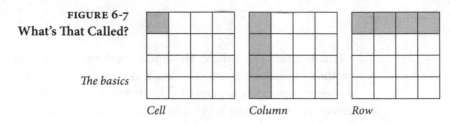

FIGURE 6-7
What's That Called?

The basics

Cell   Column   Row

|Heading row made up of merged cells

A somewhat more complex example

Table border ——

These cells have been filled with a tint.

Rotated merged cells make up these side headings.

I Gelosi (1500-1604)	
CHARACTER	ACTOR
Pantalone *or* Magnifico	Giulio Pasquati
Zanobio da Piombino	Girolamo Salimboni
Dottore Gratiano Forbisoni	Ludovico *of Bologna*
Capitano Spavento della Valle Inferna	Francesco Andreini
Prima Donna	Isabella Andreini
Burattino	Unknown
Arlecchino	Simone *of Bologne*
Franchechina	Silvia Roncagli
Lesbino	Silvia Roncagli
Riccciolina	Maria Antonazzoni
Olivetta	Unknown

(Side headings: PRINCIPAL ROLES, SERVANTS)

of inline frame. Like a character, a table changes position as you add or delete text preceding it in its parent story; like an inline frame, you can't apply character formatting (point size, font, or leading) to the character containing the table.

▶ Like text, tables can flow from column to column, text frame to text frame, and from page to page. Table header and footer rows can automatically repeat when the table breaks across multiple text objects. An individual table row cannot be broken from one text frame to another or from one column to another.

▶ Table cells are something akin to text frames: they can contain text, which can contain inline graphics, text frames, or tables. Any and all of InDesign's typesetting features can be used on the text in a table cell, including character and paragraph styles, indents, tab stops, and character formatting.

▶ Table cells can automatically expand (vertically) to display their content.

▶ Tables are not only for formatting tabular data—they're useful for a number of other things. Want to put a box around a paragraph? Convert the paragraph to a single-cell table. Want to compose paragraphs "side by side"? Use a two-column table (note that this can be one way to create hanging side heads). The number of possible uses are, as the cliché goes, "limited only by your imagination" and/or good sense/taste. But we're getting ahead of ourselves, as usual.

Creating a Table

There are (at least) four ways to create a table.

▶ **"From scratch."** Click the Type tool inside an existing text frame, then choose Insert Table from the Table menu. InDesign displays the Insert Table dialog box. Enter the number of rows and columns you want in the corresponding fields and click the OK button. InDesign creates the table (see Figure 6-8).

Once you've created a table using this approach, you can add text or graphics to the table the same way you would add text to any text frame—click the Type tool inside a cell, then enter text, or paste text or graphics, or place text or graphics into the cell.

FIGURE 6-8
Creating a Table
"From Scratch"

Click the Type tool in a text frame.

Choose Insert Table from the Table menu (or press Command-Option-T/ Ctrl-Alt-T).

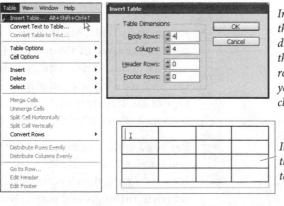

InDesign displays the Insert Table dialog box. Enter the number of rows and columns you want and click OK.

InDesign inserts the table into the text frame.

▶ **Converting Text to a Table.** To turn a range of text into a table, select the text and choose Convert Text to Table from the Table Menu. InDesign displays the Convert Text to Table dialog box. Select the delimiter characters you want to use, and specify the number of columns, if necessary (InDesign will only display this field when it cannot determine the number of columns in the table, given the specified delimiter characters). Click OK, and

InDesign converts the selected text to a table, using the delimiter characters to split the text into table rows and columns (see Figure 6-9).

FIGURE 6-9
Converting Text to a Table

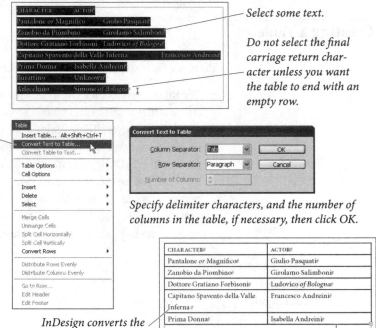

Select some text.

Do not select the final carriage return character unless you want the table to end with an empty row.

Choose Convert Text to Table from the Table menu.

Specify delimiter characters, and the number of columns in the table, if necessary, then click OK.

InDesign converts the text to a table.

► **Importing a Table.** Another way to create a table is to import a table you've saved in a Word, Excel, or RTF document. There's no trick to this—select a file containing a table in the Place Document dialog box and place it, just as you'd place any other type of file. If there is a table in the document, InDesign will convert it to an InDesign table as you flow the text onto a page.

► **Pasting a table.** You can also copy and paste tables from Word and Excel, and from HTML pages displayed in your web browser. Again, there's no trick—select the table, then copy, return to InDesign, and paste. (Not all HTML tables seem to convert, nor are the results identical from browser to browser, but it does work, at least some of the time. It won't work unless your browser copies the table to the system clipboard as RTF. David cannot get this to work at all.)

When you create a table, InDesign sets the width of the table to the width of the text frame. But you're not limited to that width—InDesign tables can be narrower or wider than their containing text frame. As you'd expect, tables take on the alignment of the paragraph containing them (though the text inside the table can be of any alignment). To change the position of the table in (or relative to) the text frame, change the paragraph alignment.

Overset Cells

Sometimes, when you create or edit a table, you'll see a red dot in one or more of the cells in the table (see Figure 6-10). This means that the content of the cell (the text or graphic inside the cell) has become overset—it's exactly the same as having overset text in a text frame. What can you do? Either resize the cell or set the cell to automatically expand (as described later in this chapter).

FIGURE 6-10
Overset Cell

The dot (you have to imagine it in red) indicates that the cell content is overset.

Converting Tables to Text

To convert a table to text, follow these steps (see Figure 6-11).

1. Select the table, or a cell, row, or column in the table, or click the Type tool anywhere inside the table.

2. Choose Convert Table to Text from the Table menu. InDesign displays the Convert Table to Text dialog box.

3. Enter the delimiter characters you want to use, if necessary, then click the OK button. InDesign converts the table to text.

Editing Tables

Once you've created a table, you can't just sit and *admire* it (as tempting as that might be for longtime page layout users); you've got to *do something* with it.

Before we talk about that, though, we'd better lay down a few ground rules about cells, rows, and columns.

▶ A column is always the width of the widest cell in the column. When you change the width of a cell, you're really changing the width of the column containing the cell.

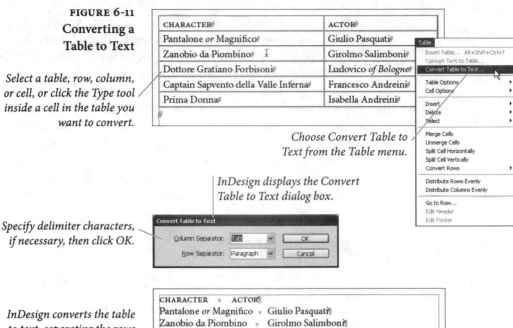

FIGURE 6-11
Converting a
Table to Text

Select a table, row, column,
or cell, or click the Type tool
inside a cell in the table you
want to convert.

Choose Convert Table to
Text from the Table menu.

InDesign displays the Convert
Table to Text dialog box.

Specify delimiter characters,
if necessary, then click OK.

InDesign converts the table
to text, separating the rows
and columns with the delim-
iter characters you specified.

▶ A row is always the height of the tallest cell in the row. Just as changing the width of a cell changes the width of a column, so changing the height of a cell changes the height of a row.

▶ In spite of the above restrictions, you can create tables containing cells that are wider than their parent columns or taller than their parent rows. You do this by merging cells, which we'll discuss later, in "Merging Cells."

Selecting and Editing Table Items

To select elements in a table, or to edit a table's content (text, rows, or columns), click the Type tool in one of the cells of the table. This activates InDesign's table tools. Once you've done this, you can enter and edit text in the cell, paste or place text or graphics in the cell, or even create another table inside the cell.

It's easy to tell when you're in this mode, because the cursor changes shape as you position it above cell, row, column, and table boundaries. What do these different cursors mean? What can you do with these tools? To find out, take a look at Table 6-1.

TABLE 6-1
Table Editing Cursors

When you see:	Your cursor is:	And you can:
↘	Above the top-left corner of the table	Click to select the table.
→	Above the left edge of a row	Click to select the row.
↓	Above the top of a column	Click to select the column.
↔	Above the right or left edge of a cell	Drag to resize the column containing the cell.
↕	Above the top or bottom of a cell	Drag to resize the row containing the cell.

In addition, the Context menu changes to display options related to working with tables (see Figure 6-12).

To select a range of cells, drag the text cursor through them. You cannot select non-contiguous cells. Note that dragging the cursor through multiple cells selects *all* of the text in the cells, regardless of the starting or ending position of the cursor.

FIGURE 6-12
Context Menu Options for Working with Tables

When you click the Type tool in a table cell, or select text in a table cell, InDesign adds options to the Context menu.

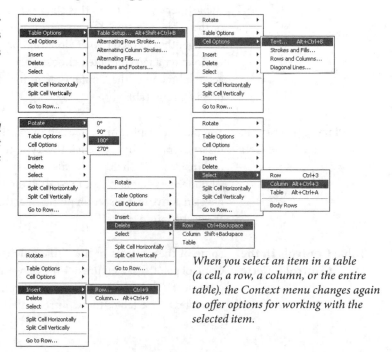

When you select an item in a table (a cell, a row, a column, or the entire table), the Context menu changes again to offer options for working with the selected item.

To select a row, position the cursor above the left edge of the first cell in the row, then click; for a column, move the cursor above the top of the first cell in the column, then click (see Figure 6-13).

You select text inside a table cell using the same methods you use to select text in a text frame.

FIGURE 6-13
Selecting Rows and Columns

Position the cursor above the top of a column…

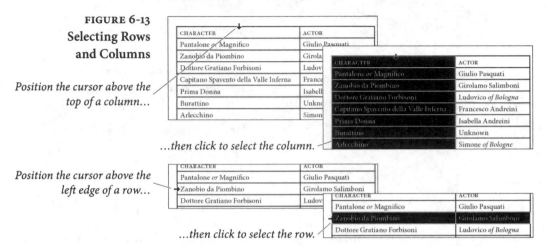

…then click to select the column.

Position the cursor above the left edge of a row…

…then click to select the row.

Entering Tab Characters

How the heck can you enter a tab character in a table cell? When you press Tab, InDesign moves the cursor to the next cell in the table (see "Table Shortcuts," later in this chapter). If the cursor is in the last cell of the table, pressing Tab creates a new table row. Either way, you don't get the character you're looking for.

To enter a tab character, choose Tab from the Insert Special Character submenu of the Context menu (or, if you're using the Mac OS, press Option-Tab).

Placing a Graphic in a Table Cell

You place a graphic in a table cell in exactly the same fashion as you insert a graphic in text: click the Type tool in a cell, or select some text inside a cell, then place a file or paste a graphic you copied to the Clipboard earlier (see Figure 6-14). Note that you must select text or have an active text insertion point; selecting the cell itself will not get the graphic into the cell.

Table Controls in the Control Palette

Some of the controls in the Table palette can also be found in the Control palette (see Figure 6-15). You won't see these controls unless you select a table item—a cell, a row, a column, or a table—when you select text in a table, the Control palette displays text formatting options.

FIGURE 6-14
Placing a Graphic in a Cell

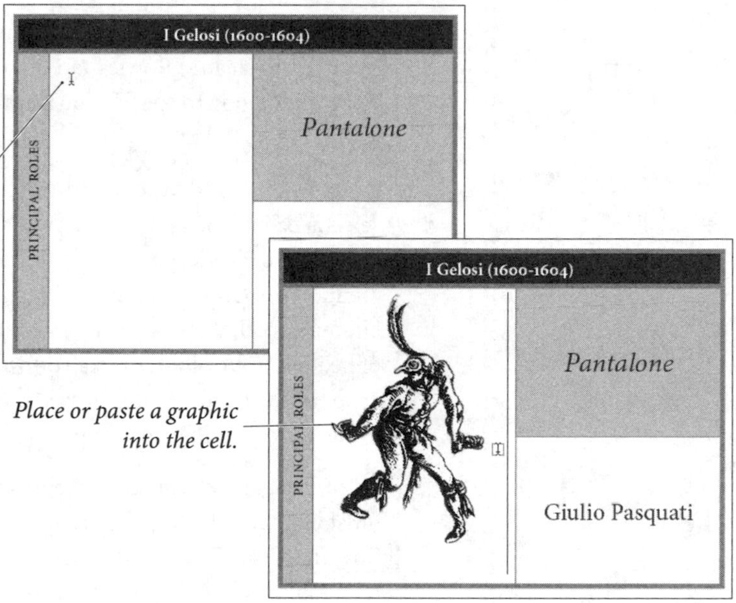

Click the Type tool inside a table cell.

Place or paste a graphic into the cell.

FIGURE 6-15
Table Controls in the Control Palette

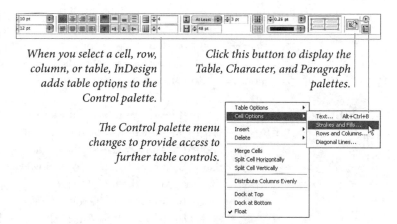

When you select a cell, row, column, or table, InDesign adds table options to the Control palette.

Click this button to display the Table, Character, and Paragraph palettes.

The Control palette menu changes to provide access to further table controls.

In most of the table-related illustrations in this chapter, we'll show the Table palette, rather than the Control palette, because the Control palette's width makes it difficult to fit into our page layout. This doesn't mean that we prefer the Table palette—in fact, we use the Control palette whenever the options we need are available there.

Adding Table Headers and Footers

InDesign tables can include header and footer rows, which can repeat as the table breaks across text frames, text columns, or pages. You can add header and footer rows when you create the table, or you can add them to existing tables, or you can convert table body rows to header or footer rows.

▶ If you're using the Insert Table command to create a table, you can use the Header Rows and Footer Rows fields in the Insert Table dialog box to specify the number of header or footer rows as you create the table.

▶ If you want to add header and/or footer rows to an existing table, select a cell in the table (or a row, or a column, or the table itself) and choose Headers and Footers from the Table Options submenu of the Context menu. InDesign displays the Headers and Footers panel of the Table Options dialog box. Enter the number of header and/or footer rows you want, specify the repeat properties of the header/footer rows, and click OK to apply the rows to the table (see Figure 6-16).

▶ To convert an existing row to a header row, select the row (it must be the first row in the table) and choose Convert to Header Row from the Context menu (see Figure 6-17). To convert multiple table body rows to header rows, select the rows—again, the first row in the table must be included in the selection (if it's not, the option won't appear on the Context menu). Converting a row (or rows) to a footer row (or rows) works the same way—select the last row (or rows) in the table and choose Convert to Footer Row from the Context menu.

Editing Header and Footer Rows

The first header and footer rows can be edited just as you'd edit any other row—the only difference is that the changes that you make are applied to all instances of the header or footer throughout the table. Subsequent header/footer rows, however, will defy your efforts to get the cursor into them (InDesign coyly displays a lock icon when you move the cursor over the row).

InDesign provides a pair of shortcuts, however, that will take you back to the first header or footer row—Edit Header and Edit Footer on the Context menu.

Changing the Size of a Table

To resize a table by dragging, follow these steps (see Figure 6-18).

1. Click the Type tool inside the table.

2. Move the cursor over the left or right edge of the table (to change the table's width), or over the top or bottom of the table (to change its height). Position the cursor above the lower-right corner of the table to resize the width and height of the table.

3. Drag the cursor to resize the table. Hold down Shift as you drag to resize the table proportionally.

FIGURE 6-16
Adding a Header Row

*Select a cell, then choose
Headers and Footers from
the Table Options submenu
of the Context menu.*

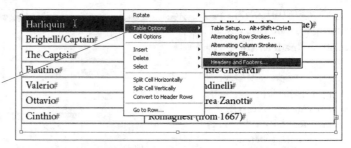

*Enter the number of header
rows you want, then define
the rate at which the rows
should repeat.*

*Click OK to apply the
header rows.*

*InDesign adds the header
rows. Enter the header text.*

*Format the header rows.
In this example, we've
merged the cells of the
first header row.*

When you resize the table by dragging the lower-right corner of the table, or when you hold down Shift as you drag, InDesign applies the changes in size equally to all of the cells in the table. If you drag the sides of the table without holding down Shift, InDesign only changes the row or column nearest the edge you're dragging. Resizing the table using this technique does not scale the text in the table.

What? You've resized the table and now want all of the columns to be the same width? Don't start dragging columns around. Instead,

FIGURE 6-17
Converting a Table Body
Row into a Header Row

Select the first row in the
table, then choose Convert
to Header Rows from the
Context menu.

Rotate	▶	
Table Options	▶	
Cell Options	▶	
Insert	▶	
Delete	▶	
Select	▶	
Merge Cells		
Split Cell Horizontally		
Split Cell Vertically		
Convert to Header Rows		
Distribute Columns Evenly		
Go to Row…		

CHARACTER	ACTOR
Harlequin	Domenic...
Brighelli/Captain	Spinetta
The Captain	Francois
Flautino	Giovanni
Valerio	Hyacinth
Ottavio	Giovanni

Cinthio	...om 1667
Leandro	...si (from 1675)
Eularia	Ursula Cortezzi
Marinetta	Lorenza Elisabetta Del Campo (from 1664)
Marinetta	Angelica Toscano (from 1675)

InDesign converts the se-
lected row to a header row.

CHARACTER	ACTOR
Harlequin	Domenico Biancolelli (called Dominque)
Brighelli/Captain	Spinetta
The Captain	Francois Mansac
Flautino	Giovanni Evariste Gherardi
Valerio	Hyacinthe Bendinelli
Ottavio	Giovanni Andrea Zanotti

If the table spans multiple
text frames or text columns,
the header row will appear
at the top of each table section. (You can turn this off,
if you like, using the Headers
and Footers panel of the
Table Options dialog box.)

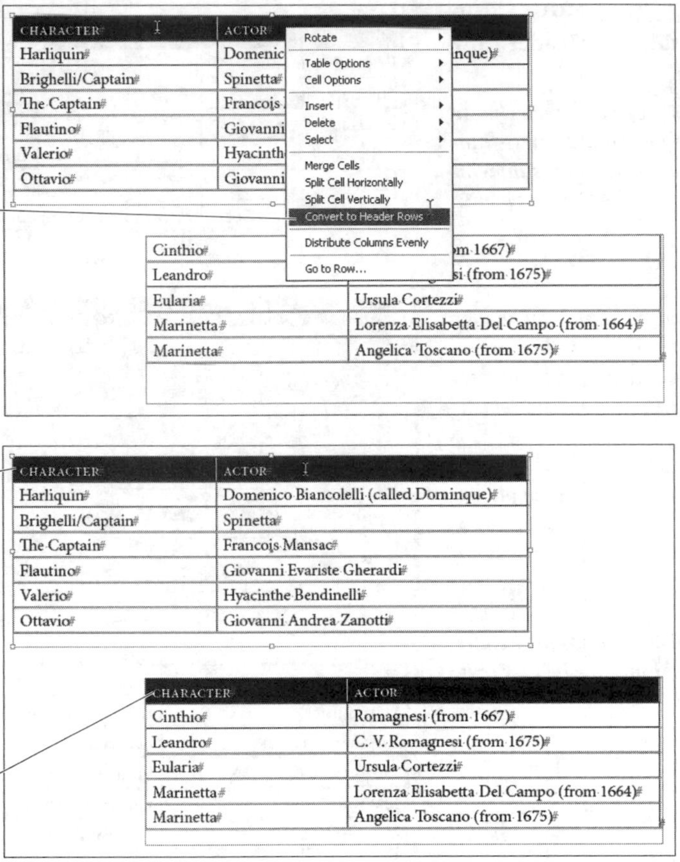

CHARACTER	ACTOR
Cinthio	Romagnesi (from 1667)
Leandro	C. V. Romagnesi (from 1675)
Eularia	Ursula Cortezzi
Marinetta	Lorenza Elisabetta Del Campo (from 1664)
Marinetta	Angelica Toscano (from 1675)

FIGURE 6-18
Resizing a Table

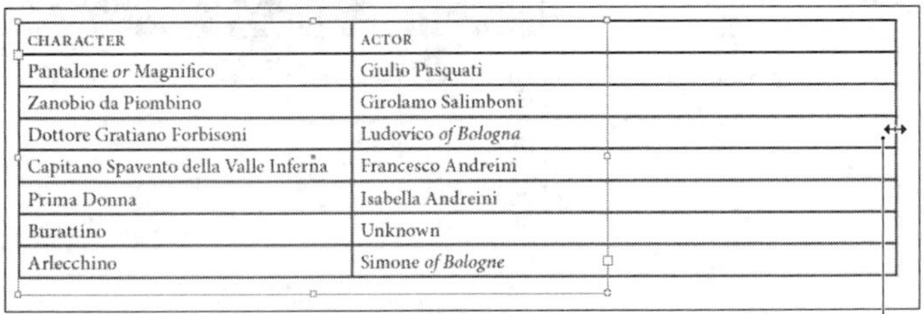

CHARACTER	ACTOR
Pantalone *or* Magnifico	Giulio Pasquati
Zanobio da Piombino	Girolamo Salimboni
Dottore Gratiano Forbisoni	Ludovico *of Bologna*
Capitano Spavento della Valle Inferna	Francesco Andreini
Prima Donna	Isabella Andreini
Burattino	Unknown
Arlecchino	Simone *of Bologne*

Position the cursor over one of the tables edges…

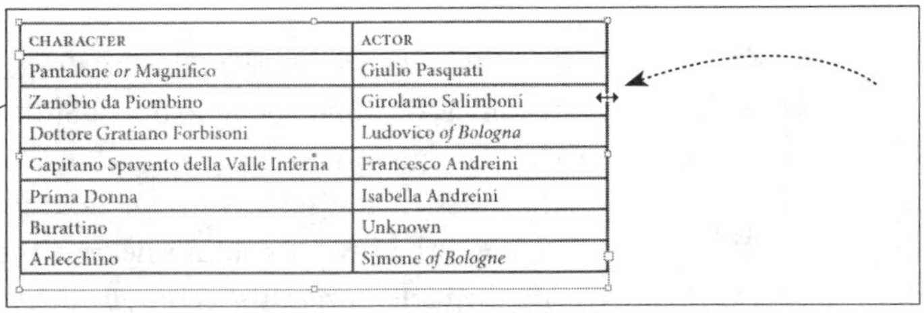

CHARACTER	ACTOR
Pantalone *or* Magnifico	Giulio Pasquati
Zanobio da Piombino	Girolamo Salimboni
Dottore Gratiano Forbisoni	Ludovico *of Bologna*
Capitano Spavento della Valle Inferna	Francesco Andreini
Prima Donna	Isabella Andreini
Burattino	Unknown
Arlecchino	Simone *of Bologne*

*…and drag. InDesign resizes the table. To resize the table
proportionally, hold down Shift as you drag.*

select the table and choose Distribute Columns Evenly from the Table palette menu or Table menu (see Figure 6-19). If you've changed the height of the table and want to make all of the rows in the table the same height, select the table and choose Distribute Rows Evenly (again, from the Table menu or from the Table palette menu).

FIGURE 6-19
Distributing
Columns Evenly

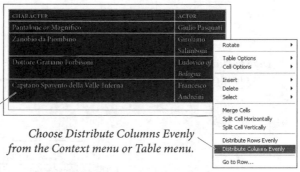

Select the columns you want to make equal in width. In this example, we've selected the entire table.

Choose Distribute Columns Evenly from the Context menu or Table menu.

InDesign makes the selected columns equal in width.

Changing the Size of Rows and Columns

To change the height of a row or the width of a column by dragging, follow these steps (see Figure 6-20).

1. Click the Type tool inside a cell.

2. Move the cursor over the top or bottom of the cell to change the height of the row containing the cell, or over the left or right of the cell to change the column width.

3. Drag the cursor up or down to resize a row, or right or left to resize a column.

To change the height of a row or the width of a column using the Table palette, follow these steps (see Figure 6-21).

1. Click the Type tool inside a cell.

2. Adjust the values in the Row Height and Column Width fields (you can type values in the fields, or use the arrow buttons associated with the fields to "nudge" the height or width up or down).

FIGURE 6-20
**Changing Row
Height by Dragging**

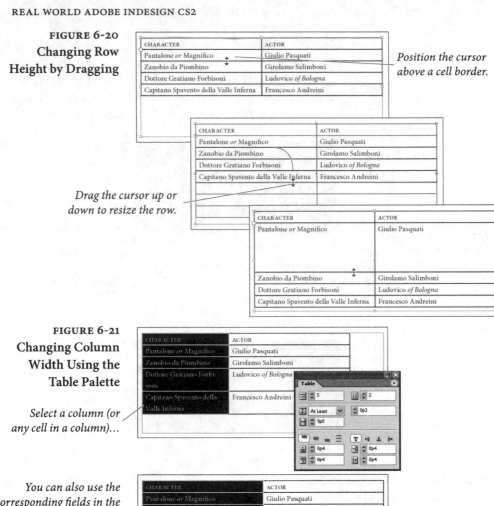

*Position the cursor
above a cell border.*

*Drag the cursor up or
down to resize the row.*

FIGURE 6-21
**Changing Column
Width Using the
Table Palette**

*Select a column (or
any cell in a column)...*

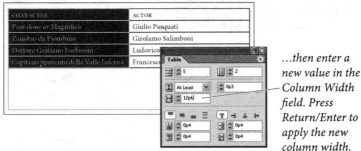

*You can also use the
corresponding fields in the
Control palette to change
column width. To get them
to appear, select a cell
or column.*

*...then enter a
new value in the
Column Width
field. Press
Return/Enter to
apply the new
column width.*

To change the height of a row or the width of a column using the Cell
Options dialog box follow these steps (see Figure 6-22).

1. Select a cell, a row, a column, or the entire table.

2. Choose Rows and Columns from the Cell Options submenu of
   the Context menu (or from the Table menu). InDesign displays
   the Cell Options dialog box.

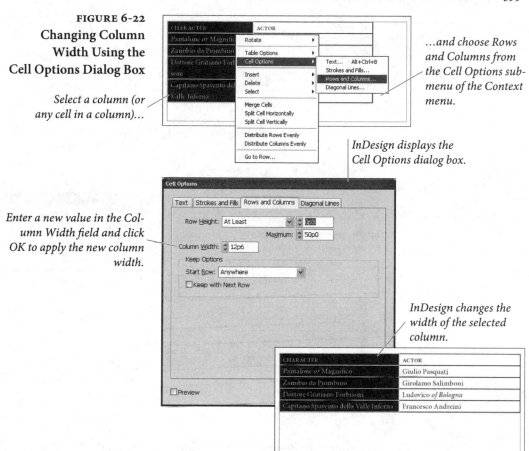

FIGURE 6-22
**Changing Column
Width Using the
Cell Options Dialog Box**

*Select a column (or
any cell in a column)...*

*...and choose Rows
and Columns from
the Cell Options sub-
menu of the Context
menu.*

*InDesign displays the
Cell Options dialog box.*

*Enter a new value in the Col-
umn Width field and click
OK to apply the new column
width.*

*InDesign changes the
width of the selected
column.*

3. Enter a new value in the Row Height field to change the height of
   the row, or in the Column Width field to change the width of a
   column.

**Adding Rows
Or Columns**

If you're entering text in a table, and have reached the cell of the last
row, you can add a row by simply pressing Tab—InDesign assumes
that this means that you want to add a row to the table. If you need to
add rows inside an existing table, it's a little bit more complicated.

To add a row or a series of rows to a table, follow these steps (see
Figure 6-23).

1. Click the Type tool in a cell in a row that is above or below the
   point at which you want to add the new rows.

2. Choose Row from the Insert submenu of the Context menu.
   InDesign displays the Insert Row(s) dialog box.

FIGURE 6-23
Adding Rows

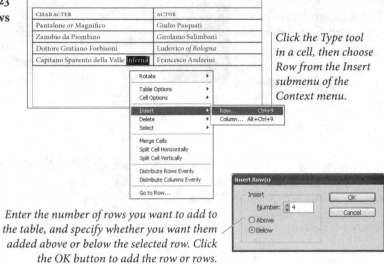

Click the Type tool in a cell, then choose Row from the Insert submenu of the Context menu.

Enter the number of rows you want to add to the table, and specify whether you want them added above or below the selected row. Click the OK button to add the row or rows.

New rows added below selected row.

3. Enter the number of Rows you want to add in the Number field, and choose the Above or Below option to tell InDesign where to put the rows (relative to the selected row).

4. Click the OK button. InDesign adds the empty rows.

To add a column or a series of columns to a table, follow these steps (see Figure 6-24).

1. Click the Type tool in a cell in a column that is adjacent to the point at which you want to add the new columns.

2. Choose Column from the Insert submenu of the Context menu. InDesign displays the Insert Column(s) dialog box.

3. Enter the number of Columns you want to add in the Number field, then choose the Left or Right option to tell InDesign where to put the rows (relative to the selected row).

4. Click the OK button. InDesign adds the empty columns.

FIGURE 6-24
Adding a Column

*Click the Type tool in a cell
(or select text in a cell).*

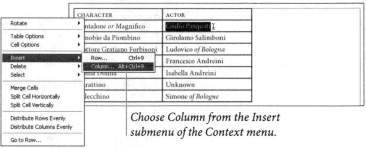

*Choose Column from the Insert
submenu of the Context menu.*

*Enter the number of columns
you want to add, and specify
the location (to the right or
left of the selected column) at
which you want to add them.*

*Click the OK button to
add the columns.*

*InDesign adds the
columns to the table.*

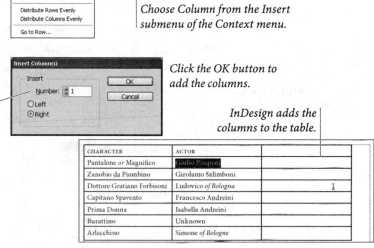

You can also add a row or column by dragging. To do so, follow these steps (see Figure 6-25).

1. Click the Type tool in a cell.

2. To add a column, position the cursor over the left or right side of the cell; to add a row, position the cursor above the top or bottom of the cell.

3. Hold down the mouse button, then press Option/Alt and drag. InDesign adds a row or column to the table.

FIGURE 6-25
**Adding a Column
by Dragging**

CHARACTER	ACTOR	
Pantalone *or* Magnifico	Giulio Pasquati	
Zanobio da Piombino	Girolamo Salimboni	
Dottore Gratiano Forbisoni	Ludovico *of Bologna*	

*Postion the cursor over a column edge. Hold down the
mouse button, then press Option/Alt and drag.*

*Stop dragging, and InDesign
adds a column to the table.*

CHARACTER	ACTOR	
Pantalone *or* Magnifico	Giulio Pasquati	
Zanobio da Piombino	Girolamo Salimboni	
Dottore Gratiano Forbisoni	Ludovico *of Bologna*	

To add a row to a table using the Table palette, follow these steps (see Figure 6-26).

1. Click the Type tool in a cell.

2. Display the Table palette (press Shift-F9), then change the value displayed in the Rows field or the Columns field.

When you add a row using this technique, the new row appears below the row you selected; when you add a column, the new column appears to the right of the selected column.

FIGURE 6-26
Adding a Row Using the Table Palette

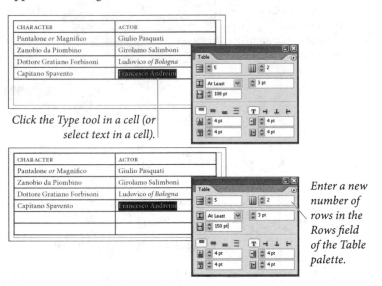

Click the Type tool in a cell (or select text in a cell).

Enter a new number of rows in the Rows field of the Table palette.

Deleting Rows, Columns, and Tables

To delete a single row, click the Type tool in a cell in the row, then choose Row from the Delete submenu of the Context menu (see Figure 6-27). There's no need to select the row or cell. To delete more than one row, select at least one cell in each row you want to delete, then choose Row from the Delete submenu of the Context menu.

To delete a single column, click the Type tool in a cell in the column, then choose Column from the Delete submenu of the Context menu (see Figure 6-28). To delete more than one column, select a cell in each column you want to delete, then choose Column from the Delete submenu of the Context menu.

To delete a table, click the Type tool in any cell in the table, and then choose Table from the Delete submenu of the Context menu. InDesign deletes the entire table containing the cell.

Alternatively, you can use the Type tool to select the character containing the table (remember: though it can be a very *large* character, it's still a single character) and press Delete.

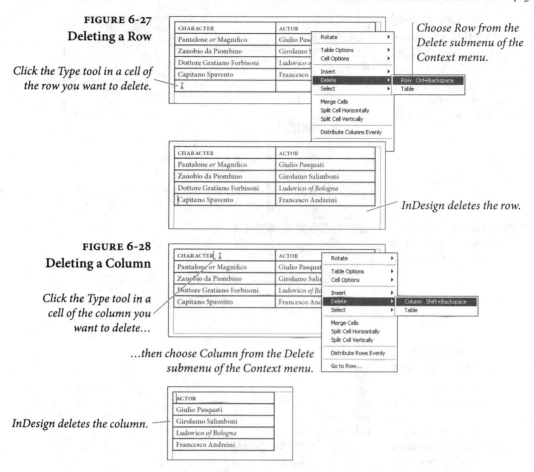

FIGURE 6-27
Deleting a Row

Click the Type tool in a cell of the row you want to delete.

Choose Row from the Delete submenu of the Context menu.

InDesign deletes the row.

FIGURE 6-28
Deleting a Column

Click the Type tool in a cell of the column you want to delete...

...then choose Column from the Delete submenu of the Context menu.

InDesign deletes the column.

To delete rows or columns using the Table palette, follow these steps (see Figure 6-29).

1. Click the Type tool in a cell.

2. Display the Table palette (press Shift-F9) if it isn't already visible, then reduce the value in either the Rows field or the Columns field. InDesign asks if you're certain you want to remove the row(s). You are certain, so click the OK button.

Merging and Unmerging Table Cells

To merge a series of selected table cells into a single cell, select the cells and choose Merge Cells from the Context menu or Table menu (see Figure 6-30). The text and graphics in the selected cells are placed in the new merged cell.

To unmerge a cell that has been created by merging cells, select the cell and choose Unmerge Cells from the Context menu or Table menu. Note that unmerging a merged cell is very different from splitting the cell, which only divides the cell in half along its horizontal

FIGURE 6-29
Deleting a Column Using the Table Palette

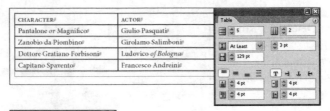

Click the Type tool in a cell (or select text in a cell, or select a cell, row, or table).

Decrease the value in the Columns field by one or more and press Return/Enter to apply the change.

InDesign asks if you want to delete the column. You do, so click the OK button.

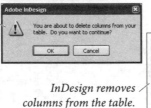

InDesign removes columns from the table.

FIGURE 6-30
Merging Cells

Select a range of cells.

Choose Merge Cells from the Context menu (or Table menu).

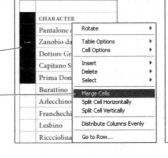

InDesign merges the cells. Any content in the merged cells is retained in the new cell.

or vertical axis. Unmerging a cell actually returns the cells in the merged cell to their original geometry, though it does not restore their original content.

Splitting Table Cells

To split a cell, select the cell and choose Split Cell Horizontally or Split Cell Vertically from the Context menu (see Figure 6-31).

If you have selected an entire column of cells, you won't see the Split Cell Horizontally option; if you've selected a row of cells, InDesign turns off the Split Cell Vertically option.

Rotating Table Cells

Cells in an InDesign table can be rotated in 90-degree increments (see Figure 6-32). To rotate a cell, select the cell and then choose one of the options (0, 90, 180, 270) on the Rotate submenu of the Context menu (or click the corresponding button in the Table palette).

FIGURE 6-31
Splitting a Cell

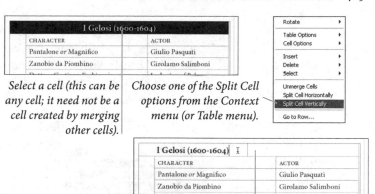

Select a cell (this can be any cell; it need not be a cell created by merging other cells).

Choose one of the Split Cell options from the Context menu (or Table menu).

InDesign splits the cell into two cells.

FIGURE 6-32
Rotating a Cell

Select a cell.

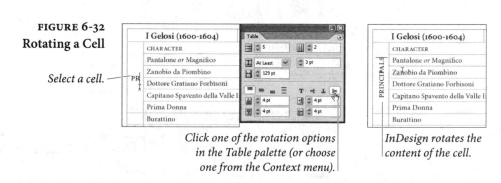

Click one of the rotation options in the Table palette (or choose one from the Context menu).

InDesign rotates the content of the cell.

Two Table Tricks

Earlier, we mentioned two of our favorite uses for tables—hanging side headings and boxed paragraphs. This section is our "best guess" attempt to find a place for these tricks in this chapter's structure.

Using a Table to Create a Box Around a Paragraph

Sometimes, you need to place a box around a paragraph—you often see this formatting used to set off notes and warnings in technical manuals. While you could always draw a box behind the paragraph, you would then have to move the box when the paragraph changes its position on the page due to text editing or layout changes. What you really need is a way to "stick" the box to the paragraph, so that it will follow the paragraph wherever it goes.

In the interest of completeness, we've shown two other methods for accomplishing this end elsewhere in this chapter (involving paragraph rules and inline frames)—but the best way to put a box around a paragraph is to convert the paragraph to a single-cell table. We do not know if single-cell tables can reproduce by fission, as other single-cell animals can, but they're certainly useful nonetheless.

To convert a paragraph to a single-cell table, select all of the text in the paragraph up to, but not including, the return at the end of the paragraph. Then choose Convert Text to Table from the Table menu (see Figure 6-33). Apply whatever formatting you want to the fill and stroke of the table's single cell.

FIGURE 6-33
Placing a Box
Around a Paragraph
(Table Method)

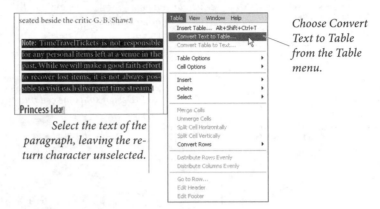

Choose Convert Text to Table from the Table menu.

Select the text of the paragraph, leaving the return character unselected.

InDesign displays the Convert Text to Table dialog box. Click the OK button.

InDesign creates a table containing a single cell.

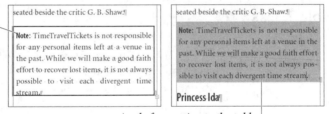

Apply formatting to the table.

Using a Table to Create a Hanging Side Head

To create a hanging side head (like the one attached to this paragraph) using a table, follow these steps (see Figure 6-34).

1. Enter the heading and the body text as separate paragraphs.

2. Replace the return between the two paragraphs with a tab character.

3. Select the text in the paragraph. Do not include the return in the selection.

4. Choose Convert Text to Table from the Table menu.

5. Format the table.

FIGURE 6-34
**Creating a
Hanging Side Head
(Table Method)**

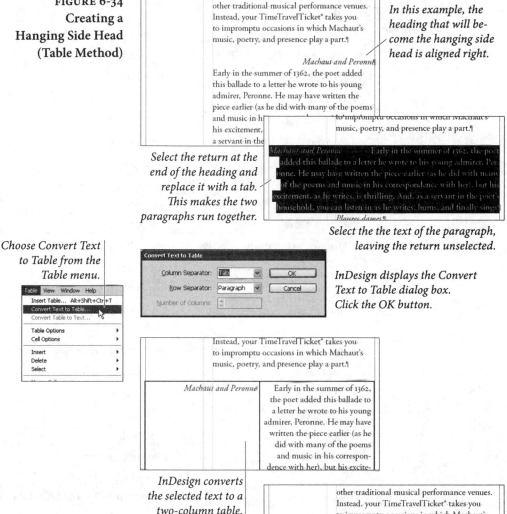

*In this example, the
heading that will be-
come the hanging side
head is aligned right.*

*Select the return at the
end of the heading and
replace it with a tab.
This makes the two
paragraphs run together.*

*Select the the text of the paragraph,
leaving the return unselected.*

*Choose Convert Text
to Table from the
Table menu.*

*InDesign displays the Convert
Text to Table dialog box.
Click the OK button.*

*InDesign converts
the selected text to a
two-column table.*

*InDesign applies the (boring)
default table formatting, so
you'll probably need to format
the table to fit your layout.*

Table Shortcuts

As you might expect, InDesign has a number of keyboard shortcuts related to working with tables (see Table 6-2). Note that there
are some very cool shortcuts that, by default, have no key assigned

Function	Shortcut
Diagonal Lines Options	not defined
Rows and Columns Options	not defined
Strokes and Fills Options	not defined
Text Options	Command-Option-B/Ctrl-Alt-B*
Convert Table to Text	not defined
Convert Text to Table	not defined
Delete Column	Shift-Backspace*
Delete Row	Command-Backspace/ Ctrl-Backspace*
Delete Table	not defined
Distribute Columns Evenly	not defined
Distribute Rows Evenly	not defined
Go to Row	not defined
Insert Table	Command-Shift-Option-T/ Ctrl-Alt-Shift-T
Insert Column	Command-Option-9/Ctrl-Alt-9*
Insert Row	Command-9/Ctrl-9*
Merge Cells	not defined
Next Cell	Tab
Previous Cell	Shift-Tab
Select Cell	Command-/(slash)/ Ctrl-/ (slash) or Esc*
Select Column	Command-Option-3/Ctrl-Alt-3*
Select Row	Command-3/Ctrl-3*
Select Table	Command-Option-A/Ctrl-Alt-A
Split Cell Horizontally	not defined
Split Cell Vertically	not defined
Alternating Column Strokes	not defined
Alternating Fills	not defined
Alternating Row Strokes	not defined
Table Setup	Command-Option-T/Ctrl-Alt-T*

* This command is only active when you have an active text
   insertion point in a text frame or table cell.

to them. Go to Row, in particular, is worth sacrificing an existing default shortcut for.

Formatting Tables

Earlier, we mentioned that table cells are similar to InDesign text frames—and we now want to point out that that similarity extends to the realm of formatting, as well. Table cells can be filled using any fill you could apply to a frame, and can use all of the strokes in InDesign's Stroke palette (including custom stroke styles).

To format table cells, however, you don't (usually) use the same controls you use to format text frames, rectangles, ellipses, or other page items. Instead, you use a special set of table formatting controls, most of which you'll find in the Table Options (see Figure 6-35) and Cell Options dialog boxes (see Figure 6-36).

Table Cell Strokes and Fills

Before we start talking about table formatting, it's important that you understand that applying a stroke to a column is exactly the same as applying a stroke to the left and right edges of all of the cells in that column. There are not separate stroke properties for rows and columns. If you change the stroke property of a column, the strokes on the corresponding cell borders in the column also change. The same is true for table border strokes—these properties apply to the outside edges of the cells at the top, right, bottom, and left edges of the table.

Applying Strokes to Cells. InDesign offers a number of different ways to set the fill or stroke of a cell. You can set the stroke weight using the Stroke palette, or the Strokes and Fills panel of the Cell Options dialog box, or from the table controls in the Control palette. You can set the fill of a cell using the Swatches palette, the Color palette, or the Strokes and Fills panel of the Cell Options dialog box. This is not a complete listing of the different methods you can use to format cells, but we think you get the idea.

When you want to apply a stroke to all of the borders of a cell or cells, follow these steps (see Figure 6-37).

1. Select a range of cells.

2. Display the Stroke palette or display the Strokes and Fills panel of the Cell Options dialog box (choose Strokes and Fills from the Cell Options submenu of the Context menu), or display the Control palette.

FIGURE 6-35
Table Options

*To open the Table Options
dialog box, select a cell and
choose one of the items on
the Table Options submenu
of the Context menu (or
Table menu).*

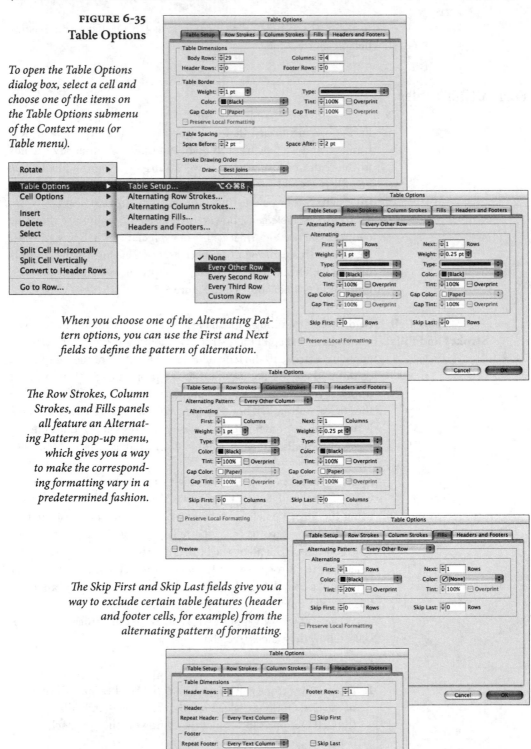

When you choose one of the Alternating Pattern options, you can use the First and Next fields to define the pattern of alternation.

The Row Strokes, Column Strokes, and Fills panels all feature an Alternating Pattern pop-up menu, which gives you a way to make the corresponding formatting vary in a predetermined fashion.

The Skip First and Skip Last fields give you a way to exclude certain table features (header and footer cells, for example) from the alternating pattern of formatting.

FIGURE 6-36
Cell Options

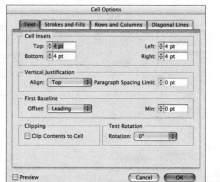

To open the Cell Options
dialog box, select a cell and
choose one of the items on
the Cell Options submenu
of the Context menu (or
Table menu).

The options in the Text
panel control the way that
InDesign composes text in the
cell—they're very similar to
the options in the Text Frame
Options dialog box.

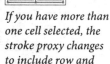

Use the Strokes and Fills
panel to set the formatting
of the selected cells.

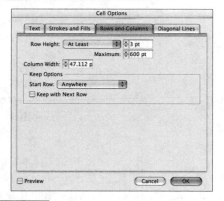

The stroke proxy gives you
a way to specify which cell
borders are affected by the
formatting.

If you have more than
one cell selected, the
stroke proxy changes
to include row and
column strokes.

The controls in the Rows and Columns panel set the
number of rows and columns in the table and their
height/width. As most of these controls are duplicated in the Table palette, the main reason you'll need
to come here is the Keep Options section, especially
Keep with Next Row, which you can use to force a
row to the next page or text frame.

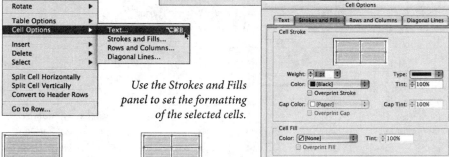

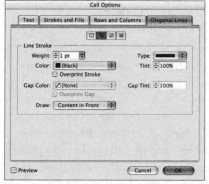

Diagonal lines are often
used to fill in empty
cells in some table
designs—the Diagonal
Lines panel, as you'd
expect, provides for-
matting options for this
feature.

*Click the Type tool in the
table, then choose Table
from the Select submenu of
the Options menu.*

*There are many ways to
apply cell formatting; we
usually use the options
in the Control palette.*

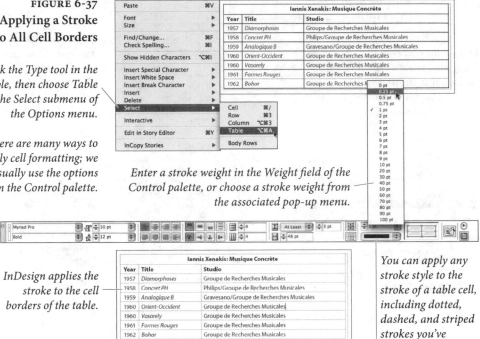

*Enter a stroke weight in the Weight field of the
Control palette, or choose a stroke weight from
the associated pop-up menu.*

*InDesign applies the
stroke to the cell
borders of the table.*

*You can apply any
stroke style to the
stroke of a table cell,
including dotted,
dashed, and striped
strokes you've
defined.*

3. Enter a stroke weight in the Weight field and press Return/Enter
   (or otherwise apply the new value).

4. Apply a stroke color. If you're applying the stroke using the
   Stroke palette or the Control palette, you can use the Swatches
   palette, the Color palette, the Gradient palette, or any of the
   other color controls. If you're using the Strokes and Fills panel of
   the Cell Options dialog box, you can use the Color pop-up menu.

Each border of a cell in an InDesign table can have a different
stroke. Note, however, that cells share borders with adjacent cells.
Applying a stroke to the right border of a cell affects the left border of
the next cell in the row.

The Cell Proxy (in the Strokes panel of the Cell Options dialog
box, or in the Control palette or Stroke palette) is the way that you
tell InDesign which border you want to work with (see Figure 6-38).
Just as the Proxy in the Transform palette "stands in" for the current
selection, the Cell Proxy represents the selected cell or cell range.

When the borders in the Cell Proxy are highlighted (in light blue),
changes you make to the stroke color or stroke weight will affect the
corresponding cell borders. To prevent formatting from affecting a
cell border, click the corresponding active border in the Cell Proxy.
To make an inactive border active again, click it again.

FIGURE 6-38
Cell Proxy

Actually, we don't know what this control is supposed to be called—we could find no reference to it in any "official" documentation. So we're calling it the "Cell Proxy." You got a problem with that?

Cell Proxy in the Cell Options dialog box

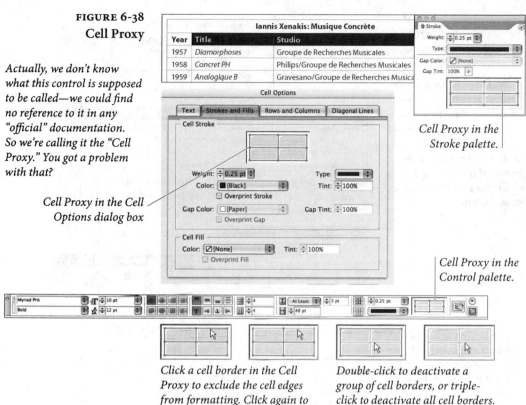

Cell Proxy in the Stroke palette.

Cell Proxy in the Control palette.

Click a cell border in the Cell Proxy to exclude the cell edges from formatting. Click again to activate the cell border.

Double-click to deactivate a group of cell borders, or triple-click to deactivate all cell borders.

If you want to apply a stroke to some, but not all, of the borders of a cell, follow these steps (see Figure 6-39).

1. Select the cell or range of cells you want to format.

2. Display the Stroke palette or display the Strokes and Fills panel of the Cell Options dialog box (choose Strokes and Fills from the Cell Options submenu of the Context menu).

3. Use the Cell Proxy to select the cell borders you want to format.

4. Apply stroke formatting using the Strokes and Fills panel of the Cell Options dialog box, or the Stroke and Swatches palettes.

Applying Fills to Cells. To apply a fill to a cell, follow these steps (see Figure 6-40).

1. Select a cell or a range of cells.

2. Display the Strokes and Fills panel of the Cell Options dialog box (to display this panel, choose Strokes and Fills from the Cell Options submenu of the Context menu).

FIGURE 6-39
Applying a Stroke to Selected Cell Borders

In this example, we want to remove the strokes around the outside edges (top, left, and right) of the first row in the table, but we don't want to remove the stroke at the bottom of the row. To do this, we use the Cell Proxy in the Stroke palette.

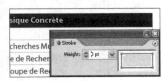

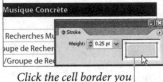

Select the cell you want to format.

InDesign displays the Cell Proxy in the Stroke palette.

Click the cell border you want to protect from formatting.

Apply the stroke.

The top, left, and right borders of the first row have been set to zero point strokes, but the bottom border of the row retains its original stroke weight.

Iannis Xenakis: Musique Concrète		
Year	**Title**	**Studio**
1957	*Diamorphoses*	Groupe de Recherches Musicales
1958	*Concret PH*	Philips/Groupe de Recherches Musicales
1959	*Analogique B*	Gravesano/Groupe de Recherches Musicales

3. Choose a color swatch from the Color pop-up menu, and enter a tint value in the Tint field, if necessary. Note that you can also set the fill to overprint using the Overprint option.

4. Click the OK button to close the dialog box and apply the fill to the selected cells.

Alternatively, you can apply a fill to a cell using the Swatches palette or Color palette (see Figure 6-41).

1. Select a cell or range of cells.

2. Click the Fill selector at the top of the Swatches palette or Color palette to make it active (if it's not already active).

3. Click the swatch (if you're using the Swatches palette) or define a color (if you're using the Color palette) to apply it to the background of the cell.

FIGURE 6-40
Applying a Fill to a Cell
(Dialog Box Method)

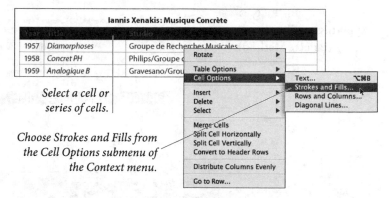

Select a cell or
series of cells.

Choose Strokes and Fills from
the Cell Options submenu of
the Context menu.

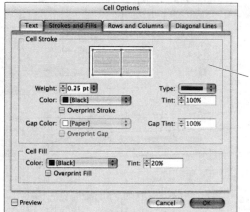

Specify fill options in
the Strokes and Fills
panel of the Cell Op-
tions dialog box. Click
the OK button to apply
your changes.

Year	Title	Studio
1957	*Diamorphoses*	Groupe de Recherches Musicales
1958	*Concret PH*	Philips/Groupe de Recherches Musicales
1959	*Analogique B*	Gravesano/Groupe de Recherches Musicales

Iannis Xenakis: Musique Concrète

InDesign applies the fill to the selected cells.

Applying Gradients to Table Cells. You can apply a gradient to the fill and stroke of a cell, but the results might not be what you'd expect (see Figure 6-42).

1. Select the cells.

2. Display the Gradient palette, if it's not already visible.

3. Click in the Gradient Ramp to apply a gradient to the selected cells. Adjust the gradient settings to define the type, color, and angle of the gradient (as discussed in Chapter 5, "Drawing").

Note that the gradient is based on the width and height of the table, rather than on the selected cell or cells. This may or may not give you the effect you're looking for. To gain more control over the

FIGURE 6-41
Applying a Fill to a Cell
(Palette Method)

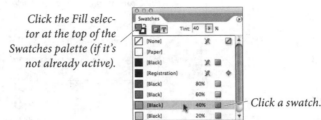

Select a cell or a range of cells.

Click the Fill selector at the top of the Swatches palette (if it's not already active).

Click a swatch.

Iannis Xenakis: Musique Concrète		
Year	Title	Studio
1957	Diamorphoses	Groupe de Recherches Musicales
1958	Concret PH	Philips/Groupe de Recherches Musicales
1959	Analogique B	Gravesano/Groupe de Recherches Musicales

InDesign applies the fill to the selected cells.

start/end points of the gradient, create and fill a rectangle, then paste the rectangle into the cell.

Applying Diagonal Lines. To apply diagonal lines to a cell, use the options in the Diagonal Lines panel of the Cell Options dialog box (see Figure 6-43).

1. Select a cell, row, column, or table (table border strokes apply to the entire table, so you need only select part of the table).

2. Display the Diagonal Lines panel of the Cell Options dialog box (choose Diagonal Lines from the Cell Options submenu of the Context menu).

3. Turn on one of the diagonal lines options. Choose a stroke weight, stroke type, color, and tint. If you want the diagonal lines to overprint, turn on the Overprint option. If you want the diagonal lines to appear in front of the table, turn on the Draw in Front option.

4. Click the OK button to apply the diagonal lines.

FIGURE 6-42
Applying a
Gradient to a Cell

*Note that InDesign positions
the start and end of the
gradient (in this example,
the center point of a radial
gradient) based on the width
and height of the entire
table—not the width of
the cell itself.*

*Display the Gradient palette
and click the Gradient Ramp
to apply a gradient fill.*

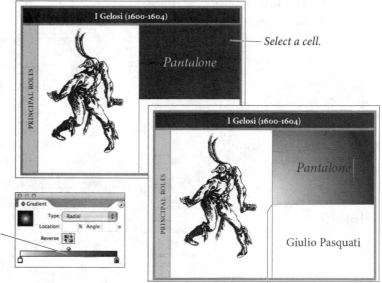

Select a cell.

Center point of a radial gradient applied to the cell.

Formatting Table Borders. To apply a stroke to the edges of a table, use the options in the Table Border section of the Table Setup panel of the Table Options dialog box (see Figure 6-44).

1. Select a cell, row, column, or table (table border strokes apply to the entire table, so you need only select part of the table).

2. Display the Table Setup panel of the Table Options dialog box (press Command-Option-T/Ctrl-Alt-T).

3. Choose a stroke weight, stroke type, color, and tint. If you want the stroke to overprint, turn on the Overprint option.

4. If you want to prevent the table border formatting from overriding formatting you've applied to the cells in the table (i.e., any formatting other than the default table formatting), turn on the Preserve Local Formatting option.

Applying Alternating Fills and Strokes. The options in the Row Strokes, Column Strokes, and Fills panels of the Table Options dialog box provide a way for you to vary the formatting of rows and columns in a table according to a predefined pattern. Shading table rows or columns is often a more visually pleasing way to format a table than using strokes (this depends on the design of the piece in which the table appears).

FIGURE 6-43
**Applying Diagonal
Lines to a Cell**

*In this example table,
a diagonal line in a cell
indicates that the seats in
that section are no longer
available. TimeTravelTickets
has run out of seats for the
November 11, 1882, premiere
of "Iolanthe," so we have to
apply diagonal lines to the
corresponding cell.*

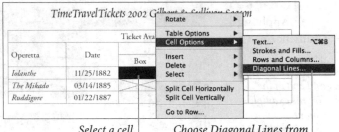

Select a cell.

Choose Diagonal Lines from
the Cell Options submenu of
the Context menu.

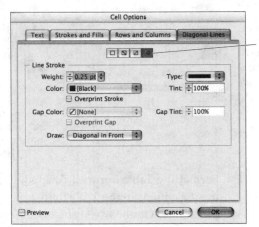

Turn on one of the
diagonal lines options
and specify the format-
ting of the lines.

*InDesign applies the
diagonal lines to the cell.*

All of these panels work the same way—you select a pattern from
the Alternating Pattern menu, and then you specify the formatting
applied by that pattern. If the pattern you've chosen is None, InDesign
does not alternate the corresponding fill or stroke properties in the
table. Otherwise, InDesign applies one of two formats to the rows
and columns in the table. Formatting you apply using alternating
fills or strokes overrides any cell formatting you've already applied to
the cells in the table (this has no effect on text formatting).

To apply an alternating fill or stroke pattern to a table, follow
these steps (see Figure 6-45).

FIGURE 6-44
**Applying Strokes to
Table Borders**

*Example table without
a table border.*

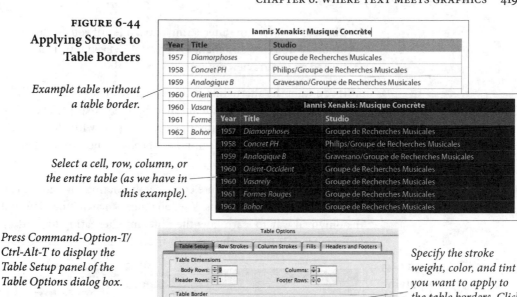

*Select a cell, row, column, or
the entire table (as we have in
this example).*

*Press Command-Option-T/
Ctrl-Alt-T to display the
Table Setup panel of the
Table Options dialog box.*

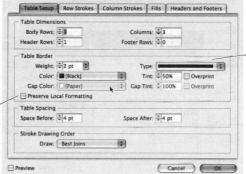

*Specify the stroke
weight, color, and tint
you want to apply to
the table borders. Click
the OK button to apply
your changes.*

*Turn this option on if you
want to retain any formatting you might have applied
to the cells in the table.*

*InDesign applies the stroke
to the outside borders of
the cells at the outside (left,
right, top, or bottom)
of the table.*

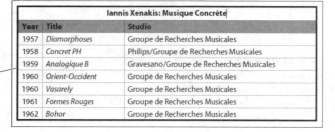

1. Select a cell, row, column, or table (this formatting applies to the
    entire table, regardless of the selection, so do whatever is easiest
    for you).

2. Display the panel of the Table Options dialog box that cor-
    responds to the attribute you want to work with (i.e., Row
    Strokes, Column Strokes, or Fills). You might want to turn on
    the Preview option—it can help you understand the effect of the
    formatting options.

3. Choose an option from the Alternating Pattern pop-up menu.

4. Choose a color for the alternating pattern (until you do this, you probably won't see any changes to the table, even if you have turned on the Preview option).

5. If you want the alternating pattern to ignore rows at the beginning or end of the table (for alternating row strokes) or at the left or right edges of the column (if you're working with alternating column strokes), enter the number of cells in the Skip First and Skip Last fields.

It should be clear that quite complex alternating formatting can be applied using these options. We don't mean to avoid the topic, but the only real way to learn how the different alternating formatting features work is to experiment with the settings. No, really. Create

FIGURE 6-45
Applying
Alternating Fills

Select a cell.

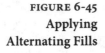

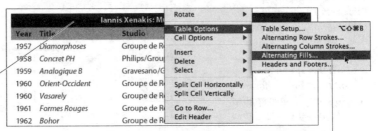

Choose Alternating Fills from the Table Options submenu of the Context menu.

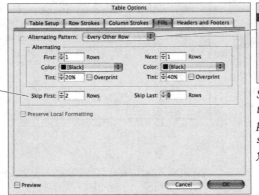

Note that we've directed our alternating pattern to skip the first two rows in the table (to avoid the table header row and title).

Select a pattern from the Alternating Pattern pop-up menu, then specify the formatting you want to apply.

InDesign applies the alternating fill pattern to the rows in the table.

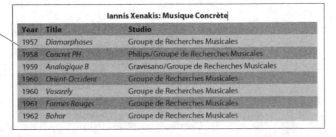

an example table, open the Table Options dialog box, turn on the Preview option, and play!

Making Table Styles. By the way, you may have noticed that nowhere in this discussion do we mention the ability to create table "styles" or "presets" which can be quickly applied to a table. That's because, inexplicably, InDesign has no such feature. However, if you create a lot of tables, you're going to want something like this. Fortunately, there are a few third-party solutions that can help. For example, TableStyles from Teacup Software (*www.teacupsoftware.com*) or SmartStyles from Woodwing (*www.woodwing.com*) are both worth looking at.

Text Wrap

Any independent object in an InDesign publication can have a text wrap—a boundary that repels text—applied to it. Wrapping text around an object is something like the opposite of flowing text inside a text frame. When you flow text inside a frame, you want text to stay inside a path; when you apply a text wrap, you want to keep it out. To set the text wrap for an object, follow these steps (see Figure 6-46).

1. Select an object—any frame or group—on an InDesign page.

2. Display the Text Wrap palette, if it's not already visible (press Command-Option-W/Ctrl-Alt-W).

3. Click one of the Text Wrap buttons in the Text Wrap palette. InDesign displays the text wrap boundary around the selected object, and pushes any text falling inside the text wrap boundary to the outside of the boundary. If you applied the text wrap to a text frame, the text in that frame is unaffected by the text wrap boundary.

4. Set the text wrap offset distances using the Top, Left, Bottom, and Right fields in the Text Wrap palette. If you've selected anything other than a rectangular frame, you'll only be able to adjust a single field (the Left field) to set the offset distance.

Note that when it comes to inline or anchored objects (objects that are anchored to a position in a text story), text wrap doesn't always play by the same rules. We cover that in more detail in "Inline Frames and Anchored Objects," later in this chapter.

FIGURE 6-46
Text Wrap

To wrap text around an object, select the object and then click one of the text wrap options in the Text Wrap palette (we've listed the "official" name of the text wrap type below each example).

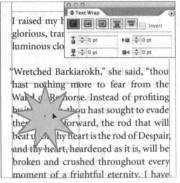

No Text Wrap

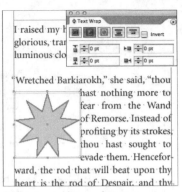

Wrap Around Bounding Box

Wrap Around Object Shape

Jump Object

When you choose one of the rectangular text wrap options (Wrap Around Bounding Box, Jump Object, or Jump to Next Column), you can adjust the offset values for the top, right, left, and bottom independently. If you choose Wrap Around Object Shape, you can only enter a single offset value that applies to all sides of the text wrap.

Jump to Next Column

The Jump Object text wrap option causes text in any column touching the text wrap boundary to jump over the text wrap—it's as if the wrap extends to the width of the column. The Jump to Next Column text wrap option pushes any text in the column below the top of the text wrap boundary to the top of the next column.

Enter a value in one of the offset fields...

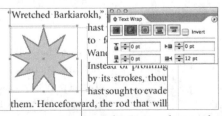

...and InDesign changes the offset for the corresponding side.

Contour Options

When you choose the Wrap Around Object text wrap type, and have an imported graphic selected, InDesign adds a new section to the bottom of the Text Wrap palette (if you don't see it, choose Show Options from the Text wrap palette menu). You can create the text wrap contour from paths or an alpha channel stored in a graphic, or detect the edges of objects in an image (see Figure 6-47). It's very similar to the clipping path options.

FIGURE 6-47
Contour Text
Wrap Options

This image includes a path saved in Photoshop.

When you first apply a contour text wrap, InDesign bases the text wrap on the image bounding box.

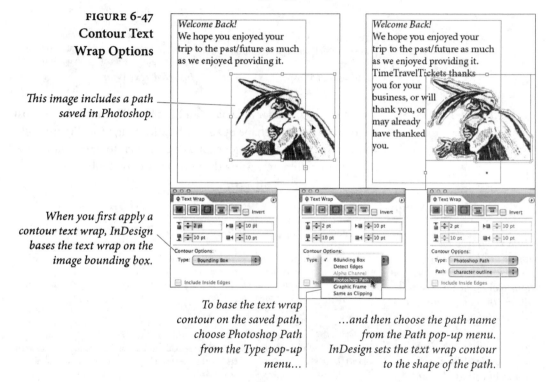

To base the text wrap contour on the saved path, choose Photoshop Path from the Type pop-up menu...

...and then choose the path name from the Path pop-up menu. InDesign sets the text wrap contour to the shape of the path.

Ignoring Text Wrap

As we pointed out in the "Composition Preferences" section of Chapter 1, "Workspace," many people aren't used to the fact that applying text wrap to an object affects the text below *and* above that object in the stacking order. Fortunately, you can make individual text frames immune to text wrap: Select the frame, choose Text Frame Options from the Object menu (or press Command/Ctrl-B) and turn on the Ignore Text Wrap checkbox.

Inverted Text Wrap

InDesign can apply an inverted text wrap to an object, which causes text to wrap to the inside of the text wrap (see Figure 6-48). We find this very helpful when... well, actually, almost never. But it's nice to have options.

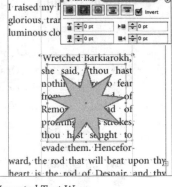

Regular Text Wrap   *Inverted Text Wrap*

Editing a Text Wrap   The text wrap boundary is a path, and can be edited and adjusted just as you'd change the shape of any path in InDesign (see Figure 6-49). You can draw new line segments using the Pen tool, or change the location of path points using the Direct Selection tool.

The text wrap boundary appears in a tint (we think it's 50 percent) of the selection color of the layer containing the object—this can make it difficult to see.

You can also use the Pen tool to add points, delete points, or change the control handles of points of a text wrap boundary.

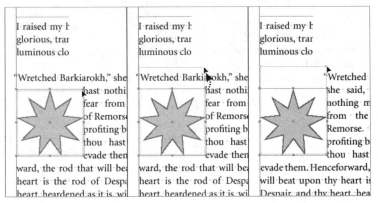

Select points on the text wrap boundary just as you would select points on any path.

Drag the points to a new location.

InDesign wraps the text around the edited text wrap boundary.

Converting Text to Outlines

When you work in graphic design, you frequently need to alter character shapes for logos or packaging designs. For years, we dreamed about the ability to turn type into paths (or "outlines") we could edit. Finally, applications such as FreeHand and Illustrator added the feature. And, as you'd expect in a modern page layout program, InDesign has it.

You can convert characters from just about any font (including TrueType, PostScript Type 1, and OpenType fonts) for which you have the printer (outline) font.

Once you've converted the characters into outlines, you lose all text editing capabilities, but you gain the ability to paste things inside the character outline, to use the path as a frame, and to change the shapes of the characters themselves.

To convert characters of text into paths, follow these steps (see Figure 6-50).

1. Select the text you want to convert. You can select text using either the Type tool, or select the text frame using the Selection tool or the Direct Selection tool.

2. Choose Convert to Outlines from the Type menu (or press Command-Shift-O/Ctrl-Shift-O). InDesign converts the characters into paths. If you selected the characters using the Type tool, InDesign positions the paths on the current line as an inline graphic; if you selected the text frame using the Selection tool or the Direct Selection tool, InDesign joins the resulting outlines into a compound path.

When you convert individual characters containing interior space (such as "P" or "O") into paths, InDesign turns them into composite paths (see "Compound Paths" in Chapter 5, "Drawing"). This is handy. Not only are multiple-part characters (such as i, é, and ü) treated as single paths, but characters with interior paths (such as O, P, A, and D) are transparent where they should be, and fill properly.

You can always make the characters into normal (not composite) paths. To do this, select the character and choose Release from the Compound Paths submenu of the Object menu (see Figure 6-51).

If Your Characters Won't Convert If you weren't able to convert the text into paths, make sure that you have the outline (printer) fonts and that they're somewhere InDesign can find them. If you don't have the outline fonts, InDesign won't be able to convert your text into paths.

Inline Frames and Anchored Objects

It was the Dark Age of page layout. The flame of classical desktop publishing knowledge flickered but dimly, kept barely alive by devoted acolytes in isolated monasteries. Pestilence and famine stalked the narrow aisles between our unheated cubicles. And, almost worst of

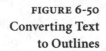

FIGURE 6-50
Converting Text to Outlines

Select a text frame with the Selection tool...

...and choose Create Outlines from the Type menu.

InDesign converts the characters in the selected text frame into a compound path.

To see the individual paths and points, select the compound path using the Direct Selection tool.

You can also select text using the Type tool, then convert the selected text to outlines.

To convert the selected characters to independent graphics (i.e., not an inline frame), hold down Option/ Alt as you select the command from the menu.

When you do this, the resulting compound path will be inserted into the text as an inline frame.

all, page layout programs could not paste graphics into text. Producing publications featuring graphics "anchored" to a specific piece of text was a nightmare. It went something like this. Scroll. Zoom in. Measure. Pull a guide down from a ruler. Select a graphic. Drag the graphic until it snaps to the guide. Sigh heavily. Repeat.

FIGURE 6-51
Working with Character Outlines

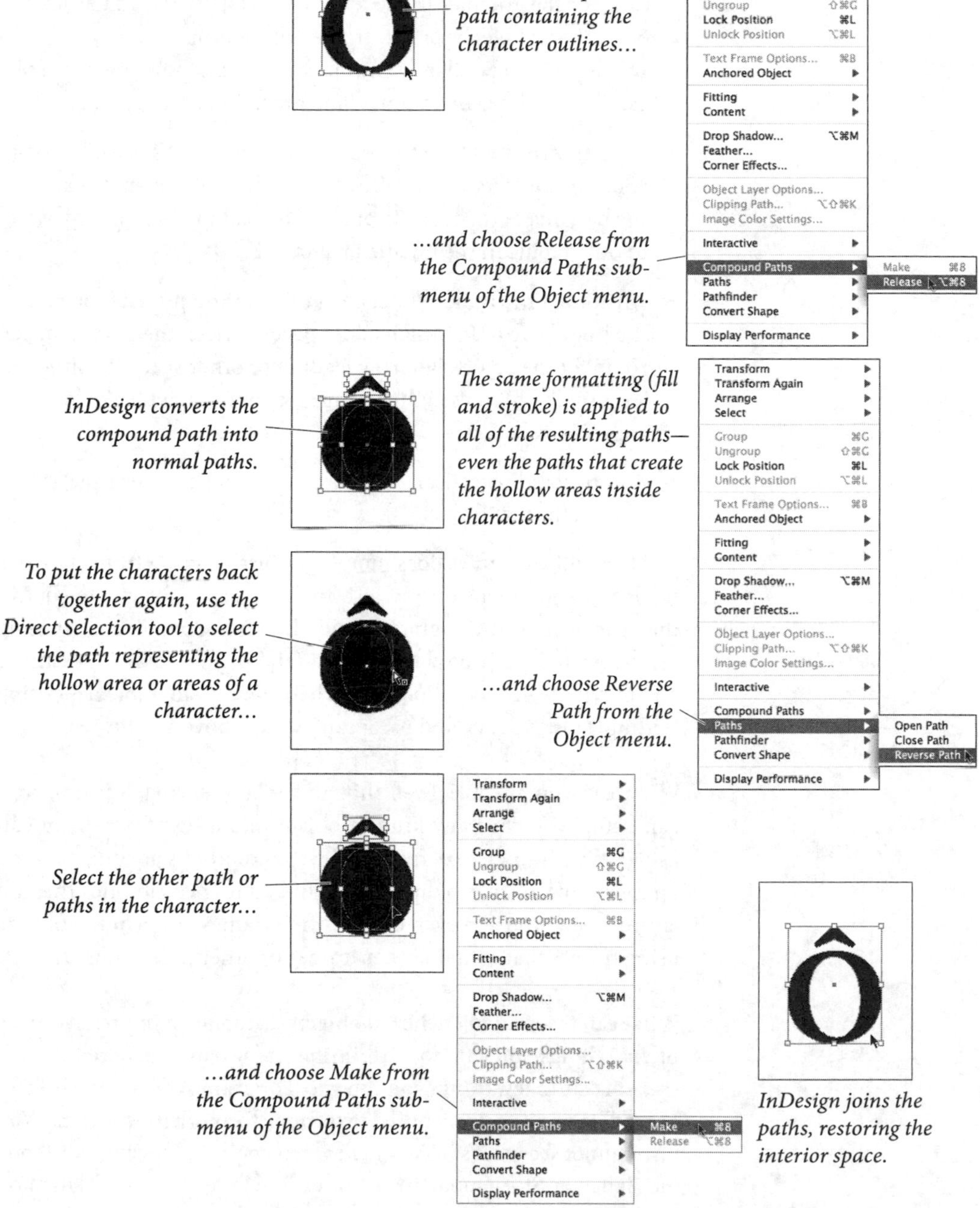
Select the compound path containing the character outlines...
Transform
Transform Again
Arrange
Select
Group ⌘G
Ungroup ⇧⌘G
Lock Position ⌘L
Unlock Position ⌥⌘L
Text Frame Options... ⌘B
Anchored Object
Fitting
Content
Drop Shadow... ⌥⌘M
Feather...
Corner Effects...
Object Layer Options...
Clipping Path... ⌥⇧⌘K
Image Color Settings...
Interactive
Compound Paths
Paths
Pathfinder
Convert Shape
Display Performance
Make ⌘8
Release ⌥⌘8
...and choose Release from the Compound Paths submenu of the Object menu.
InDesign converts the compound path into normal paths.
The same formatting (fill and stroke) is applied to all of the resulting paths—even the paths that create the hollow areas inside characters.
To put the characters back together again, use the Direct Selection tool to select the path representing the hollow area or areas of a character...
...and choose Reverse Path from the Object menu.
Open Path
Close Path
Reverse Path
Select the other path or paths in the character...
...and choose Make from the Compound Paths submenu of the Object menu.
InDesign joins the paths, restoring the interior space.

These days, we embed graphics in lines of text whenever the graphics have a defined relationship to the text. You know what we we're talking about—illustrations that should appear immediately after a paragraph (think of the screen shots in a manual), or icons "hanging" to the left of a column of text, or graphic symbols in a line of text. If you anchor the graphics in the text, they'll follow the text as it flows through the text blocks or text frames containing the story.

InDesign CS offered only "inline frames," but now you can create inline frames, above line frames, and anchored objects, too.

▶ An inline frame sits in the text position where it's placed, though you can adjust its vertical offset (how far up or down it sits from the baseline of the text around it). For example, you might want to put graphic in the middle of a line of text.

▶ An above line frame sits between the line you placed it on and the line above it. InDesign adds space between the lines to make room for the object, ignoring leading or other spacing you've set. We usually call these inline frames, even though they're technically different.

▶ An anchored object can be placed anywhere on your page, even outside the text frame.

Using inline frames does more than just "stick" a frame to a particular location in a story—it also makes it easier for you to control the space between the graphic and the text. Complicated spacing arrangements that would be difficult (and involve lots of measuring and moving) without inline frames become easy to implement using leading, tabs, indents, and paragraph space above and below.

What can you anchor? Even though we keep saying "frames," you can actually anchor any kind of object into a text frame. You can use graphic frames, text frames, lines, and groups as well, opening up new ways to solve old problems and adding capabilities that are entirely new. You can even create inline frames or anchored objects using frames that contain other frames or other inline frames.

What can't you do to anchored objects? Despite an impressive array of cool things you can do with inline frames and anchored objects, there are still a few things you can't do. For example, you can't link (or "thread") an inline or anchored text frame to another text frame. You also cannot see what's inside them when you're in Story Editor mode (or Galley or Story mode in InCopy). The latter is especially annoying. In fact, we're typing this in Story Editor right now and can't see the heading in the next paragraph because it's already anchored. Just another good reason to buy a another monitor so that you can have Story Editor and the document layout visible at the same time.

Creating an Inline Frame

You can use any of the following methods to create an inline frame (see Figure 6-52).

▶ Paste a frame or group into text.

▶ Place a graphic when you have an active text insertion point.

▶ Position the text cursor where you want the inline frame and choose Insert from the Anchored Object submenu (under the Object menu or the context menu). Then choose Inline or Above Line from the Position popup menu. We virtually never use the Insert Anchored Object feature, but it's nice to know it's there. Instead, we usually paste an existing object, or place a file.

▶ Use the Type tool to select a character or a range of characters and choose Convert to Outlines from the Type menu. InDesign creates a path for each character in the selection and embeds the paths, as a compound path, in the text.

InDesign treats each inline frame as a single character of text. When you view the text in Story Editor, you can see the "anchor marker" (a little anchor symbol) in the text.

FIGURE 6-52
Creating an Inline Frame

1. Select the object (graphic frame, text frame, or group) you want to embed in the text and cut or copy it to the Clipboard.

2. Select the Type tool and click inside a text frame.

3. Paste the object into the text. At this point, you can select the object using the Selection tool (or select object contents using the Direct Selection tool) and adjust the object's vertical position relative to the line of text.

You can also select the object as if it were a single character of text by using the Type tool.

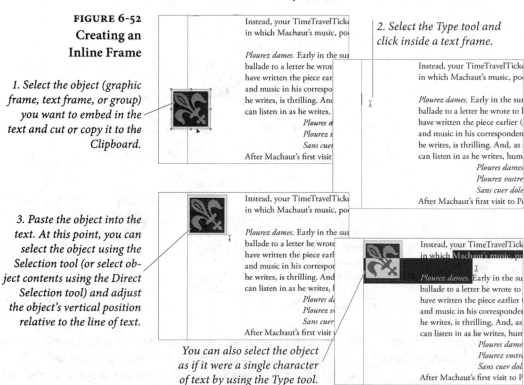

You can select an inline frame using the Type tool and adjust its leading and baseline shift using the Character palette. You can adjust the horizontal distance between the inline frame and the other characters on the line using kerning or tracking—you can even kern text following the inline frame back into the frame (you can't, however, kern the frame back into characters preceding it on a line).

You can select an inline frame using the Selection or Direct Selection tools, and you can edit the shape of the inline frame using the path drawing tools (the Pen, Add Point, Delete Point, and Convert Point tools). You can also drag an inline frame up or down in the text frame using either of the selection tools (see Figure 6-53), or you can apply a baseline shift to the character containing the inline frame.

Another way to adjust the vertical offset of a selected inline object is to choose Options from the Anchored Objects submenu (under the Object menu or the context menu) and change the Y Offset value. This is a particularly good way to get the offset back to zero if you have accidentally nudged it up or down.

FIGURE 6-53
Adjusting the Position of an Inline Frame

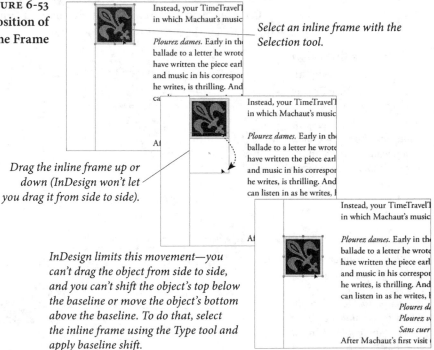

Select an inline frame with the Selection tool.

Drag the inline frame up or down (InDesign won't let you drag it from side to side).

InDesign limits this movement—you can't drag the object from side to side, and you can't shift the object's top below the baseline or move the object's bottom above the baseline. To do that, select the inline frame using the Type tool and apply baseline shift.

Inline Frames and Leading

When you insert an inline frame into a text frame, InDesign gives it the leading value of the surrounding text. If you're using "auto" leading, and if the inline frame is taller than the height of the text, InDesign pushes the line down to prevent the inline frame from overlapping the text on the lines above it. If, on the other hand, you're using a fixed leading value, you'll see the inline frame overlap the text. By default, InDesign positions the bottom of the inline frame at the baseline of text.

This works perfectly for us—when the inline frame shares a line with other text, we usually want the leading of the line to stay the same as the other lines in the paragraph—and we can get this effect using fixed leading values. When we place an inline frame in a paragraph by itself, however, we usually want the height of the paragraph to equal the height of the inline frame—and we can get that effect by using "auto" leading for the paragraph.

The rules are a little different when an inline frame falls on the first line of text in a text frame. In that case, the position of the baseline of the inline frame is controlled by the First Baseline option in the Text Frame Options dialog box.

If the height of the inline frame is greater than the height of the characters in the line (and it usually is), choosing "Ascent" positions the top of the inline frame at the top of the text frame. This pushes the first line down to accommodate the height of the inline frame. If you adjust the vertical position of the inline frame, the position of the first line of text moves up or down. The same thing happens when you choose "Cap Height" (note that these two settings produce different results for text, but are the same for inline frames).

When you choose "Baseline," however, InDesign positions the baseline of the first line of text according to the largest leading value in the line. If you're using a fixed leading value, and you've set the leading of the inline frame to the leading of the surrounding text, the position of the baseline of the first line of text won't change, regardless of what you do with the inline frame.

We always use the "Baseline" option for our first baseline position, and we always set the leading of a graphic that shares a line with text characters to the leading of those characters. This way, we always know where the first baseline of text will fall, and we don't have to worry that changes to the shape, size, or baseline position of the inline frame will mess up the leading.

The only time we use "auto" leading is when we're working with a paragraph that contains only an inline frame. The only trouble is that we want the vertical distance taken up by the paragraph to be exactly equal to the height of the inline frame—no more, no less. By default, InDesign's "auto" leading value is equal to 120% of the point size of the type (or, in this case, the height of the inline frame). How can we get the base "auto" leading percentage down to 100%?

The percentage used to calculate "auto" leading, as it turns out, is a paragraph-level attribute. To view or adjust this percentage, choose Justification from the Paragraph palette's menu. InDesign displays the Justification dialog box. Enter 100 in the Auto Leading field and click OK to close the dialog box (see Figure 6-54). Once you've done this, the leading of the paragraph will equal the height of the inline frame. If you want, you can add this to a paragraph style definition.

FIGURE 6-54
Inline Frames and
"Auto" Leading

Height of inline graphic:
*56 points (4 * 14)*

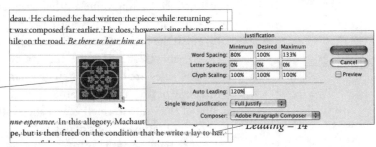

In this example, the leading of the paragraph containing the inline frame is set to "Auto," and the Auto Leading value is set to 120 percent, which means that the lines following the graphic do not align to the 14-point baseline grid.

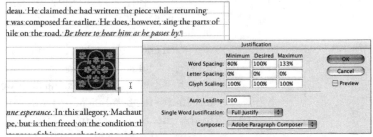

Set the Auto Leading value to 100 percent, and InDesign makes the vertical space occupied by the inline frame equal to the height of the frame.

Creating Hanging
Side Heads

If there's one thing that inline frames make easier, it's hanging side heads. You know—the headings that appear to the left of a column of text (like the one to the left of this paragraph). In InDesign, you can create a hanging side head that follows a paragraph of text as it flows through a publication—no more dragging the headings to a new position when text reflows. You use a hanging indent and an inline frame, as shown in the following steps (see Figure 6-55).

1. Create a hanging indent. To do this, set a left indent that's the width of the "companion column" you want to the left of the paragraph, then set a negative first line indent equal to the width of the left indent. Place a tab stop at the left indent.

2. Enter a tab character before the first character of the paragraph. This pushes the text to the left indent.

FIGURE 6-55
Creating a
Hanging Side Head

This paragraph has a negative first line indent to accommodate the heading, and I've already entered a tab character before the first line of the paragraph.

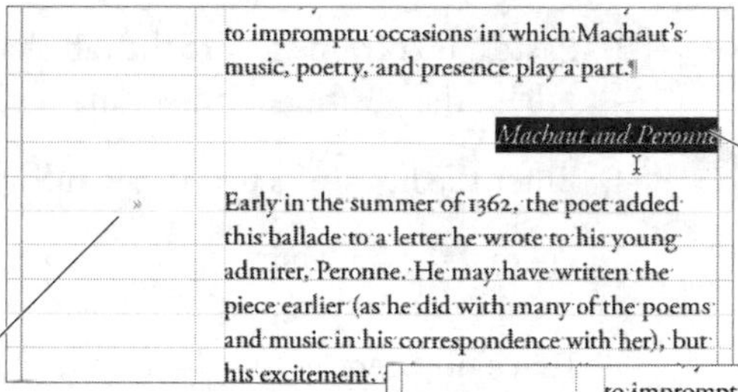

to impromptu occasions in which Machaut's music, poetry, and presence play a part.

Machaut and Peronne

Early in the summer of 1362, the poet added this ballade to a letter he wrote to his young admirer, Peronne. He may have written the piece earlier (as he did with many of the poems and music in his correspondence with her), but his excitement.

Use the Type tool to select the text you want to format as a hanging side head.

Cut or copy the heading to the Clipboard, then press Command-Shift-A/ Ctrl-Shift-A (to deselect all), and then paste. InDesign places the text from the Clipboard in a new text frame.

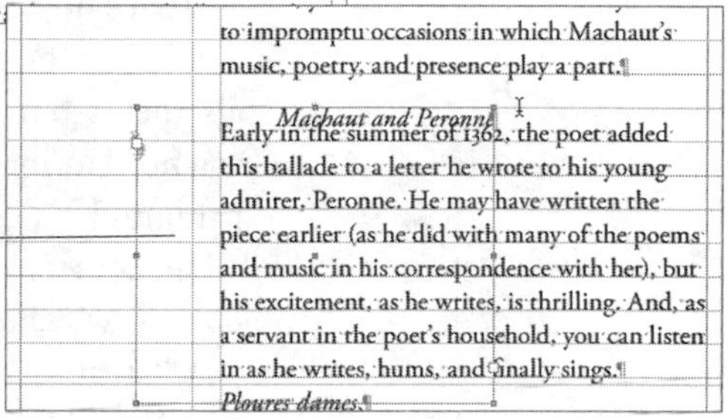

to impromptu occasions in which Machaut's music, poetry, and presence play a part.

Machaut and Peronne
Early in the summer of 1362, the poet added this ballade to a letter he wrote to his young admirer, Peronne. He may have written the piece earlier (as he did with many of the poems and music in his correspondence with her), but his excitement, as he writes, is thrilling. And, as a servant in the poet's household, you can listen in as he writes, hums, and finally sings.
Ploures dames.

Adjust the size of the text frame, if necessary.

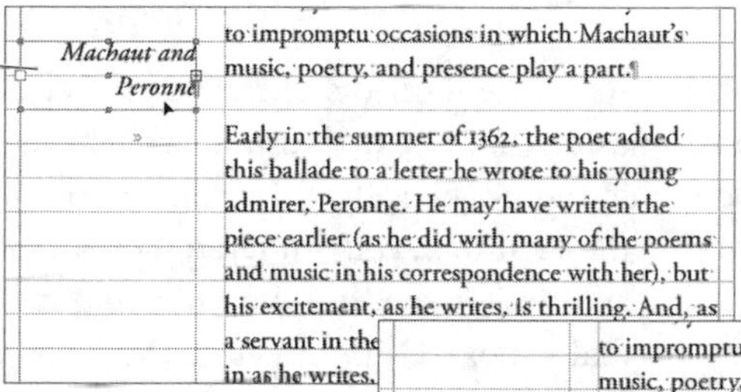

Machaut and Peronne

to impromptu occasions in which Machaut's music, poetry, and presence play a part.

Early in the summer of 1362, the poet added this ballade to a letter he wrote to his young admirer, Peronne. He may have written the piece earlier (as he did with many of the poems and music in his correspondence with her), but his excitement, as he writes, is thrilling. And, as a servant in the in as he writes,

Cut or copy the text frame to the Clipboard, then click the Type tool in the text (before the tab character) and paste the text frame from the Clipboard.

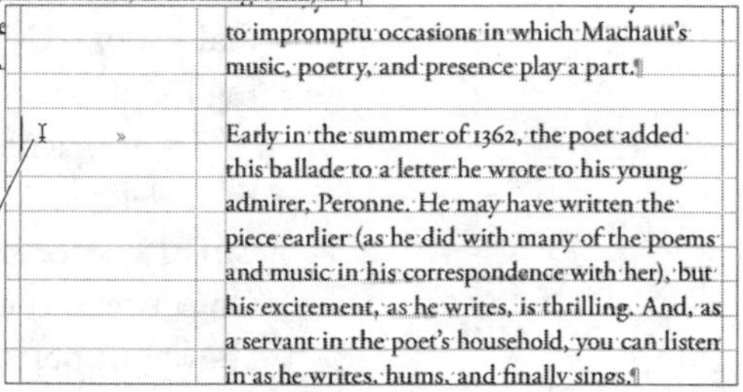

to impromptu occasions in which Machaut's music, poetry, and presence play a part.

Early in the summer of 1362, the poet added this ballade to a letter he wrote to his young admirer, Peronne. He may have written the piece earlier (as he did with many of the poems and music in his correspondence with her), but his excitement, as he writes, is thrilling. And, as a servant in the poet's household, you can listen in as he writes, hums, and finally sings.

Adjust the size and/or position of the inline text frame until it looks the way you want it to.

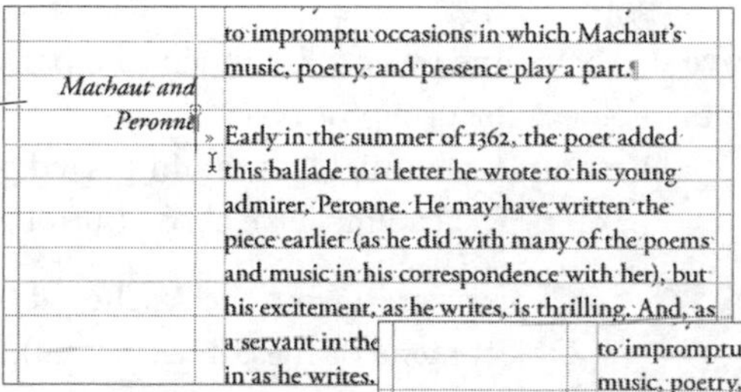

Machaut and Peronne

to impromptu occasions in which Machaut's music, poetry, and presence play a part.

Early in the summer of 1362, the poet added this ballade to a letter he wrote to his young admirer, Peronne. He may have written the piece earlier (as he did with many of the poems and music in his correspondence with her), but his excitement, as he writes, is thrilling. And, as a servant in the in as he writes,

You've created a hanging side head that will move with the paragraph of body text as that paragraph moves in response to editing or layout changes.

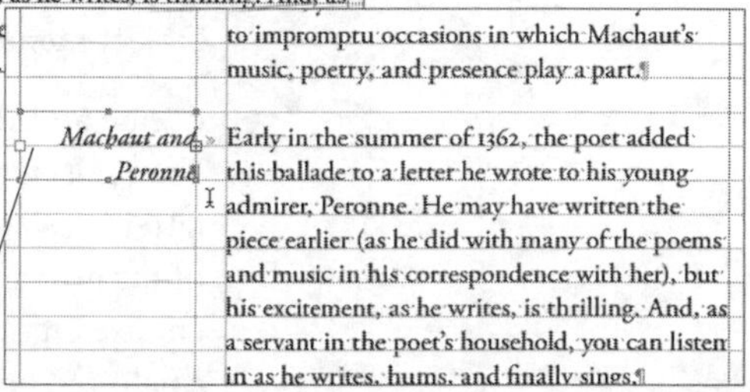

Machaut and Peronne

to impromptu occasions in which Machaut's music, poetry, and presence play a part.

Early in the summer of 1362, the poet added this ballade to a letter he wrote to his young admirer, Peronne. He may have written the piece earlier (as he did with many of the poems and music in his correspondence with her), but his excitement, as he writes, is thrilling. And, as a servant in the poet's household, you can listen in as he writes, hums, and finally sings.

3. Paste a text frame before the tab character you just entered. Adjust the position of the inline text frame, if necessary.

4. Enter the heading's text in the inline text frame.

5. Format the heading.

That's all there is to it—you now have a hanging side head that will follow the paragraph anywhere it goes. This same technique can also be used to position graphics frames, and comes in handy when you need to "hang" an icon or a vertical rule to the left of a particular paragraph.

Of course, you can accomplish the same thing with an anchored object—which can actually sit in the margin outside the text frame (see "Creating an Anchored Object," later in this chapter). But some people find inline frames easier to work with.

Selecting and Removing Inline and Anchored Objects

As we mentioned earlier, you can select an inline or anchored object using the Type tool (the object behaves as if it were a single character in the story) or the Selection tool or Direct Selection tool. If you use the Type tool, you can select more than one inline or anchored object at a time (to control their position in the Anchored Object Options dialog box). Using either method, you can delete the object by pressing Delete.

To "unanchor" an inline frame or anchored object, select it using the Selection tool, then cut and paste. If it's an anchored object, you can also select Release from the Anchored Object submenu (on the Object menu or context menu). Release doesn't work for inline or above line objects.

Creating Above Line Objects

Above line objects are much like paragraph rules, but can use any object (or group of objects), to create a wider range of effects. For example, you might use an imported graphic as a rule above a paragraph. You can make an above line object in one of two ways.

▶ Choose Insert from the Anchored Object submenu (from the Object menu or the context menu), and then choose Above Line.

▶ Create an inline frame as we described earlier in this section. Then select it using either the Selection tool or the Type tool (the latter is especially helpful when you want to convert a number of inline frames to above line objects at the same time) and choose Options from the Anchored Object submenu. When the Anchored Object Options dialog box appears, turn on the Above Line option.

Once you create an above line object, you can use the Anchored Object Options dialog box to control where the object will appear in the space between the current line and the line before it (see Figure 6-56). The Alignment popup menu lets you choose Left, Center, Right, Toward Spine, Away from Spine, and Text Alignment. The last item simply means use the same alignment as the horizontal alignment of the paragraph the above line object is sitting in (left, center, or right).

You can also adjust the space before or after the object. Increasing these values adds vertical space around the above line object. You can also use negative values for Space Before and Space After (up to the height of the object itself), which will cause the object to overlap

FIGURE 6-56
Creating an Above Line Object

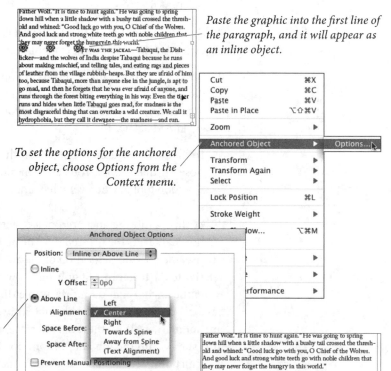

Select a graphic.

Paste the graphic into the first line of the paragraph, and it will appear as an inline object.

To set the options for the anchored object, choose Options from the Context menu.

InDesign displays the Anchored Object Options dialog box.

Turn on the Above Line option, then select an alignment and enter the space before and space after distances you want.

Here's the final anchored object, with space above and below added.

the preceding or following line. InDesign changes the Space Before and Space After values whenever you drag the object up or down. (As you'd expect, you won't be able to drag the object if you have turned on the Prevent Manual Positioning option or if you have enabled Lock Position on the Object menu. Turning either of these features on enables the other.)

**Creating
Anchored
Objects**

Unlike inline frames and above line objects, anchored objects can appear anywhere the page or spread containing their text anchor. Just like above line objects, you can create an anchored object using either the Insert Anchored Object dialog box or by creating an inline object and then converting it to an anchored object by copying and pasting (see Figure 6-57).

1. Select the inline frame (or group or line, or whatever it is) by clicking on it with the Selection tool or by dragging over it with the Type tool.

2. Choose Options from the Anchored Object submenu (under the Object menu or the context menu).

3. Choose Custom from the Position popup menu at the top of the Anchored Object Options dialog box. The dialog box now offers a dizzying array of options. Don't panic. All will be explained below.

4. To manually position the object on the page, just click OK (to close the dialog box). You can then move the object with the Selection tool to wherever you want it.

At this point, the anchored object acts as if it is tethered to the anchor marker As the text reflows, the object moves, too. To be more precise, the horizontal location of the anchored object remains fixed relative to the text frame (it only moves when the text frame moves or when the anchor marker moves into a different frame), but its vertical location moves with the line of text itself (the line containing the anchor marker). With these default settings, the anchored object will also stay within the top and bottom boundaries of the text frame—you can't drag it above or below the frame.

But the default settings are only the beginning. Let's look at what else you can do in the Anchored Object Options dialog box.

Relative to Spine. If you want to position an anchored object precisely (as opposed to just dragging it somewhere), the first decision you need to make is whether to turn on the Relative to Spine option.

FIGURE 6-57
Creating an
Anchored Object

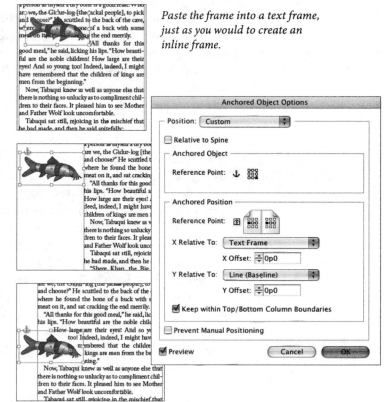

*Paste the frame into a text frame,
just as you would to create an
inline frame.*

*Open the Anchored Object
Options dialog box and turn
on the Preview checkbox.
The object will appear to
the left of the text frame by
default.*

*Drag the object to a new
location and turn on text
wrap. The object will remain
positioned in relation to
the frame and the anchor
marker in the story.*

When this option is on, InDesign positions the object differently depending on whether it sits on a left hand (verso) or on a right hand (recto) page. This option is similar to the Align Toward Spine and Align Away from Spine paragraph alignment feature, and is useful when you want an object to appear in the outside or inside margin of a page.

Anchored Object. The next step is to tell InDesign what part of the anchored object you're positioning. When Relative to Spine is off, you'll see a single Reference Point proxy from which you can choose a corner, side, or center point. If you choose the lower-right corner of this proxy, you're telling InDesign to position the lower-right corner of the anchored object at a particular place on the page. (We'll get to where it'll be positioned in a moment.)

If you've turned on the Relative to Spine checkbox, you'll see two proxies in the Reference Point section. When you choose a point on one proxy, it'll be mirrored on the other. What InDesign is trying to tell you is that you're no longer choosing the left or right sides of the anchored object, but rather the inside (toward spine) or outside (away from spine) sides. Click the lower-right corner point of the left Reference Point proxy, and you're telling InDesign that you want the lower-inside corner to be positioned at a particular place on the page.

Turn on the Preview checkbox! You will likely go insane if you try to figure out all these controls without it. With the Preview checkbox turned on, you can see the effect of each change you make.

Anchored Position. The final step to positioning an anchored object is in some ways the most complex: Telling InDesign where you want the object to appear on the page using the Anchored Position section of the Anchored Object Options dialog box. We find that it helps to learn to "read" the dialog box (see Figure 6-58).

The Reference Point control in this section (note to Adobe: Please don't give two different settings the same label) makes no sense until you look at the X Relative To and Y Relative To sections, so skip it for a moment. The X Relative To popup menu sets the horizontal position of the anchored object. You can choose Anchor Marker, Column Edge, Text Frame, Page Margin, or Page Edge.

If you click the left point in the Reference Point proxy (the one in the Anchored Position section) the default setting of Text Frame means, "position the anchored object relative to the left side of the current text frame." If you select the right point of the Reference Point proxy, it means "position the anchored object relative to the right side of the current text frame." If you have turned on the Relative to Spine checkbox, these mean, "relative to the outside/inside of the text frame."

The Y Relative To popup menu determines the vertical position of the anchored object. Your options are: Line (Baseline, Cap Height, or Top of Leading), Column Edge, Text Frame, Page Margin, or Page Edge. The default setting is "Line (Baseline)," which means, "position the anchored object on the page so that it aligns with the baseline of the line that includes the anchor marker." As the line shifts up or down, so does the anchored object.

When you choose one of the Line options from the popup menu, the Reference Point proxy limits your choices to left, center, or right. The reason is obvious: There is no "upper left" corner of the anchor marker's baseline. However, if you choose a Y Relative To setting having to do with the frame, column, or page, the Reference Point proxy changes to allow you to choose more points (upper left corner of the page, lower left corner of the page, and so on).

You can also specify X Offset or Y Offset values in order to precisely position the anchored object. If you select the right-center point of the Reference Point proxy and select Page Edge from the X

FIGURE 6-58
"Reading" the Anchored Options Dialog Box

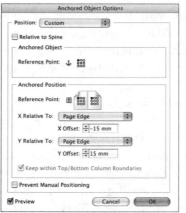

The upper left corner of the anchored object is placed 15 mm in from the upper left corner of the page.

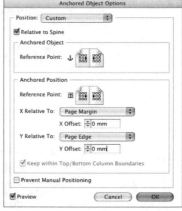

The inside center edge of the object sits halfway down the page and against the inside margin.

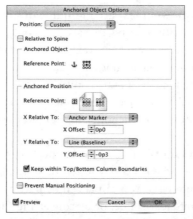

The object is centered around the anchor marker and raised 3 mm. As the marker moves, so does the object.

The object is always placed in the center of the opposite page in a letter-sized spread.

Relative To popup menu, and then type 20 mm in the the X Offset field, what you're saying is, "Place the anchored object 20 mm from the right edge of the page." You can enter negative numbers for all kinds of positioning tricks (such as putting an object on the page *opposite* the page containing the anchor marker).

The last control in the Anchored Position section is the Keep within Top/Bottom Column Bounds. (It'll be grayed out unless you have chosen one of the Line options from the Y Relative To popup menu.) The idea here is that if the line containing the anchor marker gets too close to the top or bottom of the text frame, the anchored object might extend past the frame's top or bottom edge. If you don't want this to happen, turn this option on.

Prevent Manual Positioning. As we noted earlier, turning on the Prevent Manual Positioning checkbox is exactly the same as choosing Lock Position from the Object menu. It's just a good way to ensure that your anchored objects don't get accidentally moved.

Seeing Markers. Once you've set up an anchored object, you may not remember where, exactly, the anchor marker is located. Choose Show Hidden Characters from the Type menu, and you'll see a little anchor marker symbol in the story—it's a light blue yen character (¥). Similarly, if you open Story Editor, you can see a black anchor symbol at that location. But perhaps the most useful indicator appears when you choose Show Text Threads from the View menu—select the text frame or the anchored object with the Selection tool and you'll see a dashed line connecting the two.

Text Wrap and Inline and Anchored Objects

You can wrap text around inline or anchored objects. This feature comes with three big caveats. First, only the story in which the object is anchored is affected. Text in other frames ignore anchored objects. Second, if you anchor an object inside a table cell, text wrap is completely ignored. Finally, only the lines *following* the line containing an anchored object are affected by the object's text wrap. The line containing the anchored object ignores the text wrap.

Drop Cap Wrap. One of the most frustrating aspects of drop caps is that there is no way to tell InDesign to wrap the subsequent text around them. You can fake it by putting the drop cap character in a separate text frame, or by converting the character to outlines, but then the drop cap wouldn't travel with the text, right?

Enter inline frames. As David first documented in his book with Anne-Marie Concepción, *Adobe InDesign CS/CS2 Breakthroughs*, you can place a drop cap character in a separate frame, paste it at the end of the paragraph *before* the paragraph in which it's supposed to appear (you can put the frame in a blank paragraph when the drop cap appears at the beginning of the story), and then adjust the text wrap boundaries with the Direct Selection tool to get the effect you want (see Figure 6-59).

Ole notes that this is a heck of a lot of work to go through to achieve a design effect that makes your text harder to read (as varying the starting position of successive text lines always does). Further, he notes in his irritating, pedantic fashion, there's a reason that the drop caps in beautiful old books almost always place the ornamental drop cap in a rectangular frame—to avoid this very temptation.

FIGURE 6-59
Wrapping Around an
Anchored Drop Cap

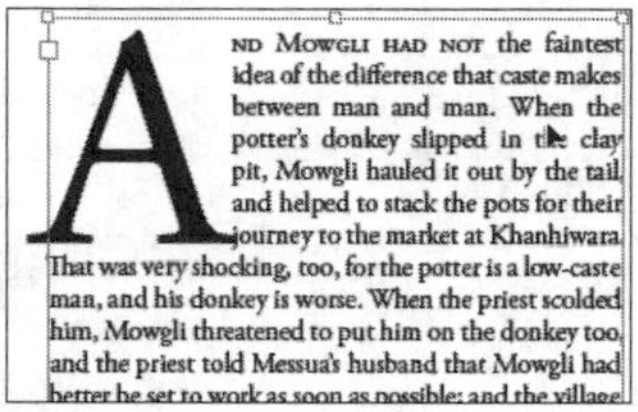

*The original paragraph
with a drop cap*

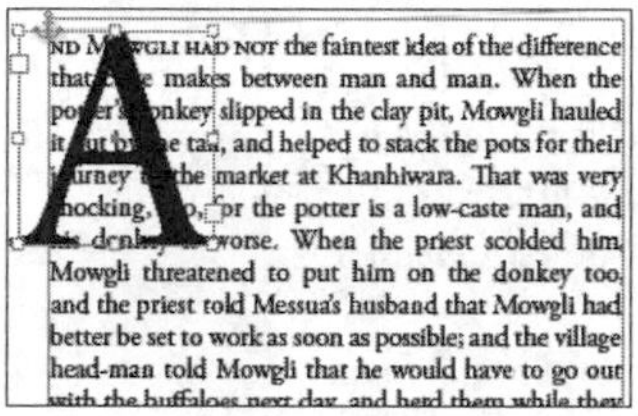

*Cut the drop cap, remove the drop cap
formatting from the paragraph, and
then paste the drop cap into a new text
frame. Choose Fit Frame to Content,
then use the Selection tool to cut the
drop cap frame and paste it into the
line before the paragraph.*

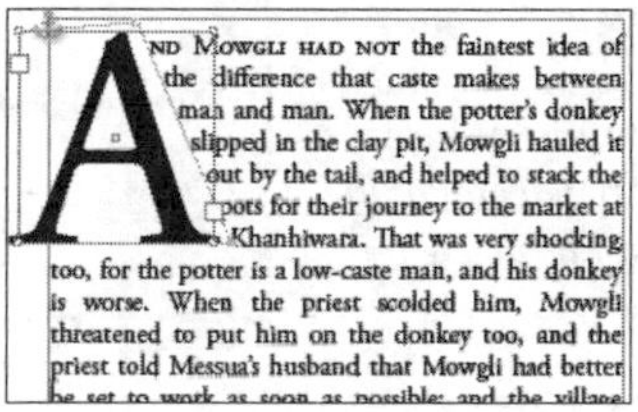

*Choose Wrap Around Bounding Box
in the Text Wrap palette, increase the
wrap a few points (so you can see them)
and then use the Direct Selection tool to
create a custom wrap.*

Anchored Object
Recipe: Hanging
Side Heads

Earlier, we mentioned that inline frames are the best way to create hanging side heads (such as the one loitering to the left of this paragraph), but we were telling only half of the story. By experimenting on ourselves (as any good pair of mad scientists should), we've found that the best approach to hanging side heads is to create inline frames by copying and pasting and then convert them to anchored objects.

We did this because we found that changes in InDesign between CS and CS2 make it much more difficult to control the vertical position of inline frames—which, in turn, made managing our hanging side heads a bit of a challenge. The good news is that anchored objects offer a level of precision that inline frames just can't match. We found a set of anchored object settings that worked well with our hanging side heads, and then created a script to apply the changes to our chapters.

We set up the hanging side heads—most of which were already inline graphics—as shown in Figure 6-60. The horizontal location of the top left corner of the hanging side head is set to the left edge of the text frame, and the vertical location is 13 points above the baseline of the line of text containing the anchor (our leading grid is based on 13 point increments).

We want the frame to remain within the vertical bounds of the text frame, and we allow manual positioning (because we need to be able to adjust the height of the frame as we add or delete text).

FIGURE 6-60
Hanging Side Heads as
Anchored Objects

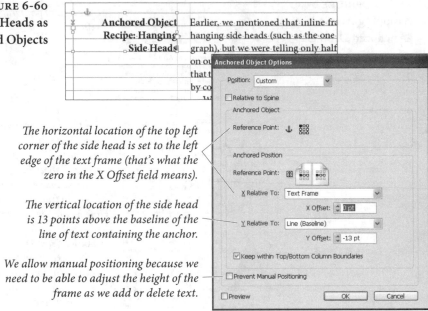

The horizontal location of the top left corner of the side head is set to the left edge of the text frame (that's what the zero in the X Offset field means).

The vertical location of the side head is 13 points above the baseline of the line of text containing the anchor.

We allow manual positioning because we need to be able to adjust the height of the frame as we add or delete text.

Putting a Box Around Text

How can you put a box around a paragraph that will follow the paragraph as it flows from column to column or page to page? As shown earlier in this chapter, you can use paragraph rules or a single-cell table (we prefer the table approach), or you can use an inline rectangle, as shown below (see Figure 6-61).

1. Create a paragraph above the "box" paragraph.

2. Draw a rectangle, then paste the rectangle into the empty paragraph you just created.

3. Set the leading of the paragraph and the inline frame to some fixed value (anything other than "auto").

4. Adjust the size and baseline position of the inline frame so that it falls around the following paragraph.

5. Use the Keep With Next option to "stick" the paragraph containing the inline frame to the following paragraph.

You could also do this with an anchored object rather than an inline frame, which means you don't need a separate empty paragraph. However, the anchored object will obliterate the text behind it unless is has a fill of None. One solution is to set the transparency blending mode for the anchored object to Multiply in the Transparency palette. Or, as we said earlier, use the table method.

FIGURE 6-61
**Yet Another Way
to Put a Box Around
a Paragraph**

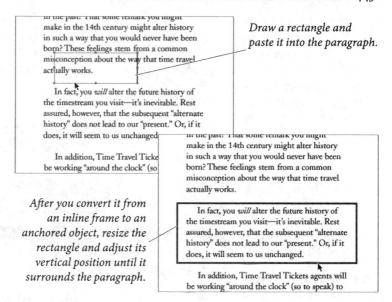

Draw a rectangle and
paste it into the paragraph.

After you convert it from
an inline frame to an
anchored object, resize the
rectangle and adjust its
vertical position until it
surrounds the paragraph.

Object Styles

The sidebars in your magazine have a twenty percent cyan fill and a soft drop shadow. How many thousand times must you apply that same fill and shadow before you go mad and throw someone else's computer out the window? (You wouldn't throw your own out the window; your favorite games are there.) One solution would be to keep an example object in a library (see Chapter 1, "Workspace"). A more flexible and powerful solution is to create an object style.

Object styles are just like paragraph and character styles, except that they apply to objects instead of text. An object style is basically just a bunch of object formatting with a name. You can apply that style to a frame or path on your page and all the appropriate formatting is applied. If you later change the definition of the style, the change immediately ripples through to all the objects tagged with that style.

**Creating
Object Styles**

To create an object style, hold down Option/Alt and click the New Object Style button at the bottom of the Object Styles palette (press Command-F7/Ctrl-F7 to display the palette if it is not already visible). If you have an object selected, the new object style takes on the formatting attributes of the object. If you don't have anything selected on the page, then the object style takes on the default formatting of the document, and you will have to define the style from scratch. We strongly urge you to use the "create style by example" approach, as shown in Figure 6-62).

FIGURE 6-62
Creating an
Object Style

Select an object that has
the formatting attributes
you want to assign to the
object style.

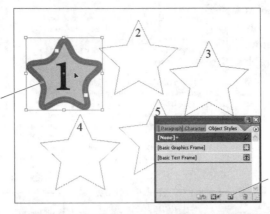

Hold down Option/Alt
and click the New
Object Style button.

InDesign displays the New
Object Style dialog box.

Make any changes you want
in the panels associated
with the dialog box. In this
example, we chose to associate a paragraph style with
the object style.

Uncheck sections to prevent
the style from affecting
the corresponding object
properties.

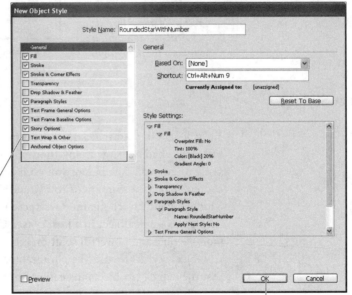

Click OK, and InDesign adds the new
object style to the list of available styles.

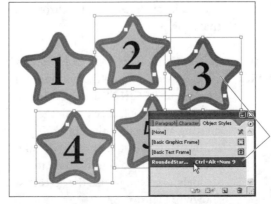

Select an object or
objects and apply the
style, and you'll see
that the formatting
attributes of the
original object
are applied to the
selected objects.

The New Object Style dialog box consists of 11 panels (count 'em!), including Fill, Stroke, Transparency, and Anchored Object Options. You can turn the checkbox next to each panel on or off. On means "apply this formatting as part of the style." Off means "ignore this formatting." That is, if you turn off the Fill checkbox, it doesn't mean that the fill should be set to None; it means that this object style has no effect on the fill of objects (see Figure 6-63).

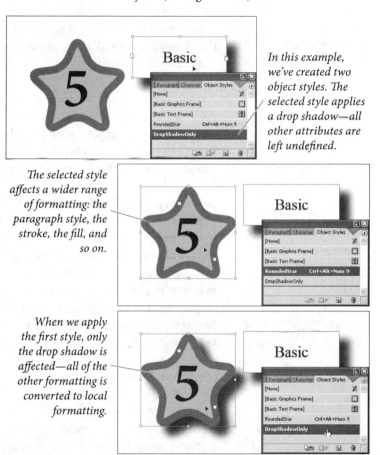

FIGURE 6-63
Selectively Applying Formatting with an Object Style

In this example, we've created two object styles. The selected style applies a drop shadow—all other attributes are left undefined.

The selected style affects a wider range of formatting: the paragraph style, the stroke, the fill, and so on.

When we apply the first style, only the drop shadow is affected—all of the other formatting is converted to local formatting.

You can create one object style that applies only a specific text wrap to an object, and a different style that applies only a stroke and a drop shadow. If you draw a frame and apply the first style, only the text wrap would be applied. Then you can apply the second style, changing only the stroke and drop shadow. At this point, the object is tagged with the second style, not the first, which means that if you redefine the first object style, this object will not be updated.

Note that you can press Tab to jump to the list of panels, and then press the up and down arrow keys on your keyboard to move among them. You can also Option/Alt-click on a checkbox to toggle the other categories: Option/Alt-click on an "on" checkbox to turn all the others off, and vice versa.

Style Settings. At the bottom of the General panel of the New Object Style dialog box is a list of Style Settings. You can use this as a summary of settings the object style will apply. But to be honest, we never use this. It's just easier to use the shortcuts to flip through each panel. If you do use it, you should Option/Alt-click on the little triangles so that they fully expand. (Otherwise, you have to click over and over again, which is annoying.)

Keyboard Shortcuts. You can assign a keyboard shortcut to an object style in the General panel. Like keyboard shortcuts for paragraph styles and character styles, the shortcut must use the numeric keypad keys (make sure that Num Lock is on), not normal numbers, characters, or function keys.

Basing One Object Style on Another. You can also choose another object style from the Based On popup menu in the General panel to create a "parent/child" relationship between styles. If you change the definition of the based on ("parent") style, that change is passed along to this style, too—provided that the child style didn't already override the parent style's formatting.

To clear the formatting in an object style that differs from its parent style, click the Reset to Base button. This makes the attributes of the style identical to those of the parent style.

The Default Styles

Every new document you create contains three initial object styles: None, Basic Graphics Frame, and Basic Text Frame. (They're listed in the palette with brackets so you know that they're special and can't be deleted.) When you create a path or an empty frame (one with an "X" through it), the None style is applied—that is, no style at all. When you make a text or graphics frame, the relevant style is applied. You can redefine these styles (see "Editing Object Styles," later in this section), and once you create new object styles, you can even tell InDesign to use those as your defaults instead.

For example, you might need to create a bunch of similarly-formatted text frames. You could change the Default Text Frame Style to one with the appropriate formatting, draw the frames, and then restore the original settings to the default style. To change the default text frame style, choose a style from the Default Text Frame Style submenu in the Object Styles palette menu. (Or the Default Graphics Frame Style submenu to change that default.)

Actually, it's even easier than that: See the little icons to the right of the default styles in the palette? Just drag one of them to the style you want to set as the default (see Figure 6-64). Alternatively, you can deselect everything and then select a style. In general, this sets the default graphics frame style; but when you have the Type tool selected, this sets the default text frame style.

FIGURE 6-64
Setting a Default Object Style

Drag the default icon (for either the graphics frame or text frame) to a new object style.

The object style you drop the icon on becomes the default object style for the corresponding frame type.

Applying Object Styles   You can apply an object style in any of several ways.

▸ Select an object or series of objects and click the object style name in the Object Styles palette (or choose it from the object style popup menu in the Control palette).

▸ Drag an object style name from the Object Styles palette and drop it on an object (the object need not be selected).

▸ Select one or more objects, then press Command-Return/Ctrl-Enter to invoke the Quick Apply feature, and then type a few characters of the object style name (see "Quick Apply," later in this chapter).

Note that if you have a lot of object styles, you can rearrange them in the palette by dragging them up or down. To reset them to alphabetical order, choose Sort by Name from the palette menu.

Clearing Local Formatting. Just as you can apply local text formatting to text over a paragraph or character style, you can apply local object formatting over an object style. You might apply an object style that fills a frame with cyan, and then manually override that to make the frame yellow. To remove all of the local overrides, click the Clear Overrides button in the Object Styles palette (or choosing the feature of the same name from the palette menu). Or you can Option/Alt-click on the style name to reset it and remove all overrides.

There's another "clear" button in the palette: Clear Attributes Not Defined by Style. Clicking this button (or choosing it from the palette menu) is basically the same as applying the None object style and then reapplying the style. InDesign sets all the object formatting that isn't described in the style definition (all of the panels without checkmarks next to them) to equal what you'd get with the None style (no fill, no stroke, no text wrap, and so on).

Breaking the Link. As we mentioned earlier, applying an object style creates a link between the object and the style. To convert the formatting applied by the object style to local formatting and break the link between the object and the style, choose Break Link to Style from the Object Styles palette menu. The object's appearance will not change, but future changes to the style definition will have no effect on the object.

Editing Object Styles

There are a whole mess o' ways to edit an object style.

▶ Double-click the style name in the Object Styles palette. If an object is selected on the page when you do this, the style will be applied to it.

▶ Right-click (or Control-click until you come to your senses and buy a two-button mouse) the style name in the Object Styles palette and choose Edit. This has the advantage of not applying the style to any selected objects.

▶ Select an object that has the style applied to it and then double-click the object style icon in the Control palette (this icon is the one to the left of the object style popup menu).

▶ Press Command-Return/Ctrl-Enter to bring up Quick Apply, type enough of the style name so that it is highlighted, and then press Command-Return/Ctrl-Enter again.

▶ Change the formatting of an object that is already tagged with the style, and then choose Redefine Object Style from the Object Styles palette menu. This updates the style definition to match the current formatting of the selected object.

Deleting Object Styles

To delete an object style, select the style in the Object Styles palette and click the Delete Style button, or drag the style name on top of the button. If the style is in use (if any objects are tagged with it), InDesign asks you which style it should apply in its place. If you choose None, you also have the option to Preserve Formatting. When this checkbox is on, objects that were tagged with the style will still appear the same, but all the formatting will be converted to local formatting. If you turn off Preserve Formatting, the objects will be completely cleared of formatting: no fill, stroke, and so on.

Importing Object Styles

How can you move your carefully-constructed object styles from one document to another? One easy way is to copy any object tagged with the style and then paste it into the target document—the style comes with it and you can then delete the object if you want.

If you want to import a bunch of styles, it may be easier to choose Load Object Styles from the Object Style palette menu. InDesign asks you to select another InDesign document, and then asks you which object styles you want to import from it. If there are object styles that have the same name in the two documents, you have a choice whether to use the incoming definition or to rename the style.

Placing Text on a Path

InDesign can place text *on* a path, as well as place text *inside* a path (which is what a text frame is, after all). Once you've added text to a path, you can select the text just as you would select any other text—select the Type tool and drag it through the characters you want to select, or click the Type tool in the text and use keyboard shortcuts. To select the path, use the Selection tool or Direct Selection tool.

To attach text to a path, follow these steps (see Figure 6-65).

1. Select the Path Type tool.

2. Move the tool over a path. The cursor changes to indicate that InDesign is ready to place text on the path.

3. Click the tool on the path. InDesign places the cursor on the path. The position of the cursor depends on the document's default paragraph alignment (if the default alignment is left, for example, the cursor will appear at the start of the path).

    Instead of clicking, you can drag the tool along the path to define the area of the path you want to fill with text.

    If InDesign cannot fit all of the text onto the path, the extra text is stored as overset text.

4. Add text to the path just as you would add text to a text frame—by typing, pasting text from the Clipboard, or importing text from a text file. This creates a new kind of object—not a text

FIGURE 6-65
Adding Text to a Path

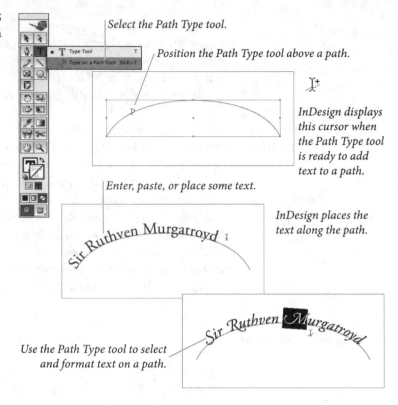

Select the Path Type tool.

Position the Path Type tool above a path.

InDesign displays this cursor when the Path Type tool is ready to add text to a path.

Enter, paste, or place some text.

InDesign places the text along the path.

Use the Path Type tool to select and format text on a path.

frame, not a path, but a blending of the two we'll refer to as a "path text object" from here on out.

Once you've attached text to a path, you can change its position on the path by dragging the Start Indicator or the End Indicator (see Figure 6-66), or change its orientation relative to the path using the Center/Flip Direction Indicator (see Figure 6-67).

Like text frames, path text objects feature an in port and an out port you can use to link the text to other text containers (text frames or other text path objects). You can even link text from a path text object to the interior of the path text object. InDesign does not apply paragraph rules to text in path text objects.

Path Text Options   You can control both the baseline position of text on a path and the relationship of the text to the shape of the path. To do this, select a path text object (or some of the text on a path) and then choose Options from the Type on a Path submenu of the Type menu (or Context menu). InDesign displays the Type on a Path Options dialog box (see Figure 6-68).

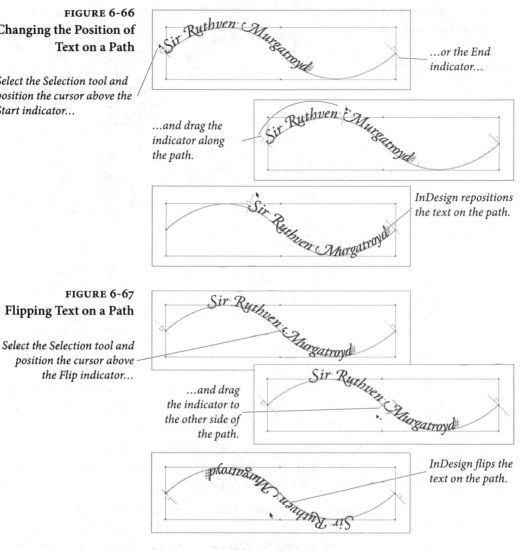

FIGURE 6-66
Changing the Position of Text on a Path

Select the Selection tool and position the cursor above the Start indicator...

...or the End indicator...

...and drag the indicator along the path.

InDesign repositions the text on the path.

FIGURE 6-67
Flipping Text on a Path

Select the Selection tool and position the cursor above the Flip indicator...

...and drag the indicator to the other side of the path.

InDesign flips the text on the path.

Effect. Do the character shapes distort in some way, or do they remain unchanged? That's the question you're answering when you make a choice from the Effect pop-up menu (see Figure 6-69). What, exactly, do these oddly named options do?

► Rainbow rotates the center point of each baseline to match the angle of the path at the location of the character.

► Skew skews the horizontal axis of the character to match the angle of the path at the location of the character, but leaves the vertical axis of the character unchanged.

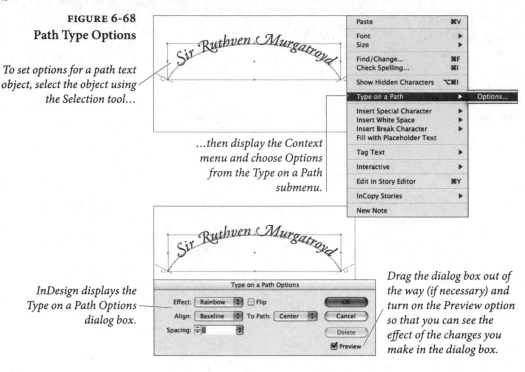

FIGURE 6-68
Path Type Options

*To set options for a path text
object, select the object using
the Selection tool...*

*...then display the Context
menu and choose Options
from the Type on a Path
submenu.*

*InDesign displays the
Type on a Path Options
dialog box.*

*Drag the dialog box out of
the way (if necessary) and
turn on the Preview option
so that you can see the
effect of the changes you
make in the dialog box.*

▶ 3D Ribbon skews the vertical axis of each character to match the
angle of the path at the location of the character, but leaves the
character's horizontal axis unchanged.

▶ Stair Step aligns the center point of each character's baseline to
match the angle of the path at the location of the character, but
does not rotate the character.

▶ Gravity rotates the center of the baseline of each character to
match the angle of the path at the character, skews the horizontal axis of the character to match that angle, and skews the
vertical axis of each character around the geometric center point
of the path.

Flip. You've probably noticed that path text follows the direction of
the path—the first character of the text typically appears at (or, if
you've dragged the Path Type tool, nearest) the first point in the path.
Given this, you'd think that you could select the path and choose
Reverse Path from the Options menu to make the text read from the
opposite end of the path. But you can't (not without first removing
the text from the path, anyway). To do what you're trying to do, turn
on the Flip option (see Figure 6-70).

FIGURE 6-69
Effect Option

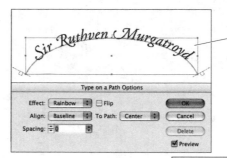

Rainbow rotates the characters around the path.

Skew skews the horizontal axis of each character to match the angle of the path, but leaves the vertical axis of the character unchanged.

3D Ribbon skews the vertical axis of each character to match the angle of the path, but leaves the character's horizontal axis unchanged.

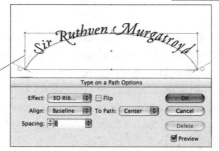

Stair Step moves the characters along the path, but does not skew or rotate the characters to match the path.

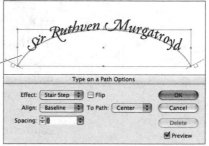

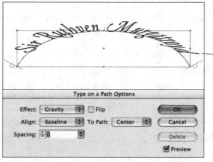

Gravity is like a combination of Rainbow and Skew—it rotates the characters around the path and skews the horizontal axis of each character.

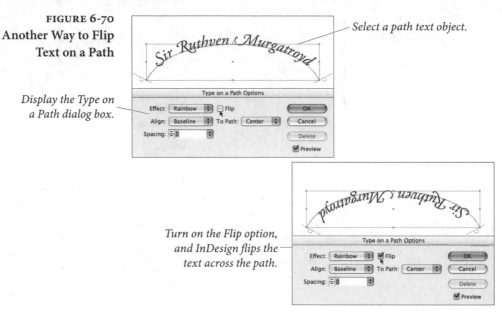

FIGURE 6-70
Another Way to Flip
Text on a Path

Select a path text object.

Display the Type on
a Path dialog box.

Turn on the Flip option,
and InDesign flips the
text across the path.

Align. These options control the way the text aligns to the path itself. Choose Ascender to align the top of the capital letters in the text (more or less) to the path, or choose Descender to position the bottoms of the characters on the path. Choose Center to align the text to the path at a point that's half of the height of the capital characters in the font, or choose Baseline to align the baseline of the characters to the path (see Figure 6-71).

To Path. The options on the To Path pop-up menu control the way that the text aligns to the *stroke* of the path. Choose Top to place the alignment point (whatever it was you chose from the Align pop-up menu) of the text at the top of the stroke; or Bottom to place it at the bottom of the stroke; or Center to align the alignment point of the text with the center of the path (see Figure 6-72). For more precise control of the text position, use baseline shift.

Spacing. The Spacing field (and attached pop-up menu) control the spacing of text around curves in the path. Enter a value (in points) in this field to tighten or loosen character spacing around curves (see Figure 6-73). Note that this setting has no effect on the kerning or tracking of text on straight line segments.

Removing Type
from a Path

To remove the text from a path type object and convert the object back into a "normal" path, you need to do more than simply delete

FIGURE 6-71
Align Options

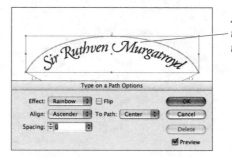

Ascender aligns the top of
the capital letters in the text
to the path.

Descender positions the
characters' descenders
on the path.

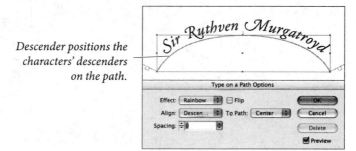

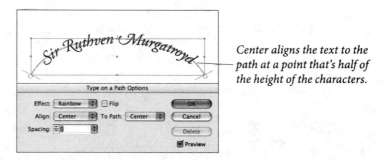

Center aligns the text to the
path at a point that's half of
the height of the characters.

Baseline aligns the baseline of
the characters to the path.

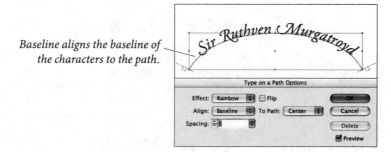

the text characters. If you do this, the object remains a path type
object. Instead, select the path (or some of the text on the path) and
choose Delete Type on a Path from the Type on a Path submenu (of
the Type menu or Context menu). See Figure 6-74.

FIGURE 6-72
To Path Options

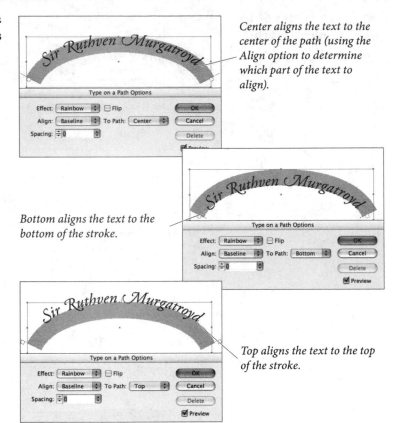

Center aligns the text to the center of the path (using the Align option to determine which part of the text to align).

Bottom aligns the text to the bottom of the stroke.

Top aligns the text to the top of the stroke.

FIGURE 6-73
Spacing

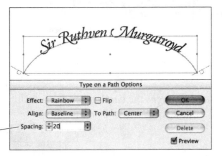

Enter a value in the Spacing field...

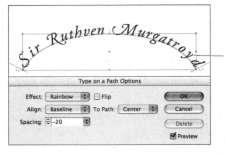

...and InDesign adjusts the spacing of text on curved line segments.

FIGURE 6-74
Removing Text
on a Path

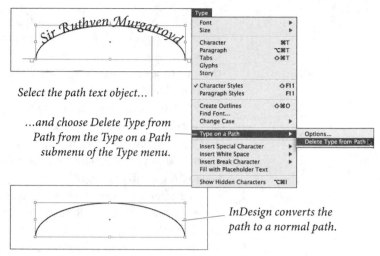

Select the path text object...

...and choose Delete Type from Path from the Type on a Path submenu of the Type menu.

InDesign converts the path to a normal path.

Quick Apply

There are some InDesign features that make a huge difference in the way that we work, but seem, in some ways, very small. They don't take long to describe, and, once you're used to them, you barely have to think about them. Take unlimited undo, for example—it's hard to imagine doing without it, but you hardly notice it. It just works. The same is true for the Quick Apply feature, which feels to us as if it's become part of our autonomous nervous systems (see Figure 6-75).

FIGURE 6-75
Quick Apply

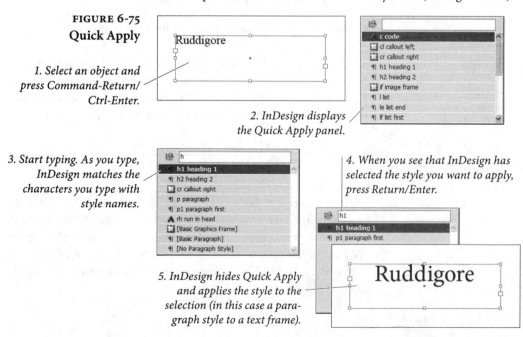

1. Select an object and press Command-Return/ Ctrl-Enter.

2. InDesign displays the Quick Apply panel.

3. Start typing. As you type, InDesign matches the characters you type with style names.

4. When you see that InDesign has selected the style you want to apply, press Return/Enter.

5. InDesign hides Quick Apply and applies the style to the selection (in this case a paragraph style to a text frame).

Quick Apply gives you a way to apply paragraph styles, character styles, and object styles. So what? You can already use the palettes, keyboard shortcuts, and menus to apply styles. The trouble is that these methods *cost something*. Palettes are use up precious screen real estate. Keyboard shortcuts are limited by available keys and by our overstressed memories. And using menus to do anything expends a precious commodity—human patience.

Quick Apply takes up no space on screen when it's not in use, requires that you remember only one shortcut, and doesn't require you to drag a cursor around.

Whenever you have an object or text selected and need to apply a style, press Command-Return/Ctrl-Enter. InDesign displays the Quick Apply panel. Type the letters of the style name until InDesign selects the style, or use the up and down arrow keys to scroll through the list of style names. Once the style name is selected, you can:

▶ Press Return/Enter to apply the style to the selection. This closes the Quick Apply panel; to apply the style and leave the panel open, press Shift-Return/Shift-Enter.

▶ Press Command-Return/Ctrl-Enter to edit the selected style.

▶ Press Option-Return/Alt-Enter to apply the style and override any local formatting. (If you're applying a paragraph style and want to override all formatting, including character styles, press Option-Shift-Return/Alt-Shift-Enter.)

▶ Press Escape to close the panel without applying a style.

Quick Apply is very clever in how it matches what you type to the list of available style names. For example, if you have a style named "Heading 3" you can just type "h3" or even just "3" (if you have more than one style with the number three in it, they'll all appear).

Alternate Reality

What wonders—or horrors—exist in this weird place, where the boundary between text and graphics breaks down? Where magic works, and previously immutable laws of physics no longer apply? We have been there, reader, and, as it turns out, we have discovered new and useful techniques that can be put to immediate use in the "normal" world.

Importing and Exporting

Someday you'll need to do something that's beyond the drawing and typesetting capabilities of InDesign. You'll need to edit large amounts of text, adjust bitmap images, render 3-D objects, or create Web pages. Other applications do these things better than InDesign does. But you can add the files you create in other applications to your InDesign publication. And you can export InDesign pages for use in other page-layout and drawing programs.

That's what this chapter is all about: importing files from disk, controlling the way that they appear in your document, and exporting your document (or pieces of it). For the most part, our discussion of importing focuses on graphics because we cover importing text in Chapter 3, "Text." Note that you won't find an exploration of InDesign's XML import and export features here; we'll cover that in Chapter 14, "XML."

Importing

InDesign offers three ways to bring files from other applications into your publications. Here are your options:

▶ **Place the file.** The Place feature (in the File menu) is the most common method for getting files onto your pages. When you place a file, InDesign creates a link to the file on disk. In the case of graphics, InDesign stores only a low-resolution, "proxy" (or "preview") image in the publication. When you print, InDesign uses the high-resolution version of the graphic from the file on your disk. You can choose to link to text files—or not, depending on the setting of the Create Links when Placing Text and Spreadsheet Files option in the Text panel of the Preferences dialog box. We'll discuss managing links later in this chapter.

▶ **Copy and paste.** The most obvious, simplest, and least reliable method of getting information from another application is to copy it out of the application and paste it into InDesign. While this technique can work reasonably well for small amounts of text, it can spell disaster for graphics and images created in other programs. We don't mean to imply that you should *never* use copy and paste, just that you should approach it with caution.

You shouldn't, for example, copy an image out of Photoshop and paste it into InDesign. This actually embeds the pixels into InDesign in an upleasant (and we think unsanitary) way that is likely to result in headaches down the road. If you want to embed an image, place it normally and then see "Linking and Embedding" later in this chapter.

A good reason to use copy and paste, however, appears when you're working with Illustrator or FreeHand: When you copy paths out of these programs and paste them into InDesign, you get editable InDesign paths. Actually, in Illustrator, this only works if you have turned on the AICB setting in Illustrator's Preferences dialog box (it's obscure, but just look around for something called AICB)—otherwise you just get an embedded, uneditable PDF file when you paste.

▶ **Drag and drop.** As we mentioned in Chapter 2, "Page Layout," you can drag objects out of one InDesign publication and drop them into another. You can drag files from your desktop (the Macintosh Finder or the Windows Explorer) and drop them into your InDesign publication window. This is essentially the same as importing the files using the Place command (except that you won't be able to set import options for the files, as you can if you place them). Even better, dragging from the desktop is a great way to import more than one file at a time (you can even drag a whole folder full of images into your document, if you want).

You can also drag one or more images from Adobe Bridge into your InDesign page to import them.

Or you can drag objects from some other programs (Illustrator comes to mind) and drop them into InDesign. This, in general, is the same as copying and pasting, and comes with the same cautions.

If you have a file open on the Mac OS, you can drag the file icon in the title bar (to the left of the document title) and drop it into an InDesign document. This is identical to dragging the file from the desktop. Note that this trick only works if you've saved the file first, and if the file is of a type that InDesign can place.

Note that you can also open QuarkXPress and PageMaker files—that's covered in Chapter 2, "Page Layout."

Placing Anything

To get a graphic file into an InDesign publication, follow these steps (see Figure 7-1 and Figure 7-2).

1. Before you leap to the Place command on the File menu, take a second to think about where you want the graphic to appear.

    ▸ Do you want the graphic to fill an existing frame? If so, select the frame.

    ▸ Do you want the graphic to appear as an inline frame in a text frame? If so, select the Text tool and click it inside the text frame.

    ▸ Do you want to place the graphic in a new frame? If so, press Command-Shift-A/Ctrl-Shift-A to deselect everything before placing the graphic.

2. Press Command-D/Ctrl-D (or choose Place from the File menu). The Place dialog box appears.

3. Locate and select a file. You can control certain import options for some file formats. To view the available import options, turn on the Show Import Options checkbox.

FIGURE 7-1
**Placing a Graphic
into a Frame**

*This is similar to the
QuarkXPress "Get
Picture" method.*

*Create a frame using one of
the frame drawing tools.*

*Choose Place from the
File menu (or press
Command-D/Ctrl-D).*

*InDesign displays the
Place dialog box.*

Locate and select a file.

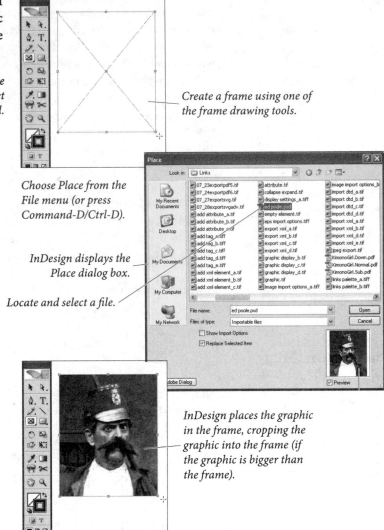

*InDesign places the graphic
in the frame, cropping the
graphic into the frame (if
the graphic is bigger than
the frame).*

4. If you have a frame selected, and want to place the file inside
    the frame, make sure you turn on the Replace Selected Item
    checkbox. If you don't want to replace the selection (perhaps you
    forgot to deselect all before selecting Place), turn this option off.
    When importing graphics, you can ignore the Retain Format
    and Convert Quotes checkboxes; those are only applicable to
    text files.

5. Click the Open button. If you turned on the Show Import
    Options checkbox, InDesign displays the Import Options
    dialog box, which looks slightly different depending on the file
    type you've selected. In many cases, the options are grayed out

FIGURE 7-2
Placing a Graphic
Without First
Making a Frame

Choose Place from the File menu (or press Command-D/Ctrl-D). InDesign displays the Place dialog box. Locate and select a file, then click the Open or Choose button.

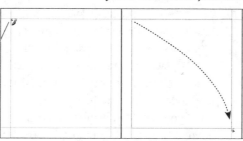

InDesign displays a graphic place icon.

Click the graphic place icon on the page or pasteboard.

InDesign places the graphic on the page, creating a frame that is exactly the size of the graphic.

When you position the place icon near a ruler guide or grid line, InDesign changes the appearance of the place icon to show that clicking or dragging the icon will "snap" the incoming graphic to the guide or grid.

If you drag the place icon as you place a graphic…
…InDesign places the graphic inside a frame that's the width and height you define by dragging. This does not scale the graphic itself.

When you position the place icon over an existing frame, InDesign changes the appearance of the icon to indicate that clicking the icon will place the file inside the frame.

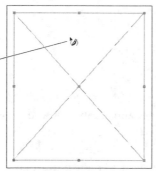
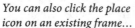

You can also click the place icon on an existing frame…

…to place the graphic inside the frame.

because they aren't relevant (the clipping path option is grayed out when there is no clipping path embedded in the file, for example). Make any changes you want (or can) in this dialog box and then click the OK button (we discuss the import options for each file type in "Working with Images," later in this chapter).

What happens after you click OK depends on the choice you made in Step 1. If you had a frame selected, and turned on the Replace Selected Item option, the graphic appears inside that frame. If you had an active text insertion point in a text frame, and if you turned on the Replace Selected Item option, InDesign places the graphic into the text frame (at the location of the cursor) as an inline graphic.

The Place Icon   If you deselected everything before placing, or if you turned off the Replace Selected Item option, InDesign displays the place icon (some folks call this the "place gun"). Click the place icon on a page or on the pasteboard, and InDesign imports the file you selected and positions the upper-left corner of the file at the point at which you clicked the place icon. InDesign places the graphic on the page or pasteboard at its original size.

Instead of clicking, you can *drag* the place icon. This produces a frame that's the width and height you define by dragging. Note that this does not scale the graphic itself.

To place the graphic inside an existing, empty frame, click the place icon in the frame. This frame doesn't have to be a graphic frame, and it doesn't have to be selected.

If you accidentally placed the graphic inside a frame, don't panic. Remember that Command-Z/Ctrl-Z will "undo" the action and display the place icon again, ready to place the graphic somewhere else. At this point, you can cancel the Place operation by pressing Command-Z/Ctrl-Z again, or by clicking the place icon on any tool in the Tools palette.

About Graphic File Formats

InDesign can import a range of graphic file formats, including Adobe Illustrator (AI) and Adobe Photoshop (PSD) formats, TIFF images, JPEG images, GIF images, EPS files, and PICT or WMF-type graphics. From InDesign's point of view, there are certain limitations and advantages to each of these file formats.

Just to refresh everyone's memory, here are a few quick definitions, rules, and exceptions regarding graphic file formats. There are three fundamental graphics file format types:

▶ Bitmap files store pictures as matrices (rows and columns) of squares known as pixels, with each pixel having a particular gray or color value (also known as a gray depth, color depth, or bit depth). Bitmap files are typically created by image editing programs such as Adobe Photoshop, or by the software you use to run your scanner. TIFF, JPEG, BMP, and GIF are all bitmap graphic file formats. Bitmaps are also called "raster data."

▶ Vector files contain sets of instructions for drawing graphic objects—typically geometric shapes, such as lines, ellipses, polygons, rectangles, and arcs. The drawing instructions say, "Start this line at this point and draw to that point"; or, "This is a polygon made up of these line segments." PostScript paths, such those as you'd find in an EPS, are another example of a vector format, but they're usually contained in a hybrid (see below).

▶ Hybrids can contain both vector and bitmap graphics. Macintosh PICT, Adobe Illustrator, PDF, EPS, and WMF (Windows metafile) formats are all examples of metafiles. (Adobe Photoshop files look like hybrids, as they can also contain a combination of vector and raster graphics, but InDesign rasterizes any visible Photoshop vector data so we don't count it as a true hybrid.) Metafiles don't have to contain *both* vector and bitmap objects. Sometimes you'll find metafiles that contain only an image, or metafiles that contain only vector artwork.

There are a lot of different ways to talk about the files saved in these three format types. We usually refer to bitmap files as "images" and vector files as "drawings."

Note that these formats are all "interchange" formats—they're for moving information from one application to another. All programs support their own "native" file format, but many can read or write files in other formats. Some programs can open or import files saved in the native formats of other programs. InDesign can also place native Illustrator and Photoshop files—which might mean that you don't have to use an interchange format at all.

Some programs are real "Swiss Army knives," and can open and save files in lots of different formats. Photoshop, for example, can open and save files in a dozen different bitmap formats. Photoshop is a great program to have around even if you use it for nothing more than file conversions.

A Philosophical Note

Whether you're an explaining parent or a computer book author, there's always a temptation to simply say, "Because we say so." We feel that you deserve better. At the same time, a basic explanation of the problems inherent in, say, the Macintosh PICT vector format would consume all of the pages of this chapter. And then there's WMF, PICT's Windows counterpart, to think about. There's just not room to talk about the advantages and disadvantages of each graphic file format, so we'll try to be brief.

The biggest problem is that many graphics file formats, in spite of their being designed as "interchange" formats, make too many assumptions about the system they'll be viewed on or printed from. Most hybrid and vector formats—except EPS and PDF—assume that the font list of the system they're created on will remain the same, and refer to fonts by their *number* (as they appear in the list of fonts at the time the file was created) rather than by their *name*. This can cause problems when you move to another system, or even when you install a new font. For this reason among others, we eschew WMF and PICT in favor of EPS and PDF.

It all comes down to using the formats for what they were intended for. BMP files were intended to be viewed onscreen, in Windows—not printed. PICT and WMF files were intended for printing on (different types of) non-PostScript printers. EPS and TIFF were designed to work well on high-resolution PostScript printers; GIF and JPEG were designed to carry a great deal of image information in the smallest possible package—which makes them ideal for on-line publishing. In addition, PDF, EPS, TIFF, JPEG, and GIF were designed for interchange between different computing environments and platforms—something you can't say of the others.

WMF is a file format for saving commands written in the Windows Graphic Device Interface (or GDI)—the language Windows uses to draw objects onscreen (or print to non-PostScript printers). PICT is based on QuickDraw, the native drawing language of the Macintosh. When you send files in these formats to a PostScript printer, they have to be translated into PostScript commands. This process isn't perfect, which means that what you see on your screen may not be what you get from your printer.

EPS and PDF Files

How did PDF and EPS get to be the industry-standard graphic file formats for vector graphics and type? It's because they're both based on the PostScript language—which, as you'll recall, is the language of high-resolution imagesetters. When you have to convert drawing instructions from another vector format—WMF, for example—into PostScript, you're asking for trouble. And trouble is expensive when you're printing on film at 3600 dots per inch.

Vector graphics saved in the PDF or EPS formats are *resolution independent*, and so paths print as smoothly as possible on whatever printer you happen to be printing to. Both formats can include color definitions (including spot colors), and store the positions of graphics and type with a very high degree of precision. All of the above make these formats ideal for prepress use.

There are two important differences between the two formats. First, PDF files can be viewed using the free Acrobat Reader and edited using tools such as Acrobat Professional or Enfocus' Pitstop

Professional utility. Second, EPS graphics can contain "active" PostScript code—routines that generate paths when the graphic reaches a PostScript interpreter.

For instance, a graduated fill from FreeHand or a gradient from Illustrator is really a piece of PostScript code that tells a PostScript interpreter to fill a path with a series of paths filled with varying colors. This means that the PostScript interpreter has to work a bit—calculating the positions of the points on the generated paths, setting their color, and so on. By contrast, a gradient in a PDF is literally a series of paths—all the PostScript interpreter has to do is draw them into the image of the page it's creating in the printer's memory.

Which File Format to Use?

We could talk about the pros and cons of various graphic file formats all day, but deciding which file format is best for you comes down to two things: what works in your particular workflow and which features you need.

We use TIFF for almost every (bitmapped) image and PDF or EPS for almost every vector graphic. However, there are times when we have to deviate from the norm.

Vector artwork is pretty straightforward. We usually import Adobe Illustrator files as native AI files, because they're essentially PDF files. We save graphics from Macromedia FreeHand as EPS or PDF—either one works just fine in our experience.

When it comes to Photoshop, you have to be careful, because Photoshop files can contain so much more than simple image data. A Photoshop file can contain images, layers, transparency, vector artwork, and text objects. There's no one-size-fits-all solution—what you should do with your Photoshop files depends on *what is in them*.

If you don't use vector artwork (text layers, shape layers, or layer clipping masks), transparent backgrounds, or spot colors in your Photoshop file, then it hardly matters what you pick. Again, we usually use TIFF, but native PSD, PDF, DCS, or EPS works fine. But if you use one or more of these features, choose a file format carefully.

For example, DCS files are often used for images with spot color channels. InDesign CS and CS2 handle DCS files much better than earlier versions—as long as the DCS file does not contain a vector layer, you can now use transparency effects with DCS files, and InDesign can even recombine a DCS file into a composite color PDF! However, DCS files cannot contain transparency (Photoshop's transparency feature, that is). And, as soon as you have a vector layer in a DCS, you can no longer use InDesign's transparency effects on it.

The native Photoshop PSD file format seems as if it should be the perfect format for all your images, but while InDesign can read spot colors, duotones, and transparency from PSD files, it can't read vector layers. Well, it *can* read them, but the vector layers become rasterized (turned into a bitmap). This means that InDesign has to maintain a separate, flattened version of the file inside your document, which adds significantly to the document size. Also, InDesign can't handle PSD files when they're in Photoshop's Multichannel mode—you'll have to use DCS files for that.

PDF files are actually more versatile than PSD files when it comes to importing layered and/or transparent images from Photoshop into InDesign. Certainly, when it comes to saving vector layers (such as text layers), PDF is our favorite. However, for technical reasons we barely understand, Photoshop won't let you save a file that has both spot color channels and background transparency as a PDF file.

Layered vs. Flattened, Photoshop vs. TIFF. How do you want to deal with layered or 16-bit Photoshop files? Do you want to import each file into InDesign as a single, layered image? Or would you rather import a separate, flattened, 8-bit version of the file (saving the layered version for archival purposes)?

If you use layers, your decision comes down to file size. If your layered file size in Photoshop is 200 MB, then it's probably better to flatten it and save it as a TIFF. (Tip: If the file has a transparent background, then use Photoshop's Merge Visible feature rather than Flatten Layers, because the latter always flattens to an opaque background.)

If you never use layers in Photoshop files, or if your layered files are relatively small, then you don't have to worry about it—you can use either Photoshop's native PSD format or as save them as layered TIFF files (yes, TIFF files can contain layers and transparency in Photoshop 6 and later) and then place them in InDesign. InDesign can also turn on and off layers (make them visible or not) in layered PSD or PDF files, but not layered TIFF files.

Compression. The native Photoshop PSD file format uses its own compression scheme to make the files smaller. Other file formats can use built-in compression, too. For example, Photoshop can save TIFF files using LZW, Zip, or JPEG compression. Few programs other than InDesign can read Zip or JPEG TIFFs, but if you're just using Photoshop and InDesign, you should definitely give Zip-compressed TIFFs a try. Often, using Zip compression in a layered Photoshop file for both the image data and the layer data makes a file smaller than a flattened, non-compressed TIFF. And Zip is a lossless compression scheme, so no image data will be lost.

We're less impressed with JPEG-compressed TIFF files, as JPEG is a lossy compression scheme (your image degrades each time you save it). You never know when you'll need those pixels.

If all this has your head spinning, check out Table 7-1, which Matt Phillips (Adobe software engineer extraordinaire and nice guy to boot) created.

TABLE 7-1
Matt's Matrix

Vectors	Spots	Transparency	PDF	PSD	DCS	EPS
No	No	No	✓	✓	✓	✓
No	No	Yes	✓	✓	•	•
No	Yes	No	✓	✓[1]	✓	•
No	Yes	Yes	•	✓[1]	•	•
Yes	No	No	✓	•	✓[2]	✓
Yes	No	Yes	✓	•	•	•
Yes	Yes	No	✓	•	✓[2]	•
Yes	Yes	Yes	•	•	•	•

[1] Except in Multichannel mode

[2] Works as long as you print separations from InDesign and the DCS file is not affected by transparency on the page.

Creating Your Own EPS Graphics

InDesign can interpret almost any PostScript file you throw at it, as long as it's in the form of an EPS (Encapsulated PostScript) file. You could, for example, take a PostScript output file from a Unix system and place it in your InDesign document. Because InDesign can interpret the PostScript, it can give you an accurate preview of what the graphic will look like when you print.

Similarly, some folks write their own PostScript code. We happen to be two of them, and if you think PostScript programming is fun, that makes three of us. You can create EPS graphics using a word processor or text editor, but you've got to remember two things.

▸ Try printing the file before you import it. If it doesn't print outside InDesign, chances are good it won't print inside InDesign, either. Always test every change you make in your word processor by downloading the PostScript file to the printer and seeing what you get before you bring the file into an InDesign publication, or at least before you take the file to a service bureau.

▸ InDesign can create a preview for any EPS graphic.

Why would you want to create your own EPS graphics? There are lots of things you can do with PostScript that InDesign doesn't do (yet). And it's fun. For example, check out the cool effects you can get from Teacup Software's PatternMaker plug-in (there's a free version available at www.teacupsoftware.com). Teacup manages the PostScript behind the scenes, so you don't have to.

Because an EPS file is a text-only file, InDesign (and other programs) need some way to distinguish it from other text-only files. They get their clues from the first few lines of the EPS (also known as the file "header"). These lines should look something like this:

```
%!PS-Adobe-2.0 EPSF-1.2
%%BoundingBox x1 y1 x2 y2
```

The values following the "BoundingBox" comment are the measurements of the EPS graphic in the following order: left, bottom, right, and top. Points are the measurement system used in an EPS graphic (unless you make other arrangements), so the bounding box of an example U.S. letter-sized EPS graphic would be:

```
%%BoundingBox 0 0 617 792
```

Figure 7-3 shows an example of a hand-coded EPS graphic, and what it looks like when you place it in InDesign.

Operators to Avoid. The PostScript you use inside an EPS should not include any of the following PostScript operators.

banddevice	copypage	erasepage	exitserver
framedevice	grestoreall	initclip	initgraphics
initmatrix	legal	letter	note
nulldevice	quit	renderbands	setpageparams
setsccbbatch	stop		

Graphic Display Properties

Once you import a graphic into InDesign, the quality of its onscreen appearance depends almost entirely on the Display Performance setting in the View menu. You can choose among three settings: Optimized Display, Typical Display, and High Quality Display. By default, these reflect low-, medium-, and high-quality displays. However, if you hate these terms you can change each setting's meaning so that Optimized is higher quality than Typical, or whatever (see "Display Performance Preferences," in Chapter 1, "Workspace").

FIGURE 7-3

Writing Your Own EPS Graphics

In case you ever need such a thing, this PostScript code will fill any shape with a wave pattern.

```
%!PS-Adobe 2.0 EPSF-1.2
%%BoundingBox: 0 0 200 200
%%Creator: D.Blatner
%%EndComments
%-- This Is The Main Waves Subroutine --
/waves {        %on stack: length of wave, width (height),
                %space between lines, linewidth
         setlinewidth
         /vert exch def  /height exch def  /width exch def
         /Y1 height 1.8 mul def  /Y2 Y1 neg def  /Y3 0 def
         gsave getpathbox grestore
         clip newpath
         llx lly height 4 div sub
         translate 0 0 moveto
         ury lly sub vert div 4 add cvi{   %repeat # of lines
                urx llx sub width div 2 add cvi{  %repeat # of curves
                /X0 oldX3 def
                /X3 width X0 add def
                /X1 width 2 div X0 add def
                /X2 X1 def
                /oldX3 X3 def
                X1 Y1 X2 Y2 X3 Y3 curveto
                }bind repeat
         stroke
         0 vert translate 0 0 moveto /oldX3 0 def
         }bind repeat
}bind def

%-- Some Support Routines --
/oldX3 0 def
/getpathbox {{flattenpath} exec pathbbox /ury exch def /urx exch def
/lly exch def /llx exch def /middlex urx llx add 2 div def /middley
ury lly add 2 div def /pathradius urx middlex sub dup mul ury
middley sub dup mul add sqrt def}bind def
```

This is the code that actually draws the triangular box.

```
%-- Draw The Box --
0 0 moveto 0 200 lineto 200 200 lineto closepath

%-- Then Call The Fill Routine --
24   % length of the wave pattern
6    % height of the wave pattern
4    % distance between lines
.5   % thickness of lines
waves
```

Here's what the above PostScript code looks like when you place it in InDesign or print it.

The default settings follow these basic rules:

▶ When you choose Optimized Display, InDesign grays out both vector and bitmapped images and turns off all transparency effects. The display of these gray boxes is very fast, but somewhat lacking in detail.

▶ When you choose Typical Display, InDesign uses a proxy image—either one embedded in the image or one InDesign generated when you placed the file. (InDesign always creates a proxy preview when it imports TIFF and JPEG; it's an import option for EPS files.) InDesign uses this proxy to display the graphic at all magnification levels—which means that images are going to get pretty ugly as you zoom in on them. The advantage? The screen display of proxy images is much faster than generating new previews for every magnification change. In this setting, transparency effects are visible, but only at a reasonable quality (drop shadows and feathering are displayed at low resolution, for instance).

▶ When you choose High Quality display, InDesign gets image data from the original file on your hard drive to render the best possible preview for the current screen magnification. For an EPS, it means that InDesign reinterprets the file to create a new preview (this is where those beautiful EPS previews come from). As you'd expect, either process takes more time than simply slamming a fixed-resolution preview onto the screen (which is what the Proxy option does). The anti-aliasing of vector images (so they look smooth on screen) and high-quality transparency effects is also calculation-intensive.

Remember, all of these settings affect only the way that graphics appear on screen, not in print.

Local Display Overrides You can also vary the display quality for individual graphics. This can come in handy when you need to see more detail in one graphic than in others, or when you want to speed up the redraw of a specific slow-drawing graphic. To control the display properties of a graphic, select the graphic, and then display the context menu (hold down Control before you press the mouse button on the Macintosh; press the right mouse button in Windows). Choose one of the display options from the Display Performance submenu (see Figure 7-4). You can also choose from the Display Performance submenu in the Object menu if you have a bizarre aversion to context menus.

FIGURE 7-4
Setting the Display Resolution for a Graphic

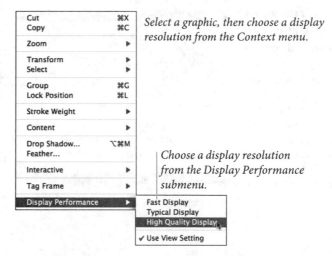

Select a graphic, then choose a display resolution from the Context menu.

Choose a display resolution from the Display Performance submenu.

InDesign displays the graphic using the display setting you selected.

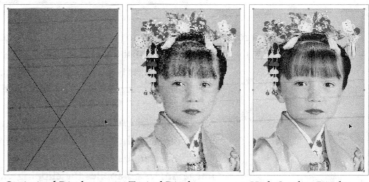

Optimized Display   *Typical Display*   *High Quality Display*

Later, after applying local display overrides to various images throughout your document, you can turn all these local overrides on and off with the Allow Object-Level Display Settings from the Display Performance submenu. As with any other feature in InDesign, you can assign a keyboard shortcut to these local override features.

Image Import Options

When you place an image, you can turn on the Import Options checkbox and use the subsequent Image Import Options dialog box to specify a number of important things about the image (see Figure 7-5). The settings in this dialog box change depending on the file format of the graphic. Note that if you later drag and drop a graphic from the desktop into InDesign, the program remembers the import options from the last file you placed.

FIGURE 7-5
**Import Options for
Bitmapped Images**

*If the file contains one or
more alpha channels, you
can choose to apply transparency to the object using
one of the alpha channels.*

*Turn this option on to apply
the first clipping path defined
in the incoming file. If you
want to use a different
clipping path, you can
choose Clipping Path
from the Object menu
after placing the file.*

*The options in this dialog box only
become active when the file you selected
contains the corresponding features.*

*If the file has an embedded
color management profile,
you can choose whether to
use that profile or to use
some other profile.*

Bitmapped Images   If you are importing a bitmapped image, such as a TIFF, JPEG, GIF,
or native Photoshop documents, InDesign displays four options in
the Image Import Options dialog box: apply a clipping path, pick an
alpha channel, enable color management, and choose layer visiblity.

Apply Photoshop Clipping Path. If the image you're placing contains
a clipping path, InDesign makes the Apply Photoshop Clipping Path
checkbox available. When you turn this option on as you place the
image, InDesign applies the clipping path to the image. If this isn't
what you want, you can always change the clipping path (see "Working with Clipping Paths," later in this chapter).

   If the image does not contain a clipping path, this option won't
be available. You can always create a clipping path for the image in
InDesign, or choose another path saved with the image as the clipping path (again, we cover this later in this chapter).

Alpha Channel. InDesign can apply transparency to an image if you
have one or more alpha channels saved within the file. (An alpha
channel is just any additional channel beyond the standard red,
green, blue, cyan, yellow, magenta, or black channels.) For example,
you could make three extra channels in Photoshop—each with a different sort of blurry vignette around the image's subject—and then
choose which one you want to use in InDesign when you import
the file. Unfortunately, InDesign doesn't give you any sort of visual
feedback inside the Import Options dialog box, so you'd better use
descriptive names for the channels. Also, once you have imported

the image, there's no way to switch to a different transparency mask to the picture other than reimporting it and revisiting this dialog box (though you can use the alpha channel to generate a clipping path).

Enable Color Management. When you're importing a color image, InDesign activates the options in the Color panel of the Image Import Options dialog box. Color management is a very complicated topic, and the following control descriptions do not attempt to discuss the finer points of each topic. For more on color management, see Chapter 10, "Color."

▸ **Profile.** If the image file you've selected contains a color management profile, InDesign selects Use Embedded Profile from the Profile pop-up menu. If you know that the embedded profile is not the one you want, choose a different profile from the menu.

Note that if you have chosen the Preserve Numbers (Ignore Linked Profiles) option in the CMYK Policies section of the Color Settings dialog box, InDesign acts slightly differently. Instead of displaying an embedded profile name in the Image Import Options dialog box, it will show Use Document Default, pointing out that the embedded CMYK profile is being ignored and the document profile is being used instead.

▸ **Rendering Intent.** Choose the gamut scaling method you want to use to render the colors in the image. For most photographic images, you'll probably want to choose Perceptual (Images).

Layer Visibility. When you import a Photoshop document or PDF file that contains layers, InDesign offers a third panel in the Import Options dialog box: Layers. This panel lets you turn the visibility on or off for each layer, or choose a layer comp (if you used Photoshop's Layer Comp palette to make comps). We discuss these options further in "Object Layer Options," later in this chapter.

EPS Files   When you import an EPS graphic with Import Options turned on in the Place dialog box, InDesign displays the EPS Import Options dialog box (see Figure 7-6).

Read Embedded OPI Image Links. Open Prepress Interface (OPI) is a standard for maintaining image links between desktop page layout and illustration software using dedicated color prepress systems, such as some of the systems manufactured by Kodak and Creo. When you work with an OPI system, you typically work with low-resolution proxy images as you lay out a page, and then link to

FIGURE 7-6
Import Options
for EPS Files

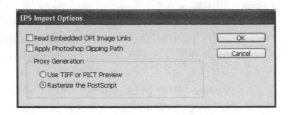

high-resolution images saved on the prepress server when you print (or otherwise hand the job off). OPI concerns imported images only, and has nothing to do with vector graphics or type.

Turn this option off if the prepress system will take care of replacing any OPI images in the EPS; turn it on if you want InDesign to replace the images as you print. (In this case, InDesign itself is acting as an OPI server.) InDesign will store the OPI image information regardless of the setting of this option.

Apply Photoshop Clipping Path. Turn on this option when you want to apply the first clipping path saved in the EPS graphic. This only affects Photoshop EPS images.

Proxy Generation. EPS graphics usually contain an embedded, low-resolution preview image. However, because InDesign can interpret almost any PostScript file, you can ask it to create a new preview image for you by selecting Rasterize the PostScript in the EPS Import Options dialog box. If you want to use the file's built-in preview, select Use TIFF or PICT Preview. We think these should have been labeled, "Use Cruddy Preview" and "Make It Look Good." We almost always make it look good by selecting Rasterize the PostScript (even though it takes a little longer to import the file). On the other hand, if you need to import 250 EPS files and onscreen quality doesn't matter, then save yourself some time and use the embedded previews.

PDF Files   When you import a PDF graphic, and have turned on the Import Options checkbox in the Place dialog box, InDesign displays the Place PDF dialog box (see Figure 7-7).

Pages. PDF files can contain multiple pages (unlike EPS, which is, by definition, a single-page-per-file format), so you need some way to select the page you want to place. You can scroll through the pages until you find the one you want. When you place a PDF without displaying the Place PDF dialog box, InDesign places the first page in the PDF.

FIGURE 7-7
Place PDF Dialog Box

The Place PDF dialog box can display a preview of the pages of the PDF you've selected.

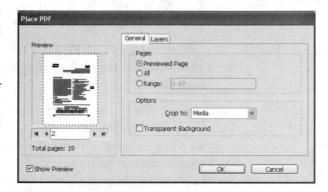

If you want to import more than one page, choose All or type in the page numbers (using commas or hyphens to denote multiple pages) in the Range field. To import the page displayed in the preview, select Previewed Page.

When you import more than one page from a PDF, InDesign loads the Place cursor as usual, but each click places one PDF page. Alternatively, you can Option/Alt-click and InDesign will place all the PDF pages on the same page. It would be nice to have the option to place each page of the PDF on a different page of the InDesign document, but there isn't. That's why Ole wrote the PlaceMultipage-PDF script (see Chapter 12, "Scripting," for more on where to find scripts and how to use them.)

Crop To. Do you have to import the whole page? No—you can use this pop-up menu to define the area of the page you want to place. Choose one of the following options (depending on the PDF, some options may be unavailable).

▸ Choose Bounding Box to crop the incoming PDF graphic to an area defined by the objects on the PDF page.

▸ Choose Art to place the area defined by an art box in the PDF graphic (if no art box has been defined, this option will not be available). For a PDF exported from InDesign, the art box is the same as the Trim area (see below).

▸ Choose Crop to crop the area of the incoming PDF graphic to the crop area defined in Acrobat (using the Crop Pages dialog box). If the PDF has not had a crop area defined, this area will be the same as the Media setting (see below).

▸ Choose Trim to import the area defined by any trim marks in the PDF.

▸ Choose Bleed to import the area defined by any bleed marks in the PDF.

▸ Choose Media to import the area defined by the original paper size of the PDF.

Transparent Background. Turn this option on when you want to be able to see objects behind the imported PDF, or turn it off to apply an opaque white background to the PDF graphic. In general, we think you should leave this option turned on—if you want an opaque background, you can always apply a fill (of any color) to the frame containing the PDF graphic. If you turn this option off, on the other hand, the white background applied by InDesign cannot be changed by setting the fill of the frame.

Placed PDFs and Color Management. InDesign can't apply color management profiles to PDF graphics, but profiles embedded in the PDF will be used when you color separate the publication. If your PDFs require precise color matching, apply and embed the appropriate color profiles before saving the PDF for import into InDesign.

PDF Layer Options. If you're placing a PDF that includes layers (such as from Illustrator or InDesign), you can choose to show or hide individual layers using the Layers panel of the Place PDF dialog box (see Figure 7-8).

The options in this panel are self-explanatory except, perhaps for the When Updating Link pop-up menu. This controls what happens if, down the line, you update or relink the graphic to a newer version (see Object Layer Options," later in this chapter). Choose Keep Layer Visibility Overrides if you want to make sure the changes you make here are respected if the image gets updated.

FIGURE 7-8
PDF Layer Options

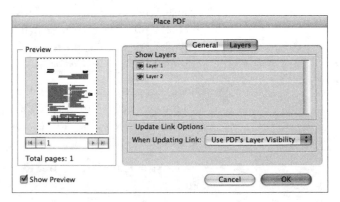

Linking and Embedding

In InDesign, you can choose to embed (that is, store) imported graphics in your publication, or you can choose to store them externally and link to them.

When you link to a graphic, InDesign doesn't include the graphic file in your publication, but establishes a link between the publication and the imported file. InDesign creates a low-resolution screen preview of the graphic, and uses that preview to draw the image on your page. Linking means you don't have to store two copies of the original file—one on disk, and one in your InDesign publication—thereby saving disk space.

When you print, InDesign includes data from linked graphics in the stream of PostScript sent to your printer or to disk. This means that you need to take any externally stored graphics with you when it's time to print your publication at an imagesetting service bureau.

Which method should you use? It's up to you. When you embed graphics, your publication size increases, but you don't have to keep track of the original files. When you link to externally stored graphics, your publications will take up less space on disk, but you'll have to keep track of more than one file. We generally recommend linking, partly because that is what the industry has come to expect (that's the way QuarkXPress works), and partly because we don't like our InDesign files becoming tens (or hundreds) of megabytes larger.

If you import a bitmapped image smaller than 48K, InDesign embeds a copy of the graphic in your publication. This "automatic" embedding differs from "manual" embedding—you can maintain links to automatically embedded files, but not to manually embedded graphics.

The Links Palette

When you move a linked file or change its name, you break the link between the file and any InDesign publication you've placed it in. You can also break the link when you move the publication file to another volume.

When you open a publication, InDesign looks in the folder containing the document for the linked file, and in a folder inside that folder named "Links." If InDesign can't find the linked file there, it displays an alert stating that the publication contains missing or modified linked graphics. Click the Fix Links Automatically button to locate and link to the file or files (see Figure 7-9). If InDesign cannot find a file, it will display the Relink dialog box—you'll have to find the file yourself.

FIGURE 7-9
Fixing Missing Links
As You Open a File

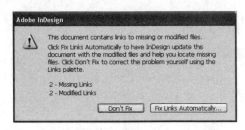

When InDesign can't find
a linked file in a docu-
ment, you'll see the Fix
Links dialog box.

Click the Fix Links Auto-
matically button to have
InDesign attempt to fix the
links for you, or click Don't
Fix to fix them yourself.

If InDesign cannot locate a missing link
it will display the Relink dialog box.

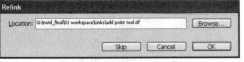

Click the Browse button
to display a standard
file dialog box, then
locate and select the
appropriate file.

To skip the file, click the Skip button; to stop
looking for missing links altogether, click Cancel.

The key to InDesign's linking and embedding features is the
Links palette (see Figure 7-10). To display the Links palette, press
Command-Shift-D/Ctrl-Shift-D, or choose Links from the Window
menu. The Links palette displays the names of the linked files in the
publication along with various icons.

▶ If a graphic has been modified since its last update, you'll see a
Caution icon (a yellow triangle with an exclamation mark).

▶ If a graphic is missing, you'll see the Missing link icon—it's a red
circle with a question mark in it. This means that InDesign can't
find the file—it's been moved or deleted (or maybe you've lost
your connection to the server that holds the file).

▶ If you have embedded a graphic (see "Embedding a Graphic,"
later in this section), a square with two shapes in it (another
square and a triangle) appears.

You can change the order of the links in the Links palette—to do
this, choose Sort by Status, Sort by Name, or Sort by Page from the
Links palette menu.

**Getting Link
Information**

Where the heck is that graphic file stored, anyway? Do we need it
to print the publication? What color profile is attached to it, if any?
The answers to these and other questions can be found in the Link
Information dialog box. To display the Link Information dialog box,
select the graphic's file name in the Links palette, then choose Link
Information from the Links palette menu (or just double-click the
file name in the palette).

FIGURE 7-10
Links Palette

*Press Command-Shift-D
or Ctrl-Shift-D to display
the Links palette.*

Out-of-date link (note icon)

Missing link icon

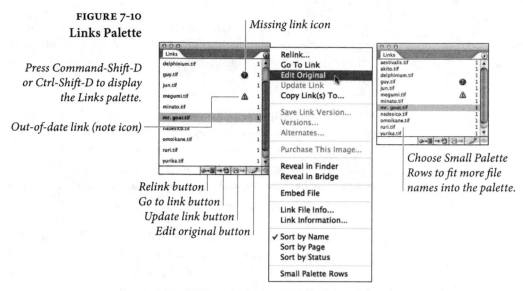

Relink button
Go to link button
Update link button
Edit original button

*Choose Small Palette
Rows to fit more file
names into the palette.*

*Choose Link Information
(or double-click a link)
to display the Link
Information dialog box.*

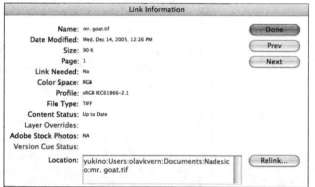

*Choose Link File Info to
display the XMP data
(Photoshop File Info)
associated with the
linked file, if any.*

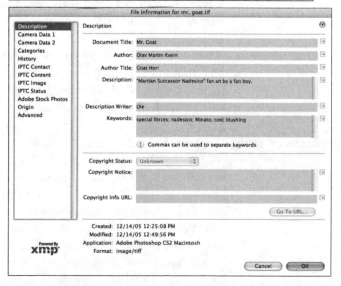

The meaning of most of the items in the Link Information dialog box is fairly straightforward—the Size field shows the amount of disk space taken up by the graphic, for example—but a few of the fields deserve further explanation.

Link Needed. Is the linked file needed to print the publication? If the graphic has been embedded by InDesign, you won't need the original file to print the publication, so InDesign displays N/A. Very small bitmapped images (smaller than 48K) are automatically linked *and* embedded; because you don't need the original file in order to print the document properly, the Link Needed field says "No."

Location. Note that the Location field is the only editable field in the Link Information dialog box. While we say it's an "editable" field, we don't mean that you can change the path name in the field—you can't. But you can select the text and copy it out of the Links Information dialog box.

Version Cue Status. The Version Cue status field at the bottom of the Link Information dialog box will be blank and grayed out unless the file is being managed by Adobe Version Cue.

Next/Previous. The Next and Previous buttons display link information on the next or previous file shown in the Links palette. Note that the order of the links shown in this list does not necessarily have anything to do with the location of the graphics—the "next" link could be separated from the current link by many pages (unless you've chosen Sort By Pages from the Links palette menu).

Link File Info

Choose Link File Info to display the XMP information (known as File Info in Photoshop) associated with the link. If the file does not contain any XMP data, InDesign does nothing (see "File Info and Metadata," later in this chapter").

Finding Links on Disk

Someone hands you an InDesign file, and now you need to find one of the imported images on disk. The Link Information dialog box shows you the path, but it's much faster just to select the image on your page, then right-click on it (or Control-click on a one-button Mac) and choose Reveal in Finder (in Mac OS) or Reveal in Explorer (in Windows) from the Graphics submenu in the context menu. Or, you could choose Reveal in Bridge, if you want to launch Adobe Bridge and view the image there.

You can also find the Reveal features in the Links palette menu.

Updating a Link

InDesign checks the status of your graphics when you open a document or when you switch from another application back into InDesign. As soon as it notices a linked file is modified or missing, it displays an icon in the Links palette. To update the link of an imported graphic that has been modified since you last updated it or placed it, follow these steps (see Figure 7-11).

1. Display the Links palette, if it's not already visible.

2. Select the graphic you want to update, or select the corresponding link in the Links palette.

3. Choose Update Link from the Links palette menu (or click the Update Link button at the bottom of the Links palette). InDesign updates the link to the graphic file.

To update all of the modified links in a publication, deselect all of the file names in the Links palette (by clicking in the blank space at the bottom of the list, or clicking a linked file and then Command/Ctrl-clicking it). Then choose Update Link from the Links palette menu (or click the palette's Update Link button). InDesign updates all of the links.

To replace missing links, use the Relink command.

FIGURE 7-11
Updating a Link

When the link to a graphic is out of date, InDesign displays an icon next to the filename in the Links palette.

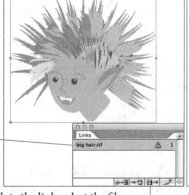 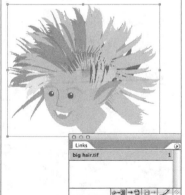

To update the link, select the filename and click the Update Link button.

InDesign updates the link to the graphic.

Linking to Another File

Modified files are easy to update; *missing* files are quite another matter. To link to another file, or relink to the original file in a new location, follow these steps (see Figure 7-12).

1. Display the Links palette, if it's not already visible.

2. Select the graphic you want to update, or select the corresponding link in the Links palette.

FIGURE 7-12
Linking to Another File

Select an imported graphic.

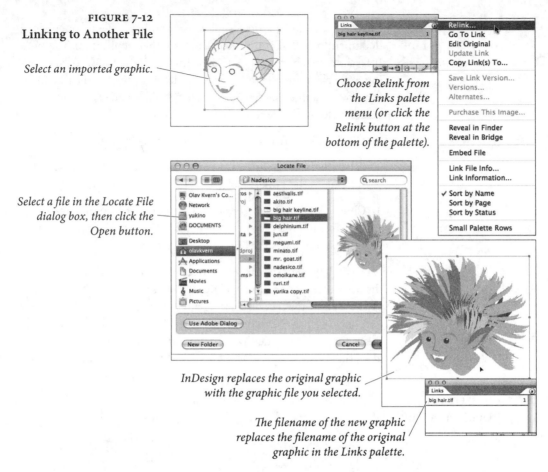

*Choose Relink from
the Links palette
menu (or click the
Relink button at the
bottom of the palette).*

Select a file in the Locate File
dialog box, then click the
Open button.

*InDesign replaces the original graphic
with the graphic file you selected.*

*The filename of the new graphic
replaces the filename of the original
graphic in the Links palette.*

3. Click the Relink button (or choose Relink from the Links palette menu). InDesign displays the Relink dialog box.

4. Locate and select a file.

5. Click the OK button.

As we noted above, relinking to a new image retains the same transformations (scaling, rotating, and so on), which is often—but not always—what you'd want. Note that you should not use the Relink button to change the link to an image that was set up as an OPI link in an imported EPS file.

By the way, if a bunch of images are listed as missing and they all exist in the same folder on disk, you can relink to them all by deselecting all the file names in the Links palette (click in the blank area at the bottom of the list) and then clicking Relink. InDesign will ask you to find the first missing file; after you locate it and click OK, wait for a few moments and the program should notice that the other files are there, too.

Edit Original One of the most useful features in the Links palette is the Edit Original button (or the Edit Original command from the palette menu), which opens the selected graphic in an editing application. If you select a TIFF image (on the page or in the Links palette) and choose Edit Original, that image typically opens in Photoshop. We have to add the caveat "typically" because InDesign relies on the operating system to know which application to use. If the Mac OS or Windows is set to open TIFF files in Photoshop, then that's where Edit Original will take you.

Some graphics don't work well at all with Edit Original—such as an EPS from FreeHand or CorelDraw—because the original application isn't designed to open the exported file. Nevertheless, in most cases, Edit Original is a great way to make quick changes. Also, if you use Edit Original, when you return to InDesign, the graphic is automatically updated, so you don't have to update the link manually.

By the way, there's an even faster way to invoke Edit Original: Option/Alt-double-click on the graphic with the Selection or Direct Selection tool.

Embedding a Graphic To store a graphic inside the publication, select the name of the graphic in the Links palette and choose Embed from the Links palette menu. When you embed a graphic, InDesign displays an embedded graphic icon next to the graphic's filename. Embedding a graphic has the following effects.

▸ It breaks the link to the external file, which means you won't be able to update the embedded graphic when you make changes to the original file (except by replacing the embedded graphic using the Relink command).

▸ The size of your publication file increases by the size of the graphic file. If you copy the embedded graphic and paste it elsewhere in your document, the publication grows again by the same amount. It's not true that an embedded graphic on a master page increases a publication's file size by the size of the embedded file for each use of that master page (we've seen other authors state this myth). However, file size does increase by the size of the graphic if you apply a manual override to the master page item (this is as you'd expect, as an override *copies* the master page item to the document page).

► You can't use the Edit Original command to open and edit the graphic file.

Ultimately, you shouldn't embed a graphic just because you want to take your publication to another system or to an imagesetting service bureau; instead, you should try using InDesign's Package and Preflight features (see Chapter 11, "Printing"). Embedding confuses service bureaus, who are used to working with QuarkXPress (which cannot embed graphics).

Unembedding a Graphic Embedding a picture into PageMaker documents was almost always a dead-end street, but InDesign is smarter: You can unembed graphics, too, by selecting the graphic in the Links palette and choosing Unembed File from the palette menu. The program gives you a choice of linking to the original file on disk (if it's still there) or saving the embedded file to disk and linking to it.

Navigating with the Links Palette One very nice feature of the Links palette is the Go to Link button. To display any file that appears in the Links palette, select the file and click the Go to Link button. InDesign selects and displays the graphic, centered in the publication window (jumping to another spread, if necessary, to do so).

Working with Images

We don't think too much about the process of taking a photograph, scanning it, incorporating it into a page layout, printing color separations of the publication, and then printing it on a commercial offset printing press. But it's an amazing process.

First you record the visible light that's bouncing off of physical objects. To do this, you use a lens to project the light onto a piece of film that's coated with a chemical compound that changes on contact with light. After you expose the film to some other chemicals, an image appears. Next, you turn the photographic image into pixels using a scanner. Or you skip the film altogether and take the picture with a digital camera.

When you print from your page layout program, you turn the pixels into color halftone screens—overlapping patterns of dots, which, when printed using certain inks, produce something that resembles what you saw in the first place.

Given all of the above, is it any surprise that there's a lot to think about when it comes to images?

**Images and
Halftoning**

Most commercial printing equipment can only print one color per printing plate at one time. (There are some short-run printing systems can print colors in other ways, but they're still pretty rare.) We can get additional "tints" of that color by filling areas with small dots; at a distance (anything over a foot or so), these dots look like another color. The pattern of dots is called a halftone (for more on digital halftoning and commercial printing, see Chapter 10, "Color").

We use halftoning to print the different shades inside images, or the different colors in vector artwork. The eye, silly and arbitrary thing that it is, tells our brain that the printed photograph is made up of shades of gray (or color)—not different patterns of large and small dots.

About Gray Levels

When we refer to "gray levels," we're not necessarily talking about the *color* gray—we're talking about halftone screen values less than 100 percent and greater than 0 percent that appear on a printing plate. You still need gray levels when you're printing color separations, because almost all of the colors you'll find in a typical printed color image are made up of overlapping tints of two or more inks.

**Halftone Screen
Frequency and
Resolution**

Let us introduce you to the image resolution balancing act (in case you haven't already met). It's natural to assume that scanning at the highest resolution available from your scanner will provide the sharpest images. The truth, however, is that this isn't so. Because of the way that digital halftoning works, the resolution of an image and the halftone screen frequency interact—with the net result that some information is not needed or used when an image reaches your printer. In short, for grayscale and color images, your image resolution should be no higher than twice the halftone screen frequency you intend to use. All higher scanning resolutions give you are larger file sizes, longer printing times, and bigger headaches.

In fact, you can almost always get away with resolutions only 1.5 times your screen frequency. For instance, at 133 lpi your images need not be any greater than 200 pixels per inch(ppi); at 150 lpi you probably don't need more than 225 ppi images. The difference between a 300 ppi image and a 225 ppi image is more significant than you might think: A four-by-five-inch CMYK image is 6.9 Mb at 300 ppi and only 3.8 Mb at 225 ppi—about half the size. That means it takes less time to transfer across the network (to a server or to a printer), less disk space to store, faster printing times, and so on.

We like to scan at the optical resolution of our scanner (usually 600 dpi or so), resize and downsample the image in Adobe Photoshop, and then sharpen it using Photoshop's Unsharp Masking filter (all scanned images need some sharpening if you intend to print them using halftone screens). David wrote about this process in greater detail in his books *Real World Photoshop* (co-authored with Bruce Fraser) and *Real World Scanning and Halftones, 3rd Edition* (co-authored with Glenn Fleishman, Conrad Chavez, and Steve Roth).

Line Art   Line art images (which have only black and white pixels, saved using Photoshop's Bitmap mode) obey different rules than grayscale or color images. These monochrome (or bi-level) bitmapped images do not use halftone screening. This means that they're exempt from the resolution balancing act mentioned above, but it also means that they require higher resolutions to avoid jaggy (pixelated) edges.

If your final artwork will be printed on a desktop laser printer, you probably don't need to use resolutions greater than 600 ppi. Imagesetter output rarely requires more than 1200 ppi (though for a sheetfed art book, we might bump this up to 1500 ppi). Printing on uncoated stock requires a lower resolution because of halftone spots spreading; you can easily get away with 800 ppi for newsprint.

Scaling in InDesign   Ideally, you should import your bitmapped images at the same size as you intend to print them. Resolution changes when you change the size of the image in InDesign. For instance, doubling the size of a 300 dpi picture on your page cuts the effective resolution in half, to 150 dpi (because each pixel in the image has to be twice as wide and twice as tall as before, so fewer of them fit "per inch"). Conversely, making this graphic 25-percent smaller increases to 400 dpi. (If you really care why the resolution increases by a third instead of by 25 percent, e-mail us and we'll explain the unpleasant math.)

We don't mind scaling images 5 or 10 percent up or down in InDesign. However, if the design requires any more scaling than that and we really care about the image quality, we'd rather resample in Photoshop and then apply a little more sharpening, to offset the blurriness that scaling or resampling introduces.

(Actually, for the sake of full-disclosure, we should note that we do *not* resize screen captures—such as the ones in this book—in Photoshop. When it comes to synthetic images like this, resizing on the InDesign page is usually better.)

Working with Graphic Frames

Getting used to the way that InDesign works with graphics and graphics frames can take some time—especially for users of FreeHand and

PageMaker (where graphics are not obviously stored inside frames). So, while this doesn't strictly have anything to do with importing or exporting images, we hope that the following sections help.

Selecting Frames and Graphics

You can modify the size, shape, and formatting of a graphic frame, or you can modify the frame's contents, or you can change both at once. The key to making these adjustments lies in the selection method you use (see Figure 7-13).

▶ When you click the frame or frame contents using the Selection tool, or when a selection rectangle created by dragging the Selection tool touches the frame, you're selecting both the frame and its contents. At this point, any changes you make (using the Transform palette or transformation tools) affect both the frame and its contents (see Chapter 9, "Transforming").

▶ When you click the edge of the frame with the Direct Selection tool, you're selecting the frame only—not its contents. Select the frame when you want to edit the shape of the frame using the drawing tools, or transform (scale, rotate, skew, or move) the frame using the transformation tools or the Transform palette

FIGURE 7-13
Selecting a Graphic

Click the Selection tool on the frame or graphic to select the frame and the graphic (note solid selection handles).

Click the Direct Selection tool on the frame to select the frame (note hollow selection handles).

Click the Direct Selection tool inside the frame to select the graphic. When the frame and the graphic are exactly the same size, it can be difficult to tell which is selected (in this example, it's easy, because the selected graphic is larger than the little frame). After you select the image, you can direct-select the frame by Option/Alt-clicking the image.

without transforming its contents. To drag the frame without moving the picture, drag its center point with the Direct Selection tool. (If you drag a point or a segment on the edge of the frame, you're likely to move just a portion of the frame.)

▶ When you click *inside* the frame with the Direct Selection tool, you're selecting only the frame contents—not the frame itself. Select the graphic when you want to transform (rotate, scale, move, or skew) the graphic alone, or when you want to apply color to the graphic. If you then Option/Alt-click inside the frame again with the Direct Selection tool, InDesign selects the "parent" frame of the graphic instead.

▶ You can also use the Position tool to drag an image inside the frame or resize the frame itself. (See "Panning a Graphic," below, for more on this.)

Resizing Imported Graphics

When you select a graphic frame with the Selection tool and drag the corner handle, InDesign resizes the frame *but does not scale the graphic.* To scale the graphic inside the frame as you scale the frame, hold down Command/Ctrl as you drag the corner handle (see Figure 7-14). Hold down Command-Shift/Ctrl-Shift as you drag to proportionally resize the frame and graphic.

FIGURE 7-14
Scaling a Graphic with the Selection Tool

When you simply drag one of the selection handles of a frame containing a graphic, InDesign scales the frame, but does not scale the graphic.

Hold down Command/Ctrl as you drag a selection handle, and InDesign will scale the graphic as it scales the frame.

You can also resize both the frame and the graphic using the Scaling tool or the Scale Horizontal and Scale Vertical fields in the Transform palette, provided you've selected the frame using the Selection tool. Or use the Free Transform tool or the Scale dialog box (see Chapter 9, "Transforming").

**Panning
a Graphic**

When you "pan" a graphic, you move the graphic without moving the graphic's frame. To do this, select the graphic with the Direct Selection tool, then drag. As you drag, InDesign repositions the graphic inside the frame (see Figure 7-15). If you hold down the mouse button for a moment before you drag, you'll see the part of the image outside the frame, too—it's tinted to differentiate it from the part of the graphic inside the frame.

**FIGURE 7-15
Panning a Graphic**

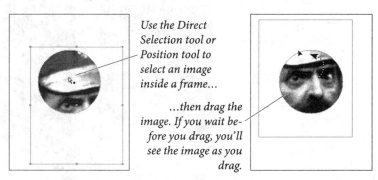

Use the Direct Selection tool or Position tool to select an image inside a frame...

...then drag the image. If you wait before you drag, you'll see the image as you drag.

You can also use the Position tool (which you can select under the Direct Selection tool in the Tool palette or press Shift-A) for this task. The Position tool is cool because it has attributes of both the Selection and the Direct Selection tool: You can pan an image inside a frame by dragging it around, or you can change the image's crop by dragging the edge or corner handles of the frame itself.

Of course, no matter what tool you use, if you pan the contents too far, the graphic won't even be visible in the frame, which makes it frustrating to select again later. Select the frame and choose Center Content from the Fitting submenu (in the Object menu, or the context menu) to recover the picture.

Note that it's possible to move the graphic entirely outside the frame, off the page, and beyond the edge of the pasteboard. Don't.

**Fitting Frames
and Graphics**

After importing a graphic, you can adjust its size within the frame, or the size of the frame in several ways. You can choose each of the following from the Fitting submenu (under the Object menu or in the context menu). These commands also appear as somewhat cryptic buttons on the right side of the Control palette (see Figure 7-16).

FIGURE 7-16
**Fitting Frames
and Images**

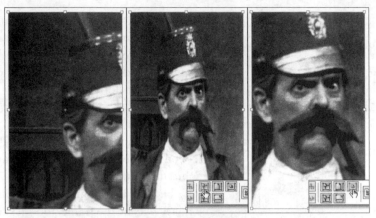

Fit Content to Frame   *Center Content*

*Fit Frame to
Content expands or
contracts the frame
to fit the content.*

Fit Content Proportionally   *Fill Frame Proportionally*

▶ **Fit Content to Frame.** The Fit Content to Frame feature resizes the graphic to fit into the current frame size. However, unless the graphic already has the same height/width proportions as the frame, it will be stretched non-proportionally.

▶ **Fit Content Proportionally.** If you want to ensure your image is resized with the same X and Y percentages, choose Fit Content Proportionally. The image is sized so that the entire image fits inside the frame. In most cases, there will be an empty portion of the frame.

▶ **Fill Frame Proportionally.** Choosing Fill Frame Proportionally will resize the image so that it completely fills the frame, cropping out a portion of the graphic if necessary (which it usually is). The upper-left corner of the resized image is placed in the upper-left corner of the frame, and whatever doesn't fit gets cropped out.

- **Fit Frame to Content.** When you select Fit Frame to Content, InDesign resizes the frame to match the size of the graphic. The size or position of the graphic itself does not change.

   Note that the Fit Frame to Content feature also works for text frames (as long as they're not linked to other frames). When there is only a single line of text in the frame, InDesign adjusts the height and width of the frame. When there is more than one line of text, only the height is adjusted.

- **Center Content.** Choose Center Content to position the center point of the graphic at the geometric center of the frame. This is especially helpful if you accidentally position an image outside of the frame boundaries (so that you can no longer see it).

File Info and Metadata

Metadata (which literally means "data about data") isn't a new thing. Photoshop's File Info dialog box has allowed you to add metadata such as captions, copyright info, and routing or handling instructions for years. But the Adobe Creative Suite applications are beginning to incorporate metadata features more seriously now (based on the open standard XMP structure, which is based on XML, if you care). Metadata can be almost any kind of information about your file, and it travels invisibly behind the scenes with the file as it moves from machine to machine. We think you'll find that the more time you take to add metadata to your files now, the happier you'll be in the long run.

Adding Metadata to InDesign Files

You can add metadata to an InDesign files by selecting File Info from the File menu (see Figure 7-17). The File Info dialog box contains several panels of fields and pop-up menus, though you'll likely just use the Description panel most of the time. Some panels—such as Camera Data 1 and 2—aren't applicable to InDesign documents at all. See *Real World Photoshop CS2* for more information on image-related metadata.

Another, less intuitive way to add metadata to InDesign documents is to use Adobe Bridge. (You can do this in Photoshop CS's File Browser window, too, but first, you have to choose Unreadable Files from the File Browser View menu.) Just select an InDesign document and choose File Info from Bridge's File menu. To apply metadata to more than one InDesign file at a time, choose the documents and use Bridge's Metadata and Keyword palettes. (Beware, though—this action isn't undoable.)

Metadata in an InDesign file travels not only with the file itself, but also with PDF files exported from the document. When you export a PDF file of your InDesign document, InDesign automatically includes the metadata, too. (If you include any sort of personal or trade information in your metadata, you may need to strip it out manually with Acrobat or Bridge before sending a PDF file to someone else.)

Reading Metadata in Imported Images

Both Illustrator and Photoshop let you add metadata in the same way. But while it's all well and good to add metadata to your files and images, it doesn't do you a lot of good unless you can read the metadata out again. You can always revisit the File Info dialog box again to see the metadata, but what about retrieving metadata from imported images? There are two ways to see this hidden information: After selecting an imported graphic, you can select File Info from the Info palette menu, or you can select Link File Info from the Links palette menu.

Even better, you can extract the metadata from the imported image by selecting a field and copying it to the Clipboard. For example, if someone added a caption to an image from within Photoshop, you could copy that caption out and paste it into a text frame in InDesign—no more PostIt notes with captions passed from person to person!

Searching for Metadata   One of the most important reasons to add metadata to your images and documents is so that you can search for that data later. For example, you might want to find all the InDesign documents on your hard drive that include the phrase "square the circle" in the Description field or the word "frogs" as a keyword. InDesign doesn't have a built-in way of doing these kinds of searches, but several asset management utilities do. The most obvious one is Adobe Bridge: Choose a folder, click Bridge's Search button, and select from the Criteria pop-up menu.

When you find the InDesign file you're looking for, you can select it in Bridge and then choose Open with InDesign from the context menu (right-click in Windows or Control-click on the Macintosh).

By the way, if you're searching for a PDF file that contains metadata, you can also use Bridge, but Acrobat's own Search feature may be even faster. It's not obvious that the Searches feature looks for file metadata, but it does. You just need to set it to look through documents on disk rather than the currently open file.

Object Layer Options

We've long loved InDesign's ability to import native Photoshop (PSD) files, layers and all. Now, our favorite page-layout program goes one step beyond by letting us turn those layers on and off (making them visible or hidden). You can control layer visibility in either PSD and PDF files that contain layers. Ironically and sadly, it won't work for Photoshop PDF files or native AI files, but Adobe Illustrator PDF files work great, as long as you turn on the Create Acrobat Layers option when making the PDF from Illustrator.

You can turn layers on or off when you first import a file into InDesign by turning on the Show Import Options checkbox in the Place dialog box (see "Image Import Options," earlier in this chapter). Or, if you have already imported the image, select it on your page and choose Object Layer Options from the Object menu (or the context menu). In either case, you're presented with the same three options (see Figure 7-18).

Show Layers. It's unclear whether a feature could be any simpler than this: To make a layer visible or invisible, click in the column to the left of the layer's name. If you've used layer sets in Photoshop, you can view the individual layers within those by clicking the triangle next to the layer set name. Also, you can Option/Alt-click on an eye

FIGURE 7-18
**Changing
Layer Visibility**

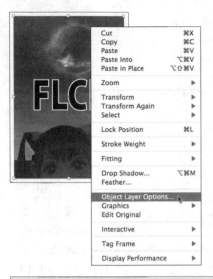

*Select an imported graphic
that contains layers and choose
Object Layer Options from the
Context menu (or from the
Object Menu).*

*Change layer visibility in the
Show Layers section of the
Object Layer Options dialog
box...*

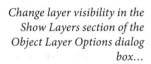

*...and InDesign displays or hides
layers as you've specified.*

icon to toggle all the other layers. That is, if all the other layers are
visible when you do this, they'll all become hidden, and vice versa.

Layer Comps. Photoshop's Layer Comp palette lets you create "comps"
of layer settings. For example, you might have one layer comp that
shows layers A, B, and C; and another layer comp in which A, C,
and D are visible. Or you might make a layer comp in which some
of the layers have layer styles (like drop shadow or emboss) turned
on, and another comp in which they're turned off. Layer comps are
great when you have a lot of ideas in Photoshop but you're not sure
what will look best when the image hits the page. The good news is
that you can choose any of your layer comps from the Layer Comps
popup menu. Of course, if a PSD file has no layer comps saved in it,
this menu is unavailable.

Update Link Options. After you override the native layer visibility settings (what the file was saved with) with the Object Layer Options dialog box, InDesign displays a small eye icon in the Links palette next to that image's name. This helps alert you that someone did something to those layers. However, what if you go back, change the layer visibility in Photoshop or Illustrator, and then save the file again? InDesign offers two options: If you choose Use Photoshop's Layer Visibility (or Use PDF's Layer Visibility, depending on what kind of image it is) from the When Updating Link popup menu, InDesign will throw out any layer visibility overrides as soon as you Relink or Update the image link. Alternately, if you choose Keep Layer Visibility Overrides, then your overrides will be maintained even after the image is modified and updated.

This feature bit David recently on the book he co-authored with Conrad Chavez, *Adobe Photoshop CS/CS2 Breakthroughs*. Conrad had imported several PSD files with layers into InDesign, used Object Layer Options to control the layers, and then sent the InDesign file and linked images to David. When David opened the InDesign file, the images appeared as modified, he automatically updated the links, and then wondered why the images were all different than expected. (We actually don't know why the files appeared modified when they hadn't actually changed. We think that compressing the image files and then sending them from one computer to another confused the operating system into thinking the files had been modified recently.)

Unfortunately, after the "modified" images were updated, there was little recourse other than to manually change the layer visibility for each image. The moral of the story: Pay attention to the the When Updating Link popup menu.

Working with Clipping Paths

Earlier in this chapter, we talked about InDesign's ability to use a clipping path stored in a graphic as you place the graphic—but what about creating a clipping path for a graphic that doesn't have one? First, there's nothing magical about clipping paths. In fact, you could say that every graphic you place in InDesign is inside a clipping path—its graphic frame.

A clipping path is a PostScript path, much like other Bézier lines in InDesign, Illustrator, or QuarkXPress. However, a clipping path acts like a pair of scissors, cutting out an image in any shape you want. Clipping an image is actually the same as cropping it, but because InDesign makes a distinction, we will, too: The shape of a graphic frame crops the picture, but the clipping path (if there is one) clips it.

Why Use Clipping Paths?

Remember that InDesign can read transparency in imported images. Even if you don't want to use any of the transparency effects, you still may want to take advantage of this feature because it means you might avoid using clipping paths altogether. Save yourself a bundle of time and just make the background of the image transparent in Photoshop.

Nevertheless, some people will still want to use clipping paths. For example, clipping paths are always drawn at the resolution of the output device, so you can get very sharp edges. If you like this sharp-edged effect, use a clipping path. Also, those folks who want to avoid the transparency flattener might still want to use clipping paths. As for us, we haven't bothered with a clipping path for months.

Selecting an Existing Clipping Path

If the selected graphic contains a clipping path—or, in the case of a Photoshop image, *any* path saved in Photoshop's Paths palette—you can select the clipping path you want to apply. To do this, select the graphic or its frame, then display the Clipping Path dialog box (choose Clipping Path from the Object menu or press Command-Option-Shift-K/Ctrl-Alt-Shift-K). Select Photoshop Path from the Type pop-up menu. If there are multiple paths, choose one from the Path pop-up menu (see Figure 7-19).

Creating a Clipping Path

You can ask InDesign to create an "automatic" clipping path using the following steps (see Figure 7-20). However, to be honest about it, we tend to shy away from this option unless we're building a quick comp for a client or we're planning on spending some time editing the resulting path. In general, you'll just get better results making clipping paths by hand in Photoshop.

1. Select a graphic. You'll have the best luck with a graphic against a white background. In addition, it's a good idea to select the graphic using the Direct Selection tool (as opposed to selecting the frame). We know this seems odd, but bear with us.

2. Choose Clipping Path from the Object menu (or press Command-Option-Shift-K/Ctrl-Alt-Shift-K). InDesign displays the Clipping Path dialog box.

FIGURE 7-19
**Using an Existing
Clipping Path**

*Place a graphic contain-
ing a clipping path (in
this example, we've used
a Photoshop file).*

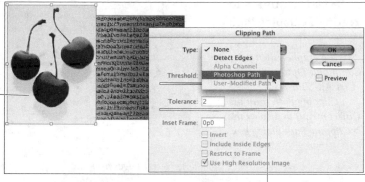

*Select the graphic, then press
Command-Option-Shift-K/
Ctrl-Alt-Shift-K (or choose
Clipping Path from the
Object menu) to display the
Clipping Path dialog box.*

Choose Photoshop Path from the Type pop-up menu.

Choose a path from the Path menu.

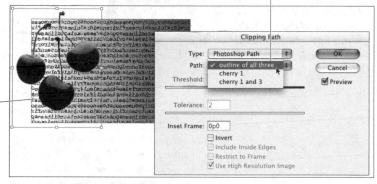

*InDesign applies
the first clipping
path defined in
the graphic.*

*If that's not the path
you wanted, choose a
different one. Here, we've
chosen "cherry 1 and 3."*

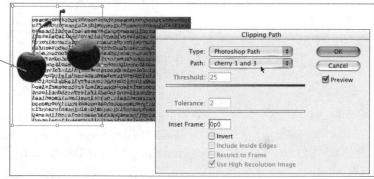

3. Choose Detect Edges from the Type pop-up menu. Turn on the
   Preview option, if it's not already on, and drag the Clipping Path
   dialog box out of the way (if necessary) so that you can see the
   selected image. Look at the clipping path that InDesign has built
   around the image. What? You can't see the clipping path? That's
   because you didn't select the image using the Direct Selection
   tool, like we told you to in Step 1. If you had, you'd be able to see
   the clipping path as you adjust the settings in the Clipping Path
   dialog box.

FIGURE 7-20

Creating a Clipping Path

Select a graphic, then press Command-Option-Shift-K/ Ctrl-Alt-Shift-K (or choose Clipping Path from the Object menu) to display the Clipping Path dialog box.

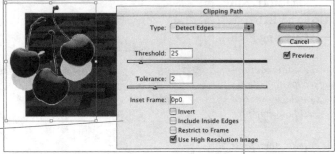

Choose Detect Edges from the Type pop-up menu.

InDesign attempts to find the edges in the graphic. Of course, InDesign does a better job of this when the graphic has a simple outline and a simple background.

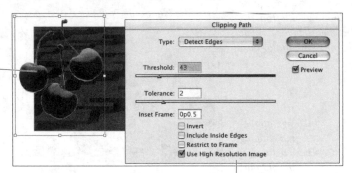

You can fine-tune the clipping path using the controls in the Clipping Path dialog box. Here, we've adjusted the Threshold and Inset Frame values to remove some off-white areas.

4. Work with the controls in the dialog box.

   ▸ Adjust the values in the Threshold and Tolerance fields (either enter values in the fields or drag the associated sliders) until the clipping path looks the way you want it to.

   ▸ Turn on the Include Inside Edges option to create "holes" inside the clipping path for any blank (as defined by the value you entered in the Threshold field) areas inside the graphic.

   ▸ Turn on Invert to turn the clipping path "inside out."

   ▸ Turn on Restrict to Frame to limit the clipping path to the boundaries of the graphic frame. (Since the image can't extend past the edges of the graphic frame anyway, this is reasonable. However, if you change your frame cropping, you'll have to rebuild your clipping path, so we leave this turned off.)

   ▸ Most of the time, you'll probably want to turn on the Use High Resolution Image option—it uses data from the image file on disk (rather than simply using the screen preview image) to create a more accurate clipping path.

▸ If necessary (and it usually will be), enter a value in the Inset Frame field to shrink (enter positive values) or expand (enter negative values) the clipping path. We often use a small inset value, like .5 points.

5. Once the clipping path looks the way you want it to, click the OK button.

Don't worry about making a mistake; you can always open up this dialog box again and change the values, or change the clipping path using the Direct Selection tool or the various Pen tools.

Note that you can also create a clipping path based on an alpha channel if one has been saved in an imported image. To do this, select Alpha Channel from the Type pop-up menu. The problem is that alpha channels (saved selections) can have soft anti-aliased or feathered edges, and clipping paths cannot. So, InDesign has to convert soft edges into hard-edged Bézier paths using the features above. It's hardly worth the trouble in our opinion.

Removing a Clipping Path

To remove a clipping path, select the image, display the Clipping Path dialog box, and choose None from the Type pop-up menu. InDesign removes the clipping path.

Convert Clipping Path to Frame

You can convert a clipping path into a frame of the same shape by selecting any image with a clipping path and choosing Convert Clipping Path to Frame from the context menu (right-click in Windows or Control-click on the Mac OS). This works for all clipping paths, including clipping paths generated by the Detect Edges feature.

One reason you'd want to convert a clipping path to a frame is to print a spot varnish over a silhouetted image, or emboss the image.

1. Copy the image to a new layer (remember that holding down Option/Alt and dragging the Layer palette object proxy to another layer duplicates the selected object).

2. Convert the clipping path of the duplicated image to a frame.

3. Select the image inside this new frame with the Direct Selection tool and delete it.

4. Set the fill color of the empty frame with a spot color that simulates the varnish. For instance, you could pick a light yellow Pantone solid color.

5. In the Attributes palette, turn on Overprint Fill so that this spot color doesn't knock out the image beneath it.

Of course, you won't be able to see the image until you turn on Overprint Preview from the View menu. Now, when you print color separations, you'll get a spot plate for this page in exactly the same shape as the clipping path.

Applying Color to an Imported Graphic

You can't apply color to just any imported graphic—but you can apply colors to bi-level (*i.e.*, black-and-white) and grayscale TIFF images. To apply a color to an image, select the image using the Direct Selection tool, then apply a color as you normally would—probably by clicking a swatch in the Swatches palette (see Chapter 10, "Color").

If you want the image to overprint any objects behind it, select the image using the Direct Selection tool, display the Attributes palette (if it's not already visible), and then turn on the Overprint Fill option. You can use this technique to create duotones from grayscale images you've placed in a publication, as shown in Color Figure 7. Or, instead of using the Overprint Fill trick, you can simply set the image to Multiply mode in the Transparency palette.

Exporting Documents

Sometimes, you've got to get your pages out of your InDesign publications and into some other application or format. You can export InDesign pages as EPS, PDF, HTML, SVG, or XML (in addition to the text export options described in Chapter 3, "Text"). We explore each of these in depth in the following sections—except XML, which we cover in Chapter 14. In each case, the first step is always to select Export from the File menu (or press Command-E/Ctrl-E).

Exporting JPEG

The best way for someone else to see a page from your document if they don't own InDesign (or you don't want to give them your InDesign file) is to export and send them a PDF file. However, a JPEG image of your document page often works just as well—and not only is a JPEG file usually much smaller than a PDF, but it's also much easier to view (any Web browser can display a JPEG, file, but not everyone has Acrobat Reader). Of course, a JPEG file is a bitmapped image, so whoever you send it to can't really zoom in on the file.

InDesign can export a low-resolution (72 ppi) JPEG file of any page or object in your document—you can even export a series of JPEG files for more than one page at a time. To export a JPEG file, choose Export from the File menu and pick JPEG from the Format pop-up menu. The Export JPEG dialog box is pretty simple (see Figure 7-21). You can control which page or pages you want to export (use commas and hyphens to type ranges of pages). To export one or more objects from a page or spread, select them before choosing Export and then turn on the Selection option in the dialog box

The Image Quality pop-up menu offers a handful of choices, from Low to Maximum—the lower the quality you choose, the smaller the file will be on disk. Unfortunately, there's no way to preview the quality difference before saving the file. Use the Format Method pop-up menu to choose Baseline or Progressive—we recommend Baseline unless you need people to see the image progressively appear in stages (low resolution, then higher resolution) when they view it.

If you need more control over how your InDesign files get saved as JPEG (such as choosing a higher resolution), or you want to save them as GIF instead, we suggest exporting the page or pages as a PDF or EPS file, opening it in Photoshop, and then choosing Save for Web from the File menu.

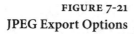

FIGURE 7-21
JPEG Export Options

Exporting EPS

To export an InDesign page (or series of pages) as an EPS graphic (or series of graphics, as EPS is, by definition, a single-page-at-a-time format), choose EPS from the pop-up menu in the Export dialog box or the Save as Type field (Windows), pick a location for the file, and then click the Save button. InDesign displays the Export EPS dialog box. This dialog box has two panels: General and Advanced. Here's a quick description of the options in each panel.

General. The controls in the General panel define the way that InDesign exports objects to the EPS file (see Figure 7-22).

▶ **Pages.** Which pages do you want to export? Bear in mind, as you work with the controls in this panel, that each page in the page range you specify will be exported as a separate EPS file. To export pages one, two, three, seven, and twelve, for example, enter "1-3,7,12" into the Ranges field. See "Page Ranges" in Chapter 11, "Printing," for more information. When you turn on the Spreads checkbox, InDesign exports the pages in readers spreads, just as they appear in your document window. For instance, pages 2 and 3 are combined into one wide EPS file.

▶ **PostScript.** Choose the PostScript version of the printer you expect to use to print the EPS. If you're sure you're printing on a PostScript 3 printer, choose Level 3. Choose Level 2 if your printer could be PostScript Level 2 or PostScript 3. InDesign no longer supports PostScript Level 1 printers; a Level 2 EPS file may or may not print on one of these old beasts.

▶ **Color.** Do you want to convert RGB images in your publication to CMYK as you create the EPS? If so, choose CMYK from the Color pop-up menu. The method InDesign uses for this conversion depends on the setting of the Enable Color Management

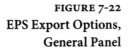

FIGURE 7-22
EPS Export Options,
General Panel

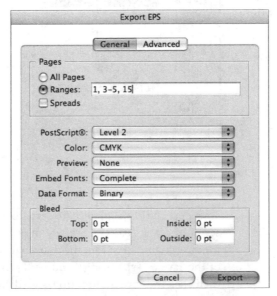

option in the Color Settings dialog box (see Chapter 10, "Color," for more on color management). If the option is on, and you've assigned a color profile to an image, InDesign uses that profile to create separations of the image. If the option is turned off, or if you have not turned on color management for the image, InDesign uses its internal RGB to CMYK conversion method.

While it's pretty rare that you'd need to choose Gray or RGB, these options will convert all colors to their grayscale or RGB equivalents.

If you're using some other software to handle the EPS's color separation, you can choose Leave Unchanged. When you do this, InDesign leaves RGB and CMYK images alone during the export process.

▸ **Preview.** EPS files usually have low-resolution, built-in previews, which applications use to display the EPS on screen; Macintosh EPS files typically have PICT previews, Windows EPS files must use TIFF previews. If you're re-importing the EPS file back into an InDesign document, you can leave the Preview pop-up menu set to None, because InDesign actually creates a preview on the fly when you import the file. Similarly, if you're going to open the EPS file in Photoshop (rasterizing it into a bitmapped image), Illustrator (converting it into paths), or process the EPS file with some software that doesn't require a preview image, you can leave Preview set to None. If the EPS will be used in any other program (like QuarkXPress), select PICT or TIFF (the latter is more flexible because most Macintosh programs can read both PICT and TIFF).

▸ **Embed Fonts.** To make sure that the EPS contains all of the fonts you've used, choose Complete from the Embed Fonts pop-up menu. Why not do this every time? Because your EPS files can become huge, bloated, and swollen with included fonts. To reduce the size of the EPS, choose Subset to include only the characters needed to print the text in the EPS. Choose None when you don't want or need to include any fonts in the EPS.

Some fonts cannot be embedded—the font manufacturer has included information in the font that prevents embedding. When InDesign reads this information, it will not include the fonts in the EPS, regardless of the choice you make from the Embed Fonts pop-up menu. If you find you're missing a font in an EPS, return to the InDesign publication and convert all of the characters that use the missing font to outlines and then export the EPS again.

- **Data Format.** Choose ASCII if you expect to print the EPS on a system connected to a printer via a serial cable, or if you plan to edit the EPS using a text editor or word processor—otherwise, choose Binary to create a compressed version of the file. Binary files are smaller and therefore transmit to the printer faster, but they sometimes choke really old networks.

- **Bleed.** If you do not enter values in the four Bleed fields (Top, Bottom, Inside, and Outside—or Left and Right, in a non-facing-pages document), InDesign sets the edge of the EPS bounding box to the edge of the page you're exporting. Enter a value in the Bleed fields to expand the area of the page. See Chapter 11, "Printing," for more on bleeding off the edge of the page.

Advanced. Just because it's called the Advanced tab of the Export EPS dialog box doesn't necessarily mean that these options are any more advanced or tricky. These features let you control how images and transparency are handled in EPS files (see Figure 7-23).

- **Send Data.** In most cases, you want the full resolution of your bitmapped images to be included in your EPS files (so they can later be printed properly). On occasion, however, you may want only a low-resolution version of your images in the EPS file. For example, let's say you were going to rasterize the EPS in Photoshop in order to save it as a GIF or JPEG and place it on the Web; there's no need for the full-resolution images, so you could choose Proxy from the Send Data pop-up menu. If you're planning to print the EPS through an OPI system, and plan to replace the images, or if you're creating the EPS for onscreen viewing only, choose Proxy.

- **OPI Image Replacement.** Turn this option on to have InDesign perform OPI image replacement as you export the EPS. If you're exporting a page containing EPS graphics with OPI image links, you'll probably need to turn this option on (unless your EPS will later be processed by an OPI server).

- **Omit For OPI.** To keep InDesign from including a certain type of imported graphic file in the EPS, turn on the corresponding option in the Omit section (to omit placed TIFF images, for example, turn on the TIFF option). We discuss OPI in more detail in Chapter 11, "Printing."

- **Transparency Flattener.** In order for transparency effects to print on most devices, InDesign must "flatten" them. We discuss flattening and transparency flattening styles in great detail in

FIGURE 7-23
EPS Export Options,
Advanced Panel

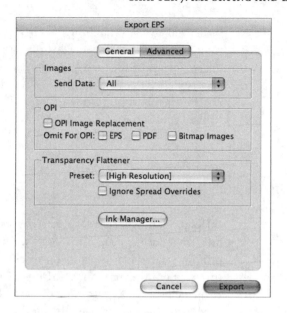

FIGURE 7-23
EPS Export Options,
Advanced Panel

Chapter 11, "Printing." Suffice it to say that you can choose a flattener style here, as well as tell InDesign to ignore any flattener style spread overrides that you (or someone else) may have made in the document (by turning on Ignore Spread Overrides).

► **Simulate Overprint.** If you've set various objects in your document to overprint (using the Attributes palette), but you're not going to print this EPS file on a device that can handle overprinted colors, then you may want to turn on the Simulate Overprint checkbox. However, this radically changes your EPS file, so while it may be useful for proofing, you probably shouldn't use it for final output.

► **Ink Manager.** The Ink Manager manages how colors trap with each other and how spot colors interact (for instance, you can use the Ink Manager to alias one spot color to another). We cover the Ink Manager in Chapter 10, "Color."

An EPS-Related Rant   It's inevitable—some of you are going to be asked by your imagesetting service provider to give them EPS files of your InDesign pages. This is because they want to import the EPSs into QuarkXPress 3.32. Why would they want to do this? Because they were probably raised by hyenas and this is the only way they know how to print *anything*. In spite of the output disasters that this approach can cause, it's what they're familiar with, and is the only way they'll print your job. You're laughing now, but, believe us, these guys are out there.

So, while you're searching for a new imagesetting service bureau, you might as well give them what they want. (And, in fact, it's better to give them EPS file than PDF files. Some of these folks think that placing PDF files into QuarkXPress is a good idea. Not so. XPress is not really a robust PDF reader/printer. If you know someone is going to place your exported files into XPress, you should almost certainly give them EPS files rather than PDF.)

Exporting PDF

InDesign can export Adobe Acrobat Portable Document Format files (what normal people call "PDF"), which can be used for remote printing, electronic distribution, or as a graphic you can place in InDesign or other programs. InDesign's PDF files can even include "rich" media, such as buttons, movies, and sounds. InDesign doesn't need to use the Acrobat Distiller (or the Distiller Assistant) to create PDF files.

Note, however, that Distiller usually makes more compact PDF files than exporting directly from InDesign, which may be important if your PDF files are destined for the Web. If you want to use Distiller to make PDF files instead of creating them directly using the Export feature, you must use the Print dialog box to write PostScript to disk first (we discuss how to do that in Chapter 11, "Printing").

While PDF is great for putting publications on the World Wide Web, or for creating other sorts of online publications, most of us ink-on-paper types care more about making PDF files suitable for print. Fortunately, InDesign can export PDFs for just about any purpose, onscreen or on-press. It all depends on how you set up the export options.

When you export a PDF (by selecting Export from the File menu and choosing PDF from the Type pop-up menu), InDesign displays the Export PDF dialog box. This dialog box contains seven panels for setting PDF export options: General, Compression, Marks & Bleeds, Output, Advanced, Security, and Summary. Remember that in all paneled dialog boxes like this one, you can jump to the second panel by pressing Command-2/Ctrl-2, the third panel with Command-3/Ctrl-3, and so on. (Actually, as we go to press, there is a bug in CS2 that stops these keyboard shortcuts from working in this particular dialog box. With luck, that will be fixed by the time you read this.)

Above all these panels sits the Style pop-up menu, which lets you select a PDF export preset (each of which is a collection of various export options). You may be familiar with these styles, as they're basically identical to those found in Illustrator and Distiller. We discuss creating your own in "Defining a PDF Export Preset," later in this chapter.

General   The General panel of the Export PDF dialog box (see Figure 7-24) is a hodge-podge of options, controlling everything from what pages get exported to whether InDesign should launch Acrobat after saving the file.

Standard (PDF/X). InDesign fully supports several important international ISO standards, including PDF/X-1a and PDF/X-3. You can select either of these from the Standard pop-up menu or the Preset menu. However, if you're going to use PDF/X, we strongly recommend you choose from the Preset menu instead of the Standard menu—otherwise, it's easy to make a PDF/X file that, while technically valid, will make the recipeient of the file unhappy.

PDF/X-1a is for a straight CMYK-only (or spot color) workflow, and is relatively popular in the United States. PDF/X-3 is used in color managed workflows, especially in Europe. Both of these standards aren't some weird, proprietary flavor of PDF; they're just regular PDF files that specify the sorts of things that can be included. For example, you can't put a button or movie or even an RGB image in a PDF/X-1a file, and all fonts must be embedded. You can see why many magazines and newspapers now insist that you send them a PDF/X file—they have to worry much less about whether you exported the

FIGURE 7-24
Export PDF Options,
General Panel

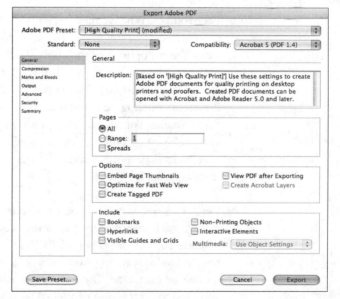

file correctly. Note that you can make a PDF/X compliant PDF file without choosing from the Standard or Preset pop-up menus; these just make it easier.

Compatibility. Who is your audience for this PDF file? Acrobat 7 has been out for over a year now, so we usually assume that most professionals have it but many of the general public may only have Acrobat 5 (or at least the free Acrobat 5 Reader). On the other hand, if there's any chance your recipient only has Acrobat 4, you'll need to choose Acrobat 4 from the Compatibility pop-up menu. Unfortunately, the PDF version numbering can be confusing: Version 1.3 is Acrobat 4, 1.4 is Acrobat 5, 1.5 is Acrobat 6, and version 1.6 is Acrobat 7.

There's another reason you want to pay attention here: If you have used any transparency effects in your document, the Compatibility pop-up menu controls who does the flattening. Choosing Acrobat 4 means you want InDesign to flatten the file (see "Transparency Flattener" later in this section, and "Printing Transparency" in Chapter 11, "Printing"). Acrobat 5, 6, and 7 can read the unflattened transparency effects. If we're sending files to our printer or an imaging bureau that we trust knows about flattening, then we'd much rather send them Acrobat 6 or 7 PDF files.

Similarly, if you want your PDF to have interactive elements (like buttons and movies), there's a good chance you'll want to save this as an Acrobat 6 or 7 file. (See Chapter 13, "Interactive PDF," for all the reasons why.)

Page Ranges. Which pages do you want to export? Just as in the General panel of the Print dialog box, you can export all document pages (click the All option) or specify individual page ranges (135-182) or noncontiguous pages (3, 7, 22) in the Range field. Note that unless you have Absolute Numbering selected in the General panel of the Preferences dialog box, you'll need to type page ranges with their actual names. For instance, if you want to export the first four pages and you're using roman numerals, you'll have to type "i-iv". If you've specified a page number prefix, like "A", you'll have to include that in the Range field, too.

Reader's Spreads. When you turn on the Spreads option, InDesign exports each spread in the page range you've specified (see above) as a single page of the exported PDF. This is called "reader's spreads" because the spread appears as it would to a reader flipping through a book or magazine. This does not create "printer spreads," which you need to print a saddle-stitched booklet. You need a separate plug-in to do that. Personally, when we want to view a PDF in reader's spreads, we don't turn on this feature; we just turn on the Facing option in Acrobat's View menu—the effect is basically the same.

Embed Page Thumbnails. Creates a preview image, or "thumbnail" of each page or spread (if you're exporting reader's spreads) you export. You can display thumbnails when you view the PDF using Acrobat or Acrobat Reader. They don't do much for us, and they increase the size of the file.

Optimize for Fast Web View. The key word here is "Web." The only time you'd want to turn this on is when you're creating a document that will only be viewed on the Web. When this option is off, InDesign includes repeated objects (such as objects from master pages) as individual objects on each page of the PDF. When you choose Optimize PDF, InDesign exports a single instance of each repeated item for the entire PDF. When the item appears on a page in the PDF, InDesign includes a reference to the "master" item. This reduces the file size of the PDF without changing the appearance of the exported pages. When this option is on, InDesign also overrides the settings in the Compression panel with its own Web-appropriate settings, and restructures the file so that it can be downloaded one page at a time from a Web server rather than having to download the whole megillah.

View PDF after Exporting. When you turn this option on, InDesign opens the file in Acrobat Reader or Acrobat after exporting the PDF.

Create Acrobat Layers. Acrobat 6 introduced the idea of hiding and showing layers within a PDF file. If you turn on the Create Acrobat Layers checkbox, all your InDesign document's layers (even hidden layers) are converted into Acrobat layers and can be controlled from within Acrobat. In a stroke of brilliance, even the page marks (like crop and registration marks) are put on their own layer. Obviously, this only works when exporting in the Acrobat 6 (PDF 1.5) format or later.

Include Bookmarks. If you've used the table of contents feature (which we discuss in Chapter 8, "Long Documents"), you can tell InDesign to automatically build bookmarks for your PDF file based on the table of contents. Just turn on the Include Bookmarks checkbox. Or, if you used the Bookmarks palette to add custom bookmarks to your document (see Chapter 13, "Interactive PDF") you have to turn this checkbox on to actually see them in the PDF file. Again, this is a feature suitable for PDFs destined for onscreen viewing, not prepress.

Tagged PDF. The Include Tagged PDF checkbox determines whether InDesign adds structure tags inside your PDF files. These tags tell Acrobat (or the Acrobat Reader) about the structure of the document, including what constitutes a paragraph. For instance, if you turn this option on, open the resulting PDF file in Acrobat 5 or 6, and then save it as an RTF (Rich Text Format) file, you can see that each paragraph is preserved. If you turn off Include eBook Tags, your final RTF file ends up with each line as a separate paragraph. After all, without structuring tags, Acrobat can't possibly know what constitutes a paragraph.

While there is hardly ever a need for these tags in documents that are simply being printed, they don't affect file size or export time much, so we typically just leave this option turned on. We discuss tagging structure and the Tags palette further in "Form and Function: XML," later in this chapter.

Hyperlinks. You can use the Hyperlinks palette to add as many hyperlinks to your document as you want, but unless you turn on this checkbox they won't appear in your PDF file. When you turn this option on, InDesign also creates hyperlinks in your table of contents and indexes (see Chapter 8, "Long Documents," for more on these features). Of course, it's not really appropriate to include hyperlinks when sending off a PDF for high-resolution printing. See Chapter 13, "Interactive PDF," for more on hyperlinks.

Interactive Elements. If your document contains buttons, movies, or sounds, you need to turn on the Interactive Elements checkbox to include them in the PDF file. Like the Hyperlinks option, there's no reason to turn this on for documents bound for press. When you do turn it on, however, you can also tell InDesign (in the Multimedia pop-up menu) whether to embed all sounds and movies into the PDF or leave them linked to the disk file. See Chapter 13, "Interactive PDF," for more on these sorts of things. The setting in the Multimedia pop-up menu overrides any object-level settings you have chosen for movies and sounds.

Non-printing Objects. Ordinarily, nonprinting objects (items on your page for which you've turned on the Non-printing checkbox in the Attributes palette) won't appear in exported PDF files. However, you can force them to export (overriding the Attributes palette) by turning on the Export Non-printing Objects checkbox in the Export PDF dialog box. Why would you do this? We bet someone can think of a good reason.

Visible Guides and Baseline Grids. If you turn on this export option, InDesign exports all visible guides (margins, ruler guides, baseline guides, and so on), which may be helpful for designers who are collaborating on a project. The only guide type that doesn't export is the document grid (even if it's visible).

Compression

The options in the Compression panel define the compression and/or sampling changes applied to the images in your publication as it's exported as a PDF (see Figure 7-25). Compression is almost always a good thing, but you need to choose your compression options carefully, depending on where your PDF is headed. PDFs for onscreen viewing can handle more compression, and those destined for the Web typically *need* a lot of compression to keep file sizes down. A PDF file that you're sending to a printer for high-resolution output requires very little compression, if any (unless you have to e-mail the file or it won't otherwise fit on a disk for transport).

Bitmapped images are almost always the largest part of a document, so PDF's compression techniques focus on them. InDesign has two methods of making your files smaller: lowering the resolution of the images and encoding the image data in clever ways.

FIGURE 7-25
Export PDF Options,
Compression Panel

Resampling. If you place a 300 ppi CMYK image into your document and scale it down 50 percent, the effective resolution is 600 ppi (because twice as many pixels fit in the same amount of space). When you export your PDF, you can ask InDesign to resample the image to a more reasonable resolution. If your final output is to a desktop inkjet printer, you rarely need more than 300 or 400 ppi. Printing on a laser printer or imagesetter (or any device that uses halftone screens, as explained earlier in this chapter) requires no more than 1.5 to 2.0 times the halftone screen frequency—a 150 lpi halftone rarely needs more than 225 ppi of data to print beautifully.

Monochrome (or bi-level) bitmapped images do not have halftone screens applied to them by the printer and, therefore, are not subject to the same rules that govern grayscale and color images. In a monochrome image, you never need more resolution than the resolution of the printer. If your final output is your 600 dpi laser printer, you certainly never need more than 600 dpi monochrome images. Imagesetter output rarely requires more than 1200 dpi (though for a sheetfed art book, we might bump this up to 1500 dpi). Printing on uncoated stock requires less resolution because of halftone spots spreading; you can easily get away with 800 dpi for newsprint.

If you're exporting a PDF for online viewing, you can get away with 72 or 96 ppi, unless you want the viewer to be able to zoom in on the image and not see pixelation.

InDesign only downsamples when exporting PDF files. That is, it throws away data to decrease image resolution (it won't add resolution). Downsampling works by turning an area of pixels into a single, larger pixel, so the method you use to get that larger pixel is crucial. When you *downsample* an image, InDesign takes the average color or gray value of all of the pixels in the area to set the color or gray value of the larger pixel. When you *subsample* an image, on the other hand, InDesign uses the color or gray value of a single pixel in the middle of the area. This means that subsampling is a much less accurate resampling method than downsampling, and shouldn't be used for anything other than proofing (see Figure 7-26). We rarely use Downsample or Subsample; instead, the best option is Bicubic Downsample, which provides the smoothest sampling algorithm.

Ultimately, however, we much prefer to just get the resolution right in Photoshop before placing the image, rather than relying on InDesign to downsample it. That way, we can see the result of resampling on the screen, and undo the change if necessary. Otherwise, we won't see the result until we view the PDF.

Normal   *Downsampled to 300   Subsampled to 300
                  pixels per inch   pixels per inch*

Encoding. The PDF specification supports both ZIP and JPEG encoding for grayscale and color bitmapped images; and CCITT Group 3, CCITT Group 4, ZIP, and Run Length encodings for monochrome bitmapped images. In Acrobat 6 or 7, you can even use JPEG 2000. It's enough to make your head spin! Which method should you use? Again, it depends on where the PDF is going and what kind of images you've got.

Scanned images generally compress better with JPEG, and synthetic images (such as screen captures that have a lot of solid colors and sharp edges) compress better with ZIP. However, JPEG compression, even at its highest quality setting, removes data from an image file (it's "lossy"). Most designers find that some JPEG compression for scanned photographs is an acceptable compromise, as it results in dramatically smaller file sizes. JPEG 2000 compresses even smaller and results in less degradation. But, ultimately, when we don't need to worry about file size, we prefer to use ZIP for everything because ZIP compression does not discard image data (it's "lossless"). You never know when you might need that image data!

If we are using JPEG, then we make a choice from the Quality pop-up menu: You get the best compression with Minimum quality, but who wants to look at the results? Unfortunately, the only good way to choose from among the Quality options is to save two or three to disk, look at them in Acrobat, and compare their file sizes.

Exporting PDF files for print is easier: We usually just choose ZIP for both color and grayscale images, and then specify 8-bit from the Quality pop-up menu (4-bit describes fewer colors, so it's half the size but lousy quality). However, if you need to save some disk space (again, like if you're emailing the file to your output provider), it's usually reasonable to use Automatic compression with the Quality pop-up menu set to Maximum quality—the resulting JPEG images are usually indistinguishable from uncompressed images. Or, if you know that the recipient has Acrobat 6 or later, then consider using the better-quality JPEG 2000 encoding.

As for monochrome image encoding, it's rare to see much of a difference among the choices (they're all lossless and provide reasonable compression). We usually use Run Length or ZIP encoding, but only because we don't like the sound of CCITT. Say it aloud a few times, and you'll see what we mean.

Compress Text and Line Art. The Compress Text and Line Art option applies to text and paths you've drawn in InDesign—we cannot think of any reason you should turn this option off.

Crop Image Data to Frames. When you turn this option on, InDesign sends only the visible parts of the images in the publication. This sounds reasonable, and can result in a much smaller file for publications that contain cropped images. But it also means you won't have access to the image data if you edit the image in the PDF. Most of the time, this isn't a problem, but you might want to turn this option off if your PDF includes images that bleed (so that you or your service provider can later increase the bleed area, if necessary).

Marks & Bleeds   In a desperate attempt at reducing the redundancy in our overly complex lives, we're going to skip a detailed analysis of the Marks & Bleeds panel of the Export PDF dialog box and instead point out that these features are exactly the same as the features in the Print dialog box (see "Marks and Bleeds" in Chapter 11, "Printing").

Output   In order to maintain consistency among the Creative Suite applications, Adobe moved several features from the Advanced panel to the Output panel in CS2 (see Figure 7-27).

Color Conversion. Choose No Color Conversion from the Color Conversion pop-up menu if you don't want InDesign to mess with your colors and just write them into the PDF as specified. That is, RGB colors will remain RGB, and CMYK colors will stay CMYK. This is what you get with PDF/X3, because in that standard, colors are managed at print time from Acrobat.

If you do want InDesign to manage the colors, you should choose either Convert Colors or Convert Colors (Preserve Numbers). In either case, all RGB colors get converted to CMYK based on the CMYK profile you choose in the Destination popup menu. However, when you choose the "preserve numbers" option, any CMYK colors

FIGURE 7-27
**Export PDF Options,
Output Panel**

that you have specified in your InDesign document (such as colors you have applied to text or frames) are left alone—that is, they are not converted from your document CMYK profile to the destination CMYK profile. For example, this stops 100-percent black text changing to four-color CMYK text, or 100-percent cyan changing to a mix of cyan, yellow, and magenta (which a problem in earlier versions of InDesign).

However, whether or not you choose "preserve numbers," if your CMYK image is tagged with a color profile *and* that profile was preserved when you placed it (which is typically not the case with CMYK images), it will get cross-converted to the new CMYK space. (See Chapter 10, "Color," for more on color management.)

Note that choosing CMYK does not separate spot colors to CMYK in the PDF file; if you want to do that, you should use the Ink Manager (see below).

If you have turned on color management (that is, you chose Emulate InDesign 2.0 in the Color Settings dialog box), then you have only three choices here: do nothing, Convert to CMYK, or Convert to RGB. Either way, InDesign uses its internal RGB-to-CMYK conversion method (the default CMYK space is based on SWOP inks—technically, it's the default CMYK settings from Photoshop 5; the default RGB space is AdobeRGB).

Profile Inclusion Policy. When you're converting colors, you can tell InDesign whether or not to embed ICC profiles into your PDF file. In a color-managed workflow, it is important to include profiles, or else other programs (or InDesign, if you're re-importing the PDF into another InDesign document) cannot color-manage the file. However, if you are simply creating a CMYK files (such as a PDF/X1-a workflow), there is no reason to include your profiles. Also, turn this option off when exporting PDF files for the Web, since the Web isn't color managed and ICC Profiles increase file size.

Simulate Overprint. Acrobat 4 has no way to preview overprinting instructions, so if you need to use Acrobat 4 and you need to proof overprinting, you can turn on the Simulate Overprint option. Because everyone we know is using Acrobat 5, we never have to worry about this feature. Note that Simulate Overprint should not be used for final artwork, as it radically changes your document (spot colors are changed to process colors, for instance). It's just a proofing tool.

Ink Manager. Have a spot color that should be a process color? Or two different spot colors that really should be one? The Ink Manager handles these kinds of troubles (for more information, see "Ink Manager" in Chapter 10, "Color").

PDF/X. If you have chosen one of the PDF/X options in the Standards popup menu at the top of the dialog box, InDesign offers you the option of specifying the final output destination profile in the mysteriously named Output Intent Profile Name. Fortunately, this is almost always exactly the same as the Destination profile you chose above. You can also add a short description in the Output Condition Name field if you think anyone downstream at the printer will care (seems doubtful to us). If the profile you choose is registered somewhere (such as the International Color Consortium at www.color.org), you can specify a name and URL in the final two fields of this section. That information simply gets embedded in the PDF file so someone can later decode what you've done.

Advanced   There's nothing particularly "advanced" about any of the options in this panel, and while you probably won't spend much time messing with these settings, it is important to understand what they do and why you'd want to change them (see Figure 7-28).

Subset Fonts Below. InDesign can always embed font information in exported PDF files, so it doesn't matter whether the person you give the file to has the font. The exception to this is when the font manufacturer has specified that their font should not be embedded. Many

FIGURE 7-28
Export PDF Options,
Advanced Panel

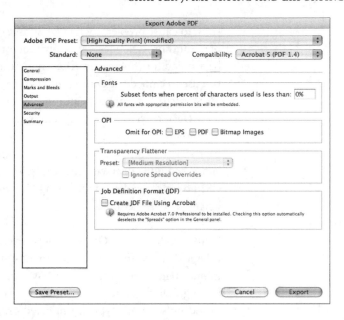

Asian fonts cannot be embedded, for instance. This is a political and legal hot-potato that we're not going to touch, other than to say that if your fonts cannot be embedded, complain to the font developer, not Adobe (or us). Or, better yet, if there isn't a lot of text in that font, convert the text to outlines before printing or exporting.

Anyway, usually the question isn't whether to embed your fonts, but rather how much of the font you want to embed. The value you enter in the Subset Fonts Below field sets the threshold at which InDesign includes complete fonts in the PDF you're exporting. When you "subset" a font, you include only those characters that are used on the pages you're exporting, which keeps file size down. Enter 100 to force InDesign to always save a subset of the font's characters, or enter 0 to force InDesign to include the entire font (or fonts) in the PDF. You can also enter some other percentage value to strike a balance between the two extremes, but we generally find that either we want subsets or we don't.

One reason you might not want to subset your fonts is to maximize the potential for editing the PDF later. Let's say you subset your fonts, and later need your output provider to edit the PDF (perhaps to change a typo). If they need to change "karma" to "dharma" and you haven't used the letter "d" elsewhere in the document, they can't do it (unless they have the font installed on their system).

Another reason not to use font subsetting is if you expect users on a platform other than your own to view and print your exported PDFs. We know, it's supposed to work. In our experience, it doesn't. Platform-specific character encoding and printer driver issues always seem to cause problems when we subset fonts in a PDF. At least one of the authors (Ole!) feels strongly that font subsetting should always be avoided for this reason. The small amount of (cheap!) disk space you use to embed the entire font is a small price to pay, compared to (expensive!) last-minute print production problems.

InDesign CS unfortunately embedded its fonts in a format called "CID" (which is usually reserved for Asian fonts). This wouldn't have been so bad except that some laser printers (notably PostScript "emulators") couldn't deal with CID fonts. The good news is that InDesign CS2 no longer embeds fonts using CID encoding, so this should no longer be a problem.

Omit for OPI. In an OPI workflow, the high-resolution image data is kept separate from your document until it's merged in at the last minute before printing. If you have an OPI server capable of processing PDF files with OPI comments, you can keep InDesign from including a certain type of imported graphic file in the PDF file by turning on the corresponding option in the Omit section (to omit placed EPS images, for example, turn on the EPS option). We discuss OPI in more detail in Chapter 11, "Printing."

Transparency Flattener. While Acrobat 5 can handle InDesign's transparency effects, Acrobat 4 is clueless. So if you're exporting an Acrobat 4 file, InDesign must "flatten" all transparency effects. We discuss flattening and the Transparency Flattener Style pop-up menu in great detail in Chapter 11, "Printing." Suffice it to say that you can choose a flattener style here, as well as tell InDesign to ignore any flattener style spread overrides you may have made in the document (by turning on the Ignore Spread Overrides checkbox).

Job Definition Format. The Job Definition Format (JDF) is talked about a lot, but most people don't realize that it all just comes down to adding some metadata about your document to the file (in this case, the PDF file). Adobe wants you to think that InDesign directly supports JDF, but if you turn on the Create JDF File Using Acrobat checkbox, all you really get is a regular PDF file plus a tiny JDF file in the same folder. Plus, InDesign launches Acrobat Professional (which you have to have installed to make use of this feature) and lets you use its JDF tools to fill in the details—such as who is the primary contact person for this print job, what kind of paper stock should it be printed on, and so on.

Security   Digital Rights Management (DRM) is all the rage these days. The basic issue is who gets to do what with your content? When it comes to PDF files, you have several DRM options set out in the Security panel of the Export PDF dialog box (see Figure 7-29).

In our view, most of the PDF security features are for PDFs you're exporting for online distribution (that is, the PDF is the final product of your production process), and not for prepress use. We might have our paranoid moments, but our practicality gets the better of them most of the time—and it's just not practical to lock up a PDF that's headed for printing and prepress work. Think about it—do you want your imagesetting service bureau calling you at four in the morning to ask for the password you used to lock up a PDF?

On the other hand, if you're exporting a PDF to send to a client or a printer who you don't have a close relationship with, you might want to activate some of these settings.

Passwords. You can give your PDF file two different passwords: one to limit who can open the document (User Password), and one to limit who can change the security settings in the document (Master Password). The two passwords must be different. If you're going to turn on *any* security settings in the PDF—even if you don't require a User Password—then we strongly encourage you to provide a Master Password (just in case you need to make changes to the PDF later).

Note that if you choose to export in Acrobat 4 (PDF 1.3) format, InDesign only uses the older 40-bit RC4 encryption, which isn't

FIGURE 7-29
Export PDF Options,
Security Panel

nearly as powerful as the newer 128-bit encryption—you get better encryption when you export as Acrobat 5 or 6 (PDF 1.4 or 1.5).

Permissions. The two popup menus and three checkboxes in the Permissions settings are self-explanatory: They let you control whether the file can be printed (or at what resolution), whether it can be altered, whether content can be copied or extracted, whether screen readers for the visually impaired should be supported, and whether your metadata should be readable by databases or search systems (see "File Info and Metadata," earlier in this chapter). These are useful if you're sending a file to a client and you don't want them to do anything but add comments, or if you're sending a file to be printed, and you want to make sure the output provider doesn't "accidentally" change anything. However, note that the security settings can also play havoc with some non-Adobe PDF readers (like Mac OS X Preview).

Summary   The last panel of the Export PDF dialog box, Summary, lists all the settings in all the tabs in one long text list (see Figure 7-30). Do we ever sit and read through this? Nope; it's more time-consuming to read through this unformatted list of settings than it is to skip through each of the panels. However, it's nice that you can click the Save Summary button to save this list to disk as a text file. If you're exporting a PDF file to send to someone else, consider including this summary along with it, so that they know how you set up the dialog

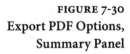

FIGURE 7-30
Export PDF Options,
Summary Panel

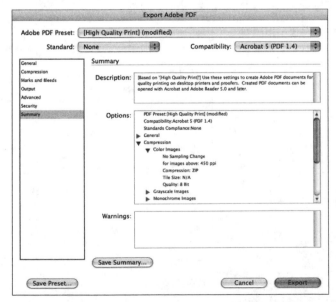

box (and can see whether you did anything inappropriate). You can also use this saved summary as a log of what you did to later refer to if something prints in an unexpected fashion.

Defining a PDF Export Preset

PDF export presets are like paragraph styles—they're bundles of attributes that can be applied in a single action. Almost all of the attributes in the PDF Export dialog box are included in a PDF export preset (the Ink Manager and the Security settings aren't). It's easy to create a PDF export preset; set up the Export PDF dialog box with the options the way you want them, click the Save Preset button at the bottom of the dialog box, and then give the style a name. You can then go ahead and export, or just cancel out of the Export PDF dialog box (if you just wanted to set up the preset without exporting).

InDesign also has a second method for making PDF export presets, though we find it slightly more cumbersome (see Figure 7-31).

1. Choose PDF Export Presets from the File menu. InDesign displays the PDF Export Presets dialog box with a list of the current PDF export presets.

2. Click the New button. InDesign displays the PDF Export dialog box, but with a few differences: there's a Name field at the top, there's no Security panel, and Ink Manager and page ranges are grayed out. Note that if you select an export preset before clicking New, this dialog box will be based on the preset you selected.

3. Enter a name for the PDF export preset in the Name field, then set up the PDF export options using the panels of the dialog box. Click the OK button when you're done. InDesign returns you to the PDF Export Presets dialog box and adds the new preset to the list of available presets.

To export a PDF using the settings in a PDF export preset, choose the preset name from the Preset pop-up menu in the Export PDF dialog box. InDesign applies the settings of the PDF export preset to the controls in the Export PDF dialog box. You'll still need to enter a page range in the General panel—the export preset does not include that information.

Note that you can also make PDF presets in Acrobat Distiller or any other CS2 application. InDesign and the other Creative Suite programs share PDF presets, which makes consistent PDF creation much easier.

Managing PDF Export Presets

You can use the PDF Export Presets dialog box to add, delete, rename, edit, and import or export PDF export presets.

*Choose PDF Export
Presets from the File menu.
InDesign displays the Adobe
PDF Presets dialog box.*

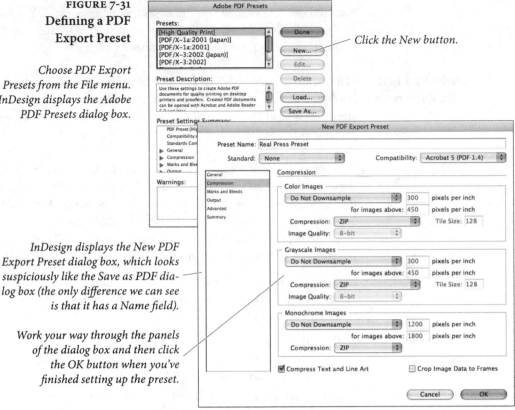

Click the New button.

*InDesign displays the New PDF
Export Preset dialog box, which looks
suspiciously like the Save as PDF dialog box (the only difference we can see
is that it has a Name field).*

*Work your way through the panels
of the dialog box and then click
the OK button when you've
finished setting up the preset.*

*After you've saved the PDF
export preset, InDesign adds
it to the list of available
presets. You'll be able to
choose it from the Preset
pop-up menu to export
the PDF using the settings
defined in the preset.*

▶ To delete a PDF export preset, select the preset name
and click the Delete button. (You can't delete the default
presets: eBook, Screen, Print, Press, PDF/X-1a, PDF/X-3,
and Acrobat 6 Layered.)

▶ To export PDF export presets, select the presets and click the
Save button. InDesign displays the Save PDF Export Presets
dialog box. Specify a file name and location and click the OK
button.

▶ To import a PDF export preset or set of presets, open the PDF
Export Presets dialog box and click the Load button. InDesign
displays the Load PDF Export Presets dialog box. Locate and

select a file containing the saved presets and click the OK button. If the PDF export presets you're importing already exist in the publication, InDesign will create copies (InDesign appends a number—usually "1"—to the duplicate presets).

▸ To edit or rename a PDF export preset, select the preset name in the PDF Export Presets dialog box, then click the Edit button.

Data Merge

It's hard to be creative when you're faced with hundreds (or thousands) of pieces of data from a database or spreadsheet that need to be formatted. Fortunately, there are tools that can help you automate mundane formatting tasks like this, and one of them is built right into InDesign: Data Merge. Note that Data Merge is not as powerful as some other database publishing tools—such as Em Software's InData—but it's far better than doing the work by hand.

In order for Data Merge to work, you need two things: a file with all the raw, unformatted data; and an InDesign file that has template information that says where the data should go and how to format it. You'll also need the Data Merge palette, which you can find in the Automation submenu (under the Window menu).

Setting up the Data   Virtually every database and spreadsheet program lets you export your data as a comma-delimited (.csv) or tab-delimited (.txt) file. The difference is in what's used between each field and record (or column and row, in a spreadsheet), but Data Merge can read both. Note that if you're exporting a .csv file and a single cell or field includes one or more commas (such as "Yoyodyne, Inc."), then you need to make sure that that field is surrounded by double straight quotes, or else InDesign will get confused as to which comma should be in the text and which one is a delimiter. This is one reason we almost always opt for tab-delimited files.

By the way, the first line of the data file must list the names of each field. You'll use these same names in the InDesign template.

Using variable images. You can also import images along with your text data by including the file path to each image (on your hard disk) as one of the fields. The trick is to place an "at" symbol (@) before the field's name in the *first line* of the data file (see Figure 7-32). Then, when you enter add each field, specify a file path to the graphic. File

FIGURE 7-32
Setting Up the
Data File

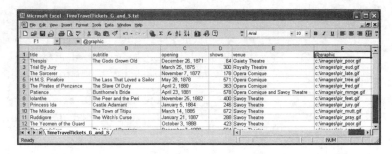

paths are written differently between the Mac OS and Windows: In Windows, you need to use backslashes between folder names, while on the Mac, you use a colon.

Setting up the Template

Once you have your data in a file that InDesign can import, it's time to set up a prototype (or template, or proxy, or whatever you want to call it) in InDesign (see Figure 7-33).

1. Open the Data Merge palette (choose Data Merge from the Automate submenu, under the Window menu).

2. Choose Select Data Source from the palette menu and pick the file you created on your disk. InDesign is smart enough to tell whether the text is comma-delimited or tab-delimited, but if you felt a strong need to tell it (lets say the import wasn't working properly and you wanted to check the settings), you could turn on the Show Import Options in the dialog box. If the data file isn't set up properly (for instance, if the first line in the data file ends with some extra tab characters), you'll see an error alert.

3. A list of all the data field names appears in the Data Merge palette.(This is why the first line of the data file needs to list those names.) If something looks terribly wrong, you can always select Remove Data Source from the palette menu to reset the palette.

4. Place the flashing text cursor in a text frame and click on one of the field names in the palette. InDesign inserts the field name at that position, surrounded by double angle brackets. (Or drag the field name on top of any frame. If the frame is empty, it becomes a text frame and the field name appears in it; if the frame has text in it, the field name is appended at the end of that text.) No, you cannot just type the field name surrounded by angle brackets—you have to use the palette. You may want to insert these in text frames on a master page; we'll explain why in just a moment.

   To place an image label (something that was specified as an image path in the data file) as an inline graphic, place the text

FIGURE 7-33
**Creating the
Data Template**

*Choose Select Data
Source from the Data
Merge palette menu.*

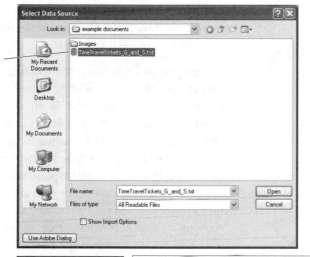

Locate and select a data file.

*InDesign loads the field
names from the first record
in the file and displays them
in the Data Merge palette.*

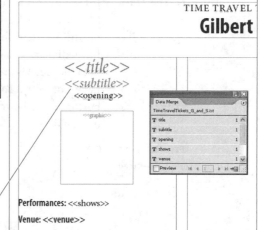

*You can drag fields from the Data Merge palette and
drop them into your layout, or you can position the
cursor in text and double-click to insert a field name.*

*Format the field
names as you would
any other text.*

cursor where you want it and click the label in the palette. To
place an image in its own frame on the page, choose an emtpy
frame with the Selection tool before clicking on the image name
in the Data Merge palette.

5. Continue adding field names until you've used all the fields you
want. You do not have to use all the fields in the data source. You
can put the fields in as many text frames as you want, even on

more than one page of your document. You can also put text around the field names. For example, you might want to insert a <<LastName>> field, followed by a comma and a space, followed by a <<FirstName>> field, followed by a paragraph return.

6. Apply text formatting to each field name in the text frame. For example, if you want the <<company>> data to appear in bold, just select that field name and apply the bold style or a bold character style or paragraph style.

Using a Master Page. You don't have to insert the data labels on your master page, but we usually do because it makes the final merged document more flexible. Specifically, if you need to make a change or reimport the data, you can do so from the document InDesign is about to create rather than having to go back to this original document and more or less start the import process over. However, if you do put this stuff on the master page, make sure it's on the right side of a facing page document. For example, you probably want to put it on the right-hand page of a master page spread, or else nothing will show up on page 1 (which is a right-hand page).

Merging the Data

InDesign now knows where the data is and what it's supposed to look like in your InDesign document, so it's time to merge the two. Turn on the Preview checkbox in the Data Merge palette and InDesign immediately replaces the data labels with the first record from the data file (see Figure 7-34). This way you can see if you set up the template correctly. To preview another record, click the Next Record button at the bottom of the palette, or type a record number in the text field.

FIGURE 7-34
Data Merge Preview

Click the Preview option at the bottom of the palette, or choose Preview from the Data Merge palette menu...

...and InDesign will display a preview layout of the first record (or any other record you specify using the controls at the bottom of the palette.

When you're certain you've got everything arranged just right, it's time to choose Create Merged Document from the Data Merge palette menu (or click the button in the lower-right corner of the palette) to create a merged document (see Figure 7-35). .

FIGURE 7-35
Doing the
Data Merge

Choose Create Merged Document (or click the button at the bottom of the Data Merge palette).

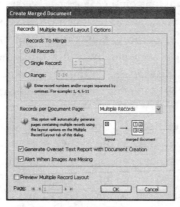

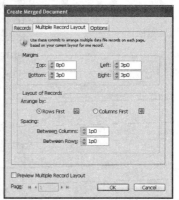

InDesign displays the Create Merged Document dialog box. Set up the data merge using the controls in this dialog box and click the OK button.

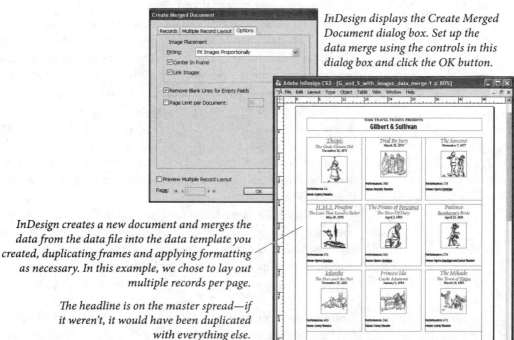

InDesign creates a new document and merges the data from the data file into the data template you created, duplicating frames and applying formatting as necessary. In this example, we chose to lay out multiple records per page.

The headline is on the master spread—if it weren't, it would have been duplicated with everything else.

Data Merge Layout Options

InDesign then offers you a number of options in the Create Merged Document dialog box.

Records. The first panel of this dialog box lets you choose which records you want to import from the data file. You can also choose whether you want each data record to appear on its own page (choose Single Record from the Records per Document Page popup menu) or whether you want more than one record (like a sheet of mailing labels). We'll cover the more-than-one record choice below.

If you turn on the Generate Overset Text Report with Document Creation checkbox, InDesign will save a text file to your hard disk if the import process causes any text frames to become overset. That's handy so we generally turn it on. Similarly, we turn on the Alert When Images are Missing checkbox, because we want to know if something has gone wrong during the import process.

Multiple Record Layout. If you choose Multiple Records from the Records per Document Page popup menu, InDesign attempts to duplicate your page objects in a grid on your page. For example, let's say you were making name tags for several hundred people. You could create one or more text frames on your page (it doesn't matter where on the page you put them), insert the data merge labels, and then specify Multiple Records. The Create Merged Document dialog box has a Preview checkbox that shows you what the layout will look like before you commit to the data merge procedure. It takes a little time to process, but it's well worth the wait, as you'll inevitably find you need to tweak something the first time you try it.

You can control how InDesign lays out the frames on your page in the Multiple Record Layout panel of the dialog box, including how much space you want between the rows and columns. The Margins fields here simply overrides those in the Margins and Columns dialog box. We wish we could save these settings as a preset to recall them quickly later, but no can do.

Note that if you have laid out your initial template with more than one frame, InDesign treats them all as a single "group" that gets duplicated multiple times across the page. Also, if you have more than one page in your template file, you can't do multiple record layout (n-up layout) because... well, because it'll just get too confusing.

Options. The Options panel of the Create Merged Document dialog box lets you control how Data Merge handles imported images, blank lines in the data file, and large number of imported records. Choose a method from the Fitting popup menu to control what happens to images that don't match the frame size you've drawn in the template. For instance, you might want to choose Fill Frame Proportionally to get the largest image possible in the frame, but that will crop out a portion of the image if the image height/width ratio isn't the same as the frame. If you want imported images to be placed in the center of the frame rather than in the upper-left corner, turn on the Center in Frame checkbox. (Of course, if you have no images in your data file, then you can ignore both of these.)

What should InDesign do when a whole line ends up being blank? For example, let's say you're inserting someone's name on one line, their company name on the second line, and their address on the third line. If someone isn't affiliated with a company, then you'd normally end up with a blank line. However, if you turn on the Remove Blank Lines for Empty Fields checkbox, InDesign will simply delete that line from the final merged document. Note that this only works when there would be *no* text on that line—even a blank space after the text label will foil this feature.

The last option, Record Limit Per Document, lets you control how large the final document will be. InDesign will import records and keep adding pages until this limit is reached. However, if you wanted a different InDesign document for each record, you could change this number to 1. (That's a good way to max out InDesign's resources and possibly cause mayhem.)

Doing the Merge. When you're confident that all is well and you've chosen your options wisely, click OK. InDesign creates a new document based on the one you built (the template) and the settings you made. If your data merge labels were placed on the master page, they will also be on the master page of this new document, which will allow you to update the data, should the need arise.

Updating Your Data   When you first import the data source into the Data Merge palette, InDesign creates a link between the InDesign file and the .txt or .csv file—you can even see this link in the Links palette. Then, when you create the new merged document, it, too, has that link (as long as the template fields were sitting on the master page rather than the document page). That means if some of the data changes, you don't necessarily have to go back to the original and create a new merged file. Instead, you can choose Update Content in Data Fields from the Data Merge palette menu. However, this appears to work only when the data fields appear in a single text frame—if you used more than one text frame, it gives you an error message. We think this is probably a bug.

(You might think that clicking the Update button in the Links palette should do the same thing as Update Content in Data Fields. No such luck.)

If the names or number of fields in each record change in the data source (perhaps you decided to export from the database with more fields), you should to be able to choose Update Data Source from the palette menu. We have never gotten this to work correctly. Unfortunately, it appears that the best solution is to remove all of the data fields from your original template, choose Update Data Source (or Select Data Source again), and then reapply the data fields manually.

Ultimately, we find Data Merge very handy for small or simple jobs, but it's buggy enough and limited enough that we try not to lean too hard on it.

InDesign Interchange Format (INX)

What if you could describe your whole InDesign document as a compact text file? That's what the InDesign Interchange (INX) format is: An XML representation of each and every object on every page of your document, as well as the styles, colors, margins, and all other document information. You can export an INX file, send it to someone else, and, when they open your INX file, InDesign creates a new file that looks exactly like the one you made.

Why would you want to do this? One reason is backward compatibility—INX is the only way that you can "save back" from InDesign CS2 to InDesign CS. This works as long as you have upgraded to the free "April 2005" update of InDesign CS, which gives the program the ability to read the InDesign CS2 INX format files. INX format is not supported by InDesign 2 at all, so you can't go back that far.

Another reason to use INX is to remove corrupt data that may have snuck into your file. For example, some folks have reported that they cannot delete unwanted color swatches in their Swatches palette. In most (but not all) cases, simply exporting the document in the INX format and then reopening it clears out the trouble.

In one case we saw, we had to dig deeper to get rid off the problem: We opened an INX file that had the can't-delete-color problem, opened it with a text editor (BBEdit, in this case), searched through it for the code that defined the color in question, deleted it, saved the file, and opened it back in InDesign. The color was gone. Do we recommend this kind of editing? No, not really, and we certainly can't guarantee that it won't ruin your day (and file). But it worked that time, and it's a good example of the power of INX.

One last reason to use INX: It's a very compact way to describe a file. David recently exported a 20 Mb InDesign file as a 1.5 Mb INX file, which. Compressed, this document became 200 Kb. It was easy to email to a colleague, who unzipped it and then opened it in InDesign to recreate the file without any loss of data or quality. Note that this depends on the recipient of the file having the linked graphics used in the file—if not, expect gray boxes in place of the graphics and "Missing" icons in the Links palette.

To export a file in the INX format, choose Export from the File menu, then select InDesign Interchange from the Format popup menu. You can open an INX file just as you would open any other InDesign document.

Snippets   What happens when you select one or more objects on your page and drag them to the desktop? InDesign creates a snippet file with the .INDS file name extension. A snippet is a file written in the InDesign Interchange (INX) language that describes just one or more objects from a page or spread. (As opposed to an INX file, which describes an entire document.)

You can also create a snippet file by dragging one or more objects into Adobe Bridge, or by selecting and exporting the objects on the page and choosing InDesign Snippet from the Format popup menu in the Export dialog box.

Snippets are great for sending InDesign objects to someone else via email, or for saving objects that you want to reuse. In fact, the Library feature (see Chapter 1, "Workspace") actually saves objects internally as snippets. Because snippets are just small XML files, you could easily place a bunch of them in a database, and then use some program to build your InDesign pages on the fly by pulling just the snippets you need from the database.

To place a snippet into your InDesign file, you can use the Place command from the File menu, or simply drag the snippet file in from the desktop or Bridge. Note that when you import a snippet file, each object in the snippet remembers its original page location. If the object was in the upper-left corner of the page when you created the snippet, it will be placed at the same location when you import it.

Package for GoLive (Exporting HTML)

What in Thor's name was Adobe thinking? They removed a perfectly reasonable feature—exporting your document's content as HTML—from InDesign 2. Sure, Export as HTML wasn't perfect; it had its problems, like the best of us. But that's no reason to remove the feature entirely. Fortunately, they replaced it in InDesign CS and CS2 with something that is pretty darn cool, though it's not as versatile and it has plenty of problems of its own.

The feature is called Package for GoLive, and as you're probably suspecting, it'll be great if you use GoLive and significantly less impressive if you use something else (such as Dreamweaver). Package for GoLive lives in the File menu, and it works like this.

1. After you save your InDesign file, choose Package for GoLive. Or, if you want to package up a whole book (multiple files in a Book palette), select Package Book for GoLive from the Book palette menu.

2. InDesign asks you where to save the package. The name you type in the Save Package As dialog box will be the name of the folder. If you're already working with a GoLive site, go ahead and save the package into the site's Web-packages folder (in the Web-data folder). That way, GoLive can manage the packaged files more easily.

3. InDesign then displays the Package for GoLive dialog box (see Figure 7-36).

    The Pages section determines which pages of the document are exported.

    The choice you make from the Encoding pop-up menu tells InDesign how to save "special" text characters (such as curly quotes, em dashes, non-Roman text characters, and so on). The default setting, UTF-8, is appropriate for most English text. You might want to use UTF-16 for larger character sets, or Shift-JIS for Japanese (double-byte) text. The important thing is that the encoding you pick is the same as the encoding of the HTML file in GoLive, or else those characters may not appear correctly. (You can change a GoLive file's encoding from the Document Content submenu in the Edit menu.)

    The Images, Movies, and Sounds section lets you tell InDesign what to do with any imported media in your document. If you turn on the Original Images checkbox, it copies all the images into the package folder. Choose Formatted Images to omit image information that is not visible in the InDesign layout (for cropped images, for example). Note that these are checkboxes, so you can choose more than one at a time. But if you do choose both, GoLive always uses the original, so we're not sure why anyone would want to turn on more than one

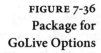

FIGURE 7-36
**Package for
GoLive Options**

checkbox. In general, we would *much* rather just use Photoshop to optimize these images before they get to GoLive than mess with these latter two options.

4. Click Package, and InDesign collects the various files it needs. The longer and more complex your document, the longer this will take—sometimes it can take quite a long while indeed.

What to Do in GoLive   We obviously can't teach you how to use GoLive in this book, but here's the quick-and-dirty rundown on what to do once your packaged document shows up in GoLive. Keep in mind that the resulting document might bear little resemblance to your laid-out publication—if maintaining control over the appearance of your material is important, you should use PDF or SVG, rather than HTML.

To get a text story or an image from the package into your GoLive file, drag it from the window that is displaying the PDF. You can navigate to a different page using the buttons at the bottom of the PDF window. If two or more objects are overlapping, choose the one you want in the Select submenu in the context menu (right-click on a PC or Control-click on a Macintosh). Note that you can zoom in temporarily on an object by double-clicking on it in this package window; double-click on it again to zoom back out.

For really complex pages, you might be better off clicking the Assets button at the top of the package window and choosing the story or graphic from the list. When you choose Assets, GoLive's Inspector palette displays the page to give you visual feedback.

Text Components. When you drag a text story onto your page, GoLive won't let you edit it because what you've actually imported is a *component*—like placing a graphic in InDesign, this component is just linked to a file on disk. The benefit is that if you later change the component, the HTML page updates automatically. However, if you want to be able to edit the text, you have to detach it from the original XML file. You can do this before dragging the story into your GoLive page by selecting the object in the package window, clicking Settings in GoLive's toolbar, and changing the Content Usage pop-up menu from Component to Direct.

Or, if you have already added the story to your GoLive page, you can select it on the page, then choose Detach Selected Components from the context menu.

As you know, HTML can't reproduce a lot of the text formatting you can apply in InDesign. CSS style go a long way to help (InDesign and GoLive create CSS styles for your text automatically, based on the paragraph and character styles in your InDesign document). However, many features just don't translate, including baseline shift, ligatures, kerning, paragraph rules, justification, tabs, drop caps, wrapped text, and so on. If you need some text to appear the same on your Web page as it does in print, you might consider converting the text to a graphic by holding down the Shift key while dragging the story out of the package window.

Importing Images. Drag images on to your page in the same way. You can choose Settings in GoLive to adjust how your original image will be converted to a JPEG or GIF. If you've ever used the Save for Web feature in Photoshop or Illustrator you'll feel right at home in this GoLive feature. However, for some bizarre reason, no matter how you packaged them, GoLive always seems to import graphics and movies much smaller than they're supposed to be. To set the image (or movie) back to its original size, select it and click the Set to Original Size button in the Inspector palette (that's the button with no name, that just looks like a square within a square).

Updating the File   If (or, more likely when) you later change the InDesign document, you can update your Web files by choosing Package for GoLive again—just save the package in the same place with the same name and InDesign will update the package. Unfortunately, InDesign won't get rid of any image files already in the package folder; if you package a document, then later change the images and package again, the original images are still there. It's a good way to slowly fill up your hard drive with unecessary data.

Also, before selecting Package for GoLive again, make sure the package window (the PDF file) is closed in GoLive; otherwise,

InDesign won't be able to replace it with the new one and you'll hang your head in shame and failure.

As long as you haven't detached the components from their original files on disk, GoLive can automatically update your HTML pages based on the new package files.

There's another way to update the Web page: Change the components yourself (again, as long as you haven't detached the components). The text files are saved in XML, which is just a text file that can be opened in any text editor. You can even edit a story in GoLive's own text editor by double-clicking on the component on the GoLive page. (To see the XML text, choose the Source tab in the window that opens when you double-click on the component.)

As we said earlier, the story XML files are saved in the Adobe InCopy file format, so if you have InCopy, you can use it to edit your stories, too. Very slick.

Other Techniques   Do you really want to use Package for GoLive? Sure, it's nifty, but it presents some significant challenges, too. For instance, if you have a 100-page document, how do you get a single story that jumps from page 5 to 50 into GoLive? While you can package individual pages, it can be difficult to get a single story. There's also no way to tell InDesign (or GoLive) to import some of the formatting but omit other formatting; usually you just get too much, as GoLive tries to faithfully re-create as much text formatting as it can with CSS styles. This can be quite annoying.

How can you export a story as HTML? David often resorts to copying and pasting stories from one application to the other, even though he loses text formatting as he does so. You could also export an RTF file from InDesign, open it in Microsoft Word, export that as HTML, and then open that file in GoLive. Or you could write a script that exports text as HTML, as Ole has done. Scripts are quite good at writing text files, and HTML is text.

Exporting SVG

SVG (Scalable Vector Graphics) is a vector-based file format that combines much of the power of the PostScript page-description language with the brevity of PDF (Portable Document Format), and is written using the standards of XML and CSS (Cascading Style Sheets).

SVG is probably best known as an up-and-coming alternative to the Flash (.swf) format for Web graphics. True, SVG will likely be most used on the Web, but because it's built in XML, the format is useful for all sorts of things. XML can be manipulated much more flexibly than Flash, PostScript, or PDF. For example, you can open SVG files in a text editor to edit them, easily mix them with HTML codes, or search for text within them using standard search engines—none of these are easy to do with other formats.

In order to view SVG files, you have to have a program capable of reading SVG, or an SVG plug-in that works with a Web browser. An SVG plug-in comes free from Adobe (one was probably installed on your system with InDesign or any other Adobe product) or other sources. Note that SVG is *not* an Adobe file format; it's an international standard written by a number of different companies, including Quark, Microsoft, and others.

To export SVG files from InDesign (you can only export them; InDesign can't import SVG yet), select SVG from the Formats pop-up menu in the Export dialog box (or the Save as Type pop-up menu in Windows), give the file a name, click Save, and then choose from among the various SVG options. You can also choose SVG (Compressed) from the Formats pop-up menu; this creates a non-text version (also called an SVGZ file), encoded in such a way as to be much smaller (useful for Web viewing) but less editable.

Basic SVG Export Options

The Export SVG dialog box has a cool little feature, which we hope to see someday in other InDesign dialog boxes: a Description field at the bottom that changes depending on what your mouse is hovering over (see Figure 7-37). The descriptions are brief but really help when you've forgotten what one of these export options does.

Pages. An SVG file can only describe a single page, but you can export multiple pages from your InDesign document as individual SVG files. Select All, or choose one or more pages in the Range field. For instance, "3, 5-7" exports pages three and five through seven.

Export Selection. If you turn on the Export Selection checkbox, InDesign only exports those items on your page that are selected (you have to have first selected one or more objects, of course). This, too, is a feature that we wish other export dialog boxes would have.

Spreads. The Spreads option tells InDesign to export the entire spread (like page two and three in a facing pages document) as a single SVG page. It's pretty rare that you'd want this, but it's nice that they give you the option.

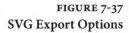

FIGURE 7-37
SVG Export Options

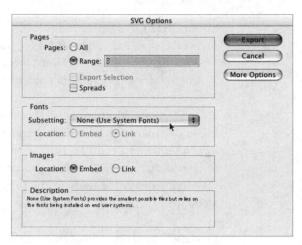

Fonts. SVG files, like PDF files, offer the option to embed fonts, or subsets of fonts, in case your audience doesn't have the same fonts you've used. You have five choices for font embedding in the Export SVG dialog box.

▸ **None (Use System Fonts).** If you're sure your audience has the proper fonts, or it's okay for the fonts to change, then choose None to turn off font embedding.

▸ **Only Glyphs Used.** To ensure that anyone looking at this SVG file sees the fonts you specified, choose Only Glyphs Used. This embeds a subset of each font with only the characters you used, so the file size stays relatively small. However, if you later edit the SVG file and include some previously unused character, you'll be in trouble.

▸ **Common English.** Choosing Common English tells InDesign to embed a subset of the font with all the normal characters in English (numerals, lowercase and uppercase characters, common symbols). Generally, if you're going to do this, it's better to choose Common English & Glyphs Used, just in case you type something that isn't in the normal Common English subset.

▸ **Common Roman.** Common Roman includes a few more characters than Common English—characters that Americans would consider "foreign," such as the ç (cedilla), characters with accents, and so on. Again, Common Roman & Glyphs Used is a better choice, so other characters (like symbols) still show up properly.

▶ **All Glyphs.** For maximum editability of the SVG file down the road, choose All Glyphs. However, note that this makes your SVG files much larger. We don't recommend using this option when you are working with double-byte fonts (such as Japanese).

The SVG specification allows for both embedding fonts and linking to external fonts. Linking to external fonts is useful when you have a bunch of SVG files that use those fonts (so you don't have to embed them in each file). If you choose the Link radio button, InDesign exports the fonts in the properly encoded XML format along with your SVG file (.cef files).

Images. The only thing that bulks up SVG files more than a font is a bitmapped image. If you use the same bitmapped image in multiple SVG pages, it's much more efficient to link to it (rather than embed it in the SVG file itself). You can tell InDesign whether you want to embed bitmapped images or link to them externally in the Images section of the Export SVG dialog box. If you choose Link, InDesign saves your images to disk separately, converting them to JPEG files on the fly and giving them names that relate to the SVG file. Vector artwork does not get linked separately; it's always embedded.

More Options Adobe appears to be worried that you'll be scared off SVG if they show you all the options at once. We have no such concern. You can see all the controls by clicking the More Options button. True, you rarely need to actually change anything here, but it's good to know about these features, just in case (see Figure 7-38).

Transparency Flattener. Although the SVG specification can handle basic transparency, InDesign chooses to flatten all tranparency effects when you export an SVG file. We discuss flattening and transparency flattener styles in Chapter 11, "Printing."

CSS Properties. XML is a very flexible method for describing things. You can tell InDesign to write its SVG files in one of four methods—each of which is very slightly different—in the CSS Properties pop-up menu. Ultimately, the default method, Presentation Attributes, is the one you're most likely to use. If you're planning on transforming your SVG files using an XSLT (Extensible Stylesheet Language Transformation), you should choose Style Attributes, even though the file is a teensy bit larger. (We discuss XSLT later in this chapter, though the specifics of using it with SVG files is outside the purview of this book.)

FIGURE 7-38
Even More SVG
Export Options

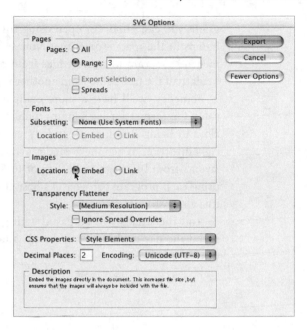

If you're just trying to get the smallest, fastest SVG file you can (for Web viewing, typically), then choose Style Attributes (Entity References). The last method, Style Elements, breaks down each element into CSS elements, which can be used by multiple HTML and SVG files (if you're into hand-coding and editing files).

Decimal Places. How precise do you want InDesign to be in describing your objects? We think the default Decimal Places value of 3 (thousands of a point) is plenty precise enough for us. In a very complex page, you can shave a tiny bit of file size off by decreasing this to 1 or 2 decimal places.

Encoding. Because SVG is a regular text file, you need to tell it how to describe special characters (those outside the normal ASCII range). You've got three choices: ISO 8859-1 (ASCII), Unicode (UTF-8), and Unicode (UTF-16). The default, UTF-8, is the best choice, unless you have any double-byte characters (like Japanese or Chinese) in your file. In that case, you'd want the 16-bit version of Unicode.

The Best of All Possible Worlds

Can you get there from here? When you're working with InDesign, you can almost always export or save files in a form you can use in another program, and you can usually produce files in other programs you can import or open using InDesign. There are definitely bumps in the road—sometimes, you've got to go through an intermediate program to convert files from one format to another (particularly if the files came from another type of computer).

Someday, we'll have a more complete, universal, and sophisticated file format for exchanging publications. PDF is getting very close to being that format, and it's certainly making steps in the right direction. When the great day arrives, we'll be able to take page layouts from InDesign to Illustrator to QuarkXPress to Photoshop, using each program for what it's best at without losing any formatting along the way.

And the streets will be paved with gold, mounted beggars will spend the day ducking winged pigs, and the Seattle Mariners will win the World Series.

CHAPTER 8

Long Documents

What constitutes a long document? Die-hard denizens of the Frame-Maker universe insist that if a document isn't over a thousand pages, it's not a long document. Poster designers, on the other hand, maintain that folded flyers and newsletters qualify.

We're not sure what our definition of a "long document" is, but we think that anyone building a book, a magazine, a newspaper, a journal, or a catalog—just about any document, really, of any number of pages—can benefit from the long document features in InDesign.

There are three features in InDesign that relate directly to publishing long documents.

▶ **Books.** You can tie multiple documents together into a book, which appears in the form of a palette in InDesign. From here, you can control page numbering, printing, and such document attributes as styles and colors.

▶ **Table of Contents.** If you use paragraph styles regularly, you're going to love the Table of Contents feature, which can build a table of contents (or a list of figures, or a table of advertisers, or any number of other things) quickly and easily.

▶ **Indexes.** Building an index is a hardship we wouldn't wish on anyone (we've done enough of them ourselves), but InDesign's indexing features go a long way toward making it bearable.

Again, even if you don't currently create what you'd consider to be "long documents," take a gander at these features; they're flexible enough to be used in documents as small as even a few pages.

Books

Even though an InDesign document can be thousands of pages long, it's best to split long documents up into smaller parts. InDesign performs better with shorter documents. Splitting a large project into smaller parts is generally more efficient, especially when more than one person is working on the project at the same time. The burning question is: if you break up your project into small documents, how can you ensure style consistency and proper page numbering among them? The answer is InDesign's Book feature.

Most people think of a book as a collection of chapters bound together to act as a single document. In InDesign, a book is a collection of InDesign documents on your disk or network that are loosely connected with each other via the Book palette. In other words, just because it's called a "book" doesn't mean it's not relevant for magazines, catalogs, or any other set of documents.

There are five benefits to using the Book palette.

▶ It's a good way to organize the documents in a project, and it's faster to open them using the Book palette than it is to use the Open dialog box.

▶ If you use automatic page numbering in your document (see "Numbering Pages" in Chapter 2, "Page Layout"), InDesign manages the page numbering throughout the entire book, so if the first document ends on page 20, the second document starts on page 21, and so on (assuming that the numbering and section options settings in that document agree, of course).

▶ You can print or export one or more documents from the Book palette using the same settings without even having the documents open.

▶ The Synchronize feature helps you ensure that styles, colors, and other settings are consistent among the documents.

▶ By associating files together as a book, you can mix page sizes and page orientations in a publication—which you can't do in a single InDesign document.

The more documents there are in your project, and the more pages, styles, colors, and whatnot are used in each document, the more useful the Book feature will be to you. Even if you're juggling two or three documents, it may be worth the minor inconvenience it takes to build a book.

Building a Book To build a new book, select Book from the New submenu of the File menu. At this point, InDesign displays the New Book dialog box. Tell the program where to save your new book file (you can put it anywhere you want on your hard drive or network, but you should put it somewhere easy to find—because you'll be using it a lot).

Book files appear in InDesign as palettes. When you've saved your new book, InDesign displays a new Book palette (see Figure 8-1).

FIGURE 8-1
Creating a New Book

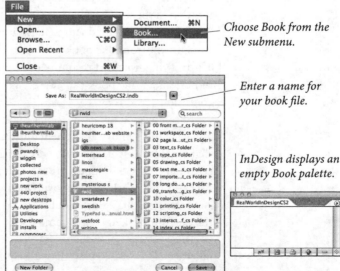

Choose Book from the New submenu.

Enter a name for your book file.

InDesign displays an empty Book palette.

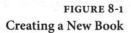

Book palette controls

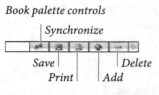

Synchronize

Save

Delete

Print   Add

Adding and Removing Book Documents

To add a document to your Book palette, click the Add Document button in the palette and choose a document from your disk or network (see Figure 8-2). If no documents on the palette are selected when you add a new document, the new document is added at the end of the list. If you select a document first, the new document is added after the selected document. You can also drag files directly from Windows Explorer or the Macintosh Finder windows into a book palette; this is often the fastest way to get a folder full of files into a book.

FIGURE 8-2
Adding a
Book Document

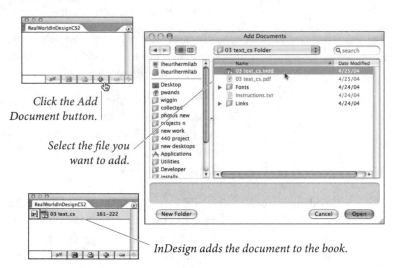

Click the Add
Document button.

Select the file you
want to add.

InDesign adds the document to the book.

If you accidentally insert a document in the wrong place in a Book palette, don't worry—you can move a document up and down on the list. To do this, select the book document and drag it to a new location in the list (see Figure 8-3).

Although Adobe's documentation points out that you can copy a document from one book palette to another by Option-dragging/Alt-dragging, we don't recommend this. Having the same document in more than one book can cause pagination problems and general confusion.

To remove a document from a Book palette, select the document and click the Remove Document button. If you want to remove more than one document, select the documents (use Shift for contiguous selections, or Command/Ctrl for discontinuous selections on the list) and then click the Remove Document button (see Figure 8-4). Note that deleting a document from the Book palette does *not* delete the file from disk; it simply removes it from the list.

To replace a book document, select the document in the Book palette and choose Replace Document from the Book palette menu.

FIGURE 8-3
**Moving a
Book Document**

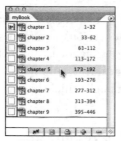 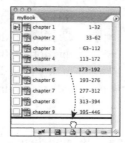 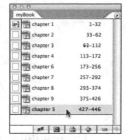

*To change the position
of a book document in
the book list, select the
document...*

*...and drag it up or
down in the list.*

*Drop the document,
and InDesign moves
the document to a new
position in the list.*

FIGURE 8-4
**Deleting a
Book Document**

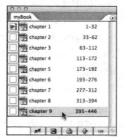 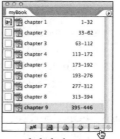 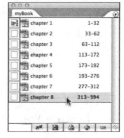

*To remove a book
document, select the
document...*

*...and click the
Remove Document
button.*

*InDesign removes the
document from the
book.*

InDesign displays the Replace Document dialog box. Locate and
select the file you want to replace the document with, then click the
OK button to close the dialog box and replace the document.

**Converting Books
from InDesign 2**

InDesign CS2 can open and convert books saved in InDesign 2 or CS.
It's pretty straightforward—just open the book. There are, however,
a couple of options that can help you—or hurt you—during the process of converting the book and the documents in the book.

► If, after opening the book, you choose Save Book from the Book
  palette menu, InDesign will over write the InDesign 2 book file
  with the converted book. Unless you have a backup copy of the
  book file, we think that you should save the converted book to
  a new book file by choosing Save Book As. Our experience is
  that every time we save over a previous version file—in any
  program—we end up regretting it at some point.

► After you've opened and converted an InDesign 2 or CS book,
  you can select the Automatic Document Conversion option
  from the Book palette menu. While this sounds like a great idea,
  it will over write every InDesign document in the book with an

InDesign CS2 version of the document. Again, unless you have a backup of the previous version files, we think you should avoid this option. If you do not use this option, however, you'll need to save each document in the book to a new file, which can be tedious if your book contains a large number of documents.

Using a Book As a Navigational Tool

Because there is only a very loose connection among the various documents in the Book palette, you could use this feature as an informal database of documents. For instance, let's say you've built 15 different product data sheets and three small brochures for a client, and the client is forever updating them. Even though the documents may each use very different colors, styles, and so on, you could put them all on one Book palette and save this collection under the client's name. Next time the client calls for a quick fix, you don't have to go searching for a document; just open the Book palette and double-click the document name to open it.

Editing Your Book

Once you've added documents to your Book palette, you can go about your regular routine of editing and preparing the documents. There are, as usual, a few things you should keep in mind.

▶ Whenever possible, you should open your book's documents while the Book palette is open. (The fastest way to open a document is to double-click the document name in the Book palette.) When you open and modify a document while the palette is not open, the palette isn't smart enough to update itself (see "File Status," below). If InDesign can't find your document (perhaps it's on a server that is not mounted), it'll ask you where it is.

▶ If you want to print more than one document in a book at a time, you should use the Print button on the Book palette (see "Printing and Exporting Books," later in this section).

▶ You should use caution when using the Numbering and Section Options feature to renumber any of the documents in the book (see "Page Numbering and Sections," later in this section). In general, if you're going to use automatic page numbering, you should let the Book palette handle your page numbering for you.

▶ We use the Save As feature to track revisions of our documents. Each time we use Save As, we change the name slightly ("mydocument1," "mydocument2," and so on), so we can always go back to an earlier version if necessary. If you do this, however, note that the Book palette doesn't catch on to what you're doing; it just lists and keeps track of the original document. So every time you use Save As, you have to select the original file and select Replace Document from the Book palette's menu.

Note that you cannot Undo or use Revert to Saved for changes in the Book palettes, so be careful what you do in these beasts. Also, the changes you make to your Book palette, including adding, removing, and reordering documents, aren't saved until you close the palette, quit InDesign, or select Save Book from the palette's menu.

File Status　As you work with book documents, the Book palette monitors and displays the status of each document in the book. There are five possible icons in the Status column of the palette: Available, Open, Modified, Missing, or In Use (see Figure 8-5).

▸ **Available.** The normal status of a document is Available (no icon). This means that no one has the document open for editing and that the document has not changed since the last time it was open on the computer you're using.

▸ **Open.** When you have a document open on your Macintosh or Windows system, the status of that file is listed as Open (an open book icon).

▸ **Modified.** When you or anyone else who has access to the file opens and changes a document while the Book palette is not open, the status will be listed as Modified in the Book palette (triangle icon). It's easy to change the status from Modified back to Available: open the file while the Book palette is open, then close the document again. Or, even easier: select Repaginate from the palette's menu.

▸ **Missing.** If you move a document after adding it to the Book palette, InDesign won't be able to find it, and the status is listed as Missing (red stop sign icon). To "find" a file again, double-click

FIGURE 8-5
Book Palette
Status Icons

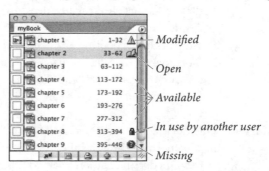

the chapter name in the Book palette; InDesign displays the Replace Document dialog box in which you can tell it where the document now resides.

▶ **In Use.** If someone else on your network opens one of the documents in your book via the Book palette, the Status field of the Book palette lists that chapter as in use (padlock icon).

It's important to pay attention to the Status column readings, because documents must be either Available or Open in order to synchronize, print, or renumber properly.

Books and Networks

People are increasingly working on projects in groups rather than individually. Adobe anticipated this, and if you put your book file and documents on a server, more than one person can open the palette at the same time. (Only one person can open an InDesign document at a time, however.) While this isn't nearly as powerful as a full-blown document management system, it's certainly useful if a group of people have to work on different documents in the book at the same time.

We don't like working on documents when they're on a server. It makes us nervous, and it's also really slow. Instead, we prefer to copy the file to our local hard drive, edit it at our leisure, and then return the file to the server when we're done with it.

There are two problems with this. First, the Book palette doesn't update properly. Second, other people on your network might not realize that you've got the "live" file, so make it clear to them: hide the document on the server, or put it in another folder called "work in progress" or something like that.

Synchronizing Your Book Documents

The more documents you're working with, the more likely it is that one or more of them contain settings inconsistent with the others in the book. Perhaps you decided to change a style definition in one document out of 20, and then forgot to change it in the other 19. Or perhaps your art director decided to change a Pantone color in a document and you now need to update the color in all of the other documents in the book.

Fortunately, the Synchronize Book button on the Book palette lets you ensure that all styles and color settings are consistent throughout the documents in a book. Here's how it works.

The Master Document

One document on the Book palette is always marked as the *master document* (by default, it's the first document you add to the palette; InDesign's documentation refers to this document as the *style source document*). The master document—which has a cryptic little icon to the left of it—is the document to which all the other documents will be synchronized. That means that if you add a new color to the master document and click the Synchronize Book button, the color will be added to all of the other documents in the book. If you add a new color to a document that is not the master document, the color won't be added when you synchronize the documents.

You can always change which document is the master document. To do that, click in the left column of the Book palette next to the document you want to set as the master document.

Synchronize   In order to synchronize your book documents, you must first select which files you want to synchronize in the Book palette; remember that you can Shift-click to select contiguous documents or use Command-click/Ctrl-click to select discontinuous documents. Or, if you want to synchronize all the files, make sure that no documents (or all documents) are selected in the palette.

▶ A style or color swatch that is defined in the master document but not in another document gets added to that other document.

▶ If a setting is named the same in both the master document and another document, the definition for that setting in the master document overrides the one in the non-master document.

▶ If a setting is not defined in the master document but exists in some other document, it's left alone. (This means you can have "local" settings that exist in one document that don't have to be copied into all the others.)

▶ By selecting Synchronize Options in the Book palette's menu, you can choose which settings will be synchronized among the documents (see Figure 8-6). However, if the master document contains table of contents styles (which we talk about later in this chapter) and you turn on the TOC Styles check box in the Synchronize Options dialog box, all the character and paragraph styles are synchronized, even if you've turned off the Character Styles and Paragraph Styles check boxes.

Note that synchronizing a document can be a time-consuming process—the more documents and the more settings there are, the longer it takes.

**Page Numbering
and Sections**   Perhaps the most helpful aspect of the Book feature is that it keeps track of your page numbering for you and updates the page numbers

FIGURE 8-6
Synchronization Options

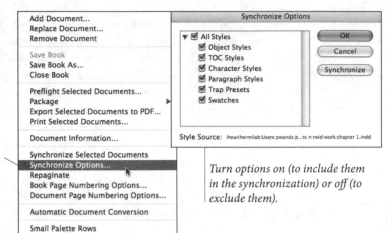

Choose Synchronize Options from the Book palette menu.

Turn options on (to include them in the synchronization) or off (to exclude them).

when you add pages to or delete them from a document, or if you add a new document between two other documents in a book. Of course, this only works if you've placed automatic page numbers on your document pages (see "Numbering Pages" in Chapter 2).

Let's say you've got one 16-page document in your Book palette already. When you add another document, InDesign automatically sets its first page number of the new document to 17 (provided you had not already specified the first page as a section start in the Numbering and Section Options dialog box). If you later open the first document and add two pages, InDesign automatically renumbers the second document—the next time you open it, you'll see that it starts on page 19.

If, on the other hand, you use the Numbering and Section Options dialog box (you can jump to this feature quickly by double-clicking on the page numbers in the Book palette) to create a section start, the Book palette respects that. Any subsequent documents in the Book palette continue the page numbering from where the previous document's page numbering left off.

If you don't use automatic page numbers, or you have manually specified page numbers for each document in your book, you will probably tire of watching InDesign repaginate your book. Fortunately, you can turn this feature off by selecting Book Page Numbering Options from the Book palette's menu, and unchecking Automatic Pagination (see Figure 8-7).

Odd Versus Even Page Numbers

When chapter 2 ends on page 45, what page number does InDesign assign to the first page of chapter 3? If you're in the book business, you probably want chapter 3 to start on page 47, because it's a right-hand page (though at least one of the authors would edit and/or adjust the

FIGURE 8-7
**Book Page
Numbering
Options**

*Choose Book Page
Numbering Options from
the Book palette menu.*

*Select page numbering options
in the Book Page Numbering
Options dialog box.*

layout to avoid a blank left-hand page). Catalog and magazine publishers would want the third file to begin on page 46, even though
it's a left-hand page. You can specify what you want InDesign to do
by choosing Book Page Numbering Options from the Book palette's
menu. You've got three choices: Continue from Previous Document,
Continue on Next Odd Page, and Continue on Next Even Page.

When you turn on the Insert blank page option, InDesign adds
a page to fill any gaps between chapters. For example, if chapter 2
ends on page 45 and you turn on the Continue on Next Odd Page,
then InDesign adds a blank page at the end of chapter 2. This page is
truly blank—it's not based on any master page. If you want a running
head on that page, you'll have to apply the master page yourself. (By
the way, David once almost drove himself mad trying to figure out
why he couldn't delete the last page from a document. The answer, of
course, was that he had forgotten this feature was on.)

**Printing and
Exporting Books**

Even though we cover printing documents in Chapter 11, "Printing,"
we should take this opportunity to mention a few things that are
specific to printing books.

First, each chapter in a book must be listed as Open, Available,
or Modified on the Book palette in order for the document to print.
This is because InDesign invisibly opens each document at print time
(you don't see the document open on screen, but it does).

Second, if you only want certain documents in a book to print,
select them in the Book palette. Remember that you can select contiguous documents on the list by holding down the Shift key, and
discontinuous documents with Command/Ctrl. If no documents
are selected, then they'll all print. When you're ready to print, click
the Print Book button in the Book palette or select Print Book (or
Print Selected Documents) from the palette's menu. The settings you
choose in the Print dialog box apply to every document in the book.

Similarly, you can export your book as an Acrobat PDF file by choosing Export Book to PDF (or Export Selected Documents to PDF) from the palette's menu.

Table of Contents

Don't get fooled into thinking the Table of Contents feature (under the Layout menu) is only for making book tables of contents. This feature lets you build collections of paragraphs that have been tagged with specific styles. For instance, if you use even two styles when you're formatting a book—one for the chapter name and another for your first-level headings—you can build a basic table of contents by collecting all the paragraphs tagged with these two styles. But if you use paragraph styles to tag your product names, you could just as easily build an index of products for a catalog. Anything you can tag with a paragraph style, you can build into a "table of contents." (While QuarkXPress can also make these kinds of lists based on character styles, InDesign currently only works with paragraph styles.)

This all depends entirely on your using styles. You should be using styles anyway—if you're not, you're working way too hard. If you don't currently use styles, refer to Chapter 4, "Type," to see why you should.

Making a Table of Contents

Making a table of contents (or a list of figures, or whatever) is easy, but it requires a methodical approach to the Table of Contents dialog box (see Figure 8-8).

1. If you only have one list (table of contents, list of figures, etc.) in your document, you can leave the Style pop-up menu set to [Default]. We'll cover table of contents styles later in this section.

2. Fill in a name for your list in the Title field. InDesign places this title at the beginning of the list, so you might want to type "Table of Contents" or "Advertisers" or something like that. To be honest, we usually leave this field blank and later make our own titles on the document page. If you do include a title, choose a paragraph style for it from the Style pop-up menu to the right of the Title field. (InDesign automatically adds a paragraph style called "TOC title" to your document when you open this dialog box, but you don't have to use that style if you don't want to.)

*Select a paragraph style from
the Other Styles list and click
the Add button.*

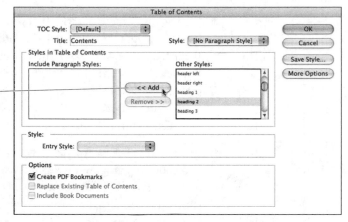

*InDesign adds the style to
the Include Paragraph Styles
list (the list of styles included
in the table of contents).*

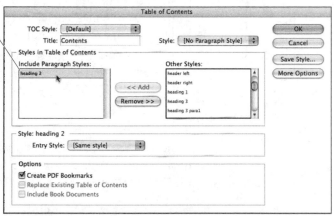

*Choose a paragraph
style to use to format
the selected table of
contents style.*

*Add other paragraph styles
to the list as necessary.*

*When you're ready to build
your table of contents, click
the OK button.*

*Unless you've chosen to
replace an existing table of
contents, InDesign displays
a place icon. Click the place
icon to place the table of
contents story.*

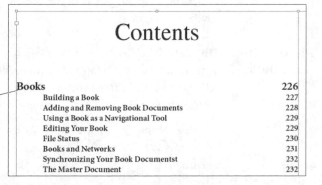

Contents

3. Choose the paragraph styles that you want included from the list on the right. You can click the Add button to add them to the list, but double-clicking the style names is faster. You can also select more than one style (by Command/Ctrl-clicking each one) and then click Add to add them all at once (in which case they're added alphabetically—if you want to rearrange the order, just click and drag the style names after adding them).

4. One by one, click each style in the Include Paragraph Styles list and choose a paragraph style for it from the Entry Style pop-up menu. This is helpful because you'd rarely want a heading from your document to appear in your table of contents in the actual Heading style; instead, you'd probably create a new style called "TOC-head" or something like that. If you want certain paragraphs to be indented on your final list, you should apply styles here that include indentation. Note that InDesign adds a paragraph style called "TOC body text" to your document when you open this dialog box, but you don't have to use it—we typically just roll our own.

5. If your document is included in a Book palette, you can choose to include the entire book in your list by turning on the Include Book Documents check box. We'll talk about the Replace Existing Table of Contents check box below.

6. Finally, when you click OK, InDesign builds the table of contents (which might take a little while, especially if you have many documents in a book). When it's done, InDesign displays the text place icon, just as if you had imported a text file (see Chapter 4, "Text," if you need to know more about placing text).

That's it! Note that InDesign captures only the first 255 characters of each paragraph when it builds a table of contents, something you should keep in mind as you think of uses for this feature (255 characters make about 40 words—more than enough for most headlines, bylines, and such).

More Table of Contents Options

The default Table of Contents dialog box gives you the basic controls you need for a simple table of contents, but for most lists we make we click the More Options button, which gives us more options for fine-tuning the table of contents (see Figure 8-9).

▶ **Page Number.** You may not want every entry in your table of contents to be followed by a page number. For instance, you might want page numbers after the headings, but not after the

FIGURE 8-9
**More Table of
Contents Options**

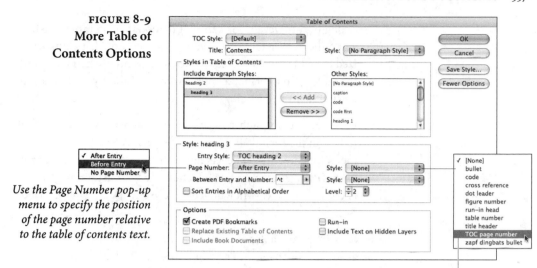

*Use the Page Number pop-up
menu to specify the position
of the page number relative
to the table of contents text.*

*You can select a character style to apply to the
page number and/or to the separator character.*

chapter titles in a book. You can control how page numbers
will appear on your printed page with the Page Number pop-
up menu. You've got three options for numbering: After Entry,
Before Entry, and None. The first two tell InDesign to include
the page number (either before or after the entry), separated
from the text of the paragraph by a tab character. We typically
create a character style for the page numbers and select it from
the Style pop-up menu to the right of the Page Number menu.
This way, all the page numbers appear the same rather than
appearing in the Entry Style.

▶ **Between Entry and Number.** By default, InDesign places a tab
character between the entry and the page number (whether the
page number is before or after the entry). However, you can
change this to some other character or characters. For instance,
we usually replace the ^t character (which is code for a tab) with
^y (a right-indent tab, which always sits flush on the right margin,
even if you haven't placed a tab stop). If you're planning on
including dot leaders between the entries and the page numbers
(which you would set up in the Tabs palette), you may want to
pick a character style from the Style pop-up menu. A regular
dot leader looks too much like periods in a row (which is exactly
what it is), so we often make a character style of 7-point text with
500 units of tracking, then apply this style to the leader.

▶ **Sort Entries in Alphabetical Order.** If you turn on the Sort
Entries in Alphabetical Order option in the Table of Contents

dialog box, InDesign sorts the list in alphabetical order when you build it. Whether or not you want your final list alphabetized is up to you; you probably wouldn't want it when you build the table of contents for a book, but you might if you're creating a list of items in a catalog.

▶ **Level.** Each paragraph style you include appears with a different indent in the Include Paragraph Styles list. You can control how much indent with the Level feature. This only adjusts the display in this dialog box; it has no effect on the final list unless your list is alphabetized—in which case, the entries are alphabetized by level.

▶ **Run-in.** Some tables of contents, such as those found in academic journals, are "run-in"—that is, the headings are all in one paragraph, separated by semicolons. If you want this sort of list, turn on this option (see Figure 8-10).

▶ **Include Text on Hidden Layers.** This option is pretty self-explanatory. If you have multiple layers in your document, you can choose whether to include the text on those layers even when the layers are hidden. While it's rare that you'd turn this on, you might do so if you have made a layer that contains keywords or explanatory text that you want in the table of contents but don't want in print (see the next section).

FIGURE 8-10
The Run-in Option

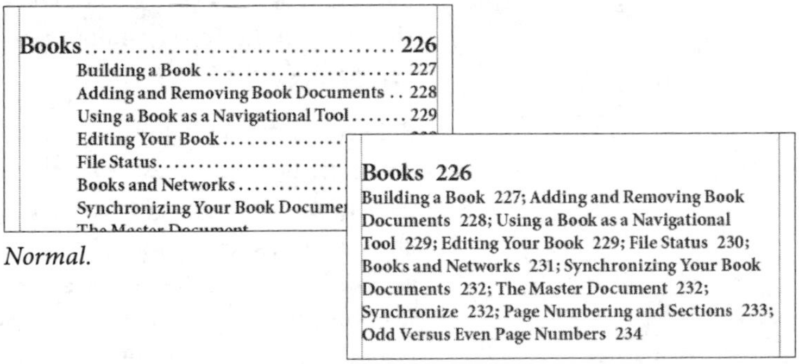

Books 226
 Building a Book 227
 Adding and Removing Book Documents . . 228
 Using a Book as a Navigational Tool 229
 Editing Your Book . . . .
 File Status . . . .
 Books and Networks . . . .
 Synchronizing Your Book Docume
 The Master Document

Normal.

Books 226
Building a Book 227; Adding and Removing Book Documents 228; Using a Book as a Navigational Tool 229; Editing Your Book 229; File Status 230; Books and Networks 231; Synchronizing Your Book Documents 232; The Master Document 232; Synchronize 232; Page Numbering and Sections 233; Odd Versus Even Page Numbers 234

Run-in.

Using Dummy Text for Lists

One of the things we like most about tables of contents is that they're document-wide rather than simply story-wide. That means that any text in any text frame can be included in a table of contents—even text in a nonprinting text frame. With this in mind, you can add "tags" to items on your page that don't appear in print, but do appear in your table of contents.

One of the best examples of this is an advertiser index. You can place a text frame with an advertiser's name on top of that company's ad in your document. Set the text frame's color to None and turn on Nonprinting Object in the Attributes palette (or put the frame on a hidden layer), and it's almost as though this were a "non-object"—the text won't print, and it won't affect the ad underneath. But if that advertiser's name is tagged with a style, you can include it on a list of advertisers.

The same trick applies to building a list of pictures in a catalog, or for any other instance where what you want on the list doesn't actually appear on the page.

Building and Rebuilding Tables of Contents

There is nothing magic about the text or page numbers in your table of contents—they're just regular text and numbers. That means if you update the document on which the list is based (such as adding pages or changing the text), the entries and page numbers in the table of contents don't automatically update, and you will have to rebuild it. We find that we build and rebuild a table of contents several times for each document or book. It isn't that we're having so much fun with the feature—it's that we make mistakes.

To update a table of contents, use the Selection tool or Text tool to select the text frame containing the list, then choose Update Table of Contents from the Layout menu. Or, if you want to make a change to the Table of Contents dialog box settings, you can choose Table of Contents from the Layout menu, make the changes, turn on the Replace Existing Table of Contents check box, and click OK.

Table of Contents Styles

Everything we've said about table of contents so far is based on the idea that you have only one of these in your document. However, you can define lots of different table of contents styles in a single document—one for headings, one for figures, one for bylines, and so on. The easiest way to do this is to build various table of contents styles, which are simply saved collections of settings. Once you set up the Table of Contents dialog box just the way you want it, you can click the Save Style button to save this setup as a style (see Figure 8-11). Later, you can reload those settings by choosing your style from the TOC Style pop-up menu at the top of the dialog box.

A second way to build a "style" is to select Table of Contents Styles from the Layout menu and click New. You get a nearly identical dialog box, but when you click OK your settings are saved for use later. You can also use the Table of Contents Styles feature to delete and edit styles, or load them from other InDesign documents.

FIGURE 8-11
Creating a Table of Contents Style

To save the current settings of the Table of Contents dialog box as a table of contents style, click the Save Style button.

Enter a name for the style in the Save Style dialog box and click the OK button.

InDesign adds the style to the list of available styles.

Note that if you save your table of contents style after building a table of contents in your document, InDesign isn't smart enough to match your built list to the style name. That means you can't use the Replace Existing Table of Contents feature. Instead, you'll have to delete the already-built list and replace it with a new one.

Indexes (Or Indices)

Sitting down and indexing a book is—in our experience—the most painful, horrible, mind-numbing activity you could ever wish on your worst enemy. And yet, where this is the kind of task that a computer should be great at, it's actually impossible for a computer to do a good job of indexing a book by itself. A good index requires careful thought, an understanding of the subject matter, and an ability to keep the whole project in your head at all times. In short, it requires *comprehension*—a quality computer software, at this early stage of its evolution, lacks. Until recently, it also required a large stack of note cards, highlighter pens, Post-It notes, and serious medication.

Fortunately, InDesign has a built-in indexing feature, which, while it won't make the index for you, does remove the note card and highlighter requirements.

Some people ask us, "Why can't a computer build an index? InDesign should just give me a list of all the words in my document and what page they're on." Unfortunately, this is not an index; it's a concordance. A concordance records the location of *words*; an index records the location of *ideas*. There are times when a concordance can be useful, especially in catalogs. In those cases, you might want to use a plug-in such as Sonar Bookends, which can build concordances automatically and very quickly. But in general, if you're looking for an index, you're going to have to do it manually with InDesign's indexing features.

You can index a document at any time in the production cycle, but it's almost always best to wait until the text has become fixed—until no text in the document will be deleted, copied, cut, pasted, and so on. The reason: as you edit the text, you may accidentally delete index markers.

The Index palette (choose Index from the Type & Tables submenu, under the Window menu) lets you add either single words or whole phrases to the index, and it displays a list of currently indexed words and phrases (see Figure 8-12). First we're going to discuss how to add, edit, and remove index entries with the Index palette. Then we'll explore how to collect all the tagged entries and build a finished index on your document pages.

FIGURE 8-12
The Index Palette

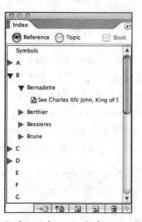
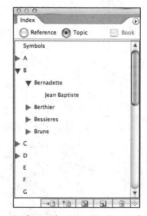

Index palette in Reference mode.   *Index palette in Topic mode.*

Go to Selected Marker

Update Preview
Generate Index

Delete Selected Entry
Create a New Index Entry

A Note to the Author Contemplating Self-Indexing. Hire a professional indexer. The author of a text is *the worst person* for the job. You simply know the material too well (or, if you don't, why in the world did you write the book?) to create a useful index. A professional indexer will read and understand your text, and will create an index that opens it up to a wider range of possible readers than you ever could. It's what they do.

Adding a New First-Level Index Entry

There's very little that is automatic about building an index. Again, it's not difficult, but you have to be methodical about it. Here are the steps you should go through for each new index entry. (Note that we always differentiate between a new index entry or topic and a new reference to an index entry. For example, "Pigs" might be a new entry for page 34, but when it appears again on page 59, it would simply be a new reference to your already added index entry—see "Adding a New Reference to an Entry," later in this section.)

To add an index entry, follow these steps (see Figure 8-13).

1. If the word or phrase you want indexed appears on the page, select it and click the New Entry button at the bottom of the Index palette, or select New Page Reference from the palette's menu (or better yet, just press Command-U/Ctrl-U). If the index entry isn't found on the page, place the text cursor anywhere in the text related to the topic and click the New Entry button. For example, a page may include a discussion of cows, but you want to index the word under the phrase "Farm animals." In this case, you would simply insert the cursor in the text and click New Entry (or press the keystroke).

2. In the New Page Reference dialog box, edit the entry under the Topic Levels heading, if needed. Whatever you type here will be what shows up in the index. Since we're focusing on first-level entries right now, you can just skip over the other two Topic Levels fields. (We'll discuss the finer points of second-level entries in "Adding a New Second-Level Index Entry," later.)

3. Index entries always appear in alphabetical order. However, occasionally you may not want your index entry to appear where it would normally be alphabetized. For instance, the famous "17-Mile Drive" would ordinarily be placed at the beginning of the index, before the "A"s. You can place it along with other words that begin with "S" by typing "Seventeen" in the first Sort As field of the New Page Reference dialog box. You'll probably leave this field blank most of the time.

FIGURE 8-13
Adding an Index Entry

FIGURE 8-13
Adding an Index Entry

*In this example, we've gotten
lucky: the text we want to
add to the index is present
on the page.*

I knew only too well. I raised my head and saw Hamaïouna, glorious, transfigured, and seated on a luminous cloud.

"Wretched Barkiarokh," she said, "thou hast nothing more to fear from the Wand of Remorse. Instead of profiting by its strokes, thou hast sought to evade them. Henceforward, the rod that will beat upon thy heart is the Rod of Despair, and thy heart, hardened as it is, will be broken and crushed throughout every moment of a frightful eternity."

Select the text...

...and click the New Entry button.

*If necessary, edit the text in the
Topic Levels field (or fields).
For this example, we don't
need to edit the text.*

*Choose an indexing range
from the Type pop-up menu.*

*Turn on the Number Style
Override option if you want
to apply a specific character
style to the page number in
the index (we don't, so we left
the option unchecked).*

*If our index contained more
than this single index entry,
we'd see a list of other topics
in this field.*

*InDesign adds the page
reference to the index.*

4. The Number Style Override feature is yet one more control that you will ignore most of the time. Let's say you want the page numbers that refer to an illustration (rather than to just text on the page) to appear bold in the final index. You can build a character style to define how you want the page numbers to appear and—when you're indexing that illustration—you can turn on the Number Style Override check box and choose that character style from the pop-up menu.

5. An index entry can span a range of pages or text. If, for example, your treatise on pigs and goats spans six pages of your document, you don't want to have to make a separate index entry for each and every page. Instead, you can specify one index entry and choose a range of pages in the Type pop-up menu. There are nine page-range choices in the Type pop-up menu, plus six more cross-reference choices. We cover those last six in "Cross References (X-Refs)," later in the chapter.

    In the previous edition, an online reviewer chastized us (thereby taking food away from our hungry children) for our failure to explain in detail when and why we might use each of these index entries. We admit that we thought it was self-evident.

    We still think so. You, the indexer, know the text. Knowing the text means that you understand that a given topic covers a specific range of pages or paragraphs (you'd use the For Next # of Pages option or the For Next # of Paragraphs option), or runs from one heading to another (you'd use the To Next Use of Style option and choose the paragraph style of the heading).

    ▶ Current page, the default page range, indexes the page that includes the index marker.

    ▶ To Next Style Change tells InDesign to index from the paragraph containing the index marker to the next paragraph style change.

    ▶ To Next Use of Style is the option we use most often. This indexes from the paragraph containing the index marker to the next use of a specific style, which you can choose in a pop-up menu next to the Type pop-up menu. For instance, let's say you've got a book about farm animals where each animal's heading is tagged with a paragraph style called "Heading-A." You could select the heading "Rabbit" and set the Type to "To Next Use of Style." Then you could choose Heading-A from the pop-up menu of styles. If the "Horse" section starts three pages after the Rabbit section, the page range in the index will span three pages; if it starts 14 pages after, the page range will span 14 pages, and so on.

    ▶ To End of Story tells InDesign to index from the paragraph containing the index marker to the end of the current story. Note that InDesign assumes that the story falls on every page. If your story starts on page 1, then skips to page 9, and ends on page 12, the index will display pages 1–12, ignoring the skipped pages.

► To End of Document is the same as To End of Story, but it spans from the paragraph containing the index marker to the end of the file. In the example of the farm animals chapter, you could index the entire chapter by placing the cursor anywhere on the first page of the chapter, specifying an index entry labeled "Farm animals," and choosing To End of Document.

► To End of Section is the same as the previous two options, but the page range extends from the index marker to the end of the current section (see Chapter 2, "Page Layout").

► For Next # of Paragraphs works when you know exactly how many paragraphs you want indexed. Unfortunately, currently InDesign only spans to the beginning of the final paragraph, rather than the end of the paragraph—a problem if that paragraph spans two pages.

► For Next # of Pages indexes from the index entry marker for the number of pages you specify.

► Suppress Page Range. Some first-level index entries don't include page numbers at all. For instance, in the book we've been discussing, "Animals" is too broad a topic to include page numbers (every page in the book would be indexed). So you might specify Suppress Page Range for this one entry, and then follow it with 15 second-level entries, each with appropriate page numbers listed. (Again, we discuss second-level entries later.)

6. After you've chosen the scope from the Type menu, click OK and InDesign adds the index entry to the Index palette, along with the page range. If the indexed text sits on a master page or on the pasteboard, the master page label or "PB" shows up in the Index palette, but these items will not actually appear in the final index.

If you're happy with the default settings of the New Page Reference dialog box, you can streamline this process significantly by selecting a word or phrase on your page and typing Ctrl-Alt-Shift-[or Command-Option-Shift-[, which adds the selection to the index, skipping the dialog box. Or, if the selection is a proper name, press the] (right bracket) instead—that indexes the selection based on the last word in the selection (so James Joyce would show up as Joyce, James). You can control how words in a proper name show up by placing a nonbreaking space between them; for instance, if you put a nonbreaking space between "King" and "Jr.," then this keyboard shortcut will index the name under King instead of Jr.

Add and Add All   You may already have spotted the Add and Add All buttons in the New Page Reference dialog box. Clicking the Add button adds the index entry but leaves the dialog box open so that you can add more entries. This is very helpful—you frequently need to index the same text using more than one entry.

Add All searches throughout your document for every instance of the index entry and adds it automatically to the index. If you select the word "Bee" on your page and then click Add All, InDesign places another identical index entry at each instance of the word "Bee" in your file. (If you have turned on the Book option in the Index palette, InDesign also adds all instances of the index entry in other documents, too—as long as those documents are open.)

When you click Add All, InDesign uses the same scope (Type) settings for every instance of the entry text. Whether this is a great feature or a potential problem depends on the formatting of your index. If each instance of an indexed topic needs special attention (this one only showing up on this page, the next one using a To Next Use of Style scope, and so on), you should avoid this feature.

You also need to be careful with Add All because it only finds exact matches. That is, if you type "Cow" in the New Page Reference dialog box and then click Add All, InDesign won't find "Cows" or even "cows".

Cross-References (X-Refs)   As you build an index, think of all the ways that your reader might look for a topic and include those words in your index. For instance, because you're familiar with your own book, you might include an index entry called "Llamas." However, another reader might look for "Cute wool-producing animals that spit." Fortunately, InDesign lets you add cross-references in your index such as "Spitting animals. *See* Llamas" and "Wool 34–46. *See also* Llamas."

To add a cross-reference to your index, you go through the same steps as you would to add a normal index entry. The one difference is that you set the Type pop-up menu to one of the six cross-reference settings: See [also], See, See also, See herein, See also herein, and Custom Cross-Reference. When you select any of these, InDesign provides a text field in which you can enter the cross-referenced word or phrase. If you want your index entry to be "Koi. *See* Carp" you would type "Koi" in the first Topic Levels field, and type "Carp" in the Referenced field (see Figure 8-14).

FIGURE 8-14
Adding a
Cross-Reference

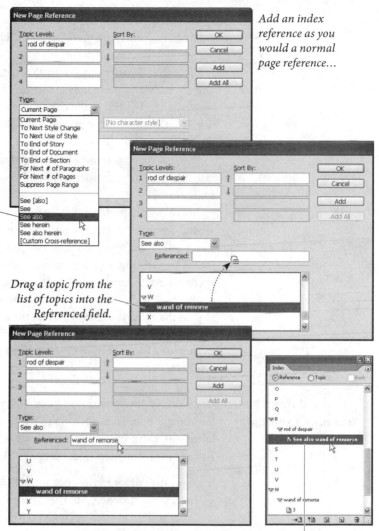

Add an index reference as you would a normal page reference…

…and then choose one of the cross reference options from the Type pop-up menu.

Drag a topic from the list of topics into the Referenced field.

InDesign adds the cross-reference to the index.

▶ *See* is generally used when an index entry has no page number references, such as "Supermarket. *See* Grocery."

▶ *See also* is used when an index entry does have page references, but you also want to refer the reader to other topics, such as "Grocery 34–51. *See also* Farmer's Market."

▶ We like the *See [also]* option best, because it uses either See or See also, depending on whether you've specified page references.

▶ *See herein* is a special case in which you are cross-referencing to a second-level entry within the same entry as the cross-reference itself, and it's used more in legal indexes than anywhere else.

▶ If you choose Custom Cross-Reference, you can type any kind of cross-reference you prefer, such as "Hey dude, go look at page".

Note that if you're cross-referencing to an index entry that you've already added to your index, you can find that entry in the list of entries at the bottom of the dialog box and drag it to the Referenced field. That's certainly faster (and probably more accurate) than typing the words again.

Because no page number is involved in a cross-reference, it doesn't matter where in your document you specify it (though it must be in a text frame).

Some people prefer to put cross-references at the end of a list of second-level index entries rather than directly after the first-level entry. InDesign won't do this for you automatically, but you can fake it by creating a dummy second-level entry (see "Adding a New Second-Level Index Entry," below) and setting its Type to a cross-reference. The dummy second-level entry should just be named with "zzz" so that it automatically falls at the end of the alphabetized list of second-level entries. Later, once you build the index onto your document pages, you will have to perform a Find/Change to remove these symbols.

Adding a New Reference to an Entry

Once you've got an entry on your Index palette, you can easily add more page references to it. Let's say you added the name "Farmer Jones" to your index back on page 13 of your document. Now, "Farmer Jones" appears again on page 51.

1. Place the cursor in the appropriate place in the text story. In this case, you'd probably put the cursor next to the word "Farmer" on page 51.

2. Click the entry in the Index palette. Here, you'd select "Farmer Jones."

3. Alt/Option-click the New Entry button. Make sure that the Type pop-up menu is set up according to how you want your new reference to appear, and then click OK. If you want to use the default New Page Reference dialog box settings, you can just drag the index entry on top of the New Entry button instead.

Note that while you don't necessarily have to click the entry in the Index palette in step 2 (you could just retype the entry in the New Page Reference dialog box or select it on the page), we recommend clicking because it ensures consistency. For example, if you relied on your typing ability, you might create the index entry "Chickens" and then later—meaning to type the same thing—create a new entry, "Chicken," causing two different entries to be made when you only meant to make one.

Adding a New Second-Level Index Entry

Now that you've specified first-level index entries, you can—if you wish—add second-level entries. As we mentioned earlier, second-level entries are subcategories of the first-level entries. For example, under the first-level index entry "Grape Varieties," you might find the second-level entries "Merlot," "Chardonnay," and "Syrah." You can make a second-level index entry just as you would make the first-level index entry, but with two added steps.

After you open the New Page Reference dialog box, click the down arrow button to move your index entry to the second Topic Level field. Then, double-click the first-level entry in the list at the bottom of the dialog box (which enters it in the first Topic Level field).

Once you've created a second-level entry, you can place a third-level entry under it. Similarly, you can put fourth-level entries under third-level entries.

Importing Topics

Many people prefer to index their text in Microsoft Word before placing the text in InDesign. Fortunately, InDesign can import Word's index markers, adding the index entries to the Index palette automatically. In fact, if you delete the Word file after importing it, the index topics remain in the Index palette. This is one good way to import a list of topics into the palette without having to type them manually in InDesign. Another way to import index topics is to choose Import Topics from the Index palette's menu, which lets you select any other already-indexed InDesign document.

Index entries in your palette that don't have corresponding index markers in the text won't show up in your final index. If you don't want to see these topics in your Index palette, select Hide Unused Topics in the palette's menu to them. To view the topics you've hidden, choose Show from the palette menu.

Deleting Entries

There are several ways to delete an entry from your index.

▶ To delete an entire entry, including all its page references, select it in the Index palette and click the Delete button. Note that this also deletes all the subcategories under it and their page references, too.

▶ To delete a single page reference, you can select it in the Index palette (click the gray triangle next to the index entry to display its page references) and click the Delete button.

► To remove a particular page reference in your index, delete the index marker. The marker is a zero-width character, but it is a character nevertheless. To view the character, choose Show Hidden Characters from the Type menu. To delete it, put the text cursor immediately after it (you may have to use the arrow keys to accomplish this) and press Backspace/Delete.

Editing Entries

We make mistakes, so it's a good thing that InDesign gives us a way to edit our flubbed index entries. When you're editing an index entry, you have to decide whether you want to edit the entry itself or a particular page reference of the entry.

Let's say that halfway through indexing your document, you realize that the index entry "Martha Washington" should have been indexed as "Washington, Martha." You can select the entry in the Index palette and choose Topic Options from the palette's menu—or even faster, you can just double-click the entry. In this case, you'd change the first Topic Level field to "Washington, Martha," and then click OK.

One of the most common entry edits is capitalizing an entry, so the folks at Adobe snuck a Capitalize feature into the Index palette's menu (see Figure 8-15). While this is nice, we wish there were a further option to change an entry to lowercase (useful for level 2 entries, which are usually set in lowercase). Maybe next version.

FIGURE 8-15
Capitalizing Index Topics

Choose Capitalize from the Index palette menu to display the Capitalize dialog box.

Editing References

You can also change the scope (type) or style of a particular page reference. For instance, let's say the reference to Martha Washington on page 47 should have spanned nine paragraphs, but you accidentally set it to Current Page instead. To fix this, click the gray triangle next to the index entry; this displays the page references for the entry. Double-click the page reference that corresponds to the one you want to change (in this case, you'd double-click the number 47). Change the index entry options, and when done, press Return/Enter.

If you actually wanted the above reference to begin on page 48 instead of page 47, you have to select the entry, cut it to the Clipboard, and then paste it in the new location. Selecting entries can be difficult, so make use of the arrow keys and the Shift key.

Finding Entries

Know you indexed "bugs" as a second-level entry, but can't remember which first-level entry it was under? Select Find from the Index palette's menu to display the palette's Find field. After typing "bugs" into the field, you can click the down arrow to see the next instance of this entry in your palette. (Or click the up arrow to see the previous instance.)

Building the Index

You've reached the finish line—and it's finally time to place your index on a document page so you can see it in all its glory. This is the fun part, because you can just sit back, choose Generate Index from the Index menu's palette, and let InDesign do the work of collecting the index entries and page numbers for you. There is still one more dialog box you need to pay attention to: the Generate Index dialog box (see Figure 8-16).

The Generate Index dialog box presents a (somewhat bewildering) array of choices you need to make in order to get the index of your dreams. InDesign shows you a few controls by default; you can see the others by clicking More Options. Fortunately, once you make your choices in this dialog box, InDesign will remember them the next time you build an index for this document.

FIGURE 8-16
Generate Index
Dialog Box

Generate Index dialog box with options hidden. Click More Options...

...and InDesign displays this monster. Daunting though they may be, these options give you a tremendous amount of control over the appearance of your index.

Title. Fill in a name for your index in the Title field. InDesign places this title at the beginning of the list, so you might want to type "Index" or "My Indexio Grandioso" or something like that. We leave this field blank and make our own titles. If you do include a title, choose a paragraph style for it from the Style pop-up menu to the right of the Title field. (InDesign automatically adds a paragraph style called "Index Title" to your document when you open this dialog box, but you don't have to use that style if you don't want to.)

Replace Existing Index. InDesign knows when you've already built an index in a document, and it automatically replaces that index with a new one unless you turn off the Replace Existing Index option. Probably the only time you'd turn this off would be if you wanted to compare two indexes to find differences between them.

By the way, note that when InDesign replaces one index with another, it doesn't just replace the text. It actually deletes all the index pages and then rebuilds them from scratch. If you've spent two hours adding extra formatting to the index, or adding boxes or lines to the pages, those additions are removed when you build the new index.

Include Book Documents. If your document is part of a book (see "Books," earlier in this chapter), you can choose to build an index for the book by turning on the Include Book Documents option. Note that InDesign can generate the index from all the documents even if they're not currently open, as long as they're available in the Book palette (not missing or opened by someone else on the network).

Include Entries on Hidden Layers. If you have multiple layers in your document, you can choose whether to include the text on those layers even when the layers are hidden. While it's rare that you'd turn this on, you might do so if you have made a layer that contains keywords or explanatory text that you want in the index but don't want in print (see "Using Dummy Text for Lists," earlier).

Nested versus Run-In. There are two primary types of index formats: nested and run-in (see Figure 8-17). In a nested index, each entry occupies its own paragraph; in a run-in index, the second-level entries merge with their first-level entry to form one big paragraph. Which you choose is entirely up to you, though it should depend in part on the content of the index. Run-in indexes make no sense when you have third- or fourth-level entries. On the other hand, run-in indexes typically conserve space, especially when they're set in wide columns (because more than one entry fits on a single line).

FIGURE 8-17
**Nested and Run-in
Index Formatting**

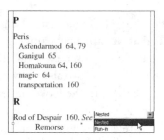
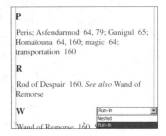

Include Index Section Headings. In this context, "section" doesn't have anything to do with page numbering sections (which we discuss in Chapter 2, "Page Layout"). Rather, the section heads refer to index sections: "A", "B", "C", and so on. Even when you turn on Include Index Section Headings, InDesign only includes the headings for which you have made index entries. If you have no entries that begin with "b", the index won't include a "B" section heading. If you really want the empty sections, you can turn on the Include Empty Index Sections check box. We're not sure why you'd want to do that, but it's nice to know you can.

Level Style. The Level Styles section of the Generate Index dialog box lets you apply a paragraph style to each entry in the index. In a run-in index, there's only one kind of paragraph: the first-level entry (all the second-level entries are merged into the same paragraph). In a nested index, however, each entry level is tagged with its own paragraph style. If you want all your second-level index entries to be slightly indented from the first-level entries (you probably do), make a new style that includes indentation, and choose it from the Second Level pop-up menu (see Figure 8-18).

Once again, designing a readable index is as much an art as a science. Take some time to peruse other people's indexes, checking for details such as indentation (what does a first-level entry do when it's longer than one line, for example?) and punctuation.

Note that InDesign builds styles for you called "Index Level 1", "Index Level 2", and so on. If you haven't already created your own styles, then use these and adjust their definitions in the Paragraph Styles palette later.

FIGURE 8-18
Selecting Level Styles

*You can use the Level Style
pop-up menus to assign
any style you've defined to a
specific index level.*

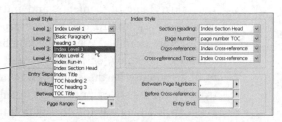

Index Style. One of our favorite things about making indexes in InDesign is that we can apply paragraph or character styles to every index element, down to the page numbers and the cross-reference words (such as "See" or "See also"). By assigning styles, you can later make global changes to the look and feel of the index by changing the style definitions. While we often apply styles in the Section Heading and Cross-reference pop-up menus, we usually leave the Page Number and Cross-referenced Topic settings alone. It all depends on the index.

Entry Separators. Index formatting is as varied as art directors' whims—or the whims of the indexers, which tend to be even more obscure. One of the main differences revolves around the incredibly picayune art of choosing punctuation. Do you want an en dash between numbers in a page range or a hyphen? An en dash is more appropriate, but the ends of the dash bump up against some numbers. Fortunately, you can type thin spaces on each side of the en dash in the Page Range field in the Generate Index dialog box. (Actually, we never type these characters themselves; we just select them from the menu to the right of the field.)

You can change the punctuation for Following Topic, Between Entries (which only applies in run-in indexes or where there are multiple cross-references per line), Page Range, Between Page Numbers, Before Cross-reference, and Entry End (see Figure 8-19).

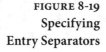

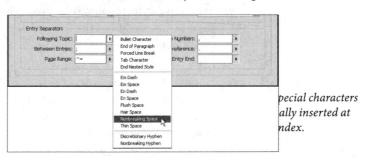

pecial characters
ally inserted at
ndex.

Putting It Together

The Book, Table of Contents, and Indexing features in InDesign go a long way toward making the process of creating long documents more bearable. Whether you're building a magazine, a book, a journal, a catalog, or even a newsletter, we're sure you'll be able to find good use for these features. Remember that a little work up front—building styles, putting documents in a Book palette, and so on—can go a long way to saving lots of time in the long run.

CHAPTER 9

Transforming

In the previous chapters, we've covered the process of getting text and graphics into your InDesign publication. This chapter is all about what you can do with those elements once you've wrestled them onto your pages. The process of moving, rotating, scaling, reflecting, or shearing an object is called *transformation*.

Many of the topics in this chapter have been touched on in the preceding chapters—mainly because everything you can do in InDesign is interconnected. In the old days, software was entirely linear and modal: one had to proceed from this screen to that screen following a particular sequence of steps. These days, software is extremely non-linear and non-modal (that is, you can do things many different ways in many different orders), and, therefore, much harder to write about. It's enough to drive one mad! Your purchase of this book will make our time at Looney Farm that much more pleasant. Thank you.

Transformation Basics

There are many ways to transform an object on an InDesign page or pasteboard. Select the object using the Selection tool, then:

▸ Drag one of the object's selection handles to scale the object (but not necessarily the contents of that object).

▸ Select a transformation tool from the Tools palette, set the center of transformation (if necessary), and drag the tool.

▸ Display the Transform palette or Control palette and enter values in the palette field corresponding to the transformation you want to apply—or choose a preset value from the pop-up menu associated with that field.

▸ Choose one of the "preset" rotation or reflection options from the Transform palette menu or Control palette menu.

▸ Double-click one of the transformation tools in the Toolbox to display the corresponding transform dialog box (double-click the Rotate tool, for example, to display the Rotation dialog box).

▸ Select the Free Transform tool, then apply a transformation by dragging inside the object, outside the object, or on the object's selection handles. See "Using the Free Transform Tool," later in this chapter.

▸ Scale an object by pressing keyboard shortcuts. See "Scaling with Keyboard Shortcuts," later in this chapter.

There's no "right" or "best" way to do transformations—you can experiment with the different methods and see which you like best. We change methods depending on the situation (and our mood).

Setting the Center of Transformation

When you select an object and then choose one of the transformation tools from the Tools palette, InDesign displays the center of transformation icon (it looks something like a small registration mark) on or around the object (see Figure 9-1). The initial position of the icon is determined by the point selected in the Proxy in the Transform palette or Control palette (by default, it's in the center).

When you scale, rotate, or shear an object, InDesign transforms the object around the center of transformation. To reposition the center of transformation icon, either drag it to a new position (with whatever transformation tool you have selected) or click a point on the Proxy in the Transform palette or Control palette.

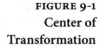

FIGURE 9-1
Center of
Transformation

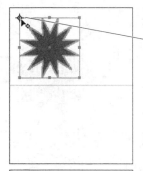

When you select an object and choose a transformation tool, InDesign displays the center of transformation icon.

When you move the cursor over the icon, InDesign changes the cursor to show that dragging will move the icon.

Drag the center of transformation icon to a new location, if necessary.

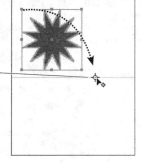

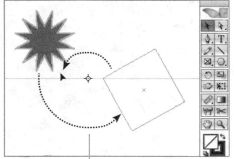

Drag the tool to transform the object. As you drag, InDesign transforms (in this example, rotates) the object around the center of transformation.

Transforming Line Segments and Points

To transform a point or line segment on a path, select the path or point using the Direct Selection tool, then transform it as you would any other object (drag it, or enter values in the X and Y fields of the Transform palette or Control palette, or press the arrow keys, or display the Move dialog box, or use any of the other transformation techniques). This can produce interesting effects (see Figure 9-2).

You can also select the points and/or line segments of a path and then copy as you transform the object by holding down the Option/Alt key after you start dragging or clicking the Copy button in the any of the transformation tool's dialog boxes. In this case, InDesign splits the path at the unselected points on the path. This takes a little getting used to, but might come in handy. If you want to transform line segments or points of a copy of a path, copy the path first, then apply the transformation.

Transforming Path Contents

When you transform a path that contains other objects (an image frame with a picture in it, for example), you can control whether the content is transformed, too. By default, dragging the handles of a frame to scale it does not scale the content, but using any of the transformation tools in the Tools palette or using the Transform palette to alter a frame *does* scale the content.

FIGURE 9-2
Transforming
Points, Not Paths

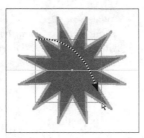

Select some points using the Direct Selection tool.

In this example, the points on the inside of the star polygon are selected; the outside ones aren't.

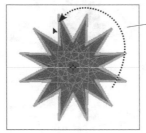

Apply a transformation. In this example, we've rotated the selected points.

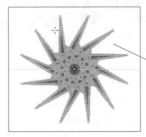

InDesign applies the transformation to the selected points, not to the entire path.

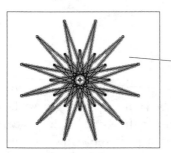

Note: If you're transforming selected points using one of the transformation dialog boxes and click the Copy button...

Rotate

Angle: 180°   OK
              Cancel
Options   Copy
☑ Rotate Content
              ☑ Preview

Copy button

...InDesign splits the path at the location of the unselected points.

To transform a frame without its contents when you're scaling (or rotating or skewing) an object using the Transform palette, turn off the Transform Content option on the Transform palette menu or Control palette menu (see Figure 9-3). You can transform a frame without its contents using the tools by first Option/Alt-clicking on the edge of the frame with the Direct Selection tool—this way the frame is selected but the content is not. Or you can turn off the Transform Content check box in the transform tool's dialog box (double-click on the tool in the Tools palette).

FIGURE 9-3
Transforming
Path Contents

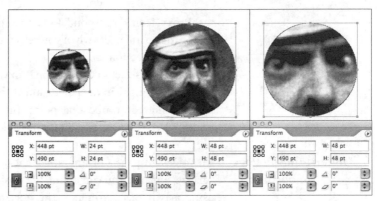

Untransformed object.

Object scaled with the
Transform Content
option turned off.

Object scaled with the
Transform Content
option turned on.

Numbers Are Your Friends

If numbers scare you, you're going to be scared by the Transform palette and Control palette. Don't give in to math anxiety—these palettes are simply too useful to avoid. The first step in taming them is to understand what it is these controls are called, and what they can do for you (see Figure 9-4). To display the Transform palette, press F9; to display the Control palette, press Command-Option-6/Ctrl-Alt-6.

The Proxy   A "proxy" is something that stands in for something (or someone) else. The Proxy in the Transform and Control palettes stands in for the object or objects you've selected (see Figure 9-5). The points on

FIGURE 9-4
Friendly Numbers

*Coordinates of the point
correspond to the point
selected on the Proxy,
and are measured
relative to the current
zero point on the ruler.*

*The Control palette has all of the
controls found in the Transform
palette, and offers a few additional
options, as well.*

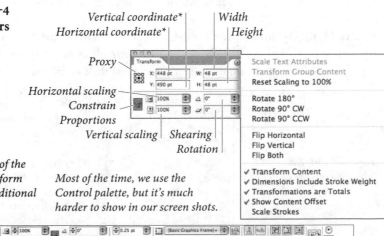

*Most of the time, we use the
Control palette, but it's much
harder to show in our screen shots.*

the Proxy icon correspond to the selection handles InDesign displays around an object when you select it with the Selection tool (not the Direct Selection tool).

When you select a point on the Proxy, you're telling InDesign that changes you make in the palette affect that point (the X and Y fields), or are centered around that point (the Width, Height, Horizontal Scaling, Vertical Scaling, Rotation Angle, and Shear Angle fields).

Understanding Page Coordinates

An InDesign page—or any other flat object—is a two-dimensional surface; a plane. You can define the position of any point on a plane using a pair of coordinates: the horizontal location (traditionally referred to as "X") and the vertical location ("Y"). The numbers you see in the X and Y fields of InDesign's Transform and Control palettes represent the horizontal and vertical distance of the selected point on the Proxy from the zero point.

As you move farther to the right of the horizontal zero point, the value in the X field increases; move the object to the left, and the value in the X field decreases. Horizontal locations to the left of the zero point are represented by negative numbers. As you move farther down on the page, the value in the Y field increases. Vertical locations above the zero point are represented by negative numbers. Note that this means that InDesign's vertical coordinate system is *upside down* relative to the two-dimensional coordinate system you learned in junior high school geometry class (see Figure 9-6).

Duplicating As You Transform

Hold down Option/Alt as you press Return/Enter to apply a change you've made to any of the Transform or Control palette fields, and InDesign copies the object and then applies the transformation to the duplicate (see Figure 9-7).

Palette Menu Options

The options in the Transform palette and Control palette menus apply preset transformations and control the way that transformations affect objects and their contents.

FIGURE 9-5
The Proxy

The point you select on the Proxy also sets the center of transformation.

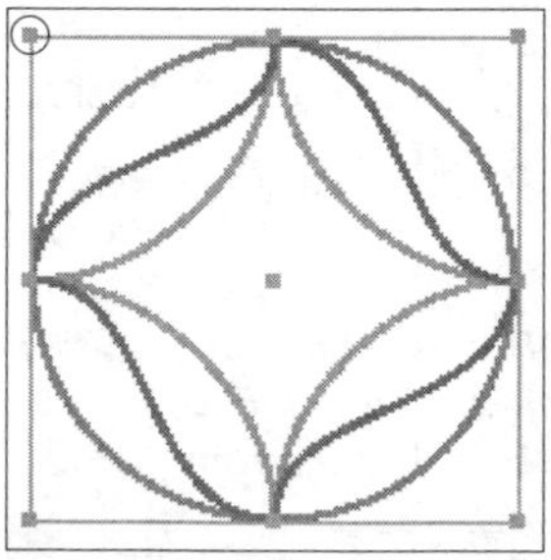

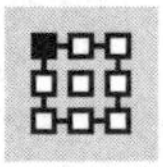

The points you see on the Proxy correspond to the selection handles you see when you select an object.

The point you select in the Proxy determines the content of the X and Y fields in the Transform palette or Control palette—select the upper-left corner (as in this example), and you'll see the coordinates of that corner of the selection.

FIGURE 9-6
Page Coordinates

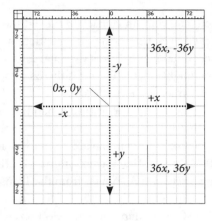

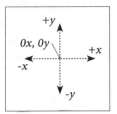

FIGURE 9-6
Page Coordinates

InDesign's two-dimensional coordinate system. All coordinates are measured from the zero point. x represents the horizontal location of a point; y represents the vertical location.

Traditional two-dimensional coordinate system (note that values on the y axis increase as you go up—the opposite of InDesign's approach).

FIGURE 9-7
Duplicating As
You Transform

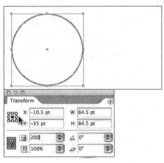

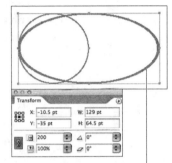

Enter a value in the Horizontal Scaling, Vertical Scaling, Width, or Height fields...

...and press Option-Return (Macintosh) or Alt-Enter (Windows). InDesign applies the transformation to a copy of the selected object.

While these features give you unprecedented control over your objects, they can seem a little overwhelming at first. Fortunately, the default settings are good enough most of the time. But the more you understand these, the more power you'll have.

Scale Text Attributes. Transforming text frames in InDesign 1.x was incredibly frustrating because the program would scale the frame (and the text in it), but the Character and Paragraph palettes would still display the original point size. For example, if you used the Scale tool to double the size of a text frame containing 12-point text with a two-pica indent, the Point Size field in the Character palette would still show "12 pt", the Left Indent field in the Paragraph palette would show "2p", and the Transform palette would show "200%".

Fortunately, Adobe changed this behavior. When you select a text frame with the Scale tool and scale it, InDesign immediately applies the transformation to the text, and the Transform palette and Control palette scaling fields revert to 100%. In the example above, the text size would show "24 pt" and the indent would appear as "4p". If

you like, you can go back to the old ways by turning off the Adjust
Text Attributes When Scaling option in the Type panel of the Preferences dialog box (press Command/Ctrl-K, then Command/Ctrl-2).
You might want to do this if there's a good chance you'll need to set
the frame back to 100% later.

Now back to the feature at hand: If you have set the preferences
so that InDesign works the old way, you can force the program to
apply the scaling to the text (effectively resetting the scaling field to
100%) by selecting the text frame with the Selection tool and choosing Scale Text Attributes from the Transform palette menu.

Transform Group Content. Select several objects on the page, group
them together (Command-G/Ctrl-G), and then apply a transformation (scale, rotate, etc.). InDesign transforms the group as a whole
around the *group's* point of transformation and displays the change
in the Transform palette and Control palette. For instance, if you
rotate the group 30 degrees, the palette fields show "30°". You can
reset the transformation to zero degrees by selecting Transform
Group Content from the Transform palette menu or Control palette
menu. Each item in the group stays transformed, but the group as a
whole is no longer considered transformed.

Rotate and Flip. Some transformations are so common that Adobe
added the following presets to the Transform and Control palettes:
Rotate 180 degrees, Rotate 90 degrees clockwise, Rotate 90 degrees
counter-clockwise, Flip Vertical, Flip Horizontal, Flip Both (see
"Rotating Objects," and "Reflecting Objects," later in this chapter).

Transform Content. As we noted earlier, the Transform Content
option (in the Transform and Control palette menus) determines
whether InDesign scales, rotates, or skews the *content* of frames
(either nested pictures or other nested objects) as you make changes
to the frame. This setting only affects transformations you apply
using the palettes, and it has no effect on text frames.

Dimensions Include Stroke Weight. What defines the dimensions
of a path? Is it the geometric representation of the path itself? Or is it
the area taken up by the path, including the stroke weight applied to
the path? We prefer to work with the geometric bounds of a path, so
we turn off the Dimensions Include Stroke Weight option. You might
prefer to work with the visible bounds of objects—if you do, turn this
option on (it's on by default).

Transformations Are Totals. When you select an object that's contained by a frame, should the palette fields reflect the state of the selected object relative to the pasteboard, or relative to the frame containing the object? That's the question you answer by turning the Transformations are Totals option on the Transform palette or Control palette menus on or off (it's on by default). When you turn this option on, InDesign displays the rotation, scaling percentages, and shear angle of the selection relative to the pasteboard. Turn this option off to display the information relative to the containing frame (see Figure 9-8).

Show Content Offset. If you nest one object inside another (like a picture in a graphic frame), and then select that nested item with the Direct Selection tool, what should appear in the X and Y fields of the Transform palette and Control palette? By default, the Show Content Offset option is turned on in either palette menu, so the X and Y fields display the offset of the nested object from the "parent" frame. For example, if you simply place an image on the page and then select

The frame containing this image has been rotated 20 degrees, as you can see by looking at the Rotation field in the Transform palette. If you use the Direct Selection tool to select the image...

...InDesign displays its rotation relative to the parent frame...

...unless you turn on the Transformations are Totals option on the Transform palette menu.

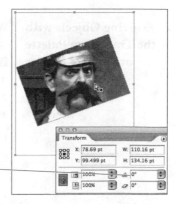

When you do that, InDesign displays the angle relative to the pasteboard or the scaling percentages relative to the original size of the image.

it with the Direct Selection tool, the fields will both show 0 (zero) because the image has not moved relative to the frame. If you turn off this option, the X and Y fields display exactly where the image sits on the page, relative to the ruler's zero point.

Moving Objects

There are (at least) four ways to move objects in InDesign—select the object and then try any of the methods shown here. (To move the content of a frame without moving the frame itself, select the Direct Selection tool and click inside the frame.)

▶ Drag the objects with the Selection or Direct Selection tool.

▶ Enter values in the X and Y fields in the Transform palette or Control palette.

▶ Drag the object using the Free Transform tool.

▶ Press the arrow, or "nudge" keys.

Moving Objects by Dragging

InDesign is just like any other program: If you want to move an object, select the object with the Selection tool or the Direct Selection tool and drag. Hold down Option/Alt as you drag to duplicate the object.

If you select an object and then immediately start dragging, you'll see only a box representing the object. If, on the other hand, you hold down the mouse button for a second before dragging, you'll see the object as you drag it. Dragging quickly is great for snapping objects into position by their outlines; waiting a second before dragging is best when you want to see the objects in a selection as you position them on the page.

Moving Objects with the Transform Palette or Control Palette

When we need precision, we always move objects by entering numbers in the X and Y fields of the Transform or Control palette (see Figure 9-9). And it's not just because we're closet rocket scientists; it's because we don't trust the screen display, even at 4000 percent magnification. You shouldn't either, when it comes to making fine adjustments in your InDesign publication.

1. Select the object you want to move.

2. Display the Transform palette or Control palette.

FIGURE 9-9
**Moving Objects Using
the X and Y Fiields**

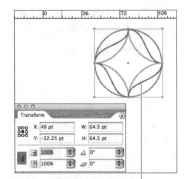

*To move an object to a
specific location on the page
or pasteboard...*

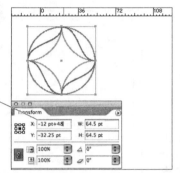

*...enter the position
in the X or Y field.*

*Press Return/Enter, and InDesign moves
the object to the location you entered.*

*To move an object by
a certain amount add (to
move to the right or down)
or subtract (to move to the
left or up) the amount to the
value in the the X or Y field.*

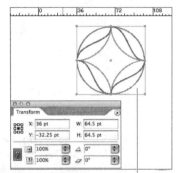

*Press Return/Enter, and InDesign moves
the object relative to is current position.*

3. Enter values in the X field (to move the object horizontally) and
   the Y field (to move the object vertically). If you want to move
   the object to an *absolute* position (relative to the current position of the zero point), enter a new value in the field; to move
   the object some distance *relative* to its current location, add or
   subtract that distance from the value in the palette field.

4. Press Return/Enter. InDesign moves the selected object.

**Moving Objects with
the Move Dialog Box**

To move objects using the controls in the Move dialog box, follow
these steps (see Figure 9-10).

1. Select an object.

2. Double-click the Selection tool (or choose Move from the Transform submenu of the Object menu). InDesign displays the Move
   dialog box.

3. Set movement options using the controls in the dialog box.
   Values here are always relative to the current position. If you

FIGURE 9-10
Moving Objects with the
Move Dialog Box

*Choose Move from the
Transform submenu of the
Object menu to display the
Move palette (or double-click
the Selection tool in the Tools
palette), and InDesign will
display the Move dialog box.*

*Turn on the
Preview
option to see
the effect of
your settings.*

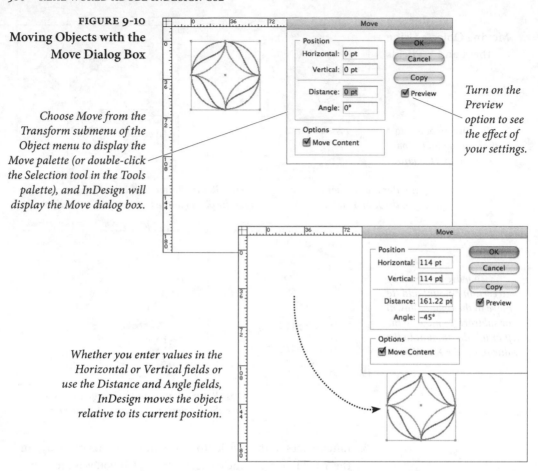

*Whether you enter values in the
Horizontal or Vertical fields or
use the Distance and Angle fields,
InDesign moves the object
relative to its current position.*

want to move a frame but not its contents, turn off the Move
Content option. To see the effect of the current settings, turn on
the Preview option.

4. Press Return/Enter to move the object, or click the Copy button
   to move a copy of the object.

Using the Free
Transform Tool

You can use the Free Transform tool to move objects—position the
tool over any part of the object other than the selection handles, and
the Free Transform tool will work just like the Selection tool. Drag
an object by its center point, and InDesign snaps the center point
to any active grids or guides. Hold down Option/Alt as you drag to
duplicate the object as you move it.

Moving Objects by Pressing Arrow Keys

As if dragging by eye and specifying coordinates weren't enough (in terms of movement options), InDesign also sports "nudge" keys. Select an object and press one of the arrow keys, and the element moves in that direction, using the increments you set in the Cursor Key field in the Units & Increments Preferences dialog box.

To move the selected object by ten times the distance you entered in the Cursor Key field, hold down Shift as you press the arrow key. To duplicate the selection as you move it, hold down Option/Alt as you press the arrow key.

Duplicating and Moving Objects with Step and Repeat

When you want to duplicate an object and move the duplicate to a new location, or create a series of duplicates, turn to InDesign's Step and Repeat feature. Select an object, then choose Step and Repeat from the Edit menu. InDesign displays the Step and Repeat dialog box. Enter the number of duplicates you want in the Repeat Count field, then enter the horizontal and vertical offsets for each duplicate. Click the OK button, and InDesign duplicates the original object, and move each duplicate as you specified (see Figure 9-11).

Note that you can create a duplicate of an object on top of the original object by entering one in the Repeat Count field and zeros in the Horizontal Offset and Vertical Offset fields.

InDesign's Duplicate command remembers the offset settings from the Step and Repeat dialog box, so the next time you select an object and choose Duplicate, the duplicate will be offset from the original by the same distance.

FIGURE 9-11
Step and Repeat

Select an object and choose Step and Repeat from the Edit menu (or press Command-Option-U/ Ctrl-Alt-U).

Enter the number of duplicates you want.

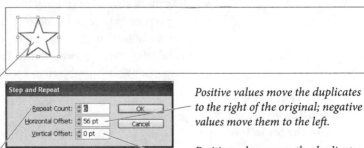

Positive values move the duplicates to the right of the original; negative values move them to the left.

Positive values move the duplicates down the page; negative values move them up.

InDesign duplicates the object, spacing the duplicates according to the values you entered in the Horizontal Offset and Vertical Offset fields.

Scaling

To change the size of an object, select the object and then use any of the following techniques.

▸ Drag the Scale tool.

▸ Drag a selection handle with the Selection tool or the Free Transform tool.

▸ Enter values in the fields of the Transform or Control palette.

▸ Enter values in the Scale dialog box.

▸ Press a keyboard shortcut.

You can also change the width of text frames by changing the width of the columns in the text frame (see Chapter 3, "Text").

Scaling with the Scale Tool

When you want to scale an object until it "looks right," use the Scale tool (see Figure 9-12).

1. Select the object you want to scale.

2. Select the Scale tool from the Tools palette (or press S).

3. Change the location of the center of transformation icon, if necessary. To do this, either drag the icon to a new location or click one of the points in the Proxy in the Transform palette.

4. Drag the Scale tool horizontally to scale the object's width, or drag vertically to scale the object's height. Dragging diagonally sizes the object's width and height. Hold down Shift as you drag to scale the object proportionally. Hold down Option/Alt as you drag to duplicate the object and scale the duplicate.

FIGURE 9-12
Scaling an Object with the Scale Tool

Select an object, move the center of transformation icon (if necessary), and then drag the Scale tool on the page or pasteboard.

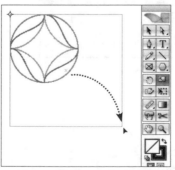

Hold down Shift to scale the object proportionally, or Option/Alt to scale a duplicate.

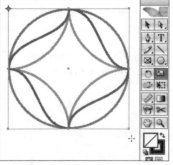

Once the object reaches the size you want, stop dragging.

**Scaling with
the Selection Tool**

As in almost any other drawing or page-layout application, you can change the size of objects by dragging their corner handles with the Pointer tool (see Figure 9-13). As you drag, the object you're dragging gets larger or smaller. Hold down Shift as you drag to resize the object proportionally.

When you scale a frame, InDesign, by default, does not scale the frame's contents. To do this, hold down Command/Ctrl as you drag one of the selection handles.

**FIGURE 9-13
Scaling an Object Using
the Selection Tool**

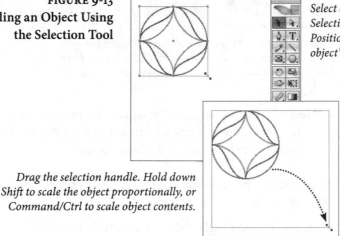

Select an object, then select the Direct Selection tool from the Tools palette. Position the cursor over one of the object's selection handles.

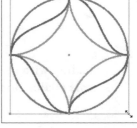

Drag the selection handle. Hold down Shift to scale the object proportionally, or Command/Ctrl to scale object contents.

Once the object reaches the size you want, stop dragging.

**Scaling with the Free
Transform Tool**

To scale an object using the Free Transform tool, follow these steps.

1. Select an object.

2. Select the Free Transform tool from the Tools palette.

3. Position the tool above one selection handles, then drag. Hold down Option/Alt to scale the object proportionally around its center point, or hold down Shift to scale proportionally.

**Scaling with the
Transform Palette or
Control Palette**

When you know you want to make an object larger or smaller by an exact percentage, or to scale the object to a specific width or height, use the Transform palette or Control palette (see Figure 9-14).

1. Select the object you want to scale.

2. Display the palette if it's not already visible.

3. Enter a new value in the Width or Height field (or in both fields), or enter a scaling percentage in the Horizontal Scaling field or the Vertical Scaling field.

FIGURE 9-14
Scaling an Object Using the Transform Palette

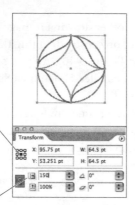

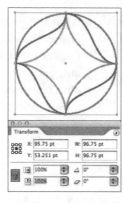

Off   On

Set the center of transformation by selecting a point on the Proxy, if necessary.

Enter a scaling percentage in the Horizontal Scale or Vertical Scale field, or enter a new value in the Width or Height field.

Turn on the Constrain Proportions control option, and InDesign applies scaling changes proportionally; turn it off to scale the object nonproportionally.

Press Return/Enter to apply the scaling change. If you hold down Command/Ctrl as you apply the change (as we have here), InDesign scales the object proportionally.

4. Press Return/Enter to scale the object. To apply proportional scaling, hold down Command/Ctrl as you press Return/Enter, or turn on the Constrain Proportions option.

Scaling with the Scale Dialog Box

To scale using the Scale dialog box, select one or more objects and follow these steps (see Figure 9-15).

1. Double-click the Scale tool (or choose Scale from the Transform submenu of the Object menu). InDesign displays the Scale dialog box.

2. Set scaling options using the controls in the dialog box. To scale the object proportionally, turn on the Uniform option and enter a scaling percentage in the Scale field. To scale an object non-proportionally, turn on the Non-Uniform option, then enter scaling percentages in the Horizontal and Vertical fields. To scale the contents of a path, turn on the Scale Content option. To see the effect of the current settings, turn on the Preview option.

3. Press Return/Enter to scale the object, or click the Copy button to scale a copy of the object.

Scaling with Keyboard Shortcuts

You can also scale the selected object by pressing keyboard shortcuts. Note, however, that these changes don't appear in the scaling percentages of the Transform palette (except for when you select an image with the Direct Selection tool).

► Press Command-. (period)/Ctrl-. to increase the size of the object by one percent.

FIGURE 9-15
FIGURE 9-15
Scaling an Object Using
the Scale Dialog Box

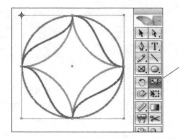

Double-click the Scale tool in the Tools palette (or choose Scale from the Transform submenu of the Object menu)...

...and InDesign displays the Scale dialog box.

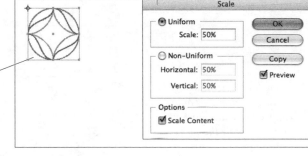

Enter a scaling percentage. If you've turned on the Preview option, you'll see the result of the scaling. Click OK to apply the scaling.

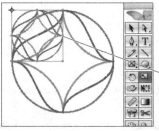

If you click the Copy button, InDesign duplicates the selected object (or objects) and applies the scaling to the copy.

▶ Press Command-, (comma)/Ctrl-, to decrease the size by one percent.

▶ Press Command-Shift-. (period)/Ctrl-Shift-. to increase the size by five percent.

▶ Press Command-Shift-, (comma)/Ctrl-Shift-, to decrease the size by five percent.

Scaling Strokes

We often want to scale a page item without scaling its stroke. This is especially true when we're scaling frames containing images—we want to resize the frame and the image, but leave the stroke of the frame the same width. To do this, turn off the Scale Strokes option on the Transform Palette or Control palette menu before you scale the frame (see Figure 9-16).

Resetting Stroke Scaling

You goofed. You scaled a page item (a rectangle, ellipse, polygon, or graphic line) while the Scale Strokes option was on. To reset the stroke of a scaled InDesign page item, select the item, then choose

FIGURE 9-16
Scaling Strokes (or Not)

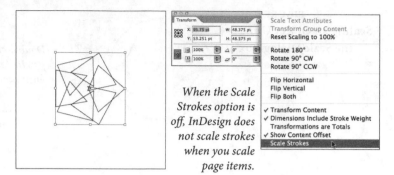

*When the Scale
Strokes option is
off, InDesign does
not scale strokes
when you scale
page items.*

*Note that resizing a page
item by dragging or by
using a keyboard shortcut
does not scale the stroke.*

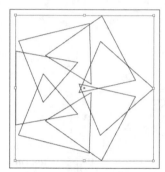

Scale Strokes option off.   *Scale Strokes option on.*

Reset Scaling to 100% from the Transform palette menu or the Control palette menu. At that point, you can apply the stroke weight you really want, rather than the scaled weight.

Rotating Objects

InDesign can rotate any object on a page, in .001-degree increments. The rotation angle is always shown relative to the pasteboard (where 0 degrees is horizontal) or to the frame containing the rotated object (unless you've turned on the Transformations are Totals option). If you rotate an object by 30 degrees, entering that rotation value again in the Rotation Angle field will not change the rotation of the object. To do that, you'd need to enter "+30" following the value shown in the Rotation Angle field—or use the Rotate dialog box.

**Rotating with
the Rotate Tool**

To rotate an object "by eye," select the object or objects and follow these steps (see Figure 9-17).

1. Select the Rotate tool from the Tools palette (or press R).

FIGURE 9-17
Rotating an Object Using the Rotate Tool

Select the Rotate tool from the Tools palette.

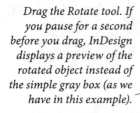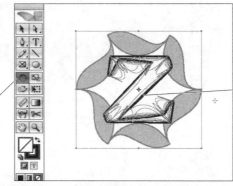

Move the center of transformation icon, if necessary, to set the point you want to rotate around.

Drag the Rotate tool. If you pause for a second before you drag, InDesign displays a preview of the rotated object instead of the simple gray box (as we have in this example).

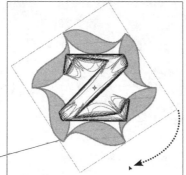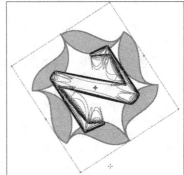

When the object looks the way you want it to, stop dragging.

2. Drag the center of transformation to the point you want to rotate around, or click a point in the Transform palette's Proxy. To rotate around the geometric center of an object, click the center point in the Proxy.

3. Drag the Rotate tool.

4. When the object looks the way you want it to, stop dragging.

Rotating with the Free Transform Tool

To rotate an object using the Free Transform tool, follow these steps (see Figure 9-18).

1. Select an object and then choose the Free Transform tool from the Tools palette (or press E).

2. Position the tool anywhere outside of the object's selection handles, then drag. InDesign rotates the object around its center point, or hold down Shift as you drag to constrain rotation to 45-degree increments.

FIGURE 9-18
**Rotating an Object with
the Free Transform Tool**

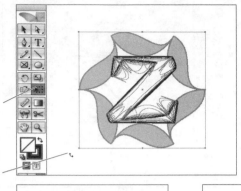

*Select the Free Transform
tool from the Tools palette.*

*Position the cursor
outside one of the
object's selection
handles.*

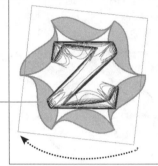

*Drag the Free Transform
tool. If you pause for a
second before you drag,
InDesign displays a preview
of the rotated object rather
than a simple bounding box
preview.*

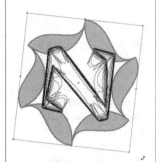

*When the object looks the way
you want it to, stop dragging.*

**Rotating with the
Transform Palette**

To rotate an object using the Transform palette or Control palette, follow these steps (see Figure 9-19).

1. Select the object or objects you want to rotate.

2. Click a point on the Proxy to set the point you want to rotate around, if necessary.

3. Enter a new value in the Rotation Angle field. To rotate the object to a specific angle, enter that angle in the field. To rotate the object relative to its current rotation angle, add to or subtract from the value in the Rotation angle field.

    You can enter positive numbers (such as "45") or negative numbers (such as "-270") between -360 and 360 degrees. Positive rotation angles rotate the selected object counterclockwise; negative values rotate the object clockwise. You enter rotation angles in .001-degree increments.

4. Press Return/Enter to rotate the object, or Option-Return/ Alt-Enter to rotate a copy of the object.

FIGURE 9-19
Rotating an Object
Using the Transform
Palette or Control
Palette

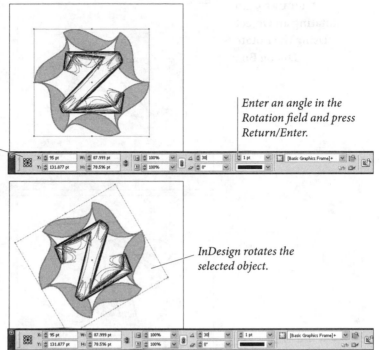

Set the center of
transformation by clicking
a point on the Proxy.

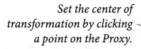

Enter an angle in the
Rotation field and press
Return/Enter.

InDesign rotates the
selected object.

Rotating with the
Rotate Dialog Box

To rotate an object using the Rotate dialog box, follow these steps (see Figure 9-20).

1. Select an object.

2. Double-click the Rotate tool. InDesign displays the Rotate dialog box.

3. Set rotation options using the controls in the dialog box.

   ▶ Enter a rotation angle in the Angle field.

   ▶ To rotate the contents of a frame or path, turn on the Rotate Content option.

   ▶ To see the effect of the current settings, turn on the Preview option.

4. Press Return/Enter to rotate the object, or click the Copy button to rotate a copy of the object.

Rotating Multiple
Selected Objects

When you rotate more than one object (we're counting groups as single objects), the objects rotate around a single point. This point can be their joint geometric center, or around any other point you've specified. They don't all rotate around their individual center points.

FIGURE 9-20
**Rotating an Object
Using the Rotate
Dialog Box**

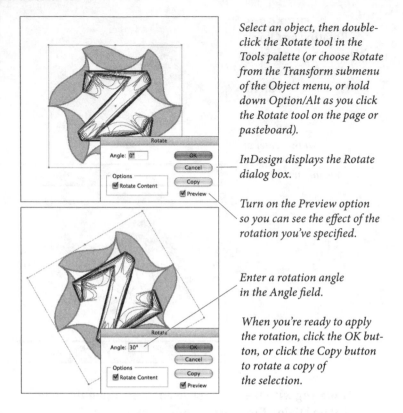

Select an object, then double-click the Rotate tool in the Tools palette (or choose Rotate from the Transform submenu of the Object menu, or hold down Option/Alt as you click the Rotate tool on the page or pasteboard).

InDesign displays the Rotate dialog box.

Turn on the Preview option so you can see the effect of the rotation you've specified.

Enter a rotation angle in the Angle field.

When you're ready to apply the rotation, click the OK button, or click the Copy button to rotate a copy of the selection.

Reflecting Objects

Reflecting—or mirroring—objects in InDesign is very simple, and you can reflect, or "flip" an object over its vertical axis, its horizontal axis, or both its vertical and horizontal axes at once. That's it. There's no reflection tool, no need to enter a reflection angle anywhere (reflecting an object across an angle is the same as reflecting the object across its horizontal or vertical axis and then rotating).

To reflect an object, follow these steps (see Figure 9-21).

1. Select the object you want to reflect.

2. Choose Flip Vertical, Flip Horizontal, or Flip Both from the Transform palette menu. InDesign reflects the selected object.

Shearing Objects

Shearing (or skewing) an object makes it appear that the plane the object's resting on has been rotated away from the plane of the page. It's good for creating perspective effects—but it's not a replacement for a serious 3D rotation program (see Figure 9-22).

FIGURE 9-21
Reflecting an Object

Select an object…

…and then choose one of the reflection options from the Transform palette or Control palette menu.

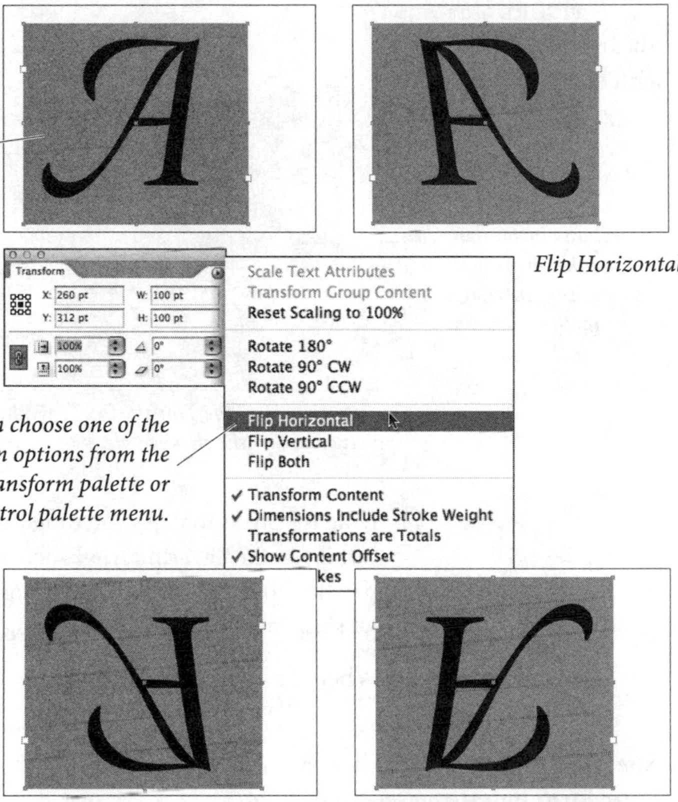

Transform
X: 260 pt
Y: 312 pt
W: 100 pt
H: 100 pt
100%
100%
0°
0°
Scale Text Attributes
Transform Group Content
Reset Scaling to 100%
Rotate 180°
Rotate 90° CW
Rotate 90° CCW
Flip Horizontal
Flip Vertical
Flip Both
✓ Transform Content
✓ Dimensions Include Stroke Weight
Transformations are Totals
✓ Show Content Offset

Flip Horizontal

Flip Vertical

Flip Both

FIGURE 9-22
Shearing an Object

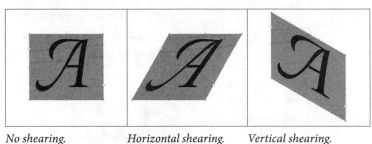

No shearing. *Horizontal shearing.* *Vertical shearing.*

Shearing with the Shear Tool

To shear an object using the Shear tool, follow the steps below (see Figure 9-23).

1. Select an object.
2. Choose the Shear tool from the Tools palette (or press O).
3. Change the location of the center of transformation icon, if necessary (you can either drag the icon to a new location, or click one of the points in the Transform palette Proxy).

FIGURE 9-23
FIGURE 9-23
Shearing an Object
with the Shear Tool

Select an object, then
drag the Shear tool.
As you drag, InDesign
shears the selection.

As you drag, the Transform
palette displays the shear angle.

When the object looks the way you
want it to, stop dragging.

4. Drag the Shear tool. As you drag the cursor, the skewing angles display in the Shearing Angle field of the Transform palette. The palette shows that vertical shearing is actually done by horizontal shearing (skewing) *and* rotating the object.

5. When the object looks the way you want it to, stop dragging.

Shearing with the
Transform Palette

To shear an object using the Transform palette, follow these steps (see Figure 9-24).

1. Select the object you want to shear.

2. Display the Transform palette, if it's not already visible.

3. Click one of the points on the Transform palette Proxy. This sets the center of transformation.

FIGURE 9-24
Shearing an Object
Using the Transform
Palette

Select an object...

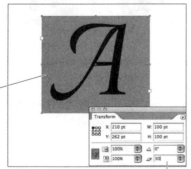

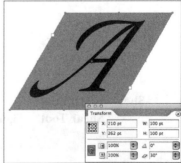

...enter a shear angle
in the Shear field of the
Transform palette.

Press Return/Enter to shear the
selection. Press Option-Return/
Alt-Enter to apply the shear to a
copy of the selection.

4. Enter an angle in the Shear Angle field, or add or subtract a value from the current content of the field.

5. Press Return/Enter to shear the selected object.

Typing value in the Shear Angle field only lets you skew (horizontal shear) the object. To create a vertical shear, type the same angle into the Rotation angle field.

Shearing with the Shear Dialog Box

To shear an object using the Shear dialog box, follow these steps (see Figure 9-25).

1. Select an object.

2. Double-click the Shear tool (or choose Shear from the Transform submenu of the Object menu). InDesign displays the Shear dialog box.

3. Set the shearing options using the controls in the dialog box. Enter an angle in the Shear Angle field, and pick an axis (the options are horizontal, vertical, or a specified angle). To rotate the contents of a path, turn on the Shear Content option.

4. Press Return/Enter to shear the object, or click the Copy button to shear a copy of the object.

FIGURE 9-25
Shearing an Object Using the Shear Dialog Box

Select an object, then double-click the Shear tool in the Tools palette (or choose Shear from the Transform submenu of the Object menu, or hold down Option/Alt as you click the Shear tool on the page or pasteboard).

InDesign displays the Shear dialog box.

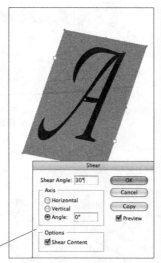

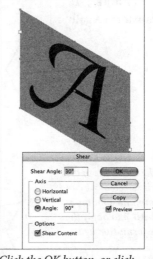

Turn on the Preview option so you can see the effect of the shearing you've specified.

Enter a shear angle in the Shear Angle field. Specify the shear axis you want to use.

Click the OK button, or click the Copy button to shear a copy of the selection.

Repeating Transformations

The options on the Transform Again submenu of the Object menu give you a way to repeat transformations you've recently applied (see Figure 9-26). You can repeat individual transformations, or you can repeat a series of transformations. InDesign will remember an individual transformation until you apply a different transformation, and will keep track of any uninterrupted sequence of transformations.

How it works: select an object and apply a transformation, then select another object and choose one of the options from the Transform Again submenu of the Object menu or use the associated keyboard shortcut. There are four ways to use Transform Again:

▶ **Transform Again.** Applies the most recent transformation to the selected object or objects.

▶ **Transform Again Individually.** Applies the most recent transformation to each object in the selection (see Figure 9-27).

▶ **Transform Sequence Again.** Applies the most recent series of transformations to the selected objects (see Figure 9-28).

▶ **Transform Sequence Again Individually.** Applies the most recent series of transformations to each object in the selection.

FIGURE 9-26
Transform Again

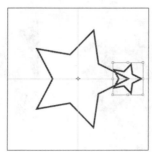

In this example, we'll select an object and rotate a copy of it (by pressing the Copy button) by a specified amount.

While the duplicate of the object is selected, we can press Command-Option-3/ Ctrl-Alt-3 to apply the transformation again.

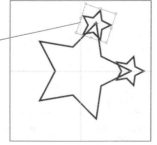

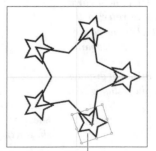

You can repeat the transformation as many times as you like, and you can apply it to other objects.

FIGURE 9-27
Transform
Sequence Again

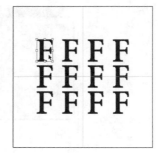
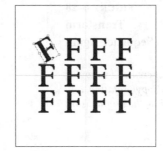

After you've selected and transformed an object...

...you can select other objects and apply the same transformation.

When you choose Transform Again, InDesign transforms all of the objects in the selection as a unit; choose Transform Again Individually to transform each item in the selection.

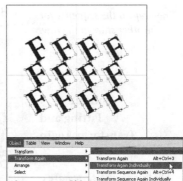

Fitting options that you apply to a frame can also be repeated using Transform again (see Figure 9-29).

Locking Object Positions

In InDesign, you can lock an object's position—which means that you can't transform it. You can, however, select the object, copy the object, or change its appearance.

To lock an object, select it and press Command-L/Ctrl-L (or choose Lock Position from the Object menu). To unlock an object, press Command-Option-L/Ctrl-Alt-L (or choose Unlock Position from the Object menu).

FIGURE 9-28
Transform Sequence Again

Object created by moving (with Copy), rotating, and scaling the original star.

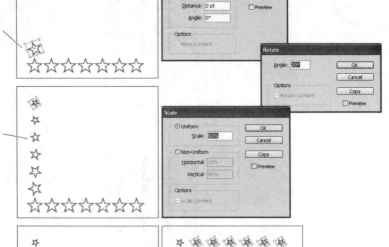

Repeat the sequence of transformations using Transform Sequence Again Individually.

Then repeat the sequence for the other stars in the row.

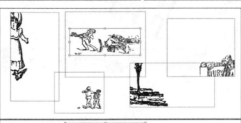

FIGURE 9-29
Fitting and Transform Again

In this example, we have a variety of images in varying degrees of distress.

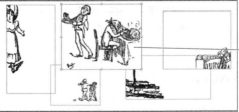

We apply proportional scaling to one of the graphics, and then apply Fit Content Proportionally and Fit Frame to Content.

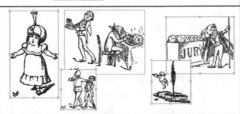

We then select all of the other graphics and choose Transform Sequence Again Individually. Much better!

Of course, another good way to lock an object is to place it on a layer and then lock the layer. An object on a locked layer is totally locked; you can't even select it.

Aligning and Distributing Objects

For many of us, MacDraw ushered in the era of object alignment. You could align the left, right, top, bottom, or center of selected objects. It was the greatest. We spent whole afternoons just aligning things. You couldn't do that in MacPaint.

We consider alignment and distribution to be transformations (in case you're wondering what the topics are doing in this chapter), by the way, because they amount to automated methods of moving objects.

InDesign features both object alignment and object distribution. InDesign aligns objects based on the object's bounding box—more or less what you see when you select the object with the Free Transform tool.

When you distribute objects you're telling InDesign to evenly arrange the selected objects. Objects can be distributed inside the area occupied by the objects, or by a specific distance.

Aligning Objects

When you've selected the objects you want to align, press Shift-F7 to display the Align palette. Click one of the the alignment buttons to align the selected objects (see Figure 9-30).

If you've locked the position of an object in the selection, InDesign does not move that object when you apply an alignment. If an object doesn't seem to be following the herd, chances are good that it's locked—choose Unlock Position from the Object menu to apply alignment to it.

If you find you're using a specific alignment frequently, why not assign a keyboard shortcut to it? While none of the alignment or distirbution options are assigned a keyboard shortcut by default, you can use the Keyboard Shortcuts dialog box to add this feature to your copy of InDesign (see Figure 9-31).

Distributing Objects

Have you ever wanted to space a bunch of objects at even distances from each other (from each other's centers, at any rate) across a particular horizontal measurement? If you have, InDesign's Distribute feature should make your day. To distribute the selected objects inside the rectangle defined by the objects' bounding box, click one

FIGURE 9-30
Aligning Objects

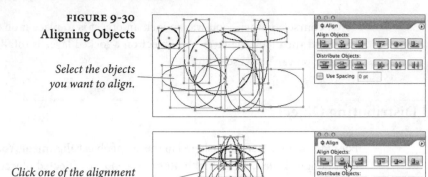

*Select the objects
you want to align.*

*You can hide or
show the Align
palette by
pressing Shift-F7.*

*Click one of the alignment
buttons. InDesign aligns the
selected objects.*

*When you want to apply
both a horizontal and a
vertical alignment, it's a
two-step process: apply
one of the alignments,
then apply the other.*

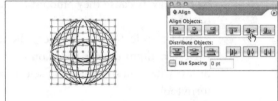

*In this example,
we've aligned the
objects to their
horizontal cen-
ters, then to their
vertical centers.*

FIGURE 9-31
Alignment Shortcuts

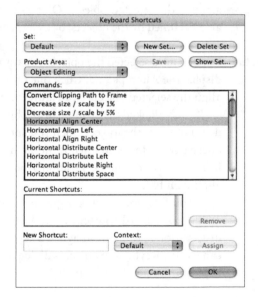

of the distribute buttons in the Align palette. InDesign distributes
the objects as you've specified (see Figure 9-32).

To distribute (or space) the objects by a specified distance, use the
Use Spacing option in either the Distribute Objects section of the
Align palette or the Distribute Spacing section (see Figure 9-33).

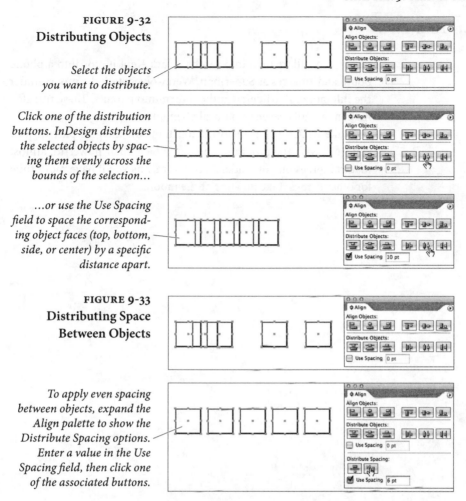

FIGURE 9-32
Distributing Objects

Select the objects you want to distribute.

Click one of the distribution buttons. InDesign distributes the selected objects by spacing them evenly across the bounds of the selection...

...or use the Use Spacing field to space the corresponding object faces (top, bottom, side, or center) by a specific distance apart.

FIGURE 9-33
Distributing Space Between Objects

To apply even spacing between objects, expand the Align palette to show the Distribute Spacing options. Enter a value in the Use Spacing field, then click one of the associated buttons.

When you click one of the buttons in the Distribute Objects section, the value you enter in the Use Spacing field sets the distance between the object sides (top, bottom, right, and left) or object centers (vertical or horizontal). If you enter 12 points, for example, and then click the Horizontal Distribute Lefts button, InDesign spaces the left edges of the objects in the selection 12 points apart.

When you use the Use Spacing option in the Distribute Spacing section, InDesign spaces the objects apart by the distance you enter in the Use Spacing field. Click the Vertical Distribute Space button to distribute the objects vertically, or click the Horizontal Distribute Space button to distribute the objects horizontally. Note, in addition, that the objects do not need to be the same shape or size—you'll still get the correct spacing between objects.

Transform Your Life!

Fuzzy caterpillars turn into moths. Clark Kent jumps into a phone booth and emerges as Superman. Werewolves stalk the moors under the full moon. Bewildered authors turn into parents. These transformations are all everyday, natural phenomena.

Make InDesign's transformation tools an integral part of how you work with the program, and you'll have their powerful, almost magical forces on your side. And that means you'll have more time for other things. Like howling at the moon.

CHAPTER 10

Color

Color communicates, telling us things about the object bearing the color. Without color cues, we'd have a hard time guessing the ripeness of a fruit or distinguishing a poisonous mushroom from an edible one. And many animals would have a hard time figuring out when to mate, or with whom.

We associate colors with human emotions: we are green with envy; we've got the blues; we see red. Colors affect our emotions as well. Various studies suggest that we think best in a room of one color, and relax best in a room of another color.

What does all this mean? Color's important. A rule of thumb in advertising is that a color advertisement gets several times the response of a black-and-white ad. Designers of mail-order catalogs tell us that color is often cited as the reason for buying a product—and it's usually the reason a product is returned.

InDesign features a formidable array of features dedicated to creating, editing, applying, and printing colors. In addition, InDesign's color management can make what you see on your screen much closer to what you'll get when you print. Before we go any further, however, we have to talk about color printing.

Seeing Color, Printing Color

It's impossible to discuss the process of creating and using colors in InDesign without first talking a little about printing and visual perception. If you already know about those topics, feel free to skip ahead, though you'll miss all the jokes if you do. Everyone else should note that this is a very simple explanation of a pair of very bizarre and complex processes.

The Color Spectrum and Color Gamuts

The colors we see when we look at the world around us are the light reflected from objects in our field of view. In our eyes, the cornea, iris, and pupil conspire to cast this light on a rejoicing multitude of photoreceptive cells—the rods and cones at the back of the retina.

These cells, in turn, use chemical and electrical signals to pass information about the light striking them on to our visual cortex. And, after a series of profoundly *weird* things happen in the visual cortex (a friend of ours is an academic studying human visual perception—we don't understand a word she says), we see a picture.

The *visible spectrum* is the range of light wavelengths visible to the human eye (not your eye, or our eyes, but an idealized, "normal" human eye) ranging from the top of the ultraviolet (wavelengths around $7 * 10^{-5}$ centimeters, or 700 nanometers) to the bottom of the infrared (wavelengths around $4 * 10^{-5}$ centimeters, or 400 nanometers). It's the job of our scanners, monitors, printers, and printing presses to reproduce the colors we see in the visible spectrum.

Alas, they all fail miserably.

The range of color a device, color model, or printing method is capable of reproducing is referred to as its *color gamut*. There's no device, apart from your eye, that's capable of reproducing the range of light that your eye is capable of seeing. And even your eye isn't consistent from day to day.

We've settled, therefore, on a reasonably well-known and well-understood set of compromises.

The Printing Process

After you've printed your InDesign publication on film and delivered it to your commercial printer (we like to walk in through the loading dock), the printer takes the film and uses it to expose (or "burn") a photosensitive printing plate. (These days, you might skip all of these steps and print directly to a printing plate.) The surface of the plate has been chemically treated to repel ink. When you expose the printing plate to light, the image areas from your film become able to accept ink. Once the plate's been exposed, the printer attaches the printing plate to the cylinder of a printing press.

As the cylinder holding the plate turns, the parts of it bearing the image become coated with ink, which is transferred (via another, rubber-covered cylinder—the offset cylinder) to the paper. This transfer is where we get the term "offset," as in "offset printing," because the printing plate itself does not touch your paper.

Printing presses put ink on paper one ink at a time. Some presses have more than one printing cylinder (also called a printing "head" or "tower") and can print several colors of ink on a sheet of paper in one pass through the press, but each printing cylinder carries only one color of ink. We can make it look like we've gotten more than one color of ink on a printing plate by using screens—patterns of dots that, from a distance, fool the eye into thinking it sees a separate color.

Spot and Process Inks

Spot-color printing is simple: your commercial printer uses inks that exactly match the color you want (or mixes inks to get the same result), then loads the press with that ink. In spot-color printing, we sometimes use "tint builds"—screens of inks printed on top of each other—to create a new color without using another ink. In process-color printing, tint builds are where it's at; we use overlapping screens of four inks (cyan, magenta, yellow, and black) to simulate part of the spectrum of visible color. If everything's gone well, the dots of the different-colored inks are placed near each other in a pattern called a rosette (see Color Figure 6 on the color pages for an example of a rosette).

Process-color printing can't simulate all the colors our eyes can see (notably very saturated colors, or metallic and fluorescent colors), but it can print color photographic images. Spot colors can print any color you can make with pigments, but aren't generally used to reproduce color photographic images (that's what process color printing was designed to be good at).

Color in InDesign

Now that you know all about color perception and color printing, it's time to get down to the process of specifying and applying colors in your InDesign publication.

Named and Unnamed Colors

InDesign has two basic methods for working with color: unnamed colors and color swatches. What's the difference? Both unnamed colors and color swatches can change the appearance of an object's fill or stroke, but swatches establish a relationship between the object and the named color swatch. Change the definition of the color swatch, and the color of all of the objects you've applied that swatch to will change as well.

Here's another way to look at it: unnamed colors are to color swatches as local character formatting is to a character style. You get the *appearance* you're looking for, but you don't get the link between the style (in this case, the color swatch) and the object.

Why do you need that link? Because people change their minds. Your publication might have started its life intended for a two-color press, but, because of a recent change in management, it's now a six-color job (lucky you!). The client's corporate color may have been Pantone 327 when you started the job, but it's now Pantone 199. You get the idea—something like this has probably happened to you.

If you've used unnamed colors, there's nothing to do but claw your way through the objects in your publication, selecting and changing each affected object. If you've used named color swatches, on the other hand, making a change of this sort is a simple task: change the definition of the swatch, and you've changed the color applied to all of the fills and strokes formatted using the swatch.

Colors and Inks

Spot colors in your publication correspond directly to the inks you'll use to print the publication; process colors are made up of some or all of the four process inks (cyan, magenta, yellow, and black). When you create, edit, or import a color in InDesign, you're working with a single ink, or a tint of that ink, or (for a process color or mixed ink swatch) a set of inks that, when printed, optically blend together to produce the color you want to see.

When it comes time to print, the ink list (in the Output panel of the Print dialog box) displays the inks needed to print the colors you have defined in your publication. You'll always see the process inks (cyan, magenta, yellow, and black) in the ink list, whether you've defined process colors or not. If you've defined spot colors, you'll see the spot inks associated with those colors in the ink list. If you want, you can print simulations of spot colors using process inks by clicking the All to Process button in the Ink Manager (we cover the Ink Manager later in this chapter). This converts the colors as you print—the color definitions are not changed in your publication.

Spot Color or Process Color or Both?

Whether you use spot colors, process colors, or both depends on the needs of your specific publication—which has to do with your printing budget, your communications goals, and, most importantly, your mood. If you plan to use color photographs in your publication, you're going to have to use at least the four process inks. If you're printing on a tight budget, you'll probably want to forgo the color images and use only one or two inks.

When you're defining a color, you're offered a variety of choices: is the color a spot color, a process color, or a tint? Which color model should you use? Should you choose a color from a swatch library, or make up your own color definition? The following sections attempt to answer these questions.

Color Models

InDesign lets you define colors using any of three color models—CMYK, RGB, and LAB. Which color model should you use? That depends on how you plan to produce your publication.

Spot colors. If you're working with spot colors, you can use RGB, LAB, or a swatch book like a Pantone color, and it really doesn't matter what the color looks like on the screen, as long as you let your commercial printer know what color of ink they need to use to print your publication. How do you know what ink to use? If you use Pantone colors (the most likely scenario), you can tell them the PMS color number. If you don't, it's trickier, but your printer can help you match the color you want to an ink they can mix.

If you plan to use Pantone spot colors, save yourself some trouble: choose swatches from the Pantone swatch libraries, rather than trying to mix the color yourself. Note that, in any case, you can't use the Color palette to create a spot color from scratch—to do that, you'll have to use the controls in the New Color Swatch dialog box or the Swatch Options dialog box (both of which we talk about later in this chapter).

Process colors. If you're working with process colors, *specify your color using the CMYK color model or a CMYK color-matching system*, or be ready for some surprises when your publication gets printed. It's always best to look at a printed sample of the process color (like those in the Trumatch or Pantone Process swatch books) and enter the values given in the sample book for the color. In other words, trust what you see on paper, not what you see on your screen.

Onscreen colors. If you're creating a publication for online distribution (on a CD-ROM or on the Web), use the RGB color model. If you're creating a publication for distribution on the Web, you may also want to stick with "browser safe" colors—colors that appear without dithering on old 8-bit color screens. For more on picking browser-safe colors, see "Swatch Libraries," later in this chapter.

Tints. If you're trying to create a tint of an existing color (process or spot), use the Swatches palette—don't try to approximate the right shade by mixing colors. You can base your tint on a spot color or a process color, but you can't base tints on another tint.

Color Conversion Errors. When you convert a color from one color model to another—from RGB to CMYK, for example—a certain amount of error is introduced by the process of conversion. This is because the color models don't cover the same color gamut, and because the color models have differing approaches to defining colors. Each time you convert the color, the rounding error is compounded: if you convert 100C 10M 50Y 0K to RGB, you'll get 0R 230G 128B—converting that RGB color back to CMYK will yield a color defined as 90C 0M 40Y 10K. There's no "round trip" in color model conversion.

Swatch Libraries

InDesign's swatch libraries support the most frequently used color-matching systems in the graphic arts industry, like Pantone and Trumatch. There's nothing magical about these color libraries—they're just sets of agreed-upon industry standards. Colors from swatch libraries are always named colors, and appear in your publication as swatches.

DICColor. A spot-color specifying system corresponding to inks manufactured by Dainippon Ink and Chemicals, Inc. It's something like a Japanese version of Pantone—and not seen frequently in North America or Europe—except in printing subsidiaries of Japanese printers. Still, it's a nice set of colors, which you might want to use if you can get a printer to match them.

Focoltone. A process-color specification system (mostly used in Europe). Colors in the Focoltone library are organized in sets of colors with common percentages of at least one process color. The idea is to create a library of colors that, when applied to objects, are easy to trap, or don't need trapping at all.

HKS_E, HKS_N, HKS_D, HKS_K. Where do these colors come from, and what do they want? No one knows (except perhaps some secret U.S. government agency, and they're not telling). There's no mention of them in the documentation, and the only information we've been able to glean from our usually reliable European sources says they're used almost exclusively by architects and industrial designers in Germany. Snooping around in the library itself, we see that they're spot colors defined using the CMYK model.

Pantone Coated, Pantone Matte, Pantone Uncoated. Sets of spot-color inks manufactured by Pantone, Inc. These inks are the industry standard for spot color in the North American printing business (as always, ask your commercial printer). The onscreen preview of the colors changes slightly in each set, attempting to simulate how this color would appear on each type of paper stock.

Pantone Process. A set of Pantone process-color tint builds. These colors have no relation to the Pantone spot colors.

System (Macintosh), System (Windows). These two swatch libraries contain the 8-bit RGB color palettes for their respective systems. We can't find any good reason to use these.

Toyo Color Finder. A spot-color library for matching inks from the Toyo Ink Manufacturing Company, Ltd., and corresponding to their Toyo 88 Color Guide ink sample book. Like DIC, Toyo is primarily used in Asian countries, and isn't seen much in Europe or North America.

Trumatch. A process-color specifying system featuring small percentage changes from one process color to another. The Trumatch swatch book gives you a good set of printed examples for specifying process color (this is David's favorite process-color swatch book because it's laid out in a very intuitive manner).

Web. In the bad old days, most computers could only display 8-bit color—only 256 different colors at any one time, and some of those colors were reserved by the operating system. Any color outside of these 256 would get dithered (like an airbrush spatter of two different colors to simulate a third). If you're choosing colors for an onscreen purpose (like the Web), you can avoid dithering on those old systems by using a color from the Web palette. However, we rarely build Web pages in InDesign, and almost no one in the industrialized nations has an 8-bit video system anymore anyway, so we usually just ignore these.

InDesign's Color Controls

InDesign's controls for working with color are found in several palettes and menus. The most important palettes are the Toolbox, because it contains the Fill selector and the Stroke selector, and the Swatches palette, because it contains tools for defining, editing, and applying swatches (which can be colors, gradients, or tints) to objects.

You can also use the Color palette and the Gradient palette to create and apply unnamed colors and gradients—but, as we've noted earlier, you'll be better off if you use named color swatches. If you apply a color to an object using the Color palette, there is no swatch associated with it—it's an *unnamed color*. Unnamed colors are a nightmare for service bureaus and printers because it's hard for them to figure out what colors you used if they need to troubleshoot your file. They can also be a nightmare for you if you ever need to go back to change a color. Given that everything you can do using the Color palette can be accomplished using the Swatches palette, we recommend just leaving the Color palette closed.

Fill and Stroke Selectors

Stroke selector active

Fill selector active

Fill text selector active

At the bottom of the Tool palette and in the upper-left corner of the Swatches palette and the Color palette, you'll see the Fill selector and the Stroke selector. These aren't labeled in any way (unless you count the tool help we always turn off), but the Fill selector is the filled square on the left (here's proof that InDesign's user interface, while easy to use, is hard to write about). When you want to work with an object's fill, click the Fill selector; to work with an object's stroke, press the Stroke selector (the outlined square). InDesign shows you which selector is active by bringing it to the front.

Honestly, we almost never actually click on those squares; rather, we use these favorite shortcuts for working with the Fill and Stroke selectors.

▸ Press X (this is another of those keyboard shortcuts that doesn't work when you're editing text) to toggle between the Fill selector and the Stroke selector.

▸ Press Shift-X to swap fill and stroke colors (this shortcut is the same as clicking the double-headed arrow Swap Fill and Stroke icon).

▸ Press D to apply the default fill and stroke colors to the selected object (black stroke and a "None" fill).

▶ To apply the currently selected swatch to an object's stroke or fill, click the corresponding selector, then click the Apply Color button (or click the swatch itself, or press comma). To remove a fill or stroke from the selected object, click the appropriate selector and then click the Apply None button (or click the None swatch in the Swatches palette, or press /). To apply the last-used gradient, click the Apply Gradient button at the bottom of the Tool palette (or press period).

Swatches Palette

The Swatches palette is InDesign's "color control center"—it's where you create, edit, and apply colors, tints, and gradients. The Swatches palette often displays a bewildering array of icons and symbols. What does it all mean? To find out, take a look at Figure 10-1.

Press Command-Option/Ctrl-Alt and click inside the Swatches palette to activate the list. Once you've done this, you can select a color by typing its name, or move up and down in the list of swatches using the arrow keys. (But note that this will change the color of any

FIGURE 10-1
Swatches Palette

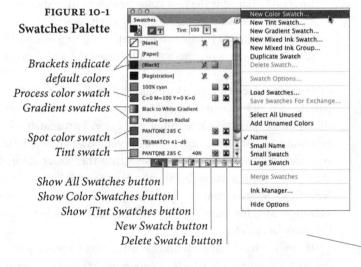

Brackets indicate default colors
Process color swatch
Gradient swatches
Spot color swatch
Tint swatch

Show All Swatches button
Show Color Swatches button
Show Tint Swatches button
New Swatch button
Delete Swatch button

To display the Swatches palette, press F5.

The colors "None" and "Black" cannot be edited.

Process color icon
Spot color icon
CMYK icon
RGB color icon
LAB color icon
Registration color icon
Mixed ink icon

Select this to hide the Tint, Object selector, and Stroke/Fill selector. (Why would you do this?)

Alternative views of the Swatches palette

Small name

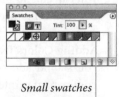

Small swatches (hover cursor over color to see title)

Large swatches

selected objects on any page. We prefer to press Command-Shift-A/ Ctrl-Shift-A to deselect all objects before messing with swatches.)

Creating a color swatch. To create a color swatch, follow these steps (see Figure 10-2).

1. Choose New Color Swatch from the Swatches palette menu. InDesign displays the New Color Swatch dialog box, set to duplicate whatever the currently selected color is. As long as None or Paper is not selected in the Swatches palette, you can also open this dialog box by Option/Alt-clicking on the New Swatch button at the bottom of the palette.

2. Enter a name for the new color swatch (it's optional—InDesign will have filled in the Name field with a default name).

3. Define the color using the controls in the New Color Swatch dialog box.

4. Click the OK button or press Return/Enter to close the dialog box. InDesign adds the new color swatch to the list of swatches shown in the Swatches palette. Alternately, you can click the Add button to add the swatch to the list and immediately start working on a new swatch (without closing the dialog box first).

Adding Unnamed Colors. As we said earlier, if you've used the Color palette to apply a color to an object, that color will not appear in the Swatches palette; it's an unnamed color. Fortunately, there are two ways to add unnamed colors to your Swatches palette. First, you can add unnamed colors by selecting the object colored with the unnamed color, then clicking the New Swatch button (or choose New Color Swatch from the Swatches palette menu, then click OK). InDesign adds the color applied to the object to the list of colors in the Swatches palette.

If you've created more than one unnamed color, or you're working with a document in which someone else applied unnamed colors, you can add all these colors to the Swatches palette at once by selecting Add Unnamed Colors from the palette's menu.

Adding Colors from a Swatch Library. Most of the time, we think you should add colors from swatch libraries. Why? Because your commercial printer wants you to (when they talk in their sleep, they call out Pantone numbers and common process tint builds), and because it's the quickest way to add a named color. To choose a color from a color library, follow the steps for adding a color, above, but

FIGURE 10-2
**Creating a
Color Swatch**

*Choose New Color Swatch
from the Swatches palette
menu...*

*...or click the Add
Swatch button.*

*InDesign displays the New
Color Swatch dialog box.*

Enter a name for the color...

*...or turn on the Name with
Color Value option to have
InDesign enter a color name.*

*Set up the color type (spot
or process) and color mode
(the model used to define the
color), then adjust the color
values.*

*Click the OK button
when you're done.*

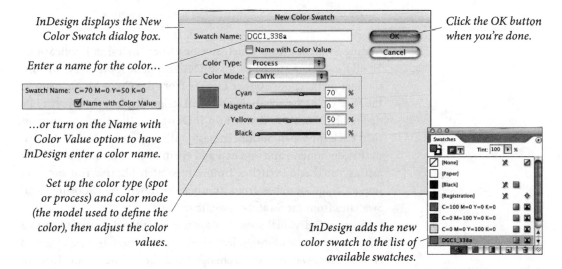

*InDesign adds the new
color swatch to the list of
available swatches.*

choose a swatch library from the Color Mode menu in the New Color Swatch dialog box (see Figure 10-3). Note that this is significantly different than in earlier versions of InDesign, which forced you to open special swatch library palettes (as in Adobe Illustrator).

In some cases, you can also change the Color Mode after selecting a color swatch. For example, if you need to simulate a Pantone spot color using process colors, first specify the Pantone color, then change the Color Mode pop-up menu to CMYK and the Color Type pop-up menu to Process. (This is based on the Pantone Spot to Process library rather than the ProSim library that you might be familiar with.) Of course, some Pantone colors don't convert to process colors particularly well because you can't make any given hue just using process colors.

FIGURE 10-3
**Working with
Swatch Libraries**

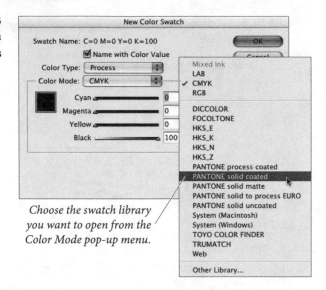

*Choose the swatch library
you want to open from the
Color Mode pop-up menu.*

Adding Swatches from Illustrator or Other InDesign Publications.
To add swatches stored in an InDesign publication or an Illustrator document, choose Other Library from the Color Mode menu in the New Color Swatch dialog box. InDesign displays the Open a File dialog box. Locate and select an InDesign or Illustrator document, then click the Open button. InDesign displays the swatches defined in that document, and you can add them to the current publication just as you'd add swatches from any swatch library. You can also import color swatches from another document by choosing Load Swatches from the Swatches palette menu.

To save individual swatches for use in other documents or Creative Suite applications, select them in the Swatches palette and choose Save Swatches for Exchange from the palette menu. This creates an .ase file which you can load with Load Swatches.

Out of Gamut Warning. InDesign constantly monitors the values of the colors you create, and when a color swatch definition falls outside the gamut defined by the default CMYK document profile, InDesign displays an alert icon next to the color sliders in the New Color Swatch or Swatch Options dialog box. To adjust the color definition so that it falls in the gamut of the separations profile, click the alert icon. We discuss document profiles in detail when we explore color management later in this chapter. Note that as long as you are choosing colors from swatch libraries or using the CMYK mode, you won't see this alert.

*Out of gamut
warning*

Creating a Tint Swatch

To create a new tint swatch, follow these steps (see Figure 10-4).

1. Select a color swatch in the Swatches palette. If you select a tint swatch, the new tint will be based on the same color as the existing tint swatch—you can't create a tint based on a tint.

2. Choose New Tint Swatch from the Swatches palette menu. InDesign displays the New Tint Swatch dialog box.

3. Enter a new value in the Tint field or drag the slider.

4. Click the OK button or press Enter to close the dialog box and add the tint to the list of swatches in the Swatches palette.

If you remove a color (see "Deleting a Swatch," later in this chapter), all tint swatches based on that color will change to tints of the color you choose in the Delete Color dialog box. If, as you remove a

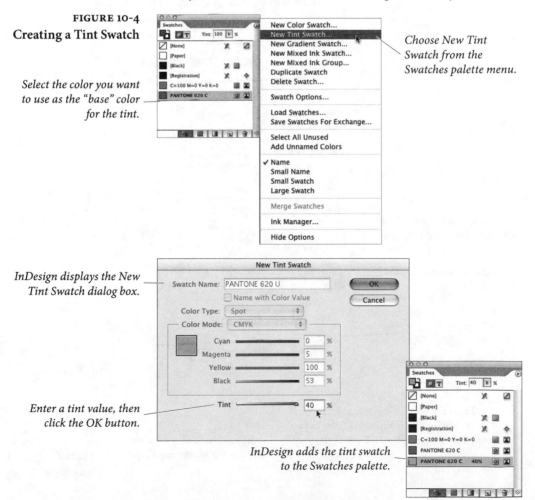

FIGURE 10-4
Creating a Tint Swatch

Select the color you want to use as the "base" color for the tint.

Choose New Tint Swatch from the Swatches palette menu.

InDesign displays the New Tint Swatch dialog box.

Enter a tint value, then click the OK button.

InDesign adds the tint swatch to the Swatches palette.

color, you choose to convert the color to the default colors "None" or "Paper," InDesign removes all of the tints based on that color from the Swatches palette. This is also what happens when you remove a color swatch and choose Unnamed Swatch as the Delete Color option.

Creating a Gradient Swatch

To create a gradient swatch, follow these steps (see Figure 10-5).

1. Choose New Gradient Swatch from the Swatches palette menu. InDesign displays the New Gradient Swatch dialog box.

2. Enter a name for the gradient (the default name of "New Gradient Swatch" isn't particularly useful). Edit the gradient's ramp and color attributes using any or all of the following techniques.

   ▶ Click on one of the gradient stops to edit it. Or, to add a new gradient stop, click below the gradient ramp.

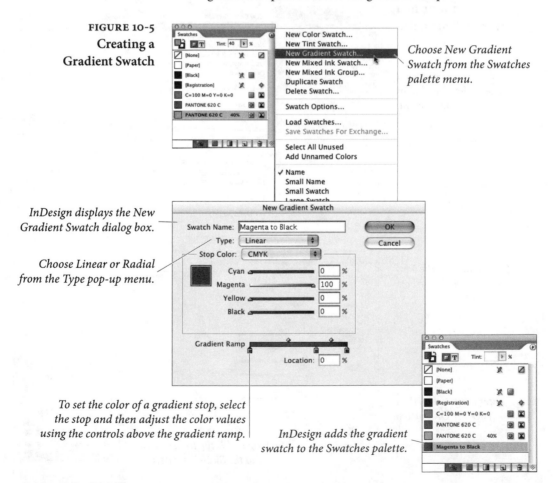

FIGURE 10-5
Creating a Gradient Swatch

Choose New Gradient Swatch from the Swatches palette menu.

InDesign displays the New Gradient Swatch dialog box.

Choose Linear or Radial from the Type pop-up menu.

To set the color of a gradient stop, select the stop and then adjust the color values using the controls above the gradient ramp.

InDesign adds the gradient swatch to the Swatches palette.

▶ To change the color of a gradient stop, select the stop, then adjust the color definition using the controls above the gradient ramp. Note that you can dial in a color or pick Swatches from the Stop Color pop-up menu (to choose a color you're already saved as a swatch). You can even pick the Paper swatch as a gradient stop color.

▶ To change the position of a gradient stop, drag it along the ramp.

▶ To delete a gradient stop, drag it away from the ramp.

▶ To change the midpoint location between any two gradient stops, drag the midpoint icon along the top of the ramp.

3. Once the gradient looks the way you want it to, click the OK button to add the gradient swatch to the Swatches palette. You can then apply this gradient to any object (or even text) as easily as applying a color swatch.

You can also build a gradient swatch directly within the Gradient palette by dragging swatches from the Color or Swatches palette on top of the gradient bar (or on top of gradient stops). When you're done with designing the blend, drag the preview swatch from the Gradient palette into the Swatches palette.

Also, once you've created a gradient swatch and applied it to an object on your page, you can fine-tune that object's gradient using the Gradient palette—reversing the order of the blend, dragging the gradient stops, and so on. Most importantly, the Gradient palette is where you can adjust a blend's angle. (Unfortunately, gradient angle can't be built in to a gradient swatch; you have to change that manually for each object or use an object style.)

Mixed Ink Swatches   If you can overlay two tints of process colors to create a third color, it stands to reason that you can do the same thing with spot colors. InDesign's Mixed Ink Swatch feature helps considerably, because it lets you build a single color based on varying percentages of other colors in your Swatches palette. However, there are some issues you need to think about when mixing spot colors (also called "tint builds" or "multi-ink colors").

▶ Most spot colors are made with inks that have a different consistency than process-color inks; the more opaque the inks, the harder it is to mix varying tints of them at the same place on a page.

▶ Some inks don't tint well; for instance, metallic and flourescent inks lose much of their special appearance unless you use a very coarse halftone.

▶ There's only one spot-color swatch book that shows what happens when you mix colors together (the Pantone Two-Color Selector), and while it's extensive, it certainly doesn't show every combination of every spot color on the market. Therefore, there's often a lot more guessing involved when you mix spot colors.

Discuss multi-ink colors with your printer before jumping in and using them. Ask them if it'll be okay to mix two particular colors on press. Perhaps they'll make a "draw-down" for you so you can see how the colors will look when they're mixed together (though this only shows you what the colors will look like when they're overprinted at 100 percent).

Making a Mixed Ink Swatch. It was painful to mix spot colors in InDesign 2 because you had to duplicate objects, apply a different color and tint to each one, and then make sure one properly overprinted the other. Now, mixing colors is as easy as one, two, three.

1. Choose New Mixed Ink Swatch from the Swatches palette menu.

2. Click in the checkbox to the left of a swatch color, then type in the percentage in the field on the right or use the color slider (see Figure 10-6). Repeat this for each color you want included in the swatch.

3. Click OK to finish, or click Add to add this swatch and start making a new one right away.

You can even mix process colors with spot colors in this dialog box. For example, you might want to create darker shades of a spot color by mixing it with a tint of black ink.

FIGURE 10-6
**Making a Mixed
Ink Swatch**

*Click in this column to add
an ink to the mix*

*Drag the sliders or enter
percentages to specify the
contribution of each ink to
the mix*

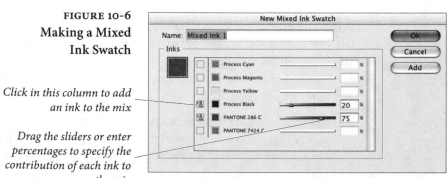

When you print color separations, each color appears on its proper plate, just as you'd expect. However, each color in a mixed ink swatch needs a correct halftone angle, or else you'll get dot-doubling (halftone spots that overprint each other, creating muddy colors) or moiré patterns when your pages come off press. We dicuss halftone angles in Chapter 11, "Printing."

Mixed Ink Groups. Once you've got the hang of mixed ink swatches, you're going to want to use them all the time because they make two- and three-color jobs look much more interesting. However, it's a pain in the *tuchus* to make a bunch of similar mixed ink swatches. That's where mixed ink groups comes in handy. InDesign can mix two or more colors together in varying percentages for you. Unfortunately, the user interface is confusing at best. Here's how you do it.

1. Select New Mixed Ink Group from the Swatches palette menu.

2. Give the group a name (preferably something descriptive).

3. Choose which inks you want in the group by clicking in the checkbox in the left column. You must pick at least two colors, of which one must be a spot color (see Figure 10-7).

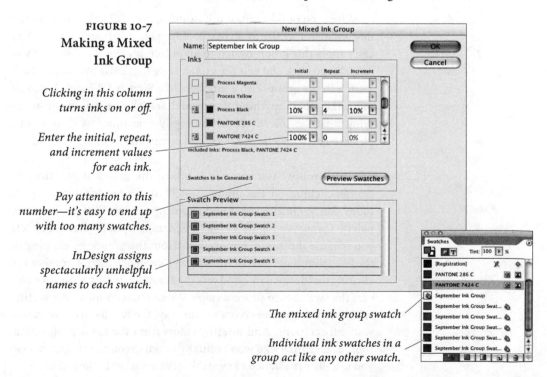

FIGURE 10-7
Making a Mixed Ink Group

Clicking in this column turns inks on or off.

Enter the initial, repeat, and increment values for each ink.

Pay attention to this number—it's easy to end up with too many swatches.

InDesign assigns spectacularly unhelpful names to each swatch.

The mixed ink group swatch

Individual ink swatches in a group act like any other swatch.

4. For each ink, pick an initial tint. For example, let's say you're trying to make darker tints of your Pantone color by adding black. The initial value for the Pantone would be 100 percent and the initial tint for black could be 10 percent.

5. The Repeat value tells InDesign how many separate ink swatches it should build. Choosing a Repeat of 4 results in five inks: the initial swatch plus four more. Set Repeat to 0 (zero) to keep the color at the initial tint throughout the group.

6. If the Repeat value is anything other than zero, you can set how much each repeat increases in the Increment field. For instance, you might want an ink to increment by 15 percent, to get swatches of 15 percent, 30 percent, 45 percent, and 60 percent.

7. Click the Preview Swatches button to see a list of all the swatches InDesign will build when you click OK. This "preview" is pretty silly, as it just shows you a bunch of little color swatches, but at least it helps you see if you made some obvious mistake (like setting Repeat to 50 instead of 5).

8. Click OK when you're satisfied.

When you build a mixed ink swatch group, InDesign adds all the new swatches to the Swatches palette, plus a "group" swatch. You can't apply this group swatch to an object; it's just there so that you can later go back and edit the group. Note that InDesign names each swatch in the group with a number (like Swatch 1, Swatch 2, and so on) rather than anything that would actually be helpful in identifying what the color is. If this annoys you as much as it annoys us, please email someone at Adobe and complain.

Editing Groups. You can edit a mixed ink group at any time by double-clicking on the group swatch in the Swatches palette (or, more slowly, clicking on it and choosing Swatch Options from the palette menu; see Figure 10-8). The Swatch Options dialog box lets you rename the group, remove inks from the group (by clicking in the left column next to the ink's name), swap one ink for another (by clicking on the ink name and picking from the pop-up menu), or convert the swatches to process color. We can't recommend converting spot colors to process colors in this way; the results may not match your expectations. And deleting colors from the list is problematic, too, because InDesign won't actually remove redundant swatches (so you usually get a bunch of swatches that are exactly the same).

FIGURE 10-8
**Mixed Ink
Group Options**

*Click in this column to
turn an ink on or off.*

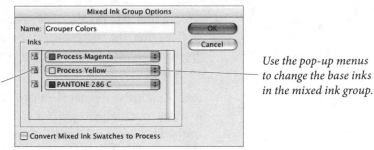

*Use the pop-up menus
to change the base inks
in the mixed ink group.*

You might want to swap one ink for another if, for instance, you have a monthly newsletter that uses a different Pantone color each month. If you used the mixed ink group swatches throughout your document, you'd simply need to change the ink in the group and the whole file's colors would change in one fell swoop.

Process Color Groups. Earlier, we noted that you must have one spot color in your mixed ink group. Fortunately, there's always a work-around. Let's say you just want various process-color green swatches. You could make a mixed ink group with cyan, yellow, and a spot color—but leave both the Initial and Repeat fields for the spot color set to 0 (zero). Then, after clicking OK, you could double-click on the group swatch and delete the spot color. This converts all the swatches to normal process-color color swatches. (But there's no way to make this a group again, other than the normal Undo feature.)

Managing Swatches

Once you've built up an armory of color, tint, gradient, and mixed ink swatches, you need to know how best to manage them.

Changing the order of the swatches in the Swatches palette. You can change the order in which colors appear in the Swatches palette by dragging them up or down in the palette. This can be handy when you've got a long list of colors and want to position frequently used colors near the top of the palette. (Be careful to deselect all objects before playing in this palette or you may apply colors accidentally.)

Editing a Swatch. To edit a swatch, do one of the following:

▶ Double-click the swatch in the Swatches palette. (We don't use this shortcut because the first click applies the swatch to the fill or stroke of any object we've selected, or applies the swatch to the default fill or stroke if no object is selected.)

▶ Select a swatch in the Swatches palette, then choose Swatch Options from the Swatches palette menu. Again, this method applies the swatch to the selection or to the document defaults, so we tend to avoid it.

▶ Press Command-Option-Shift/Ctrl-Alt-Shift and double-click a swatch to open the swatch for editing. We always use this method, as it does not apply the swatch to the selection or to the document default fill or stroke.

After any of the above actions, InDesign displays the dialog box appropriate to the type of swatch you clicked (the Edit Color Swatch, Edit Tint Swatch, or Edit Gradient Swatch dialog box). Make changes to the swatch definition, then click the OK button to close the dialog box. InDesign updates the appearance of all the objects formatted using the swatch.

Note that if you're looking for a different shade of the same basic CMYK color, you can hold down the Shift key while dragging one of the sliders. This moves the other sliders at the same time to achieve a lighter version of the same hue.

Deleting a Swatch. To delete a swatch from a publication, follow these steps (see Figure 10-9).

1. Select the swatch in the Swatches palette (you may want to deselect all objects on the page first). To select a range of swatches, hold down Shift as you click the swatch names. To select noncontiguous swatches, hold down Command/Ctrl as you click the swatch names. If you want to select all the swatches that appear in the palette but aren't used anywhere in your document, choose Select All Unused from the palette menu.

2. Click the Delete Swatch button in the Swatches palette (or choose Delete Color Swatch from the palette's menu). InDesign displays the Delete Swatch dialog box.

3. If you want to replace the color you're deleting with an existing swatch, turn on the Defined Swatch option and choose the name of the swatch from the attached pop-up menu. To replace the swatch with an unnamed color (why would you want to do this?), turn on the Unnamed Swatch option.

4. Click the OK button. InDesign deletes the swatch and applies the replacement swatch (if you selected the Defined Swatch option) or an unnamed color (if you selected the Unnamed

FIGURE 10-9
Deleting a Swatch

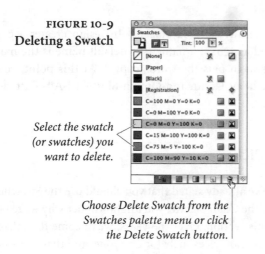

*Select the swatch
(or swatches) you
want to delete.*

*Choose Delete Swatch from the
Swatches palette menu or click
the Delete Swatch button.*

*To apply an existing swatch
to the objects colored with the
swatch you're removing, turn
on the Defined Swatch option
and choose a swatch from the
pop-up menu…*

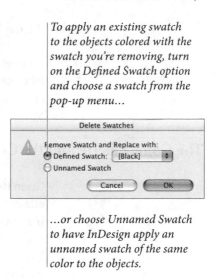

*…or choose Unnamed Swatch
to have InDesign apply an
unnamed swatch of the same
color to the objects.*

Swatch option) to all of the objects formatted using the swatch you're deleting.

As we noted earlier, when you remove a swatch that you've used as a basis for tint swatches, InDesign bases the tint swatches on the color you specified (if you selected the Defined Swatch option), or just deletes the tint swatch if you choose Unnamed Swatch, Paper, or None.

Merging Swatches. The folks at Adobe threw a rather confusing little feature into InDesign called Merge Swatches. The idea is simple: Take two or more swatches in the Swatches palette, merge them together into a single swatch, and delete the others. The problem is few people ever figure out how it works. The key is that the first swatch you select will be the one that survives, the one that the other swatches will get merged into. After clicking on one swatch (make sure nothing is selected first, or else this click will apply the color to the selected object), then Command/Ctrl-click on one or more other swatches in the palette. Finally, select Merge Swatches from the Swatches palette menu. We find this helpful only when you've got a lot of swatches you want to merge together; for one or two, we usually just use Delete Swatch.

Duplicating Swatches. If you want to base a swatch on an existing swatch, select the swatch in the Swatches palette and then choose Duplicate Swatch from the palette's menu. (You can also click the New Swatch button in the Swatches palette, but that also applies the duplicate to any selected objects.) InDesign creates a copy of the swatch and assigns it a name (the default name is the name of the original swatch plus the word "copy"). At this point, you can edit the swatch by Command-Option-Shift/Ctrl-Alt-Shift double-clicking on it.

The Color Palette and the Color Picker

Given that we've already stated that you should use the Swatches palette instead of the Color palette, you might wonder why we're bothering to write this section. Over the years, we've come to realize that our methods are not necessarily for everyone, and that some people have very different working habits from our own. For some of you, working with the Color palette and unnamed colors might be better than the process of creating named swatches—and there's nothing wrong with that.

The Color palette is always *on*—whenever you adjust the controls in the palette, you're applying them to something (either the selected object or the document's default fill and stroke formatting). For a look at the Color palette, see Figure 10-10.

The Color palette does have one thing that the Swatches palette's methods for defining colors lack: the color bar. To apply a color, drag the cursor in the Color Bar.

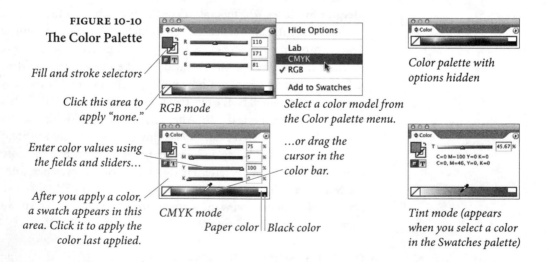

FIGURE 10-10
The Color Palette

Fill and stroke selectors

Click this area to apply "none."

Enter color values using the fields and sliders...

After you apply a color, a swatch appears in this area. Click it to apply the color last applied.

RGB mode

Select a color model from the Color palette menu.

...or drag the cursor in the color bar.

CMYK mode

Paper color | Black color

Color palette with options hidden

Tint mode (appears when you select a color in the Swatches palette)

COLOR FIGURE 1
Overprint and Knockout

Objects colored with spot color 1 set to knock out (Overprint Fill option off)

Spot color 1 plate

Spot color 2 plate

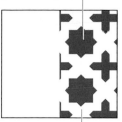

Spot color 1 knocks out spot color 2

Objects colored with spot color 1 set to overprint (Overprint Fill option on)

Spot color 1 plate

Spot color 2 plate

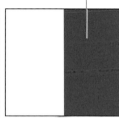

Spot color 1 overprints spot color 2

COLOR FIGURE 2
Trapping an Open Path

This cyan path needs to be trapped. Unless we've been very lucky, you'll see paper showing through around the stroke of the path.

Make sure that the stroke alignment for the paths that you're trapping is set to Align Center. If you don't do this, horrible things can happen.

To create a spread (as shown here), clone the path (by copying the path and then choosing Paste In Place from the Edit menu). Increase the stroke weight of the cloned path, then turn on the Overprint Stroke option.

To create a choke, clone the path and then decrease the stroke width of the cloned path. Set the stroke of the original path to overprint.

The thicker stroke (exaggerated in this example) overprints objects behind it.

The original path knocks out objects behind it.

Trapped path (without exaggeration)

COLOR FIGURE 3
Trapping Closed Paths and Text

Select the path you want to trap and press F10 to display the Stroke palette. Add a stroke to the object that's twice the width of the spread you want, and turn on the Overprint option.

Again, unless we've been lucky, you'll see the paper showing through around the cyan circle in this example. To prevent the paper from showing, you need to trap the object.

If you could separate the fill and the stroke, you would see something like this.

To create a choke, apply an overprinting stroke the color of the background rectangle to the ellipse.

The fill is set to knock out…

…the stroke is set to overprint.

When you print, the the stroke of the circle overprints the background square, while the fill knocks out. This creates a spread.

This example has not been trapped, so you'll probably see paper showing through around the text characters.

The cyan stroke overprints the background objects, creating a spread. In general, you want to spread the lighter color (cyan, in this example) into the darker color (magenta).

Trapped using a spread.

Because InDesign prints the fill of text over the stroke, we had to create a duplicate text frame containing characters with a magenta stroke and a fill of "None"

Trapped using a choke.

When you choke lighter characters, the apparent shape of the characters changes (not a good thing).

COLOR FIGURE 4
Overprinting and Process Colors

Background rectangle is
80C 20M 80Y 10K

 ★ 0C 80M 0Y 40K

■ ⬟ 20C 80M 20Y 40K

Overprint off
Overprint on

Where the overprinting object's percentage of a process color is zero, the background color will show through.

We've always wondered what it really means to say that you're overprinting process colors, so we created this figure to explain it to ourselves. We hope it works for you, too.

These objects contain percentages of each process color, so overprinting and non-overprinting objects print identically on each plate.

COLOR FIGURE 5
InDesign Trapping

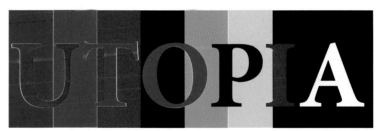

This (very beautiful) example was trapped using InDesign's default trapping settings (shown below).

Rich black (15C 15M 15Y 100K)

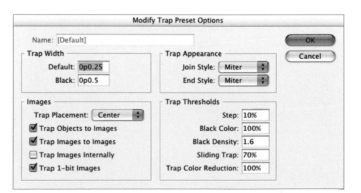

COLOR FIGURE 6
Rosettes

We can't load our printing presses with millions of inks, so we fool the eye by printing patterns of dots of (at least) four inks when we want to print scanned natural images. The pattern made by these dots is called a "rosette."

In this example, we've enlarged part of the image (of Ole's son, Max). Look at the enlarged sample from a distance, and you'll see how the dots blend together to create the appearance of more than four colors.

We've also pulled the sample apart to show the halftone screen angle used by each ink, at right.

Rosettes for an area of flat color: 10C 10M 10Y 10K (a bland gray, as shown, but good for demonstration purposes).

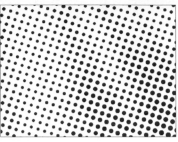

Cyan

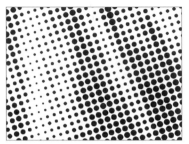

Magenta

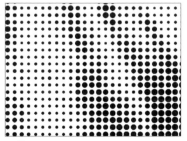

Yellow

Black

COLOR FIGURE 7
Duotones

Fake duotones: images in black ink over a background tint of cyan. The examples below do not use transparency— this comes in handy when you have to work with printers who won't or can't accept transparency in InDesign files.

Photoshop duotone. Set Photoshop duotones to 99.9% Normal Blending Mode (transparency) to get them to separate properly.

100% cyan background

50% cyan background

Grayscale image colored with a mixed ink swatch or tint build. (Use mixed ink for spot inks, tint builds for process inks.)

Fake duotone made by applying transparency to an image above a cyan colored rectangle (or vice versa).

COLOR FIGURE 8
Creating a "Neon Glow" Effect

When you need to create a "glow" effect, you typically use a blend in Illustrator or FreeHand. But, with a little help from InDesign scripting, you can create blends in InDesign. Here's one of Ole's example scripts.

Select a path in InDesign.

The path should have a fairly thick stroke (3 points or more), and you should turn on the Weight Changes Bounding Box option (on the Stroke palette menu).

Run the script. The example script on your InDesign CD has a user interface, so you don't have to edit the script to change the effect.

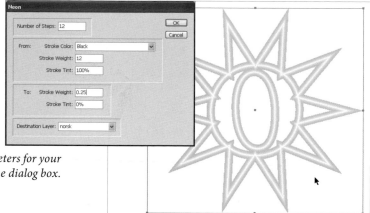

Enter the parameters for your neon effect in the dialog box.

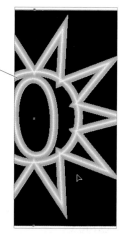

The "neon" effect looks better on a dark background.

We don't usually think of scripting as a creative tool, but this example script gives you a way to apply an effect that would be difficult to accomplish without leaving InDesign for a drawing program.

COLOR FIGURE 9
Separating Color Images

CMYK images as separated by Photoshop.

Example RGB TIFFs separated by InDesign. In this example, we used the default Adobe InDesign Default RGB profile and the Perceptual (Images) rendering intent.

COLOR FIGURE 10
Blending Modes

For each blending mode, we've shown the effect of four overlapping rectangles colored with 100% cyan, magenta, yellow, and black. We've applied the blending mode to each rectangle with an opacity of 80%.

Normal

Multiply

Screen

Overlay

Soft Light

Hard Light

Color Dodge

Color Burn

Darken

Lighten

Hue

Saturation

Color

Luminosity

Color Palette Shortcuts

The Color palette has shortcuts, too.

▶ To display (or hide) the Color palette, press F6.

▶ To change the color mode of the palette, select RGB, LAB, or CMYK from the palette menu. Even faster, just Shift-click on the color bar to rotate through these options. If you're using a named swatch, Shift-clicking will also offer you a tint bar of the current color.

▶ When you enter a value (or a mathematical expression) in one of the color value fields, you can hold down Command/Ctrl as you press Return/Enter to apply the same percentage change to all of the color value fields.

▶ To select a color that is similar in hue, but different in shade, hold down Shift as you drag a color value slider. This moves the other sliders in tandem (unless you're dragging the Black slider, or one of the other sliders is set to zero).

Out-of-Gamut Warning. The out-of-gamut warning also appears in the Color palette, too, when a color swatch definition falls outside the gamut defined by the default CMYK document profile (see Figure 10-11). To adjust the color definition so that it falls in the gamut of the separations profile, click the alert icon. (See "Color Management," later in this chapter.) Note that as long as you are choosing colors in the CMYK mode, you won't see this alert (because they're all in gamut, by default). Also, note that you won't see this icon when you've chosen Hide Options from the palette menu.

The Color Picker

You can also choose an unnamed color or create a color swatch with the Color Picker dialog box (double-click on the fill or stroke icons at the bottom of the Tool palette). The Color Picker is a sad and pathetic attempt at providing a Photoshop-like feature in a page-layout program. We don't use it.

FIGURE 10-11
Fixing Out of Gamut Colors

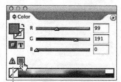 

When the current color cannot be printed by the separations printer you've selected, InDesign displays the out-of-gamut warning.

Click the icon to redefine the color so that it falls within the gamut of the output device.

Applying Colors and Gradients

Once you've selected an object, you can use any (or all) of the following techniques to apply a color, tint, or gradient to the object (see Figure 10-12).

▶ Click one of the selectors (Fill or Stroke) at the bottom of the Toolbox or in the Swatches palette, then click a color in the Swatches palette.

▶ Click the Fill selector or the Stroke selector, then click the Apply Color button, Apply Gradient button, Apply None button, swap fill and stroke icon, or the default fill and stroke icon. Or press

FIGURE 10-12
Applying a Color

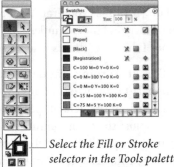

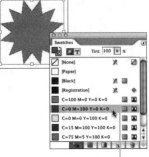

Press X to switch between the Fill selector and the Stroke selector.

Select the Fill or Stroke selector in the Tools palette or the Swatches palette.

Click a color swatch in the Swatches palette.

These three buttons apply last-used color swatch, gradient swatch, or None.

Click the Formatting Affects Text button (it looks like a little "T") to apply a color to the text inside a frame rather than the frame itself.

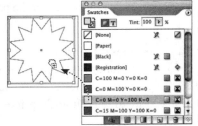

Press F5 to display the Swatches palette.

Drag a color swatch out of the Swatches palette (note that you do not need to select an object to apply a color via this method) on to an object's fill or stroke.

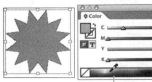

Press F6 to display the Color palette.

Click the cursor in the color bar, or adjust one of the color controls in the Color palette, and InDesign applies the color to the selected object.

any of the keyboard shortcuts corresponding to the buttons (comma, period, slash, Shift-X, or D, respectively).

▸ Select an object, then adjust any of the controls in the Color palette or open the Color Picker and choose from there.

▸ Drag a color swatch out of the Swatches palette and drop it on the fill or stroke of an object. You don't have to select the object on the page first.

▸ Use the Eyedropper tool to pick a color from an existing object, then click on another object to apply that color to it.

Applying Colors to Text

You can apply a fill or stroke to the characters of text in your publication. Characters of text act just like individual objects on your page, so to apply a color to text, select it with the Text tool, and apply a color using any of the techniques described above. Note that this means you can apply any color swatch, including gradients or None, to text. If you select the text block with the Selection tool, you can apply a color to all the text in the frame by first clicking the Formatting Affects Text button in the Tool, Swatches, or Color palette.

Applying Colors to Imported Graphics

You can apply colors to bi-level (black and white only) TIFFs, and grayscale TIFFs (or native Photoshop .PSD files). To apply a color to an imported image, select the image using the Direct Selection tool, click the Fill selector in the Toolbox, and then click a color swatch. When you print, InDesign prints the image on the appropriate separation (for a spot color) or series of plates (for a process color).

Ink Manager

One of the most common complaints among prepress service providers is that too many publishers don't understand the difference between spot and process color inks, and they're forever creating spot color inks that need to be converted to process color at print time. If you're one of those service providers, you're going to love the Ink Manager. (If you're a designer, it's still important to understand the Ink Manager, but you probably won't use it much.) The Ink Manager does three things.

▸ You can tell the Ink Manager to convert spot colors to process colors at the time of output (but it won't change the actual color swatch definitions in your document).

▶ You can alias one spot color to another, so two (or more) different spot colors will output onto the same plate.

▶ You can tell InDesign how your inks act so that the program can trap them properly.

We'll discuss converting and aliasing spot colors here, and hold off on the trapping features until later in this chapter.

The Ink Manager appears in four different places: the Output panel of the Print dialog box, the Swatches palette menu, the Advanced panel of the Export PDF dialog box, and the Advanced panel of the Export EPS dialog box. A change made in any one of these places affects the Ink Manager in all its locations.

Converting Spot Colors

The Ink Manager dialog box lists the four process colors, plus every spot color in your document, whether or not they're actually used (see Figure 10-13). When you click in the column to the left of a spot color, the color changes to a process color (the little four-color icon appears). Click again, and it's a spot color again. As we said earlier, this does not change the color's definition; the color only changes at print or export time.

If you want to output all the spot colors in the document as process colors, turn on the All Spots to Process checkbox at the bottom of the Ink Manager dialog box.

Aliasing Spot Colors

Let's say you create a document with two spot colors, but later find that you can only afford to print black and one spot color. You could replace one spot color with the other throughout your document by deleting one of them (see "Deleting a Swatch," earlier in this chapter). However, it's easier and more flexible to merge the two spot colors together at print time by *aliasing* one to the other.

To make an alias, select a spot color in the Ink Manager dialog box and choose a different color from the Ink Alias pop-up menu. Notice that the icon changes to the left of the color's icon (the icon, almost impossible to see without a loupe, is of an arrow pointing to a little ink well). You can still convert this color to a process color later if you want, using the techniques described above.

One of the coolest aspects of aliasing colors is that it works not only for spot colors applied to InDesign objects, but even to spot colors embedded in EPS graphics. Note that you can preview the spot color aliasing in your document by turning on both Overprint Preview and High Quality Display in the View menu.

FIGURE 10-13
Ink Manager

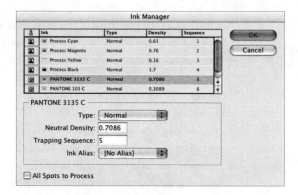

Trapping

A "trap" is a method of overlapping abutting colored objects to compensate for the imperfect registration of printing presses. Because registration, even on good presses with good operators, can be off by a quarter point or more, abutting elements in your publication may not end up abutting perfectly when the publication is printed by your commercial printer. What happens then? The paper shows through where you don't want it to (see Color Figures 2 and 3).

Do we need to tell you what happens when you take your work to a press that's badly out of register or run by turkeys? Disaster. Before this happens to you, talk with your commercial printer regarding the tolerances of their presses and/or operators. Don't ask them if they're turkeys—it's considered rude.

Manual Trapping

If you can't (or don't want to) use InDesign's automatic trapping methods (In-RIP or built-in), you can still trap your publication—you'll just have to do it yourself. We describe this process first because we believe that you should know how to add and subtract, multiply and divide before you ever use a calculator.

However, before we start describing manual trapping techniques, we need to state that InDesign's automatic trapping methods can almost always trap your publications better than you can (assuming that you have both deadlines to meet and a finite amount of patience), and if you use them, you usually won't even have to *think* about trapping. Also, many prepress shops prefer to use post-process trapping software; in this case, they'll want you to leave trapping turned off (it's off by default). As always, check with your service provider before doing anything rash.

Object-Level Overprinting. The key to trapping, in InDesign and any other software, is in controlling which objects—or which parts of objects—print on top of other objects as the printing press prints your publication. The only way to make manual trapping work is to control the overprinting characteristics of individual objects (see Color Figures 1 and 4).

Luckily, you can. Any InDesign path can be specified as an overprinting object (that is, it won't knock a hole in any objects behind it when you print), regardless of the object's color. The controls for object-level overprinting are the Overprint Fill and Overprint Stroke options found in the Attributes palette (see Figure 10-14). These controls, used in combination with InDesign's Paste Into command, can be used to create virtually any trap.

FIGURE 10-14
Attributes Palette

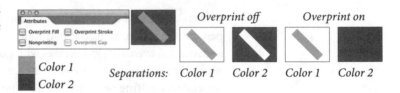

We have to stress the importance of the Weight Changes Bounding Box option on the Stroke palette menu. You cannot create traps when this option is turned off, so you'll have to make sure it's turned on as you follow any of the procedures in this section. (We don't usually have this turned on, which is one reason we prefer to use auto trapping rather than manual trapping.)

When you're working with trapping, you'll be creating *spreads* (outlines of objects, in the same color as the object, that are slightly larger than the object itself) and *chokes* (outlines of the object that are the same color as the underlying object's color). Spreads make the object larger so that the edges of the object print over the underlying object; chokes make the area knocked out of the underlying object smaller than the outline of the foreground object.

Use chokes when the foreground object is a darker color than the background object; use spreads when the foreground object is lighter. In other words, trap from light colors into darker colors. Sound subjective? It is. We use chokes when we're trapping type—text characters often look distorted when you use spreads (the eye is very critical when it comes to text). Some folks ask why you don't just always overprint every color on top of every other color. The answer is that inks are almost never fully opaque, so if you print solid cyan on top of solid magenta, you'll get purple—probably not the effect you were looking for. With trapping, you'll still get purple, but only in a tiny stripe along the edge between the cyan and magenta objects.

Overprint Preview. InDesign has a powerful feature called Overprint Preview (in the View menu), which gives you an onscreen preview of the strokes and fills that you set to overprint. You may not want to work with Overprint Preview turned on all the time because there is a slight performance hit, but it's certainly worth leaving it on when trapping, or when zooming in to 2000% or more to see if something is trapping correctly.

Overprinting Black. By default, all objects on an InDesign page knock out of all objects behind them—unless they're black. InDesign, by default, overprints black ink. Most of the time, this is a good thing. To turn off black overprinting, display the General panel of the Preferences dialog box and turn off the Overprint Black option.

Remember, however, that black ink isn't really fully opaque, even if it looks like it is on screen. Overprinting solid areas of black on an image or other page objects can look mottled, and unfortunately even Overprint Preview won't display this problem unless you have color management enabled (which we discuss later in this chapter). If you need larger areas of solid black in a full-color document, consider making a *rich black*, a CMYK black that is made of 100 percent black plus perhaps 25 percent each of cyan, magenta, and yellow.

Solid Color Trapping. It's more important to trap abutting color fields in publications when you're printing using spot colors or areas of single process colors (like where 100 percent cyan text sits on top of 50-percent magenta background) than it is in most process color publications. Usually when you're working with process colors, you'll almost always see some ink between abutting objects, so you're less likely to see paper-colored gaps showing a poor trap.

The easiest way to demonstrate how spot-color trapping works is to show you some examples. As you work through these examples, you'll trap an ellipse into a rectangle by manipulating the color, width, and overprinting specifications of the path that surrounds the ellipse. First, draw the colored objects.

1. Create a rectangle. Fill the rectangle with a spot color ("Color 1"). Set the rectangle's stroke color to None.

2. Draw an ellipse on top of the rectangle. Make sure that the ellipse is entirely inside the rectangle. Fill the ellipse with a different color from that of the rectangle ("Color 2"). Set the stroke of the ellipse to None.

3. Save the file.

The ellipse needs to be trapped, or you'll run the risk of having paper-colored lines appear up around the ellipse when you print the publication. You can either spread or choke the ellipse, or both.

To spread the ellipse, follow these steps (see Color Figure 3).

1. Select the ellipse.

2. Press F10 to display the Stroke palette.

3. Turn on the Weight Changes Bounding Box option from the Stroke palette menu, then enter a new line width in the Weight field. The line width you enter in the Weight field should be equal to twice the trap amount—if you enter "2", you'll get a stroke of one point on either side of the path. If your commercial printer has asked for a trap of .5 points, enter "1" in the Weight field.

4. While the object is still selected, turn on Overprint Stroke in the Attributes palette.

When you print, the fill of the ellipse knocks out the background, but the stroke overprints. That means the ellipse is larger than the hole that's been knocked out of the background rectangle. You've just created a spread.

To choke the ellipse, change the stroke color of the ellipse to the same as the background color (see Color Figure 3). Now when you print, the hole that's knocked out of the background rectangle is slightly smaller than the original ellipse.

Choose Revert from the File menu to get the file ready for the next procedure.

Trapping Across Color Boundaries. The techniques described above work well as long as objects don't cross color boundaries. If the objects do cross color boundaries (especially going from a color background to a white background), it's too obvious that you've changed the shapes of the objects. What do you do?

1. Drag the ellipse so that it's partially outside of the rectangle, and then press Command-Shift-[/Ctrl-Shift-[to send it to the back (behind the rectangle).

2. Press Command-C/Ctrl-C to copy the ellipse.

3. Now select the rectangle and select Paste Into from the Edit menu (or press Command-Option-V/Ctrl-Alt-V). This duplicate should appear in exactly the same place as the original, but nested inside the rectangle. If for some reason it doesn't show up in the same place, then select the original ellipse, and note the values in the X and Y fields of the Transform palette. Then use the Direct Selection tool to select the nested ellipse, turn off Show Content Offset in the Transform palette menu, and enter the X and Y values into the Transform palette fields. InDesign moves the copy of the ellipse into the same position as the original ellipse.

4. Without deselecting the duplicate ellipse, enter a stroke weight for the trap in the Weight field of the Stroke palette. Make sure that the fill and stroke colors are the same in the Swatches palette.

5. Turn on the Overprint Stroke option in the Attributes palette.

At this point, the ellipse you pasted inside the rectangle spreads slightly, while the part of the ellipse outside the rectangle remains the same size and shape. If you want the rectangle's color to choke into the ellipse, then change the color of the nested ellipse's stroke to match the rectangle's fill color.

What happens when the object you need to trap overlaps more than one other, differently colored object? In this case, you can run into trouble. The trap you use for one background color might not be the trap you want to use for the other. You might want to spread one and choke the other, depending on the colors you're using. In these cases, you can use the same basic techniques described above for the overlapping and/or abutting objects. But, at this point, we have to urge you to save yourself some trouble and use either of InDesign's automatic trapping methods.

Trapping Lines. The trapping techniques above work well for filled paths, but what open paths? After all, you can't apply two different stroke properties to a single path. Instead, you clone the path and make the width of the clone larger or smaller for the spread or choke you want. One of the strokes overprints; the other line knocks out.

Follow these steps to spread an open path (see Color Figure 2).

1. Draw a rectangle and fill it with a spot color.

2. Draw a path inside the rectangle. Create another spot color and apply it to the path. Do not set this path to overprint.

3. Select the path and clone it with Step and Repeat.

4. Increase the stroke weight of this duplicate path by twice the amount of spread you need (remember, PostScript strokes grow out from their centers) and turn on the Overprint Stroke option in the Attributes palette to make the stroke overprint.

That's all there is to it. The original path knocks a hole in the background rectangle, and the clone of the path spreads to just a little bit beyond the edges of the knockout. Of course, this doesn't create a trap around the ends of the line, just the sides.

To choke the path, follow these steps (see Color Figure 2).

1. Draw a rectangle. Create a spot color and fill the rectangle with it.

2. Draw a path inside the rectangle. Create another spot color and apply it to the line. Set this path to overprint.

3. Select the path and clone it.

4. Decrease the weight of the path by twice the amount of choke you need in the Stroke palette. Turn off the Overprint Stroke option in the Attributes palette.

This time, the cloned path is narrower than the original and knocks out an area that's slightly smaller than the original path, creating a choke.

Trapping Text. Text is usually the element in a publication that needs trapping the most. For whatever reason, it's easier to notice poor trapping around text than around other elements. At the same time, traps that are too large distort the shapes of the characters you're trapping. It tends to be a problem with small type, especially serif type.

Here's how to create a spread for text (see Color Figure 3).

1. Draw a rectangle, create a spot color ("Color 1"), and apply it to the rectangle.

2. Enter text in a text frame. Position the text frame on top of the rectangle so that the text is entirely within the area occupied by the rectangle.

3. Create a second spot color ("Color 2") and apply it to the text in the text frame.

4. While the text is still selected, display the Stroke palette. Enter the stroke weight you want (remember, it's two times the amount of trap you want) in the Weight field. Turn on the Overprint Stroke option in the Attributes palette.

The next example shows how you can choke text by making the shape the characters knock out of the background a bit smaller than the characters themselves.

1. Draw a rectangle, create a spot color ("Color 1"), and apply it to the rectangle.

2. Create a text frame. Position the text frame on top of the rectangle so that it's entirely within the rectangle.

3. Create a second spot color ("Color 2"). Select all the text in the text frame and apply "Color 2" to the fill of the text.

4. Clone the text frame using Step and Repeat with zero offsets.

5. Select the text in the duplicate frame, set its fill color to None and give it a stroke color the same as the background rectangle ("Color 1").

6. Enter the stroke weight you want for the trap in the Weight field of the Stroke palette. Turn on the Overprint Stroke option in the Attributes palette.

If text crosses color boundaries, use the techniques described earlier for trapping overlapping paths.

Process-Color Trapping. Process-color trapping is a bit simpler than spot-color trapping, because it's usually less critical that process-colored elements have traps (because many of these colors are built of multiple process colors, so there are shared colors—if one color shifts on press, then the other colors are still there to cover the white paper). However, it can be far harder to figure out exactly what color to make the stroke for a process-colored object. When you're talking about trapping two process-colored graduated fills, watch out!

The main thing to keep in mind, however, is that for each of the process inks the ink percentage used in the topmost object in any stack of objects always wins—they knock out all percentages of that ink behind them, regardless of any overprinting settings.

Unless, that is, the ink percentage is zero. If, for example, the percentage of cyan used in the fill color of the topmost object in a stack of objects is zero, turning Overprint off makes the path knock out any other cyan in the area covered by the path. Overprinting the fill, in this case, means that the area taken up by the fill disappears from the cyan plates—the percentage of cyan in the next object in the stack shows through the area where the objects overlap. If your head is spinning at this point, just go see Color Figure 4 for a visual explanation.

Another way to think of this is to think of each ink in a process color as behaving like a separate spot ink.

Simple Process-Color Trapping. In process-color trapping, you've got to make your overprinting strokes different colors from either the background or foreground objects. Why? Because process colors have a way of creating new colors when you print them over each other. It's what they do best.

As in the spot-color trapping section earlier, we'll demonstrate process-color trapping techniques by example.

1. Create a rectangle that's filled with "Color 1," which is specified as 20C 100M 0Y 10K.

2. On top of this rectangle, draw an ellipse and fill it with "Color 2," which is specified as 0C 100M 50Y 0K.

3. Select both objects and set their stroke to None.

4. Save the file.

The ellipse needs to be trapped, or you run the risk of having cyan-colored lines appearing around the ellipse when the publication is printed—which could happen if the cyan and yellow plates aren't in good register, or if your paper stretches. Whether you spread or choke the ellipse depends on its color. If the ellipse is darker than the background rectangle, choke the ellipse. If the ellipse is a lighter color than the background rectangle, spread the ellipse. In this case, the ellipse is a lighter color, so you'll use a spread. To spread the ellipse, follow these steps.

1. Create a new process color in the Swatches palette containing only those colors in "Color 2" having higher values than "Color 1." Quick quiz: what component colors in "Color 2" have higher values than their counterparts in "Color 1"? If you said 50Y, you're the lucky winner. Specify a new color: 0C 0M 50Y 0K (we'll call this "Color 3").

2. Select the ellipse.

3. Press F10 to display the Stroke palette, if it's not already visible. Enter the stroke weight you want for your stroke in the Weight field. It should be twice the width of your desired trap.

4. Apply the color swatch "Color 3" to the stroke of the ellipse and set it to overprint.

When you print, all the areas around the ellipse have some dot value inside them, and the new colors created where the objects abut won't be too obvious. Choose Revert from the File menu to get ready for the next example.

What if the ellipse is the darker color? If it were, we'd have to choke it. To choke the ellipse, follow these steps.

1. Select the ellipse and fill it with "Color 1." Select the rectangle and fill it with "Color 2."

2. Create a new color ("Color 3") that contains only the largest color component in "Color 1." That's 100M, so "Color 3" should be specified as 0C 100M 0Y 0K.

3. Use the Weight field in the Stroke palette to specify the weight of the trap you want.

4. Set the stroke color to "Color 3."

5. Turn on the Overprint Stroke option in the Attributes palette.

When you print, the stroke you applied to the ellipse guarantees that there's no gap around the ellipse, even if you run into registration problems when you print the publication.

Automatic Trapping At this point, you've read your way through the manual trapping techniques and are seriously considering hiring 20 house elves to take care of your trapping needs. But wait—InDesign includes two powerful automatic trapping methods: In-RIP trapping and InDesign built-in trapping (see Color Figure 5).

What are the differences between the two automatic trapping methods? InDesign's built-in trapping cannot do the following things (all of which can be accomplished by in-RIP trapping).

► Trap gradients created in InDesign.

► Use trap widths greater than 4 points.

► Be used with in-RIP separations.

► Be used with most OPI or DCS workflows.

► Create traps inside color images, or trap InDesign objects to images contained in DCS, EPS, or PDF files.

► Trap imported vector graphics or type within PDF or EPS files. See "Built-in Trapping and Imported Graphics," later in this chapter.

Don't let the length of the above list discourage you—InDesign's built-in trapping can take care of the trapping needs of most publications and printing processes. If, however, you see an item in the above list that is crucial to your publication, then you'd probably better use in-RIP trapping.

Of course, in-RIP trapping only works with PostScript printers that have trapping built in. All PostScript 3 devices should be able to handle this, but if you have a PostScript Level 2 printer, check with the manufacturer to see if it has this feature. In-RIP trapping also only works when you're also using in-RIP color separations. Most people don't use in-RIP separations (they separate on a host machine), so they can't use in-RIP trapping either. In that case, we recommend third-party post-process trapping software that creates traps for you.

Note that both forms of automatic trapping work best with PostScript and OpenType fonts; this is another instance where TrueType fonts may cause problems.

Built-in Trapping and Imported Graphics. When InDesign elements overlap an imported EPS or PDF graphic, InDesign won't be able to trap the InDesign elements properly and you can get odd trapping results. If the elements don't touch each other, or don't need to be trapped, this isn't a problem. If the InDesign object does touch the graphic, however, you can sometimes work around the problem by adjusting the frame that contains the graphic. If the InDesign elements overlap an empty area in the graphic, edit the shape of the frame containing the graphic so that it doesn't touch the elements.

Alternatively, you can copy and paste paths from Illustrator or FreeHand (or any other application capable of putting data on the system Clipboard in Illustrator format), thereby converting the paths into InDesign objects—but this will only work for very simple graphics.

Specifying Trapping Settings. While InDesign's default trap settings are reasonably good for most sheetfed print jobs, you will likely have to change the trap settings for different jobs or for different pages within a job (InDesign does not let you adjust the trap preset for individual objects on your page). You can do all of this with the Trap Presets palette (see Figure 10-15). Note that this is different from InDesign 1.x, which hid trapping settings in the Print dialog box.

All documents start with two trap presets: Default and No Trap Preset. We'll see how you can use No Trap Preset later when we talk about assigning trap presets to pages. If you just want to change the trapping values for the entire document, edit Default by double-clicking on it in the Trap Presets palette. Or, to create a new trap preset, Option/Alt-click on the New Trap Preset button at the bottom of the palette (or select New Trap Preset from the palette menu).

FIGURE 10-15
Trapping Settings

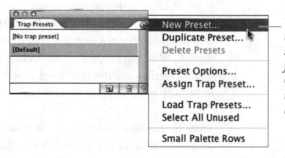

To create a trapping preset, select New Preset from the menu or Option/Alt-click the New Preset button.

InDesign displays the New Trap Preset dialog box.

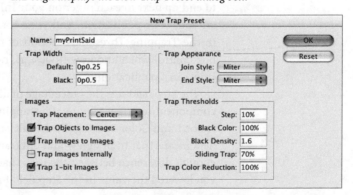

The New Trap Preset and the Modify Trap Preset dialog boxes are functionally equivalent. Here's a quick rundown of what all these cryptic features are for.

Trap Width. The value you enter in the Default field sets the trap width for all inks except solid black—you set that trap width using the nearby Black field. If you're using InDesign's built-in trapping, the trapping width is never greater than four points (regardless of the value you enter in these two fields).

If you're working with a rich black (that is, a color containing other process inks in addition to black), the value you enter in the Black Width field also sets a kind of "margin" of black ink at the edges of a rich black object. This margin is known as the "holdback" or "holdback area."

The holdback area comes in handy at the edges of a rich black object. If, for example, you've placed white text over a rich black area, the holdback area prevents the non-black inks from appearing around the edges of the white characters.

Trap Appearance. Those of you who *really* care about how your traps appear can adjust the look and feel of trap lines with the Join Style and End Style pop-up menus. Join Style determines how corner points in trap segments will appear (mitered, rounded, or beveled). End Style determines how the trap lines act at their end points (the default, Mitered, keeps the trap lines slightly away from each other, while Overlap lets the trap lines… well, overlap). We typically just leave both of these set to their default values.

Trap Thresholds. Imagine that you have two process colors in your publication. Color 1 is defined as 60C 20M 0Y 0K, and Color 2 is 65C 15M 0Y 5K. Do these two colors need to be trapped if they happen to end up next to each other on your InDesign pages? That depends on you, your publication, and your commercial printer. The fields in the Trapping Thresholds section of the New Trap Preset dialog box control when and how InDesign traps the boundaries between colors in a publication.

The Step field sets the percentage of difference between each color component to trigger automatic trapping. In the above example of Color 1 and Color 2, using the default value of 10 percent in the Step field means that InDesign would not trap the two colors—there's not enough difference between the inks that make up the two colors. If you lowered the value in the Step field to 5 percent, InDesign would trap the objects (because the C, M, and K ink components vary by that percentage).

Black Color. How much black ink has to be used in a color before InDesign applies the holdback defined by the value you entered in the Black field? That depends on what you enter in the Black Color Limit field. Enter 100 percent when you want to apply a holdback to colors containing 100 percent black ink, or lower the percentage to apply a holdback to colors containing less black ink.

Black Density. InDesign traps colors in a publication based on their ink neutral densities (see "Editing Ink Neutral Densities," later in this chapter). Lighter colors typically spread into areas of darker colors, which usually produces a less obvious trap. You can manipulate the way that InDesign traps objects by changing the neutral densities in the Ink Manager dialog box. Or you can use the Black Density field to redefine the density InDesign thinks of as black. By default, black ink is set to an ink neutral density of 1.6.

The value you enter in the Black Density Limit field also affects InDesign's application of the Black holdback area. By reducing the value in the Black Density Limit field, you instruct InDesign to apply the holdback to inks other than black.

Sliding Trap. When gradients abut, the colors at the edges of the gradients vary along the border between the two gradients. You can't use a simple spread or choke for the entire length of the boundary between gradients—at some point, the trap will just become too obvious.

One way to solve this problem is to use a centerline trap—a trap that extends equally on either side of the boundary between the gradients. Another method is to use a sliding trap—which changes from a spread to a centerline trap, and then to a choke, depending on the ink neutral densities of the colors used in the gradients.

The value you enter in the Sliding Trap Limit field defines the point (or points) at which the trap switches from a spread to a centerline trap, and from a centerline trap to a choke. This value is a percentage of the difference between ink neutral densities (note that this is unlike the percentage in the Step field, which is the difference between the color components making up a color). Enter 0% (zero percent) to force InDesign to use a centerline trap for the entire length of the trap, or enter 100% to make InDesign apply a spread along the length of the boundary between the two gradients. Other values (such as the default 70 percent) apply sliding traps.

Trap Color Reduction. The value you enter in this field defines the colors InDesign creates as it builds traps. When the value in this field is 100 percent, some color combinations can result in a trapping color (or colors) that is darker than either of the original colors. To avoid this, enter a smaller value in this field. Enter 0 (zero) to set the neutral density of the objects created by the trapping system to the neutral density of the darkest color (note that this doesn't necessarily mean it's the same color).

Image Settings. The controls in the Images section of the New Trap Preset dialog box define the way that InDesign traps InDesign page items to imported graphics. Note that "image," in the context of this dialog box, means any imported graphic—not just bitmaps.

Trap Placement. Choose Center to apply a centerline trap (see "Sliding Trap," earlier) to the boundary between the InDesign object and the imported graphic. Choose Choke to extend the InDesign objects into the area inside the imported graphic. Choose Neutral Density to apply the trap based on the ink neutral density of the abutting colors. Choose Spread to spread the colors from the image into the InDesign object.

Trap Objects to Images. Turn this option on to apply automatic trapping to areas where InDesign objects abut imported images. InDesign uses the trapping method you chose from the Image Trap Placement pop-up menu to trap the objects (see above).

Trap Images to Images. This feature lets InDesign build traps where two bitmapped images abut each other.

Trap Images Internally. Turn this option on to apply in-RIP trapping to areas of color inside imported bitmap images. Most scanned images (photographs) don't need trapping—this option is for synthetic images (such as screen shots) containing abutting areas of flat color. Turn this option off for faster trapping.

Trap 1-bit Images. Turn this option on to trap bilevel (black and white) images to InDesign objects. This affects images to which you've applied colors in InDesign.

Trapping Ranges   If the pages in your publication have differing trapping needs, you can use trapping ranges to vary the trapping presets used to trap the publication. For instance, if one or more pages don't require trapping at all (perhaps they include only black text or objects don't overlap at all), your document will print faster if you turn off trapping for those pages. To change one or more page's trap preset, select Assign Trap Preset from the Trap Presets palette menu (see Figure 10-16).

In the Assign Trap Preset dialog box, select a trapping preset from the Trap Preset pop-up menu, then enter the page range you want to trap using the style (separate individual pages with commas and page ranges with hyphens). Make sure you click the Assign button before clicking Done, or else InDesign ignores your change. To turn off trapping for a page or range of pages, select [No Trap Preset] from the Trap Preset pop-up menu.

FIGURE 10-16
Assigning Trap Presets

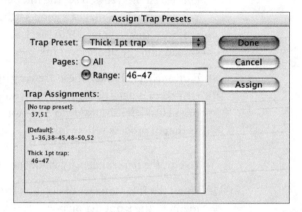

Editing Ink Neutral Densities

When you use either automatic trapping method, the trapping system (whether in InDesign or in a PostScript RIP) bases its trapping decisions on the inks used in abutting objects on an InDesign page. In general, the trapping system tries to spread lighter inks into darker inks. How can the system tell which inks are lighter or darker? By comparing the ink *neutral density* values between the objects. A color's neutral density is sort of like "how dark would the color be if this were in grayscale."

In general, InDesign assigns ink neutral density values based on the CMYK values of the colors you've used in a publication. If you've used spot colors (inks), or have created colors using the RGB or LAB color model, InDesign uses the process color equivalent of the color.

Most of the time, this approach works pretty well. But we can think of three cases in which you might want to edit the ink neutral density values.

▸ **Varnishes.** A varnish should almost always be the lightest ink on the page, so set its ink neutral density to 0 (zero). This way, the trapping system will spread the varnish into abutting objects.

▶ **Metallic Pantone inks.** Metallic inks are more opaque than other inks, and they're also somewhat reflective. Spreading a metallic ink into an abutting area of some other color is almost certain to create an obvious trap. Set the ink neutral density of metallic inks to 1.7 (the value of black ink) or higher—that way, they will be considered the darkest ink on the page by the trapping system (and all other inks will spread into them).

▶ **Pantone fluorescent inks.** Like metallic inks, fluorescent inks are more opaque than other inks, and they're also very bright. In general, you want every other ink to spread into an area of fluorescent ink, so you set the ink neutral density to a high value. We think that 1.6 makes a good setting for fluorescent inks—that way, they'll spread into black areas, but most other inks will spread into the fluorescent ink.

▶ **Pantone pastel inks.** These are very light colors and should be treated in much the same way as you'd treat a varnish. Set the ink neutral density value to .15—approximately the same value as that of process yellow ink.

To edit the neutral density value for an ink, follow these steps.

1. Open the Ink Manager dialog box from the Swatches palette menu or the Print dialog box.

2. Select the ink you want to edit.

3. To set the ink type, choose an option from the Type pop-up menu. You use these options to declare to the trapping system that a specific ink doesn't follow the usual trapping rules. This can come in handy when you're working with certain types of spot inks: varnishes, metallic colors, fluorescent colors, and pastel colors. You can also control the inks trapping behavior by manipulating its ink neutral density, as in Step 5.

   ▶ Choose Normal for all process inks and for most spot colors.

   ▶ Choose Transparent for varnishes and very light spot inks (Pantone pastels, for example).

   ▶ Choose Opaque for very opaque inks, such as Pantone metallic or fluorescent colors.

   ▶ Choose OpaqueIgnore for inks you want to have the trapping system ignore entirely—for instance, nontransparent metallic inks or varnishes.

4. Enter a new value in the Neutral Density field. Do this only if you've set the Type pop-up menu to Normal. Use this approach if your publication contains "specialty inks" (the ink types listed in Step 4) and you need to define the ways these inks trap to each other.

5. The Trapping Sequence field offers a way for you to tell InDesign the order in which the inks will be printed (this has no effect at all on the order in which the color separations will print). While it's rare that you'd need this, the Trapping Sequence feature can be useful if you're printing multiple opaque inks. For instance, InDesign can then know to spread other inks underneath the last-printed opaque ink.

6. Click the OK button to close the Ink Manager dialog box and apply your changes.

Note that changing the neutral density values for an ink has no effect on how the color appears on screen, even when Overprint Preview is turned on. This only affects InDesign's trapping behavior.

Color Management

When you aim at a target—and it doesn't matter whether you're aiming a rifle, a bow, a laser, or a camera—you have to make adjustments. You've got to consider the atmospheric conditions, the distance to the target, the characteristics of the target itself. Once you know what the variables are, and how they affect what you're trying to do, you've got a better chance of hitting the bullseye.

The same thing is true in color management. You need to understand the tools you have to work with, how they work together (or don't), and how they combine to produce the colors you see in the printed version of your publication.

It would be nice if we could make what we see on our screen exactly match what we'll get when we print. But we can't, for a variety of practical and physiological reasons (not to mention simple lack of time and money). That said, we must also add that we can get very close—and we can also make the relationship between the display and the printed piece more consistent and predictable.

The "device" (a printer, scanner, monitor, or printing press) is the key. Every device renders colors in a slightly different way. To adjust color in one environment so that it matches the color as seen in another environment, color management systems refer to a file containing information on the color characteristics of a device (how it displays or prints color). This file is called a "device profile." Device profiles for scanners and printers are usually created by the manufacturers who make the hardware, though quite a few come with InDesign. You've got to make monitor profiles yourself, because every monitor is different (just as several television sets from the same manufacturer can show the same image differently). The process of creating a device profile is called "characterizing" a device.

Once a device profile has been created for a device, you've got to maintain (or "calibrate") the device so that it doesn't vary from the profile. Imagesetter operators and commercial printers calibrate their equipment regularly (or should) to match industry standards.

InDesign's color management system uses device profiles compatible with the International Color Consortium (ICC) specification. If you're on the Macintosh, you can also use device profiles provided by Apple with the system-level ColorSync color management system (these profiles are also ICC compatible).

For more on choosing device profiles, see "InDesign's Color Management Controls," later in this chapter.

For More Information

Color management is an enormous subject and we can only focus on one aspect of the big picture here: How color management works in InDesign. If any terminology in this section is confusing to you (like gamut, ICC profile, color engines, and rendering intents), we encourage you to go look at two other sources for a truly in-depth look at getting consistent color. First, because most of what you want to manage is probably created in Photoshop, check out a book that David wrote with Bruce Fraser: *Real World Photoshop*. Then, to really see how all this fits together, see *Real World Color Management*, by Bruce Fraser, Chris Murphy, and Fred Bunting.

Do You Need Color Management?

Everyone wants consistent color from original to screen to proof print to printing press, but it's worth asking yourself whether you really need it. Managing color is not as simple as turning on a checkbox, and though it's not as hard as flying an airplane, it can still cause a fair amount of rifling through medicine cabinets trying to ease the pain in your head. You may not need to worry a lot about managing color in InDesign if you can rely on color swatch books when picking solid colors, and if you can rely on color prepress professionals to deal with your color Photoshop images.

There are other instances when it's not even worth trying to get InDesign to manage your color. For example, InDesign can't manage grayscale images or spot colors (unless you convert them to process colors). Similarly, InDesign isn't really set up to color-manage vector art when saved as an EPS file (it can do it, but we don't recommend it). Vector art saved as PDF or native Adobe Illustrator (.ai) files should work reasonably well.

Nevertheless, we must admit that it is particularly satisfying when you work through all the issues and achieve (as close as possible) parity among your screen, inkjet printer, and final press output. Being able to rely on your screen ("soft proofing") and desktop color printer is a great boost in efficiency, too. Plus, as the world becomes increasingly reliant on direct to plate technologies, bypassing film entirely, color management systems become increasingly important to ensure quality output. And if you want to import RGB images and let InDesign do the color separation for you at print time, you'll get better results if color management is turned on.

Controlling Your Color-Viewing Environment

If it's important to you that what you see on your screen looks as much like the printed version of your publication as possible, there are a few rules you need to follow.

- ► Use a monitor and video system capable of displaying at least 24-bit color.

- ► Characterize and calibrate your monitor with a tool like Gretag-Macbeth's EyeOne device. If color is of critical importance to you and your publications, find a system that works with your monitor, or buy a monitor that works with the calibration system you prefer.

- ► Control the lighting around your monitor and keep it consistent when you're working. Just about everyone agrees that the fluorescent lighting used in most of our office buildings is the worst possible lighting for viewing colors. Turn it off, if you can, and rely on incandescent lighting (desk lamps with one sort of bulb or another) to light your work area. If you can't turn it off, try getting some "full spectrum" (or "amber") fluorescent tubes to install above your monitor. These also reduce eyestrain.

- ► Control the lighting of the area where you'll be viewing your color proofs. Ideally, you'd have a room or small booth equipped with "daylight" (or 5,000-degree Kelvin) lamps—but few of us can afford the money or space required.

Why is lighting important? Basically, the temperature of the light affects what a color "objectively" looks like. You can't assume ideal viewing conditions, but you have to work in them to be able to do consistent work.

Is What You See Anything Like What You'll Get?

One of the simplest rules for getting the color you expect is also one of the least technologically advanced: Any time you're working with ink, refer to printed samples, rather than looking at the colors on your screen. Remember that, unlike the paper you'll be printing on, your screen is backlit, so it displays colors very differently from what they'll look like when printed.

If you're using uncoated paper, look at samples of the ink (spot color) or ink mix (process color) printed on uncoated stock. If you're using coated paper, look at examples printed on coated paper. If you're using a colored paper, try to find an example of the ink printed on a colored paper—though these examples are much harder to find (if it's a big enough job, your printer might be willing to make a "draw down" for you by mixing the ink and scraping it on the paper by hand).

Pantone makes a line of swatch books showing their libraries of spot and process colors (including process color equivalents of the spot colors); they're printed on both coated and uncoated stocks, and, although they're kind of expensive, they're not as expensive as pulling a job off of a press because you didn't like the press check. They're downright cheap if you consider what they must cost to print.

However, we don't recommend you use Pantone spot colors (the ones you find in the Pantone spot color library) to specify a process color. The Pantone Matching System is a spot-color specifying system, and the colors don't convert to process colors particularly well because you can't make any given hue just using process colors (see the discussion earlier in this chapter).

While Pantone also makes a swatch book with a spectrum full of process colors, we tend to like the one made by Trumatch even more; it's just easier to use for some reason.

Don't assume that color printers will automatically produce an accurate simulation of what the colors in your publication are going to look like when they're printed by your commercial printer. To do that, you'll have to do some work—you'll have to run test pages and adjust device profiles. And, at the same time, bear in mind that most color printers print using something akin to the process-color method. Your spot colors will be converted to process colors during printing. Some of the six- and seven-color inkjet printers can produce good matches for most spot inks.

Note, however, that the color proofs you print on a color inkjet printer cannot show you the way that your pages will print on a printing press. In particular, they can't show you trapping problems. For that, you need to use one of the color proofing processes (such as Chromalin or Press Match) to create your proofs from the film you've gotten out of your imagesetter. Imagesetting service bureaus frequently offer color proofing as part of their business. Some of these proofing processes can give you a proof on the paper you're intending to use, or can give you transparent overlays that you can place on top of your selected paper to get an idea of what your publication will look like when printed. If you're printing direct to plate or direct to press, then there won't be any film from which to burn proofs and you have to be all the more careful when setting up your files.

InDesign's Color Management Controls

You can control how color appears in InDesign in two places: the Color Settings dialog box (under the Edit menu), and the Proof Setup dialog box (under the View menu). These controls are similar to the features of the same name in Illustrator and Photoshop. Because proofing relies entirely on how you've set up Color Settings, we'll start with the former and then cover proofing later. You can use the Color Settings dialog box to set up your color policies and choose the device profiles for your monitor, your separations printer, and your composite printer.

By the way, InDesign offers a separate control over how the color black appears on your screen and in color proofs. In short, you can choose to view 100-percent black ink as lighter than "rich black" (black mixed with other colors). We cover that in "Appearance of Black," in Chapter 1, "Workspaces."

Application Color Settings

The choices you make in the Color Settings dialog box form the basis for how InDesign displays and prints color (see Figure 10-17). These controls all match the similarly named features in Adobe Photoshop, though the meanings are sometimes subtly different. Note that these controls are all application wide (not just for the open document). When you create a new document, it embeds the color settings that are currently in place in this dialog box.

Settings. In a valiant effort to make color management easier, Adobe has created color management "presets" that you can pick in any of the Creative Suite applications. Or, better yet, pick the same setting in all the applications, so you get consistent color as you move files from one program to another. (You can automate this by launching

FIGURE 10-17
**Color Settings
Dialog Box**

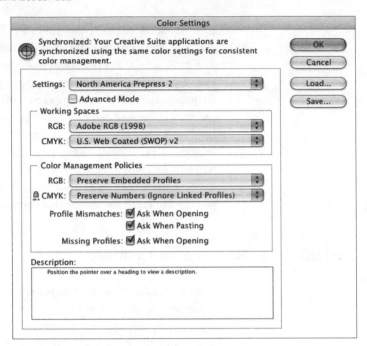

Adobe Bridge and then choosing Creative Suite Color Settings from the Edit menu.)

If InDesign's Color Settings dialog box is set up differently than other Suite applications, you'll see a message alerting you to the fact that the Suite isn't synchronized. This isn't necessarily a bad thing—for example, we typically like seeing missing profile alerts in Photoshop but not in InDesign. (We cover alerts like this in "Color Managment Policies," in a few pages.) However, for color management novices it's usually best to try to keep them all synchronized.

InDesign's color management is turned on by default in CS2. The Settings popup menu typically shows five presets.

▶ **Emulate Adobe InDesign 2.0 CMS Off.** "Off" is misleading—there is no such thing as truly turning color management off. This setting tells InDesign to hide what it's doing from you. For example, if you import an RGB image and print color separations, InDesign will still convert the RGB to CMYK (which is one of the prime uses of color management). The result may look only adequate because InDesign is making two assumptions: that the RGB image is based on the Adobe RGB profile and the CMYK ink behavior is based on SWOP inks (technically, the Photoshop 5 Default CMYK settings). The further from these descriptions your images or press—like if you're printing on newsprint—the worse the quality will be. We'd rather gnaw off our leg than choose this setting.

► **Monitor Color.** This is good for... um... well, it might have some marginal use in Photoshop (if you're creating output for video perhaps), but we can't think of any reason to use it here.

► **General Purpose.** The default setting is General Purpose, which turns off most of the color management alert dialog boxes that make people nervous, uses sRGB as the default RGB space, and uses U.S. Web Coated SWOP for the default CMYK space (or Fogra or Japan Color in Europe or Asia). This is not a terrible setting, but we tend not to use it.

► **Prepress.** If you're making pages for a printing press, we think you should choose North American Prepress 2 (or Europe Prepress 2 or Japan Prepress 2, depending on where you're reading this). This uses the same CMYK default, but standardizes on the Adobe RGB model for RGB colors. We like it because it encompasses a spectrum of colors better suited for print than sRGB.

► **Web/Internet.** If virtually all your pages are destined for the Web, you might choose the Web/Internet preset. It uses the sRGB workspace for RGB colors, but that's appropriate for Web files.

Again, these are only defaults—not necessarily what you'll use for your documents. If you have a custom CMYK profile for a project, you can use that for your document instead (see "Changing Document Spaces," later in this chapter).

Note that you can also save your Color Settings dialog box setup by clicking Save. If you save it in the location that InDesign offers, you'll find it in the Settings popup menu in the future. Plus, you can use that setting in all your other Creative Suite applications, too.

Monitor profile. While you could specify your monitor profile in early versions of InDesign, now InDesign is smart enough to pull this information from the default operating system monitor profile. The software that you use to characterize your monitor generally makes the profile it generates the default monitor profile automatically. If you don't have a hardware calibration system—like GretagMacbeth's EyeOne, or the Spyder with OptiCal—you can try to eyeball it using ColorSync (on the Mac) or Adobe Gamma (which was installed along with InDesign for Windows).

Working Spaces. Perhaps the most important features of the Color Settings dialog box are the two Working Spaces pop-up menus, which control InDesign's default color profiles for RGB and CMYK colors. Remember that an RGB value doesn't mean anything because red, green, and blue phosphors are different on different devices. Cyan, magenta, yellow, and black inks can also be radically different depending on ink manufacturer, paper stock, press conditions, and so on. So RGB and CMYK colors are all just a bunch of numbers. Profiles assign color meaning to the numbers: such-and-such CMYK value *on this particular device.*

The profiles you choose from the CMYK and RGB pop-up menus are the profiles InDesign will use for any objects you create in InDesign, and for any imported graphics that did not include a color management profile (and that you have not applied a profile to using the Image Color Settings dialog box). Also, as we'll point out in the discussion below about color policies, the default CMYK profile is also used for imported CMYK images—even those that have their own profile—when you choose the Preserve Numbers option (which you probably will).

Although we almost always recommend using Adobe RGB (1998) for the RGB working space, the choice of a CMYK working space depends entirely on your print workflow. In a perfect world, you'd have a color profile for your particular printing press or output device, with your particular paper stock, and so on. But in reality, you can typically get away with picking either a profile for the proofing system you'll be using (if you have a profile) or use something close. For most of our print jobs we just pick U.S. Web Coated or U.S. Web Uncoated. ("Web" here refers to a Web press, as opposed to a sheetfed press, and has nothing to do with the World Wide Web.) If we were in Europe, we'd choose Euroscale or Europe ISO Fogra27 (which David erroneously pronounces *fois gras*).

Note that your imported graphics don't have to share the same working space with your document; InDesign is smart enough to handle different spaces at the same time.

However, the default RGB and CMYK working spaces that you set here do not apply to any documents that already have a profile associated with them. These defaults only affect the default working space for new documents you create from now on and for documents that are not tagged with a profile. A document won't be tagged with a profile if it was created when color management was disabled, or if it was saved when the Color Mangement Policies were set to Off (more on policies below).

If you're looking for a particular profile that you know you've installed in the operating system correctly, but doesn't appear here, try turning on the Advanced checkbox (see "Advanced Color Settings," later in this section).

Color Management Policies. InDesign assigns the default working spaces to each new document you create while color management is on. But what should InDesign do when color management is turned on and you open a document that was created when color management was turned off (so no profile was associated with the document)? What if you open a document made by someone else who used a different working space? You can tell InDesign what to do in these cases with the Color Management Policies section of the Color Settings dialog box.

The Policies section also manages what happens to CMYK images that you import, which has huge implications over how they appear in print.

► **RGB.** We suggest leaving the RGB pop-up menu set to its default value (Preserve Embedded Profiles) most of the time. This means InDesign will keep track of embedded profiles in RGB images and InDesign documents that contain RGB colors—very useful if you receive RGB images or files from other people.

We can't think of any reason to set RGB to Off (which would simply ignore all profiles and stop InDesign from embedding an RGB profile in the document, causing untold horrors when it came to getting any sort of color consistency). However, choosing Convert to Working Space could be useful on occassion, if you knew you had to open 50 InDesign documents that had simply been created with the wrong RGB profile. But watch out: Any RGB colors you created in the InDesign document will look the same, but the actual RGB numbers will likely change upon conversion.

► **CMYK.** The choice for the CMYK policy is not so cut and dry. Most people will want to use Preserve Numbers (Ignore Embedded Profile), but if you're serious about color management you may want to choose Preserve Embedded Profile. The first choice (Preserve Numbers) tells InDesign to use the current CMYK document profile as the profile for all your CMYK colors and imported CMYK images. For example, let's say you make a 100-percent cyan in a CMYK TIFF that uses some wacky custom CMYK profile, then you import that into your InDesign document that uses the normal SWOP profile. InDesign ignores the wacky profile entirely and just assumes that the image uses SWOP. You can override this (see "Applying Device Profiles to Images," later in this chapter), but you wouldn't want to have to do that very often.

Preserve Numbers (Ignore Embedded Profile) sort of defeats the greater purpose of color management, because the appearance of the colors may change even though the CMYK numbers won't. Nonetheless, it usually works pretty well—especially when all your incoming CMYK images are created with the same profile (which is often the case).

On the othe hand, if you receive CMYK images that have embedded CMYK profiles from a number of sources, you're pretty sure that the sources each used different CMYK profiles, and you need to make sure they all look good when you print or export PDF, you'll want to use Preserve Embedded Profile. This tells InDesign to keep their appearance consistent with the originals (how they looked in Photoshop, for example), even if it means changing the CMYK numbers to accomplish that. For example, that 100-percent cyan swatch might change to 95-percent cyan plus 5-percent magenta.

Again, we urge people not to set the CMYK policy to Off, as it will likely only cause you heartache down the road. (If you're frustrated with your previous experiences with color management, choose Preserve Numbers rather than Off.)

In most cases, all three Profile Mismatches and Missing Profiles checkboxes in the Color Management Policies section should be turned on. That way, you're asked what to do when you open a document that doesn't contain working spaces or that has a different working space than the current application defaults. This is safe and practical, though it does get a little annoying seeing those dialog boxes all the time. So if you're relatively sure what will happen to RGB and CMYK colors when you open a document, you might want to turn off the two Ask When Opening checkboxes.

Advanced Color Settings

While the color management options we've described are enough for many workflows, you can get even more tweaky by turning on the Advanced Mode checkbox (see Figure 10-18). First, when Advanced Mode is turned on you can select any color profile installed in your operating system for your working spaces (as opposed to only the recommended Adobe profiles). Next, you can select an alternate color management engine, adjust the default rendering intent, and choose whether or not to use black point compensation.

FIGURE 10-18
Advanced
Color Settings

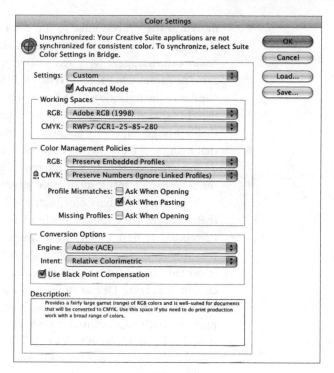

Engine. Color management engines (the actual software at the heart of the system that converts one color into another) are made by a variety of manufacturers—InDesign comes with a few: the Adobe CMS and either the Microsoft ICM (on Windows) or Apple ColorSync (on the Mac). Mac users will notice separate entries for the Apple CMM and for Apple ColorSync. Apple CMM means that the Apple CMM will always be used; Apple ColorSync uses whatever engine is set in the ColorSync control panel or System Preference. You may even have other third-party engines available. Ultimately, it's very unlikely that you would ever see a difference between any of these. However, unless you have a really good reason to switch, you should just use the Adobe CMS (which is also what Photoshop uses by default).

Intent. What happens when the color management system encounters a color that is outside of the gamut of the selected printing device? The color management system must change the color to one that's inside the printer's gamut. *How* it does that is the topic of the Intent pop-up menu. Intent is shorthand for *rendering intent*.

When you choose either Relative Colorimetric (which is the default) or Absolute Colorimetric, the out-of-gamut colors are moved to the nearest edge of the color gamut—also called gamut clipping—which means that differences between out-of-gamut colors can disappear (*very* red and *very, very* red both become the same in-gamut CMYK red). When this happens, you'll see an effect similar to posterization in the more saturated areas of images. The Perceptual rendering intent squeezes all the document's colors so that out-of-gamut colors are brought into the color gamut in a way that maintains a distinction between the colors. The Saturation rendering intent, on the other hand, moves all colors toward the edge of the color gamut, resulting in more saturated color.

In general, Relative Colorimetric is best for solid colors and synthetic images (like images made in Illustrator or FreeHand), and Perceptual is best for scanned images. Unfortunately, InDesign uses this rendering intent both for colors built in InDesign and for imported images (unless you specifically override it, which we discuss in "Applying Device Profiles to Images," below). However, for most documents and images—especially those already in CMYK mode—Relative Colorimetric probably makes the most sense. On the other hand, if you use a lot of RGB images with saturated out-of-gamut colors, and you're trying to match these colors with swatches built in InDesign, you might want to use Perceptual instead. If you want more intense color in business graphics (such as charts and graphs), you might try choosing Saturation.

Use Black Point Compensation. The Use Black Point Compensation option, when turned on, maps the black of the source profile to the black of the target profile. We usually think of black as being "just black," but of course black on different devices appears differently (for instance, solid black on newsprint is much more gray than solid black on glossy sheetfed stock). We generally recommend leaving this turned on, ensuring that the entire dynamic range of the output device is used.

Changing Document Spaces

By default the document working space is whatever Color Settings was set to when you first created the document. If you later change Color Settings, the application's default working space will be different than your document's space; that's no big deal because InDesign always uses the document space if there is one.

What if you want to change the document working space? For example, you thought you were going to print on coated stock but later found you had to cut your budget and switch to uncoated stock? You can add or change a document's working space profiles using the Assign Profiles and the Convert to Profile features in the Edit menu.

Assign Profiles lets you tag your document with another set of RGB and/or CMYK profiles, or even remove the document profile entirely (see Figure 10-19). Changing the document profiles with Assign Profiles is like saying, "The colors in this document now mean something else, because cyan now looks like this, magenta looks like this, and so on." Accordingly, the colors on screen may change, but the actual color definitions don't.

Convert to Profile is the opposite: It actually converts the colors in your document to a new profile, changing the color definitions to maintain the look of the colors (see Figure 10-20). That means a 100-percent magenta will end up as something like 96-percent magenta, 6-percent yellow (or something else, depending on what profile you're converting to). We encourage you to be very careful when using Convert to Profile; it can really mess up your documents, or it can be a lifesaver if you really know what it's doing.

Note that Convert to Profile is the only good way to find out what your document space currently is (you'll find it listed at the top of the dialog box).

FIGURE 10-19
Assign Profiles

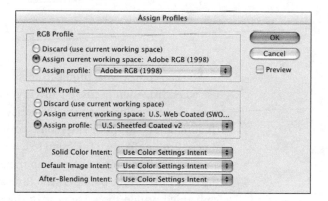

FIGURE 10-20
Convert to Profile

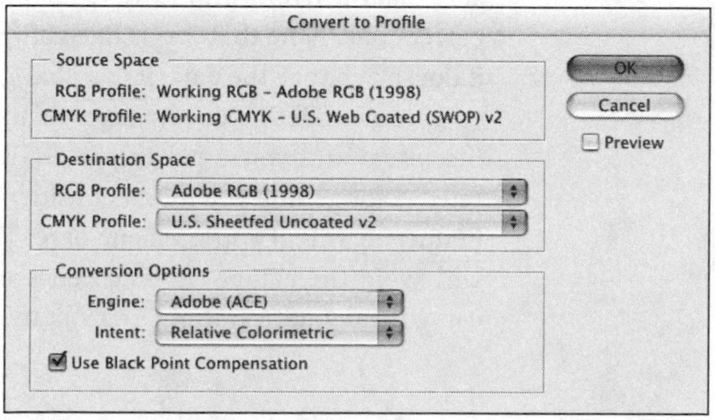

Applying Device Profiles to Images

When you save an image from Adobe Photoshop, by default the program embeds a color profile that describes the image's color space (see *Real World Photoshop* for more on Photoshop's behavior). InDesign recognizes that profile (if color management is turned on) when you place the graphic on your page, though if the CMYK policy was set to Preserve Numbers (Ignore Linked Profiles) when you created this document, any embedded profile is ignored at this point.

However you can adjust this behavior if you turn on the Show Import Options checkbox in the Place dialog box, and then click on the Color tab of the Image Import Options dialog box (see Figure 10-21). Of course, this works only with color-manageable images (that is, it's pretty much any reasonable format other EPS).

FIGURE 10-21
Applying a Profile at Import

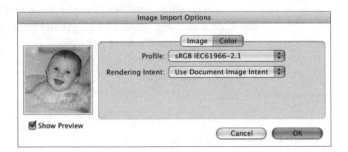

You can choose what profile to apply, and what rendering intent to use when InDesign needs to convert the colors to a different profile space. If your color management policy is set to Preserve Numbers (Ingore Linked Profiles), the Profile pop-up menu will read Use Document Profile. To force InDesign to use an embedded profile instead, you can choose it from the pop-up menu (it should be listed at the top of the list). If the policy is set to Preserve Embedded Profiles, the embedded profile should appear in the pop-up menu. But if you're sure that the wrong profile was embedded then feel free to choose the correct one. Note that this is like using Assign Profile in Photoshop; it doesn't change the data; it just changes the meaning of the data.

If your InDesign document is set to Relative Colorimetric rendering intent and you're placing an RGB image that has a large, saturated color gamut, you might consider selecting Perceptual from the Rendering Intent pop-up menu here. That way, this particular image will avoid the gamut-clipping behavior. For most images, however, using the default value of Use Document Image Intent is reasonable.

Whatever you choose upon placing the image, you can always override it by selecting the image and choosing Image Color Settings from the Object menu (or right-click on the image and choose it from the Graphics submenu in the context menu).

Soft-Proofing Controls

You probably want to get some sense of what your pages are going to look like before you commit to a $50,000 print run. Increasingly, proofing is being done not on traditional color proofing systems, but rather on desktop inkjet printers and on screen. Proofing images on screen is called soft-proofing, and the quality of soft-proofing in InDesign is limited only by the accuracy of the profiles involved.

The Proof Colors command on the View menu lets you turn soft-proofing on and off. But it's in the Proof Setup submenu that you can control what the proof is showing you. Note that the settings you make in Proof Setup are specific to the window that's in the foreground, not the document itself. This means you can create several views of the same page (by choosing New Window from the Window menu) and apply different soft-proofing settings to each view, letting you see how the page will work in different output scenarios. However, note that turning on Proof Colors slows down document redraw, so while it's good to look at, it's not particularly fun to work on your document when this is on.

The three items in the Proof Setup submenu are Document CMYK, Working CMYK, and Custom. We typically just use Custom, which displays the Proof Setup dialog box (see Figure 10-22), which gives us

FIGURE 10-22
Soft-Proofing

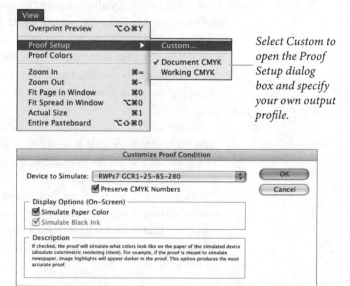

Select Custom to open the Proof Setup dialog box and specify your own output profile.

more control over the soft-proof (though not as much as Photoshop offers). First, choose the profile of the device you're trying to emulate. Then, choose whether to preserve CMYK numbers, and whether to simulate Paper White and Ink Black.

Preserve CMYK Numbers. The Preserve CMYK Numbers checkbox lets you tell InDesign what you want done with the CMYK colors you defined in the document and CMYK images that either have no embedded profile or have an embedded profile but are using the document CMYK profile because you have set the CMYK policy to Preserve Numbers (Ignore Linked Profiles). If you turn on this checkbox, these CMYK colors are simply passed through without conversion. If you turn off the checkbox, all colors are converted to the proof profile. Which you choose should depend on which you're going to pick in the Print or Export PDF dialog box (see "Color Management in Output," below).

Simulate Black/White. The two checkboxes in this section control the rendering of the document's colors from the proofing space to the monitor. When Paper White and Ink Black are turned off, InDesign does a relative colorimetric rendering, mapping the white of the proof device's paper to monitor white and the black of the device's black ink to monitor black. This isn't particularly useful; after all, for a soft-proof you're trying to see what the real paper's white and ink's blacks will look like.

Instead, we almost always turn on the Paper White checkbox (which automatically also turns on the Ink Black checkbox). This way, the monitor simulates the paper's white (which is often duller than monitor white), and you can see the compressed dynamic range of print. If you're simulating a low-dynamic-range process—like newsprint, or inkjet on uncoated paper—turning on Ink Black (or Paper White) gives you a much better idea of the actual color range you'll get in print.

Unfortunately, the effect of simulating a compressed dynamic range is so dramatic that it feels like it ruins the document's colors. It's a good idea to put the document in Preview mode (press W while not editing text), hide your palettes (press Tab), then select Proof Colors from the View menu, but before actually letting go of the mouse button, close your eyes for a few seconds. When you open your eyes, your brain can readjust its own internal white point, giving you a better sense of what the image really will look like when it comes off the printer.

It's worth noting again that you'll never get an exact match between screen and final printed output. However, like any proofing system, the key is not in getting a perfect match, but rather in getting pretty dang close, and then learning the *relationship* between screen and printed piece. The more you do this (and the more accurate your profiles are), the more accurate you'll get at predicting final color.

Color Management in Output

None of this color management stuff is relevant if you can't get your final design to print well. Fortunately, you can perform color conversions from your document space to a selected profile when you print your document or export it to PDF or EPS.

Print dialog box. When color management is on, InDesign activates the features in the Color Management tab of the Print dialog box (see Figure 10-23). The key to managing color is to specify a source space and a target space, so the color management engine knows where the color is coming from (what the color is supposed to look like) and where the color is going (how that device images color, so it can convert the colors properly).

▶ **The Source.** You have two choices for a source space in the Print section of this panel: Document (the document working space)

FIGURE 10-23
Color Management in the Print Dialog Box

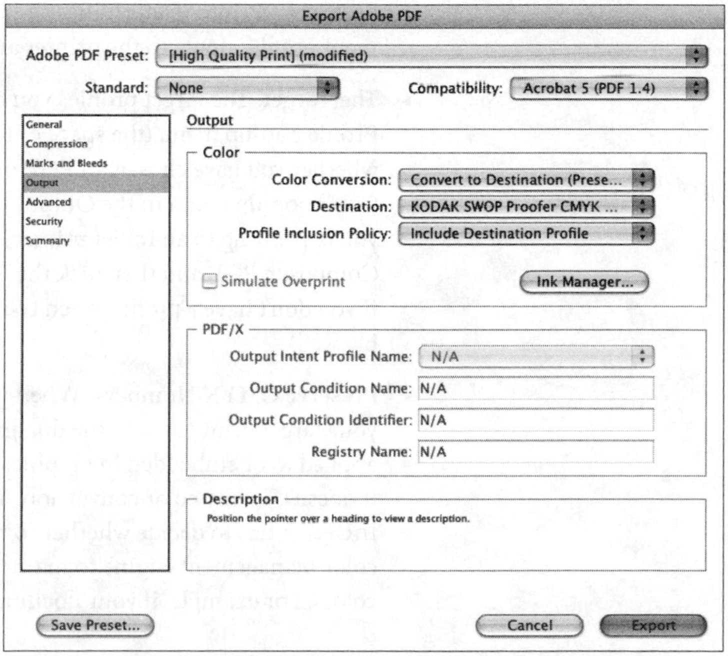

or Proof (the profile you last chose in the Custom Proof Setup dialog box). The Proof option lets you print your file to a composite printer, like a desktop inkjet, and make it simulate the CMYK output you've been soft-proofing—that is, it gives you a hard copy of your soft-proofed document.

When you choose Proof, you can also choose whether to simulate the paper color of the final target by turning on or off the Simulate Paper Color checkbox in the Options section of the dialog box.

▶ **Who Handles the Color.** You next need to determine who is going to do the color management: InDesign or your PostScript printer. You can choose one or the other from the Color Handling pop-up menu. As long as we have a reasonably good target profile for our printer, we virtually always choose Let InDesign Determine Color, as we trust Adobe's color management system more than most.

On the other hand, if you don't have a good profile for your printer, or you trust your printer's PostScript RIP to provide the color management, you can choose PostScript Printer Determines Color. Of course, this only works on PostScript devices, and it only works when you've selected one of the Composite options or InRIP Separations from the Color pop-up menu in the Output tab of the Print dialog box. When you choose PostScript Printer Determines Color, InDesign sends your document profiles down to the printer and hopes for the best.

▶ **The Target.** The target profiles you can choose from the Printer Profile pop-up menu (the space of the print device) depend on whether you have chosen an RGB or a CMYK space from the Color pop-up menu in the Output tab of the Print dialog box. If you're printing to an inkjet printer, you should probably choose Composite RGB and then pick the RGB profile for that device (or, if you don't have a profile, often the sRGB works at least reasonably well).

▶ **Preserve CMYK Numbers.** When you print, InDesign compares your target print space to the document space and the profiles applied to or embedded in graphics; if they're all the same, then it doesn't do any color conversion. Whenever the profiles differ, InDesign has to decide whether to run the colors through the color management engine to maintain visual consistency of the colors. For example, if your document CMYK setting is U.S.

Web Coated (SWOP) but you choose a Newsprint output profile, InDesign will obviously have to convert your RGB colors to the Newsprint CMYK space. But it may also convert your CMYK colors from their original space to Newsprint, too.

Converting from one CMYK space to another CMYK space is called cross-rendering, and it can be a blessing or a curse. It can really get you out of a last-minute jam if you don't have time to go back and reseparate RGB images into your new CMYK space. However, there's no way to tell InDesign to cross-render your images but not other things, so all your 100-percent black text also gets cross-rendered—resulting in four-color CMYK text—rarely what you'd expect or want.

Fortunately, you can turn on the Preserve CMYK Numbers checkbox in the Print dialog box. When this is on, InDesign won't cross-render any of your document's CMYK colors or CMYK images that either have no embedded profile or have an embedded profile but were imported with the Preserve Numbers (Ignore Linked Profiles) color policy enabled in the Color Settings dialog box. This is our new best friend in the color management wars. We suggest you turn it on unless you really know what you're doing. (Of course, if the source and target profiles are the same, it's grayed out because colors aren't in danger of cross-rendering.)

Don't forget that you can have the Preserve Numbers (Ignore Linked Profiles) policy turned on and still force InDesign to cross-render a specific image by giving it a profile with the Image Color Settings dialog box that we talked about earlier. Also, don't forget that you can change your document profile before printing with Assign Profile or Convert Profile.

Export as PDF. You can tell InDesign whether to color-manage your exported PDF files in the Output tab of the Export PDF dialog box (see Figure 10-24). You have several options here.

▶ **Color Conversion.** If you don't want InDesign to convert any colors (if you want all the document and image color data left as is) then select No Color Conversion from the Color Conversion pop-up menu in the Output tab. This is what you get when you use the PDF/X3 standard because the understanding is that the color management will be handled downstream when the PDF is printed.

However, if you want InDesign to handle the color management while generating the PDF, choose either Convert to

Destination or Convert to Destination (Preserve Numbers). For
example, if you're exporting the PDF for primarily onscreen
viewing, choose Convert to Destination from the Color Conversion pop-up menu and then choose an RGB profile from the
Destination pop-up menu—the sRGB profile is probably the
most useful, as it purports to define the "average" monitor. This
forces everything into the sRGB space.

If you're exporting for print and you want to color-manage
the entire document, then choose Convert to Destination and
choose your final output device in the Destination pop-up menu.
However, if the Destination profile is different than your document profile, your CMYK colors will likely get cross-rendered
into a different CMYK space. As we noted earlier, this is the
cause of the four-color black text problem that many people had
in earlier versions. So in most circumstances, we would recommend the Convert to Destination (Preserve Numbers) option,
which leaves document colors and untagged colors alone.

▶ **Include Profiles.** The Profile Inclusion Policy pop-up menu lets
you choose choose whether or not to embed various profiles in
your PDF. If you choose one of the two Convert to Destination

options in the Color Conversion pop-up menu, you can choose to either not embed any profiles or to embed the destination profile. If you expect your PDF to be further color managed by some other application (even to view it properly on screen), you should definitely include your profiles. But it does make a larger PDF file, so in many cases, we just leave it out.

If the Color Conversion pop-up menu is set to leave your colors alone (again, the assumption here is that your file will be color managed later), you have three different choices in the Profile Inclusion Policy dialog box: Include All Profiles, Include Tagged Source Profiles, and Include All RGB and Tagged Source Profiles. Of course, you can also just tell InDesign not to include any profile, but we're not sure why you'd do that.

Export as EPS. There is little color management interface in the Export EPS dialog box (see Figure 10-25); when you pick RGB or CMYK from the Color pop-up menu, InDesign simply assumes your document profiles are the destination profiles, and it color-manages your document—converting all imported images (at least the ones that it can, like TIFF and .PSD files) to the document working space. You can avoid this by choosing Leave Unchanged from the Color pop-up menu, or by turning color management off before saving files as EPS.

The Color "Done"

As you work with commercial printing, always remember that you're at the mercy of a series of photochemical and mechanical processes—from your imagesetter through the printing press—that, in many ways, haven't changed since 1900 (if that recently). Temperature, humidity, and ambient static electricity play large roles in the process, and the people who operate these systems are at least skilled craftspeople; at best, artists. Ask them as many questions as they'll answer, set your job up the way they want it, and then sit back and watch your job come off the press.

CHAPTER 11

Printing

Printing is an ancient art, and has been invented and reinvented many times. You can print by rolling a carved cylinder over a sheet of wet clay, as the Mesopotamians did. Or you can smear a carved block of wood with ink and then press the block into a sheet of paper, as the Chinese started doing in the eighth or ninth century. With grease, water, and ink, even a slab of limestone can learn to transfer an image to paper, as Alois Senefelder of Munich found in 1798 (thereby inventing lithography).

In the fifteenth century, Gutenberg (and possibly others) came up with moveable type made of cast metal—which, in turn, transformed printing from a craft into an industry. Scribes the world over lamented the decline in the quality of written materials.

Printing—the ability to make dozens, hundreds, thousands, millions of copies of an image—flourished. For whatever reason, we humans will go to great lengths to get our pictures, text, and advertising into the hands of our willing or unwilling audience. And, in spite of the encroachments of the Web, printing is still the best way to do that.

The InDesign Print Dialog Box

When you press Command-P/Ctrl-P or choose Print Book from the Book palette (see Chapter 8, "Long Documents"), InDesign displays the Print dialog box. There are so many features packed into this dialog box that Adobe had to break it up into eight different tabs, each listed along the left side of the dialog box: General, Setup, Marks and Bleeds, Output, Graphics, Color Management, Advanced, and Summary (see Figure 11-1).

Even if you're printing to a lowly desktop printer, it's worth at least glimpsing at each of these tabs. Fortunately, you can use keyboard shortcuts to navigate among them: Command/Ctrl-Down arrow jumps to the next tab, Command/Ctrl-Up arrow jumps to the previous tab, and holding down the Command/Ctrl key while pressing a number from 1 to 8 skips to the corresponding tab number (1 for General, 2 for Setup, and so on). We'll cover each of these tabs, in order, below.

Printers, PostScript Files, and PPDs

Before you go anywhere in the Print dialog box, you've got to make one or two important decisions. First, you must choose from the options on the Printer pop-up menu, which lists the printers you have installed on your computer. When you choose a printer, InDesign looks to the printer driver to see what PPD (PostScript Printer Description) file is associated with that printer, and it displays it—grayed out—in the PPD pop-up menu. In the case of a non-PostScript device, InDesign leaves this pop-up menu blank.

If you want to print a PostScript file directly to disk rather than to a device (also called making a "PostScript dump"), choose PostScript File from the Printer pop-up menu. In this case, you must also pick the PPD file that describes your final output device or choose Device Independent. You can typically use device-independent PostScript files—also called ".sep files" or "prepress files"—for output using imposition and trapping systems.

Writing PostScript to disk offers some advantages (you can change the PostScript with a word processor to learn about InDesign's PostScript, fix printing problems, add special design effects, or just goof around). However, most output providers now prefer receiving PDF files over PostScript files. Some companies don't even accept PostScript files anymore, except from clients that they know will create them properly (because it's difficult to make changes to your document once it's written as PostScript). We discuss exporting PDF files in Chapter 7, "Importing and Exporting."

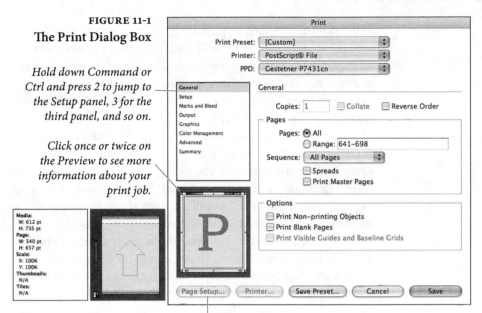

FIGURE 11-1

The Print Dialog Box

Hold down Command or Ctrl and press 2 to jump to the Setup panel, 3 for the third panel, and so on.

Click once or twice on the Preview to see more information about your print job.

Click Page Setup to open the printer driver's print options. In general, you should avoid using the printer driver dialog boxes. (It's not available in this example.)

Note that PPDs are not, and should not be confused with, printer drivers. Printer drivers are pieces of software that direct information from your system and applications to a hardware port—usually, your computer's printer port or network connection. PPDs work in conjunction with printer drivers to give applications information about the printer (what paper sizes are available? what's the resolution of the printer? what do the printer error messages mean?) and to customize the printer's operation for the application (what PostScript routine does the application use to render halftones?).

InDesign and other applications use PPDs to optimize printing for a specific printer. If you are specifying a PPD file, it's important that you choose the right one, or else your pages may not print correctly (and might not print at all). The settings you choose here determine what options you have in the rest of the Print dialog box.

By the way, if you have installed a PPD in OS X and it doesn't appear in the PPD pop-up menu, it may be a compressed PPD. Try decompressing it using StuffIt Expander first.

Printer Driver Settings

Our eagle-eyed readers will quickly find a Setup button (in Windows) or Page Setup and Printer buttons (on the Macintosh) at the bottom of the Print dialog box. These are doorways into your operating system's printer drivers. At print time, InDesign interacts with whatever printer driver you're using. However, there are very few instances when you'd need to click these buttons to change the printer driver settings. In most cases, the settings are duplicated somewhere in InDesign's Print dialog box, and it's always better to set it within this dialog box than in the driver.

However, if you know of an option in the printer driver that InDesign doesn't handle, click the appropriate button. For example, many inkjet printers require you to specify resolution, quality, and color adjustments in their own drivers. Similarly, some PostScript printers offer options like toner density, paper tray handling, and so on, which also require a trip to the printer driver dialog box.

Note that in some rare cases you may get really weird results when applying both printer driver settings and Print dialog box settings (such as trying to print color separations while, at the same time, telling the driver to print multiple document pages per printed page).

PostScript vs. Non-PostScript   While InDesign can print to non-PostScript printers reasonably well, it's really designed for PostScript devices. PostScript is a page-description language—a collection of commands that PostScript devices understand. When you tell InDesign to print a page, it writes a computer program in PostScript describing the page, and sends that program to the printer. The printer (or imagesetter, or platesetter), which has a PostScript interpreter (called a raster image processor, or RIP) inside it or attached to it, interprets the PostScript and puts marks on the paper or film.

When InDesign detects that your printer isn't equipped with PostScript (based on the driver you're using), it grays out the Print dialog box features that don't work on non-PostScript devices, such as color separations and the transparency Flattener (transparency effects print fine on these devices, but you don't need the Flattener to create them; see "Printing Transparency," later in this chapter).

Print Preview   InDesign displays a preview of the way your page fits on the selected paper size in the lower-left corner of the Print dialog box. This preview does not include a preview of the elements on your pages, unlike the print preview features found in Word, Excel, Illustrator, or FreeHand. The previews, however, do provide feedback that can save you from printing pages in the wrong orientation or printing pages that won't fit on the paper.

InDesign displays additional information "behind" the preview icon. Click once on the preview and you can see data such as the paper size, the page size, how many tiles will print (see "Tile" in "Setup," later in this chapter), and so on. Click again, and InDesign shows you how your page will print relative to the paper path through the printer. For laser printers and other printers with fixed paper sizes, this isn't very helpful, but it's great when printing to a roll-fed imagesetter or platesetter.

General

The General tab of the Print dialog box contains the lowest common denominators of printing features: what pages do you want to print, how many copies do you want, and how do you want them to come out of the printer (see Figure 11-2).

Copies
Enter the number of copies of the page you want to print in the Copies field. You can print up to 9999 copies of your publication.

Collate
When you turn on the Collate option, InDesign prints the range of pages you've specified, in order, for each copy of the publication you print. This makes for much slower printing. When you print multiple copies of a page, your printer only needs to process each page once (and then prints multiple copies of the page using the same image); when you turn on the Collate option, your printer must process each page once for every copy of the print job.

Reverse Order
When you print a multipage document, do you want the first page to come out first or last? Turning on the Reverse Order check box tells InDesign to print the last page first, then print "backwards" to the first page. You'll want to turn this on if your pages come out of the laser printer face up.

Page Ranges
Turn on the All Pages option to print all of the pages in the publication. To print a range of pages, turn on the Range option. Enter the page range in the Range field as shown in Table 11-1.

You can mix and match page ranges. To print pages one, three, six through ten, and 20, for example, you'd enter "1,3,6-10,20." The pages and ranges you specify must be in order (you couldn't, for example, print page 20 before printing page 6). Specifying "1,5,5,9" means print page 1, then two copies of page 5, and then page 9. If you want to print from page 10 to the end of the document, type "10-".

FIGURE 11-2
The General Panel
of the Print Dialog Box

Or, to print from the beginning of the file up to (and including) page 10, type "-10".

If you've used the Page Numbering and Section feature, then printing specific page ranges gets even more complicated. For example, let's say your first section uses roman numerals and is 5 pages long. To print the first six pages, you type "i-6" (you can't type "1-6" because there is no page called "1"—the first page is called "i"). However, you can change this behavior: If you select Absolute Numbering in the View pop-up menu of the General tab of the Preferences dialog box, then you should type "1-6" because the range now refers to *absolute* page numbering ("the first through the sixth page").

Note: If you've chosen Absolute Numbering from the View pop-up menu in the Page Numbering section of the General Preferences dialog box, InDesign expects you to enter absolute page numbers in the range field, rather than the number of the page as defined by the section containing the page. If page 1 of section 3 of the document is the fifteenth page in the document, you would enter "15" in the Range field (if, on the other hand, you chose Section Numbering from the View pop-up menu, you would enter "Sec3:1").

Sequence   To print even and odd pages, select the All Pages option from the Sequence pop-up menu; to print even pages, select Even Pages Only; and to print odd pages select Odd Pages Only. These choices affect all page ranges, including page ranges you've entered in the Range field. The only time we've used this pop-up menu is when we've printed

TABLE 11-1
Printing Page Ranges

To print:	Enter:	Example:
A continuous range of pages	first page - last page	12-21
Up to a specific page	- last page	-5
From a page to the end of the document	first page -	5-
Noncontiguous pages	page, page	1, 3
Mixed page ranges	page, range	-3, 6-9, 12, 15-
Pages by section	section:page	Sec1:1, Sec2:5

double-sided documents on a laser printer (print just the odd pages, then flip the pages, put them back in the printer, and print the even pages). If you've turned on the Spreads option, these options will be unavailable.

Spreads When you turn on the Spreads option, InDesign tries to print each spread in the publication on a single sheet of paper (or other output media). If the spread is larger than the selected paper size, you can turn on the Scale to Fit option in the Setup panel of the Print dialog box and/or change the paper orientation. This is also called "readers spreads." Note that this is not the same as printer spreads, which are a form of imposition, printing the first and last page together, and so on. Fortunately, you can get good printer spreads out of InDesign using the InBooklet SE feature (under the File menu). This is a "lite" version of a product from www.alap.com that Adobe licensed for InDesign CS2. (Of course, as we go to press, ALAP is now owned by Quark. So the future of this plug-in may be limited.) Or you can try any or all of the imposition scripts available for download from http://share.studio.adobe.com.

Print Master Pages Sometimes you need to print your master pages instead of your document pages. No problem: Just turn on the Print Master Pages check box. When you do this, you cannot specify page ranges—InDesign prints all the master pages in the document.

Print Non-Printing Objects When you turn on the Print Non-printing Objects check box, InDesign prints every object on your pages, regardless of the state of the Nonprinting check box in the Attributes palette. However, this feature does not print objects that are on hidden (and therefore non-printing) layers.

Print Blank Pages　What happens when you print a three-page document that has nothing on page 2? By default, only pages 1 and 3 print out. If you want the blank page 2 to print, too, you'd better turn on the Print Blank Pages check box.

Print Visible Guides and Baseline Grids　When you turn the Print Visible Guides and Baseline Grids check box on, all visible margin guides, baseline grid guides, and page guides print out (but not the document grid). We find this particularly helpful when designing templates for others to use.

Setup

When we talk about page size, we're talking about the page size you've defined for your publication using the New Document or Document Setup dialog boxes. This page size should be the same as the page size of the printed piece you intend to produce. "Paper size," on the other hand, means the size of the medium you're printing on. The Setup tab of the Print dialog box lets you specify paper size, as well as how you want the page to appear on that paper (see Figure 11-3).

Paper Size　PPDs contain information about the paper sizes that a printer can handle, and this information then shows up in the Paper Size pop-up menu. When you specify a non-PostScript printer, Paper Size changes to Defined by Driver, and you'll have to handle the paper size in the printer driver dialog box. Once again, the paper size doesn't have to be the same as your page size; if you're printing page marks (like crop marks), then the paper size will need to be larger. In the case of printers that image larger sheets of film, we usually set Paper Size to Custom, and then leave the Width and Height fields set to Auto (so InDesign figures out the proper imaging area for us).

Offset　The Offset feature controls the placement of your document on the paper, film, or plate. The printer's default paper offset, even when set to zero, is almost always large enough so that you don't have to worry about changing the value of Offset here. However, if you need the page to image farther from the paper edge, change this value.

Gap　The Gap setting, which is really only relevant for roll-fed printers, determines the amount of blank space between each page of the document as it prints out. Some output providers that print to film like to set this to about 2p, so they can cut the pages apart more easily. In most cases, you can just ignore this setting.

FIGURE 11-3
**The Setup Panel
of the Print Dialog Box**

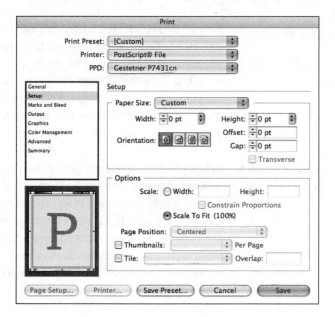

Orientation You can control the rotation of your page on the paper using the Orientation setting. The four choices (each rotated another 90 degrees) are indicated with tiny icons, but we find it easier to watch the preview page in the lower-left corner of the dialog box.

Transverse The Transverse setting is like Orientation, but is used for roll-fed imagesetters and platesetters when the Paper Size is set to Custom. When you turn on Transverse, the width of the paper is placed along the length of the imagesetter's paper roll, which can save paper or film. The best way to get a feel for the Transverse command is to click the Preview icon twice (to see the page versus the paper path), then turn on and off this check box. Of course, you have to first select an appropriate PPD.

Scale You can scale the output of your pages, from as small as one percent to as large as 1000 percent of their actual size. You can specify a scaling percentage yourself, or ask InDesign to fit the page to the size of the paper. When you use large percentages, watch the print preview to see that the enlarged page will fit on the paper you've selected.

If you're printing using a commercial printing process that distorts the printed images (flexographic printing, for example, typically stretches the axis parallel to the rotation of the printing cylinder), you can compensate for the distortion by entering different values in the Width and Height fields. To do this, turn off the Constrain

Proportions option, then enter the percentages you want in the Width and Height fields. When the Constrain Proportions option is turned on, any changes you make in one field are reflected in the other.

When Scale to Fit is on, InDesign calculates the scaling percentage necessary to fit the page (plus any printer's marks you selected in the Marks and Bleeds panel of the Print dialog box) onto the selected paper size, and uses that scaling percentage when you print.

Page Position   When you select a paper size that is larger than your document, you can specify using the Page Position pop-up menu where on the page you want your document to sit. You've got four choices: Upper Left, Center Horizontally, Center Vertically, and Centered. Upper Left is the default; the other three are self-explanatory. We find this control a matter of personal preference most of the time, though it's not uncommon for the printer's internal margins (the area of the paper where the printer simply cannot lay down toner or ink) to clip off the top or left part of your page. In this case, just change the page position to Centered and try printing again.

Thumbnails   Thumbnails are great when you're trying to print out an overview of your document. For instance, you can print nine pages on a single piece of paper—three across and three down—by turning on the Thumbnails check box and then choosing 3x3 from the Per Page pop-up menu. Note that on PostScript printers it takes as long to print this one sheet as it would to print all nine pages individually, so plan your time accordingly. We're happy to note that in CS2, InDesign now places page numbers next to each thumbnail.

Tile   If your pages just won't fit on your paper, you've got to resort to tiling and (horror of horrors) tape, wax, or glue. InDesign offers three ways to tile documents—Automatic, Auto Justified, and Manual.

Automatic Tiling. When you choose this option from the Tile pop-up menu, InDesign starts the tile at the upper-left corner of the page, and prints as much of the page as it can given the paper size. Then it starts the next tile, with an overlap as specified in the Overlap field. It goes across the page, then moves down the page by the height of the paper you're printing on, and then goes across the page again.

If you click once on the page preview, InDesign tells you how many tiles will be required to print each page. If you find that it's producing *lots* of tiles per page, try reducing the overlap. If you're just tiling together a proof, a slight reduction in the scaling percentage could save you a lot of time with scissors and tape.

Auto Justified Tiling. The Auto Justified tiling option lays out the pieces of your page on the paper so that there's no extra white space to the right or underneath the page image (as you typically get with Automatic tiling). When you use this option, the Overlap field is meaningless; InDesign is actually figuring the overlap amount itself.

Manual Tiling. When you choose Manual tiling, InDesign only prints one tile per document page, using the zero point on the ruler as the upper-left corner of the tile. To print successive tiles, you have to move the zero point and print again. We find Manual tiling much more useful than Automatic tiling—Automatic tiling always seems to split the tiles right in the middle of an important text block, so you can't read it. Or, worse, it splits an image or other tinted area—have you ever tried cutting and pasting to get the halftone dots in a photograph to line up? With Manual tiling, you can ensure that items that you want to be able to proof are positioned so they're easy to see.

Note: As far as we can tell, there's no way to turn off the tiling marks InDesign adds around the edges of pages printed using Automatic tiling.

Tiling: Just Say No. Now it's time for pure, unadulterated (no adults were used), talk-radio-style opinion. Any time anyone tells us that they plan to tile a publication, our sense of honesty and fair play forces us to ask them why they want to do that. Is it a masochistic streak they've had since childhood? A profound sense of personal inferiority? Something genetic?

If you can't find some way to print your publication without tiling, then use a copy camera or other photographic process to enlarge it to the size you want, rather than printing tiles and then trying to paste the printed tiles together. If you don't know if such a service is available in your area, get out the Yellow Pages. Even if you have to send the publication across the country to get it blown up to the size you want, do it. Sure—these services do cost money. But what's your time—or your sanity—worth?

Marks and Bleeds

When you print your publication, you can choose to include (or exclude) a number of printer's marks—crop marks, registration marks, and other information (see Figure 11-4). The preview window displays the effect (given the current page and paper sizes) of your

FIGURE 11-4
The Marks and Bleeds
Panel of the Print
Dialog Box

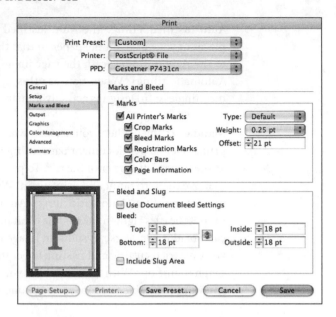

FIGURE 11-4
The Marks and Bleeds
Panel of the Print
Dialog Box

choice of printer's marks options, though they're usually too small to see well.

All Printer's Marks   Turn on the All Printer's Marks option when you want to print all of the printer's marks and page information. This is usually more than you need; for instance, if you don't have any objects bleeding off the page, then why bother with the Bleed Marks?

Crop Marks   Turn on the Crop Marks option to print lines outside the area of your page that define the area of the page (these are also called "trim marks"). Of course, if your paper size is not larger than your page size, InDesign won't (can't) print your crop marks.

Bleed Marks   Turn on the Bleed Marks option to print lines outside the area of your page that define the area of the bleed. Like crop marks, if your paper size is not larger than your page size, InDesign won't print your bleed marks. We almost always turn this option off, even when bleeding objects off the page; in our experience, it doesn't offer any useful information, and it can cause confusion.

Registration Marks   When you turn on the Registration Marks option, InDesign prints little targets around the edge of your page for your commercial printer to use when they're lining up, or registering, your color separations for printing. If your paper size is smaller than your page size, InDesign won't print the registration marks.

Color Bars   When you turn on the Color Bars option, InDesign prints small squares of color outside the bleed area of your printed page. Your commercial printer can use these samples to adjust their press as they print the publication. It's worth checking with your printer to find out if they really want these before turning on this check box.

Page Information   Turn on the Page Information option to print the file name and date of your publication on each printed page. In color separations InDesign also adds the name of the color plate. This makes it easy to tell which of several printed versions is the most current. It can also make it easier for your commercial printer to tell which pieces of film in a stack of separations go together (it's easy for you to tell, but put yourself in their shoes for a minute). We almost always leave this turned on (as long as the paper size is larger than the page size).

Type   Now here's an intriguing option—a pop-up menu offering only "Default" as a choice. The idea is that developers will be able to add different printer's marks at some point. We haven't seen any yet (apart from the specialized Japanese marks in InDesign-J).

To try to spur the development of alternative printers' marks, we'll show you how to create your own printers mark customization files later in this chapter.

Weight   You can change the thickness of the page marks by choosing from among three options in the Weight pop-up menu: .125 pt, .25 pt, and .5 pt. We're pretty happy with the default weight, .25 pt.

Offset   The Offset feature determines how far from the edge of the page the page marks should sit. The default value of six points seems a little tight to us. We don't operate a two-ton paper cutter at a bindery, but if we did, we'd sure wish people increased the space between page and trim marks (and registration marks) to at least 12 points.

Bleed   The values you enter in the Bleed fields set the real boundary of the printed page. When the value in the Bleed fields is zero, InDesign neatly clips off any page elements extending beyond the edges of the page. This leaves little room for error in trimming the resulting printed pages—usually, when you want a page element to bleed off of a page, you should allow at least 24 points of bleed to compensate for inaccuracies in printing and trimming. If objects bleed off the page to the pasteboard, you must change these Bleed values in order for the object to still bleed upon printing.

Output

Do you want to print a composite version of your publication, or do you want to print separations? If you're printing separations, which inks do you want to print? Those are among the questions you answer using the Output tab of the Print dialog box (see Figure 11-5).

Composite vs. Separations

If you've only used black ink in your document, you can ignore the Output tab. However, for those of us who create color documents, the most important setting here is the Color pop-up menu, with which you can tell InDesign to print composite color or color separations. Which of these you should choose depends on your printer and the output you're trying to achieve.

Desktop inkjet printers should generally be considered RGB devices, so you should send composite RGB data to them. Color PostScript printers usually do a better job with composite CMYK data. If you choose Composite CMYK, InDesign converts all your RGB data (including any RGB TIFF files) into CMYK at print time. You can use any of the composite choices when printing to a black-and-white desktop laser printer.

Composite CMYK is also useful for workflows in which the separations will be performed by a RIP, even if that RIP is running as software on another machine. However, in most of these instances, it makes more sense to create a PDF file, a device-independent PostScript file, or—for the adventurous—a device-dependent PostScript file using In-RIP separations, especially if you are using

FIGURE 11-5
The Output Panel of the Print Dialog Box

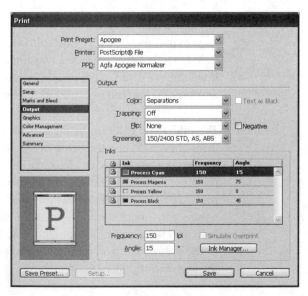

trapping (trapping is not supported in CMYK composite output). Choosing In-RIP Separations from the Color pop-up menu instructs InDesign to create a special type of composite CMYK file that will only print properly on a PostScript 3 output device and some newer PostScript Level 2 devices.

To tell InDesign to send the composite color information to the printer without changing it, choose Composite Leave Unchanged. If you do this, you will not be able to use the Simulate Overprint option.

You can also tell InDesign to separate each of your pages into four plates (or more, in the case of spot colors) by choosing Separations from the Color pop-up menu. If you select the Separations or In-RIP Separations option, InDesign activates the Inks list and its associated controls (the Flip, Frequency, Angle, Trapping settings, and so on).

Text As Black One problem with printing proofs on a desktop laser printer is that it's sometimes difficult to read colored text because it appears as a tint. Similarly, when you want to fax a black-and-white version of your document, screened text becomes almost unreadable. When you turn on the Text as Black check box, InDesign ensures all your text appears as solid black—except for text that is already set to solid white, Paper color, or None.

Trapping The Trapping pop-up menu controls whether InDesign applies automatic trapping to your documents. Choose one of the following trapping options from the Trapping pop-up menu:

► **Off.** Use this option if you've done all of your trapping manually (using InDesign's fills and strokes) or if you plan to separate and trap the publication using a post-processing program.

► **Application Built-In.** Choose Application Built-In when you want InDesign to trap your publication as it's sent to the printer (or to disk).

► **Adobe In-RIP.** Select this option when you want to leave trapping up to the RIP in your printer or imagesetter. This feature, which makes us rather nervous, only works on PostScript 3 and some PostScript Level 2 printers.

We cover trapping in greater detail in Chapter 10, "Color."

Flip and Negative   InDesign can mirror pages at print time if you choose Horizontal, Vertical, or Horizontal & Vertical from the Flip pop-up menu. Flipping an image is used for creating either wrong- or right-reading film from imagesetters, or film with emulsion side up or down. This is often handled in the imagesetter or platesetter, so be careful before you go changing this setting. The same thing goes for the Negative check box, which inverts the entire page so that everything that is set to 100-percent black becomes zero-percent black (effectively white). Never make assumptions about what your output provider wants; what you think will help might actually hinder (and cost you money in the long run).

Screening   What halftone screen frequency (in lines per inch) and screen angle do you want to use to print your publication? If you selected Composite Gray in the Color pop-up menu, you can choose either the printer's default (which is defined by the PPD you selected) or you can choose Custom and then enter your own values in the Frequency and Angle fields.

When you're printing separations, you'll see more choices on the Screening pop-up menu, and the values shown in the Frequency and Angle fields change as you select inks in the Inks list. Where the heck are these choices and values coming from? They're coming from the PPD. Every PPD contains a list of screen frequencies and screen angles optimized to avoid moiré patterns on the specific PostScript device described by the PPD. Because of the way that PostScript halftoning (or any digital halftoning, for that matter) works, a PostScript RIP cannot perfectly "hit" just any halftone screen.

On PostScript Level 1 devices, the screen angle and screen frequency you'd get would sometimes fail to match the frequency and angle you specified. This often resulted in serious output problems and severe moiré patterns. PPDs list combinations of screen angles known to be safe for a given printer at a screen frequency and angle.

While the need for these optimized screen angles has diminished somewhat with newer versions of PostScript, we strongly advise you to stick with them when you're printing separations.

To override the optimized screen settings for an ink, select the ink in the Inks list and then enter new values in the Frequency and Angle fields. Again, we don't recommend this, but you might have a very good reason for doing so that we simply haven't thought of yet (like perhaps you've lost your mind).

The optimized screen angles only cover the process inks, however. When your publication includes spot inks, InDesign sets the screen angle of every spot ink to 45 degrees.

For spot-color work—especially where you're overlaying tints of two spot colors or using duotones from Photoshop based on two spot inks—you need to specify the screen angles appropriately. Here's how to set them.

▶ If the spot inks *never* interact, set the screen angle for the inks to 45 degrees (because a 45-degree halftone screen is the least obvious to the eye).

▶ If you're creating lots of two-ink tint builds, or using duotones, you have a few choices, and two (somewhat contradictory) goals. You want both colors to print as close as possible to 45 degrees (especially the dominant, or darker, color), and you want as much separation between the angles as possible (the greater the separation between angles—45 is the maximum possible—the less patterning is visible where the screens interact). Table 11-2 lists some options.

▶ If you're printing with two spot inks and the spot colors don't overprint any process inks, use the default screen angles for Magenta and Cyan from the optimized screen you've selected.

Note that even if you set specific screen frequencies and angles for every color, you may not get what you ask for. Most imagesetters and platesetters these days strip out all screening settings and

TABLE 11-2
Screen Angles for Spot Color Work

Subordinate:	Dominant:	Notes:
15	45	Traditional. Only a 30-degree separation, but neither angle is very obvious on its own.
0	45	Avoids patterning. Ideally, the ink printed at zero degrees is a very light color—otherwise, the horizontal bands of halftone dots will be too obvious.
22.5	67.5	The complete compromise. Both angles are more obvious than 45 degrees, but less obvious than 0, and you get the full 45-degree separation to avoid patterning.
75	30	The dominant color screen is slightly less obvious than the subordinate screen. Full 45-degree separation.

replace them with their own unless you (or your output provider) turns off this process. We've been caught by this several times, when we've chosen low-frequency screens in order to create a special effect, only to find our instructions ignored and the normal 133 lpi halftone appear. Very annoying.

Inks

When you select the Separations option, InDesign activates the Inks list. In this list, you'll see at least the four process inks (yes, they'll appear even if you aren't using process colors in your publication), plus any spot inks you've defined. When you select an ink in the Inks list, InDesign displays the halftone screen properties for that ink in the Frequency and Angle fields (see "Screening," above).

To tell InDesign not to print an ink, click the printer icon to the left of the ink name in the Inks list. You can also turn on or off all the inks by Option/Alt-clicking. Don't worry about inks that aren't used in your publication—InDesign will not generate a blank separation for them. If, for example, your publication uses only black ink and a spot ink, InDesign will not create separations for Cyan, Magenta, and Yellow, even though those inks appear in the Inks list.

Simulate Overprint

As we discussed in Chapter 10, "Color," you can set various objects to overprint using the Attributes palette. However, most composite printers (like laser printers and inkjets) don't support overprinting. Fortunately, you can simulate overprinting on these output devices by turning on the Simulate Overprint check box. Because this can change color definitions (spot colors get converted to process, for example), you *don't* want to turn this on for anything other than proofing your files on composite printers.

Ink Manager

The Ink Manager manages how colors trap with each other and how spot colors interact (for instance, you can use the Ink Manager to alias one spot color to another). We cover the Ink Manager in Chapter 10, "Color."

Graphics

The options in the Graphics tab control the way that InDesign prints the fonts and graphics in your publication (see Figure 11-6).

Send Data

The Send Data pop-up menu affects what InDesign does with bitmaps in TIFF, JPEG, and other explicitly bitmapped file formats. It has no effect on images inside imported EPS or PDF graphics.

FIGURE 11-6
**The Graphics Panel
of the Print Dialog Box**

Do you want to print that 30-megabyte color scan every time you proof a document on your laser printer? Probably not. The Send Data pop-up menu gives you four options to control what InDesign does with images when you print: All, Optimized Subsampling, Proxy, and None, each of which is described below.

All. Use this option when you want InDesign to send all of the image data from the image file to the printer. We recommend that you always use this option when printing the final copies of your pages.

Optimized Subsampling. This option tells InDesign to only send as much information from the image as is necessary to produce the best quality on the given output device using the current settings. It reduces the amount of data that has to be passed over the network and imaged by the printer. It can speed up printing immensely.

How InDesign pares down the data depends on whether the image is color/grayscale or black and white.

▸ **Color/Grayscale images.** As we mentioned in Chapter 7, "Importing and Exporting," there's no reason for the resolution of grayscale and color images (in pixels per inch) to exceed two times the halftone screen frequency (in lines per inch). When you choose Optimized Subsampling from the Send Data pop-up menu, InDesign reduces the resolution of grayscale and color images to match the halftone screen frequency you've selected (in the Output tab of the Print dialog box). If you've set up a

75-line screen (for instance), InDesign won't send more than 150 dots per inch of image resolution. Note that InDesign does not change the resolution of the images in your publication—it just reduces the amount of data that's sent to the printer.

▶ **Black-and-white (bi-level) images.** When you're printing bi-level, black-and-white images, and have selected Optimized Subsampling from the Send Data pop-up menu, InDesign matches the images it sends to the resolution of the output device. So if you've got a 600-pixels-per-inch black-and-white TIFF, and you're printing on a 300-dpi laser printer, InDesign reduces the resolution of the image to 300 pixels per inch before sending it to the printer. For those who really want to know, InDesign gets the printer's resolution from the DefaultResolution keyword in the PPD.

The real value of the Optimized setting lies in printing laser proof copies of jobs that are destined for high-resolution (hence high halftone screen frequency) output. If you're producing a document that will be printed with a 133-lpi screen, for instance, you may be working with images that have resolutions of 250 or even 300 ppi. But for proofing on a 600-dpi laser printer (which has a 85-lpi default screen frequency), you only need 106 dpi—maximum. By subsampling to this lower resolution, InDesign is sending *less than one fifth* of the information over the wire. Obviously, this can save you a lot of time. With high-resolution line art, InDesign might send only a sixteenth of the data.

Printing an image using the Optimized Subsampling option produces a more detailed printed image than using the Low Resolution option, but doesn't take as long to print or transmit as would the full-resolution version of the image.

While Optimized Subsampling might sound like the universal cure for perfect (speedy, high quality) printing, it isn't. Subsampling, by its nature, blurs and distorts images, especially in areas of high contrast. Therefore, we think you should use this option for proof printing, but not for printing the final copies of your pages.

Proxy. Choose Proxy from the Send Data pop-up menu to have InDesign send only the low-resolution preview images it displays on your screen to the printer. Again, this is an option to use when you're printing proof copies of your pages, not for final output.

None. When you choose this option, InDesign prints all of the imported graphics in your publication as boxes with Xs through them. As you'd expect, this makes it print faster. Proof printing is great when you're copy-editing the text of a publication—why wait for the graphics to print?

Note that you can speed things up a bit, without completely eliminating the graphics, by using the Proxy or Optimized Subsampling option on the Send Data pop-up menu. Also, note that you can turn off the printing of a particular type of imported graphic using the Omit EPS/PDF/Bitmap Images options in the Advanced tab of the Print dialog box.

Font Downloading

One of the best ways to speed up InDesign's printing is to manage downloaded fonts sensibly. You can save many hours over the course of a day, week, month, or year by downloading fonts to your printer in advance, and by understanding the way that InDesign handles font downloading.

The basic concept is pretty simple: Fonts can be either "resident" (which means that they're stored in your printer's memory or on a hard drive attached to the printer) or "downloadable" (which means they're stored somewhere on your system or network).

When you print, InDesign checks the printer PPD to see if the fonts are available on the selected printer. If the font is available, InDesign sends a reference to the font, but does not send the font itself, which means that the text will be printed in the font available on the printer.

What happens when a font is not available in the printer's memory or on its hard drive? That depends on the option you've selected in the Fonts section of the Graphics tab of the Print dialog box.

When you choose the None option, you're directing InDesign to refrain from including any fonts in the PostScript it's sending to the printer (or to disk). If text in your publication has been formatted using fonts that are not resident on the printer, that text will be printed using the printer's default font (usually Courier).

When you choose the Complete option, InDesign checks the state of the Download PPD Fonts option. If this option is on, InDesign sends all of the fonts used in the publication to the printer's memory. If the option is turned off, InDesign downloads all of the fonts used in the publication that are not listed in the PPD (PPDs contain lists of fonts available on a given make and model printer, plus any you've added by editing the PPD). InDesign downloads the fonts once for each page that's printed. As you'd expect, this increases the amount of time it takes to send the job to your printer.

To decrease the amount of your printer's memory that's taken up by downloaded fonts, or to decrease the amount of time it takes InDesign to send the fonts to your printer, choose the Subset option. When you do this, InDesign sends only those characters required to print the publication. This can speed up printing tremendously.

At the same time, subsetting fonts can cause problems with some printers. If you find that you are losing characters, that the wrong characters print, or that your printer generates a PostScript error when you're trying to print using the Subset option, use one of the other options. If you're printing a file to disk as PostScript for delivery to a service bureau or to create a PDF using Acrobat Distiller, do not use the Subset option.

Postscript Level   Adobe would love it if everyone had PostScript 3 devices. Not only would they make tons of money from licensing fees, but their software could also take advantage of all the cool features in PostScript 3 RIPs. However, currently most people only have PostScript Level 2 devices. (Please don't ask us why "PostScript 3" omits the "Level" moniker. We can only assume that Adobe's marketing strategists have their reasons.) In most cases, InDesign reads the PostScript level from the PPD, so you don't have to think about this. However, if you're making a device-independent PostScript file you will need to choose Level 2 or Level 3. (Here Adobe *does* use "Level." We guess consistency isn't really a human trait.) If you have trouble printing to a PostScript 3 device, you might consider changing this to Level 2; that might change the PostScript enough to get it to print.

Data Format   The Data Format feature controls how bitmapped images (like TIFF and JPEG) are sent to the printer. While sending the information in ASCII format is more reliable over some older networks, binary is almost always fine and has the benefit of creating a much smaller PostScript file (the images are half the size of ASCII). We usually use binary unless we're sending files to an output provider that we know uses a PC- or UNIX-based system for output.

Color Management

The features in the Color Management tab of the Print dialog box are grayed out until you turn on Color Management in the Color Settings dialog box. We discuss color management, including all these Print dialog box settings, in Chapter 10, "Color."

Advanced

We're not sure what makes this tab more "advanced" than the others, but it's where you specify how InDesign should print gradients (blends), images in an OPI workflow, and objects that have transparency settings (see Figure 11-7).

OPI Image Replacement

When you're printing through an OPI server, you can direct the server to replace the low-resolution images you've used to lay out your document with the high-resolution images you've stored on the server. To do this, turn off the OPI Image Replacement option and turn on the appropriate Omit for OPI check boxes. This omits the images from the PostScript output, leaving only the OPI link information in their place.

Note that you can specify which types of images you want to replace with OPI comments: EPS, PDF, or Bitmap Images. When you turn on the EPS option, you're telling InDesign not to print any EPS graphics in the file, but if PDF and Bitmap Images are still turned on then the program will include that image data at print time.

When you turn on OPI Image Replacement, InDesign acts as an OPI server at print time, replacing the low-resolution OPI proxy images with the high-resolution versions. InDesign needs access to the server or drive containing the files for this to work. To retain OPI image links to images stored inside imported EPS graphics, make sure that you turn on the Read Embedded OPI Image Links option in the EPS Import Options dialog box.

FIGURE 11-7
The Advanced Panel of the Print Dialog Box

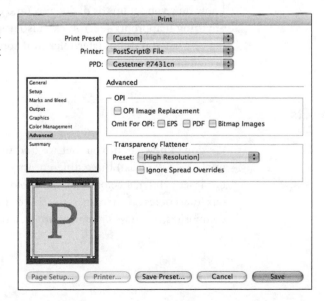

Transparency Flattener   We hate to give you the runaround, but if you're reading this hoping to learn all about how the flattener works, you're out of luck. We cover all the issues regarding printing transparency later in this chapter. We will say, however, that you can use the Transparency Flattener section of the Advanced tab of the Print dialog box to choose a default Flattener setting for your print job, and to tell InDesign whether to ignore any Flattener settings you've applied to particular spreads in your document with the Pages palette.

In general, you should use Medium Resolution when printing proofs and High Resolution when printing final artwork. But "Medium" and "High" can mean different things depending on the Flattener settings, so you still need to go read that other section. Sorry.

Summary

The last tab of the Print dialog box, Summary, simply lists all the various settings in all the tabs in one long text list. We think this is perhaps the silliest of all features in the Print dialog box; it's more difficult and time-consuming to read through this unformatted list of settings than it is to skip through each of the tabs. However, it's nice that you can click the Save Summary button to save this list to disk as a text file.

If you're writing PostScript to disk to send to someone else, it's a good idea to include this summary along with it, so that they will know how you set up the dialog box (and can check to see if you did anything inappropriate). You can also use this saved summary as a log of what you did to later refer to if something prints in an unexpected fashion.

Print Presets

We don't know about you, but we find we print a typical InDesign publication (at least) three different ways. We print a proof copy on our laser printer, a color proof on a color printer, and then we print our final copies on an imagesetter. In the first two instances, we print composites; when we print to an imagesetter, we typically print color separations. You might think that for each type of printing we have to claw our way through the settings in the Print dialog box. Instead, we save our Print dialog box settings in a *print preset*—which means that switching from proof to final printing is as easy as selecting the appropriate print preset.

Print presets are like paragraph styles—they're bundles of attributes that can be applied in a single action. Almost all of the attributes in the Print dialog box and in the printer driver dialog boxes are included in a print preset.

Creating a Print Preset   It's easy to create a print preset; set up the Print dialog box with the options the way you want them, click the Save Preset button at the bottom of the dialog box, and then give the preset a name. You can then go ahead and print, or just cancel out of the Print dialog box (if you just wanted to set up the preset without printing).

InDesign also has a second method for making print presets, though we find it slightly more cumbersome.

1. Choose Define from the Print presets submenu of the File menu. InDesign displays the Define Print Presets dialog box (see Figure 11-8).

2. Click the New button. InDesign displays the Print dialog box, except with one difference: there's a Name field at the top.

3. Enter a name for the print preset in the Name field, then set up the dialog box with the settings you want, and click the OK button. InDesign returns you to the Define Print Presets dialog box and adds the new print preset to the list of available presets.

To print using the settings in a print preset, you can choose the preset from the Print preset pop-up menu in the Print dialog box. Or, even easier, select the print preset name from the Print presets submenu of the File menu. InDesign displays the Print dialog box. Click the Print button (or the Save button, if you're printing to disk), and InDesign prints the specified pages.

To print without displaying the Print dialog box, hold down Shift as you choose the print preset name from the Print Presets submenu of the File menu.

FIGURE 11-8
Creating a Printer Preset

Choose Define from the Printer Presets submenu of the File menu.

For a fun surprise, try making any printer preset named "Friendly Alien". With that selected in the Preset popup menu in the Print dialog box, click the Preview window in the lower left corner of the dialog box.

InDesign displays the Printer Presets dialog box. Click the New button.

Enter a name for the new printer preset and set up the New Print Preset dialog box the way you want it.

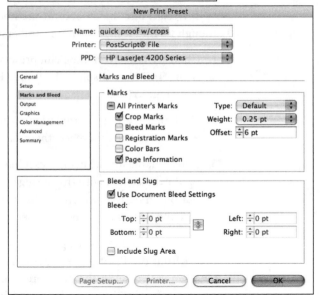

InDesign adds the new printer preset to the list of available presets.

To print using the printer preset, choose the preset name from the Printer Presets submenu of the File menu (hold down Shift if you want to print without displaying the Print dialog box).

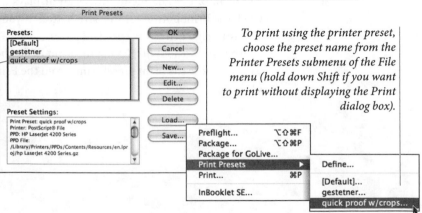

Managing Print Presets   You can use the Print Presets dialog box to add presets, delete presets, rename presets, edit presets, or import or export print presets.

- ▶ To create a new print preset that is based on an existing preset, open the Print Presets dialog box, select a print preset, and then click the New button. Enter a name for your new print preset, then modify the settings in the panels of the Print dialog box. Note that this does not link the two presets—changes made to the "parent" print preset will not affect any presets you've based on it.

- ▶ To delete a print preset, select the preset name and click the Delete button.

- ▶ To export a print preset (or presets), select one or more presets and click the Save button. Specify a file name and location for the print presets document and click the OK button.

- ▶ To import a print preset or set of presets, open the Print Presets dialog box and click the Load button. Locate and select a print presets document (or an InDesign publication containing print presets), then click the OK button. If the print presets you're importing already exist in the publication, InDesign will create copies of the presets (InDesign will append a number—usually "1"—to the duplicate print presets).

- ▶ To edit a print preset, select the preset name in the Print Presets dialog box, then click the Edit button. InDesign displays the Print dialog box. Make the changes and click the OK button to save the edited preset.

Customizing Printers' Marks

If there's one thing we've learned about our fellow desktop publishers over the years, it's that you're picky about printer's marks. You want to control the offset of the crop marks and bleed marks from the edge of the page. You want to use star targets instead of, or in addition to, the standard registration marks. You want the color bars to print at the top, the bottom, the left, or the right of the page.

There is utterly no way for a page layout program to provide for all of your individual preferences—what's right for one person is not just wrong, but is probably offensive to another.

InDesign, in recognition of this fact, provides a way for you to define your own printer's marks. The trouble is—no one knows how to do it. Until now.

InDesign uses printer's marks definition (also known as PMD) files to customize the way the program prints printer's marks. They're text files that can be edited with any text editor (BBEdit and Notepad work quite well). Once you've saved a PMD file to a specific folder on your system, a new entry will appear in the Type pop-up menu in the Marks and Bleed panel of the Print dialog box. Choose the option, and InDesign will print using the marks defined in the file.

Most previous attempts to provide custom printer's marks were based on hacking the PostScript output stream of a program—Ole wrote custom files to provide this feature for FreeHand and PageMaker. InDesign's PMD files are not only easier to create (they're not PostScript), but they'll also print on non-PostScript printers. For that matter, the custom marks will also appear in exported PDFs, if you want them to.

Inside a PMD File   InDesign PMD files have a fairly forgiving set of rules, but they have rules all the same. First, an InDesign PMD file must begin with the following line:

```
//pgmk.v02.00
```

Inside the printer's marks definition file, "//" indicates a comment—apart from the comment in the first line, all other comments are ignored by InDesign.

The body of the file is surrounded by "<", which opens a printer's mark "dictionary," and it's closed by "<". Inside the angle brackets, you set global values (if any) and then create a set of custom printer's marks with the following line:

```
MarksArray
```

Following this line, square brackets ("[" and "]") enclose the actual printer's mark definitions. The skeleton of the file, therefore, looks like this:

```
//pgmk.v02.00
<
//Global definitions go here.
MarksArray
[
//printer's mark definitions go here.
]
>
```

There are currently four global definitions you can add. They're all optional, one of them is not used, and most of them are overridden by settings in the InDesign Print dialog box. We never use them, but, just in case you do, for some reason, Table 11-3 shows the global definitions you can use.

Once you're inside the angle brackets, however, things get much more exciting (if you're as easily excited about printer's marks as we are). This is the place where you define the appearance and location of the marks that will appear when you print.

Most of the mark definitions inside the file look like this:

```
<
Type FourCropMarks
Length 24
>
```

An entry for a custom registration mark is a little bit more complicated, as shown in the following:

```
<
Type RegistrationMark
Count 4
InnerRadius 3  // no inner black-filled circle
OuterRadius 6  // radius of outer circle
OutLength 12   // half of the length of the crosshair mark
               // perpendicular to the closest edge of the page
AlongLength 24 // half of the length of the crosshair parallel
               // to the closest edge of the page
Location <
  Side [Top Bottom Left Right]
  OutAnchor MidCropMark
  OverAnchor Center
  MarkCorner MarkCenter
  >
>
```

The PMD file can support a variety of predefined mark types, and can place the marks in a variety of locations. The mark types are shown in Table 11-4, the location keywords can be found in Table 11-5, and a list of the keywords you can add to a page (date, time, separation name, and so forth) appears in figures 11-9 and 11-10.

Note: Many of the measurements in the PMD file are based on the Length and Offset settings for the FourCropMarks mark type and on the Length and BleedMarkOffset settings for the FourBleedMarks mark type, so you should define these marks at the beginning of the Marks Array section of the file.

Note: If you're using the JCornerMarks mark type, the distances will be based on the Length setting. In addition, JCornerMarks overrides

Mark Type Name:	What It Means:
Style	The name of the printers' marks file. Optional.
DefaultWeight	The default stroke weight, in points. Not used by InDesign.
DefaultCrop-MarkOffset	The default offset for crop marks. Overridden by the corresponding field in the Marks and Bleed panel of the Print dialog box.
DefaultBleed-MarkOffset	The default offset for bleed marks. Overridden by the corresponding field in InDesign. Can be overridden by using the BleedMarkOffset parameter.

both FourCropMarks and FourBleedMarks, so omit those marks in files using JCornerMarks. Finally, add the IgnoreMarkOffsets value in the Globals section of the file and set it to true if you're using JCornerMarks.

Disclaimer: Fiddling with PMD files is something that you do entirely at your own risk. Adobe does not support this practice (in fact, we're not completely certain we should be telling you about it), and is in no way responsible for any problems you might run into during the course of experimentation. That said, the authors will try to help you if you run into trouble—just drop us a line!

Saving a PMD File

Save the PMD file as a text-only file with the file extension ".mrk" to the PrintSpt folder. The location of this folder varies—the best thing to do is to search your system for a folder with this name. Once you've done this, the name of your custom printer's marks file will appear on the Type pop-up menu in the Marks and Bleed panel of the Print dialog box (see Figure 11-11).

You can also select your custom printer's marks when exporting files to PDF using the Type pop-up menu in the Marks and Bleed panel of the Export PDF dialog box.

If you want to print your custom printer's marks on another system, you'll have to take your PMD file with you and install it on that machine.

Example PMD Files

The PMD file shown in Figure 11-12 adds printer's marks in an arrangement similar to that used by QuarkXPress. Figure 11-13 shows a sleazy way to get page information for a page to print on the page itself, rather than in the bleed area. This is handy when you're printing letter-size pages on letter-size paper.

TABLE 11-4
Mark Types

Mark Type Name:	What It Means:	
FourCropMarks	Draws a vertical and horizontal crop mark at each of the four corners of the page.	
	Parameters	
	Name:	**What it is:**
	Length	Length of the crop marks, in points.
	Weight	Stroke weight of the crop marks, in points. Overridden by the Weight field in the Marks and Bleed panel of the Print dialog box.
	CropMarkOffset	Distance from the edge of the page, in points. Overridden by the Offset field in the Marks and Bleed panel of the Print dialog box.
FourBleedMarks	Draws a vertical and horizontal bleed mark at each of the four corners of the bleed area.	
	Parameters	
	Name:	**What it is:**
	Length	Length of the crop marks, in points.
	Weight	Stroke weight of the crop marks, in points. Overridden by the Weight field in the Marks and Bleed panel of the Print dialog box.
	CropMarkOffset	Distance from the edge of the page, in points. Overridden by the Offset field in the Marks and Bleed panel of the Print dialog box.

TABLE 11-4
Mark Types (continued)

Mark Type Name:	What It Means:	
JCornerMarks	Draws Japanese-style corner marks (a combination of crop and bleed marks) at the corners of the page.	
	Parameters	
	Name:	What it is:
	Length	Length of the marks, in points.
	Weight	Stroke weight of the marks, in points.
RegistrationMark	Draws a registration mark at a specified location.	
	Parameters	
	Name:	What it is:
	Count	The number of registration marks to draw.
	InnerRadius	The radius of the filled circle at the center of the registration mark.
	OuterRadius	The radius of the unfilled outer circle of the registration mark.
	OutLength	Half the length of the crosshair mark perpendicular to the edge of the page.
	AlongLength	Half the length of the crosshair mark parallel to the edge of the page.
	KnockoutWeight	The weight of the crosshair mark inside the inner circle of the registration mark.
	Weight	Stroke weight of the mark, in points.
	Location	Location of the registration marks. See Table 11-5 for a list of locations.

TABLE 11-4	Mark Type Name:	What It Means:	
Mark Types (continued)	StarTarget	Draws a star registration mark.	
		Parameters	
		Name:	What it is:
		InnerRadius	The radius of the filled circle at the center of the registration mark.
		OuterRadius	The radius of the unfilled outer circle of the registration mark.
		Spokes	Number of spokes in the star target.
		Location	Location of the registration marks. See Table 11-5 for a list of locations.
		Weight	Stroke weight of the marks, in points.
	ColorBar	Draws a range of color/gray swatches.	
		Parameters	
		Name:	What it is:
		NumberOfCells	Sets the number of cells in the bar.
		CellSize	The size of each cell.
		CMYKValues	An array whose length is equal to the NumberOfCells parameter. Each array element contains an array of four values. See the example files.
		RegistrationValues	An array whose length is equal to the NumberOfCells parameter. Each array element contains a single value between 1 (solid) and 0 (white). See the example files.
		NumberOfCells	Sets the number of cells in the bar.

Mark Type Name:	What It Means:	
ColorBar	*Continued from previous page.*	
	Parameters	
	Name:	What it is:
	CellSize	The size of each cell.
	CMYKValues	An array whose length is equal to the NumberOfCells parameter. Each array element contains an array of four values. See the example files.
	RegistrationValues	An array whose length is equal to the NumberOfCells parameter. Each array element contains a single value between 1 (solid) and 0 (white). See the example files.
	Weight	Stroke weight of the marks, in points.
	Location	Location of the color bars. See Table 11-5 for a list of locations.
	CMYKStrokeValue	The color of the stroke surrounding the cells in the color bar, as an array of four values.
	Registration-StrokeValue	The color of the stroke surrounding the cells in the color bar, as a value from 1 (solid) to 0 (white).
	Count	The number of color bars to draw.
	SeparationsOnly	If true, draw color bars; if false, omit color bars.

TABLE 11-4 Mark Types (continued)	Mark Type Name:	What It Means:	
	MarkText	Informational text, such as the date and time a page was printed.	

Parameters

Name:	What it is:
TextSize	The size of the text, in points.
Registration-TextColor	A value between 1 (solid) and 0 (white) defining the color of the text.
CMYKTextColor	An array of four values defining the color of the text.
AllPlates	Prints the text in a solid color on all plates; changes the location of the text on each plate.
SamePositionOn-AllPlates	Set this value to true to print the text in the same position on all plates when you are using the AllPlates color.
FormatString	The text to print. This can be a string ("From the Desk of") or "%s", which is a placeholder for an InfoValue. Each string must be enclosed in parentheses.
InfoValues	An array of predefined page information. You can use Date, Time, PubName, PageLabel, Screen Frequency, ScreenAngle, and Plate Color.

TABLE 11-5 Locations	Name:	What It Means:
	Side	The side of the page on which to draw the mark. You can use Top, Bottom, Left, or Right. The position of the mark on the defined side of the page is set by the OutAnchor parameter.
	OverAnchor	Sets the position of the mark along the edge of the page. You can use Center, EdgeOfPage, InnerCropMark, MidCropMark, OuterCropMark, Bleed, MidBleedMark, or OuterBleedMark (see Figure 11-9). In addition, you can adjust the location of the mark, relative to the location you specify, using the OverDirection and/or OverOffset modifiers. OverDirection moves the mark relative to the the side of the page (as defined by the Side parameter)—if the Side parameter is Top or Bottom, OverDirection can be either Left or Right; if the Side parameter is Left or Right, OverDirection can be either Top or Bottom. OverOffset moves the mark relative to the OverAnchor position. Negative values move the mark away from the center of the page; positive values move it toward the center of the page.
	OutAnchor	Defines the distance of the mark from the edge of the page using a range of predefined positions. You can use EdgeOfPage, InnerCropMark, MidCropMark, OuterCropMark, Bleed, InnerBleedMark, MidBleedMark, or OuterBleedMark (see Figure 11-10). You can adjust the position of the mark using the OutOffset parameter.
	MarkCorner	Specifies the alignment of the mark relative to the location you've defined. You can use MarkCenter, MarkRight, MarkUR (upper right), MarkTop, MarkUL (upper left), MarkLeft, MarkLL (lower left), MarkBottom, or MarkLR (lower right).

FIGURE 11-9
OverAnchor Positions

You can think of OverAnchor positions as being on the horizontal axis of the page.

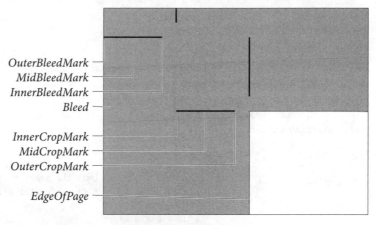

OuterBleedMark
MidBleedMark
InnerBleedMark
Bleed

InnerCropMark
MidCropMark
OuterCropMark

EdgeOfPage

FIGURE 11-10
OutAnchor Positions

You can think of OutAnchor positions as being on the vertical axis of the page.

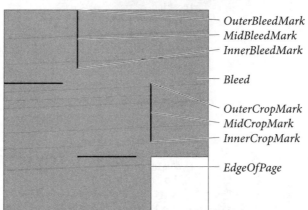

OuterBleedMark
MidBleedMark
InnerBleedMark

Bleed

OuterCropMark
MidCropMark
InnerCropMark

EdgeOfPage

FIGURE 11-11
Choosing Custom Printer's Marks

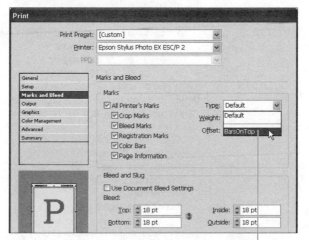

Once you've created a PMD file and have saved it to the PrintSpt folder, the new mark type will appear on the Type pop-up menu.

FIGURE 11-12

**QuarkXPress-Style
Printer's Marks**

*You can download
this text from
David's Web site:
www.moo.com/rwid/mrk.zip*

```
//pgmk.v02.00
<
Style (BarsOnTop)
MarksArray
[
  <
    Type FourCropMarks
    Length 24
  >
  <
    Type RegistrationMark
    Count 4
    InnerRadius 0  // Omit the inner target.
    OuterRadius 6  // Radius of outer circle.
    OutLength 12
    AlongLength 24
    Location <
      Side [Top Bottom Left Right]
      OutAnchor MidCropMark
      OverAnchor Center
      MarkCorner MarkCenter
    >
  >
  // Color bar, on the upper left.
  <
    Type ColorBar
    NumberOfCells 12
    CellSize 16
    CMYKValues [0  0  0  1    // black
        0  0  1  0   // yellow
       0  1  1  0 // magenta + yellow
       0  1  0  0  // magenta
       1  1  0  0  // cyan + magenta
       1  0  0  0  // cyan
       1  0  1  0  // cyan + yellow
       1  1  1  0  // cyan + magenta + yellow
       .5 0  0  0  // 50% cyan
       0  .5 0  0  // 50% magenta
       0  0  .5 0  // 50% yellow
       0  0  0  .5] // 50% black
    Weight 2 // Width of the stroke around each cell
    CMYKStrokeValue [0 0 0 0] // Color of the stroke (white)
    Location <
      Side Left
      OutAnchor MidCropMark
      OverAnchor EdgeOfPage
      OverDirection Top
      OverOffset 4
      MarkCorner MarkTop
    >
    //Threshold and AltMarkDefinition tell InDesign
    //what to do with the marks when the page size becomes
    //too small to fit the marks along the top/bottom
    //or left/right side of the page.
    ThreshHold <
```

FIGURE 11-12

QuarkXPress-Style

Printer's Marks

(continued)

```
      MinPageHeight 448
   >
   AltMarkDefinition <
     Location <
       Side Left
       OutAnchor OuterCropMark
       OutOffset 2
       OverAnchor Center
       MarkCorner MarkRight
     >
   >
 >
//End of color bar definition.
//Gray bar, at the bottom left.
 <
   Type ColorBar
   NumberOfCells 10
   CellSize 16
   //The array of tints printed in the cells:
   RegistrationValues [1 .9 .8 .7 .6 .5 .4 .3 .2 .1]
   Weight 2 // Stroke width the cells.
   RegistrationStrokeValue 0 // Stroke color of the cells (white).
   Location <
     Side Bottom
     OutAnchor MidCropMark
     OverAnchor EdgeOfPage
     OverDirection Left
     OverOffset 4
     MarkCorner MarkLeft
   >
   ThreshHold <
     MinPageWidth 448
   >
   AltMarkDefinition <
     Location <
       Side Bottom
       OutAnchor OuterCropMark
       OutOffset 2
       OverAnchor Center
       MarkCorner MarkTop
     >
   >
 >
//End of gray bar definition.
// Page information, at the top of the page.
 <
   Type MarkText
   TextSize 7
   AllPlates true
   SamePositionOnAllPlates  true
   FormatString (%s   %s   %s  - %s -   (%s\))
   InfoValues [PubName Date Time PageLabel PlateColor]
   Location <
     Side Top
     OutAnchor MidCropMark
```

FIGURE 11-12
QuarkXPress-Style
Printer's Marks
(continued)

```
       OutOffset 4
       OverAnchor EdgeOfPage
       OverDirection Left
       OverOffset 3
       MarkCorner MarkLL
     >
   >
   //End of page information definition.
 ]
 //End of MarksArray
 >
 //End of custom printer's marks file.
```

FIGURE 11-13
Printing Page
Information
on the Page

*You can download
this text from
David's Web site:
www.moo.com/rwid/mrk.zip*

```
//pgmk.v02.00
//Prints page information inside the page area.
//Not useful for prepress work, but quite useful
//when you're printing letter-size drafts on a
//laser printer. Make sure that this PMD file is NOT
//selected when you create your final printout!
<
  Style (PageInfoOnPage)
  MarksArray
  [
  <
    Type FourCropMarks
    Length   15
  >
  //Page information.
  <
    Type MarkText
    Count 2
    TextSize 6
    RegistrationTextColor 1.0
    //Feel free to replace our shameless advertising with
    //your own shameless advertising.
    FormatString [(%s   %s * Real World Adobe InDesign)(%s    %s)]
    InfoValues [PubName PageLabel Date Time]
    Location <
      Side Bottom
      OutAnchor InnerCropMark
      //Move info up--36 points is enough to
      //get it onto the page for most printers.
      //Adjust this value as you see fit.
      OutOffset -36
      OverAnchor EdgeOfPage
      OverDirection [Left Right]
      OverOffset [10 0]
      MarkCorner [MarkLL MarkLR]
    >
  >
  ]
  >
```

Separations Preview

If there's one feature we've longed for since desktop publishing programs gained the ability to print color separations (yes, Junior, there was a time when they didn't), it's a separations preview—a way that we could look at the individual separations of a document *before* committing them to expensive imagesetter film or printing plates.

We've tried all sorts of workarounds—rasterizing files in Photoshop and then splitting channels; printing separations to disk and then converting the PostScript to PDF using Acrobat Distiller...you name it, we've probably tried it in our quest to see what our separations would look like without having to print them.

That's all over now, thanks to InDesign's Separations Preview palette. With this modern marvel, you can see what your separations will look like without even having to leave InDesign.

To view your pages as separations, display the Separations palette (choose Separations from the Output submenu of the Window menu, or press Shift-F6). Choose Separations from the View menu in the Separations palette. Click the column to the left of the Ink names to turn the display of that ink off or on (see Figure 11-14). You can also use keyboard shortcuts, as shown in Table 11-6.

You can choose to display the separations in the ink color, or you can view the separations in black—to do the latter, choose Show Single Plates in Black from the Separations palette menu.

As you move the cursor over objects on the page, the Separations Preview palette displays the inks percentages used in the objects beneath the cursor.

In addition to showing separations, the Separations Preview palette can also help you watch the ink densities of objects on your

TABLE 11-6
Keyboard Shortcuts for Separations Preview

To Display:	Press:
First spot plate	Command-Shift-Option-5/Ctrl-Alt-Shift-5
Second spot plate	Command-Shift-Option-6/Ctrl-Alt-Shift-6
Third spot plate	Command-Shift-Option-7/Ctrl-Alt-Shift-7
Fourth spot plate	Command-Shift-Option-8/Ctrl-Alt-Shift-8
Fifth spot plate	Command-Shift-Option-9/Ctrl-Alt-Shift-9
All plates	Command-Shift-Option-` (accent grave) /Ctrl-Alt-Shift-` (accent grave)
Black plate	Command-Shift-Option-4/Ctrl-Alt-Shift-4
Cyan plate	Command-Shift-Option-1/Ctrl-Alt-Shift-1
Magenta plate	Command-Shift-Option-2/Ctrl-Alt-Shift-2
Yellow plate	Command-Shift-Option-3/Ctrl-Alt-Shift-3

pages. To do this, choose Ink Limit from the View pop-up menu in the Separations Preview palette, then enter an ink coverage percentage in the associated field. When the ink coverage in an area exceeds the percentage you entered, InDesign highlights the area in red (see Figure 11-15).

FIGURE 11-14
Separations Preview

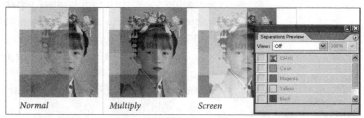

Separations preview off.

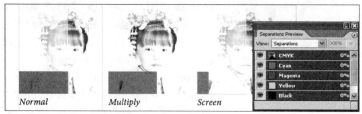

Separations preview on, Black plate displayed.

FIGURE 11-15
Ink Limit

Choose Ink Limit…

…and enter a percentage in the associated field (the percentage should match the maximum ink coverage for the type of press and paper you're printing on).

InDesign highlights the areas in which the ink concentration is greater than the percentage you've entered (shown as black here, as we don't have color to work with).

All other objects are rendered using gray values corresponding to the intensity of ink coverage in the area.

One really cool thing about the Separations Preview is that you can see the effect of overprinting, as shown in Figure 11-16. This feature alone is worth a great deal, as you can use it to preview simple text trapping and special overprinting effects without having to print the document.

FIGURE 11-16
Previewing
Overprinting

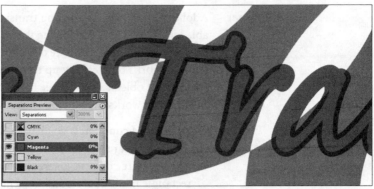

You can use the Separations
Preview palette to view overprinting before you print.

Stroke greatly enlarged for illustrative purposes!

Printing Transparency

Two of the most important figures in the desktop publishing revolution—Tim Gill (founder of Quark, Inc.) and John Warnock (co-
founder of Adobe, Inc.)—each had a blind spot that led to a tragedy
of unparalleled proportions. Well, maybe not quite that strong (they
both retired quite happily in recent years). But the blind spots did
have interesting results that caused their companies difficulties.

Tim Gill didn't believe that HTML was worth much attention, and
Quark suffered by being late to supporting the Web. John Warnock
didn't believe transparency was important and so it took PostScript
20 years to support it. Everyone knows that vector transparency is
important to designers, but because PostScript couldn't print it, programs couldn't support it.

But wait, you say, some programs have had transparency features
for many years! Photoshop supported transparency because it only
had to worry about pixels, not vector artwork. The transparency features of every other program (including Illustrator, FreeHand, and
so on) worked by faking the effects at print time, "flattening" the
transparent objects into a form that PostScript could handle.

In recent years, transparency has finally made its way into
PostScript 3 by way of the PDF 1.4 specification (PostScript 3, version 3015 or later, to be precise). RIPs that support PDF 1.4 directly
can print transparency without any chicanery. Unfortunately, as we
write this, the vast majority of RIPs—especially RIPs suited for high-
resolution imagesetters and platesetters—support only PostScript
Level 2. So most of the time programs like Illustrator and InDesign
are still forced to flatten files that include drop shadows, feathering,
or any other cool transparency effects.

The Flattener Adobe's technology for turning transparent objects into a form suitable for older RIPs is called "the flattener." (David is pleased to have finally found a word that more or less rhymes with his last name.) The flattener works by breaking up transparent objects into smaller non-transparent objects. It has three basic methods to do this. (Note that the flattener works the same in Illustrator, Acrobat, and InDesign.)

▶ **Divide and conquer.** If you have a 50-percent transparent magenta square partially over a cyan square, the flattener splits this into three objects: where the two overlapped it creates a rectangle made of cyan and magenta; where they didn't overlap, it makes two L-shaped objects, one cyan, the other magenta.

▶ **Clip it up.** Let's say you have a 20-percent transparent picture partially overlapping that cyan square (or vice versa, a partially transparent cyan square overlapping a picture). The flattener splits the picture into two (or more) pieces by drawing invisible frames (clipping paths) and putting pieces of the picture into them. The part of the picture that is inside the square gets cyan added to it to finish the effect.

▶ **Rasterize.** When all else fails, and InDesign realizes that it'll take too long to use the previous two methods (too long to flatten means the file will probably also take way too long to print), it punts and just turns the whole thing into a bitmapped picture (converting vectors into bitmaps is called rasterizing).

Again, all of this is done behind the scenes and only at print time (or when you export the file as an EPS or an Acrobat 4 PDF file, both of which also use the flattener). In most cases, you'd never know that InDesign was doing any of this if we hadn't told you, because the results are extremely clean. In some cases, primarily when InDesign ends up rasterizing part of your page, you may find the results only fine, okay, or (rarely) unacceptable.

Transparency Tricks Okay, here comes our "with power comes responsibility" talk. Transparency is all about accepting compromise, and if you can't deal with compromise then you might consider avoiding transparency altogether. The first compromise is time versus quality: the better the quality, the more time your files will take to print (or export). The next compromise is that if you want to play with transparency (or your clients want to, and you've agreed to print their documents), you need to pay attention to how your document is created and be prepared to proof the final results carefully.

Here are a few things you should pay attention to when messing with transparency:

▶ Transparency comes in all sorts of forms. If you use the Drop Shadow or Feather feature, you're introducing transparency. So does importing a native Photoshop, Illustrator, or PDF document that includes any transparent object. If the page icon in the Pages palette has a checkerboard in it, you can bet that the flattener will kick in.

▶ If you're going to use transparent objects in Adobe Illustrator (including transparent brushes, most filters, drop shadows, and so on), make sure you're using version 9.02 or later (you should probably just use version 10 or later). Also, we suggest saving files in the native .ai format, the Acrobat 5 PDF format, or an .eps format compatible with Illustrator 9 or 10 (not earlier versions). This way InDesign handles flattening at print time instead of you worrying about Illustrator getting it right.

▶ If you're importing Illustrator documents that include images and use transparency effects, it's probably a good idea to embed the images in the Illustrator file itself rather than relying on linking to the file on disk.

▶ Set the Transparency Blend Space (in the Edit menu) to CMYK rather than RGB, and—if you've turned on color management— use Convert to Profile to convert the document working space to your final output space.

▶ Spot colors offer a number of opportunities for problems, especially the flattener converting spot colors to process colors (or worse, converting part of an object to process color and leaving the rest of the object a spot color). Fortunately, this typically only happens when you use fancy transparency modes (like Color, Saturation, Difference, and so on) or when you have spot color gradients involved with transparency.

▶ The flattener must work with high-resolution images on disk, which means that DCS files and an OPI workflow—both of which rely on importing low-resolution images that get swapped out with high-resolution later—are out. (Of course, if you have DCS or OPI images that are not involved with transparency then you can still use them.) Adobe's documentation says that EPS duotones are also a no-no, but we haven't run into any problems with them.

▸ It's better not to mix overprint settings (like Overprint Stroke or Overprint Fill in the Attributes palette) with transparency. For example, if you're using transparency anyway, then consider using the Multiply blend mode rather than turning on Overprint Fill.

▸ Most PostScript RIPs can handle the flattener tricks just fine, but we have encountered some RIPs that cause problems. For example, because Scitex (now part of Creo) RIPs rely on separating continuous tone imagery from line work (vector) images, you can get some very bad results, especially where text interacts with transparent objects. Creo says they're working on a fix for this, but be extra careful when perusing your output if you (or your output provider) are using this sort of RIP.

▸ In fact, it would behoove you to always look over your final output carefully. Look for spot colors that were converted to process, overprinting instructions that were ignored, vector objects that were rasterized in unpleasant ways, unintentionally rasterized type, and text or strokes that became heavier.

Flattener Presets   As we said earlier, flattening is a matter of compromise. Fortunately, you have a say in the matter, by selecting among various flattener presets. Each flattener preset is a collection of flattening choices, such as how hard should InDesign try before giving up and rasterizing the artwork.

InDesign ships with three predefined flattener presets: Low Resolution, Medium Resolution, and High Resolution. You can mentally replace the word "resolution" with "quality." You should typically use Low or Medium when printing to a desktop laser printer and High when printing to an imagesetter or platesetter (see "Applying Flattener Presets," later in this chapter).

Occasionally we find a need to create our own flattener preset. For example, if you're doing a lot of proofs on a black-and-white desktop laser printer, you could probably get away with making a "Very Low" preset, which may print faster than Low Resolution with "good enough" quality. Or, if you're getting unacceptably slow printing, PostScript errors, or poor quality on an imagesetter with the High Resolution preset, you might want to create a custom preset that works better for you.

To make a custom flattener preset, select Transparency Flattener Presets from the Edit menu (see Figure 11-17). While you cannot edit

FIGURE 11-17
Creating a
Flattener Preset

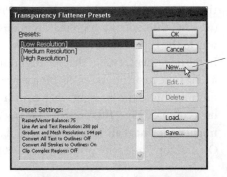

To define a flattener preset, select Transparency Flattener Presets from the Edit menu.

To base a new preset on an existing preset, select a preset and click the New button.

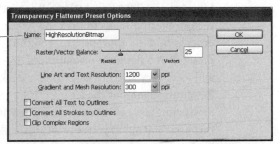

Enter a name for the flattener preset.

Set up the options for the preset, then click the OK button to save the preset.

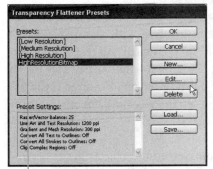

The new flattener preset appears in the list of available flattener presets.

To print using the flattener preset, choose the preset from the Preset pop-up menu in the Advanced panel of the Print dialog box.

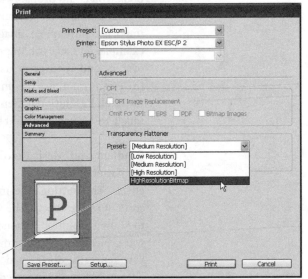

the default presets, you can base a new one on a default preset by selecting the preset, then clicking the New button, which opens the Transparency Flattener Preset Options dialog box. Beyond the name of the preset (enter whatever you want), there are six controls here.

Raster/Vector Balance. The Raster/Vector Balance slider is a graphic representation of the quality/speed compromise. Push the slider all the way to the left and InDesign rasterizes everything on the page (we can't think of any good reason to do this). Push the slider all the way to the right and InDesign tries its best to maintain every vector in the document, even if that means taking a long time to flatten and a long time to print. As left-leaning as we tend to be, we always prefer pushing this to the far right when printing on imagesetters. However, on a complex page, this creates so many clipping paths that your file might not print at all. In that case, you'd need to take it down a notch. On desktop PostScript printers, we'd set this even lower.

Line Art and Text Resolution. When InDesign ends up rasterizing a vector object, it looks to the Line Art and Text Resolution setting in order to find the appropriate resolution. The Low Resolution flattener preset uses a flattener resolution of 288 ppi (pixels per inch), which will look very slightly jagged on a desktop laser printer. The High Resolution flattener preset uses 1200 ppi. If you were printing on newsprint, you could easily get away with creating a flattener preset that used 800 ppi. If you're printing on glossy stock for an coffee table book, you could probably raise this to 1600 ppi.

The flattener resolution also acts as an "upper boundary" when imported bitmapped images are involved with transparency. For example, let's say you import a 300 ppi image, put transparent text over it, and then print using the Low Resolution flattener preset. InDesign resamples the image down to 288 ppi. However, if you use the High Resolution flattener preset, InDesign will not upsample the image to 1200 (that would be crazy).

Gradient and Mesh Resolution. Sometimes objects get rasterized no matter what happens—for instance, soft drop shadows or feather effects. This setting determines the appropriate resolution for these sorts of raster effects. The Gradient and Mesh Resolution setting in the Low Resolution flattener preset defaults to 144 ppi, even though you typically don't need more than 100 ppi on any desktop printer. You generally don't need more than 200 ppi for high-resolution output. (After all, you need resolution to capture detail in an image, and these "images" have no detail).

InDesign may upsample your bitmapped images if they're involved with a transparent areas of the page and they're lower resolution than the Gradient and Mesh Resolution setting. For example, if you import a 72 ppi image (like a JPEG saved from a Web site) and change its transparency setting, the flattener upsamples the image to the gradient resolution. Unfortunately, if you import a 200 ppi TIFF image (which is very reasonable for most printed artwork today), set its transparency, and print it using the High Resolution flattener preset, InDesign also upsamples it to 300 ppi—causing slower printing and possibly image degradation. (InDesign uses "nearest neighbor" interpolation, which results in pretty clunky images.)

Convert All Text to Outlines. When text gets involved with transparency (either it is transparent or something transparent is on top of it), the type almost always gets turned into paths that act as clipping paths. This slows down printing a bit, and sometimes that text appears heavier than the equivalent characters that aren't converted to outlines, especially on lower-resolution printers. If, for example, you had an image that was partially transparent on top of half a column of text, the text under the image might appear like it was very slightly more bold than the rest of the text. One answer would be to create a flattener preset in which the Convert All Text to Outlines option was turned on and apply that to this particular spread (we discuss applying flattener presets below). This way, all the text on that spread gets converted to outlines. The page prints even slower, but is more consistent. This is rarely a problem when imagesetting or platesetting, however, so we usually just ignore this feature.

Convert All Strokes to Outlines. The problem with type "heavying up" is also an issue around thin lines. The flattener converts lines that are involved with transparency effects into very thin boxes. These boxes may appear thicker, however, than equal lines that don't have any transparency effects. Turning this feature on ensures that InDesign will convert all of the lines in the document, making them more visually equal. Again, this is rarely an issue on high-resolution printers.

Clip Complex Regions. When InDesign does resort to rasterizing vectors, it usually does so in rectangular areas, called "atomic regions" (sort of like the smallest regions the flattener deals with). The problem with this lies along the line between a rasterized area and an area drawn with vectors—in many cases, the step from raster to vector is visually obvious (sometimes called "stitching"), which sort of ruins the whole point. When you turn on the Clip Complex Regions check box, however, InDesign works extra hard to make the transitions between raster and vector occur only along the edges of objects. The result is a better-looking page that is more complex and prints more slowly (or not at all). Ah, compromises.

Applying Flattener Presets

After reading all of this, don't you wish you had a PDF 1.4-aware PostScript 3 device that could print transparency effects without flattening? Until you have one, however, you'd better know about how to apply these flattener presets.

You can set the flattener preset to either the whole document (the "default preset") or specific page spreads (a "local preset"). To apply a default preset at print time, choose it from the Transparency Flattener Preset pop-up menu in the Advanced tab of the Print dialog box. You can also set the default preset in the Advanced tabs of the Export as PDF and Export as EPS dialog boxes, as well as the Export as SVG dialog box (if you click More Options).

To apply a local flattener preset, select one or more page spreads in the Pages palette and select from among the choices in the Spread Flattening menu in the Pages palette menu: Default, None (Ignore Transparency), or Custom. If you choose None, InDesign prints this spread without any transparency effects. You might use this as a troubleshooting technique if your page isn't printing properly: if you turn off transparency for the spread and it then prints, then it's likely a transparency-related print issue.

Choosing Custom opens the Transparency Flattener Presets dialog box. We assume there's a good reason that there's no way to select one of the flattener presets you've already built, but we can't imagine what that reason would be.

If, at print time, you want to override any and all flattener presets applied to the document with the default preset, you can turn on the Ignore Spread Overrides check box in the Print dialog box.

Flattener Preview

It's driving you crazy. You can see that a page contains transparency (or a drop shadow, or feathering), because the page icon in the Pages palette shows a checkerboard pattern. But you can't find which object is transparent. This sort of thing often happens when you're working on a file created by someone else. Wouldn't it be great if you could see the transparent areas at a glance?

Here's another example: you've set up your transparency flattener to encourage rasterization, but you want to be certain that text near transparent areas is not rasterized. Is there some way to see which areas will be rasterized?

The Flattener Preview palette is the answer to both questions. To display the Flattener Preview palette, choose Flattener from the Output submenu of the Window menu. Use the options on the Highlight pop-up menu to highlight the type of transparency you're looking for (see Figure 11-18). In the first example we described, you'd choose Transparent Objects; in the second, you'd probably want to

FIGURE 11-18
Flattener Preview

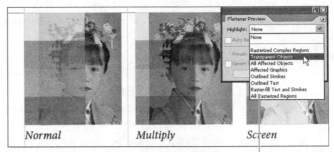

Choose a flattener preview from
the Highlight pop-up menu.

InDesign highlights transparent areas on
the page in red (shown here in dark gray).

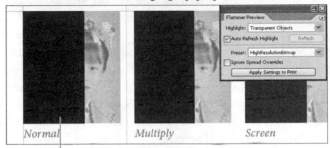

In this example, we've applied a drop shadow to the text.

Choosing All Rasterized Regions shows that the drop shadow will be
rasterized (according to the currently selected flattener preset).

When we switch flattener presets to a preset that encourages rasterization,
InDesign highlights the rasterized text.

choose All Rasterized Regions. The other options on the menu give you more specific control over the type of transparency you want to highlight.

You can choose to have InDesign refresh the transparency highlight for you by turning on the Auto Refresh Highlight option, or turn it off to speed up your screen display and click the Refresh button as needed.

The Flattener Preview palette also gives you a way to "audition" different flattener presets, which can help you decide which preset will work best for your specific document or page. Choose a preset from the Presets pop-up menu, and InDesign will highlight the appropriate areas (based on your current selection in the Highlight pop-up menu) based on the new flattener preset (if you've turned off the Auto Refresh Highlight option, you'll have to click the Refresh button to see the effect of the flattener preset change). You can turn on the Ignore Spread Overrides option to use the flattener preset you've selected, rather than using the flattener applied to the spread, if necessary.

Once the preview looks good to you, you can apply the flattener preset to your print settings by clicking the Apply Settings to Print button (you'll see this change reflected in the Advanced panel of the Print dialog box).

Preparing an InDesign File for Imagesetting

We've listened long and carefully to the grievances of imagesetting service bureau customers and operators. We've heard about how this designer is suing that service bureau for messing up a job, and we've heard imagesetter operators talking about how stupid their clients are and how they have to make changes to the files of most of the jobs that come in. We've listened long enough, and we have only one thing to say: Cut it out! All of you!

There's no reason that this relationship has to be an adversarial one. We don't mean to sound harsh. We just think that we can all cooperate, to everyone's benefit.

Designers: You have to learn the technical chops if you want to play. That's just the way it is. The technical challenges are no greater than those you mastered when you learned how to use a waxer, an X-Acto knife, or a copy camera.

Your responsibility to your imagesetting service bureau is to set your file up so that it has a reasonable chance of printing and to communicate to your service bureau exactly how it is you want your publication printed (or, if you're delivering a PostScript file or PDF, to make sure that the settings in the file are correct).

Service bureau folks, you've got to spell out the limits of your responsibility. If you don't think you should be fixing people's files, don't do it. If you do think it's your responsibility, tell your customer up front you'll fix the files, and tell them what you'll charge for your time. And if you get customers who know what they're doing, give them a discount. This will encourage everyone else.

Okay, back to the book.

Sending Your File

You have three basic choices in transporting your document to an output provider: sending the file itself, sending a PostScript dump, or sending an Acrobat PDF version of the document. While our preference has always been to send PostScript dumps or PDF files, many printers and service bureaus want the file itself. It's a question of who is in control of the final output: us or them.

When we send the InDesign file off to be printed on someone else's system, we don't know whether their fonts are different, whether they'll forget to set up registration marks, and so on. If you send them a PDF file, you can be reasonably sure that the file will print correctly. If you send a PostScript file (and you know what you're doing), you put yourself in the driver's seat. The only things that can go wrong are related to film handling and processing—the wrong film's used, the film's scratched, or the film's been processed incorrectly.

However, no matter what you're going to send to your output provider, you have to be dead certain you've thought of everything before it goes, because it's difficult to change things after that. For instance, make sure that any linked graphics in the publication are up to date, and that any embedded graphics are what you want them to be. If you're printing PostScript, make sure the Print dialog box is set up correctly: What screening are you using? Is tiling turned off? Do you need separations or composite color? What inks to print? Do you want spot colors or process colors? Your output provider should be able to help you make most of these decisions, and perhaps even give you the appropriate PPD file.

Fortunately, the Preflight feature helps with some of this. And, if you're going to send the InDesign file itself, then you should plan on using the Package feature. We discuss both of these in the next section.

Preflight and Package

Are all systems "go"? Do you know the number of kilometers, meters, and centimeters it'll take to get your publication safely in orbit around Mars? Or is it miles, feet, and inches?

Preflight To make sure that your publication is really ready for "prime time," you should use the Preflight plug-in (choose Preflight from the File menu or press Command-Option-Shift-F/Ctrl-Alt-Shift-F). When you do this, InDesign examines the publication for missing fonts, lost image links, and other conditions that might cause you problems and/or embarrassment when you take your publication to an imagesetting service bureau for printing. After it's done analyzing the publication, it displays the results in the Preflight dialog box (see Figure 11-19).

As we get along in years (David never thought he'd be saying that), we wish you could change the font size in the Preflight dialog box; it's very tiny. But it's worth taking a few minutes to squint and read everything in the Summary tab: How many fonts are used? How many images? Any in RGB that should have been CMYK? Are there spot colors that you didn't expect?

Near the bottom of the summary is a cryptic line labeled Non Opaque Objects on Page. Warning: This means this page includes transparency! If an object became partially transparent without you realizing it (maybe a colleague snuck in last night and "accidentally" changed your file), it's worth catching that now.

Even better than reading this dialog box is saving all the information to disk by clicking the Report button and then reading this exported text file in your favorite word processor using whatever font size you want.

Of course, as helpful as Preflight is, it's nowhere near as good as third-party preflighting systems such as Markzware's Flightcheck (which can also check other file formats, like QuarkXPress and Adobe Illustrator files). InDesign's preflighting has a number of limitations, including the inability to find fonts that are called for in embedded EPS files (those that are embedded using the Links palette) but which you do not currently have loaded. Well, nothing is perfect.

Package Once your publication has successfully passed the preflight check, you can assemble all of the files needed to print the publication using the Package plug-in (this is similar to QuarkXPress' "Collect for Output" feature, or PageMaker's "Save For Service Provider" plug-in).

FIGURE 11-19
Preflight Testing a Publication

The Summary panel gives you a quick look at the status of the preflight check. If anything is amiss, you'll see it reported here.

Choose Preflight from the File menu. InDesign displays the Preflight dialog box.

The Fonts panel shows the fonts you've used in the publication.

Turn on the Show Problems Only option to show only the problems the preflight check has found in the publication.

The Links and Images panel shows the status of imported graphics—and any problems the preflight check finds with any of them.

This icon means trouble—in this case, two images were saved using the RGB color model instead of CMYK.

The Colors and Inks panel lists the colors and inks used in the publication.

The Print Settings panel provides a report on the current printing settings.

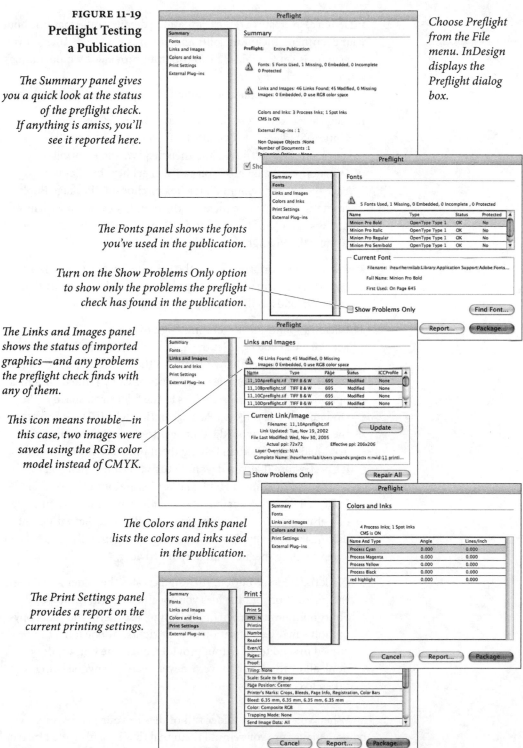

InDesign also creates a report containing detailed information about your document, including fonts and pictures you used. Then all you have to do is get the folder to your output provider by modem, messenger, or carrier pigeon.

To "package" a publication, follow these steps (see Figure 11-20).

1. Choose Package from the File menu (or press Command-Option-Shift-P/Ctrl-Alt-Shift-P). InDesign runs a preflight check on the publication and then displays the Printing Instructions dialog box. You can also get here by clicking Package in the Preflight dialog box or choosing Package Book from the Book palette menu. If the preflight came up with any possible problems (such as an RGB image), you have the choice to view the Preflight info before proceeding.

2. Enter contact information in the Printing Instructions dialog box—this information will appear in the final text report that InDesign adds to the package you're creating.

3. Click the Continue button. InDesign displays the Create Package Folder dialog box. Set the options you want and enter a name for the folder that will contain the packaged publication.

    When you turn on the Copy Fonts or Copy Linked Graphics option, InDesign copies the files to the folder you specify. The Update Graphic Links in Package option tells InDesign to set the links for non-embedded images to the images in the packaged folder (rather than leaving them linked to the original files). It's pretty rare that you'd want to turn this off. When you turn on the Use Document Hyphenation Exceptions Only option, InDesign flags this document so that it won't reflow when someone else opens or edits it on a machine that may have different dictionaries and hyphenation settings. We generally turn this on when sending the file to an output provider.

4. Click the Package button. InDesign creates the folder and copies the publication and the files you specified into it. If the Copy Fonts option was turned on, InDesign also alerts you that copying fonts may be a violation of your rights. Adobe fonts can be copied to send to an output provider, but some font vendors don't allow this (though we've never heard of anyone being taken to court for this).

When you send this folder full of files to your printer or service bureau, make sure you remind them that there is a file called Instruc-

FIGURE 11-20
**Packaging a Publication
for Remote Printing**

*When you choose
Package from the File menu
(or click the Package button
in the Preflight dialog box),
InDesign displays the
Printing Instructions
dialog box.*

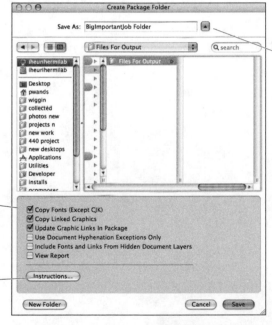

*Enter your contact information and any
notes you want to include in the fields; these
instructions will be saved as a text file.*

*After you click the Continue
button, InDesign displays
the Create Package Folder
dialog box.*

*Enter a name
and location for
the package (the
publication file and
any other files you
choose to copy).*

*Choose the files you want to
copy to the package folder.*

*You can go back to the
Printing Instructions dialog
box by clicking here.*

*If you're copying fonts,
InDesign displays this
message.*

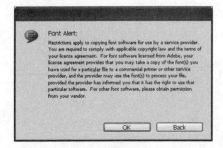

tions.txt in there that they should read. In fact, we sometimes rename this file "READ ME.txt" to make it stand out better.

Finally, if you're working on really large files with hundreds of megabytes of images, you need to be careful with the Package feature so that you don't run out of hard disk space.

All the News That Prints to Fit

Printing is all about thinking ahead. When you press Command-N/Ctrl-N to create a new publication, you really should be thinking "How the heck are we going to print this thing?" By the end of the production process, you'll be tired, cranky, and less able to deal with any problems that come up—so make your decisions about paper size, color selection, and graphic file types as early as you can.

Scripting

Most of the time, we tell a program (an application, a plug-in, or our system software) what to do by manipulating the program's user interface—we click, drag, and type. Scripting is a way of telling a program to perform the same tasks and accomplish the same things. The difference is that, with scripting, we don't have to click the buttons, type the characters, or choose the menu items. The script does it for you. Scripting is what computing is supposed to be *about*: having your computer take over boring, repetitive tasks so that you can spend more time playing *World of Warcraft*. Er, we mean, concentrating on your creative work.

Scripting also gives you the ability to add the features you need to InDesign *now*, rather than waiting for Adobe to give them to you. Even better than that, scripting gives you a way to customize InDesign to match your publications and habits to a degree that Adobe is *never* going to provide.

We're convinced that the reason many people have not taken up scripting is that they're scared. They think scripting is difficult, and is only for people with advanced computer science degrees. And they tell themselves that they're too "intuitive" and "artistic" to master the minimal analytical skills required to write a script.

Be Not Afraid

You do not need to know how to *write* scripts to be able to *run* scripts. This is a misunderstanding that prevents many people from even trying scripting, even though existing scripts might save them enormous amounts of time and trouble.

Even if you don't want to write scripts, or know anything about how they're written, you can use scripts. For that matter, chances are quite good that you know someone who *is* interested in writing scripts for you, and would be willing to do so for the occasional expression of admiration (or beer).

All you need to know is how to install scripts—and that's very simple: just put the script in the Scripts folder in the Presets folder inside your InDesign folder. When you do this, the script will appear in the Scripts palette in InDesign. To run the script, double-click the script name in the Scripts palette.

That's pretty simple, right? If not, we're not certain you should be using a computer at all (or driving a car, for that matter).

Next, we encourage everyone to consider learing to write scripts.

Ole says: "Look. I'm practically a high school dropout, and my background is in illustration, not computer science. I have never taken a single class on programming. As a rebellious teenager I did my best to ignore the sciences and to panic at the sight of even simple equations (in psychoanalytical terms this makes sense: my father was a high school algebra teacher).

"I got over it. These days, I write scripts. You can, too."

System Requirements

What do you need to write and run scripts for InDesign? The following things:

- ▶ The standard scripting system for your computer (if you plan to use the platform-specific scripting languages rather than JavaScript)

- ▶ The InDesign scripting documentation and example scripts

- ▶ A good understanding of the way InDesign works

- ▶ Confidence

It also helps to have a repetitive task that you wish you would never have to do again. This is not required, but it helps.

JavaScript InDesign supports an Adobe version of JavaScript called Extend-Script (like GoLive). ExtendScript complies with the ECMA Java-Script 1.5 standard, and adds a few features to make it more useful for scripting a desktop application (as opposed to a web browser).

InDesign JavaScripts are cross-platform—they run in both the Windows and Mac OS versions of InDesign. There are a few very minor differences between platforms—but they're limited to the way that the scripts work with files and the operating system (as you'd expect).

If JavaScript is cross-platform, why does Adobe bother support-ing the platform-specific languages? First, because scripters might prefer those languages. Adobe's goal should be to *increase* the number of languages that can be used, not to limit them. Next, because InDesign's JavaScript does not know how to communicate with other applications on your system (such as FileMaker or Access); the plat-form-specific languages do that very well.

Luckily, we can use both, and we can tie the platform-specific and platform-independent languages together with InDesign's "do script" method, which lets scripts run other scripts. A JavaScript, for example, can run an AppleScript, or a VBScript can run a JavaScript. For an example of the latter, take a look at the TextCleanup.vbs example script, where Ole uses a snippet of JavaScript to add a file browser dialog box to a VBScript.

Note: Some InDesign JavaScripts have the file extension ".js", which is the standard extension for JScripts in Windows, they will not work if run from the operating system (at best, you'll get an error message). Instead, run these scripts using InDesign's Scripts palette. Try to get in the habit of using the ".jsx" extension, rather than ".js".

Mac OS On the Mac OS, all you need is AppleScript. You almost certainly already have it installed, but in case you don't, it comes on the Mac installation CD. If you can't find your installation CD, you can download AppleScript directly from Apple (http://www.apple.com). What's the easiest way to tell if it's installed? Search for a file named "Script Editor" (this is the application you use to write and run AppleScripts). If you can't find it, you'll have to install it from the Mac OS X installation CD.

Alternative script editors are available—if you're planning to do serious AppleScript development, we strongly recommend Script Debugger, from Late Night Software (http://www.latenightsw.com). Script Debugger is an astonishingly good piece of software, well worth its purchase price. And no, we are not paid to say this.

InDesign can run uncompiled AppleScripts—script files saved as text. To use an uncompiled AppleScript, save the file with the file extension ".as" in the Scripts folder inside the Presets folder in your InDesign folder, and then run the script from the Scripts palette.

Windows   On the Windows side, you've got a number of options. There are (at least) three different scripting systems claiming to be the system standard: Visual Basic Script (VBScript), Visual Basic for Applications (VBA), and various forms of Visual Basic (VB)—including Visual Basic 6, Visual Basic .NET, and Visual Basic 5 Control Creation Edition (VB5 CCE). They're all from Microsoft, and they're all variants of the Basic programming language. Almost all of them work.

Our Recommendation: Use VBScript. To write a VBScript, all you need is a text editor. Notepad does the job quite handily. You don't need anything to run a VBScript—you can run them from Explorer or from InDesign's Scripts palette. If you run them from InDesign's Scripts palette, though, they'll run much faster.

Using VBScript makes distributing and deploying your scripts easier, too. Since they're just text, they're easy to post on web pages or send to other people.

The InDesign example scripts are provided in VBScript, so you'll have a lot of code to work with that won't require much translation (as it would if you were to try to use them in VB.NET, for example).

Our Further Recommendation: Use VB5 CCE to develop VBScripts. Troubleshooting (debugging) VBScripts can be difficult. All you can do is run the script and then note any error messages that appear—and they're not particularly useful. What you need is a real programming environment, where you can step through the lines of your script one by one, as you can when you use Visual Basic.

The Visual Basic 5.0 Control Creation Edition is available for free download from Microsoft, at http://download.microsoft.com/msdownload/sbn/vbcce/vb5ccein.exe. It moves around, though, so this URL might not be valid by the time you read this. If not, a quick Google search should yield another page download location.

VB5 CCE is an almost-complete version of Visual Basic 5.0, and works very well for developing VBScripts for use in InDesign. You can write your VBScript as a single subroutine, making certain that you don't use any part of Visual Basic that does not exist in VBScript; debug the script, and then, when everything works the way you want it to, copy the contents of the subroutine to a text editor and save it as a VBScript (.vbs) file. We'll talk more about this later in the chapter.

Something You Might Already Own: VBA. If you own Microsoft Excel, Microsoft Word, Microsoft Access, or Visio, you already own a copy of VBA. If you plan to write scripts to move data from these programs to InDesign (Access for database publishing, for example), you might want to simply write VBA scripts to control InDesign from inside these programs.

About VB.NET. VB.NET is a tremendous step backwards for the Visual Basic language in terms of performance, ease of use, and ease of learning. We could rant for hours (and have) about how messed up VB.NET is (at least from the standpoint of a scripter), but, for now, we'll content ourselves with saying that the *only* reason one should use VB.NET for InDesign script development is if your script depends on some feature of VB.NET that is not available in any of the other, better, versions of Visual Basic.

We can't think of any, right at the moment.

In addition, and though InDesign works with VB.NET, there are some InDesign scripting tasks that are much more difficult in VB.NET than they are in other versions of Visual Basic.

Finally, if you plan on deploying your scripts as VBScripts, VB5 CCE makes a better development system than VB.NET, as VB.NET does not understand the Variant data type. Because Variant is the fundamental VBScript data type, this is a problem.

Other Scripting Languages

We know of InDesign scripters who are using C#, C, C++, Perl, Python, JScript, OSA JavaScript, Delphi, and other languages to drive InDesign. If your favorite programming language can connect to the platform standard means of passing messages between applications (that's OSA/AppleEvents on the Mac OS and DDE/COM in Windows), it can probably communicate with InDesign.

We're not going to spend any time on those languages, however, because, frankly, we have more than enough to do explaining VBScript, AppleScript, and JavaScript. Forgive us.

Learning About InDesign Scripting

Once you've gathered and installed the software you need to start scripting, you need to learn about how InDesign implements scripting. You're in luck—you'll find the scripting documentation in the Scripting folder inside the Adobe Technical Information folder on your InDesign CS2 CD (it's in a similar place on the first "extras" CD in the CS2 suite CD set).

The *Adobe InDesign CS2 Scripting Guide* is a PDF that contains an introduction to scripting, and basic tutorials (including introductory scripts). The *Adobe InDesign CS2 Scripting Reference* contains reference chapters for AppleScript, JavaScript, and Visual Basic—these are simply listings of every object, property, and method in the InDesign scripting model. It's more than 2000 pages long.

In addition, the InDesign scripting forum at http://www.adobe-forums.com is a great source of scripting information—it's the center of the InDesign scripting community. The forum is a great place to find example scripts, ask questions, and generally hang out with other scripters. Do not be afraid to ask "newbie" questions—we've all been there!

How to Read the Scripting Documentation

Don't print it out! As we mentioned earlier, it's got a lot of pages, and only one third of it, at most, applies to any one scripting language. Skim the first part of the tutorial chapter in the *Scripting Guide*, up to the section "Your First InDesign Script." Try entering and running the script, and then move on to the more advanced script examples.

Once you're done with the tutorial, start thinking about the tasks in your work that you'd like to automate, and look through the example scripts for something related to the things you'd like to do.

When you need to look something up, use the bookmarks in the PDF and/or Acrobat's search feature to find likely terms. Scripting terms tend to mirror the terms you see used in the user interface.

Example Scripts

You'll find a number of example scripts in the same folder as the scripting documentation. Even if you don't intend to write scripts of your own, you might find something useful in the example scripts.

- ▶ **AddGuides.** Draws guides around the currently selected object or objects. This script shows you how to get positioning information back from InDesign, and how to create ruler guides.

- ▶ **AddPoints.** Adds points to a path: each point is added at the midpoint of each line segment in a path. This script demonstrates simple Bezier math and path and point manipulations.

- ▶ **AdjustLayout.** Moves the page items of even/odd pages by specified distances. Use this script to move objects back into the correct position after adding pages or applying master pages.

- ▶ **AlignToPage.** How many times have you wanted to position an object in the center of the page? This script does that, and many other page alignments—including the ability to align the objects relative to the page margins.

- ▶ **BreakFrame.** Removes the selected text frame and its contents from the story. This feature has been frequently requested by PageMaker users.

- ▶ **CornerEffects.** Ever want to round one or two corners of a rectangle, while leaving the other corners square? If you have, then this script is for you. The script redraws the path and applies a corner effect to a pattern of corners you specify.

- ▶ **CreateCharacterStyle.** When you create a character style in InDesign by basing the style on the selected text, InDesign records only those attributes that differ from the default formatting of the surrounding text. While this is a powerful and flexible way of working with character styles, it's also different from the way that other applications (such as QuarkXPress and FrameMaker) work. In those applications, character styles apply every formatting attribute. The CreateCharacterStyle script creates a new character style based on the selected text and defines every formatting attribute.

- ▶ **CropMarks.** Draws crop and registration marks around the selected object or objects. Like AddGuides, this script shows how to create new objects around existing objects.

- ▶ **ExportAllStories.** Exports all of the stories in a document to a specified folder using the file format of your choice (RTF, tagged text, or text only). Shows how to traverse all stories in a document and how to export text.

- ▶ **MakeGrid.** Splits the selected frame into a grid of frames. If the frame contains content, the script can duplicate the frame.

- ▶ **Neon.** Creates a simple "glow" effect by duplicating the selected path or paths. Each copy of the path is slightly smaller than the original, and slightly lighter. The final duplicate path is a white hairline. The resulting group of paths is something like an Illustrator blend.

- ▶ **PathEffects.** This script includes the ever-popular Illustrator, path effects "Bloat" and "Punk," as well as a few others. If you want to learn about scripting InDesign paths, path points, and control handles, this is a good place to start. The script also includes options for converting the selected object into a rectangle or an ellipse, which are useful features borrowed from QuarkXPress.

▶ **PlaceMultipagePDF.** InDesign CS2 can place all of the pages in a multi-page PDF, but it's a manual process—you have to click the place icon for each PDF page you want to place. This script places all of the pages of a PDF on sequential pages, placing one PDF page per page, adding pages to the document if necessary as it does so.

▶ **RandomFill.** Draws a number of rectangles, ellipses, or polygons and pastes them inside the selected path. You can control the object type, size, color, and stroke weight. This is a great script for quickly generating a random background.

▶ **SelectObjects.** Selects all of the objects on a spread that belong to a specific object type (or set of types). This script is only slightly useful by itself, but it shows you how to traverse the objects on a spread to find objects based on their type or content. As such, it's a great starting point for any graphic "search and replace" operation you might want to implement. Want to make sure that all of the graphics in your publication are scaled to the same percentage or use the same color-management profile? Modify this script (as shown later in this chapter).

▶ **SortParagraphs.** Alphabetically sorts the paragraphs in the selection. Shows how to sort text using a simple "bubble sort" algorithm, and how to move text in an InDesign story.

▶ **SplitStory.** Converts each text frame in the selected story to an independent text frame (story), retaining the content in the frames.

▶ **StepAndRepeat.** Duplicates and transforms the selected objects in a variety of ways—it's essentially a scripting version of the Step and Repeat feature, but it adds a few interesting options of its own. This script shows how to duplicate and transform objects, and how to change the color of objects.

▶ **TabUtilities.** This script automates two tasks: setting a right tab stop at the right margin of a paragraph, and setting a left tab at the current cursor position. Select some text in a single-column text frame, then click the Tab at Right button to set a tab stop at the right edge of the text column (this will also remove any existing tab stops in the paragraph). Click the Tab at Cursor button to set a left tab at the current cursor position.

▶ **TextCleanup.** Runs a sequence of find/change operations on the selected text. The find/change parameters are stored in a comma-delimited text file (it should be in the same folder as the example script). By default, these searches cover the standard stuff: changing double spaces to single spaces, changing double returns to single returns, changing double dashes to em dashes, and so on—but you can add your own favorite searches to the text file (including the ability to find/change formatting). You'll find instructions at the beginning of the script, and in the corresponding find/change file.

InDesign Scripting Philosophy

When you launch InDesign, you're probably aware that you're not really launching a single program—you probably know that you're starting a plug-in manager and several hundred plug-ins.

What you probably don't know is that each plug-in is responsible for its own scripting support, and that InDesign's scripting object model—the library of objects and the properties and methods of those objects that make scripting work—is created anew each time you change your plug-in configuration.

In other applications that support scripting, the developers try to determine what features users of their product might want to automate. They then provide scripting support for those features. The trouble with this approach, of course, is that they always miss something—and their users, in the field, are stymied. The users then complain, and are generally given the response, "Why would anyone want to do that?" (Translation: "We didn't think of that.")

InDesign scripting doesn't work that way. InDesign provides scripting access to everything (well, almost everything) you can do to the database that is an InDesign document.

Thinking About Scripting

Because scripting is a great tool for automating large, repetitive tasks, many of us think that that's *all* it's good for. But there's far more to scripting than that. Scripting is also good at little things—operations that might save you only a few seconds a day, but can make your work easier or more precise.

By "little things," we means scripts that save you only a few mouse clicks, drags, or key presses at a time. It's these tiny tasks, repeated dozens, hundreds, or even thousands of times day by day, that add up to fatigue, irritation, and repetitive motion injuries. When you take a common task that involves some number of actions and replace it with a simple double-click or keystroke (all it takes to run a script), you reduce the difficulty and complexity of your work.

Scripting, which many of us think of as being somehow *opposed* to the creative process, can be a powerful creative tool. We often imagine effects we'd like to use in a publication layout that would be difficult to accomplish by hand. When there's time, we turn to scripting for help. Frequently, in the course of working on a script, we'll find a variation on the effect that leads us in an entirely new creative direction. Scripting gives us time to experiment—and we think experimentation has a lot to do with creativity.

What we're getting at here is that scripting is what you make of it, and how you think about it. If you only think of scripting as something applicable to massive projects, you're missing out on many of the benefits—and most of the fun.

Using the Scripts Palette and the Script Label Palette

InDesign includes two scripting-related plug-ins: the Scripts palette and the Script Label palette. The Scripts palette gives you a way to run scripts without leaving InDesign, and significantly speeds script execution; the Script Label palette gives you a way to enter text into the Label property of a page item (a text frame, graphic line, a rectangle, an oval, or an ellipse).

Scripts Palette   To display the Scripts palette, choose Scripts from the Automation submenu of the Window menu (see Figure 12-1). The Scripts palette displays the scripts (or aliases/shortcuts to scripts, or folders) stored inside the Scripts folder inside the Presets folder in your InDesign application folder. If this folder does not already exist, you'll have to create it.

FIGURE 12-1
Scripts Palette

Use the Scripts palette to run scripts without leaving InDesign.

To edit a script, hold down Option/Alt as you double-click the script. Your script editor will open the script for editing.

To run a script, double-click the script name in the Scripts palette.

"Install" scripts in the Scripts palette by adding them to the Scripts folder in the Presets folder in your InDesign application folder. (Create this folder if it does not already exist.)

In general, we think it's better to store your scripts somewhere else, and place aliases (on the Mac OS) or shortcuts (in Windows) in this folder. Why? We've accidentally deleted all of our scripts by re-installing InDesign more than once. It's painful.

To run a script, double-click the script in the Scripts palette. To edit a script, hold down Option/Alt and double-click the script. InDesign will open the script in your script editor (or in the Extend-Script Toolkit, for JavaScript files). To delete scripts from the Scripts palette, open the Scripts folder on your hard drive and move the scripts to another location (or delete them).

To open the folder containing a script, hold down Command-Shift/Ctrl-Shift and double-click the script name in the Scripts palette. InDesign will open the folder containing the script in the Finder or Windows Explorer.

To open a JavaScript in the ExtendScript Toolkit (for more on debugging JavaScripts, see "Using the ExtendScript Toolkit," later in this chapter), hold down Shift as you double-click the script name in the Scripts palette.

Adding Keyboard Shortcuts to Scripts. You can now add keyboard shortcuts to scripts—when you open the Edit Shortcuts dialog box, you'll find a list of installed scripts in the Scripts section. You assign a keyboard shortcut to a script in the same way that you assign any other keyboard shortcut.

This is great—but there's a catch. The keyboard shortcut you apply is tied to a specific location in the list of scripts displayed in the Scripts section of the Edit Shortcuts dialog box. If you add scripts to, or remove scripts from, the list of scripts you have available, the shortcut could very well end up pointing to a script other than the one you intended (this doesn't always happen, but it can).

Controlling Script Order. You can control the order in which scripts appear in the Scripts palette by entering numbers (from 00 to 99) followed by a close parenthesis character (")") before the first character of the file name. The Scripts palette hides the numbers, leaving only the name of the script visible. In any folder in the Scripts folder, the file or folder with a name beginning with "00)" will appear first in the Scripts palette; the file beginning with "01)" will appear next, and so on.

Script Label Palette

To display the Script Label palette, choose Script Label from the Automation submenu of the Window menu (see Figure 12-2). The Script Label palette has only one purpose—it gives you a way to enter text into the label of an object. Once you work with scripting for a bit, you'll realize how useful the label property of a page item is. It can be difficult for a script to find the object you're looking for. By attaching a label to an object, we make finding the object a great deal easier.

But labels are useful in a wide variety of other ways, as well. An object's label can store an apparently unlimited amount of text, so you could actually store quite complex scripts (which are just text, after all) inside an object. Or a label could contain an XML representation of the object, or any other type of text data you can think of.

A page item can have more than one label, thanks to the "insert label" method and the corresponding "extract label" method. If a single label on an object isn't enough for your needs, you can always add your own.

Note: If you have converted QuarkXPress documents that contain scripting labels, those labels will be retained in the new InDesign document.

FIGURE 12-2
Script Label Palette

Select an object.

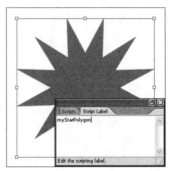
Enter a label for the object. Adding the label does not change the object in any visible way.

Getting Started

For your first script, try the "Hello World" examples in the *Scripting Guide*. They're short, they show you how to create a new document, create a new text frame, add text to the text frame, and apply formatting to that text. After that, start thinking about what you'd like to do with scripting. Is there some task you do in InDesign every day that's driving you crazy?

Wait—we've got one! When you want to get an object or series of objects *out* of a frame you've pasted them into, you end up doing a lot of selecting, cutting, and pasting. A script that could remove all of the objects from a frame (while maintaining the positions they occupied in the frame) would save you time and trouble. Right? Let's go!

This script assumes you have an object selected, and that the object contains at least one other object. The script will not ungroup a group as it processes the objects.

AppleScript

To create the script, follow these steps.

1. Start the AppleScript Script Editor and InDesign.

2. Enter the following text (note that ¬ indicates a long line—do not enter a line break in the Script Editor).

Note: You can download the text for all the scripts listed in this chapter at David's Web site: www.moo.com/rwid/ CS2scripts.zip

```
--CutContents
--An InDesign CS2 AppleScript.
set done to false
tell application "Adobe InDesign CS2"
 activate
 set mySelection to selection
 if (count mySelection) = 1 then
  set myPageItem to item 1 of mySelection
  repeat while done is false
   if class of myPageItem is not group and ¬
   (count page items of myPageItem) is greater than 0 then
    set myItem to page item 1 of myPageItem
    copy geometric bounds of myItem to myBounds
    set myX to item 2 of myBounds
    set myY to item 1 of myBounds
    select myItem
    cut
    paste
    set myPageItem to item 1 of selection
    tell myPageItem to move to {myX, myY}
   else
    set done to true
   end if
  end repeat
 end if
end tell
```

3. Save the script in the Scripts folder inside the Presets folder in your InDesign folder. If you choose to save the file as an uncompiled AppleScript (a text file), give it the file extension ".as".

JavaScript

To create the script, follow these steps.

1. Start the ExtendScript Toolkit and target InDesign. If InDesign is not already running, you'll be prompted to start it.

2. Enter the following text. Don't worry about the indents; they're just here to make it easier for you to follow—JavaScript doesn't require them.

```
//CutContents.jsx
//An InDesign CS2 JavaScript
//Cuts the contents of the selected page items and places
//them in the proper page position and stacking order.
var myObjectList = new Array;
if(app.documents.length != 0){
 if(app.selection.length != 0){
  for(var myCounter = 0; myCounter < app.selection.length;
  myCounter ++){
    switch(app.selection[myCounter].constructor.name){
      case "Rectangle":
      case "Oval":
      case "Polygon":
      case "GraphicLine":
        //If the item contains a page item,
        //add the item to the list.
        if(app.selection[myCounter].pageItems.length != 0){
         myObjectList.push(app.selection[myCounter]);
        }
        break;
    }
  }
  //If there were qualifying items in the selection, pass them
  //on to the myCutContents routine for processing.
  if(myObjectList.length != 0){
   myCutContents(myObjectList);
  }
 }
}
function myCutContents(myObjectList){
 var myPageItem;
 var myGeometricBounds;
 for(var myCounter = 0; myCounter < myObjectList.length;
 myCounter ++){
  var myDone = false;
  myPageItem = myObjectList[myCounter];
  do{
   if((myPageItem.constructor.name != "Group")&&
   (myPageItem.pageItems.length != 0)){
    myPageItem = myPageItem.pageItems.item(0);
    app.select(myPageItem, false);
    app.cut();
    app.pasteInPlace();
    myPageItem = app.selection[0];
   }
   else{
    myDone = true;
   }
  } while(myDone == false);
 }
}
```

3. Save the script as a plain text file with the file extension ".jsx" to the Scripts folder inside the Presets folder in your InDesign folder (create the Scripts folder if it does not already exist).

VBScript   To create the script, follow these steps.

1. Start InDesign and a text editor.

2. Enter the following text. Lines that end with an underscore ("_")
   are long lines that had to be broken to fit the layout (the underscore is the continuation character in VBScript). You can either
   enter the underscore character or type the long line.

```vbscript
Rem CutContents.vbs
Rem An InDesign CS2 VBScript
Rem Cuts the contents of the selected page items and places
Rem them in the proper page position and stacking order.
ReDim myObjectList(0)
Set myInDesign = CreateObject("InDesign.Application.CS2")
If myInDesign.Documents.Count <> 0 Then
 If myInDesign.Selection.Count <> 0 Then
  For myCounter = 1 To myInDesign.Selection.Count
   Select Case TypeName(myInDesign.Selection.Item(myCounter))
    Case "Rectangle", "Oval", "Polygon", "Graphic Line"
     If Not (IsEmpty(myObjectList(0))) Then
      ReDim Preserve myObjectList(UBound(myObjectList) + 1)
     End If
     Set myObjectList(UBound(myObjectList)) = _
      myInDesign.Selection.Item(myCounter)
   End Select
  Next
  If Not (IsEmpty(myObjectList(0))) Then
   myCutContents myInDesign, myObjectList
  End If
 End If
End If
Function myCutContents(myInDesign, myObjectList)
 For myCounter = 0 To UBound(myObjectList)
  myDone = False
  Set myPageItem = myObjectList(myCounter)
  Do While (myDone = False)
   If ((TypeName(myPageItem) <> "Group") _
   And (myPageItem.PageItems.Count <> 0)) Then
    Set myPageItem = myPageItem.PageItems.Item(1)
    myInDesign.Select myPageItem, False
    myInDesign.Cut
    myInDesign.PasteInPlace
    Set myPageItem = myInDesign.Selection.Item(1)
   Else
    myDone = True
   End If
  Loop
 Next
End Function
```

3. Save the script as a plain text file with the file extension ".vbs"
   to the Scripts folder inside the Presets folder in your InDesign
   folder (create the Scripts folder if it does not already exist).

Testing the
CutContents Script

Now that you've saved the script, switch to InDesign. Select a path that contains one or more objects. Double-click the script name in the Scripts palette (or, if you're using AppleScript, you can also run the script from the Script Editor). InDesign will remove each nested object inside the frame and paste it into the same position as it occupied while inside the frame (see Figure 12-3).

FIGURE 12-3
CutContents Script

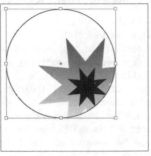 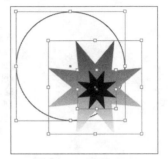

Once you've entered and saved a script, select an object you've pasted other objects into.

Run the script, and InDesign will "un-nest" the objects while retaining their original positions.

Developing VBScripts
with Visual Basic

If you've chosen VBScript as your InDesign scripting language, you need to have some way to debug (that is, step through) your scripts. VBScript, by itself, does not have this capability. Visual Basic, however, is an excellent debugging and development environment. Does this mean that you should run out and buy Visual Basic? Does this mean that you should develop Visual Basic programs rather than VBScripts?

You don't need to do either. VB5 CCE is available for download (for free) from Microsoft. Use VB5 CCE to develop your scripts, then deploy them as VBScripts and run them from the Scripts palette. The following steps show you how to get started (see Figure 12-4).

1. Start InDesign and Visual Basic.

2. In Visual Basic, create a new project. Choose Standard EXE as your project template.

3. Choose References from the Project menu. Visual Basic displays the References dialog box. Turn on the Adobe InDesign CS2 Type Library option (in the Available References list), then click the OK button to add this reference to your project.

4. Create a new form by choosing Add Form from the Project menu. Visual Basic displays the Add Form dialog box. Select the standard form template (Form) and click the Open button. Visual Basic creates a new, blank form.

FIGURE 12-4
Setting Up a Visual Basic Project

Start Visual Basic and choose New Project from the File menu. Choose Standard EXE.

Visual Basic creates a new project and displays a blank form.

Choose References from the Project menu.

Visual Basic displays the References dialog box.

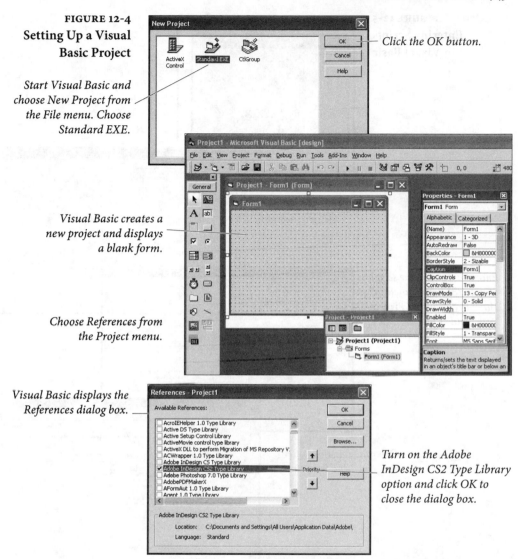

Click the OK button.

Turn on the Adobe InDesign CS2 Type Library option and click OK to close the dialog box.

5. Add a button to the form by selecting the Command Button tool and then drag the tool in the form.

6. Double-click the button to display the Code window.

Now you're ready to add a VBScript for debugging. Paste or enter the main part of the script between the lines beginning with "Private Sub" and ending with "End Sub" lines. If you wanted to debug the example script, you would paste the lines from the start of the script to the line beginning with "Function" in this area. You would then enter (or paste) any functions (such as the "myCutContents" function) following "End Sub." See Figure 12-5.

FIGURE 12-5
**Entering Scripts
in Visual Basic**

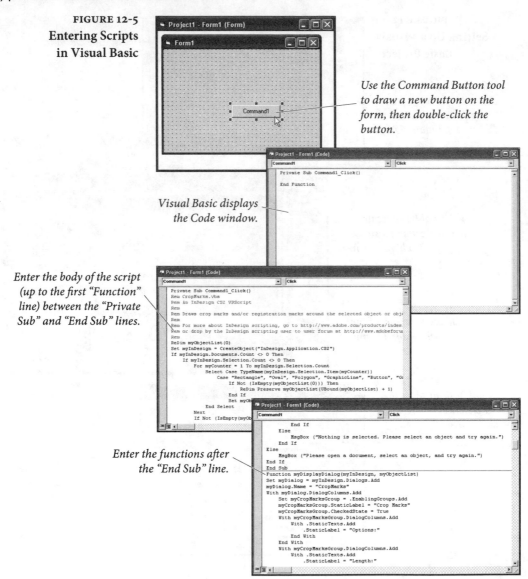

*Use the Command Button tool
to draw a new button on the
form, then double-click the
button.*

*Visual Basic displays
the Code window.*

*Enter the body of the script
(up to the first "Function"
line) between the "Private
Sub" and "End Sub" lines.*

*Enter the functions after
the "End Sub" line.*

Now you can debug the script. To set a breakpoint on a specific
line, you click in the column to the left of the line—a red circle will
appear there. Click the Run button, then click the Command button
you created earlier. Visual Basic runs the script up to the breakpoint
and stops. At that point, you can display the Locals window (choose
Locals Window from the View menu) to view the contents of the
variables you've defined in the script (see Figure 12-6). Our example
script shouldn't have any problems in it, but you'll need to use debugging when you're writing scripts of your own.

FIGURE 12-6

Debugging Scripts in Visual Basic

When you debug, you can step through your script and examine the state of variables—this makes finding problems much easier.

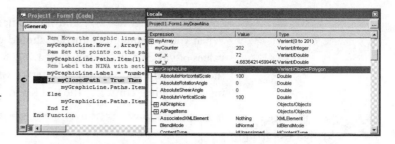

We can't devote more space to debugging scripts in Visual Basic, but you can download documentation from Microsoft (from the VB5 CCE download page) that covers the topic in detail.

Once you've got your script working the way you want it to, copy the contents of the Code window to a text file, delete the lines beginning with "Private Sub" and "End Sub", and then save the file as a text file with the file extension ".vbs".

Using the ExtendScript Toolkit

When you install InDesign CS2, you might notice that an unexpected application appears on your system. It's even...well, a bit funny looking. Its icon is a red toolbox. Above the toolbox floats the magic scroll that has come to represent a script file, hovering as if it were a genii escaping from a bottle. Its files sport the file extension .jsx, and are represented by the same scroll emerging from a coffee cup.

What the heck is this thing? And why would it be represented by symbols denoting both hard-nosed, utilitarian virtue and superstitious frivolity?

It's the ExtendScript Toolkit (or ESTK), and it's included with the Creative Suite, and/or with the individual products of the suite. The ESTK gives you a way to write, manage, and debug JavaScripts for InDesign and other CS2 applications. It's what's called an Integrated Development Environment, or IDE.

InDesign scripters working in AppleScript or VBScript have always been able to use excellent script development environments—but, before the ESTK came along, InDesign scripters working with JavaScript had to edit the scripts using a text editor and then run and debug our scripts inside InDesign. While we could debug a script using a built-in debugger, we couldn't edit text there; and, back in our text editor, we couldn't debug. It made for a very frustrating development process.

But a good IDE gives a scripter more than just a way to enter and debug a script—it should also provide editing features such as syntax coloring (see Figure 12-7) and file management (see Figure 12-8). When you're debugging, an IDE should provide a way to view the values of variables in your script, a way to step through the lines of the script, and an easy way to interact with the scripting environment through a "console." The ESTK provides all of these features.

FIGURE 12-7
Syntax Coloring in the ESTK

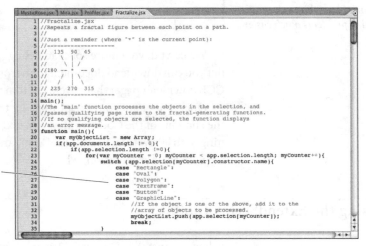

Syntax coloring shows the type of the text, which makes it easier to edit. (Since we don't have color available for this page, you'll have to use your imagination a bit.)

FIGURE 12-8
ESTK Script File Management

The Scripts panel shows the library of scripts available for the target application. To edit or debug a script, double-click the script name.

Editing and Running Scripts in the ESTK

The best way to learn about a new piece of software, of course, is to use it for something, and, to do that, you've got to start it. While you can start the ESTK as you would start any other application, the quick way to do it is to hold down Option (on the Mac OS) or Alt (in Windows) and double-click the name of a script in the Scripts palette. This starts the ESTK and opens the script for editing (see Figure 12-9). The ESTK might not become the active application--if it doesn't, you can Command-Tab (Mac OS) or Alt-Tab (Windows) to it to bring it to the front.

At this point, you can create a new script, edit a script, run a script, or debug a script. If you launched the ESTK from the Scripts palette, you'll see that the "target" application, InDesign, has been selected. If you started the ESTK some other way, you'll need to select InDesign from the drop down menu (see Figure 12-10).

FIGURE 12-9
**Setting the
Target Application**

*Choose a target application. Your
target menu might look a bit
different, but we have to deal with
pre-release craziness.*

The controls for running a script are at the top of the ESTK window, and resemble the play, pause, and stop buttons usually found on a CD or DVD player (see Figure 12-00).

As you run or debug InDesign scripts in the ESTK, InDesign's screen display is turned off. This makes your scripts run faster. To examine the state of a document while debugging a script, you'll need to stop the script and then return to InDesign.

The ESTK is a full-featured text editor, with keyboard navigation, drag and drop text editing, and standard find/change capabilities. One thing that's a bit odd on the Mac OS is that some of the keyboard shortcuts for cursor movement use the Control key, rather than the Command key. The shortcut for moving the cursor to the start of the next word is Control-right arrow, for example.

Just as text editors can check the spelling and grammar of your text, the ESTK has a way to check the syntax of your script. This is a great way to find mismatched parentheses or brackets, missing quotation marks, and other little annoyances that gremlins have inserted into or removed from your code. Choose Check Syntax from the Edit menu to perform this check—if the ESTK finds a syntax error, it'll highlight it and display an error message.

When you choose a target application, the scripts available to that application appear in the Scripts panel in the ESTK. You can open a script by double-clicking the name of the script in the panel.

FIGURE 12-10
Script Controls

Pause | *Stop*
Run | | *Step*

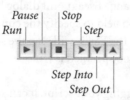

Step Into
Step Out

Setting Breakpoints

Tired of stepping through your script one line at a time? Use breakpoints. A breakpoint stops the script execution at a specific line, at which point you can examine variables in the Data Browser or Console, enter commands in the console window, step through the following lines of the script, or stop the script altogether and look at what's been going on in InDesign (see Figure 12-11).

The ESTK has two kinds of breakpoint: conditional breakpoints, which stop the script only when some condition is met; and unconditional breakpoints, which simply stop the script at the marked line.

FIGURE 12-11
Setting a Breakpoint

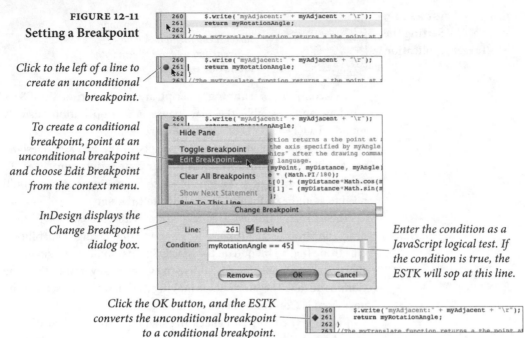

Click to the left of a line to
create an unconditional
breakpoint.

To create a conditional
breakpoint, point at an
unconditional breakpoint
and choose Edit Breakpoint
from the context menu.

InDesign displays the
Change Breakpoint
dialog box.

Enter the condition as a
JavaScript logical test. If
the condition is true, the
ESTK will sop at this line.

Click the OK button, and the ESTK
converts the unconditional breakpoint
to a conditional breakpoint.

To set an unconditional breakpoint, click to the left of the line--a red dot will appear. When you run the script, the ESTK will stop at the line you've marked. To ignore the breakpoint but leave it in place, click it once. To remove the breakpoint, click the red dot twice.

To set a conditional breakpoint, set an unconditional breakpoint, choose Edit Breakpoint from the Context menu (to display the Context menu, hold down Control on the Mac OS and click the breakpoint, or click using the right mouse button in Windows). The ESTK displays the Change Breakpoint dialog box. Enter a line of JavaScript in the Condition field to specify the condition, then click OK to close the dialog box. The ESTK will stop the script at this breakpoint when the condition you specified is true.

Writing to the Console

As you're debugging your script, it can sometimes help a great deal to write log entries to the console window. In the ESTK, you can display information in the console using the $.write() method. If you need see a the value of a number of variables at once, you'll probably use $.write() extensively during debugging (see Figure 12-12).

Using the Data Browser

Another way to view the values assigned to variables in your script as you debug is the ESTK Data Browser tab (see Figure 12-13). To view the properties of an object, click the arrow to the left of the object name to expand the object. For each property, the ESTK will display the property's value.

FIGURE 12-12

Writing to the Console

In this example, we've used $.write() to write a series of strings to the console. By doing this, you can easily watch a series of values change as you debug the script.

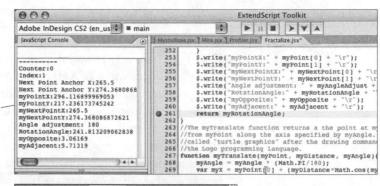

FIGURE 12-13

The ESTK Data Browser

The Data Browser shows you the values of variables in your script. If the variable is an object, as in this example, you can also see the properties of the object.

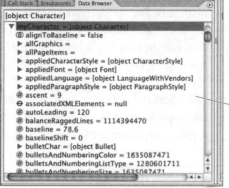

Profiling Your Script

A very interesting feature of the ESTK is the Profiler, which collects performance information about your script as it's running. We haven't had a chance to play with this feature extensively, but it's already given us useful insights into ways that we can speed up our scripts (see Figure 12-14).

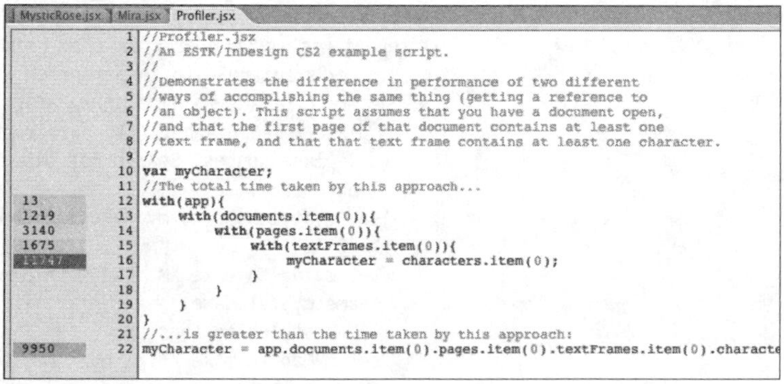

FIGURE 12-14

The ESTK Data Browser

The times listed are in microseconds; the colors indicate relative speed of execution (with green being the quickest and the red the slowest). In this example, you can clearly see that referring to a character via nested "with" statements is much slower than referring to the object directly.

More Fun with Scripting

We'll limit ourselves to a small number of further scripting examples, because we want to finish this book sometime this decade.

Automatically Creating Style-to-Tag Mappings

If you've looked through Chapter 7, "Importing and Exporting," you probably noticed the section on mapping paragraph styles to XML tags. It's a very powerful method of converting your existing InDesign documents to an XML workflow.

If your documents contain a large number of styles, and if those styles contain spaces, you probably groaned aloud thinking about the amount of work you'd have to put in to map all of your paragraph styles to tags.

Automating this process is exactly the sort of thing that scripting is very good at. The following are two example scripts (one for each platform). The script creates tags that match each paragraph style in the document, replacing invalid characters in the style names as it does so. The script then associates each paragraph style with the corresponding tag.

AppleScript. Follow the steps shown earlier in this chapter, and enter the AppleScript shown below. Note that ¬ indicates a long line in this layout—do not enter a line break in the Script Editor.

```
--MapStylesToTags.as
tell application "Adobe InDesign CS2"
 if (count documents) > 0 then
  if (count paragraph styles of active document) > 1 then
   my myMapStylesToTags(active document)
  end if
 end if
end tell
on myMapStylesToTags(myDocument)
 tell application "Adobe InDesign CS2"
  tell myDocument
   repeat with myCounter from 1 to (count paragraph styles)
    set myParagraphStyle to paragraph style myCounter
    set myStyleName to name of myParagraphStyle
    if myStyleName is not "[No paragraph style]" then
     --Replace spaces. Search for other characters if
     --necessary.
     set myStyleName to my myReplaceCharacters(myStyleName, ¬
     " ", "_")
     set myTag to make XML tag with properties ¬
     {name:myStyleName}
     --Map styles to tags
     set myMap to make XML export map with properties ¬
     {markup tag:myTag, mapped style:myParagraphStyle}
     --To map tags to styles, remove the comment from the
     --following line and comment out the line above.
     --set myMap to make XML import map with properties ¬
     --{markup tag:myTag, mapped style:myParagraphStyle}
    end if
   end repeat
```

```
        --Apply the mapping specified above.
        auto tag
      end tell
    end tell
  end myMapStylesToTags
  on myReplaceCharacters(myString, mySearchString, myReplaceString)
    set AppleScript's text item delimiters to the mySearchString
    set the myList to every text item of myString
    set AppleScript's text item delimiters to the myReplaceString
    set myString to the myList as string
    set AppleScript's text item delimiters to ""
    return myString
  end myReplaceCharacters
```

JavaScript. Follow the steps shown earlier in this chapter for creating a JavaScript, and enter the code shown here.

```javascript
//MapStylesToTags.jsx
if (app.documents.length != 0){
  if (app.activeDocument.paragraphStyles.length > 1){
    myMapStylesToTags();
  }
}
function myMapStylesToTags(){
  var myDocument = app.activeDocument;
  for(var myCounter = 0; myCounter < myDocument.paragraphStyles.
length; myCounter ++){
    var myParagraphStyle = myDocument.paragraphStyles.item(myCounter);
    var myStyleName = myParagraphStyle.name;
    if (myStyleName != "[No paragraph style]"){
      //Replace all spaces with underscore characters.
      var myRegEx = new RegExp (' ', 'gi') ;
      myStyleName = myStyleName.replace(myRegEx, '_');
      var myXMLTag = myDocument.xmlTags.add(myStyleName)
      var myMap = myDocument.xmlExportMaps.add(myParagraphStyle,
      myXMLTag)
      //To map XML tags to styles, comment the line above
      //and uncomment the following line.
      //Set myMap = myDocument.xmlImportMaps.add(myxmlTag,
      //myParagraphStyle)
    }
  }
  myDocument.autoTag();
}
```

VBScript. Follow the steps shown earlier in this chapter for creating a VBScript, and enter the code shown here.

```vbscript
Rem MapStylesToTags.vbs
Set myInDesign = CreateObject("InDesign.Application.CS2")
If myInDesign.Documents.Count <> 0 Then
  If myInDesign.ActiveDocument.ParagraphStyles.Count > 1 Then
    myMapStylesToTags (myInDesign.ActiveDocument)
  End If
End If
```

```
Function myMapStylesToTags(myDocument)
 For myStyleCounter = 1 To myDocument.ParagraphStyles.Count
   Set myParagraphStyle = myDocument.ParagraphStyles.
Item(myStyleCounter)
   myStyleName = myParagraphStyle.Name
   If myStyleName <> "[No paragraph style]" Then
    myStyleName = Replace(myStyleName, " ", "_")
    Set myXMLTag = myDocument.XMLTags.Add(myStyleName)
    Set myMap = myDocument.XMLExportMaps.Add(myParagraphStyle, _
    myXMLTag)
    Rem To map XML tags to styles, comment the line above
    Rem and uncomment the following line.
    Rem Set myMap = myDocument.XMLImportMaps.Add(myXMLTag, _
    Rem myParagraphStyle)
   End If
 Next
 myDocument.AutoTag
End Function
```

Drawing NINAs   Have you ever played with a Spirograph? Or been fascinated by one of the geometric patterns created by M. C. Escher? Both authors admit a fondness (well, more like an obsession) for geometric art. While writing this book, we stumbled across a very interesting web site: http://www.washington.edu/bibsys/mattf/nina/. Matt Freedman, at the University of Washington, invented (or is it "discovered"?) a very nifty new algorithm for drawing shapes he's named NINAs (NINA being an acronym for "Nina Is Not An Acronym"). NINAs are fascinating shapes, and we had to see if we could write InDesign scripts that make use of the NINA algorithm. Figure 12-15 shows some of the NINAs drawn by our script.

Note: This script involves a small amount of trigonometry—so we've had to add some handlers (subroutines) to the AppleScript section, because AppleScript has no built-in trigonometric functions. In addition, you should note that the Visual Basic functions return values in radians, rather than degrees, and that InDesign's vertical axis is upside down relative to traditional geometric plotting.

AppleScript   Again, follow the steps shown for creating an AppleScript earlier in this chapter. Note that ¬ indicates a long line in this layout—do not enter a line break in the Script Editor. Note, too, that this AppleScript can be very slow. If you have an AppleScript extension that supports sine and cosine functions, you could use those functions to improve script performance. In the meantime, experiment with fairly low values for the myNumberOfLines variable.

FIGURE 12-15
Various NINAs

```
--Nina.as
--An InDesign CS AppleScript
--For more on NINAs, see:
--http://www.washington.edu/bibsys/mattf/nina/index.html
--myNumberOfLines sets the number of line segments in the NINA.
set myNumberOfLines to 128
--Experiment with a_pulse and b_pulse to create different NINAs.
--values must not exceed myNumberOfLines.
set a_pulse to 33
set b_pulse to 37
--"myLength" controls the line length; the radius of the
--shape is roughly twice this value.
set myLength to 6
```

```
            --Set myClosedPath to true for a closed path; set it to
            --false to leave the path open.
            set myClosedPath to true
            tell application "Adobe InDesign CS2"
             if (count documents) > 0 then
               if (class of active window is layout window) then
                 set myOldXUnits to horizontal measurement units of view ¬
                 preferences of active document
                 set myOldYUnits to vertical measurement units of view ¬
                 preferences of active document
                 set horizontal measurement units of view preferences of ¬
                 active document to points
                 set vertical measurement units of view preferences of ¬
                 active document to points
                 my myDrawNina(myNumberOfLines, a_pulse, b_pulse, myLength, ¬
                 myClosedPath)
                 set horizontal measurement units of view preferences of ¬
                 active document to myOldXUnits
                 set vertical measurement units of view preferences of ¬
                 active document to myOldYUnits
               end if
             end if
            end tell
            on myDrawNina(myNumberOfLines, a_pulse, b_pulse, myLength, ¬
            myClosedPath)
             set myList to {}
             repeat with myCounter from 0 to (myNumberOfLines * 2)
               --Note: the "*(180/pi)" part converts radians to degrees,
               --as the sine/cosine handlers expect degrees as their input.
               set myAValue to ((-2 * pi * a_pulse * myCounter) / ¬
               myNumberOfLines) * (180 / pi)
               set myBValue to ((-2 * pi * b_pulse * myCounter) / ¬
               myNumberOfLines) * (180 / pi)
               set myASine to my sine_of(myAValue)
               set myACosine to my cosine_of(myAValue)
               set myBSine to my sine_of(myBValue)
               set myBCosine to my cosine_of(myBValue)
               set myX to (myACosine + myBCosine) * myLength
               set myY to (myASine + myBSine) * myLength
               copy {myX, myY} to end of myList
             end repeat
             tell application "Adobe InDesign CS2"
               tell active page of active window
                 set myGraphicLine to make graphic line
                 set entire path of path 1 of myGraphicLine to myList
                 if myClosedPath is true then
                   set path type of path 1 of myGraphicLine to closed path
                 else
                   set path type of path 1 of myGraphicLine to open path
                 end if
               end tell
             end tell
            end myDrawNina
```

```
--Sine and Cosine routines from Apple's
--Essential Subroutines collection.
on sine_of(x)
  repeat until x is greater than or equal to 0 and x < 360
    if x is greater than or equal to 360 then
      set x to x - 360
    end if
    if x < 0 then
      set x to x + 360
    end if
  end repeat
  --convert from degrees to radians
  set x to x * (2 * pi) / 360
  set answer to 0
  set numerator to x
  set denominator to 1
  set factor to -(x ^ 2)
  repeat with i from 3 to 40 by 2
    set answer to answer + numerator / denominator
    set numerator to numerator * factor
    set denominator to denominator * i * (i - 1)
  end repeat
  return answer
end sine_of
on cosine_of(x)
  repeat until x is greater than or equal to 0 and x < 360
    if x ³ 360 then
      set x to x - 360
    end if
    if x < 0 then
      set x to x + 360
    end if
  end repeat
  --convert from degrees to radians
  set x to x * (2 * pi) / 360
  set answer to 0
  set numerator to 1
  set denominator to 1
  set factor to -(x ^ 2)
  repeat with i from 2 to 40 by 2
    set answer to answer + numerator / denominator
    set numerator to numerator * factor
    set denominator to denominator * i * (i - 1)
  end repeat
  return answer
end cosine_of
```

JavaScript Follow the steps shown for creating a JavaScript script earlier in this chapter, and enter the following code.

```
//NINA.jsx
//For more on NINAs, see:
//http://www.washington.edu/bibsys/mattf/nina/index.html
//myNumberOfLines sets the number of line segments in the NINA.
```

```
var myNumberOfLines = 201;
//Experiment with a_pulse and b_pulse to create different NINAs.
//values must not exceed myNumberOfLines.
var a_pulse = 161;
var b_pulse = 16;
//"myLength" controls the line length; the radius of the
//shape is roughly twice this value.
var myLength = 36;
//Set myClosedPath to true for a closed path; set it to
//false to leave the path open.
var myClosedPath = true;
if(app.documents.length != 0){
 if(app.activeWindow.constructor.name == "LayoutWindow"){
  var myViewPreferences = app.activeDocument.viewPreferences;
  var myOldXUnits = myViewPreferences.horizontalMeasurementUnits;
  var myOldYUnits = myViewPreferences.verticalMeasurementUnits;
  app.activeDocument.viewPreferences.horizontalMeasurementUnits =
  MeasurementUnits.points;
  app.activeDocument.viewPreferences.verticalMeasurementUnits =
  MeasurementUnits.points;
  myDrawNina(myNumberOfLines, a_pulse, b_pulse, myLength,
  myClosedPath);
  app.activeDocument.viewPreferences.horizontalMeasurementUnits =
  myOldXUnits;
  app.activeDocument.viewPreferences.verticalMeasurementUnits =
  myOldYUnits;
 }
}
function myDrawNina(myNumberOfLines, a_pulse, b_pulse, myLength,
myClosedPath){
 var cur_x, cur_y;
 var myAnchor = new Array(2);
 var myArray = new Array;
 //Rather than draw the entire path point-by-point,
 //we'll fill an array and then use it to fill in all of the point
 //locations at once using the entirePath property.
 for (var myCounter = 0; myCounter < myNumberOfLines; myCounter++){
  cur_x = (Math.cos((-2 * Math.PI * a_pulse * myCounter) /
  myNumberOfLines) + Math.cos((-2 * Math.PI * b_pulse * myCounter)
  / myNumberOfLines)) * myLength;
  cur_y = (Math.sin((-2 * Math.PI * a_pulse * myCounter) /
  myNumberOfLines) + Math.sin((-2 * Math.PI * b_pulse * myCounter)
  / myNumberOfLines)) * myLength;
  myAnchor = [cur_x, cur_y];
  myArray.push(myAnchor);
 }
 app.activeDocument.viewPreferences.horizontalMeasurementUnits =
 MeasurementUnits.points;
 app.activeDocument.viewPreferences.verticalMeasurementUnits =
 MeasurementUnits.points;
 var myPage = app.activeWindow.activePage;
 var myGraphicLine = myPage.graphicLines.add();
 myGraphicLine.move(undefined, ["1p","1p"]);
 var myPath = myGraphicLine.paths.item(0);
 //Now set the entire path to the contents of the array.
```

```
myPath.entirePath = myArray;
if(myClosedPath == true){
  myPath.pathType = PathType.closedPath;
}
else{
  myPath.pathTYpe = PathType.openPath;
}
//Label the graphic line with the parameters used to create it.
myGraphicLine.label = "number_of_lines = " + myNumberOfLines + ",
a_pulse = " + a_pulse + ", b_pulse = " + b_pulse;
}
```

Visual Basic   Follow the steps shown for creating a Visual Basic script earlier in this chapter (as usual, "_" indicates a line break in this layout; do not break the line or type the character).

```
Rem NINA.vbs
Rem For more on NINA, see:
Rem http://www.washington.edu/bibsys/mattf/nina/index.html
Rem myNumberOfLines sets the number of line segments in the NINA.
myNumberOfLines = 201
Rem Experiment with a_pulse and b_pulse to create different NINAs.
Rem values must not exceed myNumberOfLines.
a_pulse = 161
b_pulse = 16
Rem "myLength" controls the line length; the radius of the
Rem shape is roughly twice this value.
myLength = 36
Rem Set myClosedPath to true to close the NINA, or set it
Rem to false to leave the path open.
myClosedPath = True
Set myInDesign = CreateObject("InDesign.Application.CS2")
If myInDesign.Documents.Count <> 0 Then
  If TypeName(myInDesign.ActiveWindow) = "LayoutWindow" Then
    set myViewPreferences = myInDesign.ActiveDocument.ViewPreferences
    myOldXUnits = myViewPreferences.HorizontalMeasurementUnits
    myOldYUnits = myViewPreferences.VerticalMeasurementUnits
    set myDocument = myInDesign.ActiveDocument
    myDocument.ViewPreferences.HorizontalMeasurementUnits = _
    idMeasurementUnits.idPoints
    myDocument.ViewPreferences.VerticalMeasurementUnits = _
    idMeasurementUnits.idPoints
    myDrawNina myInDesign, myNumberOfLines, a_pulse, b_pulse, _
    myLength, myClosedPath
    myDocument.ViewPreferences.HorizontalMeasurementUnits = _
    myOldXUnits
    myDocument.ViewPreferences.VerticalMeasurementUnits = _
    myOldYUnits
  End If
End If
Function myDrawNina(myInDesign, myNumberOfLines, a_pulse, b_pulse, _
myLength, myClosedPath)
  pi = 3.14159265358979
  Set myDocument = myInDesign.ActiveDocument
```

```
Set myPage = myInDesign.ActiveWindow.ActivePage
ReDim myArray(myNumberOfLines)
Rem Fill in an array with point locations.
For myCounter = 0 To (myNumberOfLines)
 cur_x = (Cos((-2 * pi * a_pulse * myCounter) / myNumberOfLines) _
 + Cos((-2 * pi * b_pulse * myCounter) / myNumberOfLines)) * _
 myLength
 cur_y = (Sin((-2 * pi * a_pulse * myCounter) / myNumberOfLines) _
 + Sin((-2 * pi * b_pulse * myCounter) / myNumberOfLines)) * _
 myLength
 myArray(myCounter) = Array(cur_x, cur_y)
Next
Set myGraphicLine = myPage.GraphicLines.Add
Rem Move the graphic line a bit to clear up
Rem page "ownership" issues.
myGraphicLine.Move , Array("1p", "1p")
Rem Set the points on the path to the array generated by the loop.
myGraphicLine.Paths.Item(1).EntirePath = myArray
Rem Label the NINA with settings.
myGraphicLine.Label = "number_of_lines = " & CStr(myNumberOfLines)_
& ", a_pulse = " & CStr(a_pulse) & ", b_pulse = " & CStr(b_pulse)
If myClosedPath = True Then
 myGraphicLine.Paths.Item(1).PathType = idPathType.idClosedPath
Else
 myGraphicLine.Paths.Item(1).PathType = idPathType.idOpenPath
End If
End Function
```

Testing the NINA Drawing Script

To test the NINA drawing script, move InDesign's ruler zero point to the point at which you want to locate the center of the shape, then run the script (we recommend setting the publication's measurement system to points before running the script). If all goes well, InDesign will draw a NINA. We urge you to experiment with the settings in the script—the number of different types of shapes you can draw is truly endless. Even very slight changes to the settings can produce wildly differing results.

This is a good script to add a user interface to—all you need is a dialog box containing four text fields (to set the myNumberOfLines, a_pulse, b_pulse, and myLength variables) and OK/Cancel buttons.

Adding a User Interface

InDesign scripts can create their own dialog boxes, and can populate those dialog boxes with static text labels, check box controls, pop-up menus, text entry fields, and a variety of number entry fields (measurement units, integers, percentages, and real numbers). Previously, adding a user interface to a script meant you had to rely on additional user interface building software, such as FaceSpan, Real Basic, or AppleScript Studio on the Mac OS, or the full version of Visual Basic in Windows. Having to rely on these add-on products made your scripts larger, and complicated sharing scripts with others.

There's good news and bad news about InDesign script dialog boxes. The good news is that InDesign takes care of all spacing and sizing issues. The bad news? InDesign takes care of all spacing and sizing issues. This means that you don't have to worry about setting pixel coordinates for every control, but it also means that you have very little control over the appearance of your dialog boxes. At the same time, it's relatively easy to create a good-looking dialog box.

Let's add a user interface to our NINA drawing script. The following sections show you how to do that in AppleScript, JavaScript, and VBScript. When you run the script, InDesign will display a dialog box (see Figure 12-16).

FIGURE 12-16
NINA User Interface

By adding a user interface to your script, you can make it much easier to use. This example dialog box was generated by InDesign—no DialogDirector, no Apple-Script Studio, no Visual Basic form. How cool is that?

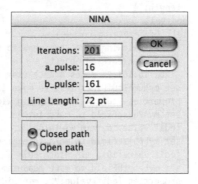

InDesign dialog boxes can include a range of controls not shown in this example, including pop-up menus, check boxes, and a variety of other number and text entry fields (only measurement edit box controls and integer edit box controls are shown here). As in all other InDesign numeric entry fields, you can do arithmetic and enter measurement overrides in these fields.

AppleScript

Open the script you created earlier, save a copy of it, and then follow these steps.

1. Delete these lines:

```
--myNumberOfLines sets the number of line segments in the NINA.
set myNumberOfLines to 128
--Experiment with a_pulse and b_pulse to create different NINAs.
--values must not exceed myNumberOfLines.
set a_pulse to 33
set b_pulse to 37
--"myLength" controls the line length; the radius of the
--shape is roughly twice this value.
set myLength to 6
--Set myClosedPath to true for a closed path; set it to
--false to leave the path open.
set myClosedPath to true
```

2. Change the line:

```
my myDrawNina(myNumberOfLines, a_pulse, b_pulse, myLength, ¬
myClosedPath)
```

to:

```
my myDisplayDialog()
```

3. Enter the following function at the end of the script.

```
on myDisplayDialog()
 tell application "Adobe InDesign CS2"
  set myDialog to make dialog with properties {name:"NINA"}
  tell myDialog
   --Add a dialog column.
   tell (make dialog column)
    tell (make border panel)
     tell (make dialog column)
      make static text with properties {static label:"Iterations:"}
      make static text with properties {static label:"a_pulse:"}
      make static text with properties {static label:"b_pulse:"}
      make static text with properties {static label:"Line ¬
      Length:"}
     end tell
     tell (make dialog column)
      --The following line shows how to set multiple properties
      --as you create an object.
      --201:16:161:72 makes a nice example NINA.
      set myNumberOfLinesField to make integer editbox with ¬
      properties {edit value:201, min width:60}
      set myAPulseField to make integer editbox with properties ¬
      {edit value:16, min width:60}
      set myBPulseField to make integer editbox with properties ¬
      {edit value:161, min width:60}
      set myLengthField to make measurement editbox with ¬
      properties {edit value:72, min width:60, edit units:points}
     end tell
    end tell
    tell (make border panel)
     tell (make radiobutton group)
      set myClosedPathButton to make radiobutton control with ¬
      properties {static label:"Closed path", checked state:true}
      make radiobutton controls with properties ¬
      {static label:"Open path"}
     end tell
    end tell
   end tell
  end tell
  set myReturn to show myDialog
  if myReturn is true then
   --Get the values from the dialog box.
   set myNumberOfLines to edit value of myNumberOfLinesField
   set a_pulse to edit value of myAPulseField
   set b_pulse to edit value of myBPulseField
   set myLength to edit value of myLengthField
   set myClosedPath to checked state of myClosedPathButton
   destroy myDialog
   my myDrawNina(myNumberOfLines, a_pulse, b_pulse, myLength, ¬
   myClosedPath)
  else
   destroy myDialog
  end if
 end tell
```

```
end myDisplayDialog
```

4. Save the script.

JavaScript   Open the script you created earlier, save a copy of the script, and then follow these steps.

1. Delete these lines:

```
//myNumberOfLines sets the number of line segments in the NINA.
var myNumberOfLines = 201;
//Experiment with a_pulse and b_pulse to create different NINAs.
//values must not exceed myNumberOfLines.
var a_pulse = 161;
var b_pulse = 16;
//"myLength" controls the line length; the radius of the
//shape is roughly twice this value.
var myLength = 36;
//Set myClosedPath to true for a closed path; set it to
//false to leave the path open.
var myClosedPath = true;
```

2. Change the line:

```
myDrawNina(myNumberOfLines, a_pulse, b_pulse, myLength,
myClosedPath);
```

to:

```
myDisplayDialog();
```

3. Enter the following function at the end of the script.

```
function myDisplayDialog(){
 var myDialog = app.dialogs.add({name:"NINA"});
 with(myDialog){
  //Add a dialog column.
  myDialogColumn = dialogColumns.add()
  with(myDialogColumn){
   with(borderPanels.add()){
    with(dialogColumns.add()){
     staticTexts.add({staticLabel:"Number of iterations:"});
     staticTexts.add({staticLabel:"a_pulse:"});
     staticTexts.add({staticLabel:"b_pulse:"});
     staticTexts.add({staticLabel:"Line length (in points):"});
    }
    with(dialogColumns.add()){
     //The following line shows how to set multiple properties
     //as you create an object.
     //201:16:161:72 makes a nice example NINA.
     myNumberOfLinesField = integerEditboxes.add({editValue:201,
     minWidth:60});
     myAPulseField = integerEditboxes.add({editValue:16,
     minWidth:60});
```

```
      myBPulseField = integerEditboxes.add({editValue:161,
      minWidth:60});
      myLengthField = integerEditboxes.add({editValue:72,
      minWidth:60});
    }
  }
  with(borderPanels.add()){
    with(radiobuttonGroups.add()){
    myClosedPathButton = radiobuttonControls.add(
    {staticLabel:"Closed path", checkedState:true});
    myOpenPathButton = radiobuttonControls.add({staticLabel:
    "Open path"});
    }
  }
  }
}
myReturn = myDialog.show();
if (myReturn == true){
 //Get the values from the dialog box.
 myNumberOfLines = myNumberOfLinesField.editValue;
 a_pulse = myAPulseField.editValue;
 b_pulse = myBPulseField.editValue;
 myLength = myLengthField.editValue;
 myClosedPath = myClosedPathButton.checkedState;
 myDialog.destroy();
 myDrawNina(myNumberOfLines, a_pulse, b_pulse, myLength,
 myClosedPath);
}
else{
 myDialog.destroy();
}
}
```

VBScript   Open the script you created earlier, save a copy of the script, and then
follow these steps.

1. Delete these lines:

```
Rem myNumberOfLines sets the number of line segments in the NINA.
myNumberOfLines = 201
Rem Experiment with a_pulse and b_pulse to create different NINAs.
Rem values must not exceed myNumberOfLines.
a_pulse = 161
b_pulse = 16
Rem "myLength" controls the line length; the radius of the
Rem shape is roughly twice this value.
myLength = 36
Rem Set myClosedPath to true to close the NINA, or set it
Rem to false to leave the path open.
myClosedPath = True
```

2. Change the line:

```
 myDrawNina myInDesign, myNumberOfLines, a_pulse, b_pulse, _
 myLength, myClosedPath
```

to:

```
myDisplayDialog myInDesign
```

3.   Enter the following function at the end of the script.

```
Function myDisplayDialog(myInDesign)
 Set myDialog = myInDesign.Dialogs.Add
 myDialog.Name = "NINA"
 With myDialog.DialogColumns.Add
  With .BorderPanels.Add
   With .DialogColumns.Add
    With .StaticTexts.Add
     .StaticLabel = "Number of iterations:"
    End With
    With .StaticTexts.Add
     .StaticLabel = "a_pulse:"
    End With
    With .StaticTexts.Add
     .StaticLabel = "b_pulse:"
    End With
    With .StaticTexts.Add
     .StaticLabel = "Line length (in points):"
    End With
   End With
   With .DialogColumns.Add
    Set myNumberOfLinesField = .IntegerEditboxes.Add
     myNumberOfLinesField.EditValue = 201
     myNumberOfLinesField.MinWidth = 60
     Set myAPulseField = .IntegerEditboxes.Add
     myAPulseField.EditValue = 16
     myAPulseField.MinWidth = 60
     Set myBPulseField = .IntegerEditboxes.Add
     myBPulseField.EditValue = 161
     myBPulseField.MinWidth = 60
     Set myLengthField = .MeasurementEditboxes.Add
     myLengthField.EditValue = 72
     myLengthField.MinWidth = 60
     myLengthField.EditUnits = idMeasurementUnits.idPoints
    End With
   End With
   With .BorderPanels.Add
    With .RadiobuttonGroups.Add
     Set myClosedPathButton = .RadiobuttonControls.Add
     myClosedPathButton.StaticLabel = "Closed path"
     myClosedPathButton.CheckedState = True
      With .RadiobuttonControls.Add
       .StaticLabel = "Open path"
      End With
    End With
   End With
 End With
 myReturn = myDialog.Show
 If myReturn = True Then
  Rem Get the values from the dialog box.
  myNumberOfLines = myNumberOfLinesField.EditValue
```

```
    a_pulse = myAPulseField.EditValue
    b_pulse = myBPulseField.EditValue
    myLength = myLengthField.EditValue
    myClosedPath = myClosedPathButton.CheckedState
    myDialog.Destroy
    myDrawNina myInDesign, myNumberOfLines, a_pulse, b_pulse, _
    myLength, myClosedPath
  Else
    myDialog.Destroy
  End If
End Function
```

End Script

Scripting is all about *empowerment*. Don't just sit around telling yourself that the reason you're working late is that InDesign can't do something you'd like it to do. Sure, there are things in every program we'd like the manufacturer to fix, but, with InDesign's scripting features, we've finally got the tools we need to *fix them ourselves*.

By urging you to take up scripting, we're urging you to take control of InDesign, your publications, your work, and your life. We know you can do it!

Interactive PDF

A hundred years ago, when David was a young pup, he turned in a school essay he had typed using an amazing new device called a personal computer and printed on that technological marvel, the dot-matrix printer. His teacher was so impressed that she wrote her copious corrections on a separate page, so as not to spoil the appearance of David's "professionally published" work. Today, a school report printed on a color laser or inkjet printer is *de rigeur,* and teachers may question a student's work ethic if they don't have a corresponding Web site and public relations team.

Communication of data has come a long way, and while print is far from dead, you can bet that the future of publishing isn't solely a matter of throwing more ink at paper. Today's communicators have to be adept at creating both print and interactive documents—files that include buttons, sounds, and movies. Fortunately, InDesign offers a number of features for the "rich media" producer. Many of these tools don't produce any visible effect on your InDesign pages, but change the content and behavior of PDF files that you export.

By the way, some of you may remember that David wrote a book about the ill-fated QuarkImmedia—a plug-in (XTension) that would turn QuarkXPress into a multimedia authoring tool. Immedia was arguably the coolest software Quark, Inc., ever released, but it died an ignoble death for a plethora of reasons. What made QuarkImmedia so great was that you could create and control interactive media with simple pop-up menus and check boxes rather than writing complicated scripts. InDesign's rich media tools take the same approach, making it easy for anyone to add interactive features to their PDFs.

Acrobat PDF Only   That said, the key thing to understand about InDesign's interactive features is that they only work when you export the file to PDF. (Or, in the case of basic hyperlinks, when you package the document for GoLive—which creates XML that GoLive can turn into HTML.) And many of the features only work when you specifically export a PDF 1.5 (Acrobat 6) file. Exporting in prior versions won't work—Acrobat 4 and 5 had some rich-media support, but it wasn't until Acrobat 6 that it started to really get good, including:

▶ Greatly improved abilities for handling sounds and movies, including internal support for file formats such as SWF ("Flash"), MPEG, and AIFF

▶ The ability to embed movies in the PDF rather than saving them as external, linked files (this is particularly important when you want to protect the movies from unauthorized copying)

▶ Support for non-RGB movies and posters, and nonrectangular posters (more on what posters are later in this chapter)

▶ Support for interactive objects on the same page as transparency effects (such as feathering and opacity), even though the media objects cannot themselves involve transparency

Acrobat 6 and 7 don't support all the rich-media tools you might want. For example, support for cool wipes or dissolves as you turn from one page to the next is quite limited. For another example, Acrobat doesn't yet support MP3 sound files. Also note that while you can usually open these interactive PDF files in other PDF-aware applications (such as Preview in Mac OS X), none of the media features work at all—you have to use Acrobat 6 or 7 to view these, too.

We cover how to export PDF files in Chapter 7, "Importing and Exporting."

Hyperlinks

What is an interactive page without links? Links help your readers explore your file, jumping between pages, to other documents, or even to Web sites. You can also add links to files that your readers can download, and you can add links for sending email. PDF files offer three kinds of links: hyperlinks, bookmarks, and buttons. Let's look at each of these in turn.

A hyperlink is essentially a button—it's a "hot" area that performs some action when you click it. There are two big differences between a hyperlink and a button made with InDesign's Button tool. First, you can apply a hyperlink directly to text—though behind the scenes, InDesign is still more or less drawing a button around that text. Second, you can save hyperlinks and use them more than once.

The key to understanding hyperlinks is to grasp the difference between a hyperlink source (what the user clicks on) and a hyperlink destination (where the link takes you). Because of the odd way in which Adobe implemented the hyperlinks feature, it's generally best to create hyperlink destinations first, name them, and then apply them to hyperlink sources in the document. But you do have a choice; you can also apply "unnamed" hyperlink destinations on the fly, directly to text or objects in your document, and then link them to hyperlink destinations later.

Making a New Hyperlink Destination

To make a new hyperlink destination, select New Hyperlink Destination from the Hyperlinks palette menu (see Figure 13-1). If you have text or an object selected, you can choose this command from the Interactive submenu in the Context menu (Control-click on the Mac OS, right-click in Windows). You can choose from among three types of hyperlink destinations: Page, Text Anchor, and URL.

Page. To link to another page within your document (but not to specific text or an object on the page), use a Page hyperlink destination. InDesign asks you which page you want to target and which zoom setting you want to use to view that page. Most of the zoom settings (such as Fit Width in Window) are pretty self-explanatory; the only two that we find confusing are Inherit Zoom and Fixed. Inherit Zoom leaves the viewer's magnification setting alone (an option we find comforting). Fixed is supposed to remember the zoom setting in InDesign when you created the hyperlink destination, but it currently seems to produce the same effect as Inherit Zoom.

Now give your Page hyperlink destination a name. Or, better yet, turn on the Name with Page Number check box, which names it

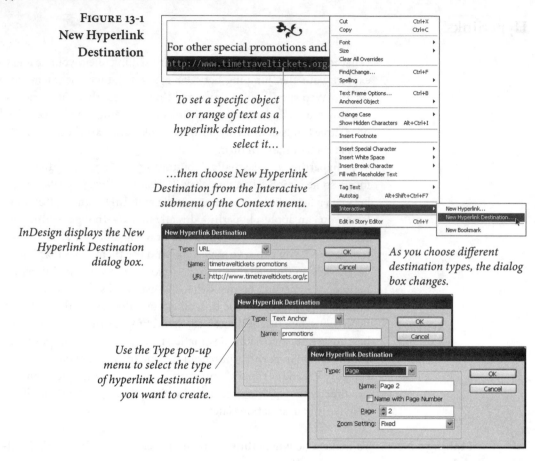

FIGURE 13-1
New Hyperlink
Destination

To set a specific object
or range of text as a
hyperlink destination,
select it...

...then choose New Hyperlink
Destination from the Interactive
submenu of the Context menu.

InDesign displays the New
Hyperlink Destination
dialog box.

As you choose different
destination types, the dialog
box changes.

Use the Type pop-up
menu to select the type
of hyperlink destination
you want to create.

automatically. This name is what you'll later use to apply this hyperlink destination to the hyperlink source on your page.

Text Anchor. If there is a particular section of text on a page you want to target, you should use a Text Anchor hyperlink destination. To do this, you must first place the cursor in the destination text (or select one or more characters of the text), or else this option will be grayed out. Then, in the New Hyperlink Destination dialog box, simply give the anchor a name. This is identical to how most HTML authoring programs create text anchors, too.

URL. To target a URL, choose URL from the Type pop-up menu, give the destination a name, and type the address into the URL field. A URL is typically a place on the Internet, like an HTTP or FTP site. However, you can use any standard kind of URL, including http://, file://, ftp://, or mailto://. If you don't know what these are, check out any good source on HTML Web links, such as webmonkey.com.

Note, however, that Acrobat 6 just passes this URL to the default Web browser (like Internet Explorer or Safari) to deal with. That's great if you're targeting a Web page, but if you're trying to jump to another PDF or some other file, using a button is probably more reliable.

Editing Hyperlink Destinations

Unfortunately, there is no obvious way to see the hyperlink destinations you've already created. Why aren't they listed in the Hyperlinks palette? Because that would be far too easy—Adobe wants to provide a little challenge in your life.

To see a list of the hyperlink destinations you've defined, choose Hyperlink Destination Options from the Hyperlinks palette menu—this displays the Hyperlink Destination Options dialog box. From here, you can view and select the existing hyperlink destinations using the Destination pop-up menu. To edit a hyperlink destination, select it from the pop-up and click the Edit button. To delete a hyperlink destination, select it and click the Delete button.

Applying a Hyperlink to a Source

You can apply a hyperlink to text selected inside a text frame, or any object on your page. While the text or object is selected, choose New Hyperlink from the Hyperlinks palette menu or click the palette's Create New Hyperlink button. The New Hyperlink dialog box can be confusing, so let's take it one step at a time (see Figure 13-2).

1. Give your new hyperlink a name. This is simply what appears in the Hyperlinks palette. (Again, the Hyperlinks palette displays a list of all the hyperlink sources, not destinations.)

2. If you have more than one document open in InDesign, choose which document contains the hyperlink destination you want to use. This is helpful when you want to link to a particular place (such as a text anchor) in a different document. However, this technique is fraught with peril: If your destination is a page or text anchor in another document, you must use that document's name as the name of the PDF (the PDF containing this hyperlink destination, not the name of the PDF containing the hyperlink source). If you don't do this, Acrobat will have no idea what file you're talking about when linking one PDF file to the another.

3. Choose a type of hyperlink from the Type pop-up menu—URL, Text Anchor, or Page—or pick All Types to see all the prebuilt hyperlink destinations.

4. Pick the hyperlink destination from the Name pop-up menu. If you neglected to make a hyperlink destination first, you can

FIGURE 13-2
New Hyperlink
Destination

Choose New Hyperlink from the Hyperlinks palette menu.

InDesign displays the New Hyperlink dialog box.

Click the OK button.

Select a hyperlink destination from the list of defined destinations.

InDesign adds the hyperlink to the Hyperlinks palette.

When you export the document as a PDF, InDesign includes the hyperlink in the PDF file.

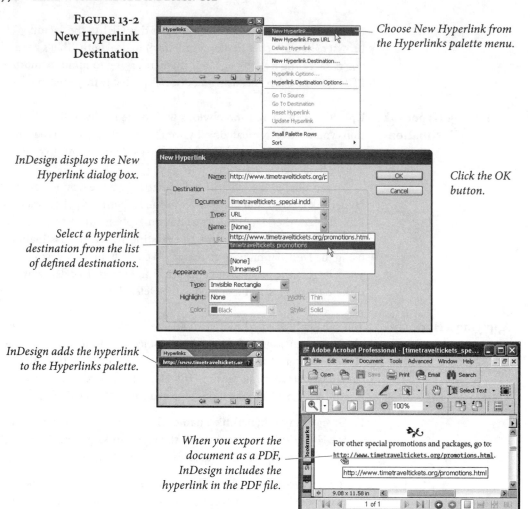

choose Unnamed from the Name pop-up menu—but only if you have URL or Page selected in the Type pop-up menu. (Obviously, you can't make a hyperlink to a text anchor without first creating the anchor.)

There's nothing wrong with setting your hyperlink source to an unnamed hyperlink destination, but it could get you into trouble later. For instance, if you make ten hyperlinks in your document to a particular URL, and then you later need to change that URL, it's a lot easier to change it once (in Hyperlink Destination Options) than in ten different places. Note that in this case, the hyperlink destination is unnamed, but the hyperlink source still has a name that shows up in the palette.

5. If you are creating an Unnamed hyperlink, choose a destination. If the Type pop-up menu is set to URL, you can now type in the URL. If it's set to Page, then choose which page you're targeting and the page magnification Acrobat should use to display it.

6. Finally, specify the appearance of the hyperlink (that is, the way it will appear in the PDF file). If you want it to be invisible, set the Appearance Type pop-up menu to Invisible Rectangle (if you do this, the only way you'll know that the link is there is that the cursor will change when it moves over the link). The Appearance options are pretty dorky, actually. Maybe someday InDesign will offer cooler hyperlink options, such as making the text highlight when you hover over it and then glow or burst into flame when you click it. Until then, only buttons provide interesting link effects (see "Buttons," later in this chapter).

After you click OK, InDesign lists your hyperlink source in the Hyperlinks palette. If you have five different sources that all point to the same target, you still get five different listings in the palette.

To edit a hyperlink source, select it in the palette or on the document page (if it's text, you can just place the cursor anywhere in the text), then choose Hyperlinks Options from the palette menu. Or, if you're in a hurry, double-click the name in the Hyperlinks palette.

Hyperlinks from URLs in the Text

If you've already typed a URL in a text frame and now you want to make that URL a hyperlink, use the Text tool to select the URL and choose New Hyperlink from URL from the Hyperlinks palette menu. This is a two-for-one: InDesign first makes a URL destination (giving it the same name as the URL itself), and then applies that destination to the selected text or object, also using the URL as the hyperlink source name that appears in the palette. Cool, huh?

Let's say you've typed http://www.google.com on your page and made it into a hyperlink. To replace the URL (on the page) with the phrase "Search Engine" you need to delete all the text in the hyperlink *except* the first and last character (in this case the "h" and the last "m"). Now type the new text between these two characters. Finally, delete the unwanted first and last characters.

Deleting and Resetting Hyperlinks

We've already mentioned that you can delete a hyperlink destination, but what about the hyperlink source? If you delete the source itself (the text or object marked as a hyperlink), the hyperlink disappears. You can also select the hyperlink source in the Hyperlinks palette and click the palette's Delete button. This leaves the text or page object alone, but it no longer has a hyperlink attached to it.

What if you applied a hyperlink to the wrong text or object? No problem—select the correct text or object, select the hyperlink name in the Hyperlinks palette, and then choose Reset Hyperlink from the Hyperlinks palette menu. The link is moved from the old source to the selected source.

Navigating Hyperlinks

Once you have a bunch of hyperlink sources in your document, you need some way to navigate through them. To view the hyperlinks (except for those whose appearance type has been set to Invisible Rectangle), choose Show Hyperlinks from the View menu. If you can't find the source of a hyperlink, select the link in the Hyperlinks palette and click the Go to Hyperlink Source button (or choose Go to Source in the palette menu).

Alternatively, you can select a hyperlink name in the palette and click the Go to Hyperlink Destination button (or choose Go to Destination from the palette menu) to invoke the hyperlink itself. This means you can use hyperlinks to navigate around your document (or documents) even if you never plan on exporting the files as PDF at all! Bonus tip: If you want "document navigation hyperlinks" but don't intend to actually export them in the PDF or have them print, then turn on Nonprinting in the Attributes palette.

Don't forget that you can put hyperlinks on a master page so that they'll show up on all the document pages based on that master.

Updating Hyperlinks

If you've used hyperlink destinations from another document and those hyperlink destinations later change (perhaps a URL changes, for instance), then you'll need to update your hyperlink source. To do that, select the hyperlink source in the Hyperlinks palette and choose Update Hyperlink from the palette menu. If the other document isn't currently open, you'll need to hold down the Option/Alt key when choosing Update Hyperlink.

Bookmarks

Any PDF file longer than a few pages should have bookmarks, which appear in the Bookmarks tab on the left side of the screen in Acrobat. Bookmarks make it easy for the viewer to find a particular section of the document. In InDesign, bookmarks appear in (surprise) the Bookmarks palette, shown in Figure 13-3 (choose Bookmarks from the Interactive submenu in the Window menu).

FIGURE 13-3
Bookmarks Palette

*Believe it or not, these are actual
bookmarks from one of David's
other book projects!*

Whenever you build a table of contents in a document, you can automatically add those entries to the Bookmarks palette by turning on the Create PDF Bookmarks check box in the Table of Contents dialog box (see Chapter 8, "Long Documents"). You can also add a bookmark anywhere in your document by selecting an object or placing the text cursor in some text and then clicking the New Bookmark button in the Bookmarks palette. You can name the bookmark anything you want.

As with the hyperlinks in the Hyperlinks palette, you can use the bookmarks to navigate around your InDesign document, even without exporting as PDF. To jump to a bookmark, double-click the bookmark name in the Bookmarks palette. Whenever you find yourself returning to a particular page in your document repeatedly, consider putting a bookmark there. You can always delete the bookmark before exporting the file if you don't want it in the final PDF.

Sorting and Editing Bookmarks

You can move a bookmark by dragging it up or down in the list. Note that, as you drag, InDesign displays a black bar indicating where the bookmark will land when you let go of the mouse button. If you drag the bookmark on top of another bookmark, the bookmark becomes a sub-bookmark (or a second-level bookmark or a nested bookmark, or whatever you want to call it). To "unnest" the bookmark, drag it out again.

If you add one or more custom bookmarks to a document and then update your table of contents, the custom bookmarks will appear at the bottom of the list again. Oops! One way to fix this is to select Sort Bookmarks from the palette menu—this sorts the list of bookmarks chronologically by page, and alphabetically for multiple bookmarks within each page.

To rename a bookmark, select it and move the cursor slightly, or wait for a second. InDesign should highlight the bookmark name so you can edit it. If that doesn't work, select it and choose Rename Bookmark from the palette menu.

Buttons

If someone asks you to list InDesign's basic building blocks, you might respond frames (which can include text or graphics or nothing at all) and lines. But there's a third type of object, too: a button. Buttons are only useful in interactive PDF files opened in Acrobat, but they can do all kinds of things—jump to another page, play a movie or sound, or hide or show another button.

There are two ways to make a button: use the Button tool or convert an object into a button.

Button Tool. The simplest way to make a button is to use the Button tool in the Tools palette (press B to get it quickly). The Button tool acts much like the Frame tool: You can drag out a button or Option/ Alt-drag to drag it out from the center point (see Figure 13-4). While the mouse button is down, you can press the spacebar to move the button; then let go of the spacebar to continue sizing the button. Or, you can click the Button tool to display the Button dialog box, where you can enter the width and height of the button.

Once you've created a button, you can fill it as you would fill any other frame—you can use the Place command, the Paste Into command, or you can enter text in the button using the Text tool.

Convert to Button. Any frame or line can be turned into a button (except for frames that contain movies or sounds). Select the object and choose Convert to Button from the Interactive submenu (in either the Object menu or the Context menu). You can also turn a button back into an object by selecting Convert from Button. An object turned into a button acts like any other object—you can even print it. But when you turn on the Interactive Elements check box in the Export PDF dialog box, the object comes to life, as it were.

The Way of Buttons It's important to remember that buttons are containers, like a special kind of frame. When you make a button using the Button tool, InDesign actually makes a button with a frame inside it. When you click the button with the Text tool and start typing, you're not typing into the button; you're typing in the text frame nested inside the button container. This means you can select that nested frame (with

FIGURE 13-4
Creating a Button

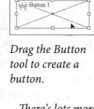

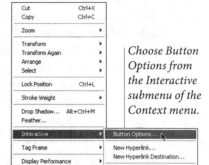

Drag the Button tool to create a button.

There's lots more to making a button than drawing the frame.

Select the Button tool.

Choose Button Options from the Interactive submenu of the Context menu.

InDesign displays the Button Options dialog box.

In the General panel, you can name the button, enter a description of the button, and set the visibility of the button in the exported PDF.

The Behaviors panel of the Button Options dialog box is where things get really interesting—it's here that you set up the behavior of the button. The Event pop-up menu lists the possible user actions that the button might respond to; the Behavior pop-up menu lists the different actions that the event might trigger.

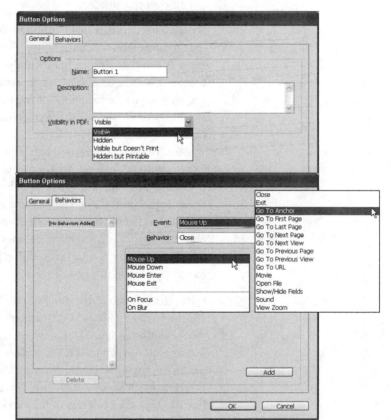

the Direct Selection tool or by clicking the Select Content button in the Control palette), move it around, delete it, replace it with something else, place a picture inside the button instead, and so on.

The same thing applies to a frame or line converted to a button: InDesign puts that object inside a button container, but you can still select and modify it.

Behavioral Modification

To make a button actually do something—react when the user clicks it—you have to change the button's behavior by selecting Button Options from the Interactive submenu (under the Object menu or the Context menu). Or, if it's not a text button (that is, there's no nested text frame in it), you can double-click on the button with the Selection tool to open the Button Options dialog box. If it is a text button, you can Command-Option/Ctrl-Alt-double-click. Here's the rundown on button behavior (see Figure 13-5).

1. Give the button a name in the General tab of the Button Options dialog box. It's also helpful to add a description of the button; this description appears as a tool tip (if the user hovers the cursor over the button).

2. Buttons are a kind of "field" (in PDF parlance), and you have four options for a field's visibility: Visible, Hidden, Visible but Doesn't Print, or Hidden but Printable. Why have an invisible button? Don't think of buttons as just something you click; if you want a picture to appear when you click a button, you make two buttons: a visible one that you click and one that has a picture in it (set to Hidden).

   Most of your buttons will either be Visible or Hidden. Occasionally, Visible but Doesn't Print can be useful—you could use it for something like a "Submit" button that you want to have appear on the screen, but not on the printed page. The Hidden but Printable option is really odd—it means that the object is invisible on screen, but shows up when you print. You might use this for special information that is only relevant for a hardcopy version of a page.

3. Select the Behavior tab of the Button Options dialog box and choose an Event: Mouse Up (that's when the user lets go of the mouse button), Mouse Down (when the mouse button is down), Mouse Enter (when the cursor is above the button), Mouse Exit (when the cursor leaves the button), On Focus (when the button is selected—either by a click or by a press of the Tab key), or On Blur (when a click or press of the Tab key moves the focus to another field).

4. Select one of the actions you want to associate with the Event from the Behavior pop-up menu.

   ▶ **Close.** This closes the current PDF file.

   ▶ **Exit.** This quits the viewer (Acrobat).

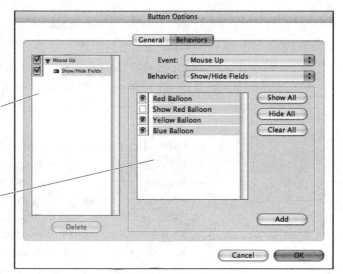

FIGURE 13-5
**Adding Behaviors
to a Button**

*As you add behaviors,
InDesign adds them to
the list in the Behaviors panel of the Button
Options dialog box.*

*Button behaviors can
affect all other buttons in a
document. In this example,
other buttons are affected
by clicking the button.*

▸ **Go to Anchor.** If you have used the Hyperlinks palette to
make a text anchor in this or any other document, you can
jump to that point with this action. If the InDesign document that contains the anchor isn't open, you can click
Browse to select it.

▸ **Go to page.** You can pick one of the four "Go to" actions:
First page, Last page (the final page of the PDF document),
Previous page (the page before the current one), or Next page
(the page following this one). For example, you might assign
these as navigation buttons, and put them on a master page
of a document. Buttons work well on master pages because
they appear on every document page tagged with that master.

▸ **Go to Previous View.** This action returns to the last page the
viewer displayed. If you jump from page 5 to page 20, Go to
Previous View would jump back to page 5.

▸ **Go to Next View.** This action only works if someone has
already invoked a "Previous page" action; it's like the Forward feature in a Web browser.

▸ Go to URL. Like a URL hyperlink, the Go to URL action
hands off the URL you specify to the default Web browser.
This can be any URL, including http://, file://, or mailto:.

▸ **Movie.** If you have placed a movie or animation file (see
"Audio and Video," later), you can control it using the Movie

action. After selecting Movie, select a movie, and then specify what you want to do to it: Play, Pause, Stop, or Resume.

▶ **Open File.** Use this action to open another file. You need to specify the file using an absolute file path; it's much simpler to click the Browse button to let InDesign figure out the path for you.

▶ **Show/Hide Fields.** While Acrobat has several different kinds of fields (such as text entry fields, check box fields, and so on), InDesign currently supports only button fields. Whenever you want objects to appear or disappear on your page, make them into buttons. Even if those buttons have no behavior of their own, they can still be controlled (made visible or hidden) using the Show/Hide Fields action. When you select Show/Hide fields, the dialog box lists all the fields (buttons) in your document (not just the fields on the current page). You can click once in the box to the left of the field name to make the button visible (you'll see a little eyeball), or click again to make the button hidden (InDesign draws a a red line through the eyeball). Click a third time to make it neutral (this action won't affect the button at all).

▶ **Sound.** After you import a sound file into your document, you can Play, Pause, Stop, or Resume it with this action.

▶ **View Zoom.** A button can control the current view settings in Acrobat. After selecting the View Zoom behavior, choose from among the many options in the Zoom pop-up menu, including Zoom In, Zoom Out, Fit in Window, Rotate Clockwise, and Single Page.

5. Very, very important: Click the Add button at the bottom of the Behaviors tab. If you don't click Add, the behavior doesn't stick and you get really frustrated.

After clicking Add, you can click OK (if you're done), or select another Event/Behavior combination and add it to the button. This means one button click can do a bunch of things at once: go to another page, show a hidden object on that page, and immediately start playing a movie.

Tab Order   When you open a PDF in Acrobat and press the Tab key, the focus jumps to the first field on the page; press Tab again, and it skips to the next field. If the field is a button, you can press Return/Enter to "click" the button. But who specifies the order of the buttons? You do. As long as you have more than one button on a page, you can choose Set Tab Order from the Interactive submenu (under the Object menu). To reorder a field in the list, select it and click the Move Up or Move Down buttons—or better, just drag it into the correct position.

Of course, InDesign only supports button fields. If you later add text and check box fields in Acrobat, your tab order may get all messed up. (There's currently no good way to order the fields in Acrobat. Oops.)

Rollovers and States

Multimedia designers love rollovers. A rollover is an image on an interactive page (like a PDF or the Web) that changes in some way when the user moves the cursor over it. The rollover may appear to change color or shape; or maybe it lights up to indicate that it's a hotspot. When you move the cursor away, the image returns to its original form. InDesign supports both normal rollovers and two-state buttons (buttons that change when you click on them). It also lets you make "two position" rollovers—where you roll over a button and an image changes somewhere else on the page.

We use the term "image," but rollovers can involve text or lines as easily as images; it's up to you. However, if you are using images, you need to create the graphics for each state of the rollover: the original image on the page (the "off" state), and the image you see when the cursor is over the image (the "on" state).

The States Palette

Remember that buttons are just containers, typically with objects nested in them—a text frame, a graphic frame, a line, or even a group of objects. The States palette (which is hiding in the Interactive submenu, under the Window menu) gives you a way to change the content of a button container depending on two events: the user moving the cursor over the button or clicking on it.

It's easy to add and change states (see Figure 13-6):

1. Select the button and open the States palette. The Name of the button appears in the palette; changing it here is the same as changing it in the Button Options dialog box.

2. Skip the Appearance pop-up menu, which offers three preset button styles so dorky that they'll make your colleagues laugh at you. Someday perhaps you'll be able to add your own presets to this menu. Until then, ignore this feature.

FIGURE 13-6

Creating Rollovers

Default (or Up) state.

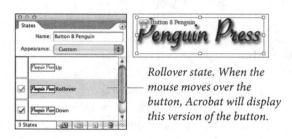

To create rollovers, you save multiple versions of a button using the States palette. It's something like a library of possible states for the button.

Rollover state. When the mouse moves over the button, Acrobat will display this version of the button.

3. Click the New State button (or choose New State from the palette menu) to add a Rollover state to the palette. If you want to add a Down state, click it again. To get a Down state without a Rollover state, click twice, and then click in the check box to the left of the Rollover state. That deactivates that state.

4. In the States palette, click the state you want to alter, and then, on the document page, make a change to the content of the button. Let's say you have a button with a picture in it. You can click on the Rollover state, and replace the picture with a different one by clicking the Place Content button in the States palette (or choosing Place Content into State feature from the palette menu). Or, you can select the picture with the Direct Selection tool and replace it using the ordinary Place feature. Or, you could make the current picture rotate ten degrees when you roll over it by selecting the nested graphic frame and rotating it.

     Here's another example: You could place text in the button instead of a picture, then add a Rollover state, and add a drop shadow to the text for that state. InDesign will remember that the text has a drop shadow for the rollover state, but no drop shadow normally. You could even change the text inside that frame so it says "Blah" most of the time, but changes to "Ha!" while the mouse button is held down on it.

5. You can test the states by exporting a PDF page and viewing it in Acrobat, or—the cheesy quick version—by clicking back

and forth among the states in the palette. Also, note that you can make the palette's thumbnail previews larger or smaller by choosing Palette Options. (The little wizard in that dialog box is Merlin from the Photoshop easter egg!)

The ability to change the content of a container is very cool and we wish InDesign would expand this to work with other kinds of containers, too. Can you imagine the ability to have five different headlines in a single text frame, and then switch from one to another with a click in a palette? But for now, it only works with buttons.

Two-Position Rollovers

Making a rollover that affects objects elsewhere on the page involves the Button Options dialog box, not the States palette. The technique is straightforward: Convert all of the relevant objects to buttons and then use the Mouse Enter and Mouse Exit behaviors to make those objects Visible or Hidden at the appropriate time(s). You could, for example, have one button that, when rolled over, makes two other buttons visible.

Audio and Video

Why on earth would anyone want to put movies, animations, and sounds into an InDesign document? Because InDesign is all about enabling you to communicate ideas in elegant ways, and sometimes movies and sounds in a PDF file do that better than plain ol' quiet, static print. For instance, watching a movie about how to change the oil in your car might help more than trying to figure it out from ten pages of printed diagrams and explanations. (Ole doubts it would, provided the diagrams and explanations were competently done.)

You can add a wide variety of audiovisual files to your files—InDesign supports WAV, AIF, and AU sound file formats, and QuickTime, AVI, MPEG, and SWF movie formats. As Acrobat evolves to support more formats (such as MP3 sound files), we're sure InDesign will follow suit. Note that you do need QuickTime version 6 or later in order for any of this to work, as it's really QuickTime doing the heavy lifting behind the scenes.

Importing Sounds and Movies

You import a sound or a movie file in the same way that you import text and graphics—use the Place feature or drag the file from a Finder/Explorer window (see Figure 13-7). If you're placing the file in an existing frame, it's important that the InDesign frame be the same size as the media file. If you're placing the file on a page, click

FIGURE 13-7

Placing a Movie

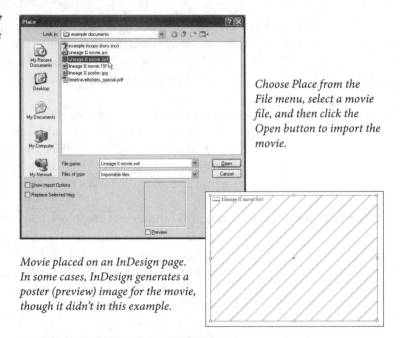

Choose Place from the File menu, select a movie file, and then click the Open button to import the movie.

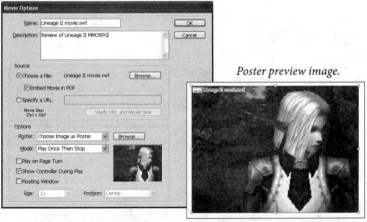

Movie placed on an InDesign page. In some cases, InDesign generates a poster (preview) image for the movie, though it didn't in this example.

To set options for the movie, double-click the movie with the Selection tool. InDesign displays the Movie Options dialog box.

To add a poster image, click the Browse button and select an image from one of your drives.

Poster preview image.

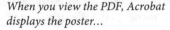

When you view the PDF, Acrobat displays the poster...

...until the movie starts playing.

the place icon to create a frame that is the size of the original file. If you do drag the place icon (to specify the size of the frame), then immediately choose Fit Frame to Content or Fit Content Proportionally from the Fitting submenu (under the Object menu). The former scales the frame; the latter scales the movie.

Here's a third way to import a movie or sound: First select any empty frame on your page and choose Movie Options or Sound Options from the Interactive submenu (under the Object menu or the Context menu). Then, in the Sound Options dialog box, click the Browse button to load a file. Or, in Movie Options, either choose a file with the Browse button or type a URL into the URL field.

You might want to link to a movie on a Web site (via a URL) if the movie will change after you export the PDF file, or if the movie is large and you don't want to transport it along with (or inside of) your PDF file. Because you want the frame to match the movie size, after specifying a URL, click the Verify URL and Movie Size button—InDesign finds the movie on the Web and gets its dimensions (you need a live Internet connection for this to work, obviously). After you click OK, use the Fitting features to make sure the frame is the same size as the movie. You can scale the movie, but don't try to clip or mask it. There doesn't appear to be any way to link to a streaming audio file; just video.

By the way, when you import a sound or a movie, make sure you don't put any other text or graphics on top of it. Acrobat isn't smart enough to play rich media behind other objects (see "Movie Limitations," late in this chapter).

A *poster* is a still image associated with a movie or sound—basically what you see on the InDesign page and in the PDF file (before you activate the movie).

Sound Options

The Sound Options dialog box (see Figure 13-8) provides controls for managing imported sound files. (There's definitely room for improvement. A way to deal with more than one sound file at a time would be most welcome.) You can open the Sound Options dialog box by choosing Sound Options from the Interactive submenu (under the Object menu or the Context menu), but it's much faster to double-click an imported sound with the Selection or Direct Selection tool.

You only need to give a sound a poster image when you want the viewer to be able to click on it to play the sound. If you have set up another button to play the sound, you can leave the Poster pop-up menu set to None. If you do want to use a poster image, choose Standard Image (which gives you a silly little speaker icon image)

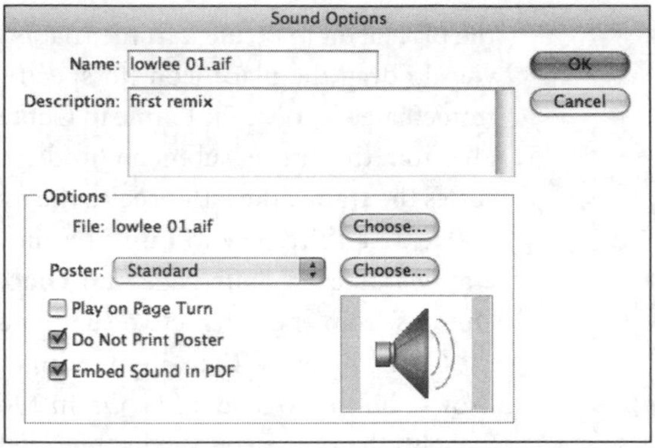

FIGURE 13-8
**Sound Options
Dialog Box**

or choose Image as Poster to select an image (and click the Browse button to display a standard file dialog box).

To change the default Standard image, save an image in the JPEG format to a file named StandardSoundPoster.jpg, and put it inside the Images folder in the Presets folder inside your InDesign folder.

We suggest giving your sounds useful names and descriptions. The name is what you use to control the sound using a button event. The description appears as a tool tip if the viewer hovers their cursor over the sound (but only if the sound has a poster).

The Sound Options dialog box offers three other controls, too.

▶ **Play on Page Turn.** When you turn on this check box, Acrobat begins playing the sound as soon as the page it's on is displayed.

▶ **Do Not Print Poster.** If you specify a poster image, then you get to choose whether that poster image appears in print or not. We're not sure why you wouldn't want this turned on.

▶ **Embed Sound in PDF.** You can embed sounds into PDF files or leave them as separate files on disk that the PDF references. We usually embed sounds. However, if the sound file might change later (perhaps you only have an "FPO" sound), linking to a file on disk might be preferable. The Export as PDF dialog box can also override this object-level setting, embedding or not embedding all your media files.

Movie Options   The Movie Options dialog box offers most of the same features found in the Sound Options dialog box, but also adds several other, movie-specific features.

▶ **Poster options.** If you choose Default Poster from the Poster pop-up menu, InDesign grabs the default poster image from the movie (which is almost always the first frame of the movie). If you prefer to use a different frame from the movie, select Choose Movie Frame as Poster; InDesign lets you scroll through the movie until you find just the right image. If you're creating a document that will be used for both print and onscreen PDF, then you should probably select Choose Image as Poster—this lets you pick a high-resolution image (like a PSD or a TIFF file) to stand in for the movie, both as a poster and when you print.

You can use any size poster you want, but posters are always cropped to the size of the movie itself. It's best to make sure that the poster and the movie have the same dimensions.

▶ **Embed Movie in PDF.** The Embed Movie in PDF check box lets you control on a movie-by-movie level whether a movie will be embedded into the PDF. If you already know that you're going to embed all the movies, you can leave this alone and just choose to embed all movies in the Export as PDF dialog box. While you can embed movies and sounds into a PDF, you cannot embed them into the InDesign document itself.

▶ **Mode.** Use the Mode pop-up menu to control what happens when the movie ends. The choices are: Play Once then Stop (the default behavior), Play Once then Stay Open (if the movie is playing in a floating window, should the window stay open or not), or Repeat Play (puts the movie into a loop).

▶ **Show Controller During Play.** Do you want the standard Quick-Time movie controller buttons to appear while the movie is play-ing? If so, turn on this check box. If you have designed your own buttons to play, pause, stop, and resume your movie, then you'd leave this turned off.

▶ **Floating Window.** Acrobat (and therefore InDesign, too) offers the choice of playing movies on the page itself or in a floating window. If you turn on the Floating Window check box, you can specify the width, height, and location of the movie.

Movie Limitations   We feel that it took ten years or so—until Acrobat 6 Professional was released—for PDF files to really get good for print production. We figure it'll be another few years until Acrobat handles onscreen multimedia as elegantly. Currently, movies and sounds are still a bit clunky. For example, there's usually a pause before and after a movie plays, making it hard to have seamless loops of movies. (This is especially a pain when you want to have a soundtrack looping in the background.)

Here are a few other limitations Acrobat has, and how they affect making interactive PDFs using InDesign:

▶ You can scale a movie on your page and it does appear scaled when you play it. However, you cannot crop a movie, even though you can crop the movie's poster image on your InDesign page—the movie will scale itself to fit inside the cropped area.

▶ Similarly, you can't clip movies into nonrectangular shapes. Acrobat can't deal with nonrectangular movies, so they'll appear as full-frame rectangles in the PDF.

▶ You can use the Hyperlinks palette to apply a hyperlink to a movie or sound frame (or to a button), but, unfortunately, they're not active in the final exported PDF document when you export using the Acrobat 6 (PDF 1.5) format. You could switch to Acrobat 5 (PDF 1.4), but then you lose other abilities.

▶ As exciting as it might feel to rotate or shear movies and sounds, all that goes away in the final PDF. Oh well.

▶ While it might appear that you can apply transparency effects to movies and buttons, these effects will not appear in the exported PDF. Drop shadows, however, work (because drop shadows are images behind the movie).

eBooks

Someday, when it's cheaper and easier to publish electronically than on paper, when you can take your eBook into the bathtub with you, and when cutting down a tree becomes illegal (because only a few of them are left), you're going to thank your lucky stars that InDesign can create rich media PDF files. Even if most of us are still making money with print projects (or trying to, anway), we still think that getting interactive PDF files, complete with buttons and movies, is pretty dang cool.

XML

XML stands for "Extensible Markup Language." What the heck does that mean? It's easy to be scared off—XML is usually mentioned in the same breath as SOAP, DTDs, XSL, metadata, structured content, and schema. With all of the buzzwords and jargon surrounding the topic, it's easy to lose track of something very basic: XML is simple.

XML is a way to mark up (or tag) information in a text file. Any application that can write text files can be used to write XML. Like HTML, XML uses tags, such as "<h1>" to mark a piece of text. Unlike HTML, XML doesn't have a limited set of predefined tags. That's what the "extensible" part of the acronym means. You're not limited to <h1>, <h2>, <p>, and so on, as you are in HTML.

Given this, it would be easy to fall into the trap of thinking that XML is something like an expanded version of HTML. This isn't the case—the two markup schemes are different in kind. HTML is all about what things *look like*; XML is about what elements *are*. The formatting of XML data—if, in fact, that data ever appears in a document—is up to you.

While we said that XML is simple (as opposed to *complex*), we never said that it couldn't be *complicated*. Indeed, the biggest problem of implementing an XML publishing workflow is figuring out the design of the XML data structures you want to work with. Users thinking about XML often end up paralyzed by the sheer number of possibilities—there are a limitless number of different ways to accomplish a given end.

In short, XML is as simple or complicated as you care to make it. Keep it simple, at least at first.

When XML Isn't XML

When you import XML into an InDesign document, *it isn't XML anymore*. It gets turned into an InDesign representation of the XML structure. If you're familiar with XML, this can be a major conceptual stumbling block.

Working with XML *outside* InDesign, one becomes accustomed to certain things: finding a given element by its content using XPath, for example, or being able to use the content of a given XML element in multiple places in a web page generated from the XML You can't do those things in InDesign—at least not directly.

XML Vocabulary

When we talk about XML, we'll be using a standard set of terms, for which we offer the following non-standard set of definitions.

Tag. A tag is a label for a piece of XML data. Tags are marked with angle brackets (also known as greater than and less than symbols), like "<title>". Tags cannot contain space characters. XML must be "well formed," which means that any "start" tag must be matched by an "end" tag. Something like this:

```
<title>Revolutionary Girl Utena</title>
```

XML Element. XML elements are the fundamental building blocks of an XML file. The title just shown is an example of an XML element (containing the data "Revolutionary Girl Utena"). XML elements may contain other elements, as shown in the following example.

```
<author>
    <name>Olav Martin Kvern</name>
    <address>4016 Francis Avenue North</address>
    <city>Seattle</city>
    <state>Washington</state>
    <zip>98103</zip>
</author>
```

Here, the "author" XML element contains the other elements. Each element, in turn, can contain other elements. We could easily change the structure to change the way that the name information is stored, for example.

```
<author>
    <name>
        <first>Olav</first>
        <middle>Martin</middle>
        <last>Kvern</last>
```

```
    </name>
    <address>4016 Francis Avenue North</address>
    <city>Seattle</city>
    <state>Washington</state>
    <zip>98103</zip>
</author>
```

XML elements are sometimes referred to as "nodes." Every InDesign document includes at least one XML element—by default, that's the "Root" element.

Using Tabs. Both of the examples above use tabs to show the nesting of elements in the file. This is not necessarily the best way to write XML for import into InDesign, depending upon the import options you choose. If you need to include white space characters, every character in the XML file will be imported (which only makes sense if you really do want tab characters in those locations).

XML Attribute. One way to attach data to an XML element is to add an element inside the element—an XML attribute is another way of doing the same thing. In general, you use attributes to add information about the element (or "metadata"). In our example, we might want to store the last time that the XML element was updated. We can do that by adding an XML attribute to the "author" tag.

```
<author last_update="11/19/02">
```

XML Structure. The structure of an XML document is nothing more than the way that the elements fit together. Don't let anyone tell you otherwise.

DTD. This is simply a description of what elements can appear, and in which order, in a defined XML structure. DTDs are not required by InDesign, but you might want to use then.

Where Should You Work with XML? Given that InDesign's Structure view (see below) gives you a way to add, delete, and rearrange XML elements in the XML structure of a document, you might think that you could take care of all XML creation and editing tasks without ever leaving the friendly confines of the program.

We urge you, however, not to do this. While InDesign's XML editing tools can be used in this fashion, they're really intended more for quick-and-dirty touch-up work than for industrial strength XML editing.

Instead, if you must create XML files from scratch, find yourself a good XML editing program. Ole likes XMLSpy for XML editing, because it also includes an XSL debugger. Oxygen is a similar XML editing package on the Mac OS.

If you can't find an XML editor you like, you can always use a text editor, such as BBEdit, Notepad, or even InDesign to enter and then save the text of an XML file (as we said, there's nothing magical about it—it's just a simple text file).

At the moment, the system platforms (Windows and the Mac OS) are adding to their XML support. There are far more system tools for working with XML (such as the MSXML parser for Windows from Microsoft) outside InDesign than there are inside InDesign.

But we expect that, most of the time, you probably won't be writing the XML yourself. Instead, you'll be getting your XML documents from some automated process, such as an Excel VBA macro, an export from FileMaker or Access, or from an InDesign document you've exported as XML.

About XML Workflow

Before we dive into the details of working with the XML structure, we'd better explain how we think XML fits into a page layout process. As usual, we risk getting ahead of ourselves by presenting a conceptual overview before we talk about the details of the feature, but there's just no other way to do it. The following is an outline of one approach we see for working with XML in an InDesign document. This approach does not include validation of the imported XML using a DTD (see the section on DTDs, later in this chapter).

1. Create an InDesign document. You can use empty placeholder frames, dummy text, fixed text (text you don't expect to have in the XML data file), or you can mark up an existing document.

2. Load XML tags from an XML file. This doesn't have to be the file containing your data, and it doesn't even have to be an XML file with the same structure as you'll be using. All it needs to include are the names of the elements you expect to have in the XML data you plan to import.

   Alternatively, you can create XML tags from scratch. You'll have to remember to make sure that the XML tag names match the element names for the XML files you'll be importing.

3. Apply XML tags to frames and text in your template document.

4. Map styles to XML tags using the Map Tags to Styles dialog box.

5. Import XML into the document. When you do this, the data in your XML file (including any graphics specified in the XML structure) will appear in your layout.

When you import a new XML file and choose to replace the existing structure, InDesign will apply the formatting you've already applied. This makes this workflow particularly useful for setting up a document with a repeating publication schedule (newsletters, product data sheets, and so on). To make certain that new XML files match the layout, you might want to export the XML from the document to use as a template (see "Exporting XML Tags") for the next iteration of the publication, or for use in a Web site or database.

Inside the Structure View

It's all about structure. No matter how crazy and free-form your layout, your brain—and the brains of your audience—impose a structure on the content of your document. This is true, whether you're conscious of it or not. So don't be afraid of the word "structure" or try to deny that your documents have it. It's there. You can choose to work with it or not. Once you're out of your "denial" phase, you'll find InDesign's Structure view a powerful ally.

Using the options in the Structure view, you can create XML elements and attributes, associate elements with InDesign page items or text, rearrange XML elements, and delete XML elements (see Figure 14-1). Even if you don't work with XML you've probably already found the Structure view—it's all too easy to expand it by accident when you're trying to add a ruler guide or reposition the zero point.

The Structure view uses icons to give you various clues about the nature of the elements in the document's XML structure, as shown in Table 14-1.

Showing/Hiding Text Snippets. To see a short passage of the text associated with the XML elements, choose Show Text Snippets from the Structure view menu (see Figure 14-2). To hide text snippets, choose Hide Text Snippets.

Tagged Frames and Tag Markers. Want to see which frames are associated with XML elements? Turn on the Show Tagged Frames option on the View menu (see Figure 14-3). To see text that's been associated with an XML element, choose Show Tag Markers from the View menu (see Figure 14-4).

FIGURE 14-1
Structure View

Drag this bar...

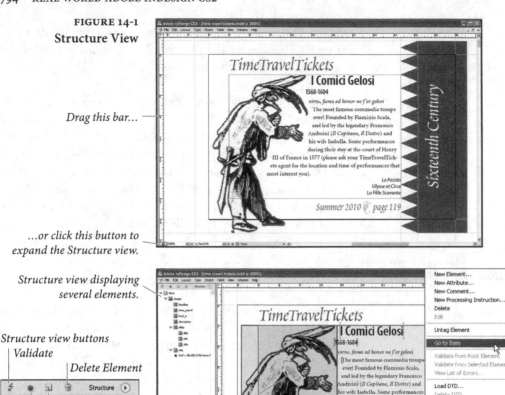

...or click this button to expand the Structure view.

Structure view displaying several elements.

Structure view buttons
Validate

Delete Element

Add Element
Add Attribute

These frames have been associated with an element in the XML structure.

Click this button again to hide the Structure view.

Structure view menu.

FIGURE 14-2
Showing Text Snippets

Without being able to see a bit of the text in each text element, it can be difficult to tell which element is which.

Choose Show Text Snippets from the Structure menu...

...and InDesign displays the first few characters of the text in each text element.

	Icon	Representing	What it means
TABLE 14-1 **Structure View Icons**	⟨⟩	The Root XML element	The Root element is the base, or top-level, XML element in your XML structure. All XML elements are contained by the Root element.
	🔲	Story element	An InDesign story.
	🔲	Text element	A range of text.
	🔲	Graphic element	A graphic.
	🔲	Unplaced text element	A text element that has not yet been associated with a page item.
	🔲	Unplaced graphic element	A graphic element that has not yet been associated with a frame.
	⊠	Empty element	An element associated with an empty frame.
	•	Attribute	An attribute of an element. Attributes are always optional, and are only visible in the Structure window.
	▽	Collapse/Expand	Click this icon to collapse or expand an element. If you hold down Command/Ctrl as you click this icon, InDesign will expand all elements contained within the element.

Adding XML Elements

There are many ways to add a new XML element to a document. You can use the Structure view to add an empty element. To do this, select the element you want to have contain the new element, then choose New Element from the Context menu (or click the New Element button). Select a tag in the Select Tag for Element dialog box, and InDesign adds a new element inside the element you selected (see Figure 14-5).

Changing XML Element Data

When you add an XML element using the Structure view, it's natural to assume that you can somehow enter the data for the element in that window. You can't. We know this, because we've clicked on the element in every imaginable way trying to do it. Remember: the data

FIGURE 14-3
Viewing Frame Tags

Some of these frames must be tagged, right? How can you tell?

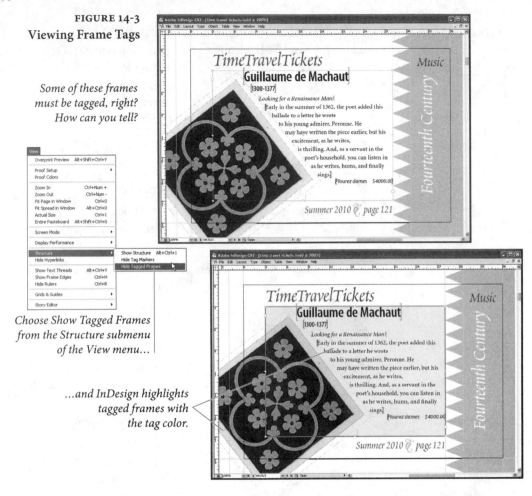

Choose Show Tagged Frames from the Structure submenu of the View menu...

...and InDesign highlights tagged frames with the tag color.

FIGURE 14-4
Viewing Tag Markers

Some of this text must be tagged, right? How can you tell?

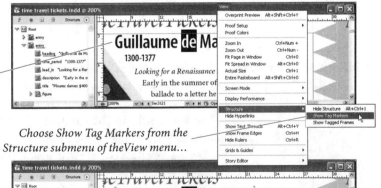

Choose Show Tag Markers from the Structure submenu of theView menu...

...and InDesign displays tag markers (brackets in the tag color) around text associated with an XML element.

FIGURE 14-5
Adding an
XML Element

Click the New Element
button. If you want to add
the element to an element
other than the Root element,
select an element first.

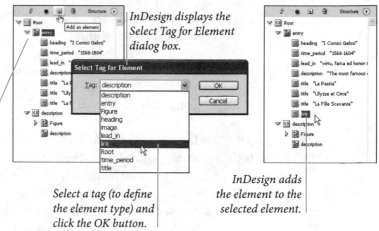

InDesign displays the
Select Tag for Element
dialog box.

Select a tag (to define
the element type) and
click the OK button.

InDesign adds
the element to the
selected element.

for an XML element in InDesign is stored in the page item or text object that the element is associated with. The only case in which you can have element data that's not associated with a frame on your page is when you've imported XML and have not yet assigned an element to a page item, or when you've deleted the object the element was originally associated with.

To change the data in an XML structure, simply edit the text or the frame that the element is associated with.

Duplicating XML Elements

To duplicate an XML element (and any elements it contains), select the element in the Structure view and copy the element. Select another XML element (such as the Root element) and paste. InDesign pastes the copied element into the selected element.

Moving XML Elements

To move an element in the XML structure (including all of the elements it contains), simply drag the element up or down in the Structure view (see Figure 14-6). To move the element inside another

FIGURE 14-6
Moving an
XML Element

You can move elements in
the XML structure without
changing their parent
element, or you can change
the parent element by
dragging an element into
another element. We'll do
the latter in this example.

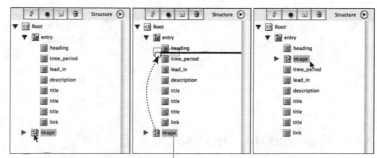

Select the element and drag it up
or down in the Structure view.
In this example, we'll drag the
element into another element.

Stop dragging, and
InDesign moves the
element in the XML
structure.

element (and thereby change the hierarchy of elements), drag the element inside another element.

**Deleting
XML Elements**

To delete an element in the XML structure, select the element and choose Delete Element from the Context menu (or click the Delete Element button).

**Working with
XML Attributes**

XML attributes are what's called "metadata"—they're information about the information in the XML element they're associated with. You can't really do much with attributes in InDesign, but you might want to add an attribute if the XML is destined to appear in a situation in which attributes are necessary.

To add an attribute to an element, select the element and choose New Attribute from the Structure view menu. InDesign displays the New Attribute dialog box. Enter a name (like XML element names, attribute names cannot contain spaces) and value for the attributes, then click OK to save the attribute (see Figure 14-7).

To change an attribute, double-click the attribute. InDesign displays the Edit Attribute dialog box. Change the name or text of the attribute and click the OK button.

To delete an attribute, select the attribute and choose Delete Attribute from the Structure view menu.

**FIGURE 14-7
Adding an Attribute to
an XML Element**

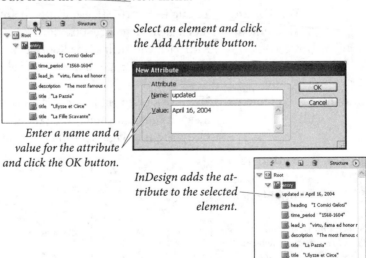

Select an element and click
the Add Attribute button.

Enter a name and a
value for the attribute
and click the OK button.

InDesign adds the attribute to the selected element.

XML Tags and the Tags Palette

XML tags provide the connection between the general name of an XML element and a specific instance of that element in the XML structure. It's important to understand that the XML tag and the

XML element are *different things.* Associating a tag with a frame or a text object adds an instance of the element type to the structure, but the tag itself has nothing to do with the structure.

The Tags palette is the key to applying and managing XML tags in InDesign (see Figure 14-8).

FIGURE 14-8
Tags Palette

When you select a tagged item, InDesign activates the Retag button.

Click the Untag button to remove a tag from a tagged object.

When you select an untagged item, InDesign activates the Add Tag button.

Tag colors give you a way of telling which tags are associated with which objects.

Click the AutoTag button to apply tags to the selected table or table cell (based on the tags specified in the Tagging Preset Options dialog box).

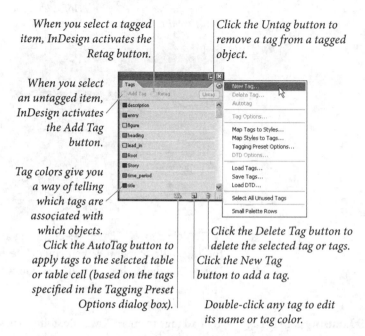

Click the Delete Tag button to delete the selected tag or tags.
Click the New Tag button to add a tag.

Double-click any tag to edit its name or tag color.

Creating an XML Tag

To create an XML tag, follow these steps (see Figure 14-9).

1. Display the Tags palette, if it's not already visible (choose Tags from the Window menu).

2. Click the New Tag button at the bottom of the palette (or choose New Tag from the Tags palette menu). InDesign creates a new tag.

3. Enter a name for the tag. You can do this by typing into the name field in the Tags palette. To change the color assigned to the tag, double-click the tag. InDesign opens the Tag Options dialog box. Choose a new color from the Color pop-up menu. Choose Other to display a color picker to define the color.

4. If you did not go to the Tag Options dialog box to change the color, press Enter. If you did, click the OK button to close the dialog box. InDesign adds the tag to the list of tags in the Tags palette.

FIGURE 14-9
Adding a New Tag

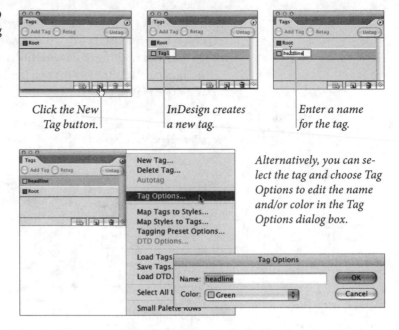

Click the New
Tag button.

InDesign creates
a new tag.

Enter a name
for the tag.

*Alternatively, you can se-
lect the tag and choose Tag
Options to edit the name
and/or color in the Tag
Options dialog box.*

To delete an XML tag, select the tag and choose Delete Tag from the Tags palette menu. When you delete a tag, InDesign displays the Delete Tag dialog box, which asks you which other tag you'd like to apply to the elements corresponding to the deleted tag.

Loading XML Tags   To load tags from an XML file, follow these steps.

1. Choose Load Tags from the Tags palette menu. InDesign displays the Open dialog box.

2. Select an XML file and click the OK button. InDesign loads the element names from the XML file and creates a tag for each.

Exporting XML Tags   To save tags to an XML file, follow these steps.

1. Choose Save Tags from the Tags palette menu. InDesign displays the Save Tags as XML dialog box.

2. Enter a name for the file and click the Save button. InDesign writes the tags to an XML file.

Tagging Objects

You use the Tags palette to manage XML tags, and to apply tags to frames and text. To apply a tag, select something—a frame or a range of text—and click a tag in the Tags palette (see Figure 14-10). If the

FIGURE 14-10
Tagging Frames and Text

Select a frame.

Click a tag in the Tags palette.

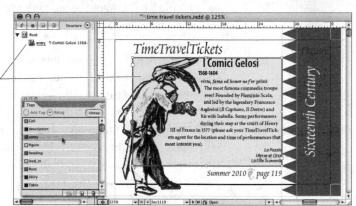

InDesign tags the frame and adds a corresponding element to the XML structure of the document. When Show Tagged Frames is on, InDesign highlights the frame.

To tag a range of text, select the text.

Click a tag in the Tags palette.

InDesign tags the text and adds a corresponding element to the XML structure of the document. In this example, the text element is added to the XML element corresponding to the frame containing the text. The brackets around the text are tag markers.

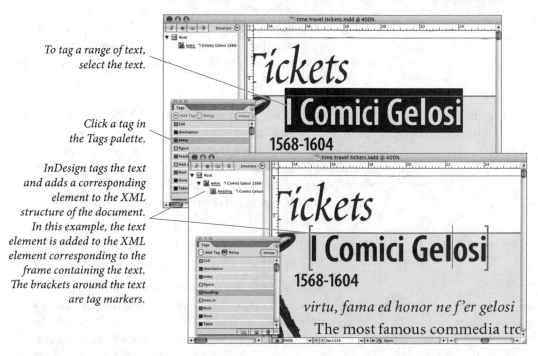

object you're tagging is not contained by an object associated with an XML element, InDesign will ask you which element you want to associate with the selection. When you apply a tag, InDesign creates an element in the XML structure. Alternatively, you can choose Tag Text or Tag Page Item from the Context menu to apply a tag to the selection (see Figure 14-11). You can also tag objects by simply dragging them into the Structure view (see Figure 14-12).

You've probably noticed the Add Tag and Retag options at the top of the Tags palette—what do they do? They answer a question: What should InDesign do when you have selected text that's already tagged and then click a tag in the Tags palette? When the Add Tag option is on, clicking a tag assigns the tag to the selected text. When the Retag option is active, InDesign switches the tag from the current tag to the tag you clicked.

To remove a tag from an object, select the object, or the corresponding element in the Structure view and then click the Untag button in the Tags palette.

Tagging Preset Options

When you apply a tag to text, and have not yet applied a tag to the text frame containing the text, InDesign applies a default tag to the text frame and adds a corresponding XML element to the document structure. You can use the Tagging Preset Options dialog box to specify the tag you want to apply as the default (see Figure 14-13).

The Tagging Preset Options dialog box also gives you a way to automate the tagging of tables and table cells. Choose the tags you want to apply from the Tables and Cells pop-up menus, and InDesign will apply those tags when you tag a table, cell, or text frame (see Figure 14-14).

Mapping XML Tags to Paragraph Styles

You've got an XML structure and a set of XML tags, and a document full of text. The task of tagging each paragraph with a specific XML tag is daunting—or is it? Not if you've used paragraph styles and character styles to format your text. If you've used styles, you can "map" those styles to XML tags, and automate the whole process.

To map XML tags to paragraph and character styles, follow these steps (see Figure 14-15).

1. Choose Map Tags to Styles from the Tags palette menu. The program displays the Map Tags to Styles dialog box.

2. For each XML tag, you can select a corresponding paragraph style or character style. You don't have to map each style to a tab, and you can map multiple styles to a single XML tag. To automatically map tags to styles of the same name, click the

FIGURE 14-11
**Tagging a Frame Using
the Context Menu**

*You can use the Context
menu to apply tags to frames
and text (when you have text
selected, the Context menu
option will read "Tag Text").*

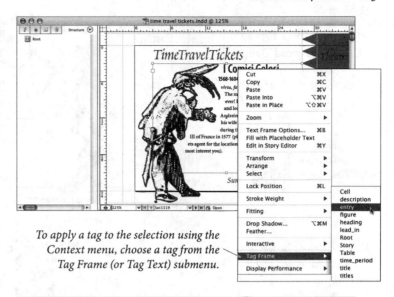

*To apply a tag to the selection using the
Context menu, choose a tag from the
Tag Frame (or Tag Text) submenu.*

*InDesign applies the tag
you selected, and creates a
corresponding XML element.*

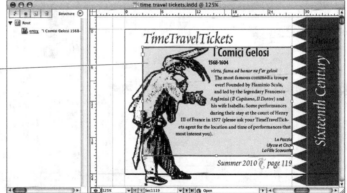

Map By Name button. This mapping is case sensitive—the style
names "Body_Text" and "body_text" will be mapped to different
XML tags. Note, also, that tag names cannot contain spaces or
punctuation (so you might want to avoid using those characters
in your style names).

3. When you've created as many tag-to-style correspondences as
    you want, click the OK button. InDesign applies the specified
    paragraph style to all paragraphs tagged with the corresponding
    XML tag.

**Mapping Styles
to XML Tags**

You've formatted all of the text in your InDesign document using
paragraph and character styles, and you've imported or created a set
of XML tags. Since you've already told InDesign what all of the text
objects are (by way of the paragraph and character styles), shouldn't

FIGURE 14-12

Tagging a Frame Using Drag and Drop

Drag objects out of your layout and drop them in the Structure view.

InDesign asks which tag you want to apply to the new XML element. Select a tag…

…and InDesign tags the objects and creates a new XML element.

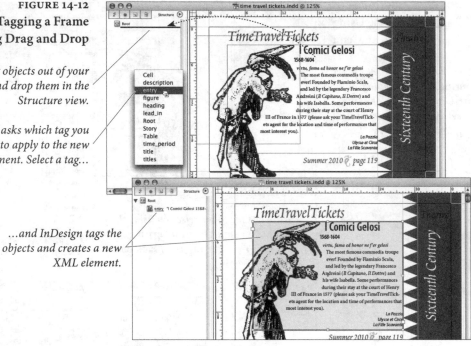

FIGURE 14-13

Tagging Preset Options

Choose Tagging Preset Options from the Structure menu, then select the default tag you want to apply to each type of object (text frames, tables, and table cells).

When you apply a tag to a text selection in an untagged text frame, for example…

…InDesign tags the text frame with the default tag you specified.

FIGURE 14-14
**Tables and Tagging
Preset Options**

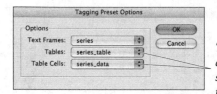

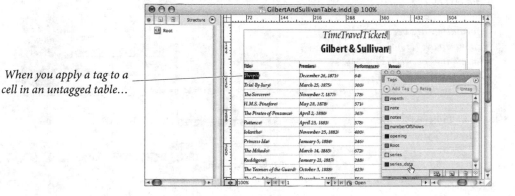

*The Tagging Preset Options
dialog box gives you a way to
specify the default tag applied to
tables and table cells.*

*When you apply a tag to a
cell in an untagged table...*

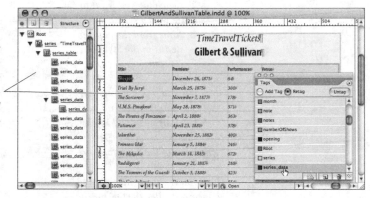

*InDesign applies the default
tag to the table and the cells
in the table. If the text frame
containing the table is also
untagged, InDesign will
apply the default tag to the
text frame.*

you be able to do so with the document's XML structure? You can, by
following the steps below (see Figure 14-16).

1. Select the Map Styles to Tags option from the Tags palette menu.
   InDesign displays the Map Styles to Tags dialog box.

2. Select an XML element for each style for which you want to
   establish a mapping. If some or all of your XML tag names are
   the same as the names of your styles, you can click the Map By
   Name button to automatically match tags and styles with the
   same names (this matching is case sensitive).

3. When you've created as many style-to-tag correspondences
   as you want, click the OK button. InDesign creates an XML
   element for all text tagged with the styles you've specified.

FIGURE 14-15
Mapping XML Tags to Styles

You've imported XML, and you've tagged frames and text objects. So why does your text look so… unformatted? It's because you haven't yet created a "mapping" between the XML tags and the styles in the document.

To do that, choose Map Tags to Styles from the Structure menu.

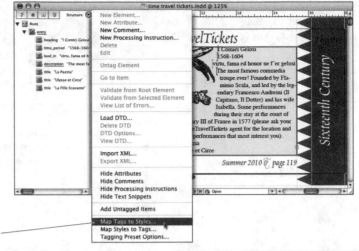

InDesign displays the Map Tags to Styles dialog box.

For each tag you want to associate with a style, choose a style name from the pop-up menus in the Style list.

If the tags and paragraph styles have the same names, you can click the Map By Name button to have InDesign do most of the work for you.

Once you've set up the mapping the way you want it, click the OK button.

InDesign applies the formatting specified in the character and paragraph styles to the corresponding text elements.

FIGURE 14-16
FIGURE 14-16
**Mapping Styles
to XML Tags**

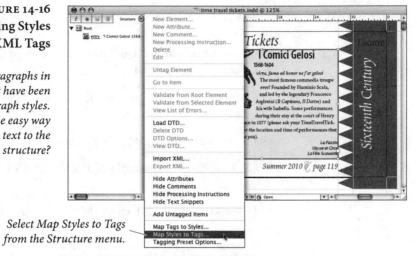

*All of the paragraphs in
your document have been
tagged with paragraph styles.
Isn't there some easy way
to add all of the text to the
XML structure?*

*Select Map Styles to Tags
from the Structure menu.*

*InDesign displays the Map
Styles to Tags dialog box.*

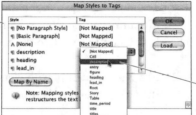

*For each style you want to
add, select a tag from the pop-
up menus in the Tag list.*

*If you've named the tags using
the same names as the paragraph
amd character styles, you can
click the Map By Name button
and save a lot of time. (Hint: This
is very much worth doing.)*

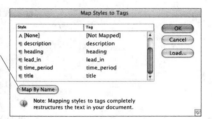

*Once you've finished creating a
mapping, click the OK button.*

*InDesign adds elements
to the XML structure
of the document based
on the mapping.*

Importing and Exporting XML

To import XML into the structure of an InDesign document, follow these steps (see Figure 14-17).

1. Choose Import XML from the File menu. InDesign displays the Import XML dialog box.

2. Locate and select an XML file to import.

3. Click the Open button. InDesign adds the XML structure to the document

When you import XML for the first time, the incoming XML data will appear in any page items that have been tagged with the Root XML element.

If you're importing XML into a document that already contains an XML structure, you can choose to replace the existing structure, or append the incoming XML to the existing structure.

Replacing XML

To replace an XML structure with elements from another XML file, follow these steps (see Figure 14-18).

1. If you want to replace any element other than the Root element, select an element in the Structure view.

2. Choose Import XML from the File menu. InDesign displays the Import XML dialog box.

3. Turn on the Replace Content option. If you want to replace the selected element, turn on the Import Into Selected Element option.

4. Click the Open button, and InDesign replaces the XML elements with the elements in the XML file.

Exporting XML

Once you've created an XML structure in an InDesign document, you can export structure to an XML file. This is a good thing, because you can then use the exported XML file as a template for future files.

To export XML, follow these steps (see Figure 14-19).

1. If you want to export a selected element (and all of the elements it contains), select the XML element you want to export in the Structure view.

2. Choose Export from the File menu. InDesign displays the Export dialog box.

FIGURE 14-17
Importing XML

*To import XML, choose
Import XML from the
Structure menu.*

*To import XML into specific
element, select the element
before importing.*

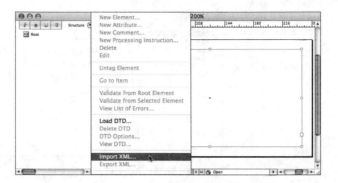

*InDesign displays the Import XML dialog
box. Locate and select an XML file, then
click the Open button to import the file.*

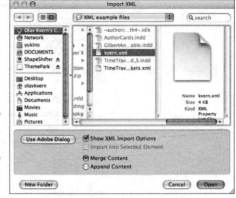

*Turn on the Merge Content option to
replace existing XML elements.*

*Turn on Import Into Selected Element to
import the elements into the selected element.*

*Choose Append Content to append the
elements in the XML file to the structure.*

*InDesign adds the elements
from the XML file to the
document structure.*

*To apply an element to a
frame, drag the element over
the frame and release the
mouse button.*

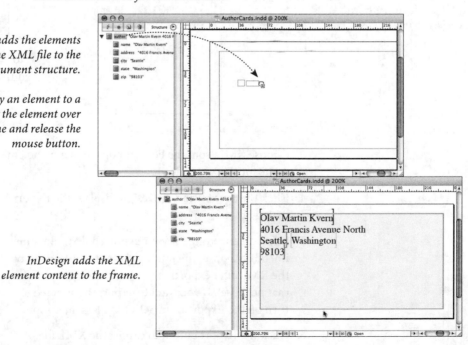

*InDesign adds the XML
element content to the frame.*

FIGURE 14-18
Replacing XML

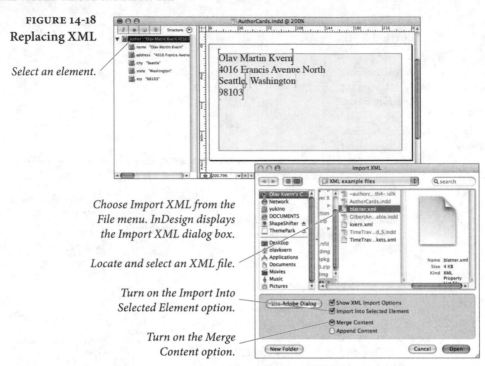

Select an element.

Choose Import XML from the File menu. InDesign displays the Import XML dialog box.

Locate and select an XML file.

Turn on the Import Into Selected Element option.

Turn on the Merge Content option.

Click the Open button, and InDesign replaces the existing elements with the corresponding elements from the imported XML file.

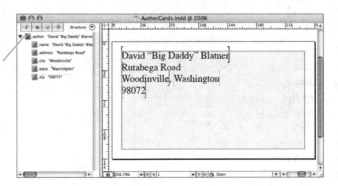

3. Choose XML from the Format pop-up menu and enter a name for the XML file.

4. Click the Save button. InDesign displays the Export XML dialog box.

5. Select an encoding for your exported XML document from the Encoding pop-up menu. If you want, you can choose to view the XML after exporting (and the browser you want to use for that purpose). If you want to export the selected element (if any), turn on the Export from Selected Element option.

6. Click the Export button to export the XML file.

FIGURE 14-19

Exporting XML

To export XML, choose
Export from the File menu
or Export XML from the
Structure menu.

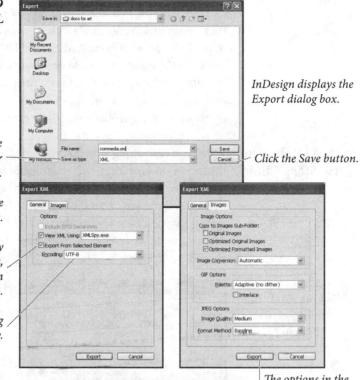

InDesign displays the
Export dialog box.

Choose XML from the
pop-up menu, then enter
a name for the file.

Click the Save button.

InDesign displays the
Export XML dialog box.

If you want to export only
the selected XML element,
turn on the Export from
Selected Element option.

Choose a character encoding
for the XML file, if necessary.

The options in the
Images panel control
the way that InDesign
exports the images
in the document.

Click the Export button,
and InDesign exports the
specified XML elements
to a file. You can view this
file using any text editor,
or you can open the file
using a Web browser.

In this example, special
characters (line end characters and carriage returns)
appear as boxes.

Exporting Structure Tags to PDF

Acrobat 5 PDF documents (PDF version 1.4 and above) can include eBook structure data. In essence, these are a defined set of XML tags that have a specific meaning to Acrobat.

The easiest way to tag the elements in your document with these tags is to choose the Add Untagged Items option from the Structure view menu. When you do this, InDesign automatically applies a tag named "Article" to untagged text frames and applies the tag "Figure" to untagged imported graphics.

If you prefer, you can create tags with these names and apply them manually. You can also use the tag name "Artifact" to mark page items you want to omit when the PDF is viewed on small-screen devices (telephones, handheld organizers, and so on).

After you've applied these tags, turn on the Include eBook Tags option as you export PDF. The PDF will then be set up to reflow when displayed by the Acrobat Reader software.

XML Tags in the Story Editor

When you're working with text you've tagged with XML tags, editing the text in the layout can become something of a chore. It can be very hard to see where one range of tagged text ends, where another tag begins, and the ways that the tags relate to each other. It can also be far too easy to delete tags inadvertently. The solution? View and edit the text in the Story Editor, which provides a better view of the text elements (see Figure 14-20).

FIGURE 14-20
Viewing XML Tag Markers in the Story Editor

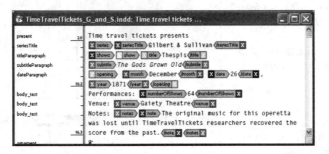

Creating Placeholders for Repeating Content

All of the techniques we've discussed so far—tagging text and frames, importing XML, replacing XML—can be used to create and populate placeholder frames for XML content. A key point, however, is that InDesign will *never* create new frames or add pages to accommodate new XML elements. InDesign will, however, duplicate text items as you import XML elements into a placeholder story. This means that you can have InDesign repeat the arrangement of placeholder elements and static text for each corresponding element in an imported XML file.

You create placeholder text by creating an XML structure that matches the structure of the XML content you plan to import (see Figure 14-21). You then use the elements from the XML structure to mark up text. The *structures* do not need to be an exact match, but the *sequence* of elements in the template and the sequence of elements in the incoming XML file must match.

FIGURE 14-21
Creating Placeholders for XML Content

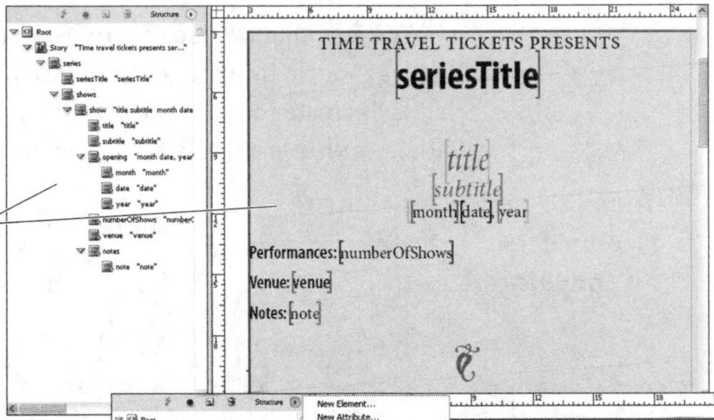

Make a text frame and use tags to create a series of XML placeholders.

In this example, the main repeating element—similar to a record in a database—is the "show" element.

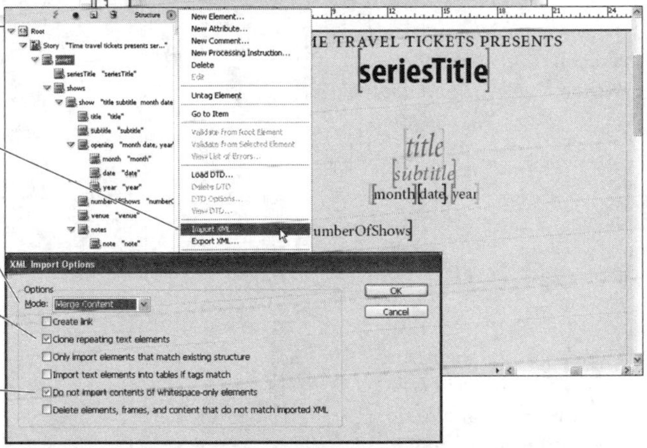

Choose Import XML from the Structure menu or the File menu.

Choose Merge Content in the XML Import Options dialog box.

Check Clone Repeating Text Elements

Turn this option on to preserve any static text you have added between placeholder elements.

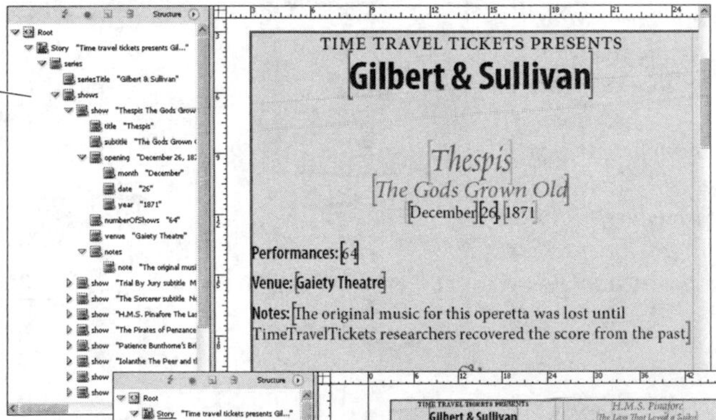

InDesign flows the XML data into the story, repeating the XML elements that match the structure of the placeholder elements.

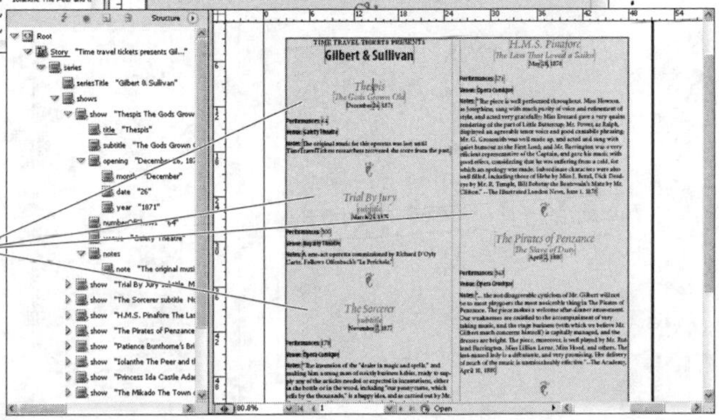

Each "show" element is laid out according to the format of the placeholder elements.

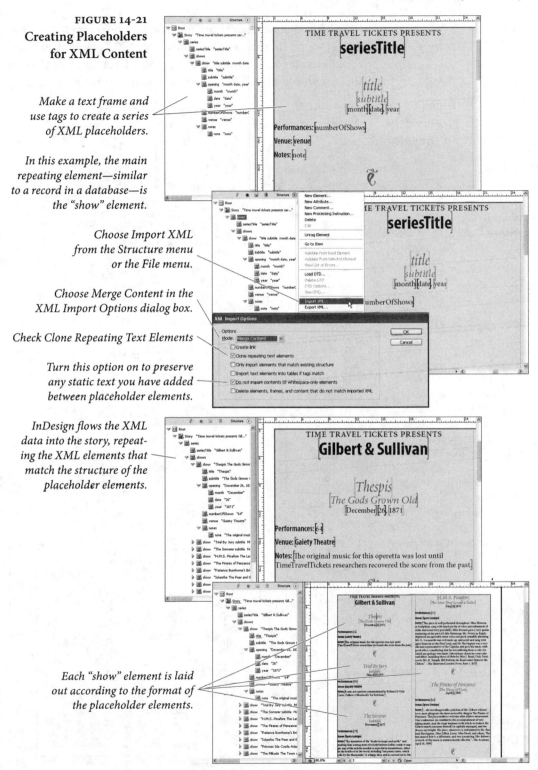

We know that we said that InDesign won't create new frames, but there is a way to incorporate graphics in your XML placeholder—and that is to create inline frames. Inline graphic frames can be filled in with a graphic just like XML placeholder text, (see Figure 14-22).

FIGURE 14-22
Inline Placeholders for Graphics

Again, set up the structure using placeholder XML elements. This time, add an anchored graphic and apply an XML tag to it.

Add graphic elements to the structure of the XML file you plan to export. For each graphic element, add the location of the graphic you want inserted for that element.

When you import the XML, InDesign will duplicate the graphic placeholder, and will import the graphic specified in the corresponding XML element.

The new graphics replace the placeholder graphic in each duplicate of the placeholder text.

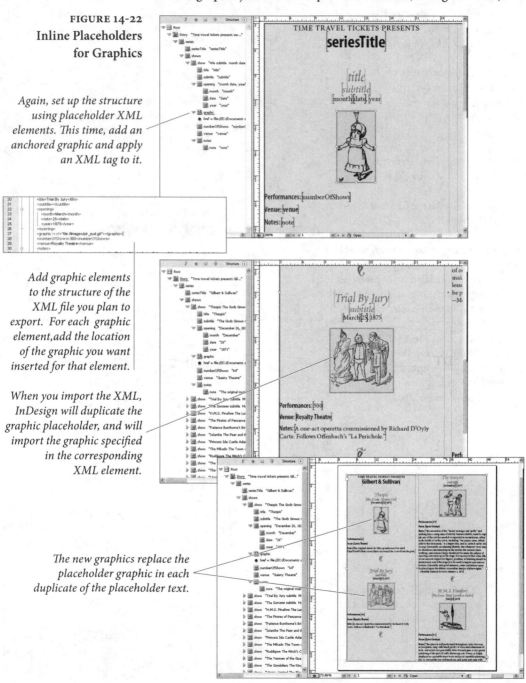

Working with DTDs

A Document Type Definition (DTD) is a text file that contains the "rules" for an XML file. There's nothing magical about these rules—there's just a formal version of the things you think about as you design and lay out a document. Heading levels, for example, follow a particular order; a numbered list must have at least two list items; last name data fields in directory data do not include middle names, and so on. Laying out documents is all about applying a structure to the data in the document (in addition to making it pretty to look at).

If, as we said earlier, an XML file can contain any data, in any order, how the heck can you work with other people? Most of us have, at one point or another, had some success training the writers and editors we work with to provide text files that are reasonably close to what we want. We've done this by giving them a detailed set of instructions on the way that they should prepare the text. And, at least for some of us, we've come up with a system that produces files that we can work with.

A DTD is something like a set of instructions for preparing a text file for page layout. But it's much more than that, and somewhat more restrictive. At their best, DTDs provide an agreed-upon set of tags and XML data structures that work seamlessly with your publication processes.

DTD Basics   Given that there are entire books larger than this one on the topic of writing DTDs, you'll have to forgive us for not going into great detail on the care and feeding of these files. (Besides, we're still learning how to write them ourselves.)

The following are a few ground rules, however.

- A DTD can exist as a separate file, or it can be inside an XML file. It's most likely you'll want to keep your DTDs as separate files, as it makes sense to work with a small set of DTDs (one or two) and apply them to a much larger number of XML files.

- DTDs have four basic parts (called declarations): document type, comments, elements, and attributes.

- If a DTD is included in a file containing XML data, the DTD is enclosed within the DOCTYPE declaration. This specifies the name of the top level (or "root") element in the XML file. If the DTD is a separate file, it does not use the DOCTYPE declaration

- Element declarations specify the name of each element—and therefore each tag—in an XML document.

▶ Attribute declarations usually contain information about the information in an element ("metadata"), but they sometimes contain other data.

A (Very Brief) DTD Primer

As we mentioned above, DTDs have four basic parts: the DOCTYPE declaration, elements, attributes, and comments. The following sections provide a a bit more detail on each part.

Document type. If the DTD appears in a file containing XML data, the DOCTYPE declaration appears at the beginning of the file, immediately following the XML declaration. The skeleton of this type of file looks something like this (in the following, the XML element "author" is the root element):

```
<?xml version="1.0" encoding="UTF-8" standalone="yes" ?>
<!DOCTYPE author [
<!-- DTD for author -->
]>
<author>
<!-- XML data-->
</author>
```

If the DTD is not included in an XML file, then you can omit the DOCTYPE declaration. We're not exactly sure *why* you would include the DTD with the XML file, but you have the option to do so, should you so desire.

Comments. Once you venture beyond simple DTDs (such as the examples in this book), you'll find that it gets difficult to keep track of all of the elements and attributes in a DTD file. When this happens, you'll want to add a note to yourself—or to anyone else who might happen to be reading the DTD—explaining what, exactly, you're trying to do with a specific line or section of the file. Comments are preceded by "<!--", end with "-->", and can be span multiple lines. Here's an example comment:

```
<!-- No more than one social security number per author -->
```

Elements. Elements are the heart of the DVD. They specify the structure of the data used by the DTD, and they correspond to the XML tags in InDesign. Each element declaration contains the name of the element and the data that the element contains. A simple element declaration looks like this:

```
<!ELEMENT first (#PCDATA)>
```

This declares that the element is named "first," and that the element contains text (that's what "PCDATA" means).

A slightly more complex element is shown below.

```
<!ELEMENT name (first middle? last)>
```

This element is named name, and is made up of three elements, "first," "middle," and "last." The question mark after the element "middle" means that this element is optional. Other marks specify other things about the content of the element—see Table 14-2.

Attributes. An attribute contains additional information about an element. Attributes are generally used for storing metadata (again, that's data about the data in the element, not necessarily data you want to print out—the date the element was created or updated would be examples of element attributes).

An example attribute looks like this:

```
<!ATTLIST address updated CDATA #IMPLIED>
```

Attribute declarations are lists with four parts: the element name, the attribute name, the attribute type, and whether or not it's required. In the above example, the attribute is associated with the "address" element, the attribute is named "updated," the attribute contains the data type CDATA (text), and it's optional.

	Symbol	What it Means
TABLE 14-2 **Element Codes**	+	Required, and may repeat (one or more of these elements may appear in the parent element).
	?	Optional, but may not repeat (only one of these elements can appear in the parent element).
	*	Optional, and may repeat.
	no mark	required, and cannot repeat.
	,	Followed by. Controls the order of appearance of elements in an element. If an element name is followed by a comma, elements following the comma must appear after the element.
	|	Or. When this mark appears between element names, it means that either or both of the elements can appear; if one of the element names is required, then one or both elements must appear.

The attribute options for the last parameter ("required") are listed below.

▶ #REQUIRED means the attribute is required.

▶ #IMPLED means the attribute is optional.

▶ #FIXED is always followed by a value; if the attribute is missing, then it's assumed to be this value.

▶ Some default value. This is really the same as #FIXED, above, in that the value provides the default value.

An Example DTD   Given our very simple XML database example, we can construct a DTD to use for validating new versions of the database. It would look something like the following.

```
<!-- DTD for author -->
<!ELEMENT author (name, address, city, state, zip)>
<!ELEMENT name (first, middle, last)>
<!ELEMENT first (#PCDATA)>
<!ELEMENT middle (#PCDATA)>
<!ELEMENT last (#PCDATA)>
<!ELEMENT address (#PCDATA)>
<!ELEMENT city (#PCDATA)>
<!ELEMENT state (#PCDATA)>
<!ELEMENT zip (#PCDATA)>
```

Importing DTDs   To import a DTD file into an InDesign document, follow these steps (see Figure 14-23).

1. Display the Structure view, if it's not already visible (choose Show Structure from the Structure submenu of the View menu, or click the Show Structure button at the lower-left corner of the InDesign window).

2. Chose Load DTD from the Structure menu. InDesign displays the Load DTD dialog box.

3. Locate and select the DTD you want to import, then click the Open button. InDesign imports the DTD.

When you import a DTD, InDesign adds the tags in the DTD file to the list of tags in the Tags palette. The tags defined in the DTD are locked—you can change the tag's color, but not tag's name.

To view the DTD, choose View DTD from the Structure menu. InDesign opens the DTD in the View DTD dialog box—something like a very simple text editor (see Figure 14-24). You can scroll through the text, and you can select and copy text out of the DTD.

FIGURE 14-23
Importing a DTD

Choose Import DTD from the Structure menu.

InDesign displays the Import DTD dialog box.

Select a DTD file.

Click the Open button.

InDesign adds the DTD to the document.

InDesign adds XML tags corresponding to the elements defined in the DTD.

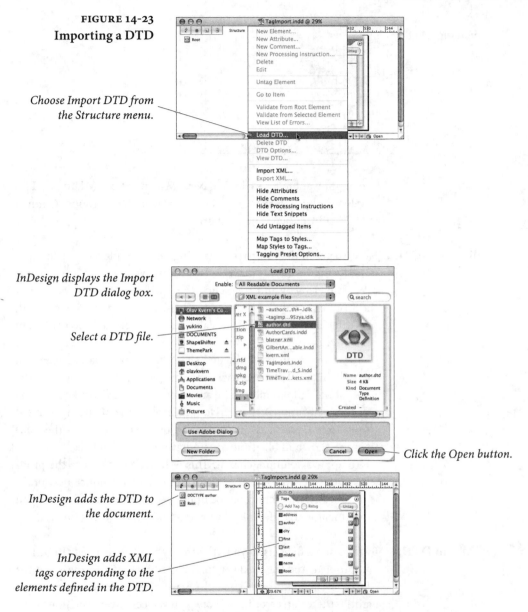

We're not exactly certain how useful this feature is, though we admit that it might come in handy during an "am I losing my mind or is that XML element really messed up" moment.

"Off the Shelf" DTDs

Before you take on the task of creating a DTD from scratch, take a look at the DTD links http://www.xml.com/pub/rg/DTD_Reposi- tories.html—you might find one there that will work for you, or at least find a good example. If you work in the newspaper industry,

FIGURE 14-24
Viewing a DTD

you might want to take a look at NewsML and SportsML, two DTDs developed by International Press Telecommunications Council (IPTC), at http://www.newsml.org.

Validating XML   Now we get to the fun part—checking an XML file to make certain it conforms to the DTD we've loaded. To validate XML elements, select the element and then click the Validate button at the top of the Structure view (see Figure 14-25). To validate a specific element, select the element and choose Validate From Selected Element from the Structure menu.

After InDesign has validated the XML, a new pane appears at the bottom of the Structure view. In this pane, InDesign displays the result of the validation. If there are errors in the XML (relative to the DTD's specifications), then InDesign displays the offending element names in red, and lists the errors and possible solutions—the solutions are shown in blue, and are underlined.

To apply a solution, click it. This will not always solve the problems with the XML file, and it will sometimes introduce new problems. Luckily, this action can be undone—which means that you can experiment with different solutions to find which works for you.

Real World DTDs   By the time a file gets to you, it's already too late. It needs to be laid out, proofed, and the final version printed by the deadline—and the editors, writers, and everyone else have already gone home for the night. If there's an error in the copy you've been given, you don't have time to go through proper channels—you just have to fix it. If the text files use the wrong styles, or if the graphics are in the wrong format, you can fix them and still have a chance of meeting your deadline.

If, on the other hand you, a file doesn't conform to the DTD you're required to use, you have a painful choice: you can start editing the XML file itself (painful and slow for all but the simplest XML files), you can turn off DTD validation and attempt to make sense of the XML structure, or you can stick to the "letter of the law" and reject the XML file because it didn't conform to the DTD.

FIGURE 14-25
Validating XML

To validate the XML in the file using the DTD you've loaded, click the Validate button.

InDesign displays the result of the validation at the bottom of the Structure view.

When the XML in the file changes, it's a good idea to validate again. You never know what you might find.

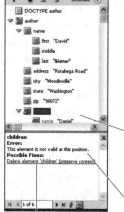

In this example, InDesign found errors in the XML—the DTD did not allow for the possibility that David would have added children.

InDesign highlights the unexpected elements in red.

InDesign lists the errors in the XML at the bottom of the Structure view.

Click the underlined blue text to attempt to fix the XML validation problem.

In the real world, the latter is not even an option. If you have really good managers, they'll probably commend you for your principled stand—and then they'll fire you.

Publishing is about deadlines, more deadlines, and ouput. Keeping a press waiting is an expensive business, as the authors know to their bitter experience. We can add all of the formal handoffs, review processes, and conform to every standard that's ever been formulated, but, in the end, we sometimes have to throw it all out the window in order to get the pages out the door. Anything that stands in the way of that fact does not belong in your workflow.

We're not saying that you shouldn't use DTDs. But we did want to caution you—if you're going to commit to a particular DTD, make certain that you build plenty of time into your process for validation and for fixing XML files that won't validate.

Transforming XML with XSL

Putting all of your data into XML presents a problem—how the heck do you get it into a form that people can look at it? InDesign is certainly one answer, but there's another, and that's XSL. XSL, or Extensible Stylesheet Language, exists to transform XML into other formats.

Once upon a time, many moons ago, there was only one Web browser (Mosaic), which ran on a single type of device (a computer). HTML did a reasonably good job of displaying data (Web pages) in that browser on that device. But the Web grew. These days, we have multiple browsers (Internet Explorer, Firefox, Safari) running on multiple platforms (telephones, Palm OS devices, Windows, the Mac OS, television sets). An HTML format that works well for one of these viewing environments probably won't work for all of the others. So Web site developers faced a problem: how could they avoid writing and maintaining multiple versions of their HTML pages?

The answer lies in the combination of XML and XSL. When you use XSL, you can store the data that makes up your Web pages as XML and transform it into HTML appropriate for viewing on whatever device and browser happens to be connecting to your Web site. If you do this, you need to write and maintain the XSL templates, but the templates change far less frequently than your Web pages.

XSL is made up of two main parts: XSL Transformations (or XSLT), which comprise the transformation language itself and XML Path Language (or XPath), a way to locate data in XML.

At this point, you're probably scratching your head and wondering just exactly what a language for transforming XML into HTML has to do with InDesign. It's this: XSL can transform XML into *any* text format, including plain text, PDF, PostScript, HTML, other forms of XML, and, our favorite, InDesign tagged text.

Why use XSL to transform XML before placing it in an InDesign document? Well, that depends on your workflow. If you need to import lots of tabular data from your XML files, converting to tagged text first can speed things up, because tables imported from XML appear in InDesign's default table formatting. This usually means that you'll have to select and reformat each table—a task that can be time-consuming, to say the least. If you transform the same XML file to tagged text using XSL, you can specify every attribute of the tables in the file.

Another point about tables—InDesign tagged text supports tables-within-tables; InDesign's XML import does not.

To transform an XML file with an XSL template, you'll have to use an XML parser (or an XML editor)—InDesign cannot apply an XSL template as it imports an XML file.

Here is a (very simple) XML fragment that we'll use in all of the following examples. Note that we're asking you to use your imagination a bit—if the XML files you are working with are really this small and simple, then you *do not need* the XSL techniques we'll talk about. But if you're looking at XML files several orders of magnitude larger and more complex—as you probably are, if you're working with XML—then you probably do.

```
<author>
    <name>
        <first>Olav</first>
        <middle>Martin</middle>
        <last>Kvern</last>
    </name>
    <address>4016 Francis Avenue North</address>
    <city>Seattle</city>
    <state>Washington</state>
    <zip>98103</zip>
</author>
```

Changing Element Order with XSL

InDesign's XML import frequently requires that the elements in the XML structure match the order of the appearance elements in the layout (this almost always true of text elements), which means that you might find that you need to re-order the elements in an XML file before you import it. The following is an example XSL template that can change the position of an element in our example XML file.

```
<?xml version="1.0" encoding="UTF-8"?>
<xsl:stylesheet version="2.0"
xmlns:xsl="http://www.w3.org/1999/XSL/Transform">
<xsl:output method="xml" version="1.0" encoding="UTF-8"
indent="yes"/>
<xsl:template match="/">
<xsl:element name="author">
<xsl:element name="name">
<!--Rearrange the order of the name elements, placing
the last name first-->
<xsl:copy-of select="author/name/last"/>
<xsl:copy-of select="author/name/first"/>
<xsl:copy-of select="author/name/middle"/>
</xsl:element>
<xsl:copy-of select="author/address"/>
<xsl:copy-of select="author/city"/>
<xsl:copy-of select="author/state"/>
<xsl:copy-of select="author/zip"/>
</xsl:element>
</xsl:template>
</xsl:stylesheet>
```

Transform the example XML using the XSL template above, and you'll get the following output XML.

```
<?xml version="1.0" encoding="UTF-8"?>
<author>
    <name>
        <last>Kvern</last>
        <first>Olav</first>
        <middle>Martin</middle>
    </name>
    <address>4016 Francis Avenue North</address>
    <city>Seattle</city>
    <state>Washington</state>
    <zip>98103</zip>
</author>
```

Duplicating Elements with XSL

It's fairly natural to expect that you could use one piece of XML data in multiple places in an InDesign layout—but that's not at all the way that InDesign works. Once you've imported XML, there is a one-to-one correspondence between the elements in the Structure view and their expression in the layout. If you want an element to appear multiple times, you've got to duplicate the element for each appearance on a document page. (Obviously, you can get around this in some cases by placing the XML element on a master page.)

Our layout requires (for whatever reason) that the author's last name appear twice. How can we duplicate the last name field? Try the following XSL template.

```
<?xml version="1.0" encoding="UTF-8"?>
<xsl:stylesheet version="2.0"
xmlns:xsl="http://www.w3.org/1999/XSL/Transform" >
<xsl:output method="xml" version="1.0" encoding="UTF-8"
indent="yes"/>
<xsl:template match="/">
<xsl:element name="author">
<!--Create a copy of the last name element
with a different element name-->
<xsl:element name="last_name"><xsl:value-of select="author/name/
last"/></xsl:element>
<xsl:copy-of select="author/name"/>
<xsl:copy-of select="author/address"/>
<xsl:copy-of select="author/city"/>
<xsl:copy-of select="author/state"/>
<xsl:copy-of select="author/zip"/>
</xsl:element>
</xsl:template>
</xsl:stylesheet>
```

When you transform the example XML file with the XSL template above, you'll get the following output XML.

```
<?xml version="1.0" encoding="UTF-8"?>
<author>
    <last_name>Kvern</last_name>
    <name>
        <first>Olav</first>
        <middle>Martin</middle>
        <last>Kvern</last>
    </name>
    <address>4016 Francis Avenue North</address>
    <city>Seattle</city>
    <state>Washington</state>
    <zip>98103</zip>
</author>
```

Transforming XML to Tagged Text

As we mentioned earlier, transforming XML into tagged text for import can offer some significant advantages for some workflows and publications. If you don't care about maintaining the XML structure in your InDesign documents, or if your use of XML involves adding text data from XML elements to other text, you might want to consider this approach.

```
<?xml version="1.0"?>
<xsl:stylesheet version="2.0"
xmlns:xsl="http://www.w3.org/1999/XSL/Transform">
<xsl:output method = "text"/>
<xsl:template match="author">&lt;ASCII-WIN&gt;&#10;&#13;
&lt;Version:4&gt;&lt;FeatureSet:InDesign-Roman&gt;&lt;ColorTable:=&l
t;Black:COLOR:CMYK:Process:0,0,0,1&gt;&gt;
&lt;DefineParaStyle:heading&gt;
&lt;DefineParaStyle:body_text&gt;
&lt;DefineCharStyle:name&gt;
&lt;ParaStyle:heading&gt;<xsl:value-of select="name/first"/
>&#32;<xsl:value-of select="name/middle"/>&#32;<xsl:value-of
select="name/last"/>
&lt;ParaStyle:body_text&gt;Once upon a time, there was an
author named &lt;CharStyle:name&gt;<xsl:value-of select="name/
first"/>&#32;<xsl:value-of select="name/middle"/>&#32;<xsl:value-
of select="name/last"/>&lt;CharStyle:&gt; who lived in a strange
little house at <xsl:value-of select="address"/> in <xsl:value-of
select="city"/>, <xsl:value-of select="state"/>.
</xsl:template>
</xsl:stylesheet>
```

When you process the XML example file using the above XSL template, you'll get the following tagged text output.

```
<ASCII-WIN>
<Version:4><FeatureSet:InDesign-Roman><ColorTable:=<Black:COLOR:
CMYK:Process:0,0,0,1>>
<DefineParaStyle:heading>
<DefineParaStyle:body_text>
```

```
<DefineCharStyle:name>
<ParaStyle:heading>Olav Martin Kvern
<ParaStyle:body_text>Once upon a time, there was an author named
<CharStyle:name>Olav Martin Kvern<CharStyle:> who lived in a strange
little house at 4016 Francis Avenue North in Seattle, Washington.
```

InDesign Interchange Format (INX)

If you've been poking around the Export dialog box, you might have noticed an option to export the file using something called the "InDesign Interchange Format." What the heck is that? In short, it's a way to save an InDesign file as an XML representation of itself. This is not the same as exporting XML from a document (which would only include the XML structure itself)—it's nothing less than an attempt to render *everything* in the InDesign file, including styles, colors, page margins, and ruler guides, out to a text file.

The InDesign Snippet (.inds) format is essentially the same as INX, but is limited to representing page items or collections of page items as XML.

The reason we're talking about INX, when we've already talked about it in Chapter 7, "Importing and Exporting," is that it's XML. All of the things you can do with XML files, you can do with INX. Yes, that means you can import them into the XML structure of a document. Don't do that! That's not what we're getting at.

Think about it. With XSL and the XML in an INX file (or snippet file), you can lay out InDesign documents *without even having InDesign open*. Sure, you'll need to open your copy of InDesign to proof, print, and export the files you've created, but a great deal of the work can be done for you while the file is in its XML form. The work can be done by a database, or by a script, on your local machine, or on a server.

If you do a large amount of template-based publishing, where the main thing that changes in your documents is text, you should really consider the approach shown in Figure 14-26. Especially in combination with scripting, this approach can bring about tremendous productivity gains for repetitive layouts such as business cards or data sheets.

As great as INX and InDesign snippet are, they are not nearly what we'd like them to be. The XML elements names are not—by any stretch of the imagination—"human readable." It's would be almost impossibly difficult to write a valid INX or snippet file from scratch using a text editor. We're not saying that that sounds like our idea of fun (actually, it *is* Ole's idea of fun), but we think that the format

FIGURE 14-26

Transforming INX with XSL

This XSL template changes the string "!!name!!" in any text frame into a specified name. In this example, we've entered the name, but a real template would pull the name or names from an XML data file. It helps to imagine that you have hundreds of these to do.

```
<?xml version="1.0" encoding="UTF-8"?>
<xsl:stylesheet version="1.0" xmlns:xsl="http://www.w3.org/1999/XSL/
Transform">
<xsl:output method="xml" version="1.0" encoding="UTF-16" indent="yes"/>
<xsl:template match="pcnt">
<!--if the content of the element is !!name!!
then change it to a specified name-->
<xsl:choose>
<xsl:when test="contains(.,'c_!!name!!')">
<xsl:element name="pcnt">c_MAX OLAV KVERN</xsl:element>
</xsl:when>
<xsl:otherwise>
<xsl:copy-of select="../pcnt"/>
</xsl:otherwise>
</xsl:choose>
</xsl:template>
<xsl:template match="*">
<xsl:copy>
<xsl:copy-of select="@*"/>
<xsl:apply-templates/>
</xsl:copy>
</xsl:template>
<xsl:template match="/">
<!--Need to add the INX header back in-->
<xsl:text disable-output-escaping="yes">&#13;&lt;?aid style="33"
type="document" DOMVersion="4.0" readerVersion="3.0" featureSet="257"
product="4.0(622)" ?&gt;&#13;</xsl:text><xsl:text disable-output-
escaping="no"/>
<xsl:apply-templates/>
</xsl:template>
</xsl:stylesheet>
```

Original business card with placeholder text.

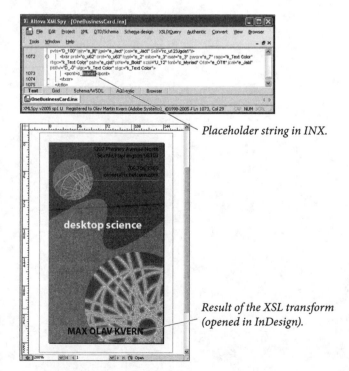

Placeholder string in INX.

Result of the XSL transform (opened in InDesign).

should be clear and robust enough that it would be possible to do so. We look forward to future development of the INX format.

Stay Tuned

As we've said, all of this is very new. Desktop publishing has not yet fully embraced XML as part of a page layout workflow, and InDesign's XML features are only a small step in the right direction. We've got a lot of experimenting to do before we find the right fit for XML—a format that is explicitly *not concerned* about formatting—and a page layout. We're convinced that they can work together, in spite of their differences, and that we'll see many more XML features work their way into InDesign in future versions.

INDEX